PHILIP'S

D0299245

STREET ATLAS

Staffordshire

www.philips-maps.co.uk

First published in 1995 by

Philip's, a division of
Octopus Publishing Group Ltd
www.octopusbooks.co.uk
2-4 Heron Quays, London E14 4JP
An Hachette Livre UK Company

Third colour edition 2005
Second impression with revisions 2007
STACB

ISBN-10   0-540-08757-2 (pocket)
ISBN-13   978-0-540-08757-0 (pocket)

© Philip's 2007

Ordnance Survey®

This product includes mapping data licensed from
Ordnance Survey® with the permission of the
Controller of Her Majesty's Stationery Office.
© Crown copyright 2007. All rights reserved.
Licence number 100011710.

No part of this publication may be reproduced,
stored in a retrieval system or transmitted in any
form or by any means, electronic, mechanical,
photocopying, recording or otherwise, without the
permission of the Publishers and the copyright
owner.

To the best of the Publishers' knowledge, the
information in this atlas was correct at the time of
going to press. No responsibility can be accepted
for any errors or their consequences.

The representation in this atlas of a road, track
or path is no evidence of the existence of a right
of way.

Ordnance Survey and the OS Symbol are
registered trademarks of Ordnance Survey, the
national mapping agency of Great Britain.

Printed and bound in Spain
by Cayfosa-Quebecor

Contents

III   **Key to map symbols**

IV   **Key to map pages**

VI   **Route planning**

X   **Administrative and Postcode boundaries**

1   **Street maps** at 2⅔ inches to 1 mile

282   **Street maps of centres of Hanley, Newcastle-under-Lyme, Longton and Stafford** at 5⅓ inches to 1 mile

286   **Index** of towns and villages

289   **Index** of streets, hospitals, industrial estates, railway stations, schools, shopping centres, universities and places of interest

Digital Data

The exceptionally high-quality mapping found in this atlas is available as digital data in TIFF format, which is easily convertible to other bitmapped (raster) image formats.

The index is also available in digital form as a standard database table. It contains all the details found in the printed index together with the National Grid reference for the map square in which each entry is named.

For further information and to discuss your requirements, please contact james.mann@philips-ma...

STAFFORDSHIRE LIBRARIES

3 8014 04344 8668

PHILIP'S MAPS
the Gold Standard for drivers

◆ **Philip's street atlases cover every county in England, Wales, Northern Ireland and much of Scotland**

◆ Every named street is shown, including alleys, lanes and walkways

◆ Thousands of additional features marked: stations, public buildings, car parks, places of interest

◆ Route-planning maps to get you close to your destination

◆ Postcodes on the maps and in the index

◆ Widely used by the emergency services, transport companies and local authorities

BEST BUY • BEST BUY
Auto EXPRESS
BEST BUY • BEST BUY

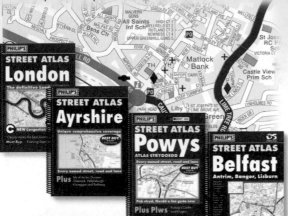

PHILIP'S

STAFFS. LIBRARY AND INFORMATION SERVICES

043448668	
HJ	07/10/2008
912.4246	£5.99
PERT	

WITHDRAWN

Street atlases currently available

England

Bedfordshire and Luton	Surrey
Berkshire	East Sussex
Birmingham and West Midlands	West Sussex
Bristol and Bath	Tyne and Wear
Buckinghamshire and Milton Keynes	Warwickshire and Coventry
Cambridgeshire and Peterborough	Wiltshire and Swindon
Cheshire	Worcestershire
Cornwall	East Yorkshire Northern Lincolnshire
Cumbria	North Yorkshire
Derbyshire	South Yorkshire
Devon	West Yorkshire

Wales

Dorset	Anglesey, Conwy and Gwynedd
County Durham and Teesside	Cardiff, Swansea and The Valleys
Essex	Carmarthenshire, Pembrokeshire and Swansea
North Essex	
South Essex	
Gloucestershire and Bristol	Ceredigion and South Gwynedd
Hampshire	
North Hampshire	Denbighshire, Flintshire, Wrexham
South Hampshire	
Herefordshire Monmouthshire	Herefordshire Monmouthshire
Hertfordshire	Powys
Isle of Wight	
Kent	**Scotland**
East Kent	Aberdeenshire
West Kent	Ayrshire
Lancashire	Dumfries and Galloway
Leicestershire and Rutland	Edinburgh and East Central Scotland
Lincolnshire	Fife and Tayside
Liverpool and Merseyside	Glasgow and West Central Scotland
London	Inverness and Moray
Greater Manchester	Lanarkshire
Norfolk	Scottish Borders
Northamptonshire	
Northumberland	**Northern Ireland**
Nottinghamshire	County Antrim and County Londonderry
Oxfordshire	County Armagh and County Down
Shropshire	
Somerset	Belfast
Staffordshire	County Tyrone and County Fermanagh
Suffolk	

How to order
Philip's maps and atlases are available from bookshops, motorway services and petrol stations. You can order direct from the publisher by phoning **0207 531 8473** or online at **www.philips-maps.co.uk**
For bulk orders only, e-mail philips@philips-maps.co.uk

Motorway with junction number	**Ambulance station**
Primary route – dual/single carriageway	**Coastguard station**
A road – dual/single carriageway	**Fire station**
B road – dual/single carriageway	**Police station**
Minor road – dual/single carriageway	**Accident and Emergency entrance to hospital**
Other minor road – dual/single carriageway	
Road under construction	**Hospital**
Tunnel, covered road	**Place of worship**
Rural track, private road or narrow road in urban area	**Information Centre** (open all year)
Gate or obstruction to traffic (restrictions may not apply at all times or to all vehicles)	**Shopping Centre**
	Parking, Park and Ride
Path, bridleway, byway open to all traffic, road used as a public path	**Post Office**
Pedestrianised area	**Camping site, caravan site**
Postcode boundaries	**Golf course, picnic site**
DY7	**Important buildings, schools, colleges, universities and hospitals**
County and unitary authority boundaries	Prim Sch
Railway, tunnel, railway under construction	**Built up area**
Tramway, tramway under construction	**Woods**
Miniature railway	**Water name** River Medway
Railway station Walsall	**River, weir, stream**
Private railway station	**Canal, lock, tunnel**
Metro station South Shields	**Water**
Tram stop, tram stop under construction	**Tidal water**
Bus, coach station	**Non-Roman antiquity** Church
	Roman antiquity ROMAN FORT

Acad	**Academy**	Inst	**Institute**	Recn Gd	**Recreation**		
Allot Gdns	**Allotments**	Ct	**Law Court**		**Ground**		
Cemy	**Cemetery**	L Ctr	**Leisure Centre**	Resr	**Reservoir**		
C Ctr	**Civic Centre**	LC	**Level Crossing**	Ret Pk	**Retail Park**		
CH	**Club House**	Liby	**Library**	Sch	**School**		
Coll	**College**	Mkt	**Market**	Sh Ctr	**Shopping Centre**		
Crem	**Crematorium**	Meml	**Memorial**	TH	**Town Hall/House**		
Ent	**Enterprise**	Mon	**Monument**	Trad Est	**Trading Estate**		
Ex H	**Exhibition Hall**	Mus	**Museum**	Univ	**University**		
Ind Est	**Industrial Estate**	Obsy	**Observatory**	W Twr	**Water Tower**		
IRB Sta	**Inshore Rescue**	Pal	**Royal Palace**	Wks	**Works**		
	Boat Station	PH	**Public House**	YH	**Youth Hostel**		

Adjoining page indicators and overlap bands
The colour of the arrow and the band indicates the scale of the adjoining or overlapping page (see scales below)

87

237

Enlarged mapping only

	Railway or bus station building
	Place of interest
	Parkland

■ The small numbers around the edges of the maps identify the 1 kilometre National Grid lines
■ The dark grey border on the inside edge of some pages indicates that the mapping does not continue onto the adjacent page

The scale of the maps on the pages numbered in blue is 4.2 cm to 1 km • 2⅔ inches to 1 mile • 1: 23810

0	¼	½	¾	1 mile
0	250 m	500 m	760 m	1 kilometre

The scale of the maps on pages numbered in red is 8.4 cm to 1 km • 5⅓ inches to 1 mile • 1: 11900

0	220 yards	440 yards	660 yards	½ mile
0	125 m	250 m	375 m	½ kilometre

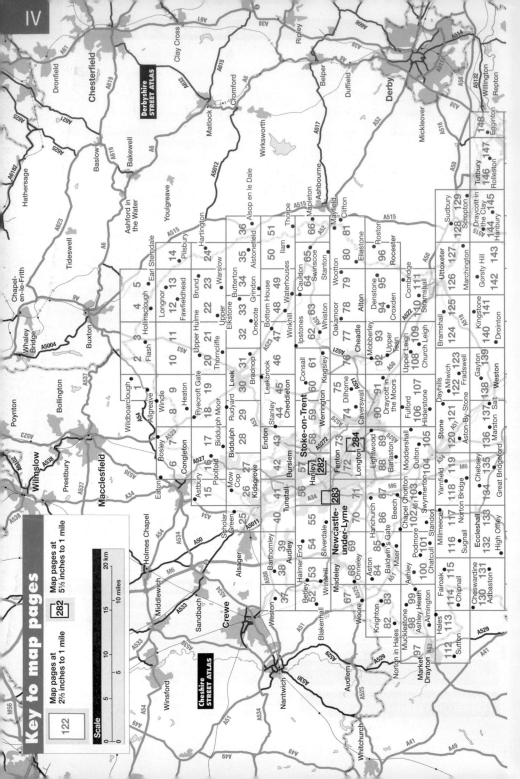

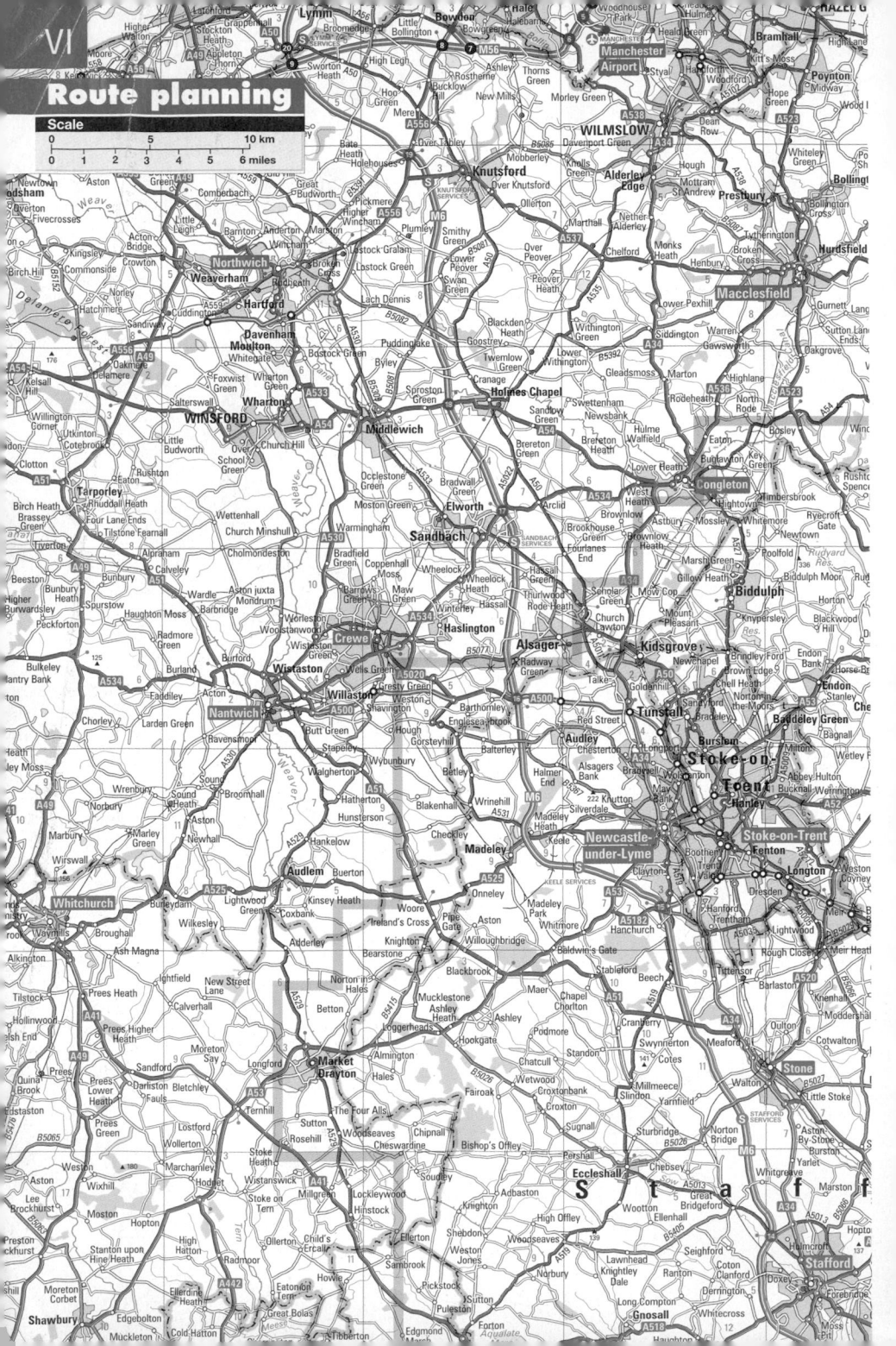

Route planning

Scale

0   5   10 km

0   1   2   3   4   5   6 miles

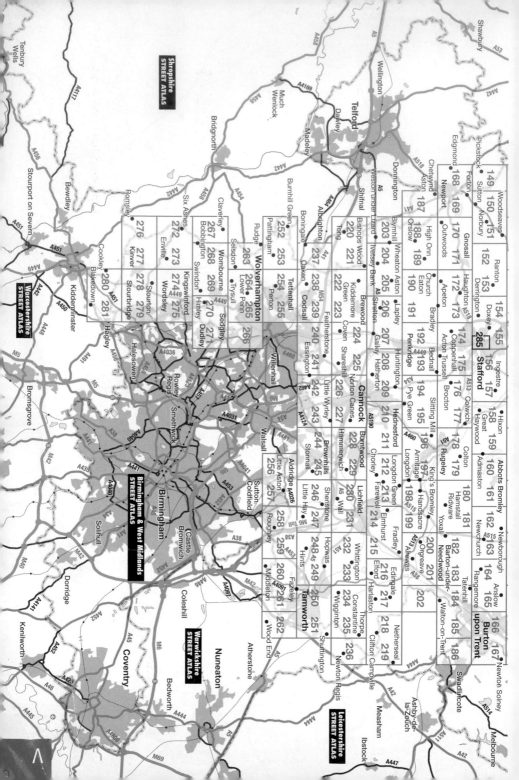

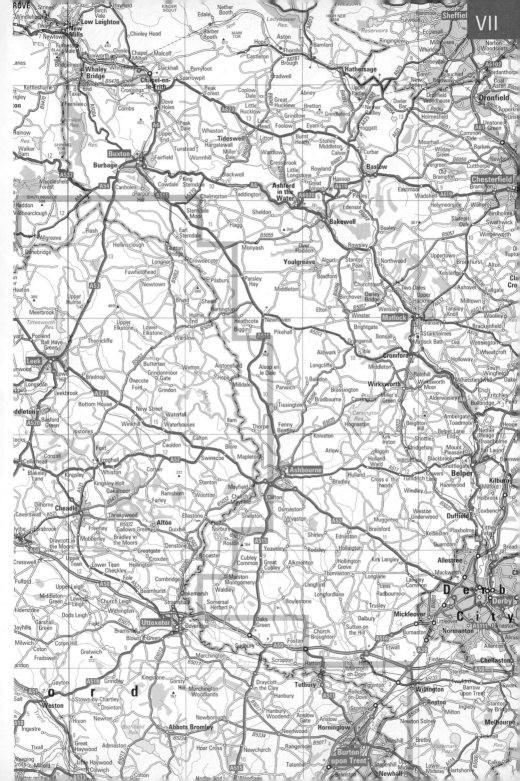

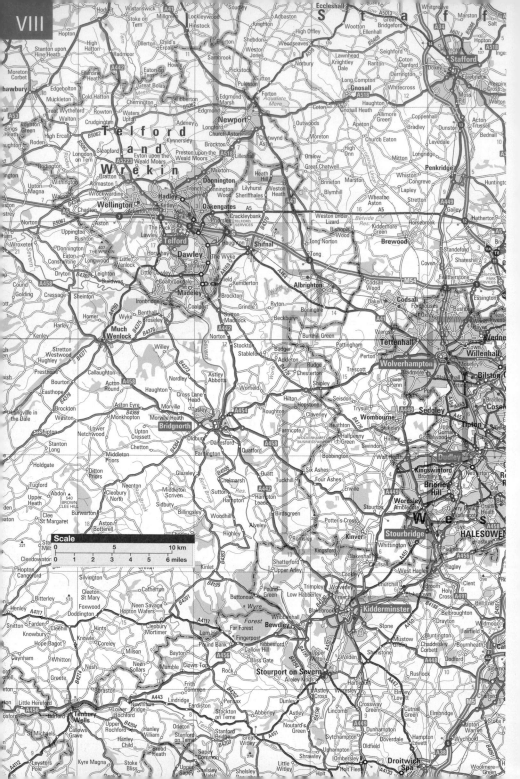

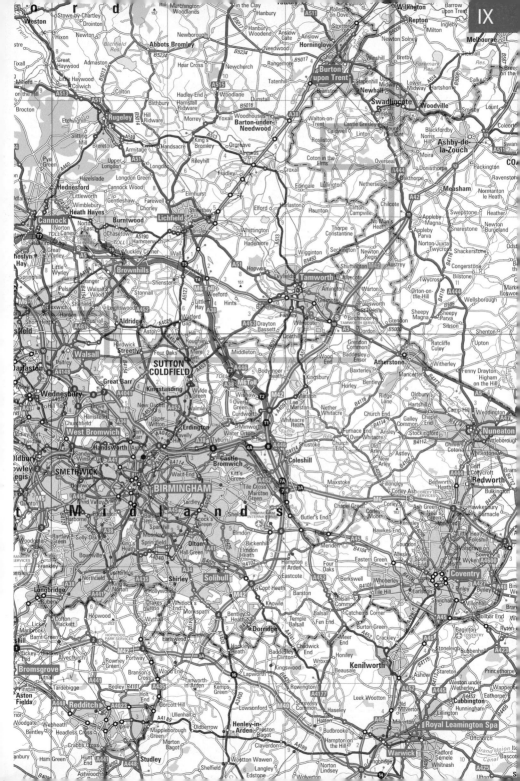

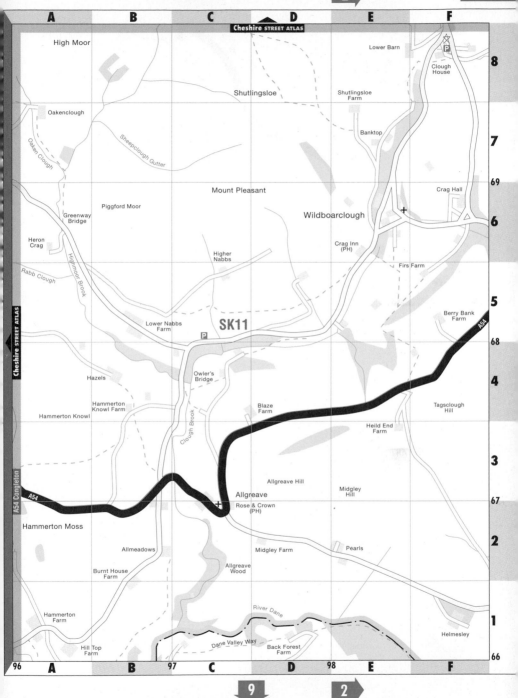

Cheshire STREET ATLAS

High Moor

Lower Barn

Clough House

8

Shutlingsloe

Shutlingsloe Farm

Oakenclough

Banktop

7

Sheepclough Gutter

69

Mount Pleasant

Crag Hall

Piggford Moor

Wildboarclough

6

Greenway Bridge

Crag Inn (PH)

Heron Crag

Firs Farm

Rabb Clough

Higher Nabbs

Highmoor Brook

Berry Bank Farm

5

Lower Nabbs Farm

SK11

68

Hazels

Owler's Bridge

4

Hammerton Knowl Farm

Blaze Farm

Tagsclough Hill

Hammerton Knowl

Clough Brook

Heild End Farm

3

Allgreave Hill

Midgley Hill

A54 Congleton

Allgreave

67

A54

Rose & Crown (PH)

Hammerton Moss

2

Allmeadows

Midgley Farm

Pearls

Burnt House Farm

Allgreave Wood

Hammerton Farm

River Dane

1

Helmesley

Hill Top Farm

Dane Valley Way

Back Forest Farm

66

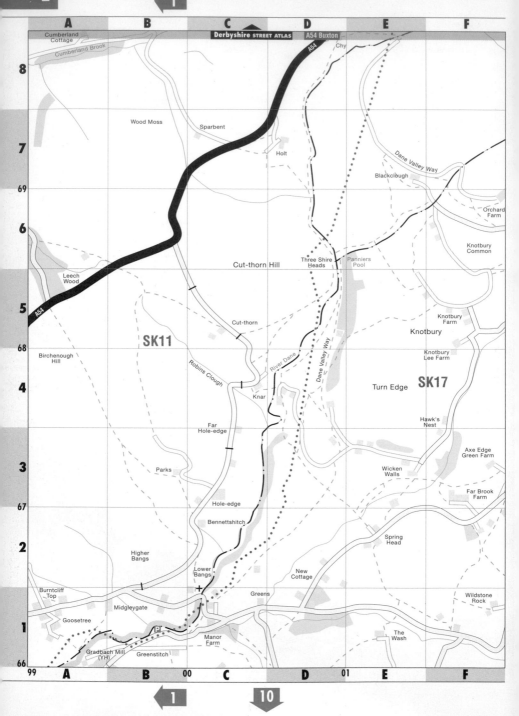

Derbyshire STREET ATLAS

A54 Buxton

Cumberland Cottage
Cumberland Brook

Wood Moss

Sparbent

Holt

Chy

Dane Valley Way

Blackclough

Orchard Farm

Knotbury Common

Leech Wood

Cut-thorn Hill

Three Shire Heads

Panniers Pool

Knotbury Farm

Knotbury

SK11

Cut-thorn

River Dane

Dane Valley Way

Knotbury Lee Farm

Birchenough Hill

Robins Clough

Knar

Turn Edge

SK17

Far Hole-edge

Hawk's Nest

Axe Edge Green Farm

Parks

Wicken Walls

Far Brook Farm

Hole-edge

Bennettshitch

Higher Bangs

Spring Head

Lower Bangs

New Cottage

Burntcliff Top

Greens

Wildstone Rock

Midgleygate

Goosetree

The Wash

Manor Farm

Gradbach Mill (YH)

Greenstitch

A54

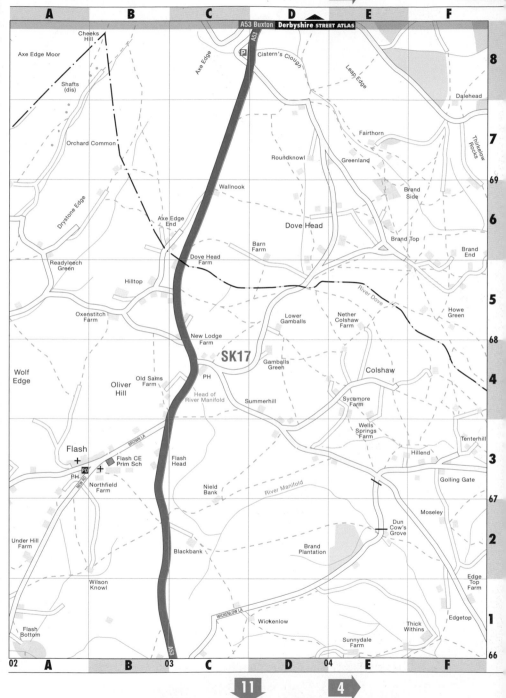

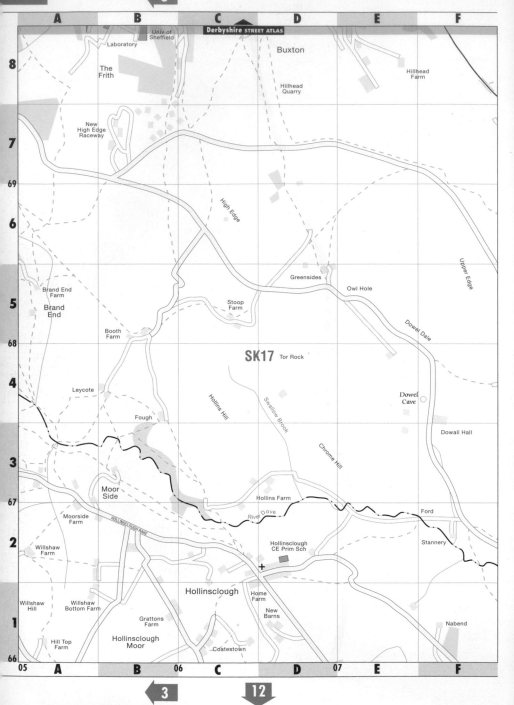

Derbyshire STREET ATLAS

A B C D E F

Univ of Sheffield
Laboratory
Buxton
The Frith
8
Hillhead Quarry
Hillhead Farm

New High Edge Raceway
7
High Edge
69

6

Brand End Farm
Greensides
Owl Hole
Brand End
5
Stoop Farm
Upper Edge
Booth Farm
68
Dowel Dale

SK17 Tor Rock

Leycote
4
Hollins Hill
Swallow Brook
Dowel Cave

Fough
Dowall Hall

Chrome Hill
3
Moor Side
Hollins Farm
67
Moorside Farm
HOLLINSCLOUGH RAKE
River Dove
Ford

Willshaw Farm
2
Hollinsclough CE Prim Sch
Stannery

Willshaw Hill
Hollinsclough
Home Farm
1
Willshaw Bottom Farm
Grattons Farm
New Barns
Nabend
Hill Top Farm
Hollinsclough Moor
Coatestown
66
05 A B 06 C D 07 E F

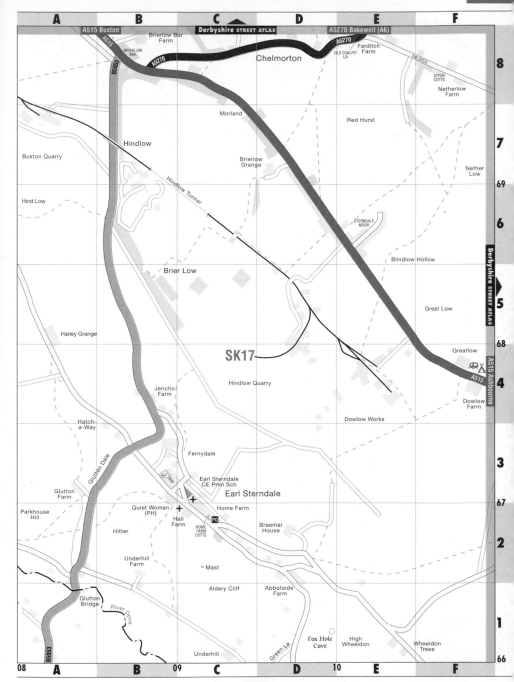

A515 Buxton
A5270 Bakewell (A6)

A | B | C | D | E | F

Brierlow Bar Farm
Chelmorton
A5270
Farditch Farm
OLD COALPIT LA
THE DITCH
DITCH COTTS

8

BRIERLOW BAR
A5270
Netherlow Farm

Morland
Red Hurst

Hindlow
7

Buxton Quarry
Brierlow Grange
Nether Low

Hindlow Tunnel
69

Hind Low
6

STERNDALE MOOR

Blindlow Hollow

Brier Low
Great Low

5

Harley Grange
Greatlow
68

SK17
4

Jericho Farm
Hindlow Quarry
Dowlow Farm

Hatch-a-Way
Dowlow Works

Fernydale
3

Glutton Dale
Earl Sterndale CE Prim Sch
67

Glutton Farm
Earl Sterndale
2

Parkhouse Hill
Quiet Woman (PH)
Hall Farm
Home Farm
PO
HOME FARM COTTS
Braemar House

Hitter

Underhill Farm
Mast

Aldery Cliff
Abbotside Farm

Glutton Bridge
River Dove
1

B5053
Underhill
Green La
Fox Hole Cave
High Wheeldon
Wheeldon Trees
66

08 | A | B | 09 | C | D | 10 | E | F

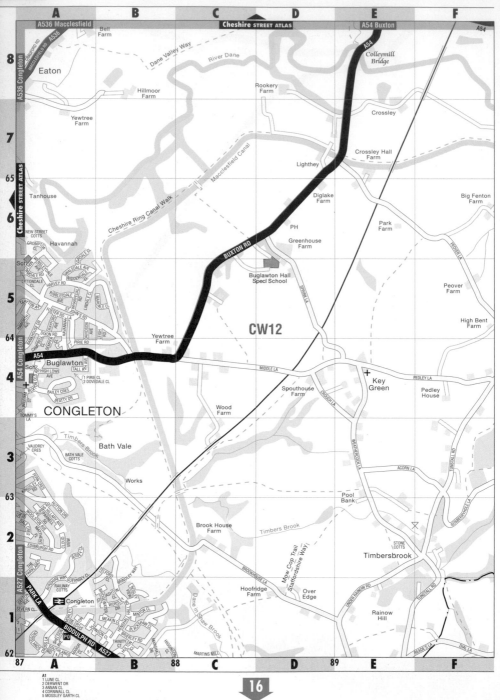

A536 Macclesfield

Cheshire STREET ATLAS

A54 Buxton

A54

Colleymill Bridge

Eaton

Bell Farm

Dane Valley Way

River Dane

Hillmoor Farm

Rookery Farm

Crossley

Yewtree Farm

Crossley Hall Farm

Lighthey

Tanhouse

Macclesfield Canal

Diglake Farm

Big Fenton Farm

Cheshire Ring Canal Walk

New Street Cotts

CROMPTON CL

Havannah

PH

Greenhouse Farm

Park Farm

Peover Farm

Sch

BUXTON RD

Buglawton Hall Specl School

SPRINK LA

High Bent Farm

CW12

Yewtree Farm

A54

Buglawton

Sch

MIDDLE LA

Key Green

PEDLEY LA

Pedley House

CONGLETON

Spouthouse Farm

CROSS LA

Wood Farm

Bath Vale

Timbers Brook

WEATHERBROOK LA

ACORN LA

TUNSTALL RD

Works

Pool Bank

Brook House Farm

Timbers Brook

STONE COTTS

A527 Congleton

PARK LA

Congleton

BIDDULPH RD

A527

Mow Cop Trail

Staffordshire Way

BROOKHOUSE LA

Hoofridge Farm

Over Edge

Dane in Shaw Brook

UNDER RAINOW RD

TUNSTALL RD

Timbersbrook

Rainow Hill

Martins Mill

READES LA

DIAL LA

A1
1 LUNE CL
2 DERWENT DR
3 ANNAN CL
4 CORNWALL CL
5 MOSSLEY GARTH CL

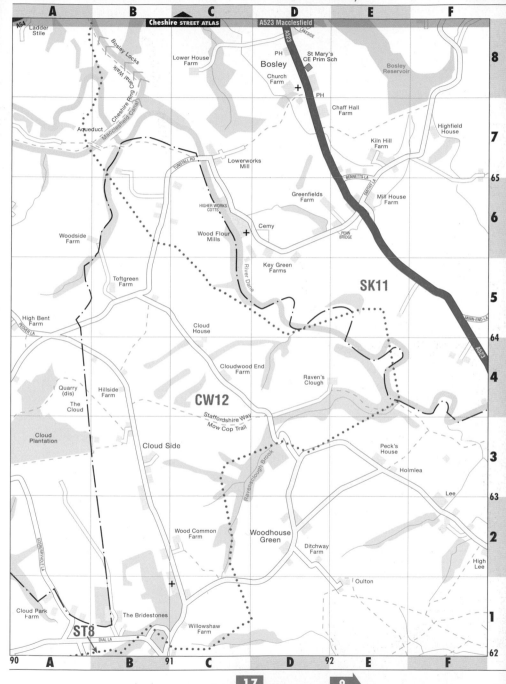

Cheshire STREET ATLAS

A523 Macclesfield

Map labels:

Ladder Stile

Bosley Locks

Lower House Farm

Bosley

St Mary's CE Prim Sch

Bosley Reservoir

Church Farm

PH

PH

Chaff Hall Farm

Highfield House

Aqueduct

Cheshire Ring Canal Walk

Macclesfield Canal

Kiln Hill Farm

TUNSTALL RD

Lowerworks Mill

BENNETTS LA

SMITH LA

Mill House Farm

Woodside Farm

HIGHER WORKS COTTS

Greenfields Farm

Wood Flour Mills

Cemy

PENN BRIDGE

Toftgreen Farm

River Dane

Key Green Farms

SK11

High Bent Farm

PEXTER LA

Cloud House

Cloudwood End Farm

Raven's Clough

A523

MINN-END-LA

Quarry (dis)

Hillside Farm

CW12

Peck's House

The Cloud

Staffordshire Way

Mow Cop Trail

Holmlea

Cloud Plantation

Cloud Side

Ravensclough Brook

Lee

Wood Common Farm

Woodhouse Green

Ditchway Farm

High Lee

GOSBERRYHOLE LA

Oulton

Cloud Park Farm

ST8

DIAL LA

The Bridestones

Willowshaw Farm

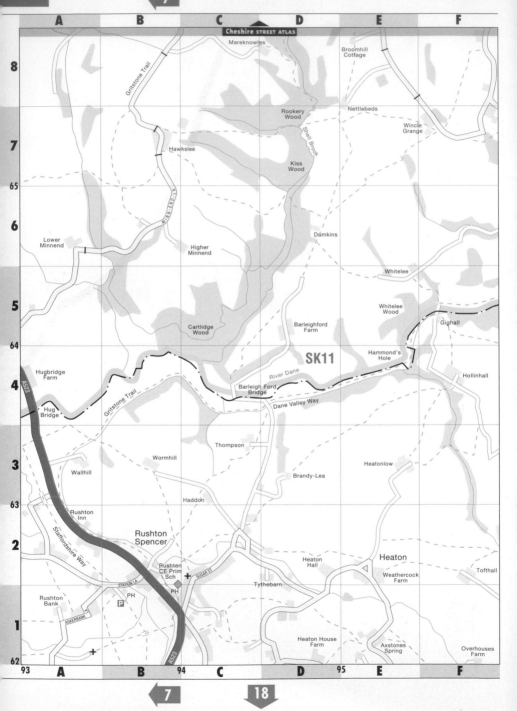

A B C D E F

Mareknowles

Broomhill
Cottage

Gritstone Trail

Rookery
Wood

Nettlebeds

Wincle
Grange

8

Hawkslee

Shell Brook

Kiss
Wood

7

65

MILL END LA

Dumkins

6

Lower
Minnend

Higher
Minnend

Whitelee

5

Whitelee
Wood

Cartlidge
Wood

Barleighford
Farm

Gighall

64

Hammond's
Hole

SK11

Hollinhall

Hugbridge
Farm

River Dane

Gritstone Trail

Barleigh Ford
Bridge

Hug
Bridge

Dane Valley Way

4

A523

Thompson

Wormhill

Heatonlow

3

Wallhill

Brandy-Lea

63

Haddon

Rushton
Inn

Rushton
Spencer

Staffordshire Way

2

Heaton

Heaton
Hall

Weathercock
Farm

Tofthall

Rushton
CE Prim
Sch

Rushton
Bank

STATION LA

PH

P

PH

SUGAR ST

Tythebarn

Heaton House
Farm

Axstones
Spring

Overhouses
Farm

ASKERBANK

1

62

A523

93 A 94 B C 95 D E F

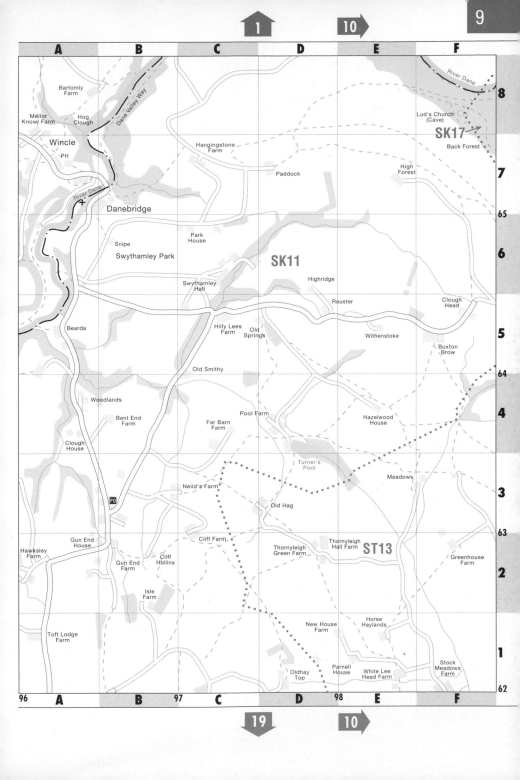

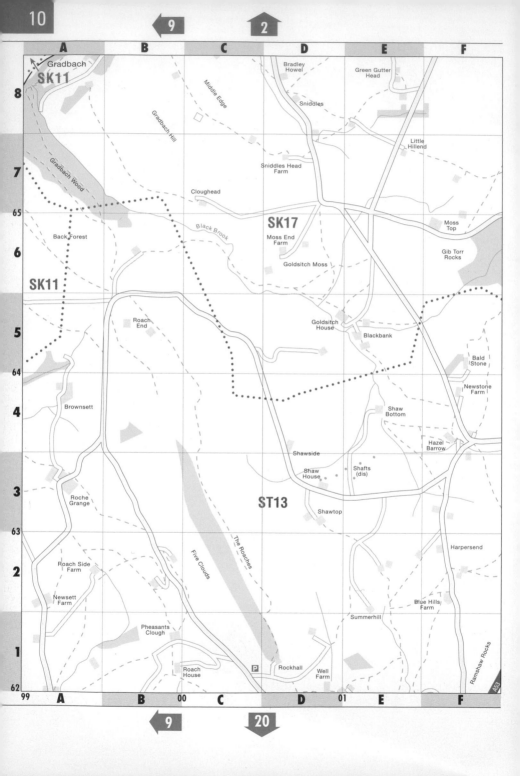

A B C D E F

Gradbach
SK11

8

Bradley
Howel

Green Gutter
Head

Middle Edge

Gradbach Hill

Sniddles

Little
Hillend

7

Gradbach Wood

Sniddles Head
Farm

65

Cloughead

Black Brook

SK17

Moss
Top

Back Forest

Moss End
Farm

6

Gib Torr
Rocks

Goldsitch Moss

SK11

5

Roach
End

Goldsitch
House

Blackbank

64

Bald
Stone

Newstone
Farm

4

Brownsett

Shaw
Bottom

Hazel
Barrow

Shawside

Shaw
House

Shafts
(dis)

3

Roche
Grange

ST13

Shawtop

63

Harpersend

Five Clouds

The Roaches

2

Roach Side
Farm

Newsett
Farm

Blue Hills
Farm

Summerhill

1

Pheasants
Clough

Ramshaw Rocks

P   Rockhall

Roach
House

Well
Farm

62

99   A   B   00   C   D   01   E   F   A53

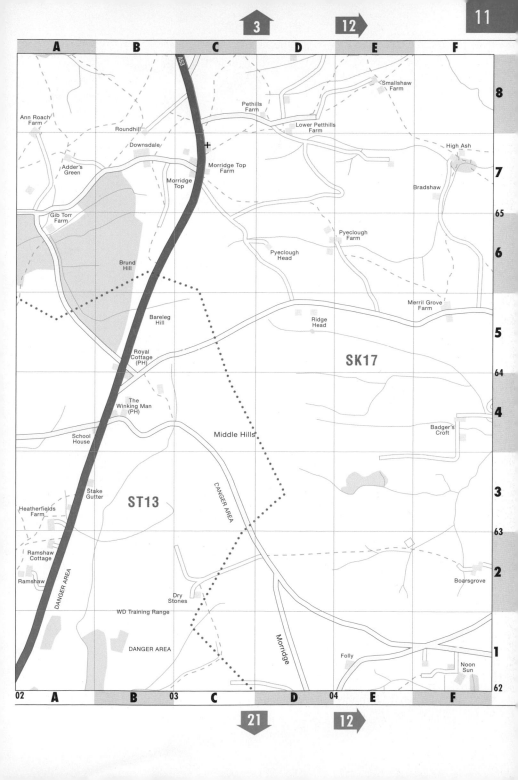

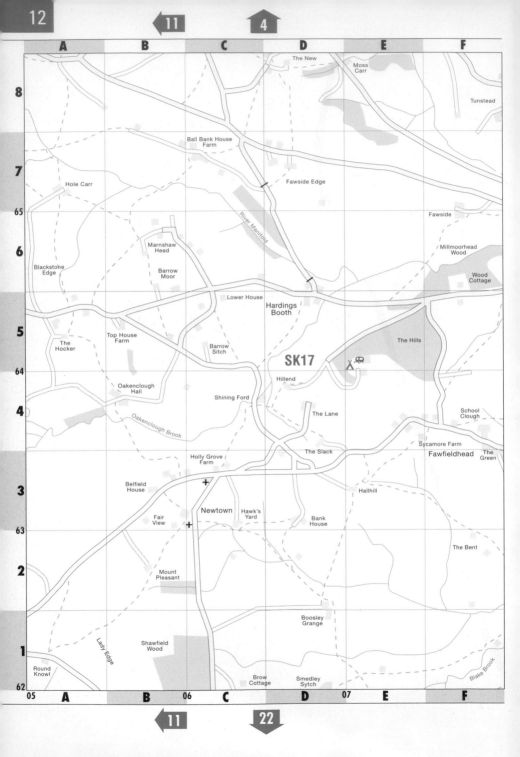

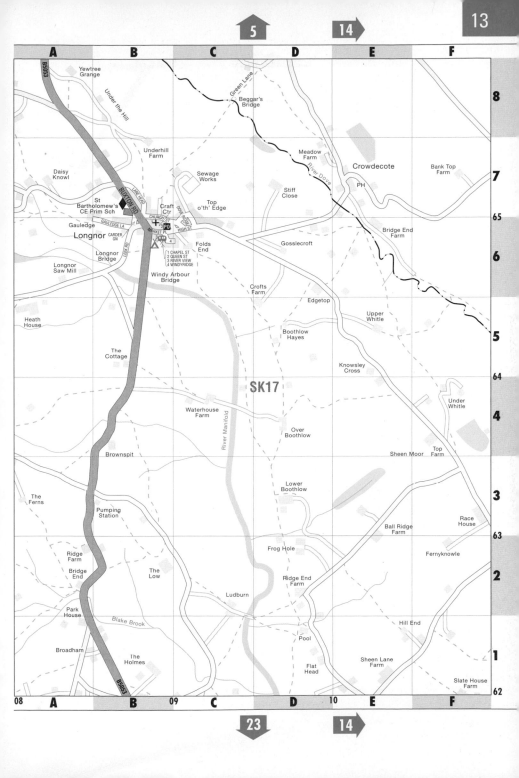

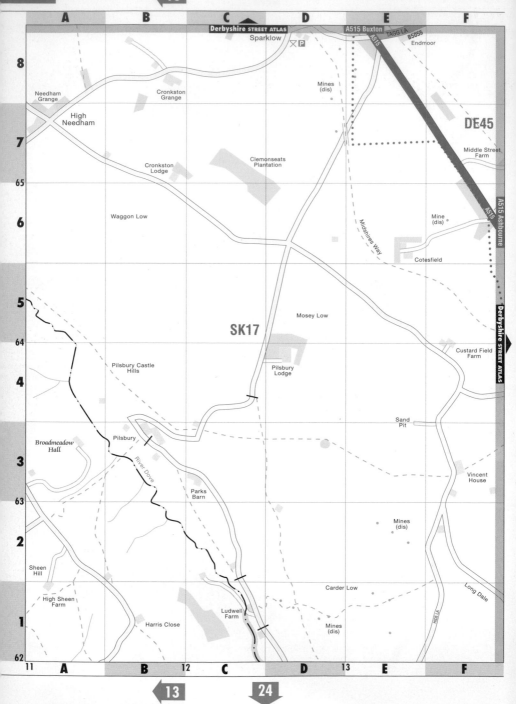

Derbyshire STREET ATLAS

Sparklow

A515 Buxton
TAGG LA
B5055
Endmoor

DE45

8

Needham Grange
High Needham
Cronkston Grange
Mines (dis)

Middle Street Farm

7

65

Cronkston Lodge
Clemonseats Plantation

Mine (dis)

6

Waggon Low

Midcshures Way

Cotesfield

A515 Ashbourne

A515

5

Mosey Low

SK17

Derbyshire STREET ATLAS

64

Pilsbury Castle Hills
Pilsbury Lodge
Custard Field Farm

4

Broadmeadow Hall
Pilsbury
Sand Pit

3

River Dove
Parks Barn
Vincent House

63

2

Sheen Hill
Mines (dis)

High Sheen Farm
Harris Close
Ludwell Farm
Carder Low
Long Dale

1

Mines (dis)
HIDE LA

62

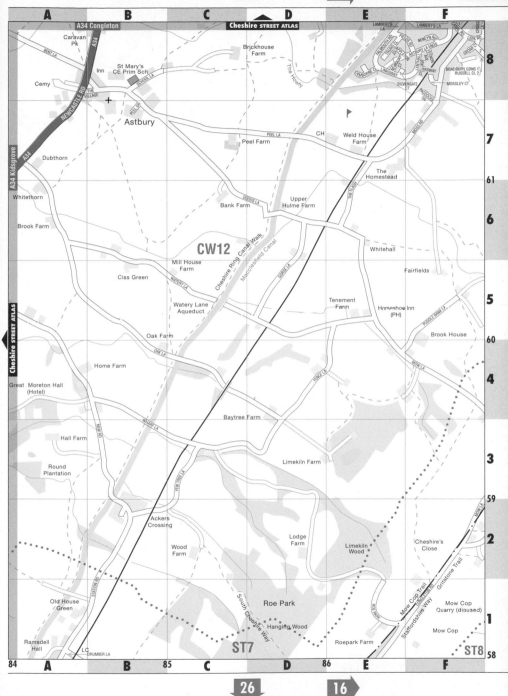

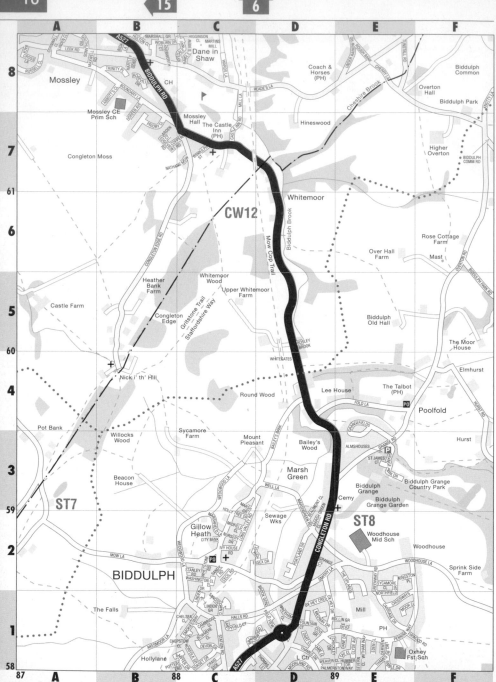

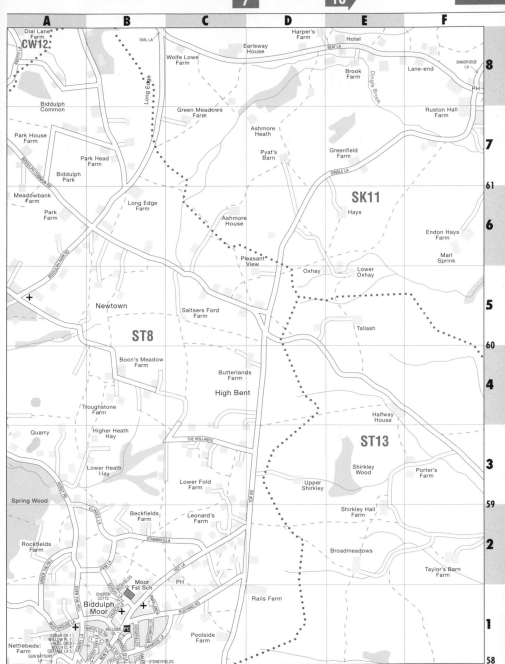

	A	B	C	D	E	F

ASKERBANK LA

A523

Mast

Overhouses Farm

Broad Moss Farm

8

Ryecroft Gate

New House Farm

Fair Edge Hill

BEAT LA

Ryecroft Farm

Rad Brook

Moss Cottage

Fold Farm

Intakes

Rotten Hole

Dingle Brook

Wolf-Dale

7

61

Lee House

High Lee Farm

Oldhill

Willott's Hill

Fairboroughs

Leeside

Barnswood Farm

6

Staffordshire Way

Barns Lee

SK11

Barnswood Scout Camp

Fairboroughs Wood

5

Garage

Blackwood Farm

60

BEACLIFFE RD

Cliffe Park

4

Rudyard Resr

Hunt House Farm

Hunthouse Plantation

A523

Birch Trees Farm

Cliffe Park Lodge

Rea Cliffe Wood

The Lady of the Lake

3

ST13

59

Brownslow Farm

Rea Cliffe Farm

Rudyard Lake Steam Rly

Rudyard Manor

Horton Brook

2

Coney Greave

St Michael's CE Fst Sch

Horton Lodge Com Specl Sch

RUDYARD VALE CVN PK

Back Wood

Greentree Farm

GREEN LA

Dairy House Bank

Dairy House

HEATH HOUSE LA

THE CRESENT

Rudyard Lake Visitors Ctr

Willgate Farm

1

Heath House

LAKE RD

Hotel

B5331 RUDYARD RD B5331

58

| 93 | A | B | 94 | C | D | 95 | E | F |

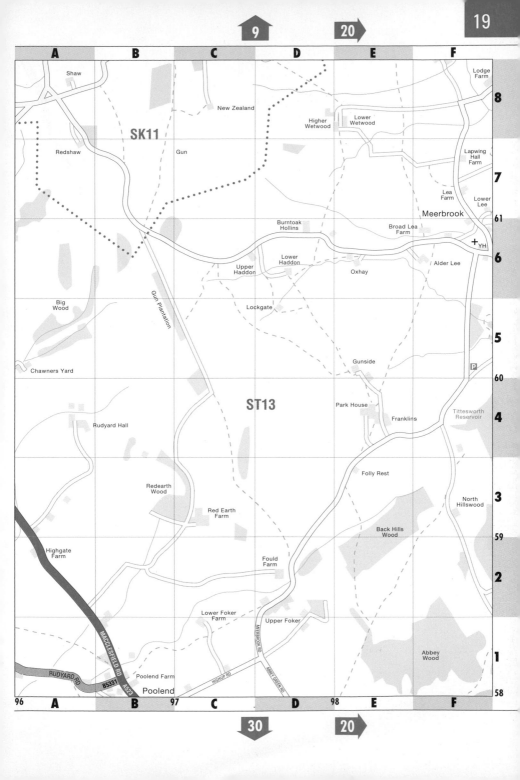

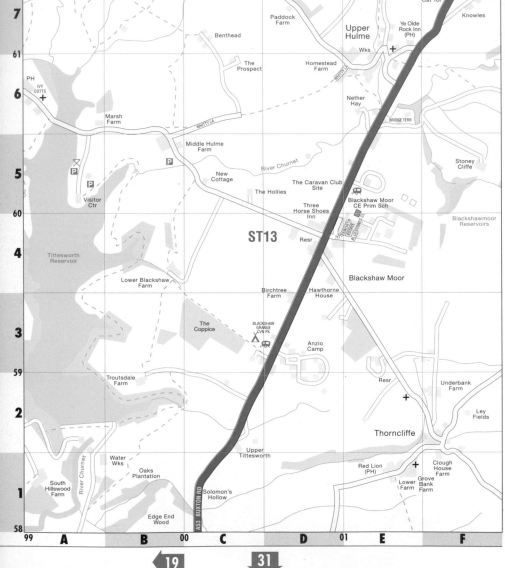

20

19 31

Greenlane

Lodge Farm
Rose Cottage

Windygates

Frith Bottom

Hen Cloud

Far House

The Roaches House

Ferny Khowl

Ramshaw Rocks

A53

Naychurch

8

Dains Mill

Cat Tor

7

Paddock Farm

Benthead

Upper Hulme

Ye Olde Rock Inn (PH)

Knowles

61

The Prospect

Homestead Farm

Wks

PH
IVY COTTS

6

Nether Hay

BRIDGE TERR

Marsh Farm

WHITTY LA

WHITTY LA

River Churnet

Stoney Cliffe

5

Middle Hulme Farm

P

P

P

New Cottage

The Hollies

The Caravan Club Site

Blackshaw Moor CE Prim Sch

Blackshawmoor Reservoirs

Visitor Ctr

60

Three Horse Shoes Inn

TITTESWORTH

BLUESTONE'S CL

ST13

Resr

4

Tittesworth Reservoir

Lower Blackshaw Farm

Blackshaw Moor

Birchtree Farm

Hawthorne House

3

The Coppice

BLACKSHAW GRANGE CVN PK

Anzio Camp

Troutsdale Farm

Resr

Underbank Farm

59

Ley Fields

2

Thorncliffe

River Churnet

Water Wks

Oaks Plantation

Upper Tittesworth

Red Lion (PH)

Clough House Farm

South Hillswood Farm

Solomon's Hollow

A53 BUXTON RD

Lower Farm

Grove Bank Farm

1

Edge End Wood

58

99 A 00 B C 00 D 01 E F

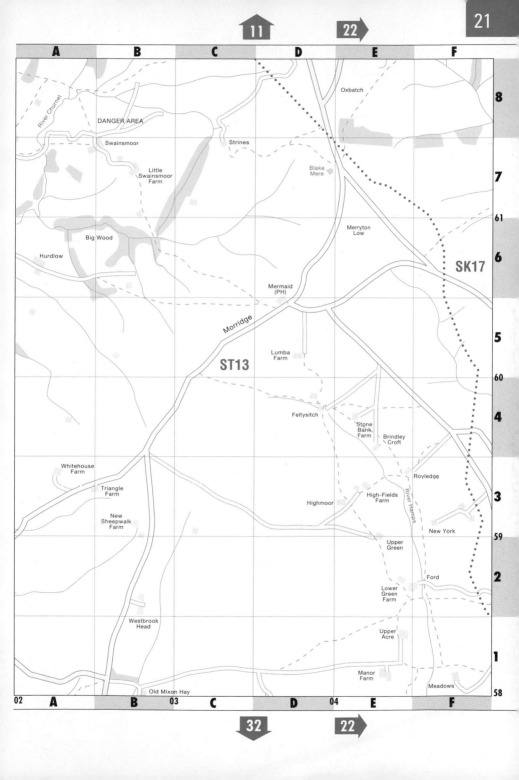

21
12

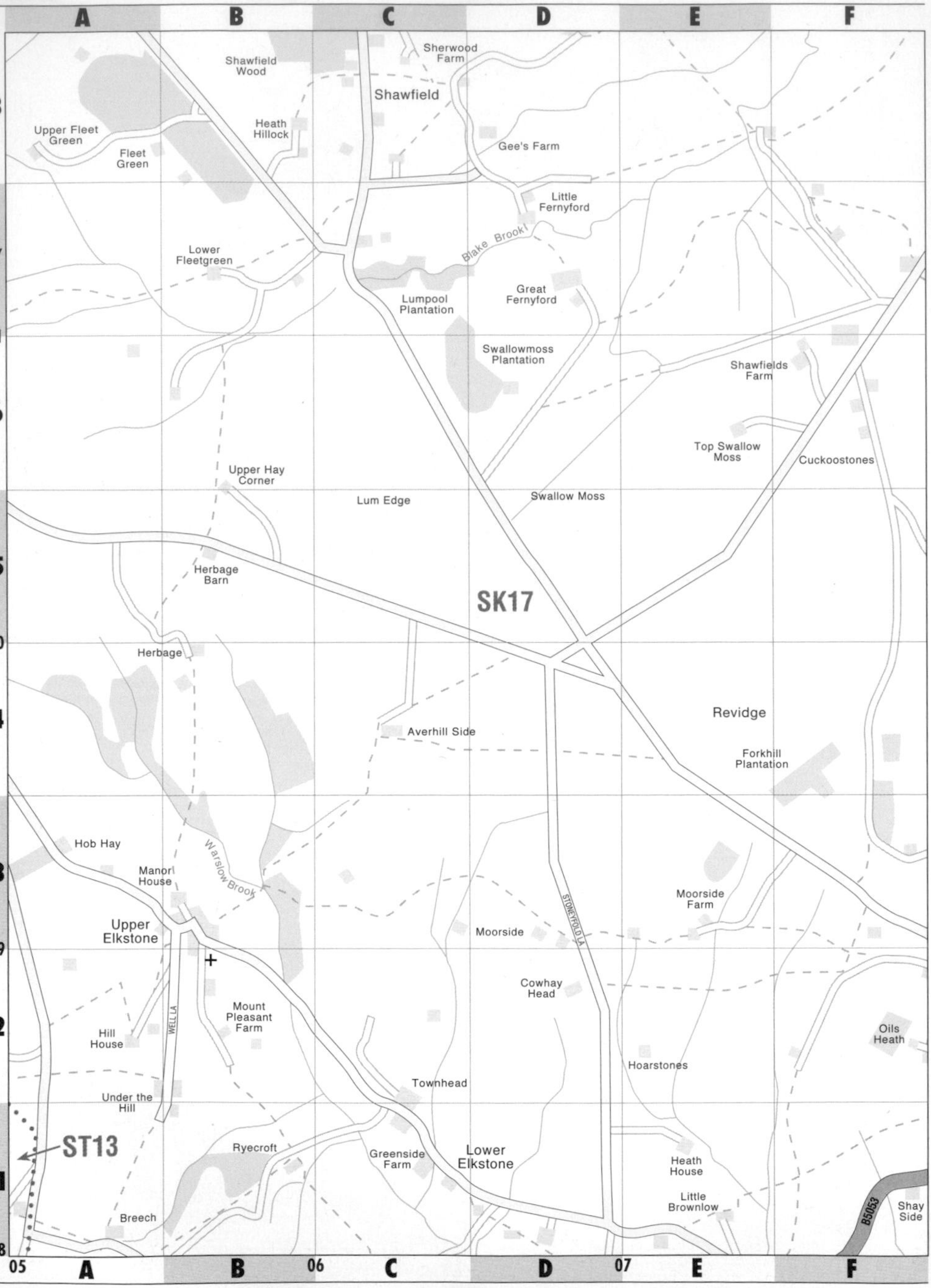

A **B** **C** **D** **E** **F**

8

Upper Fleet Green
Fleet Green
Shawfield Wood
Heath Hillock
Shawfield
Sherwood Farm
Gee's Farm

7

Lower Fleetgreen
Blake Brook
Lumpool Plantation
Little Fernyford
Great Fernyford

61

Swallowmoss Plantation
Shawfields Farm

6

Upper Hay Corner
Top Swallow Moss
Cuckoostones

Lum Edge
Swallow Moss

5

Herbage Barn

SK17

60

Herbage

Revidge

4

Averhill Side
Forkhill Plantation

Hob Hay
Warslow Brook
Manor House

3

Moorside Farm

Upper Elkstone
Moorside
STONEYWELL LA

59

Cowhay Head

2

Hill House
WELL LA
Mount Pleasant Farm
Hoarstones
Oils Heath

Under the Hill
Townhead

ST13

Ryecroft
Greenside Farm
Lower Elkstone
Heath House
B5053

1

Breech
Little Brownlow
Shay Side

58

05 **A** **B** 06 **C** **D** 07 **E** **F**

21
33

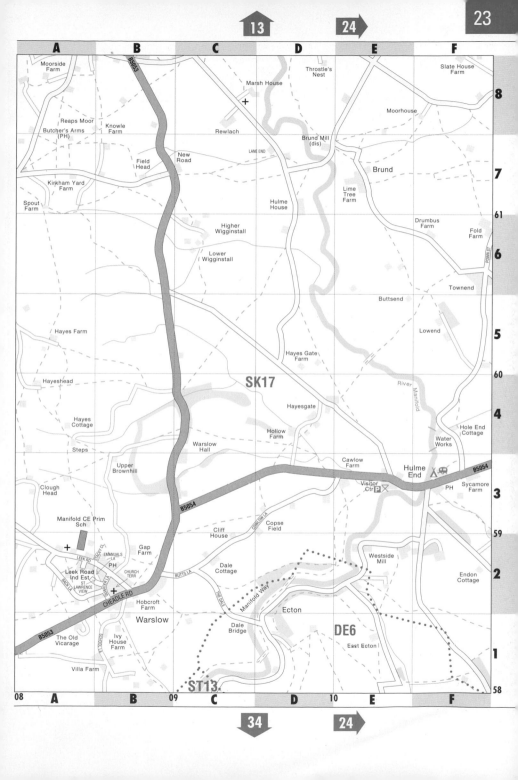

A B C D E F

8

Sprink

Manor Farm

Bank Top Farm

Madge Dale

Long Dale

7

Palace Farm

PO

Sheen

Lower House

Hide La

Walpot Lane

61

PH

Moat Hall

B5054

6

Townend

Bridge-end

Digmer Farm

Hartington Dale

Newfield

Crakelow

Market Pl

Harbott's La

Factory

Stonewell La

Church St

Hartington CE Prim Sch

Hartington Hall YH

PH

PO

5

Hartington

Parsons Cl

Hall Bank

P

High Cross

Mast

SK17

Highfield La

60

Scaldersitch

Banktop

Mill La

Lower Barn

Crossland Sides

4

The Raikes

Hartington Bridge

River Dove

Reynards La

Raikes Farm

Pennilow

B5054

3

Lower Hurst Farm

Staden Barn

Brighton

59

Tower

Beresford Dale

Upper Hurst

Beresford Cottage

2

Harecops

Barracks Farm

Beresford La

Beresford Lane Farm

1

Archford Moor Farm

Wolfscote Hill

Archford Moor

Beresford Lane

Field House Farm

DE6

Wolfscote Grange

58

11 A   B   12   C   D   13   E   F

Derbyshire STREET ATLAS

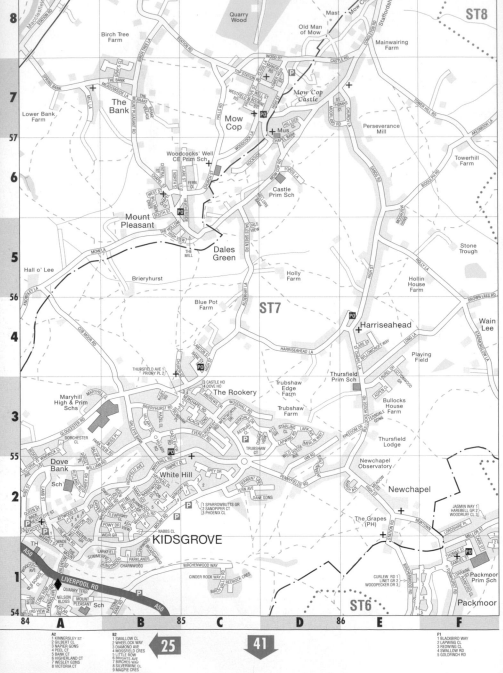

ST8

ST7

ST6

KIDSGROVE

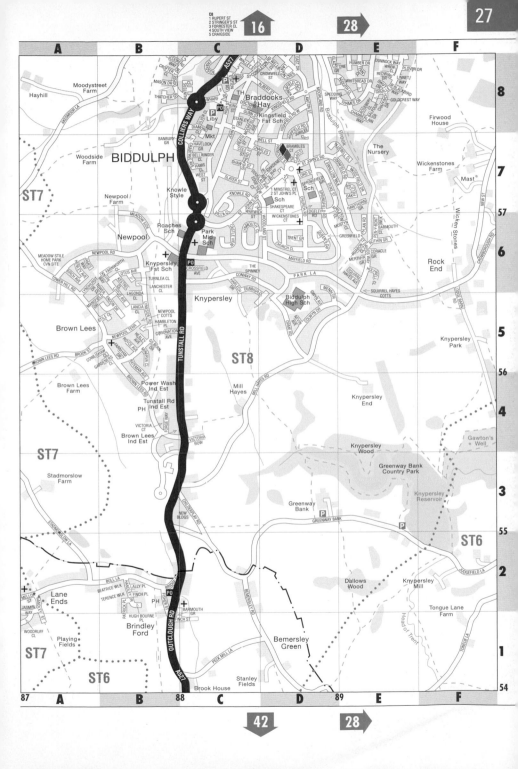

16
28
42
28

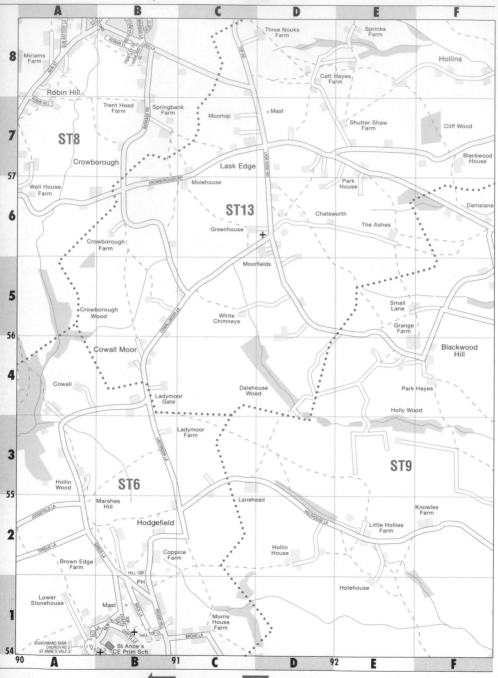

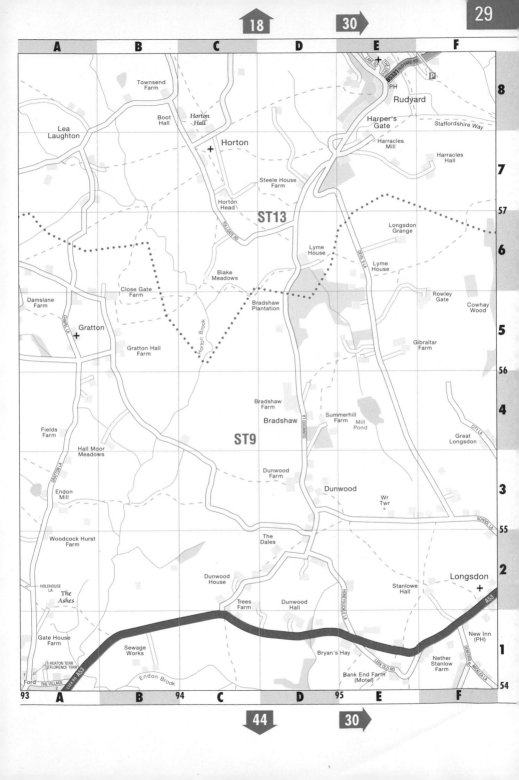

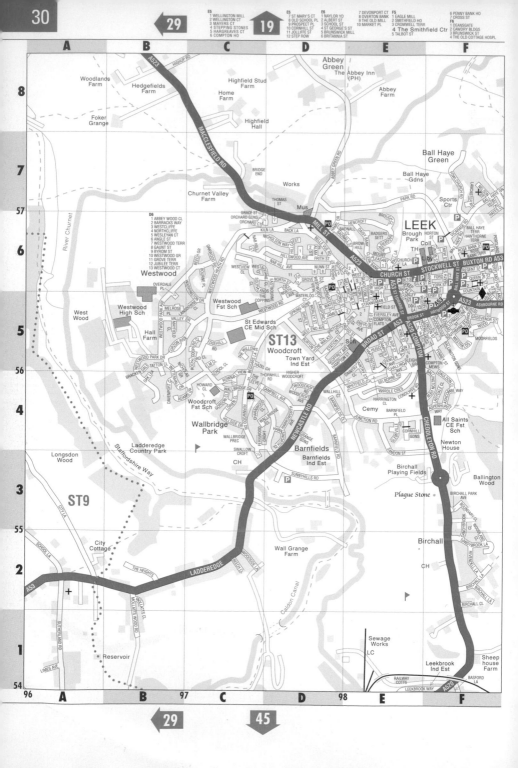

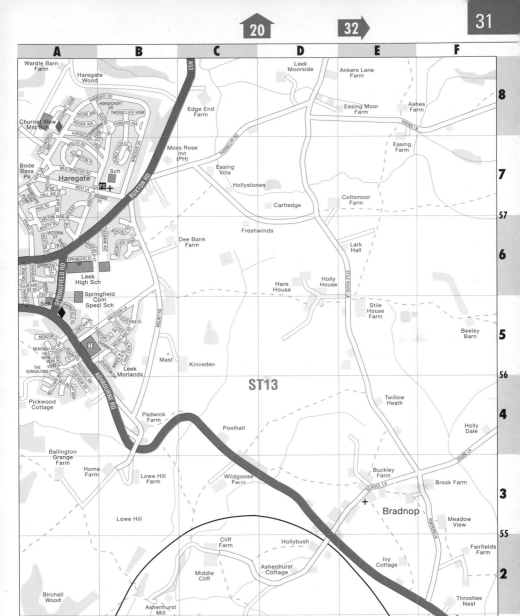

A **B** **C** **D** **E** **F**

8

EASING LA.

Old Mixon Hay

Cave

Westbrook

New Mixon Hay

7

Mixon Grange

Mixon Mines

57

Dunlea Farm

Mixon

Morridge

Wormlow Farm

6

Dale House

Harvey Gate

Newhouse Farm

River Hamps

White Lea Farm

5

Wellington Farm

Rue Hayes Farm

ST13

56

High Cross

Waterhouse

4

Onecote Lane Head

DOUSE LA.

Cemy

Onecote Grange

Intake Farm

3

Onecote Lane End

+

B5053

55

Onecote

+

Newhouse Farm

Moor Top

2

Cliffhead

Weatherworth Manor Farm

Willowmeadow

Birdsgrove Farm

Lower Moorside Farm

Moorside

WILL LA.

Hopping Head

Garstones

Slate House

New Farm

MORRIDGE SIDE

DOUSE LA.

1

Town Field Farm

A523

Astonsitch

Hobmeadows

B5053

Lane-end

54

A 02 **B** 03 **C** **D** 04 **E** **F**

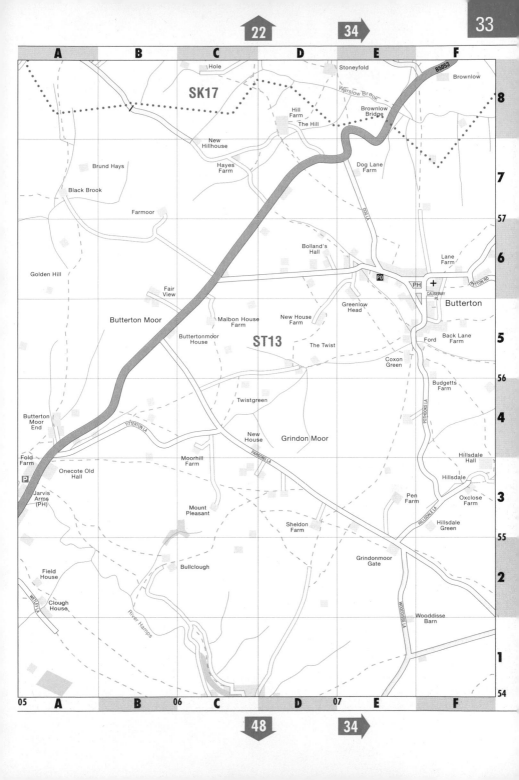

A B C D E F

SK17

Hole
Stoneyfold
Brownlow
B5053
Warslow Brook
Brownlow
8
Hill Farm
Brownlow Bridge
The Hill
New Hillhouse
Brund Hays
Hayes Farm
Dog Lane Farm
7
Black Brook
Farmoor
57
Bolland's Hall
Lane Farm
6
Golden Hill
PO
PH
+
Fair View
CAUSEWAY PL
Butterton
Greenlow Head
Butterton Moor
Malbon House Farm
New House Farm
Back Lane Farm
Buttertonmoor House
ST13
The Twist
Ford
5
Coxon Green
Budgetts Farm
56
Twistgreen
Butterton Moor End
LITTERTON LA
New House
Grindon Moor
Hillsdale Hall
4
Fold Farm
Moorhill Farm
PARSONS LA
Hillsdale
Hillsdale LA
P
Jarvis Arms (PH)
Pen Farm
Oxclose Farm
3
Onecote Old Hall
Mount Pleasant
Hillsdale Green
Sheldon Farm
55
Field House
Bullclough
Grindonmoor Gate
2
Clough House
WELSEY LA
River Hamps
WOODDISSE LA
Wooddisse Barn
1
54

05 A B 06 C D 07 E F

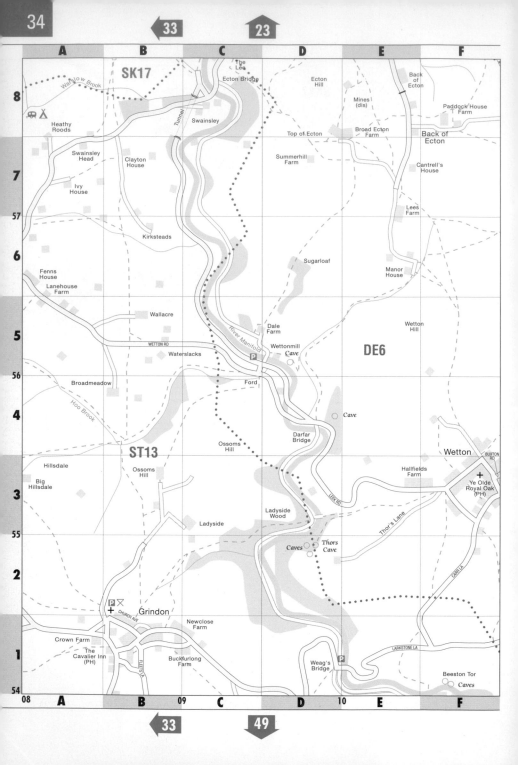

SK17

Watslow Brook

Heathy Roods

Swainsley Head

Clayton House

Ivy House

Kirksteads

Fenns House

Lanehouse Farm

Wallacre

WETTON RD

Waterslacks

Broadmeadow

Hoo Brook

ST13

Hillsdale

Big Hillsdale

Ossoms Hill

Ladyside

Crown Farm

The Cavalier Inn (PH)

Grindon

CHURCH AVE

FLEET S A

Newclose Farm

Buckfurlong Farm

The Lee

Ecton Bridge

Tunnel

Swainsley

River Manifold

Dale Farm

Ford

Ossoms Hill

Darfar Bridge

Ladyside Wood

Caves

Thors Cave

Weag's Bridge

Ecton Hill

Mines (dis)

Top of Ecton

Summerhill Farm

Sugarloaf

Wettonmill Cave

Cave

Back of Ecton

Paddock House Farm

Back of Ecton

Broad Ecton Farm

Cantrell's House

Lees Farm

Manor House

Wetton Hill

DE6

LEEK RD

Wetton

BUXTON RD

Hallfields Farm

Ye Olde Royal Oak (PH)

Thor's Lane

CARR LA

LARKSTONE LA

Beeston Tor

Caves

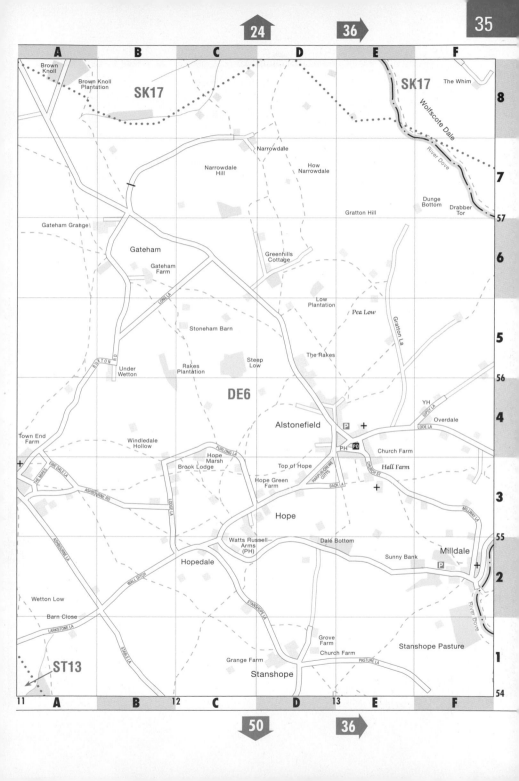

8

7

57

6

5

56

4

3

55

2

1

54

Brown Knoll

Brown Knoll Plantation

SK17

The Whim

SK17

Wolfscote Dale

River Dove

Narrowdale

Narrowdale Hill

How Narrowdale

Dunge Bottom

Drabber Tor

Gratton Hill

Gateham Grange

Gateham

Greenhills Cottage

Gateham Farm

LONG LA

Low Plantation

Pea Low

Gratton La

Stoneham Barn

Under Wetton

Rakes Plantation

Steep Low

The Rakes

BUXTON RD

DE6

YH

GIPSY LA

Overdale

LODE LA

Town End Farm

Windledale Hollow

Alstonefield

P

Church Farm

THE MIRES

GWE DALE LA

Hope Marsh

Brook Lodge

FURLONG LA

Top of Hope

PH PO

HARPUR CREWE COTTS

CHURCH ST

Hall Farm

MILLWAY LA

ASHBOURNE RD

LODGE LA

Hope Green Farm

BACK LA

Hope

Watts Russell Arms (PH)

Dale Bottom

Sunny Bank

Milldale

ASHBOURNE LA

WALL DITCH

Hopedale

P

River Dove

Wetton Low

Barn Close

STAKE LA

STANSHOPE LA

Grove Farm

Church Farm

Stanshope Pasture

LARKSTONE LA

ST13

Grange Farm

Stanshope

PASTURE LA

11

A

B

12

C

D

13

E

F

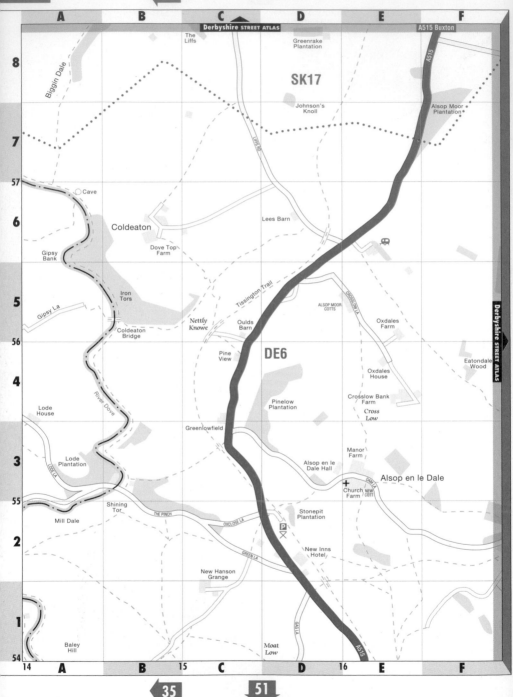

A B C D E F

8

7

57

6

5

56

4

55

3

2

54

1

SK17

A515 Buxton

A515

The Liffs

Greenrake Plantation

Johnson's Knoll

Alsop Moor Plantation

Biggin Dale

Cave

Coldeaton

Lees Barn

Gipsy Bank

Dove Top Farm

Iron Tors

Gipsy La

Tissington Trail

ALSOP MOOR COTTS

CROSSLOW LA

Oxdales Farm

Nettly Knowe

Oulds Barn

DE6

Coldeaton Bridge

Pine View

Oxdales House

Eatondale Wood

River Dove

Lode House

Pinelow Plantation

Crosslow Bank Farm

Cross Low

Greenlowfield

Manor Farm

Lode Plantation

LODE LA

Alsop en le Dale Hall

Alsop en le Dale

Church Farm

NEW COTT

DGMT LA

Shining Tor

THE PINCH

OXCLOSE LA

Stonepit Plantation

Mill Dale

GREEN LA

New Inns Hotel

New Hanson Grange

Baley Hill

Moat Low

DAG LA

A515

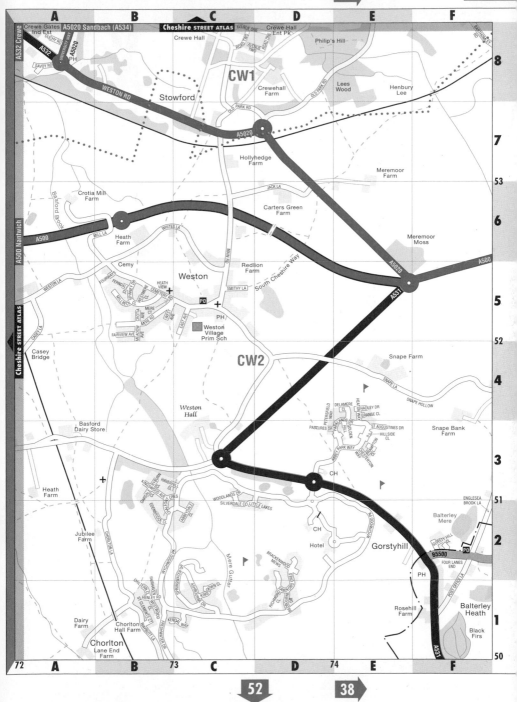

38

Cheshire STREET ATLAS

Crewe Gates Ind Est

A5020 Sandbach (A534)

A532 Crewe

DUCHY RD
UNIVERSITY WAY
A532
A5020
PH
SAVOY RD

Crewe Hall
AVENUE ONE
Crewe Hall Ent Pk.
Philip's Hill

CW1

WESTON RD

Stowford

ROAD ONE
AVENUE TWO
ROAD TWO
OLD PARK RD
DLE? PARK RD

Crewehall Farm

Lees Wood

Henbury Lee

A5020

Hollyhedge Farm

Meremoor Farm

53

Bagsford Brook

A500 Nantwich

Crotia Mill Farm

JACK LA

Carters Green Farm

Meremoor Moss

6

A500

MILL LA
WHITES LA

Heath Farm

Cemy

MAIN RD

Redlion Farm

South Cheshire Way

A5020

A500

Cheshire STREET ATLAS

WESTON LA
CASEY LA

FOURIER'S
FERNDALE AVE
FIRTREE AVE
PRIESTFIELD AVE
MALLBECK
HEATH VIEW
CEMETERY RD
MERE CT
MUSE RD
MEADOW AVE
WEST AVE
EAST AVE

Weston

SMITHY LA

A531

5

Casey Bridge

FAIRVIEW AVE

PO
PH

Weston Village Prim Sch

CW2

Snape Farm

52

SNAPE LA

4

Weston Hall

Basford Dairy Store

DELAMERE CL
HADLEY DR
GRANGE CL
HEATHVW
PETERSFIELD WAY
PASTURES DR
SANDYLANDS
EDEN
ST AUGUSTINES DR
HILLSIDE CL
HAMPTON WAY
OBSERVATION WAY
ABBEY PARK WAY

Snape Bank Farm

Heath Farm

KINGSWOOD AVE
HAVERHILL CRES
OWMILL AVE
KENSWOOD CL
EDENBRIDGE CL
MEADOW DR

WOODLANDS DR
SILVERDALE GR
LITTLE LAKES

CH

ENGLESEA BROOK LA

51

Balterley Mere

3

Jubilee Farm

CHORLTON LA

CHELFORD CL
HENLEY RD
RESTFORD
SPRINGWATER DR
RIDGWAY
FARNWORTH DR
SHERBORNE
WYCHWOOD PK

HAVERSHILL
ASHTON CL
IRWIN CL
CH

Hotel

Gorstyhill

GORSTY HILL
B5500
PO
FOUR LANES END

2

Dairy Farm

Chorlton Hall Farm

ST CLEMENT CT
WREN
KENDAL WAY

Mere Gutter

BRACKENWOOD MEWS
RISHWORTH CL
SANDHURST
SPEN GREEN

FRESHWATER DR
MEADOW LA

PH

Rosehill Farm

POST OFFICE LA
A531

Balterley Heath

1

Chorlton Lane End Farm

Black Firs

50

72   A   B   73   C   D   74   E   F

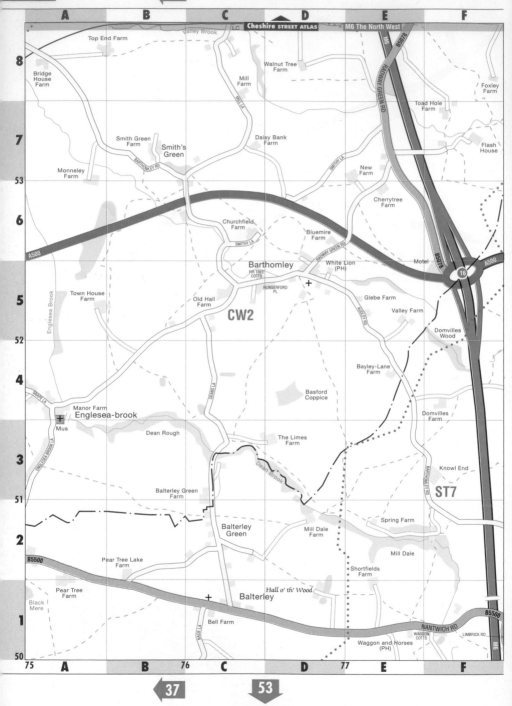

Cheshire STREET ATLAS

M6 The North West

Farms and features (as labelled on map):

Top End Farm
Valley Brook
L.C.
Walnut Tree Farm
Bridge House Farm
Mill Farm
Foxley Farm
Toad Hole Farm
Smith Green Farm
Daisy Bank Farm
Smith's Green
New Farm
Flash House
Monneley Farm
Cherrytree Farm
Churchfield Farm
Bluemire Farm
SMITHY LA
Barthomley
White Lion (PH)
Motel
FIR TREE COTTS
Town House Farm
Old Hall Farm
HUNGERFORD PL
CW2
Glebe Farm
Valley Farm
Domvilles Wood
16
Englesea Brook
Bayley-Lane Farm
Basford Coppice
Domvilles Farm
Manor Farm
Englesea-brook
Mus
Dean Rough
The Limes Farm
Knowl End
Balterley Green Farm
Dean Brook
ST7
Spring Farm
Balterley Green
Mill Dale Farm
Mill Dale
B5500
Pear Tree Lake Farm
Shortfields Farm
Pear Tree Farm
Black Mere
Balterley
Hall o' th' Wood
Bell Farm
Waggon and Horses (PH)
WAGGON COTTS
NANTWICH RD
LIMBRICK RD
B5500
M6

Roads: A500, B5078, RADWAY GREEN RD, M6, BARTHOMLEY RD, MILL LA, SMITH LA, DEANS LA, SNAPE LA, ENGLESEA BROOK LA, RUGLEY RD, BACK LA

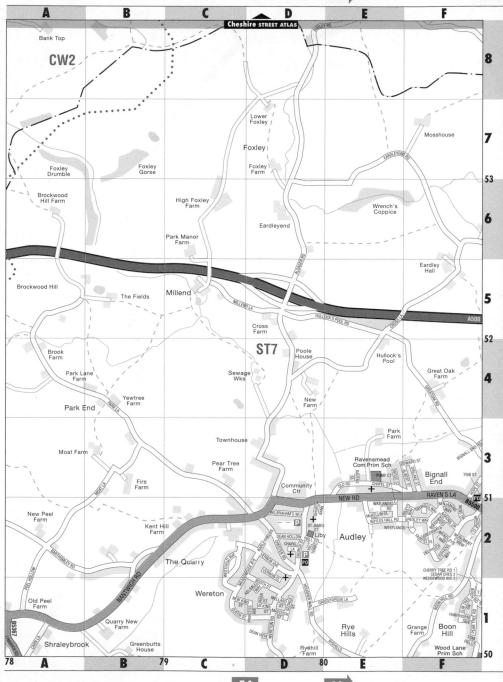

Cheshire STREET ATLAS

CW2

ST7

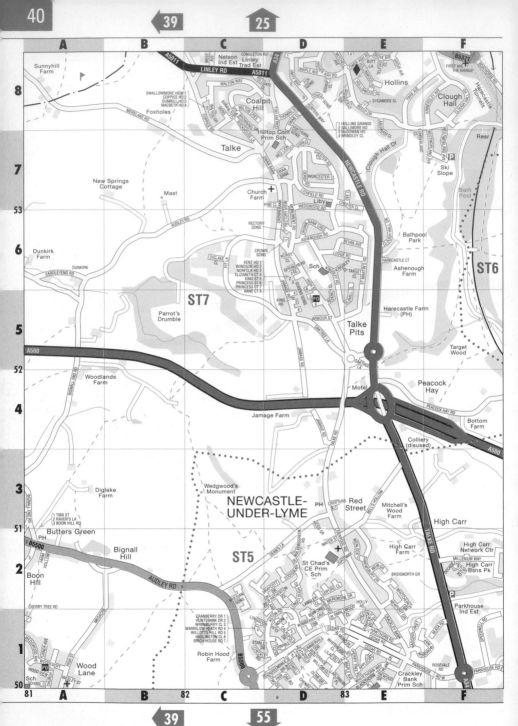

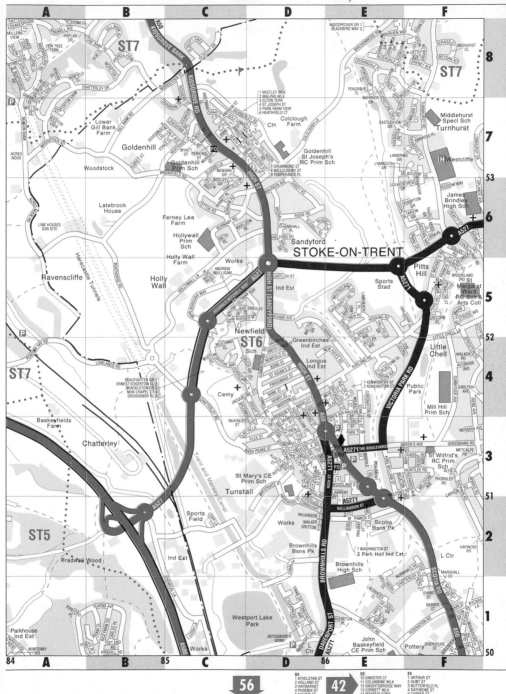

D3
1 ATHELSTAN ST
2 HOLLAND ST
3 HAYMARKET
4 PHOENIX ST
5 CALVER ST
6 PARADISE ST
7 PICCADILLY ST
8 McGOUGH ST
9 FARNDALE ST

D3
10 SIMISTER CT
11 COLUMBINE WLK
12 KNIGHTSBRIDGE WAY
13 CORBETT WLK
14 MAYFAIR GDNS
15 CORINTH WAY
16 PERSIA WLK
17 STRINGER CT
18 COOLIDGE ST

E3
1 ARTHUR ST
2 HUNT ST
3 BUTTERFIELD PL
4 RATHBONE ST
5 CAPPER ST

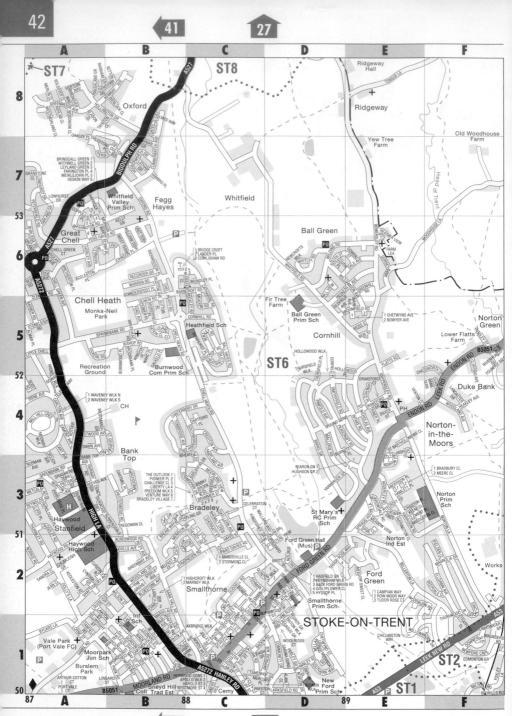

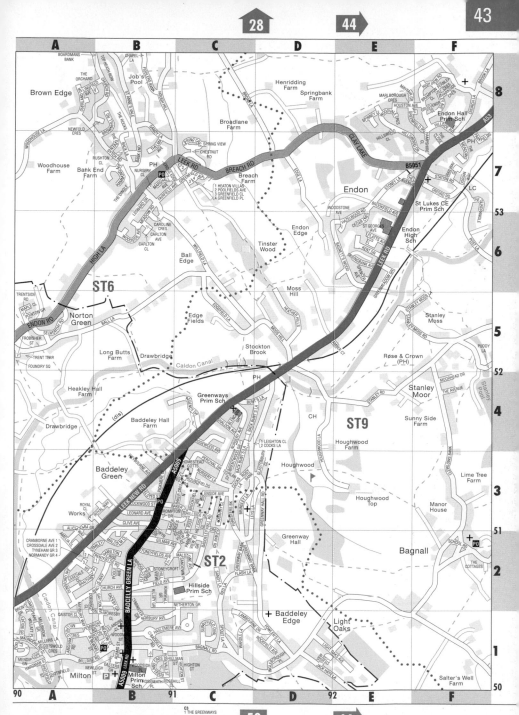

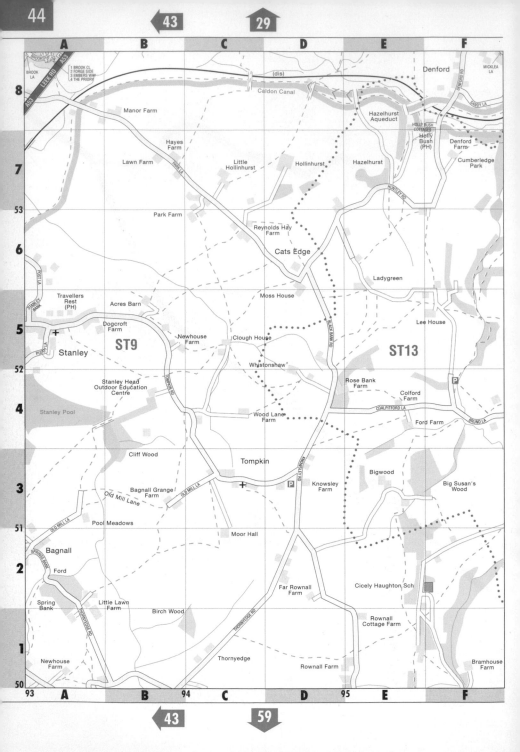

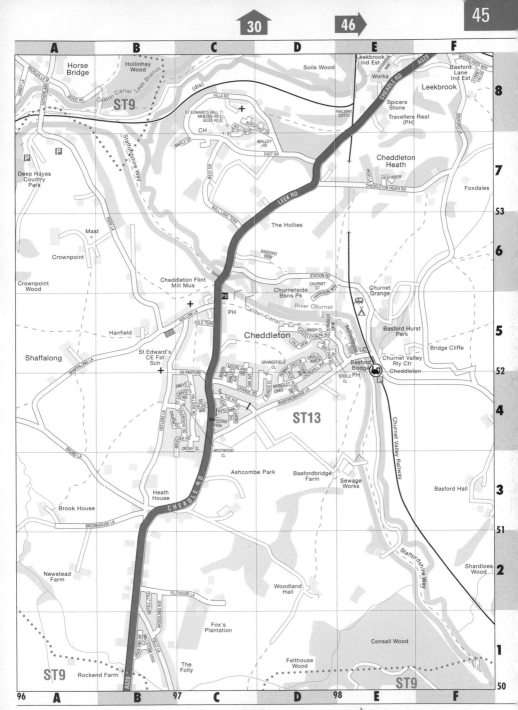

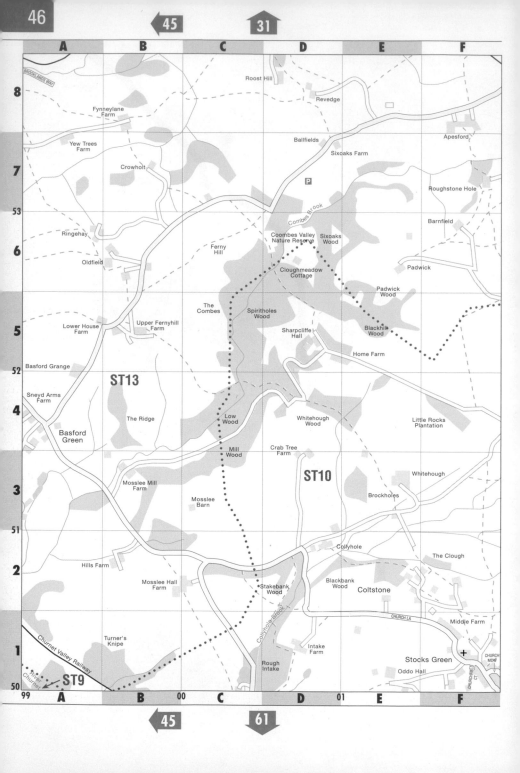

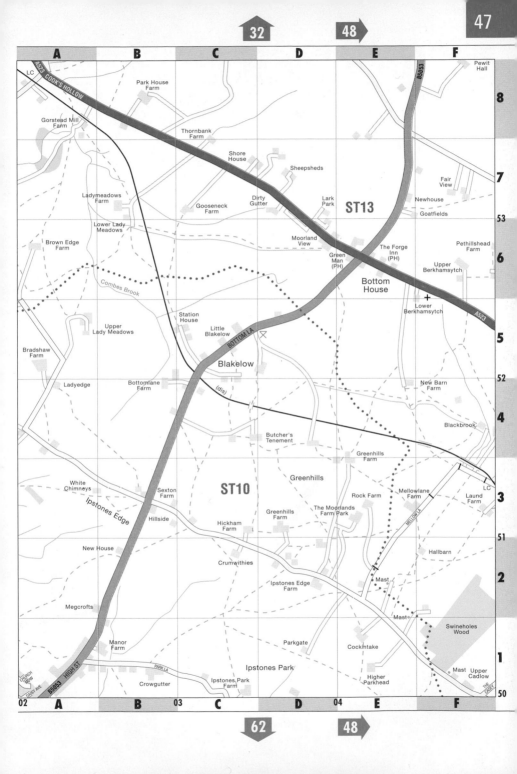

A **B** **C** **D** **E** **F**

LC
A523
COOK'S HOLLOW

Gorstead Mill
Farm

Park House
Farm

Pewit
Hall

8

Thornbank
Farm

Shore
House

B5053

Sheepsheds

Fair
View

7

Ladymeadows
Farm

Gooseneck
Farm

Dirty
Gutter

Lark
Park

Newhouse

Goatfields

ST13

53

Lower Lady
Meadows

Brown Edge
Farm

Moorland
View

Green
Man
(PH)

The Forge
Inn
(PH)

Pethillshead
Farm

Upper
Berkhamsytch

6

Combes Brook

Bottom
House

+

Lower
Berkhamsytch

A523

Station
House

Little
Blakelow

BOTTOM LA

Upper
Lady Meadows

Bradshaw
Farm

Blakelow

5

Ladyedge

Bottomlane
Farm

(dis)

New Barn
Farm

52

White
Chimneys

Butcher's
Tenement

Blackbrook

4

Ipstones Edge

Sexton
Farm

ST10

Greenhills

Greenhills
Farm

Rock Farm

Mellowlane
Farm

LC

Laund
Farm

3

Hillside

Greenhills
Farm

The Moorlands
Farm Park

MELLOW LA

New House

Hickham
Farm

Hallbarn

51

Crumwithies

Ipstones Edge
Farm

Mast

2

Megcrofts

Mast

Swineholes
Wood

Manor
Farm

Parkgate

Cockintake

Mast

Upper
Cadlow

1

CHURCH
ROW

DERBY AVE

B5053

HIGH ST

PARK LA

Crowgutter

Ipstones Park
Farm

Ipstones Park

Higher
Parkhead

THE CASEY

50

02 **A** **B** 03 **C** **D** 04 **E** **F**

A   **B**   **C**   **D**   **E**   **F**

8

Ford

Dairy House

Ford Wetley

Ford Farm

Ryebrook

7

Ten Acre Barn

Ford Grange

Sycamore Lodge

Felthouse

53

Bingham

Stonyslack

Pethills Bank Cottage

Grub Low

6

Pethillshead

Martin's Low

Backlane

Martinslow Farm

Lawnfield

5

A523

Moorside

Gibgreen

Old Hall Farm

Pethills

Ironpits

ST10

Newstreet

52

Newstreet Farm

MARTINSLOW LA

ST13

Waterfall Common

4

Blackbrook Zoological Park

Winkhillbank

Coate's Cottage

Croftshead

Bank Farm

River Hamps

Bridge Flats Farm

BROMLEYHEDGE LA

Waterfall Cross

Waterfall Common

Black Brook

Moorland View

Common Side

Green Farm

Blackbrook Bridge

WATERFALL LA

LC's

Woodbine Cottage

Winkhill

BENTYGRANGE LA

CROSS LA

3

Gutter Farm

Stonylow Farm

BREECH CL

51

Station House

Benty Grange

Waterhouses CE Prim Sch

WATERFALL LA

2

(dis)

Paper Mill Farm

Redmoorlee Farm

Crowtrees Farm Ind Est

HAMPS VALLEY RD

California

Cotton Grange

Willow House

PORTLAND PL

Swineholes Wood

Dulce Domun

MANIFOLD CL

A523

Casey Head Farm

THE CAST

ELKSTONE RD

Moorland View

Crowtrees

Steps Cottage

1

Birch Head

Broomyshaw

DUKE ST LA

New House Farm

Lee Brook

50

05   **A**   **B**   06   **C**   **D**   07   **E**   **F**

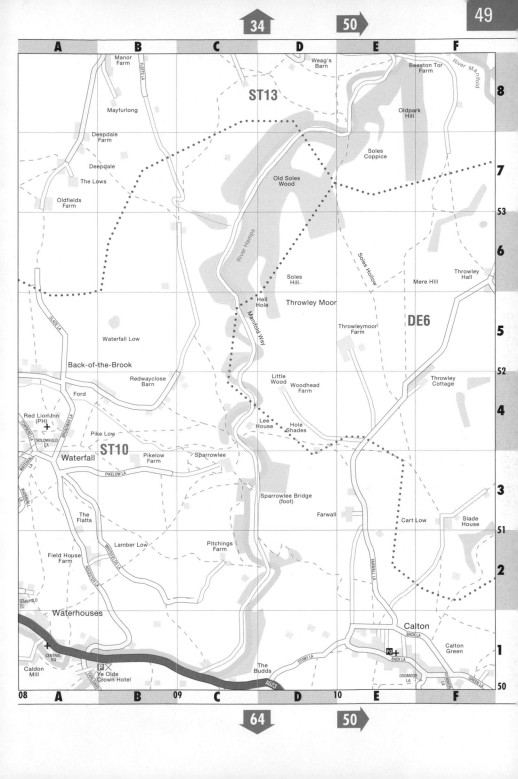

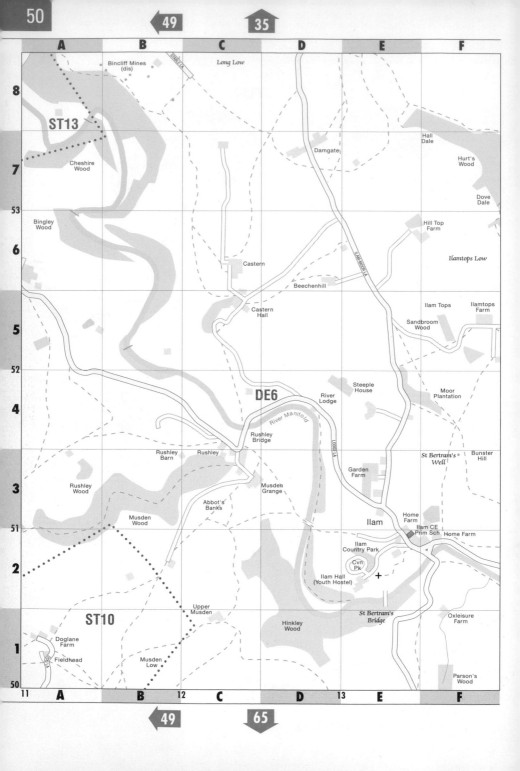

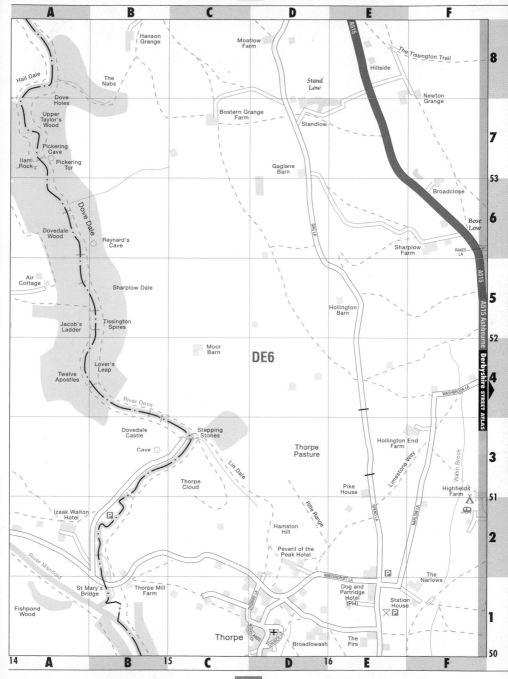

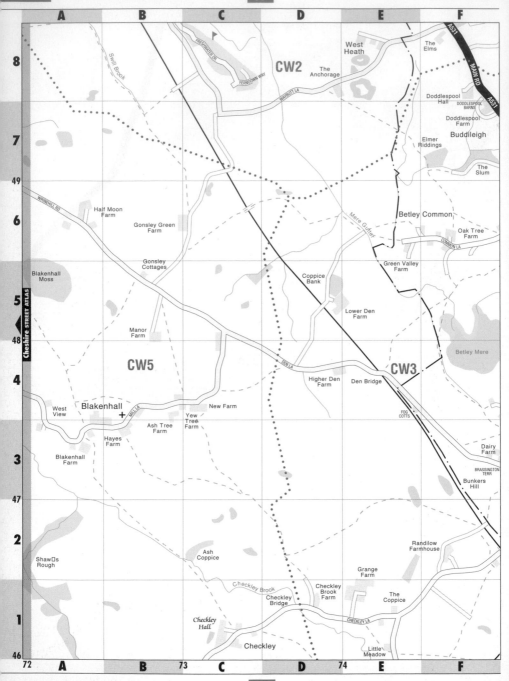

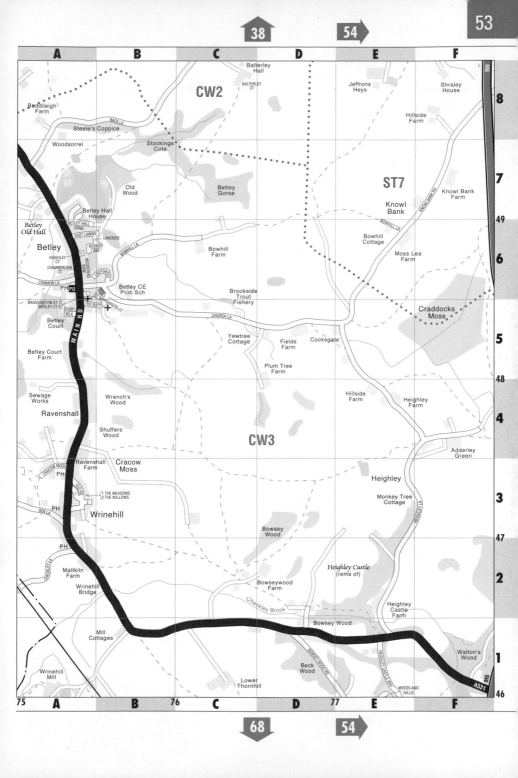

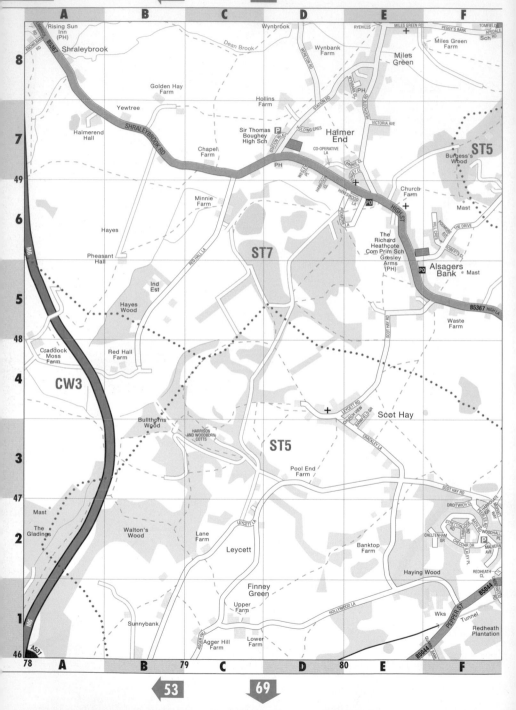

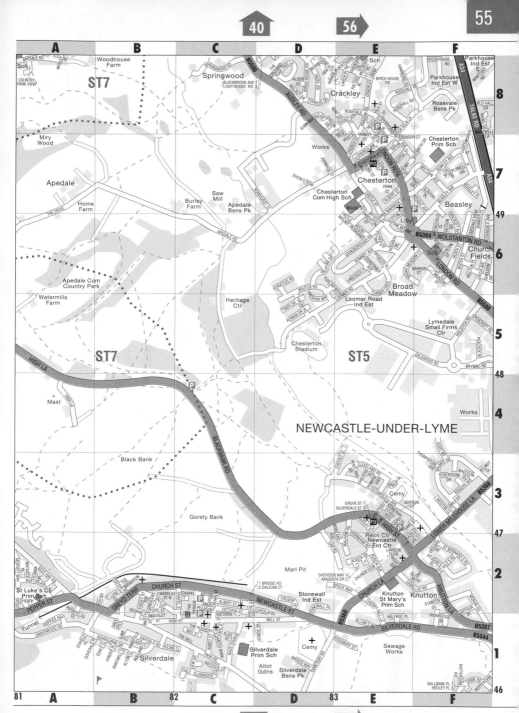

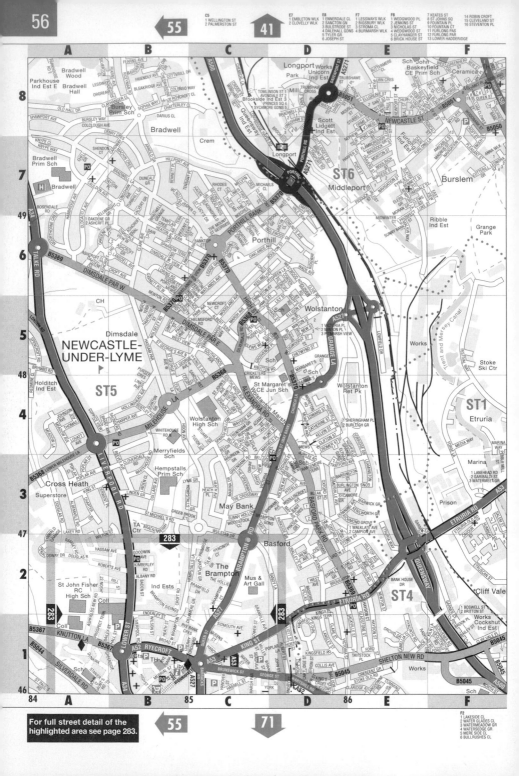

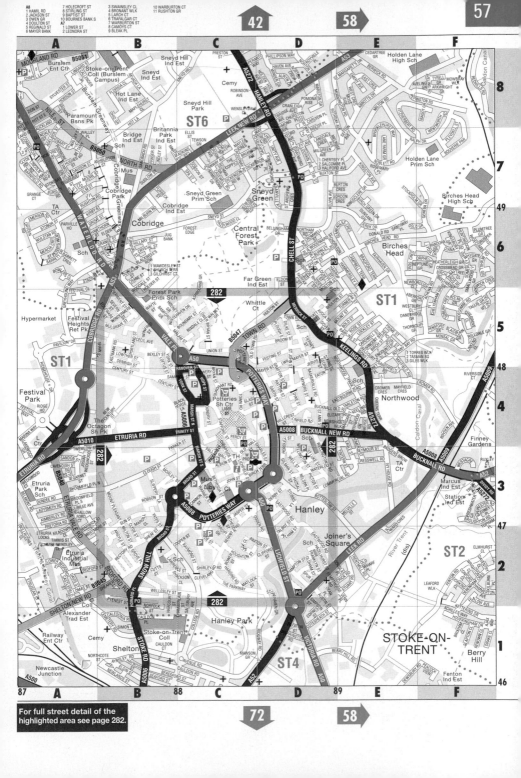

STOKE-ON-TRENT

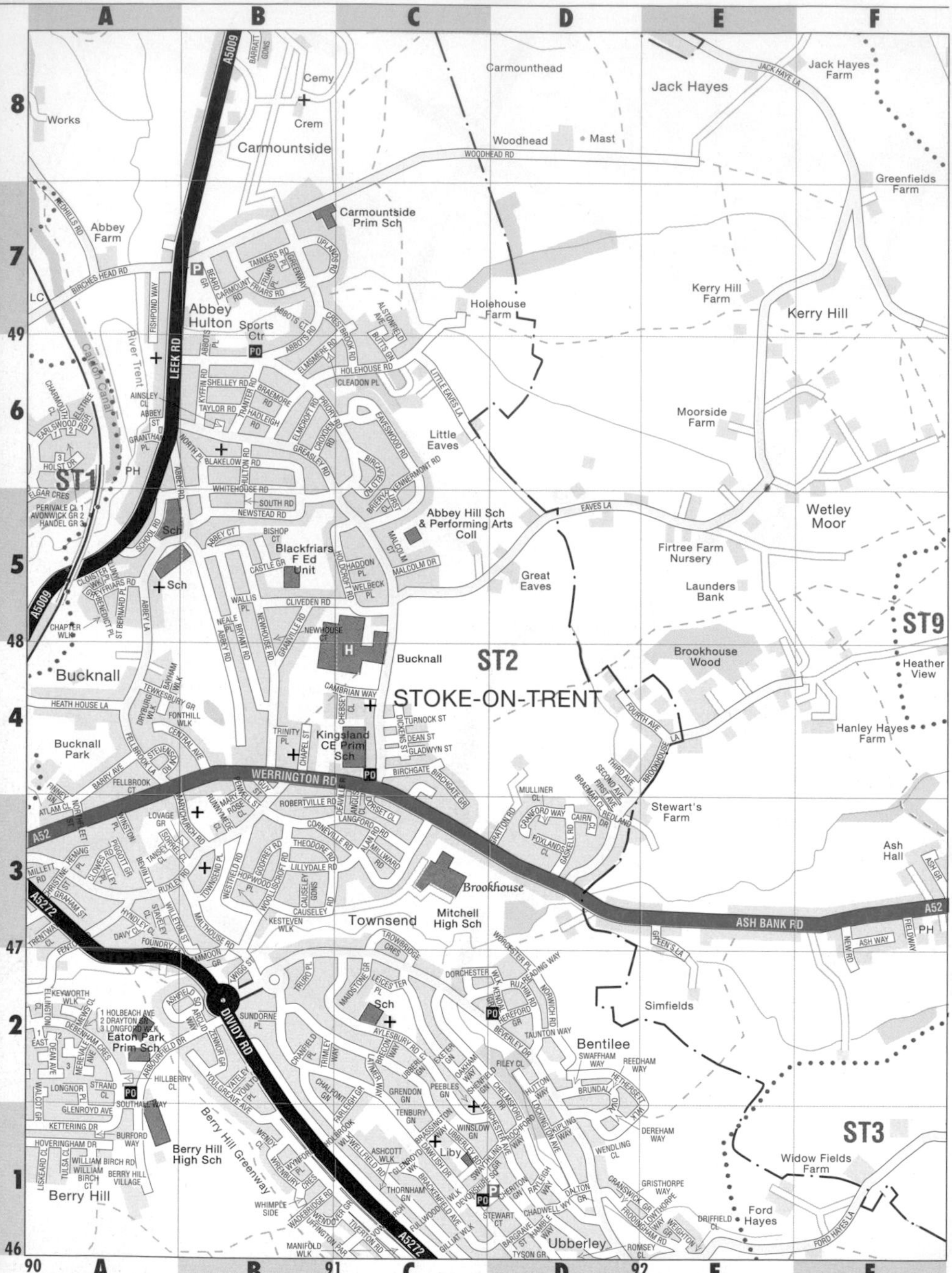

ST1
ST2
ST3
ST9

Carmounthead
Jack Hayes
Jack Hayes Farm
Carmountside
Woodhead
Mast
Greenfields Farm
Abbey Farm
Carmountside Prim Sch
Cemy
Crem
Works
Abbey Hulton
Sports Ctr
Kerry Hill Farm
Kerry Hill
Holehouse Farm
Little Eaves
Moorside Farm
Wetley Moor
Abbey Hill Sch & Performing Arts Coll
Blackfriars F Ed Unit
Great Eaves
Firtree Farm Nursery
Launders Bank
Heather View
Bucknall
Buckna ll
Brookhouse Wood
Hanley Hayes Farm
Bucknall Park
Heath House La
Ash Hall
Kingsland CE Prim Sch
WERRINGTON RD
Stewart's Farm
Brookhouse
Townsend
Mitchell High Sch
ASH BANK RD
PH
Eaton Park Prim Sch
Simfields
Bentilee
Ash Way
Berry Hill High Sch
Berry Hill Greenway
Widow Fields Farm
Berry Hill
Berry Hill Village
Ubberley
Ford Hayes

LEEK RD
DIVIDY RD
River Trent

A500
A5009
A52
A5272

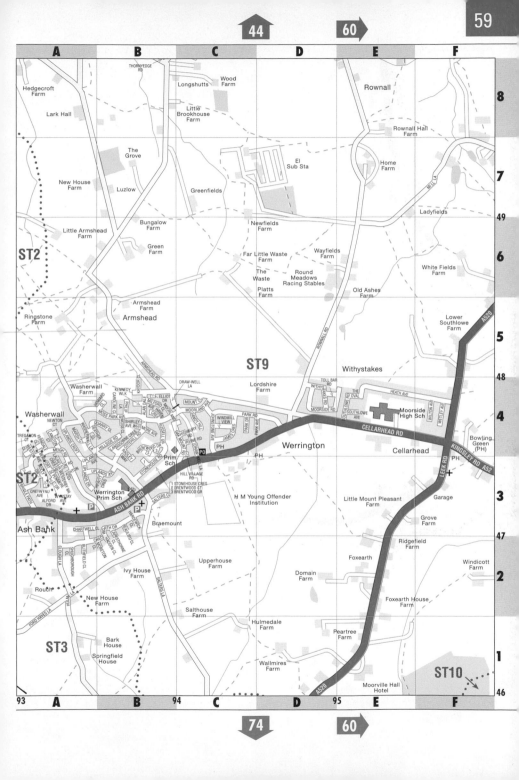

59
45

	A	B	C	D	E	F

8

Barns Farm

ST13

Park House

Consall Wood

Rock View Farm

Powys Arms (PH)

St John's CE Prim Sch

Smithy Pool

7

THE BUNTING

Wetley Rocks

Spout House

Smithy Sprink

Plough Inn (PH)

PO

Old Hall Farm

Long Meadows

MILL LA

MAIN RD

A522

CHEADLE RD

A520

POTTY LA

49

OAKLANDS CT

Knowle Bank Farm

Consall Hall

BY ROAD

6

Platt Newhouse Farm

Park House

Tunnel Farm

Consall

Darleyshire

LEEK RD

A520

MEADOW AVE

RANGELEY LA

CONSALL LA

New Farm

Middle Farm

Upper Farm

Keeper's Lodge Farm

5

Wetley Abbey

Highfields Farm

Blackbank Plantation

ST9

Lodge Spinney

Wetley Abbey Farm

CONSALL LA

48

Ivy House Farm

Upper Ladypark Wood

4

Gate House Cottage

Mast

Windyhouse Wood

Out Wood

Consall Wood

Rangemoor Farm

Broadoak Wood

3

A52

New Park Farm

LEEK RD

A522

New Farm

Blakeley Farm

Little Broadoak Farm

Broadoak Farm

KINGSLEY RD

Overmoor

MARCH LA

Richmoorhill Farm

Blakeley Lane

Youngsgreen Farm

Brough's Wood

47

2

WINDYCOTE LA

Mount Pleasant

Little Abovepark

ST10

Abovepark Farm

Greenhead Farm

Greenhead

Moor Farm

DAIRYHOUSE LA

1

Little Bank Top Farm

Bank Top Farm

Dairy House Farm

Waggon and Horses Inn (PH)

Kingsley Moor

A52

A522

46

TICKHILL LA

DAIRYHOUSE LA

Lower Above Park

96	A	B	97	C	D	98	E	F

59
75

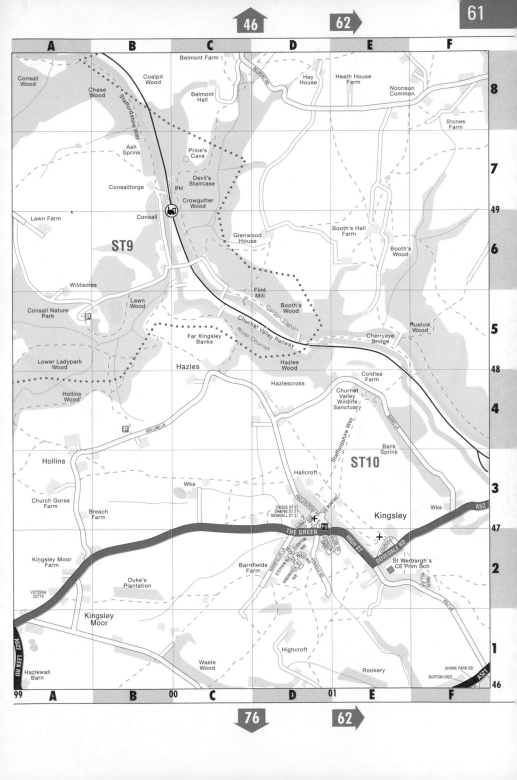

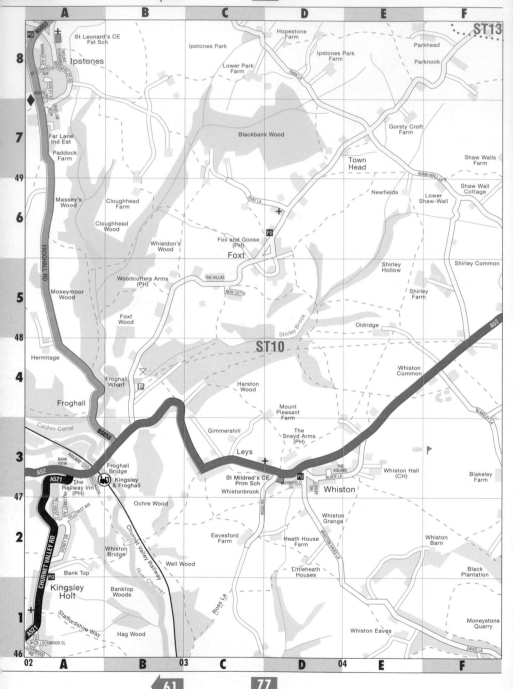

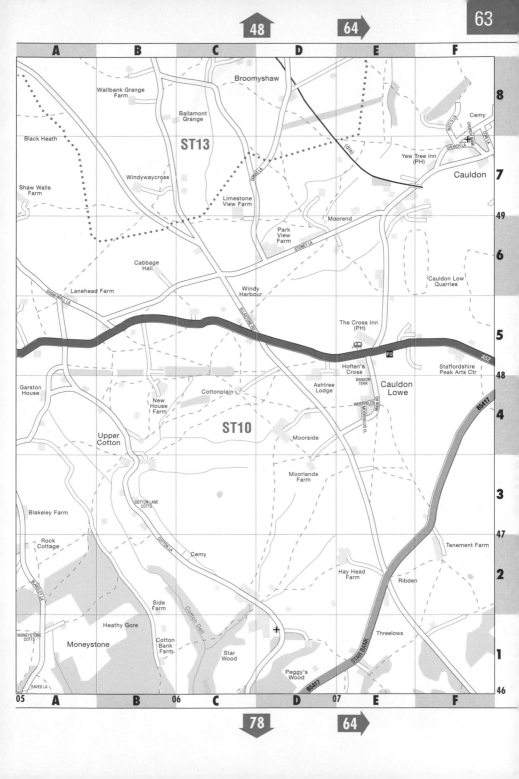

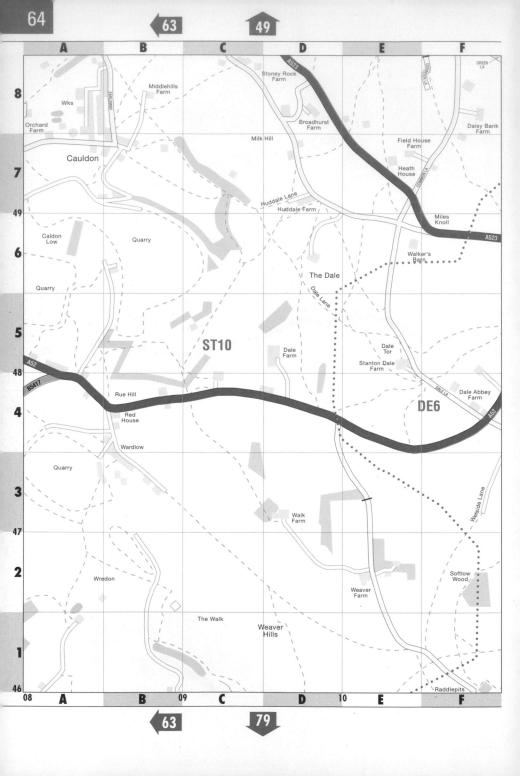

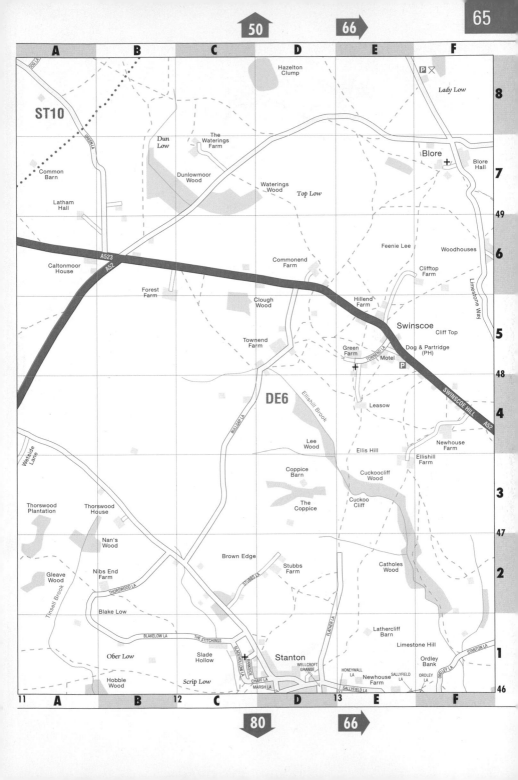

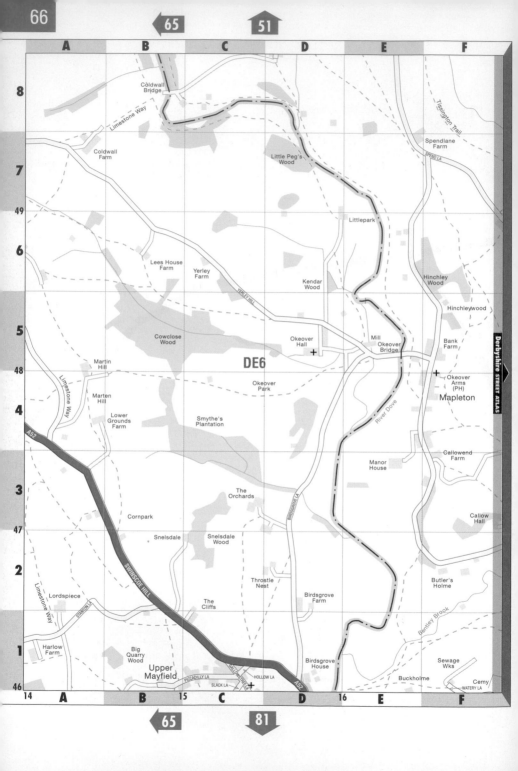

A B C D E F

8

7

49

6

5

48

4

3

47

2

1

46

Coldwall
Bridge

Limestone Way

Coldwall
Farm

Little Peg's
Wood

Spendlane
Farm

SPEND LA

Tissington Trail

Littlepark

Lees House
Farm

Yerley
Farm

Kendar
Wood

Hinchley
Wood

Hinchleywood

FENLEY HILL

Cowclose
Wood

Okeover
Hall

Mill
Okeover
Bridge

Bank
Farm

DE6

Martin
Hill

Okeover
Park

Okeover
Arms
(PH)

Mapleton

Limestone Way

Marten
Hill

Lower
Grounds
Farm

Smythe's
Plantation

River Dove

Callowend
Farm

A52

Manor
House

The
Orchards

BIRDSGROVE LA

Callow
Hall

Cornpark

Snelsdale

Snelsdale
Wood

SWINSCOE HILL

Throstle
Nest

Birdsgrove
Farm

Butler's
Holme

Bentley Brook

Lordspiece

Limestone Way

STANTON

The
Cliffs

Upper
Mayfield

Big
Quarry
Wood

Harlow
Farm

PICCADILLY LA

SLACK LA

MILLWAY LA

HOLLOW LA

A52

Birdsgrove
House

Buckholme

Sewage
Wks

Cemy

WATERY LA

14 A B 15 C D 16 E F

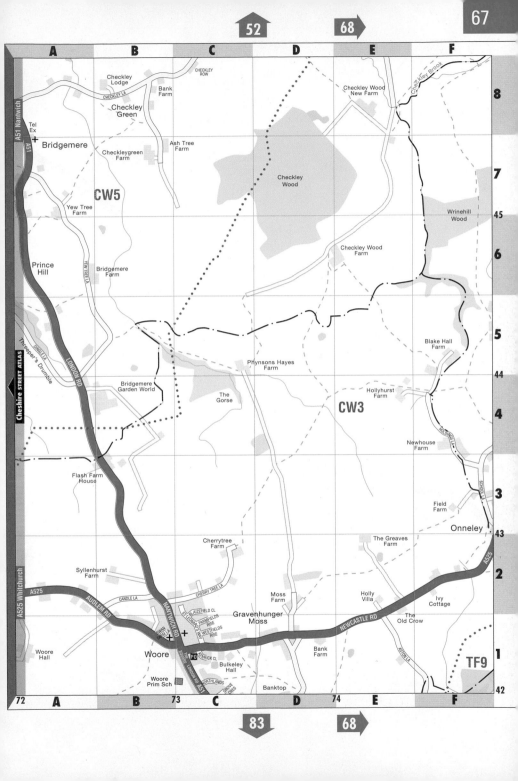

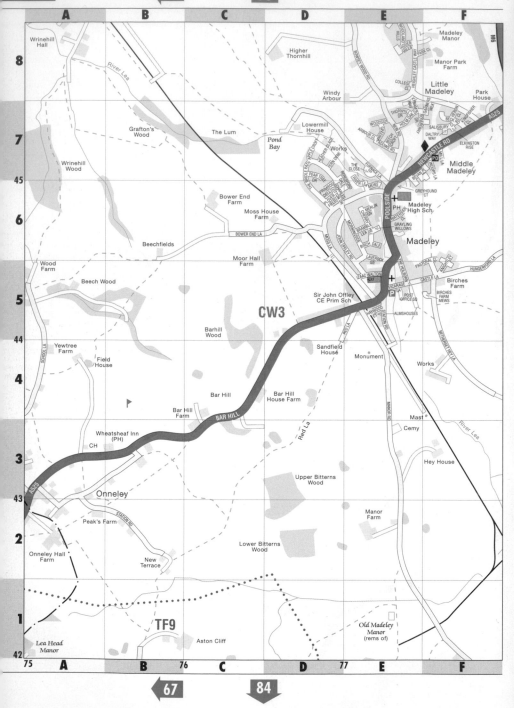

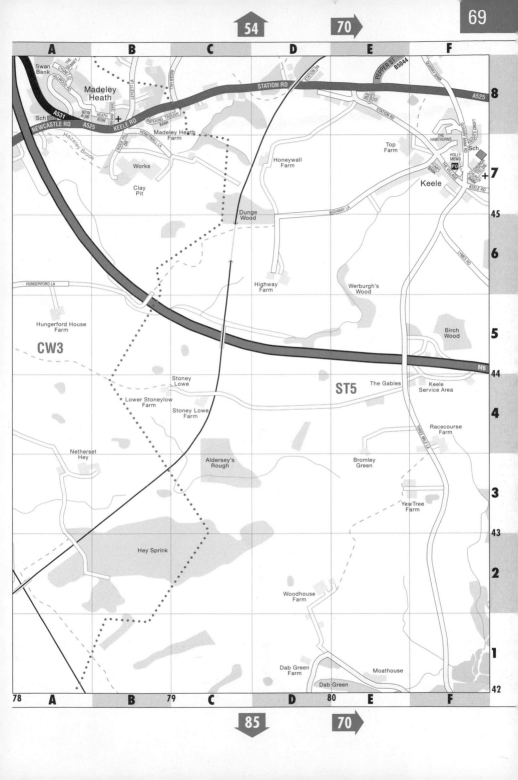

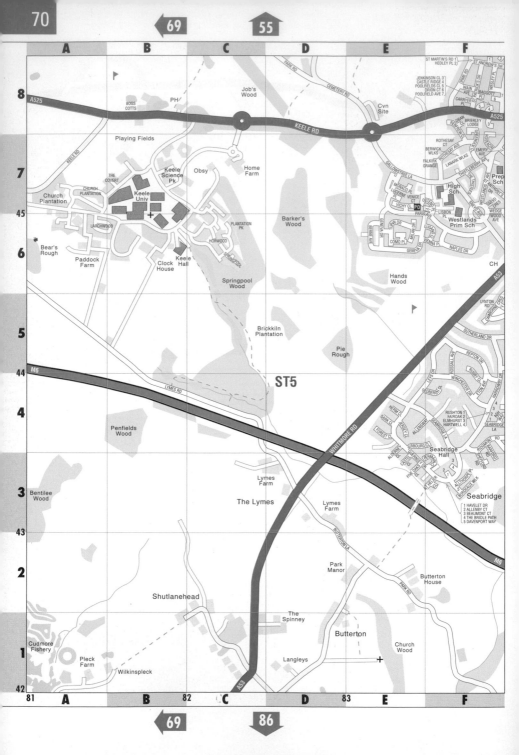

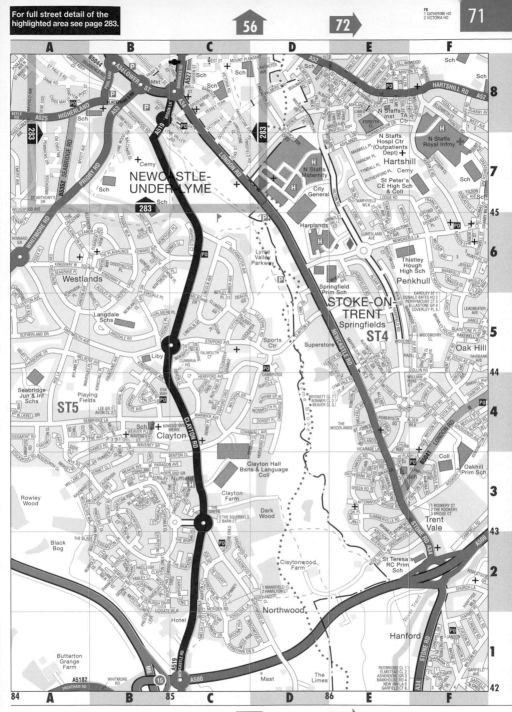

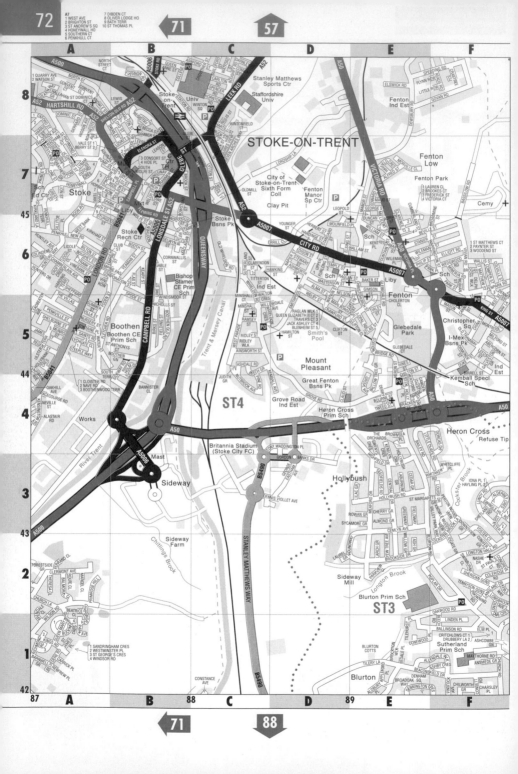

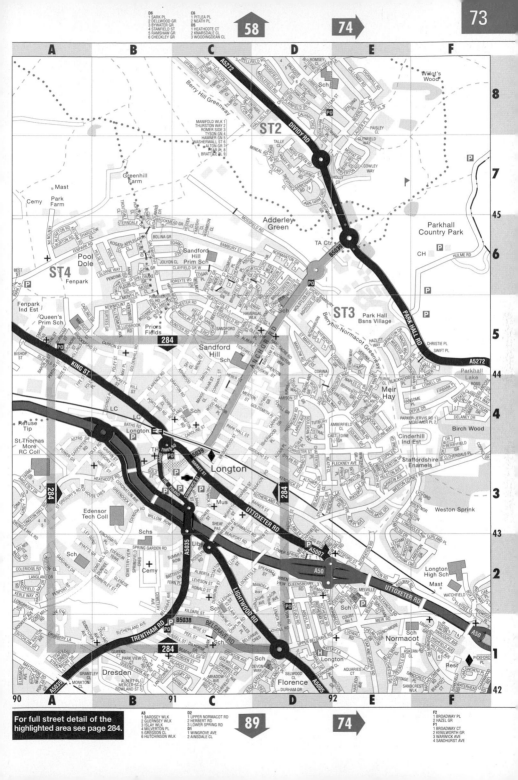

73
59

Hulme

Stonehouse Farm
HULME LA
THE COTTS
The Candlesticks (PH)
Hall Farm
HULME RD

Malthouse Farm

ST9

Creswell's Piece

ST10

Winterfield Farm
WINTERFIELD LA
MALTHOUSE LA

Smallbrook Farm

Captain's Barn

Blythe Lea

LEEK RD
A520

Sheepwash Farm
Ford
Sheepwash

Ward Hill Farm

45

Visitor Ctr

Boltongate Farm

Roughcote

Caverswall Common

Tickhill Farm

6

Parkhall Ctry Pk

COALVILLE
CARNWOOD DR
ASTER CL
DANILLA CL
EAST ST
LYNN ST
SELBY ST
BEE CL
LILAC CL
LAVENDER CL

River Blythe

Hardiwick Farm

5

Weston Coyney

WEST ST
HEATHCOTE RD
HEYSHAM CL

LILAC CL

THE CLOSE
BATTLE ST
FLINT ST

Sch

ST3

PARK HALL RD A5272

44

Weston Coyney Rd

TAME WLK
GEOFFREY PL
THE MO4

FITZGERALD CL
HAYNES GR
CATHERHALL RD

Caversall Common

Cocking Farm

Intakes Farm

ST11

ST10

4

Sch

Weston Sprink

Weston Coyney Jun Sch
DALE VIEW
DAWN VIEW
TERRY CL
MICHAEL CL
MYRTLE AVE
LANSBURY GR

QUEENS WLK
PALACE AVE
LILY VIEW

Cookshill

Green Farm

QUEENS CL
THE GREEN
FALL LADARN
NATIONAL CL
HILL TOP
TREVOR DR

Yewtree Farm

Cookshill Hall

Tunstall Sytch

3

WESTON RD

MACDONALD DRIVE
GOODWIN PL
DORSET BROADWAY
MAXTON WAY
BURNS BONDFIELD ROW

WHITCOMBE RD
BROOKHOUSE RD
WESTBURY RD

BLATCHFORD PL

THE BEVERIDGE PL
THE WOOD

The Crockett
The Red House PH
DILHORNE LA

Caverswall

43

BROADWAY

OAK PL

P0

BRIARWOOD PL
DENEWOODS PL

MAPLE
THE SQUARE LEA PL

St Peter's CE Prim Sch
THE DAMS

STOKE-ON-TRENT

Castle

GABLE COTTS

St Filumena's RC Prim Sch

2

CHERRY HILL AVE
WOODVILLE RD
WOODWILLE PL
LYME RD

Crescent Prim Sch

Wood House Farm

SCHOOL LA

BRITHE BRIDGE RD

Meir
Meir Prim Sch
GEORGE AVE

Caverswall Park

Foxfield Steam Rly

LC

1

A520
UTTOXETER RD
A50

WILLOWOOD GR
APPLEWOOD CRES
DENHURST AVE

LC

Mast

Caverswall Road

42

93   A   94   B   C   94   D   95   E   F

A1
1 DENHURST CL
2 ROWNHALL PL
3 CORNELIOUS ST
4 SMITHS BLDGS
5 REDWOOD PL
6 BROADWAY CT
7 QUEENSWAY CT
8 PICKFORD PL
9 CHATSWORTH PL
10 SARACEN WAY
11 CROSSLAND PL W
12 COBHAM PL

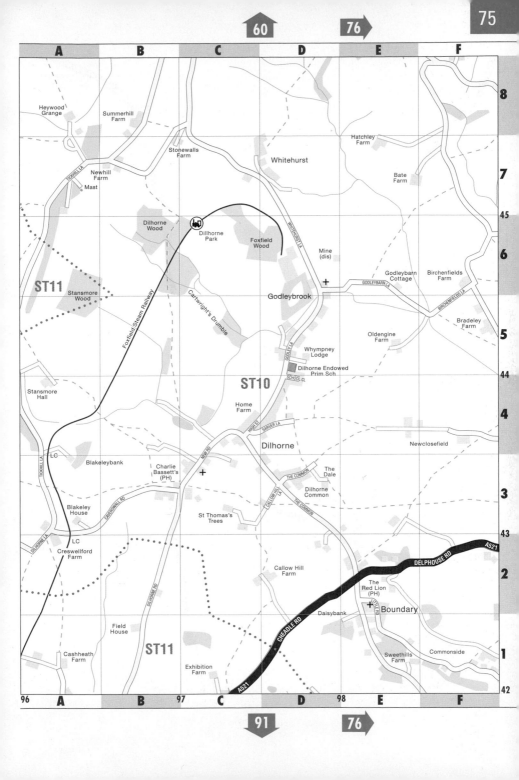

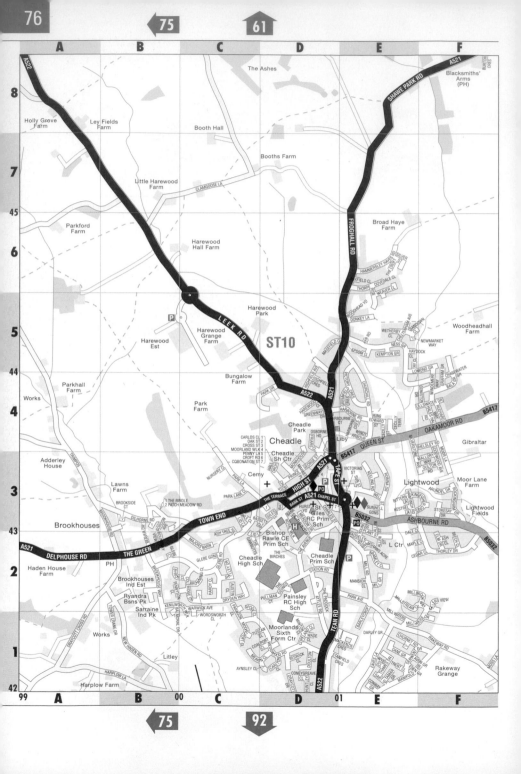

8

Kingsley Holt

Ross Bridge

Ashbourne Hey

Quarry

Crowtrees Farm

Lockwood Waste

Dustystile

Works

Lockwood Hall Farm

Jackson Wood

7

Thornbury Hall

Lock Wood

(dis)

River Churnet

Key Wood

WOODSIDE COTTS

CHURNET VIEW RD

45

LOCKWOOD RD

Woodhouse Farm

Eastwall

Newhay Wood

6

Radio Station

Gibridding Wood

Masts

Hawksmoor Nature Reserve

Staffordshire Way

Hayes Wood

Banks Farm

B5417 CHURCH BANK

LIGHTOAKS

5

Parkfields Farm

Hawksmoor Wood

Hawksmoor Cottage

P

Lightoaks Wood

ST10

CHERRY LA

Hales Hall

OAKAMOOR RD

Greendale Farm

GREENDALE LA

Sutton's Wood

STONEY DALE

44

Lower Grange Farm

Highshutt

Greendale Cotts

Oldfurnace

Dimmingsdale Wood

4

Mast

Highshutt Farm

Dimmings Dale

HABER LA

Hill Top Farm

Threap Wood

3

Monk's Wood

Lambskin Dale

43

Lightwood Farm

Counslow Cottage

Counslow Plantation

NEWTON

Fairfield Farm

Threapwood

DAVEY LA

2

B5032

MOSS LA

Highwayman Inn

Brownbank Plantation

Bradley Elms Farm

SANDY LA

1

Rakeway Castle Farm

BAKEWAY RD

The Rakeway

Gravel Pit

42

02 A B 03 C D 04 E F

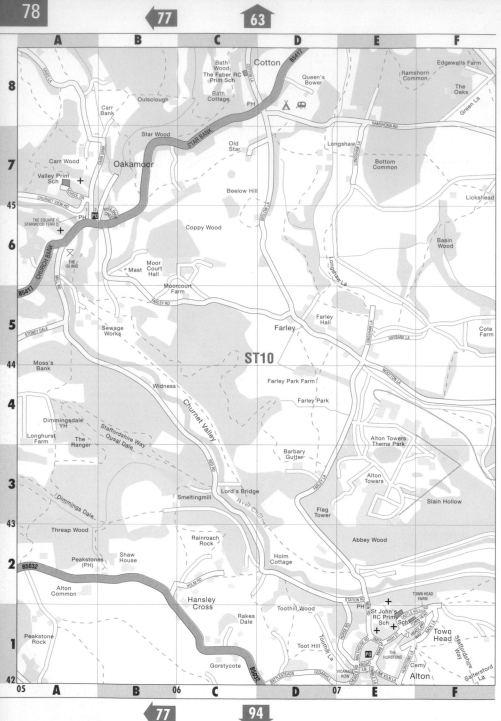

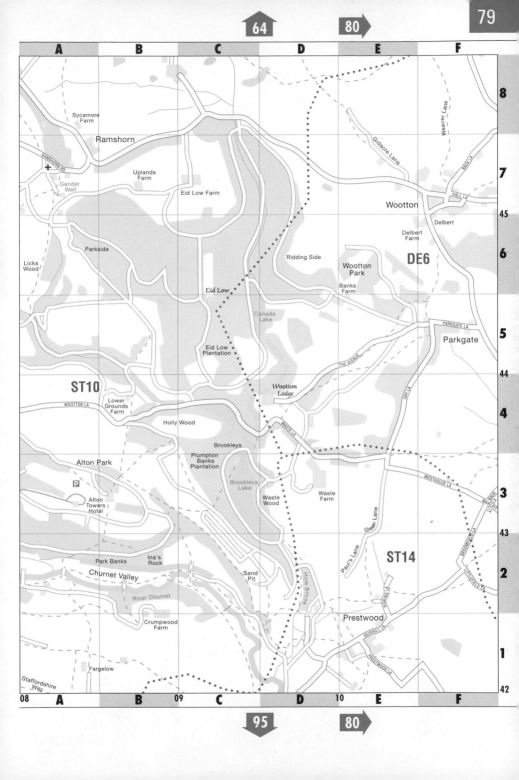

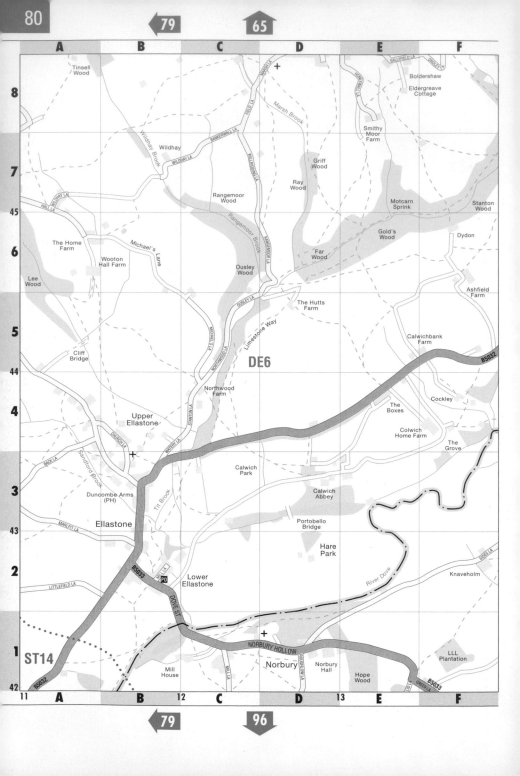

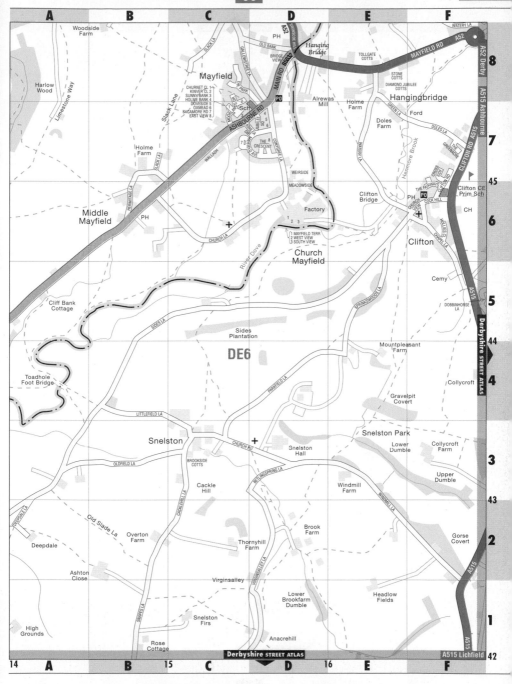

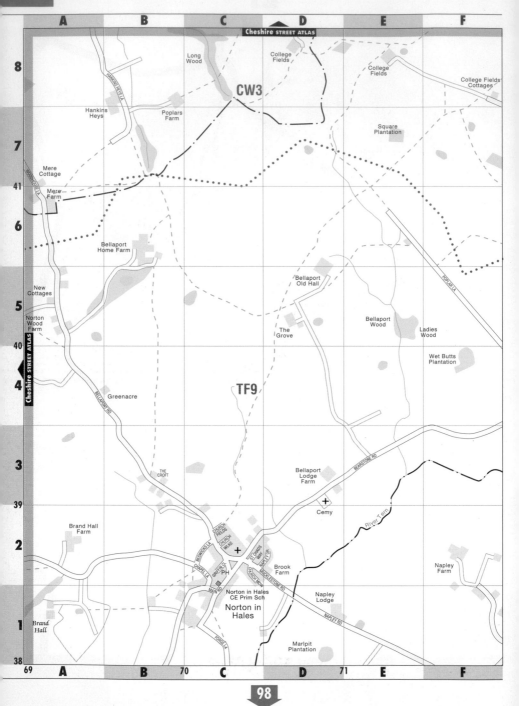

Cheshire STREET ATLAS

8
Long Wood
College Fields
College Fields
College Fields Cottages

CW3

Hankins Heys
Poplars Farm
Square Plantation

7

Mere Cottage

41
Mere Farm

6
Bellaport Home Farm

New Cottages

Bellaport Old Hall

5
Norton Wood Farm
Bellaport Wood
Ladies Wood

The Grove

40
Wet Butts Plantation

4
TF9
Greenacre

3
THE CROFT
Bellaport Lodge Farm
BEARSTONE RD

39
Cemy
River Tern

Brand Hall Farm
CHURCH FIELDS

2
PH
Brook Farm
Napley Farm

Norton in Hales CE Prim Sch
Napley Lodge

Norton in Hales

1
Brand Hall
NAPLEY RD

Marlpit Plantation

38

69 **A** 70 **C** **D** 71 **E** **F**

BELLAPORT RD
POPLAR LA

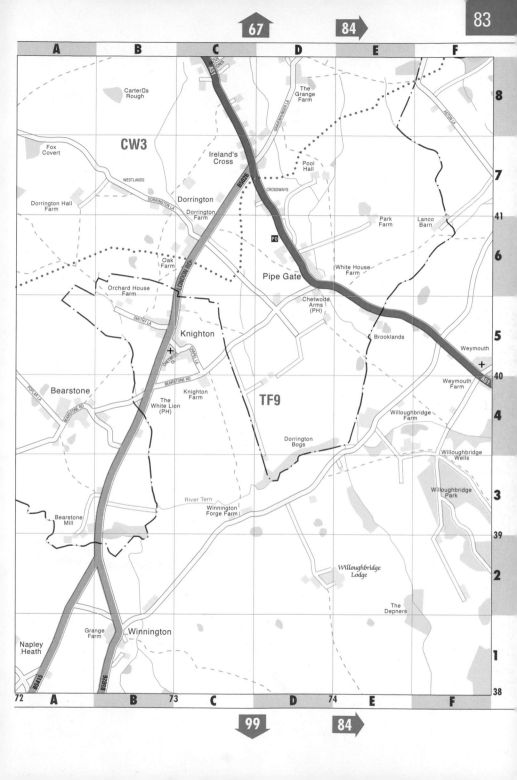

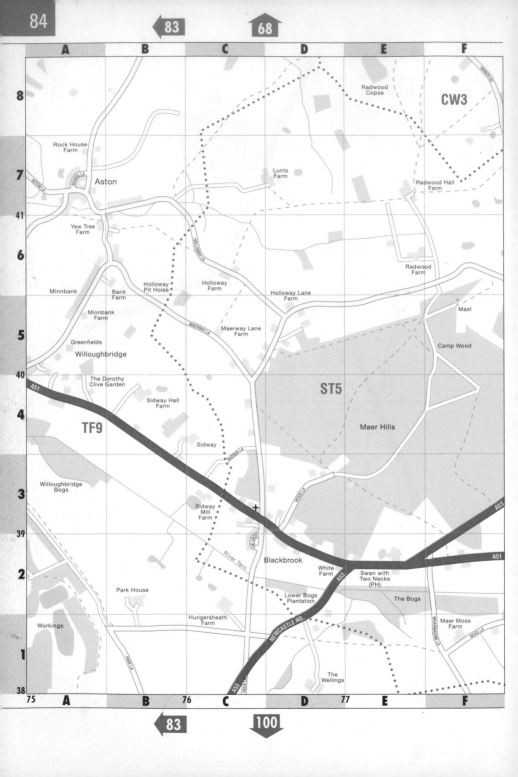

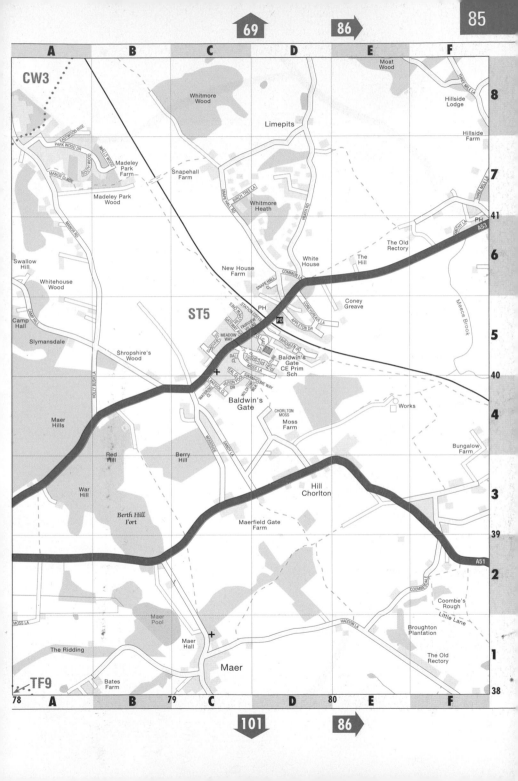

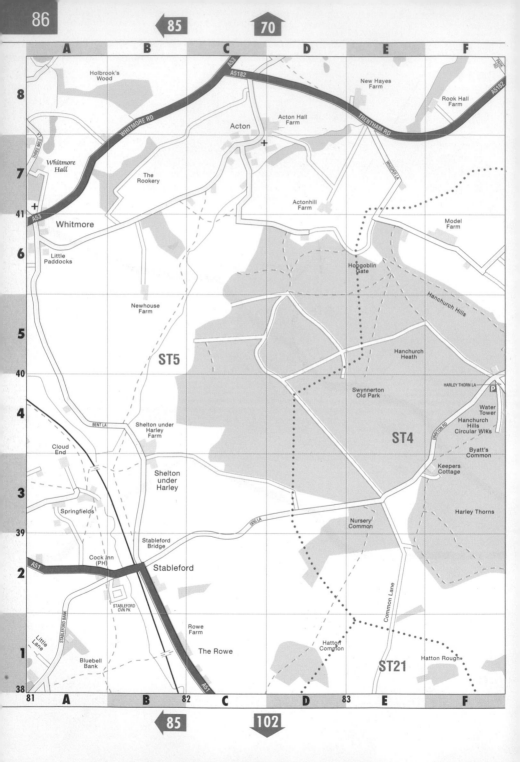

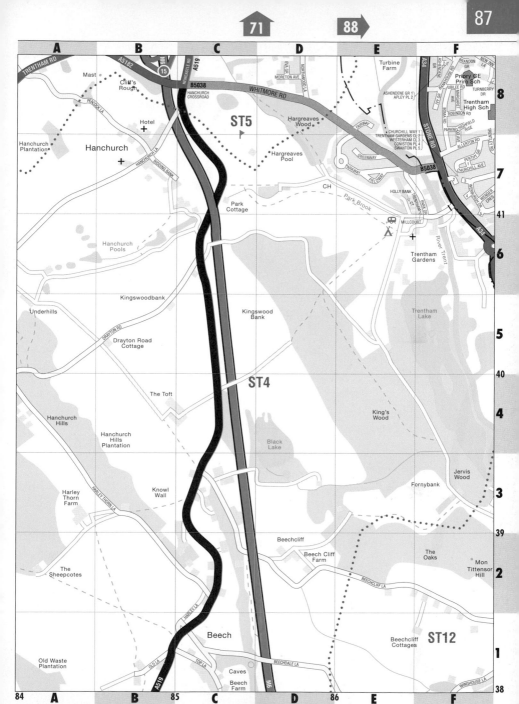

71
88
103
88

TRENTHAM RD

A5182

B5038

Mast

Cliff's
Rough

HANCHURCH
CROSSROAD

NEWCASTLE RD

A519

WHITMORE RD

Turbine
Farm

Priory CE
Prim Sch

BRANDON
GR

NEW INN
LA

A34

ASHENDENE

STONE RD

Trentham
High Sch

ASHENDENE GR 1
APLEY PL 2

TURNBERRY
DR

Hotel

ST5

Hargreaves
Wood

JUBILEE RD

MARGARET

AVE

ROMA RD

ROBINSON RD

PARKWAY

HIGHFIELD
RISE

PERTH
1

ALLERTON RD

Hanchurch
Plantation

Hanchurch

Hargreaves
Pool

CHURCHILL WAY 1
TRENTHAM GARDENS CL 2
WESTERHAM CL 3
CONISTON PL 4
SWANTON PL 5

CHURCHILL AVE

HANCHURCH LA

PUDDING BANK

CH

Park Brook

Park
Cottage

FAIRWAY

GREENWAY

PARKWAY

EVELY WAY

HOLLY BANK

PARK DR

TRENTHAM RD

TRENT VAL RD

MEYRICK RD

HUNGER
GRES

MILLCOURT

Trentham
Gardens

River Trent

41

Hanchurch
Pools

Kingswoodbank

DRAYTON RD

Drayton Road
Cottage

Kingswood
Bank

Trentham
Lake

6

Underhills

5

40

ST4

The Toft

King's
Wood

4

Hanchurch
Hills

Hanchurch
Hills
Plantation

Black
Lake

Jervis
Wood

Fornybank

3

Harley
Thorn
Farm

DARLEY THORN LA

Knowl
Wall

39

Beechcliff

Beech Cliff
Farm

The
Oaks

Mon
Tittensor
Hill

2

The
Sheepcotes

BEECHCLIFF LA

ST12

Old Waste
Plantation

Beech

OLD LA

A519

HANLEY LA

TOP LA

Caves

Beech
Farm

BEECHDALE LA

M6

Beechcliff
Cottages

WINGHOUSE LA

1

84 85 86 38

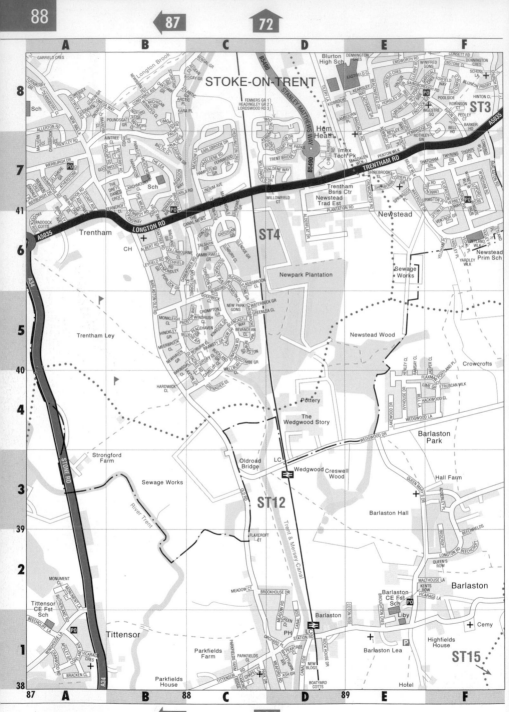

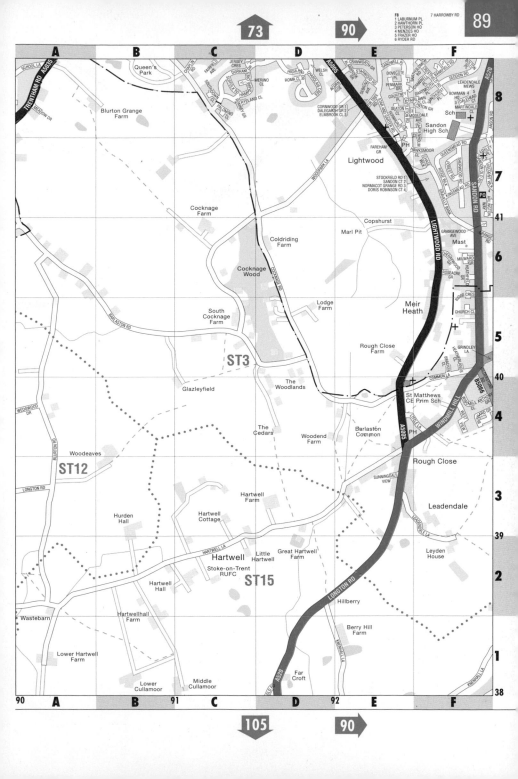

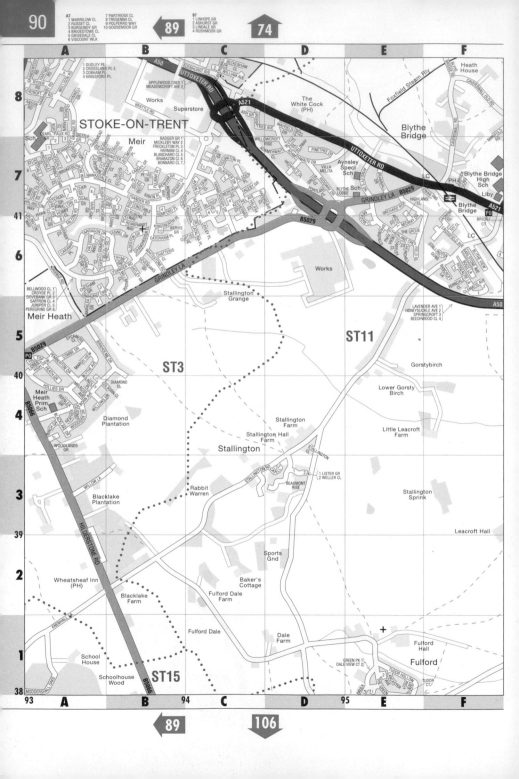

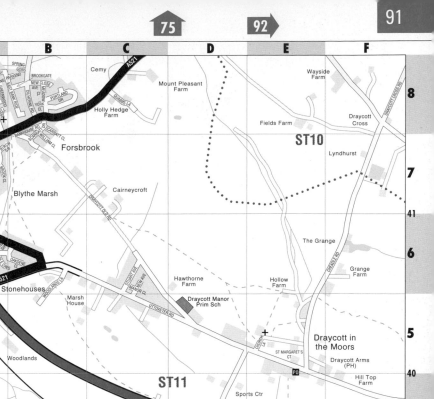

A B C D E F

8
7
41
6
5
40
4
3
39
2
1
38

Moor Green
1 MANIFOLD RD
2 STRATFORD CL
SPRING GDNS
LOW WAY
BROOKGATE
NEW CLOSE
MOOREND
PORTLAND DR
Cemy
A521
Mount Pleasant Farm
Wayside Farm
DRAYCOTT CROSS RD
Holly Hedge Farm
Fields Farm
Draycott Cross
Schs
CHEADLE RD
Forsbrook
ST10
Lyndhurst
Blythe Marsh
Cairneycroft
DRAYCOTT OLD RD
Sch
The Grange
LIMEWOOD CL
OAKDENE
Stonehouses
A521
A50
Marsh House
Hawthorne Farm
Draycott Manor Prim Sch
Hollow Farm
CHEADLE RD
Grange Farm
Draycott in the Moors
WOODLANDS LA
START AVE
NEW AVE
MANOR CL
UTTOXETER RD
St MARGARET'S CT
Draycott Arms (PH)
PO
Hill Top Farm
Woodlands
ST11
Sports Ctr
River Blithe
CRESSWELL LA
Isaac Walton (PH)
CRESSWELL OLD RD
LC (dis)
A50
LC
Cresswell
RAILWAY COTTS
Saverley Green Farm
Saverley House Farm
SANDON RD
SANDON CL
Blythe Pk
ST10
Newton
The Hollows Farm
ROOKERY CRES
LC
Saverley Green
BLYTHE VIEW
MEADVALE
The Hunter (PH)
Leese House Farm
ST15
Wastegate Farm
Paynsley Hall

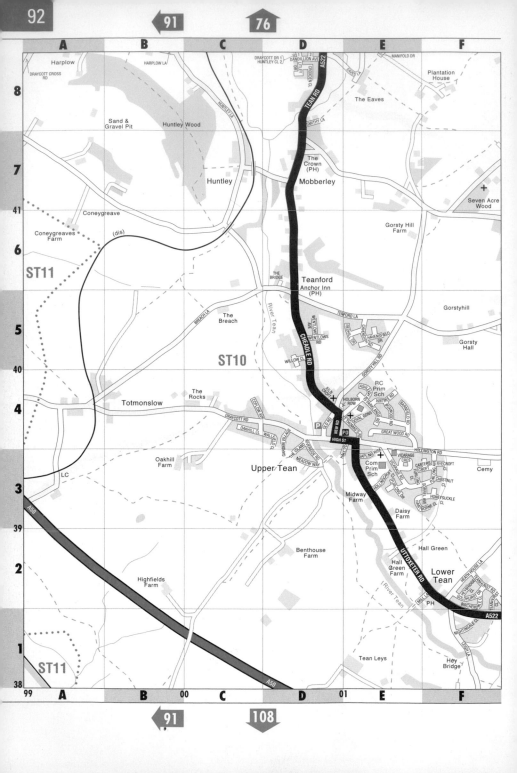

92

A **B** **C** **D** **E** **F**

8

Harplow

DRAYCOTT CROSS RD

HARPLOW LA

DRAYCOTT DR 1
HUNTLEY CL 2

DANDILLION AVE

CROKDEN CL

A522

MANIFOLD DR

Plantation House

7

Sand & Gravel Pit

Huntley Wood

HUNTLEY LA

TEAN RD

SMITHY LA

The Eaves

EAVES LA

41

Coneygreave

Huntley

The Crown (PH)

Mobberley

Seven Acre Wood

6

Coneygreaves Farm

(dis)

ST11

Gorsty Hill Farm

5

THE BRIDGE

Teanford

Anchor Inn (PH)

TENFORD LA

Gorstyhill

40

BREACH LA

The Breach

River Tean

CHEADLE RD

WEST LOWS AVE
WENTLOWS AVE

CAPEWELL DR

HAVENSFIELD

REDHILL DR

Gorsty Hill Farm

Gorsty Hall

5

ST10

WILLOW CL

GORSTY HILL RD

4

The Rocks

Totmonslow

DRAYCOTT RD

COCK LANE AVE

OAKHILL CL
WALLIS CL

GARDEN VILLAGE

NEW RD

OLD RD

WILLOW CL

HOLBORN ROW

PERCIVAL GDNS

THOMAS'S CL

ASH CL

RC Prim Sch

ASPEN CL

AINTREE RD

MANSFORD RD

MANSFIELD RD

GREAT WOOD RD

40

LC

Oakhill Farm

THE ISLAND
BRIDGE CL

MEADOW WAY

HIGH ST

P

PO

SAPLING RISE

HOLLINGTON RD

Cemy

3

A50

Upper Tean

HOLLINGCROFT

PITWOOD CL

Com Prim Sch

VICARAGE CRES

CARTERS CROFT

FURLONG

SORREL AVE

RYECROFT CL

HEART CL

CHESTNUT CL

HONEYSUCKLE CL

39

Midway Farm

Daisy Farm

2

Highfields Farm

Benthouse Farm

Hall Green Farm

Hall Green

UTTOXETER RD

River Tean

Lower Tean

HEATH HOUSE LA

HEYBRIDGE LA

TEANWEST RD 1

PH

MILL CL

BIRCHENCROFT CL

BOLDHURST

TEAN VIEW RD

A522

1

ST11

Tean Leys

Hey Bridge

NIGHTINGALE CL

A50

38

99 **A** **00** **B** **C** **00** **D** **01** **E** **F**

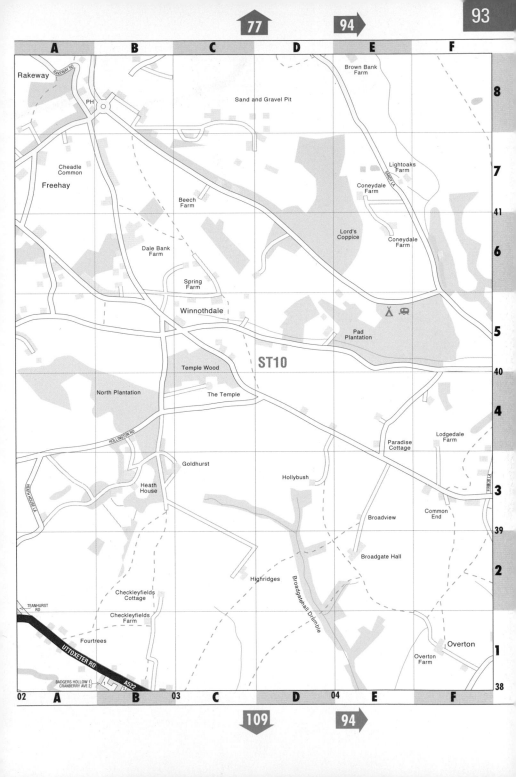

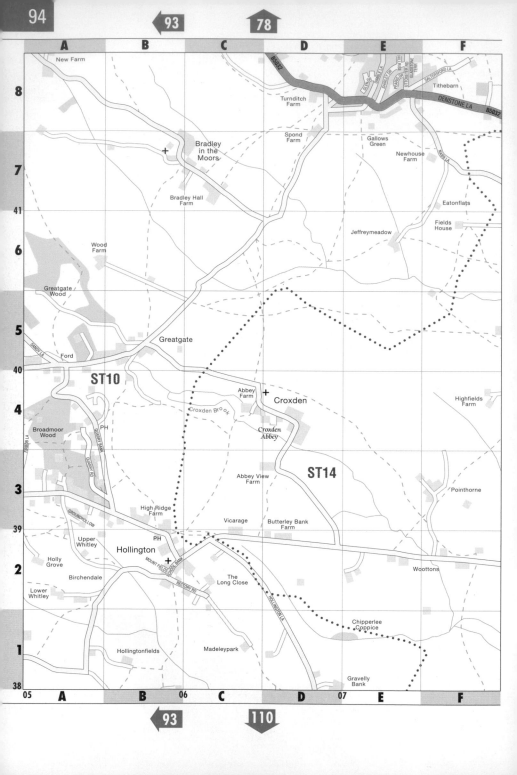

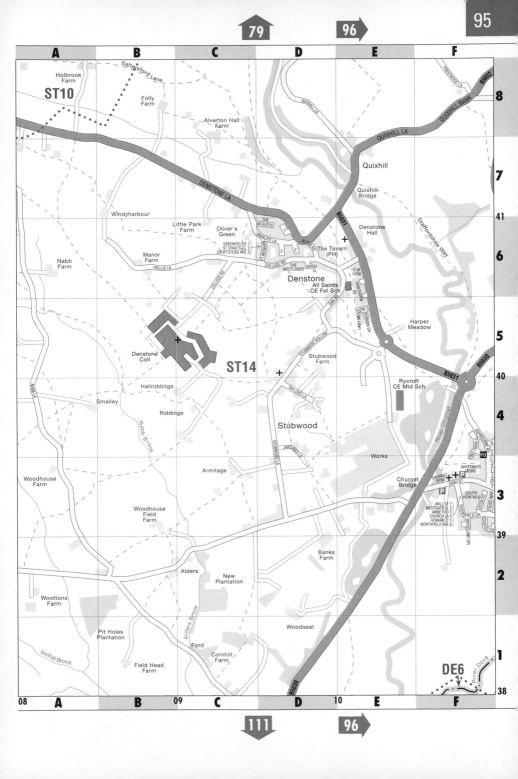

A B C D E F

B5032
B5030
B5033 GREEN LA B5033

8

Ivy Cottages
Osier Plantation
Four Acre Plantation
Green Lane Farm
Woodend

Alfross House
Norbury CE Prim Sch

Dovellys Manor Park
Leigh's Plantation
New House Farm

7

Riverside Doveleys
Roston

41

Inge Cottages
Swinholm Farm
Roston Inn (PH)
Squashly Farm

THE HOLLOW
Limestone Way
MEADOW LA
BELL LA
BACK MOSELEY LA
BACK LA
GREEN LA

6

Dalesgap
Dovecliff

UNDERTOWN LA

Barrowhill

Highfields House
DE6

5

B5030

ST14

River Dove
Shield House Farm
Hurd's Barn

Derbyshire STREET ATLAS

40

Doveflats
The Shawleys

4

Dove Fst Sch
Rocester

WOODSEAT DR
NORTHFIELD AVE
CORONATION CRES
DOVE CL
CHURCH LA
ABBEY RD
WEST AVE

Marston Park
Long Chimneys

Castrum Ct

3

VALLEY VIEW
ABBEY CL
MILL ST
MILL BANK DR
MILL LA

Park Holme
Marston Lodge

Rocester Bridge
White House

39

1 RIVERCROFT CL
2 DOVEFIELDS
3 RIVERSFIELD DR

Daisybank Farm
Alder Carrs

2

Staffordshire Way
Abbotsholme Sch
Clowneholme Farm
Marstonbank Farm
Springfield House

Thurvaston
CURLEY LA

1

Monk's Clownholme
Barway Cottages
Marston House Farm

THURVASTON RD
IVESTON RD
ALVESTON BARN

Sedsall Rough
DE6
Marstonbrook Farm

38

98

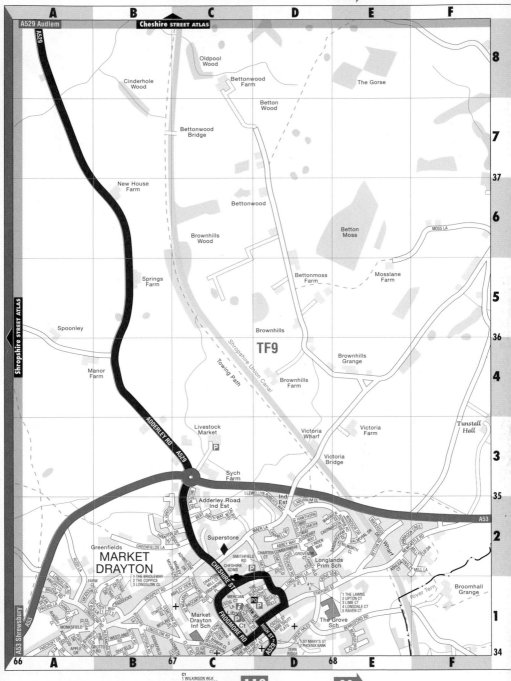

Shropshire STREET ATLAS

A529 Audlem

A529

A53 Shrewsbury

8
7
37
6
5
36
4
3
35
2
1
34

Cinderhole Wood

Oldpool Wood

Bettonwood Farm

The Gorse

Betton Wood

Bettonwood Bridge

New House Farm

Bettonwood

Brownhills Wood

Betton Moss

MOSS LA

Springs Farm

Bettonmoss Farm

Mosslane Farm

Spoonley

Brownhills

TF9

Brownhills Grange

Manor Farm

Towing Path

Shropshire Union Canal

Brownhills Farm

Livestock Market

P

Victoria Wharf

Victoria Farm

Tunstall Hall

Sych Farm

Victoria Bridge

ADDERLEY RD

A529

Adderley Road Ind Est

LLEWELLYN ROBERTS WAY

Ind Est

LABURNUM CL

A53

Superstore

Greenfields

MARKET DRAYTON

GREENFIELDS LA

Longlands Prim Sch

Wharf

Broomhall Grange

SMITHFIELD RD

CHESHIRE ST

Market Drayton Inf Sch

FROGMORE RD

P O
P

Liby

Ct

1 THE BRIDLEWAY
2 THE COPPICE
3 LONGSLOW CL

River Tern

The Grove Sch

1 THE LAWNS
2 UPTON CT
3 LIME CT
4 LONSDALE CT
5 RAVEN CT

1 ST MARY'S ST
2 PHOENIX BANK

C1
1 WILKINSON WLK
2 THE BUTTERCROSS
3 RODENHURST HOUSE FLATS
4 CORBET CT
5 WARREN CT

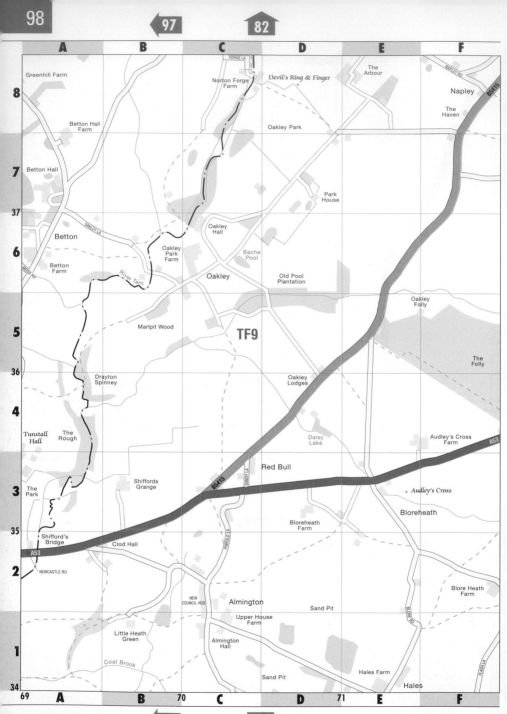

	A	B	C	D	E	F

8

Greenhill Farm

Betton Hall Farm

FORGE LA

Norton Forge Farm

Devil's Ring & Finger

The Arbour

NAPLEY RD

Napley

The Haven

B5415

7

Betton Hall

Oakley Park

Park House

37

OAKLEY LA

Betton

Oakley Hall

Bache Pool

6

Oakley Park Farm

Betton Farm

River Tern

Oakley

Old Pool Plantation

Oakley Folly

MESS RD

5

Marlpit Wood

TF9

Oakley Lodges

The Folly

36

Drayton Spinney

4

Tunstall Hall

The Rough

Daisy Lake

Audley's Cross Farm

A53

Shiffords Grange

Red Bull

Audley's Cross

Bloreheath

3

The Park

B5415

SANDY LA

Bloreheath Farm

35

Shifford's Bridge

Clod Hall

PINFOLD LA

BLORE RD

2

A53

NEWCASTLE RD

NEW COUNCIL HOS

Almington

Sand Pit

Blore Heath Farm

FLASH LA

Upper House Farm

Little Heath Green

Almington Hall

1

Coal Brook

Sand Pit

Hales Farm

Hales

34

| 69 | A | B | 70 | C | D | 71 | E | F |

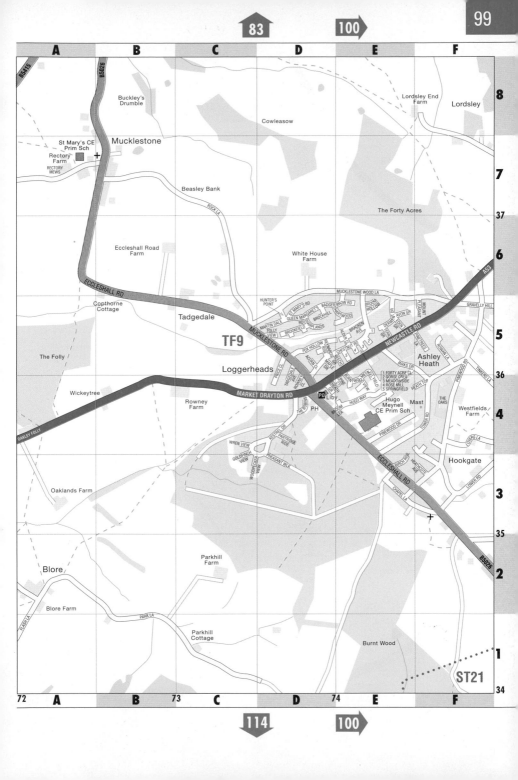

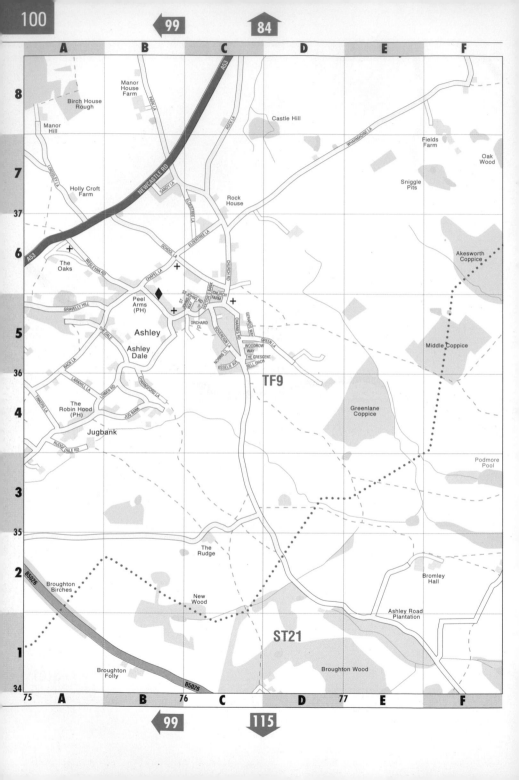

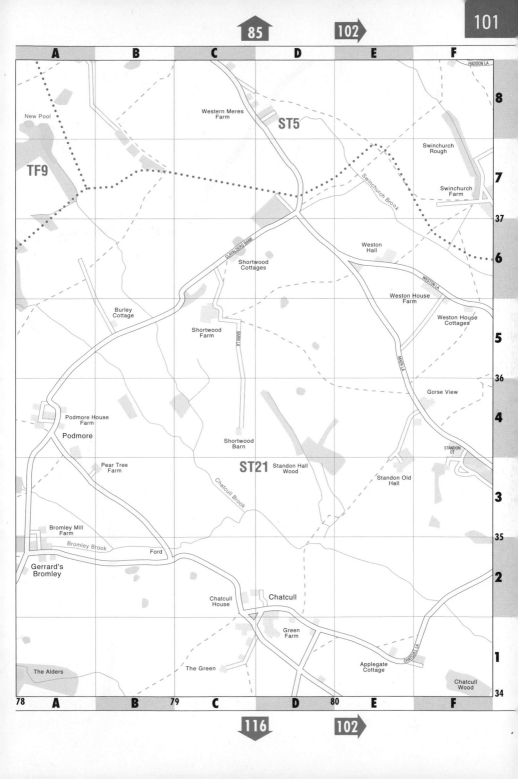

85
102

A **B** **C** **D** **E** **F**

HADDON LA

New Pool

8

Western Meres Farm

ST5

Swinchurch Rough

TF9

Swinchurch Brook

Swinchurch Farm

7

37

CLAYALDERS BANK

Weston Hall

Shortwood Cottages

6

WESTON LA

Burley Cottage

Weston House Farm

Weston House Cottages

Shortwood Farm

BARN LA

MARSH LA

5

36

Gorse View

Podmore House Farm

4

Podmore

Shortwood Barn

STANDON CT

Pear Tree Farm

ST21

Standon Hall Wood

Standon Old Hall

3

Chatcull Brook

Bromley Mill Farm

Bromley Brook

Ford

35

Gerrard's Bromley

2

Chatcull House

Chatcull

Green Farm

1

The Alders

The Green

Applegate Cottage

CHATCULL LA

Chatcull Wood

34

78 **A** **B** **79** **C** **D** **80** **E** **F**

116
102

101
86

A B C D E F

ST4

8

Chapel Chorlton

ST5

7

37

Hatton Waterworks Cotts

Upper Hatton

Hatton Bogs

Clifford's Wood

Hatton Mill

Ppg Sta
Chy

Black Bank

ST15

6

Lodgebarn

A51

Clifford's Wood Cottages

Swinchurch Brook

Lower Hatton

Butt House

BUTTHOUSE LA

Meece Brook

Marlpit Plantation

5

Beech Hill

BACK LA

The Red Lion (PH)

The Gorse Covert

GORSY LA

School Farm

36

Outdoor Education Centre

Bowers Hall Farm

ST21

Cranberry

Bowers

WESTON LA

BOWERS BENT

SANDY BANK

SANDY LA

Cotes Lodge

4

BOWERS LA

Cotes Heath

Moorfields

Bowers Farm

CHURCH LA

CRANBERRY MARSH

Westfield House

Moorfields Ind Est

3

Staun Wood

Osier Beds

Cotes Hall

HALL

NEWCASTLE RD

MHER LA

Standon House

All Saints CE Fst Sch

Mill

Railway Cotts

ST JAMES DR

35

PO

MILL LA

STATION RD

Chestnut CT

COTES LA

The Old Rectory

CHATCULL LA

ROCKS LA

Standon

Nelson Cres

1 2

Church View 1
Briar Way 2

2

Little Standon Farm

The Beeches

THE ROCKS

Ashlyn

ST15

1

Chatcull Brook

ROCK LA

Broadacres

Walford Back La

34

81 A B 82 C D 83 E F

101
117

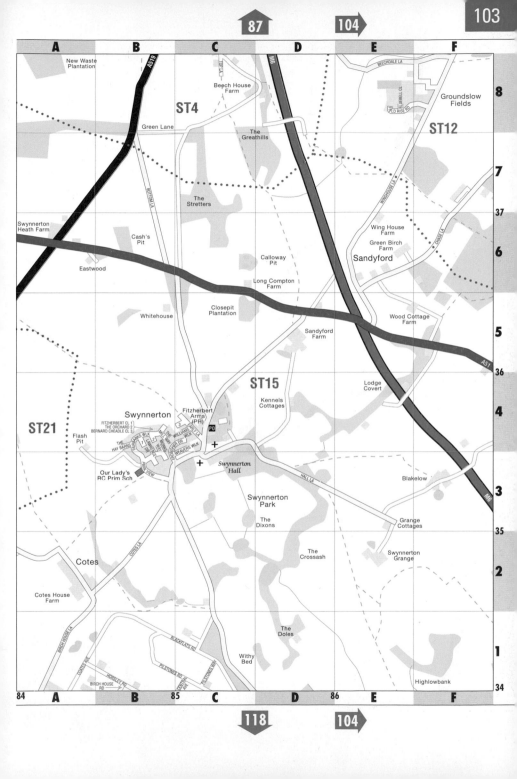

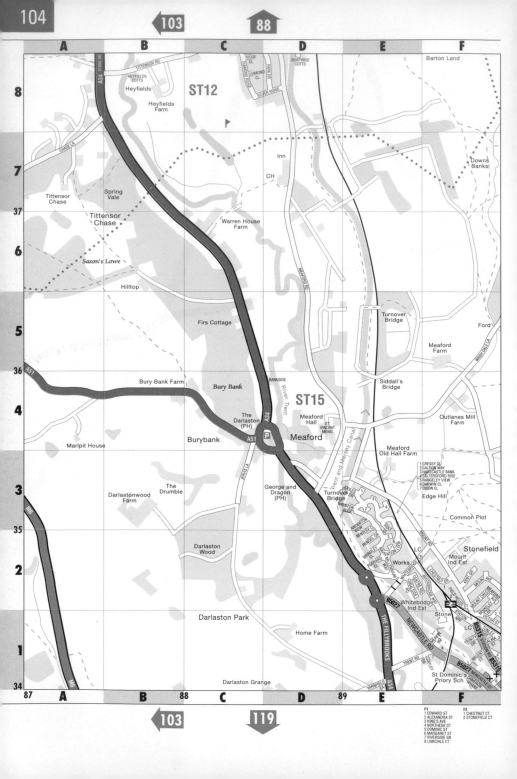

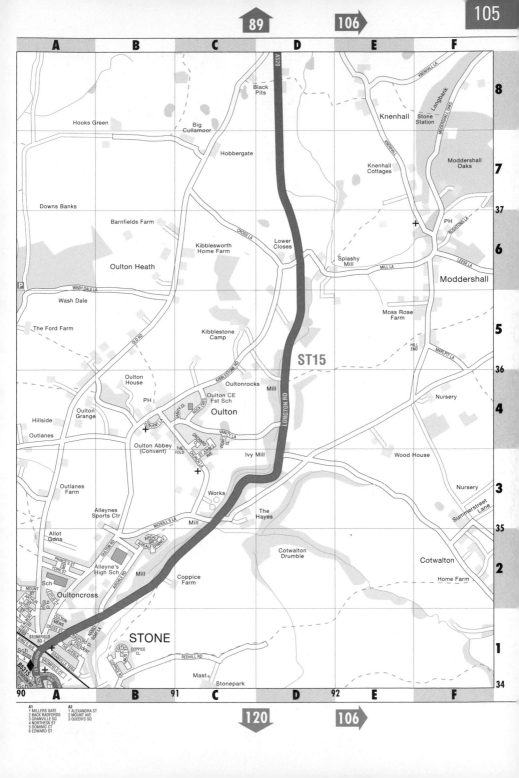

| | A | B | C | D | E | F |

8

Hooks Green

Black Pits

Knenhall

Stone Station

Longbank

Big Cullamoor

Hobbergate

Knenhall Cottages

Moddershall Oaks

7

Downs Banks

37

Barnfields Farm

CROSS LA

Lower Closes

PH

BUSHTON LA

6

Kibblesworth Home Farm

Splashy Mill

MILL LA

LEESE LA

Moddershall

Oulton Heath

WASH DALE LA

Wash Dale

Moss Rose Farm

5

The Ford Farm

OLD RD

Kibblestone Camp

ST15

HILL END

MARLPIT LA

36

Oulton House

Oultonrocks

Mill

Nursery

4

Hillside

PH

Oulton CE Fst Sch

Oulton

LONGTON RD

Oulton Grange

Outlanes

VANITY PL

ROCK CRES

CONVENT LA

ORCHARD CL

VICAR'S CL

Oulton Abbey (Convent)

THE FOLD

CHURCH LA

ST JOHN'S AVE

VANITY LA

Ivy Mill

Wood House

3

Outlanes Farm

Works

The Hayes

Nursery

Summerstreet Lane

Alleynes Sports Ctr

NICHOLL'S LA

Mill

35

Allot Gdns

OULTON RD

AIRDALE GR

AIRDALE SPINNEY

Cotwalton Drumble

Cotwalton

2

PRINCE'S ST

YORK ST

Sch

Alleyne's High Sch

AIRDALE RD

Mill

Coppice Farm

Home Farm

MOUNT ST

ARTHUR ST

OLD RD CL

Oultoncross

OULTON MEWS

KINGS GIANT LA

STONE

COPPICE CL

1

Sch

STONEFIELD SQ

KING ST

GRANVILLE TERR

RADFORD CL

THE AVENUE

COPPICE CL

COPPICE GDNS

REDHILL RD

B5315

BROMFIELD CT

CHRISTCHURCH

A520

Sch

Mast

Stonepark

34

| 90 | A | B | 91 | C | D | 92 | E | F |

A1
1 MILLERS GATE
2 BACK RADFORDS
3 GRANVILLE SQ
4 NORTHESK ST
5 DOMINIC CT
6 EDWARD ST

A2
1 ALEXANDRA ST
2 MOUNT AVE
3 QUEEN'S SQ

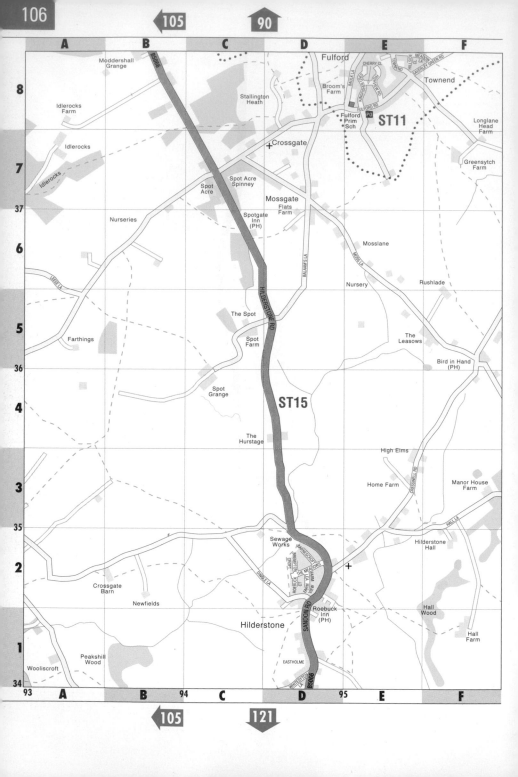

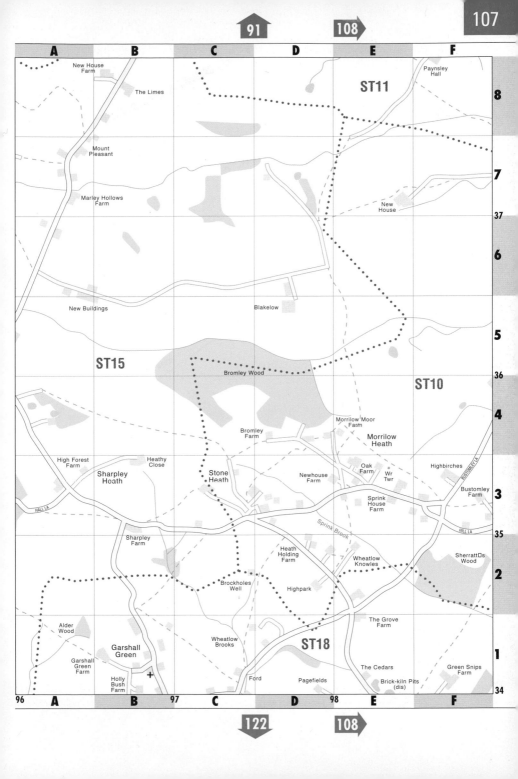

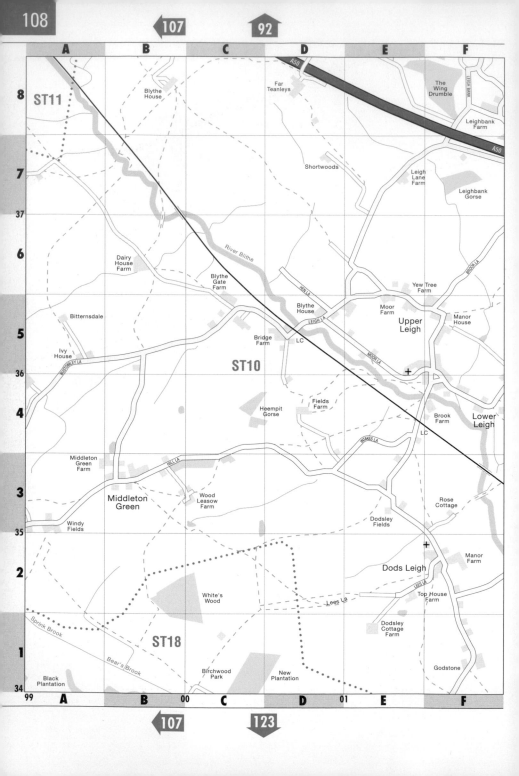

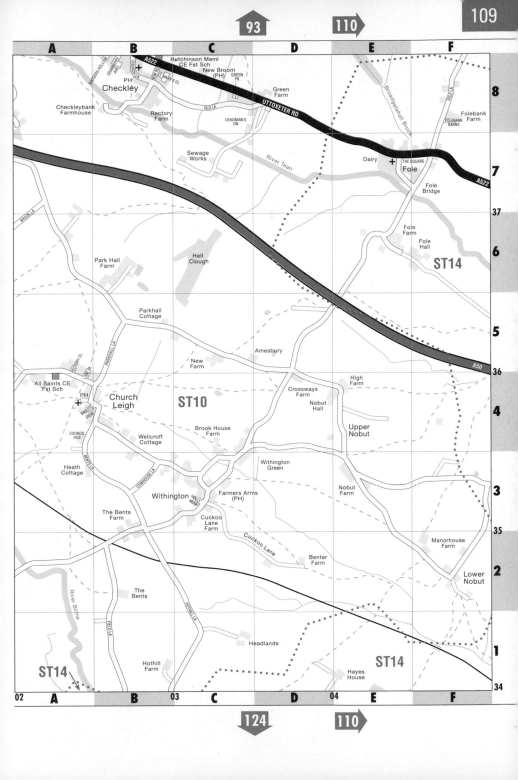

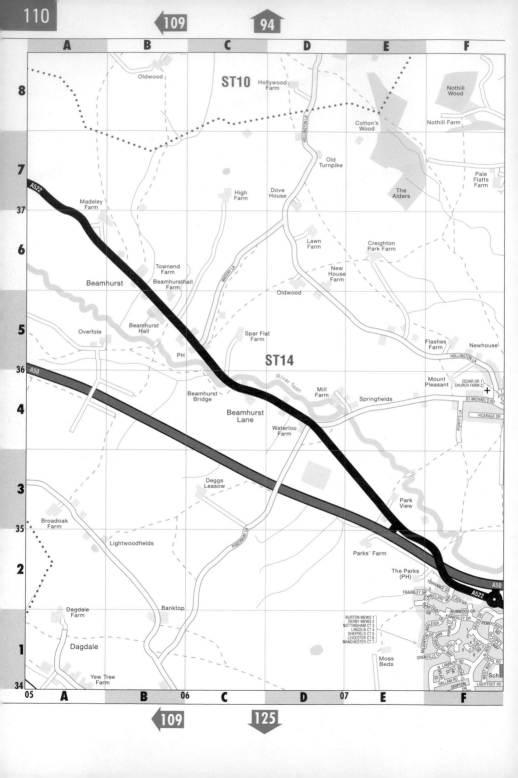

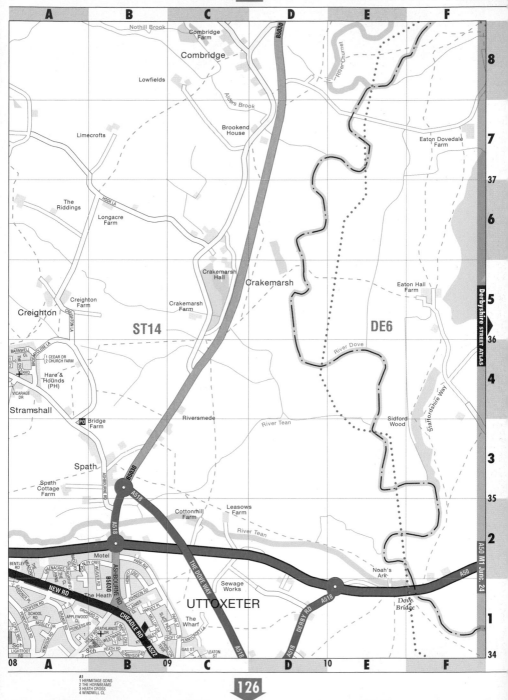

A1
1 HERMITAGE GDNS
2 THE HORNBEAMS
3 HEATH CROSS
4 WINDMILL CL

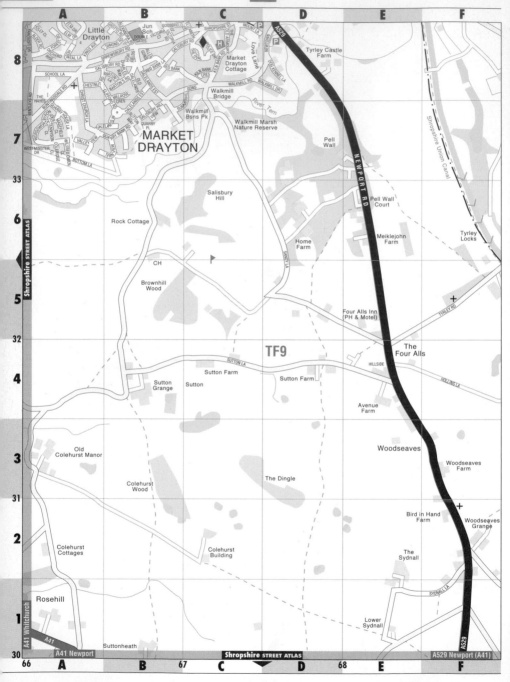

A8
1 PARKER BOWLES DR
2 GLENDON CL
3 ELLESMERE GR
4 SPRINGFIELD MOBILE HOME PK

97

Little Drayton

Jun Sch

MARKET DRAYTON

Market Drayton Cottage

Walkmill Bridge

Walkmill Bsns Pk

River Tern

Walkmill Marsh Nature Reserve

Tyrley Castle Farm

Pell Wall

NEWPORT RD

Pell Wall Court

Meiklejohn Farm

Tyrley Locks

Shropshire Union Canal

Salisbury Hill

Rock Cottage

CH

Brownhill Wood

Home Farm

SANCT LA

Four Alls Inn (PH & Motel)

TYRLEY RD

TF9

The Four Alls

SUTTON LA

Sutton Farm

Sutton Grange

Sutton

Sutton Farm

HILLSIDE

HOLLINS LA

Avenue Farm

Old Colehurst Manor

Colehurst Wood

The Dingle

Woodseaves

Woodseaves Farm

Bird in Hand Farm

Woodseaves Grange

Colehurst Cottages

Colehurst Building

The Sydnall

Rosehill

SYDNALL LA

Lower Sydnall

Suttonheath

A41 Whitchurch

A41

A41 Newport

A529

A529 Newport (A41)

Shropshire STREET ATLAS

66 A 67 B C 67 D 68 E F

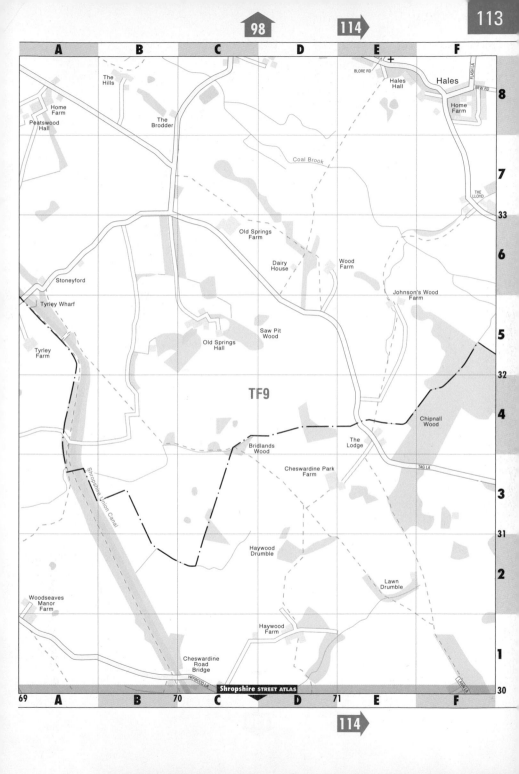

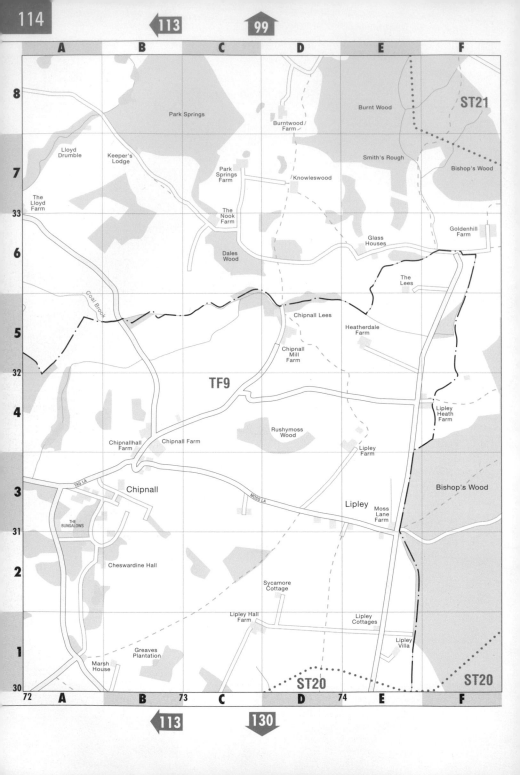

113
99

A **B** **C** **D** **E** **F**

8

ST21

Park Springs

Burntwood
Farm

Burnt Wood

Lloyd
Drumble

Keeper's
Lodge

Smith's Rough

Bishop's
Wood

7

Park
Springs
Farm

Knowleswood

The Lloyd
Farm

The Nook
Farm

33

Goldenhill
Farm

Dales
Wood

Glass
Houses

6

The
Lees

Coal Brook

Chipnall Lees

5

Chipnall Lees

Heatherdale
Farm

Chipnall
Mill
Farm

32

TF9

4

Lipley
Heath
Farm

Rushymoss
Wood

Chipnallhall
Farm

Chipnall Farm

Lipley
Farm

3

TAG LA

Chipnall

MOSS LA

Lipley

Moss
Lane
Farm

Bishop's Wood

31

THE
BUNGALOWS

2

Cheswardine Hall

Sycamore
Cottage

Lipley
Cottages

1

Lipley Hall
Farm

Lipley
Villa

Greaves
Plantation

30

Marsh
House

ST20

ST20

72 **A** **B** 73 **C** **D** 74 **E** **F**

113
130

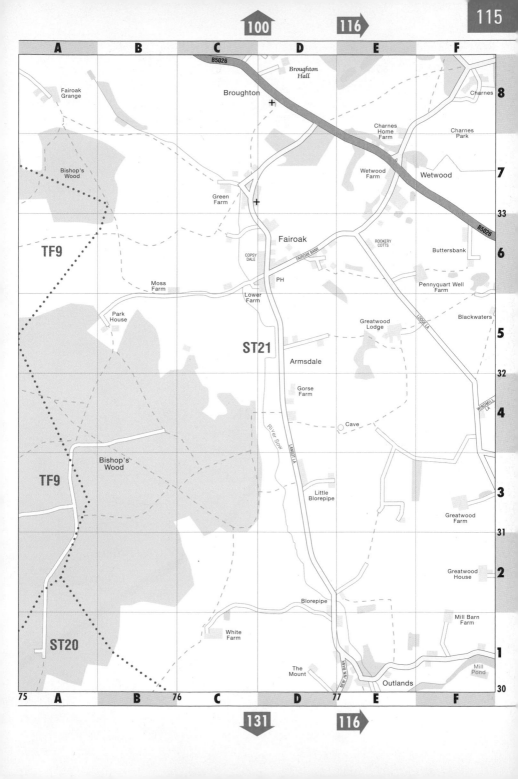

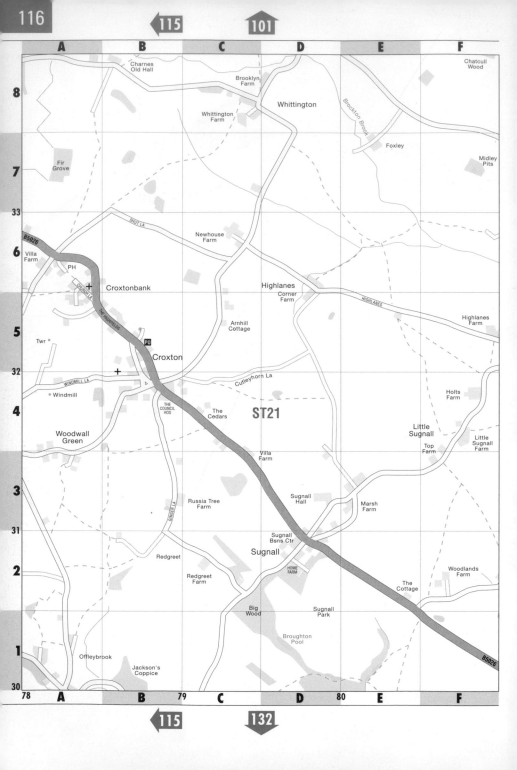

115
101

8

Charnes
Old Hall

Brooklyn
Farm

Whittington

Whittington
Farm

Brockton Brook

Chatcull
Wood

7

Fir
Grove

Foxley

Midley
Pits

33

SHUT LA

B5026

Newhouse
Farm

6

Villa
Farm

PH

Croxtonbank

Highlanes

Corner
Farm

HIGHLANES

Highlanes
Farm

CHURCH LA

THE HIGHFIELDS

Arnhill
Cottage

5

Twr

PO

Croxton

Holts
Farm

32

WINDMILL LA

Cutleyhorn La

Windmill

4

THE
COUNCIL
HOS

The
Cedars

ST21

Little
Sugnall

Little
Sugnall
Farm

Woodwall
Green

Villa
Farm

Top
Farm

3

GINGER LA

Russia Tree
Farm

Sugnall
Hall

Marsh
Farm

31

Sugnall
Bsns Ctr

Redgreet

Sugnall

2

Redgreet
Farm

HOME
FARM

Woodlands
Farm

The
Cottage

Big
Wood

Sugnall
Park

1

Offleybrook

Broughton
Pool

B5026

30

Jackson's
Coppice

78   **A**   **B**   79   **C**   **D**   80   **E**   **F**

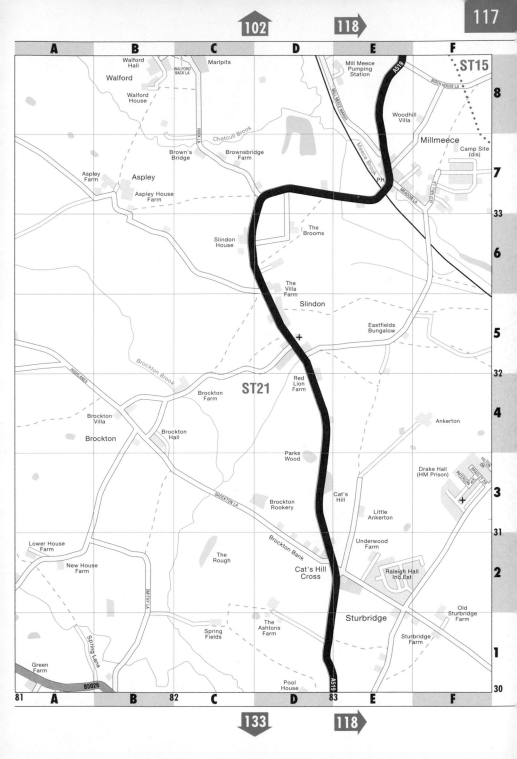

ST15

A B C D E F

8

Walford
Hall
Marlpits

Walford

WALFORD
BACK LA

Mill Meece
Pumping
Station

A519

BIRCH HOUSE LA

Walford
House

Woodhill
Villa

Millmeece

ROCK LA

Chatcull Brook

Camp Site
(dis)

7

Brown's
Bridge

Brownsbridge
Farm

Aspley
Farm

Aspley

Meece Brook

PH

OLD HILL LA

MEADOW LA

Aspley House
Farm

33

The
Brooms

Slindon
House

6

The
Villa
Farm

Slindon

Eastfields
Bungalow

5

Brockton Brook

+

32

HIGHLANES

ST21

Red
Lion
Farm

Ankerton

4

Brockton
Farm

Brockton
Villa

Brockton
Hall

Drake Hall
(HM Prison)

HILTON DR

BRINDLEY DR

PATTISON AVE

Brockton

Parks
Wood

+

3

BROCKTON LA

Cat's
Hill

31

Brockton
Rookery

Little
Ankerton

Lower House
Farm

Brockton Bank

Underwood
Farm

Raleigh Hall
Ind Est

2

New House
Farm

The
Rough

Cat's Hill
Cross

Old
Sturbridge
Farm

SMITHY LA

Spring Lane

Spring
Fields

The
Ashtons
Farm

Sturbridge

Sturbridge
Farm

1

Green
Farm

B5026

Pool
House

A519

30

81 A B 82 C D 83 E F

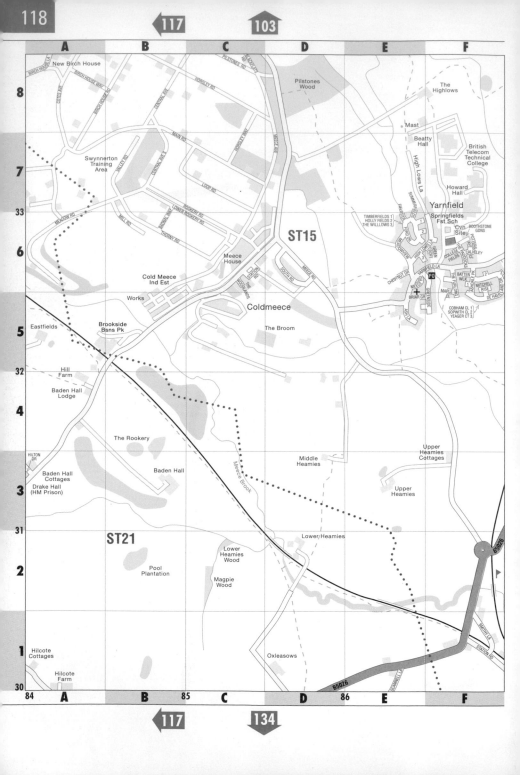

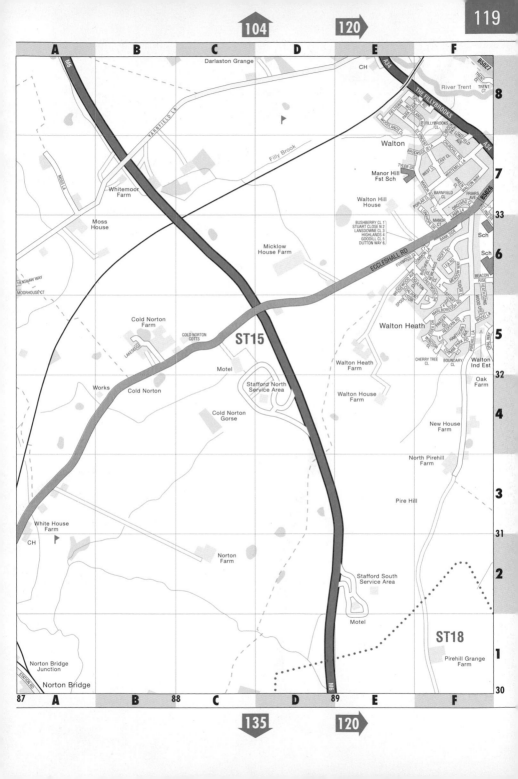

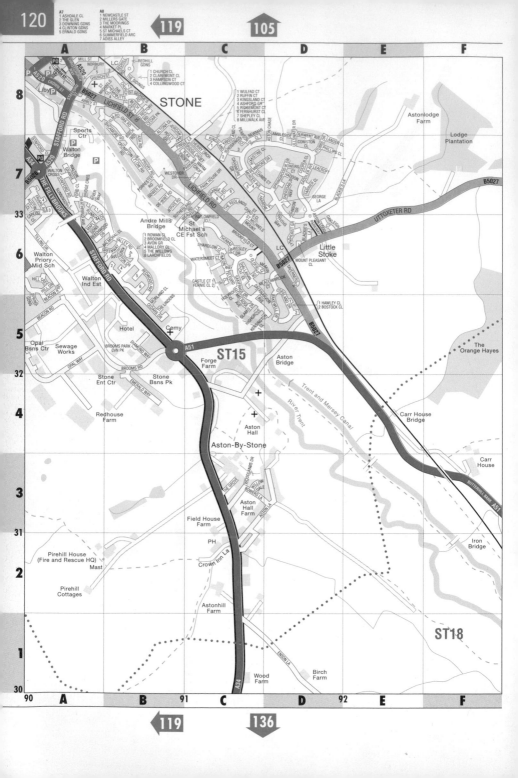

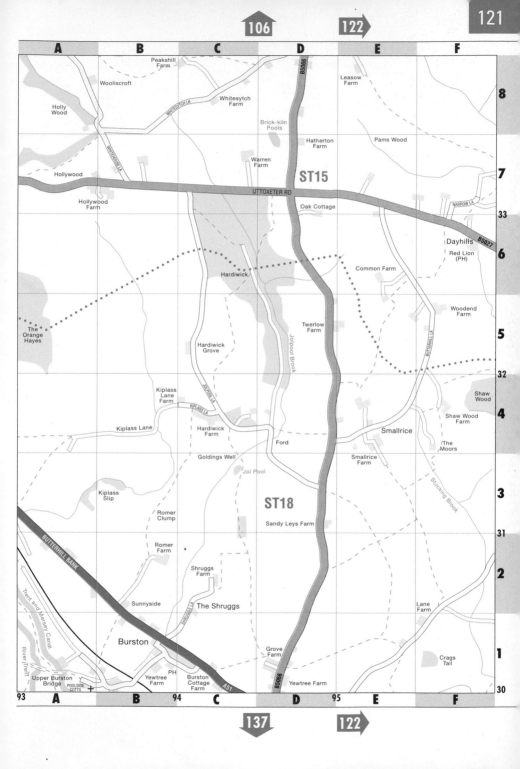

106
122

A B C D E F

8

Peakshill Farm

Wooliscroft

Holly Wood

WHITESYTCH LA

Whitesytch Farm

Brick-kiln Pools

Leasow Farm

Hatherton Farm

Pams Wood

7

Hollywood

Warren Farm

UTTOXETER RD

ST15

B5066

Oak Cottage

33

Hollywood Farm

WHITECROSS LA

NARROW LA

Dayhills

B5027

6

Red Lion (PH)

Hardiwick

Common Farm

Woodend Farm

The Orange Hayes

Hardiwick Grove

Twerlow Farm

Jolpool Brook

BUTTERHILL LA

5

32

Kiplass Lane Farm

Kiplass Lane

KIPLASS LA

JACKSON LA

Hardiwick Farm

Ford

Smallrice

Shaw Wood

Shaw Wood Farm

The Moors

4

Goldings Well

Jol Pool

Smallrice Farm

Stucking Brook

3

Kiplass Slip

Romer Clump

ST18

Sandy Leys Farm

31

BUTTERHILL BANK

Romer Farm

Shruggs Farm

Lane Farm

2

Trent and Mersey Canal

Sunnyside

SHRUGGS LA

The Shruggs

River Trent

Burston

Grove Farm

Crags Tail

1

Upper Burston Bridge

POOLSIDE COTTS

PH

Yewtree Farm

Burston Cottage Farm

A51

B5066

Yewtree Farm

30

93 A B 94 C D 95 E F

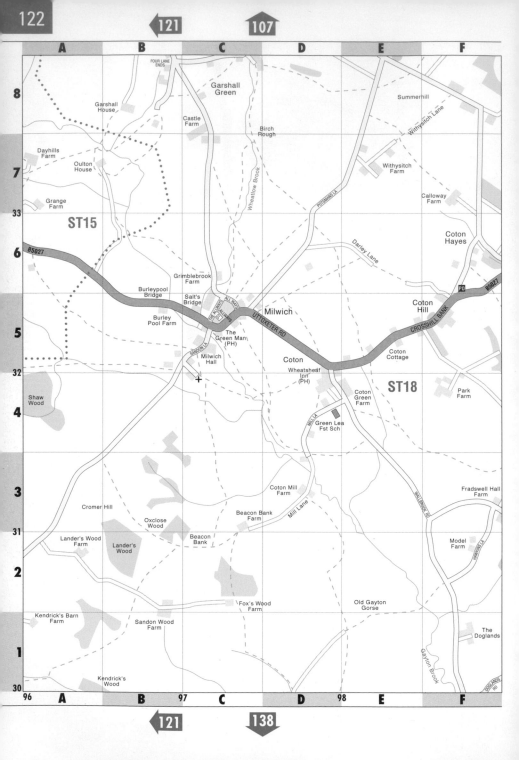

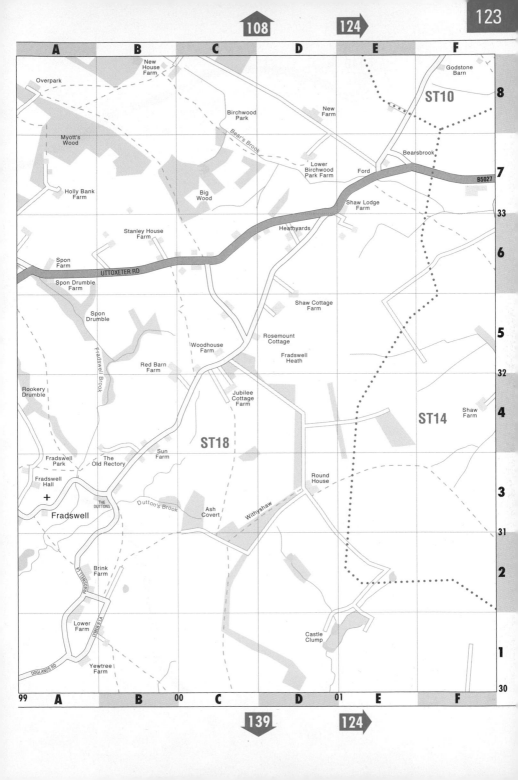

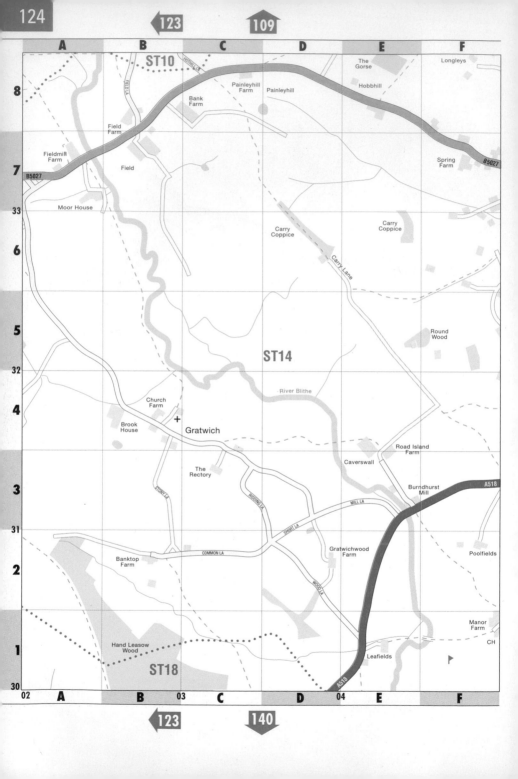

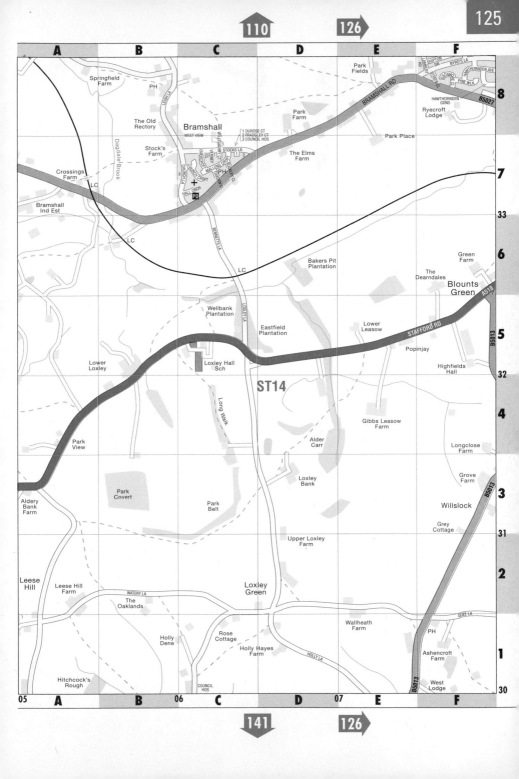

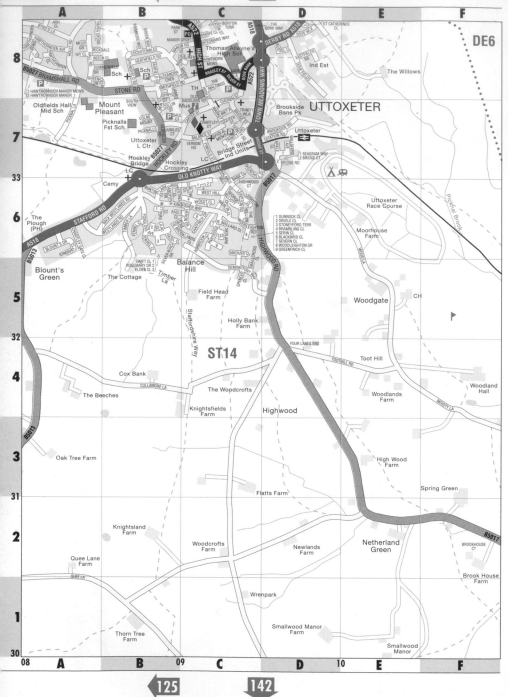

DE6

UTTOXETER

ST14

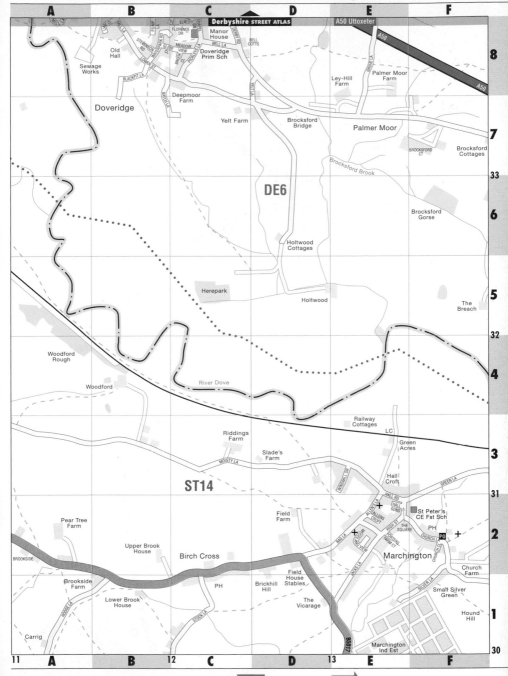

Derbyshire STREET ATLAS

A50 Uttoxeter

A   B   C   D   E   F

8

7

33

6

5

32

4

3

31

2

1

30

Old Hall

Sewage Works

Doveridge

Manor House

Doveridge Prim Sch

Deepmoor Farm

BLACKPIT LA

Yelt Farm

Brocksford Bridge

BELL COTTS

Ley-Hill Farm

Palmer Moor Farm

Palmer Moor

BROCKSFORD CT

Brocksford Cottages

Brocksford Brook

DE6

Brocksford Gorse

Holtwood Cottages

Herepark

Holtwood

The Breach

Woodford Rough

River Dove

Woodford

Railway Cottages

LC

Green Acres

Riddings Farm

Slade's Farm

MOISTY LA

ST14

Hall Croft

WINDMILL DR

GREEN LA

St Peter's CE Fst Sch

Pear Tree Farm

Field Farm

HALL RD

HALL GDNS

ALLENS CROFT

THE SQUARE

PH

CHURCH LA

PO

Upper Brook House

Birch Cross

BROOKSIDE

Brookside Farm

Lower Brook House

PH

STOCK LA

Brickhill Hill

Field House Stables

The Vicarage

BAG LA

JACKS LA

Marchington

Church Farm

SILVER LA

Small Silver Green

Hound Hill

RIDGE LA

Carrig

B5017

Marchington Ind Est

11   A   B   12   C   D   13   E   F

127

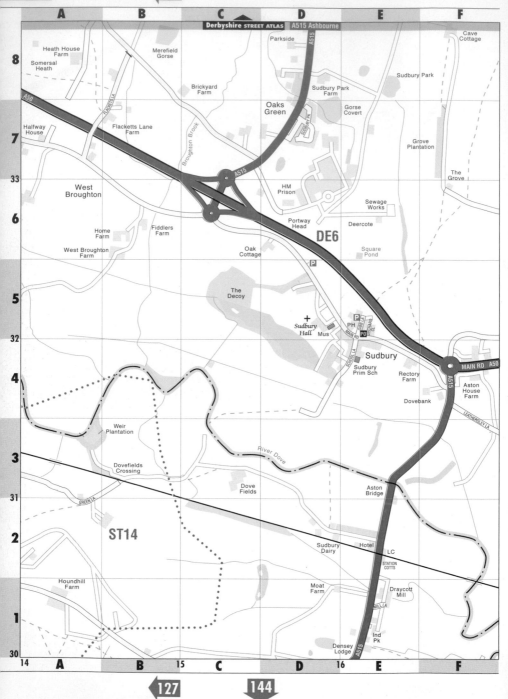

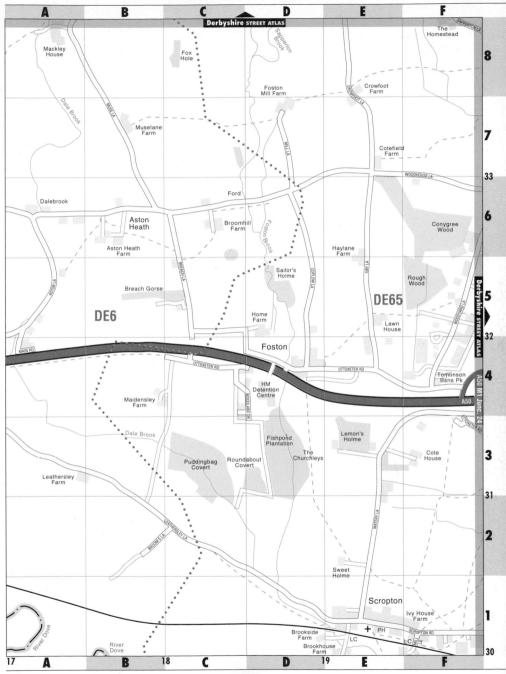

Derbyshire STREET ATLAS

The Homestead

Mackley House

Fox Hole

Foston Mill Farm

Crowfoot Farm

8

Dale Brook

MOOR LA

Muselane Farm

MILL LA

CROWFOOT LA

Cotefield Farm

WOODHOUSE LA

7

33

Dalebrook

Ford

Aston Heath

Broomhill Farm

Foston Brook

Conygree Wood

6

Aston Heath Farm

BREACH LA

Haylane Farm

HAY LA

Rough Wood

DE65

ASTON LA

Breach Gorse

Sailor's Holme

COPLOW LA

5

DE6

Home Farm

Lawn House

LITCHURCH LA

32

MAIN RD

Foston

UTTOXETER RD

UTTOXETER RD

Tomlinson Bsns Pk

4

A50

HM Detention Centre

WOODLAND DR

Maidensley Farm

Derbyshire STREET ATLAS

A50 M1 Junc. 24

UTTOXETER RD

Dale Brook

Lemon's Holme

Cote House

3

Puddingbag Covert

Roundabout Covert

Fishpond Plantation

The Churchleys

31

Leathersley Farm

WATERY LA

LEATHERSLEY LA

2

BROOM S LA

Sweet Holme

Scropton

Ivy House Farm

1

River Dove

River Dove

Brookside Farm

Brookhouse Farm

PH

LC

SCROPTON RD

LC

30

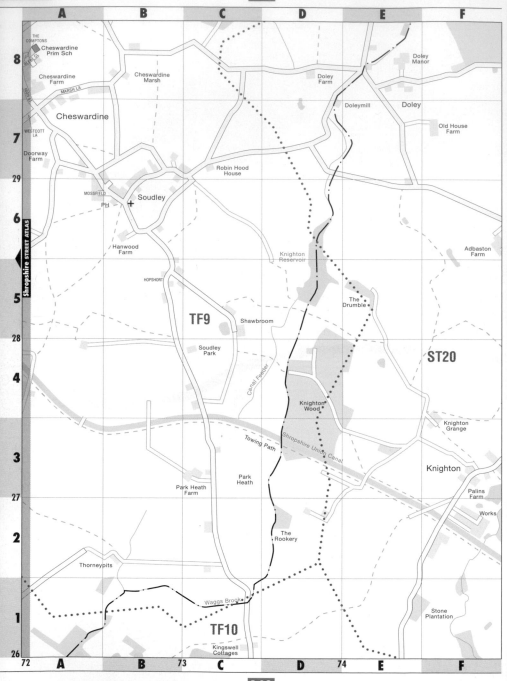

A | B | C | D | E | F

8

THE COMPTONS

Cheswardine Prim Sch

Cheswardine Farm

MARSH LA

Cheswardine

Cheswardine Marsh

Doley Manor

Doley Farm

Doleymill

Doley

Old House Farm

7

WESTCOTT LA

Doorway Farm

29

Robin Hood House

MOSSFIELD

PH

Soudley

6

Hanwood Farm

Knighton Reservoir

Adbaston Farm

HOPSHORT

5

TF9

Shawbroom

The Drumble

ST20

28

Soudley Park

Canal Feeder

4

Knighton Wood

Knighton Grange

3

Towing Path

Shropshire Union Canal

Knighton

27

Park Heath Farm

Park Heath

Palins Farm

Works

2

The Rookery

Thorneypits

1

Waggs Brook

Stone Plantation

26

TF10

Kingswell Cottages

72 | A | B | 73 | C | D | 74 | E | F

Shropshire STREET ATLAS

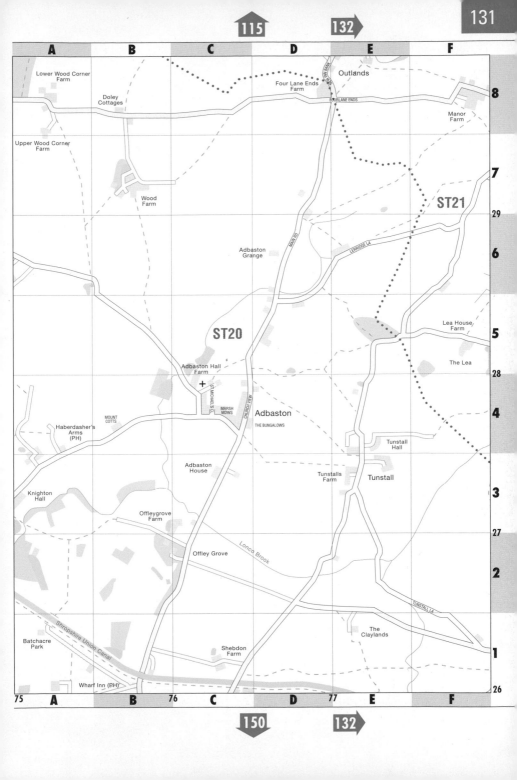

A **B** **C** **D** **E** **F**

8

Offleybrook

Walk Mill
Mill

Walk Mill

Cop Mere

Pershall
Pool

Bishop's
Offley

Offleyrock

Offleyhay

PO

Star Inn
(PH)

Villa
Farm

White House
Farm

MERE RISE

7

Copmere
End

Offleymarsh

Marsh
House

29

Brann
Farm

Rufford

The
Drumble

6

Lea
Knowl

Windsend

Peafield
Covert

The
Manor

5

ST21

Little
Horsley

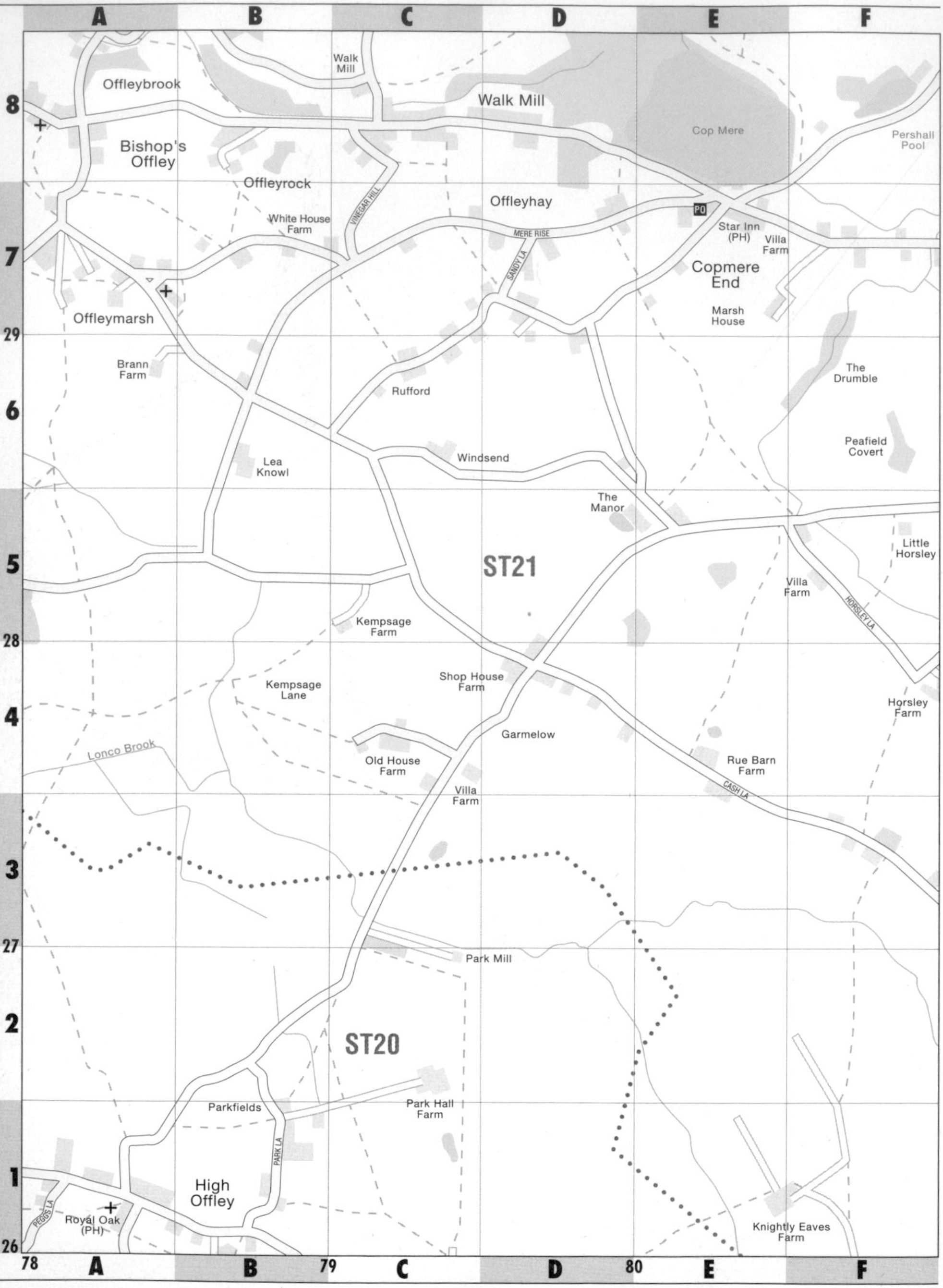

Villa
Farm

Kempsage
Farm

Villa
Farm

28

Kempsage
Lane

Shop House
Farm

Horsley
Farm

4

Lonco Brook

Garmelow

Rue Barn
Farm

Old House
Farm

Villa
Farm

CASTLE LA

3

27

Park Mill

2

ST20

Parkfields

Park Hall
Farm

PARK LA

1

High
Offley

26

Royal Oak
(PH)

Knightly Eaves
Farm

PERSHALL LA

78 **A**   **B** 79 **C**   **D** 80 **E**   **F**

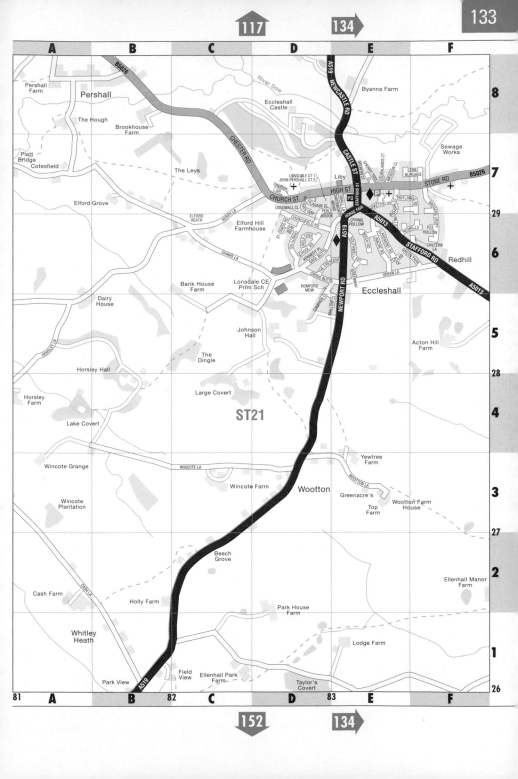

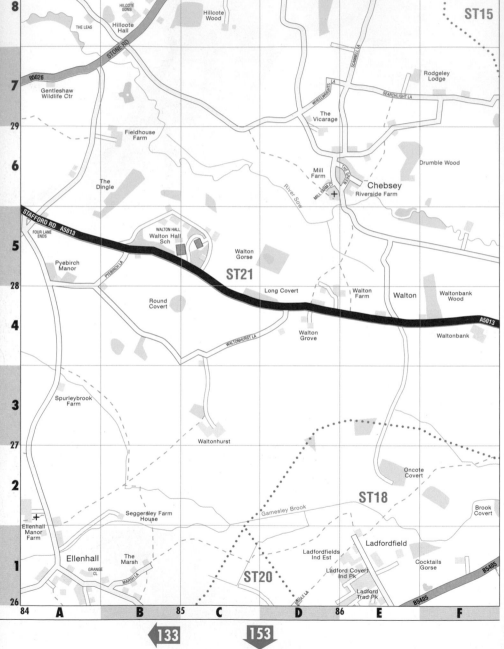

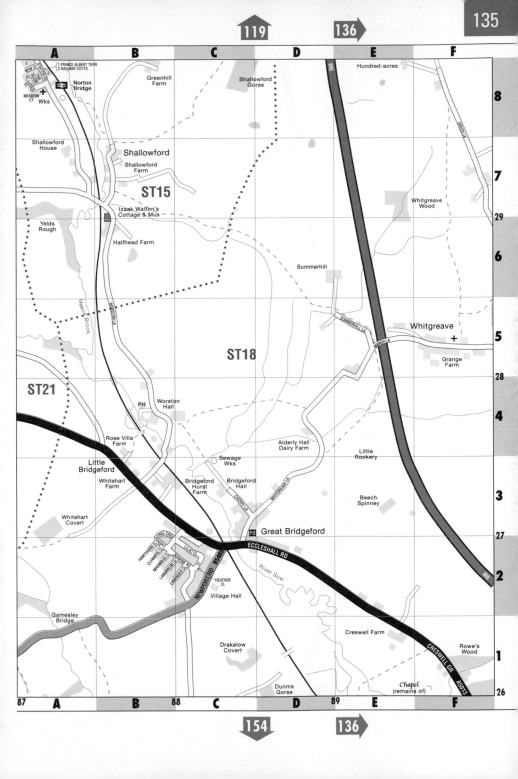

A **B** **C** **D** **E** **F**

1 PRINCE ALBERT TERR
2 RAILWAY COTTS

Hundred-acres

Greenhill
Farm

Shallowford
Gorse

Norton
Bridge

NEW ST
THE
GLEBE
CL

MEADOW
CT
Wks

8

Shallowford
House

Shallowford

GREEN LA

Whitgreave
Wood

7

Shallowford
Farm

ST15

29

Izaak Walton's
Cottage & Mus

Yelds
Rough

Halfhead Farm

Summerhill

6

Meece Brook

EGGTON LA

ST18

SUMMERHILL LA

Whitgreave

5

MILL LA

Grange
Farm

28

ST21

Worston
Hall

PH

Rose Villa
Farm

Alderly Hall
Dairy Farm

Little
Rookery

4

Little
Bridgeford

Whitehart
Farm

Sewage
Wks

Bridgeford
Hurst
Farm

Bridgeford
Hall

CHERRY LA

WHITGREAVE LA

Beech
Spinney

3

Whitehart
Covert

PO

Great Bridgeford

HAWTHORNE CL
CLEMATIS CL
CHESTNUT CL
LILAC CL

MAGNOLIA CL
LABURNUM CL

NEWPORT RD

BEACON

ECCLESHALL RD

27

LAVENDER CL

HEATHER
CL

River Sow

M6

2

Gamesley
Bridge

Village Hall

Drakelow
Covert

Creswell Farm

CRESWELL GR

Rowe's
Wood

A5013

1

Dunnis
Gorse

Chapel
(remains of)

26

87 **A** **B** 88 **C** **D** 89 **E** **F**

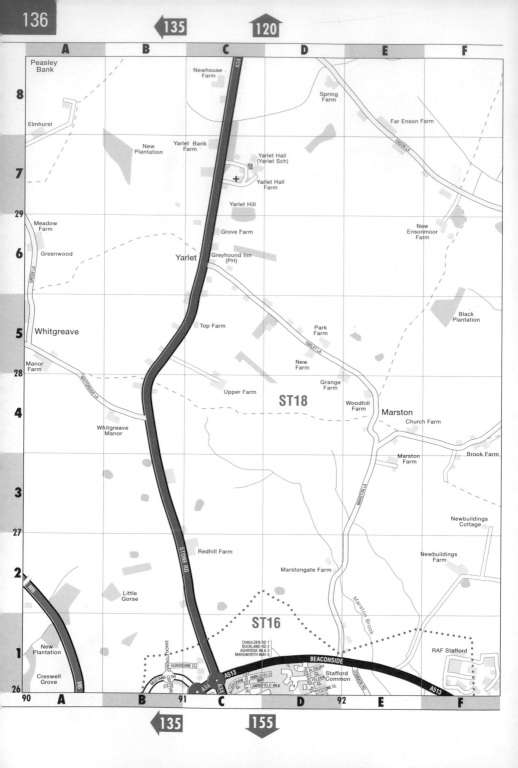

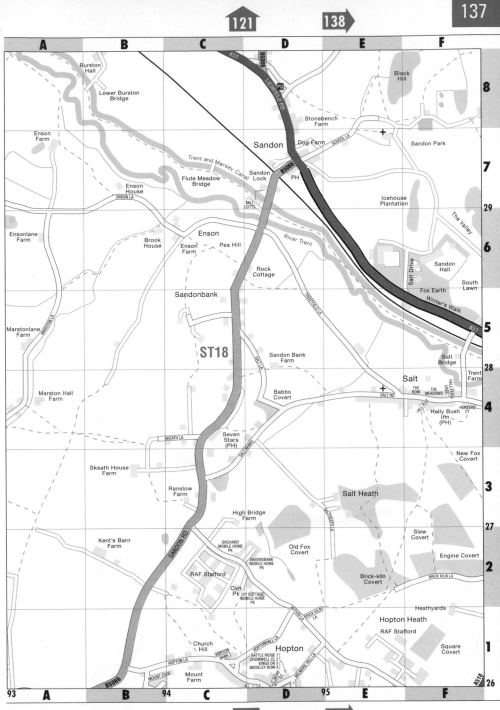

121
138

156
138

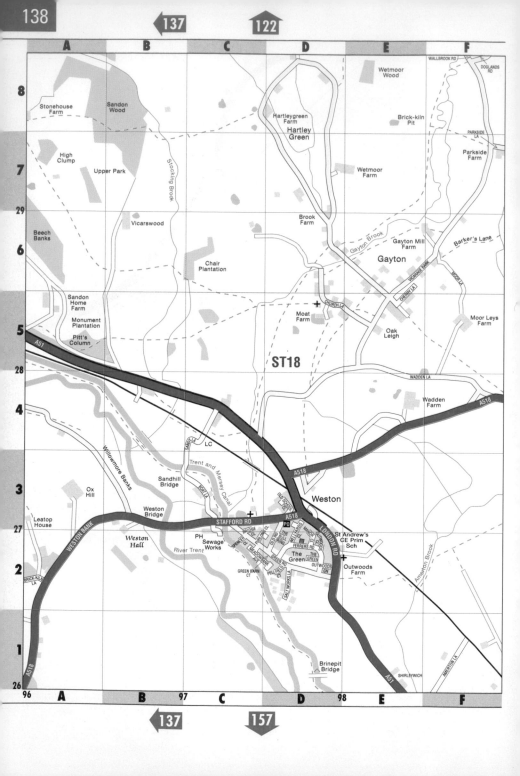

A **B** **C** **D** **E** **F**

8

Stonehouse
Farm

Sandon
Wood

Wetmoor
Wood

WALLBROOK RD

DOGLANDS
RD

Hartleygreen
Farm

Hartley
Green

Brick-kiln
Pit

PARKSIDE
LA

7

High
Clump

Upper Park

Stocking Brook

Wetmoor
Farm

Parkside
Farm

29

Beech
Banks

Vicarswood

Brook
Farm

Gayton Brook

Gayton Mill
Farm

Barker's Lane

6

Chair
Plantation

Gayton

VICARAGE BANK

MOOR LA

5

Sandon
Home
Farm

Monument
Plantation

Pitt's
Column

A51

Moat
Farm

CHURCH LA

CHERRY LA

Oak
Leigh

Moor Leys
Farm

ST18

28

WADDEN LA

4

Willowmore Banks

Wadden
Farm

A518

SANDT LA

LC

Trent and Mersey Canal

A518

3

Ox
Hill

Sandhill
Bridge

BOAT LA

Weston

Weston
Bridge

27

Leatop
House

WESTON BANK

Weston
Hall

PH

STAFFORD RD

Sewage
Works

OLD SCHOOL

A518

PO

St Andrew's
CE Prim
Sch

LONDON RD

Amerton Brook

River Trent

SPENCER RD

BRIDGE

MEADOW LA

GREEN RD

TERRERS RD

MARG...

THE
GREEN

PELL FIELD

The
Green

OUTWOODS
GDN

Outwoods
Farm

2

BRICK-KILN
LA

GREEN BARN
CT

SALT WORKS LA

1

A518

Brinepit
Bridge

A51

SHIRLEYWICH

AMERTON LA

26

A 96 **B** 97 **C** **D** 98 **E** **F**

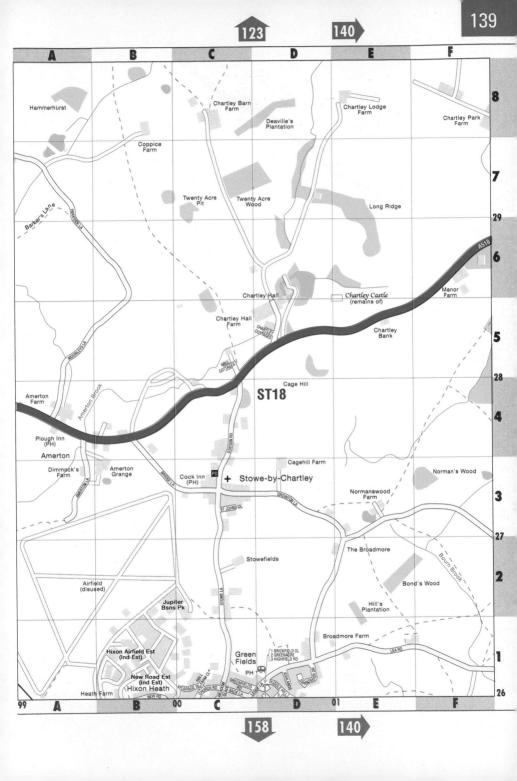

123
140
158
140

Hammerhurst

Chartley Barn Farm

Deaville's Plantation

Chartley Lodge Farm

Chartley Park Farm

Coppice Farm

Barker's Lane

PARKSIDE LA.

Twenty Acre Pit

Twenty Acre Wood

Long Ridge

A518

MOORSIDE LA.

Chartley Hall

Chartley Castle (remains of)

Manor Farm

Chartley Hall Farm

CHARTLEY COTTAGES

Chartley Bank

MILL COTTAGES

Amerton Brook

Amerton Farm

Cage Hill

ST18

Plough Inn (PH)

Amerton

Dimmock's Farm

Amerton Grange

AMERTON LA.

BRIDGE LA.

Cock Inn (PH)

PO

✚ Stowe-by-Chartley

STATION RD.

Cagehill Farm

DROINTON LA.

Normanswood Farm

Norman's Wood

St JOHNS CL.

The Broadmore

Bourn Brook

Airfield (disused)

Stowefields

STOWE LA.

Bond's Wood

Jupiter Bsns Pk

Hill's Plantation

Broadmore Farm

LEA RD.

Hixon Airfield Est (Ind Est)

Green Fields

1 BRICKFIELD CL
2 GREENACRE
3 HIGHFIELD RD

PH

GREENFIELD RD

New Road Est (Ind Est)
Hixon Heath

VICARAGE WAY

HALL CL.

MEADOW

CHURCH RD.

BACK LA.

PUDDLE HILL

JOHN'S HILL

Heath Farm

NEW RD.

99   00   01

139
124
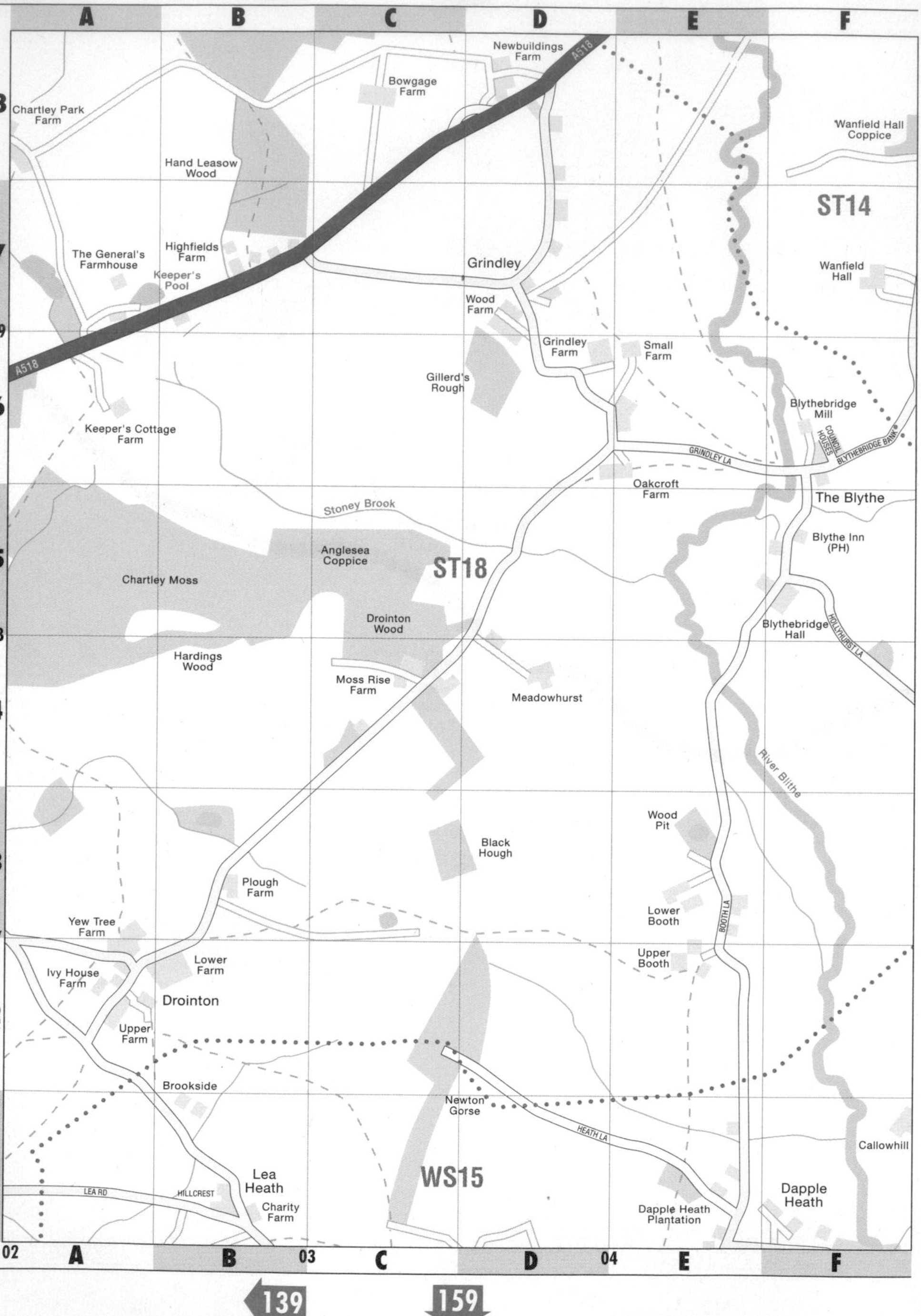

139
159

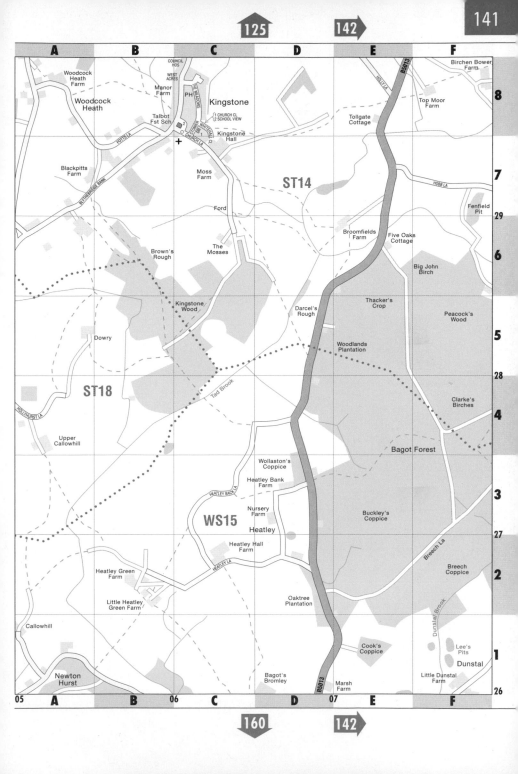

A B C D E F

8

Woodcock
Heath
Farm

Woodcock
Heath

COUNCIL
HOS
WEST
ACRES

Manor
Farm

PH

Talbot Fst Sch

Kingstone

1 CHURCH CL
2 SCHOOL VIEW

Kingstone
Hall

Tollgate
Cottage

B5013

BELLE LA

Top Moor
Farm

Birchen Bower
Farm

POTTS LA

THE MEADOWS

BIRTLE HILL RD

BIRTLE LA

CHURCH LA

7

Blackpitts
Farm

Moss
Farm

ST14

HOBB LA

Fenfield
Pit

BLYTHEBRIDGE BANK

Ford

29

Brown's
Rough

The
Mosses

Broomfields
Farm

Five Oaks
Cottage

Big John
Birch

6

Kingstone
Wood

Darcel's
Rough

Thacker's
Crop

Peacock's
Wood

Dowry

Woodlands
Plantation

5

ST18

Tad Brook

28

HOLLYHURST LA

Upper
Callowhill

Clarke's
Birches

4

Wollaston's
Coppice

Bagot Forest

HEATLEY BACK LA

Heatley Bank
Farm

Nursery
Farm

WS15

Heatley

Buckley's
Coppice

3

Heatley Hall
Farm

HEATLEY LA

27

Heatley Green
Farm

Breech
Coppice

Breech LA

2

Little Heatley
Green Farm

Oaktree
Plantation

DUNSTAL BROOK

Callowhill

Newton
Hurst

Bagot's
Bromley

B5013

Marsh
Farm

Cook's
Coppice

Lee's
Pits

Dunstal

Little Dunstal
Farm

1

26

05 A B 06 C D 07 E F

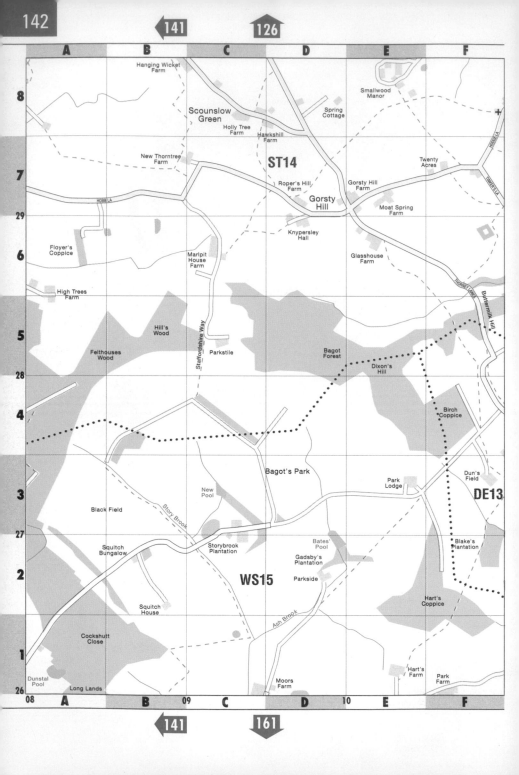

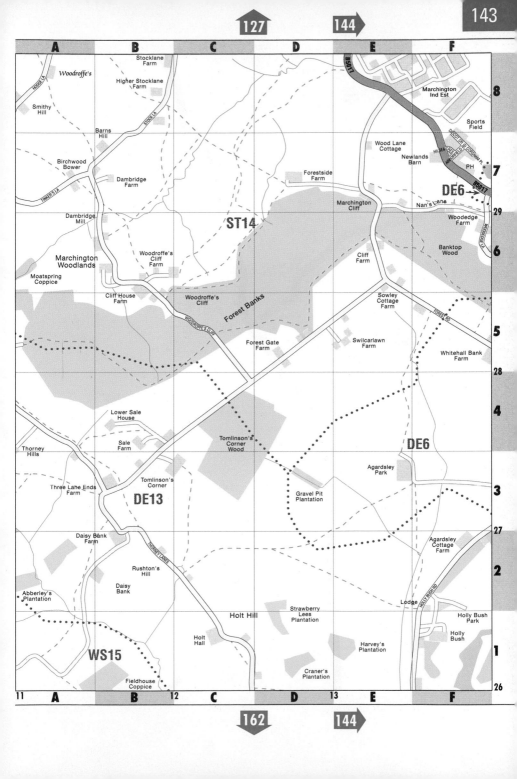

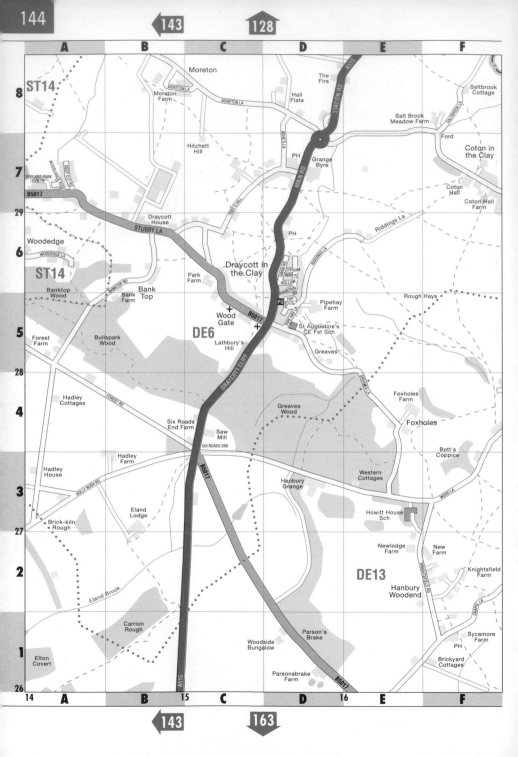

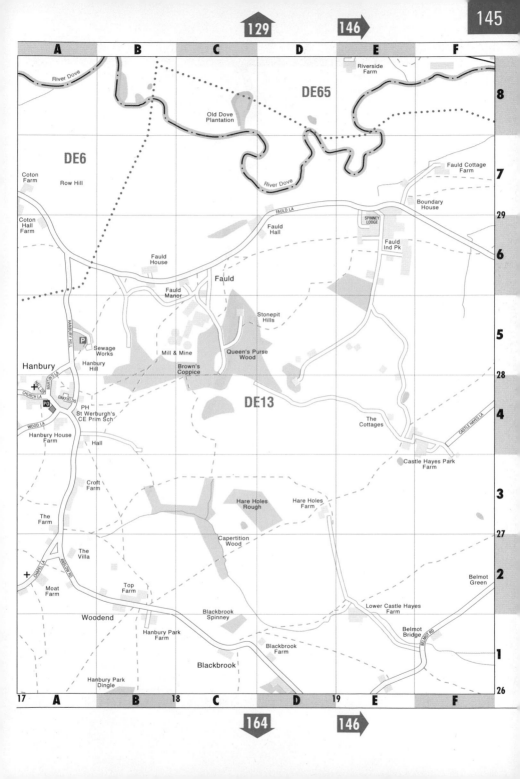

129
146
164
146

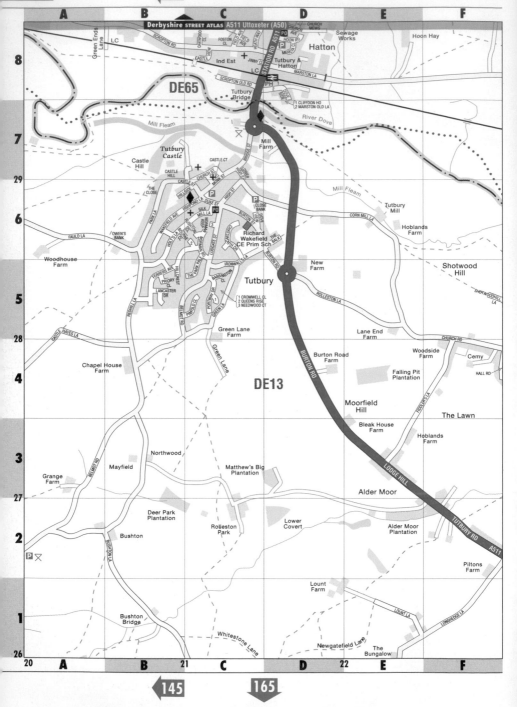
145

148

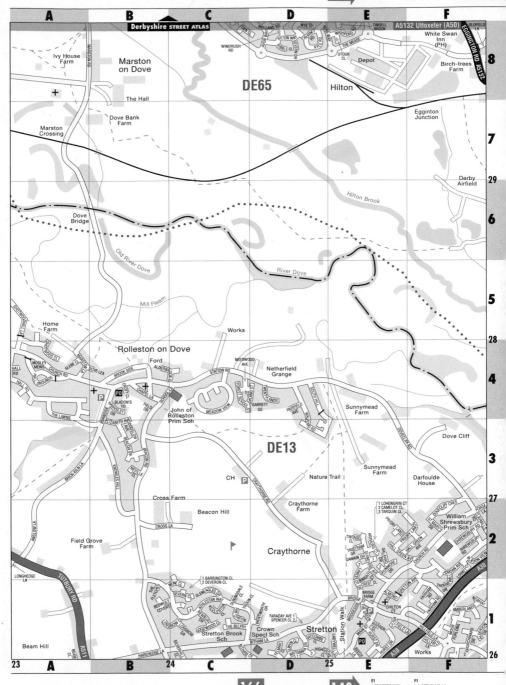

148

E1
1 PRINCESS WAY
2 CARISBROOKE DR

F1
1 ALDERHOLME DR
2 MANTON CL

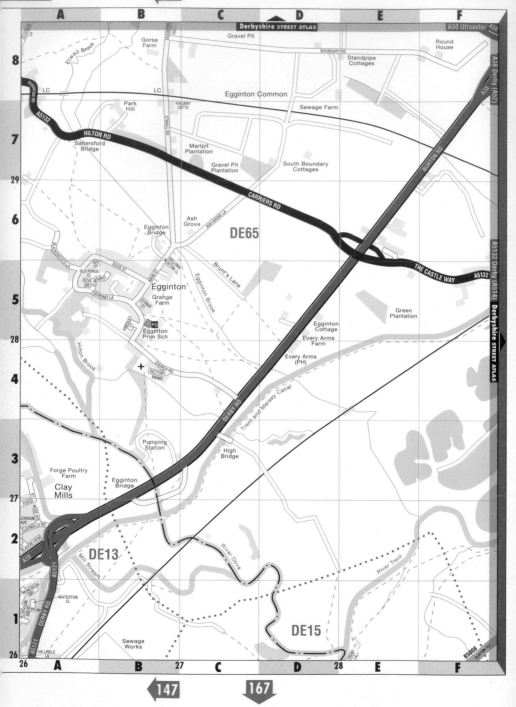

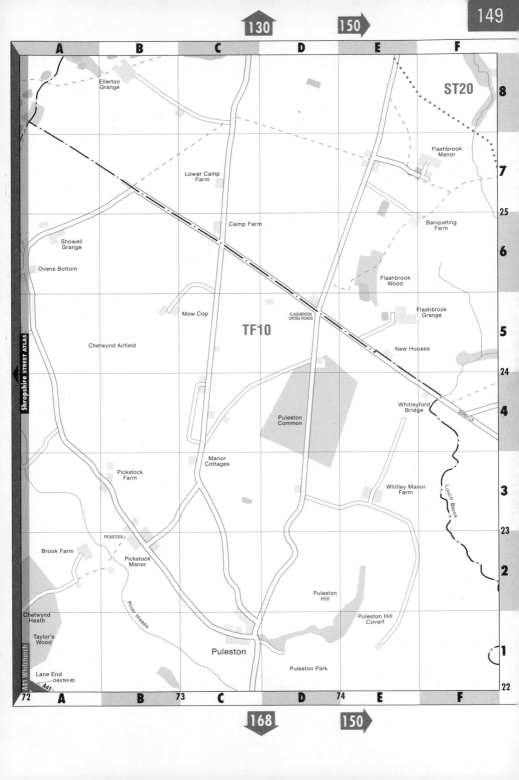

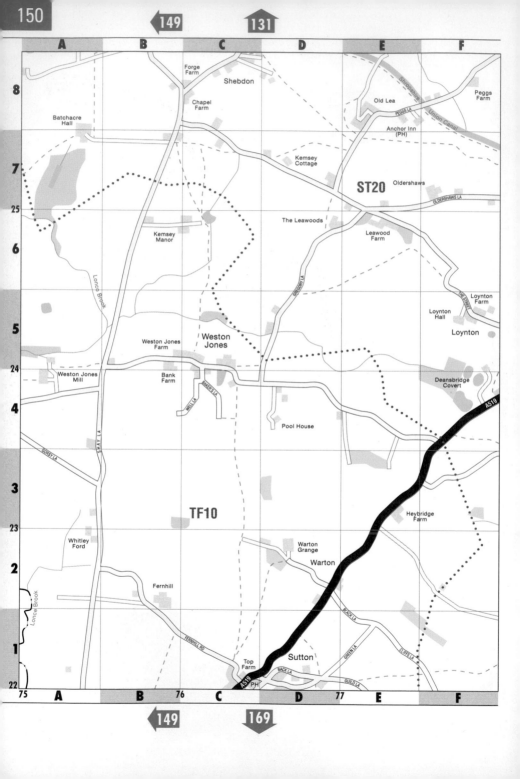

149
131

8

Forge Farm

Shebdon

Chapel Farm

Old Lea

Peggs Farm

Batchacre Hall

Anchor Inn (PH)

7

Kemsey Cottage

25

ST20 Oldershaws

OLDERSHAWS LA

The Leawoods

Kemsey Manor

Leawood Farm

6

Lonco Brook

BROGHTON LA

Loynton Farm

THE STREET

Loynton Hall

Loynton

5

Weston Jones Farm

Weston Jones

24

Weston Jones Mill

Bank Farm

WELL LA

BAKER'S LA

Deansbridge Covert

A519

4

Pool House

SHAY LA

BORSY LA

Heybridge Farm

3

TF10

23

Whitley Ford

Warton Grange

Warton

2

Fernhill

BLACK LA

GREEN LA

CLIFFE LA

1

FERNHILL RD

Top Farm

Sutton

A519

BACK LA

GUILD LA

22

PH

149
169

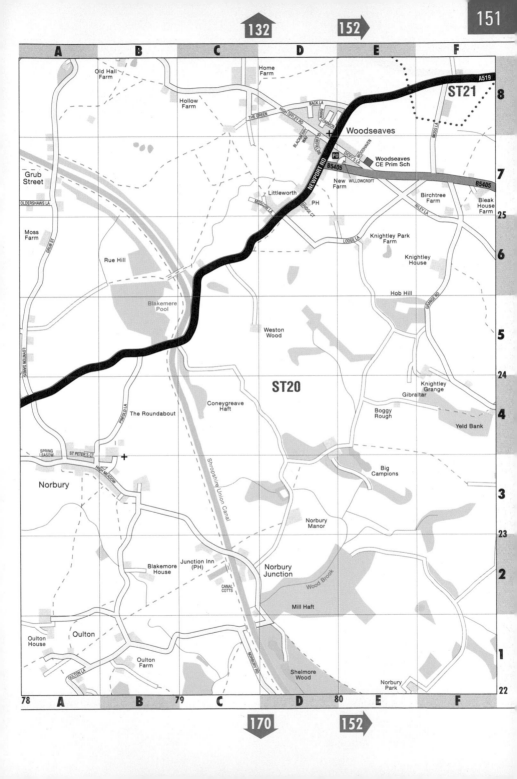

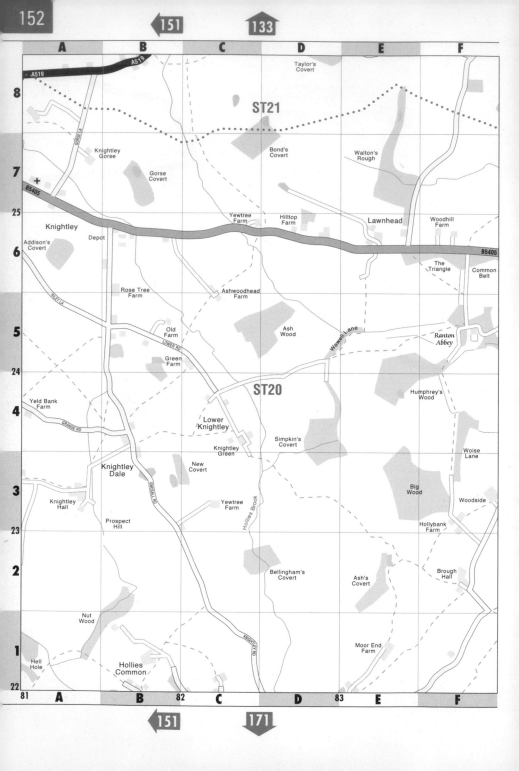

A B C D E F

8

ST21

A519

A519

Knightley
Gorse

Taylor's
Covert

Bond's
Covert

Walton's
Rough

7

Gorse
Covert

GORSE LA

B5405

25

Yewtree
Farm

Hilltop
Farm

Lawnhead

Woodhill
Farm

Knightley

Depot

Addison's
Covert

B5405

6

The
Triangle

Common
Belt

Rose Tree
Farm

Ashwoodhead
Farm

RILEY LA

5

Old
Farm

Ash
Wood

Wawell Lane

Ranton
Abbey

LOWER RD

24

Green
Farm

ST20

Humphrey's
Wood

Yeld Bank
Farm

4

GRANGE RD

Lower
Knightley

Knightley
Green

Simpkin's
Covert

Woise
Lane

Knightley
Dale

New
Covert

Big
Wood

Woodside

3

SNOSAL RD

Knightley
Hall

Yewtree
Farm

Hollies Brook

Hollybank
Farm

Prospect
Hill

23

2

Bellingham's
Covert

Ash's
Covert

Brough
Hall

Nut
Wood

KNIGHTLEY RD

Moor End
Farm

1

Hell
Hole

Hollies
Common

22

81 A B 82 C D 83 E F

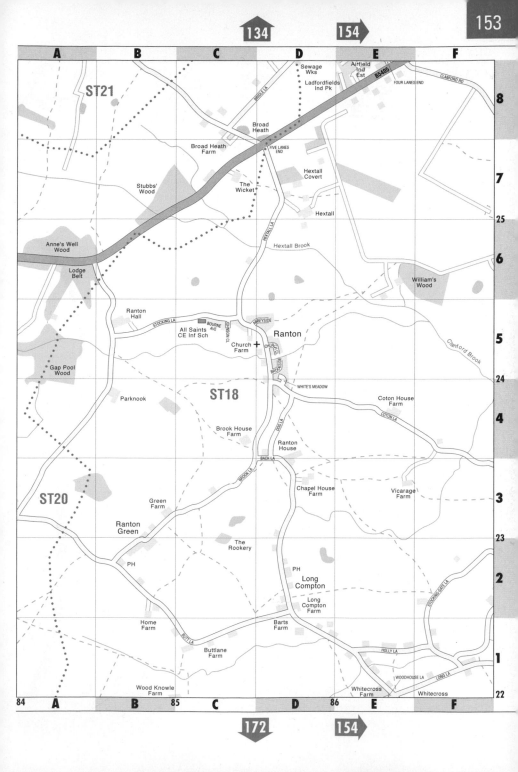

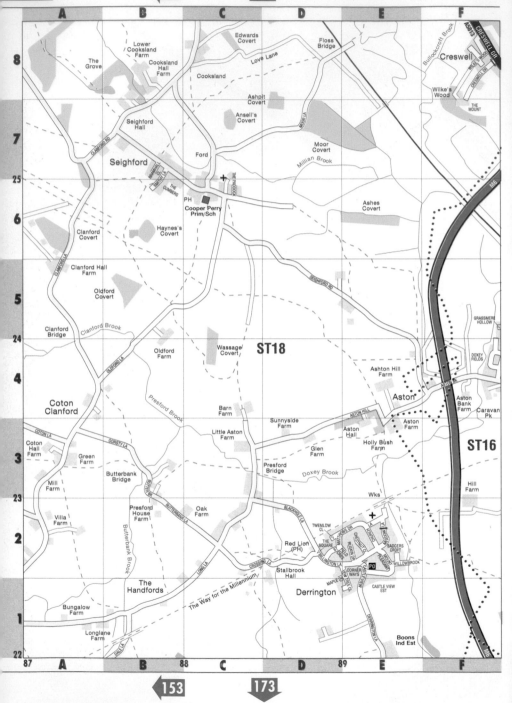

ST18

ST16

Creswell

Wilke's Wood

The Mount

Edwards Covert

Floss Bridge

Love Lane

Cooksland

Lower Cooksland Farm

The Grove

Cooksland Hall Farm

Ashpit Covert

Ansell's Covert

Seighford Hall

Ford

Moor Covert

Millan Brook

Seighford

THE CUMBERS

PH

Cooper Perry Prim/Sch

THE PADDOCK

Ashes Covert

Haynes's Covert

Clanford Covert

Clanford Hall Farm

Oldford Covert

SEIGHFORD RD

Clanford Bridge

Clanford Brook

Oldford Farm

Wassage Covert

Ashton Hill Farm

Aston

Aston Bank Farm

Caravan Pk

GRASSMERE HOLLOW

DOXEY FIELDS

Coton Clanford

Barn Farm

Little Aston Farm

Sunnyside Farm

Aston Hall

Aston Farm

Holly Bush Farm

Coton Hall Farm

Green Farm

GORSTY LA

Butterbank Bridge

Presford Brook

Glen Farm

Presford Bridge

Doxey Brook

Hill Farm

Mill Farm

Villa Farm

Presford House Farm

Oak Farm

BLACKHEATH LA

Wks

Twemlow Cl

MATTHEWS DR

THE SQUARE

Red Lion (PH)

BADGERS CROFT

WILLOWBROOK

PO

The Handfords

Stallbrook Hall

CROSSING LA

The Way for the Millennium

Derrington

CASTLE VIEW EST

Bungalow Farm

Longlane Farm

Boons Ind Est

BERRINGTON LA

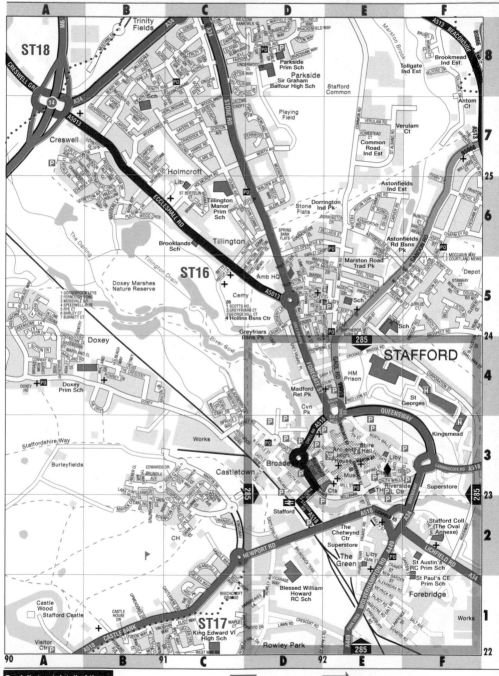

For full street detail of the highlighted area see page 285.

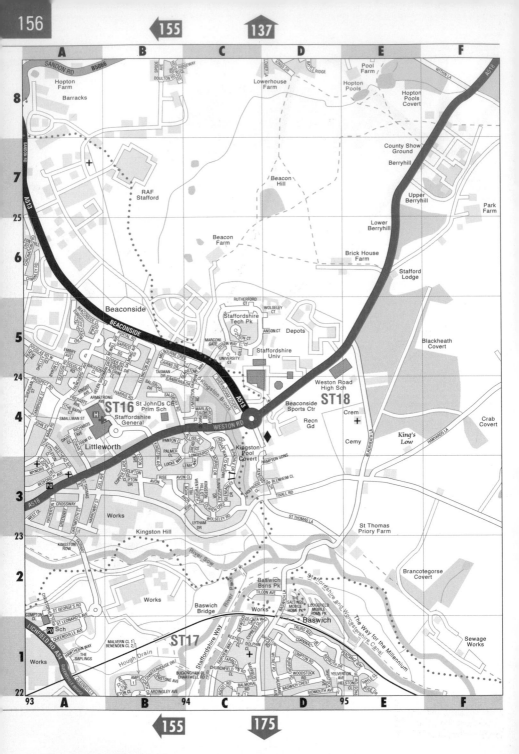

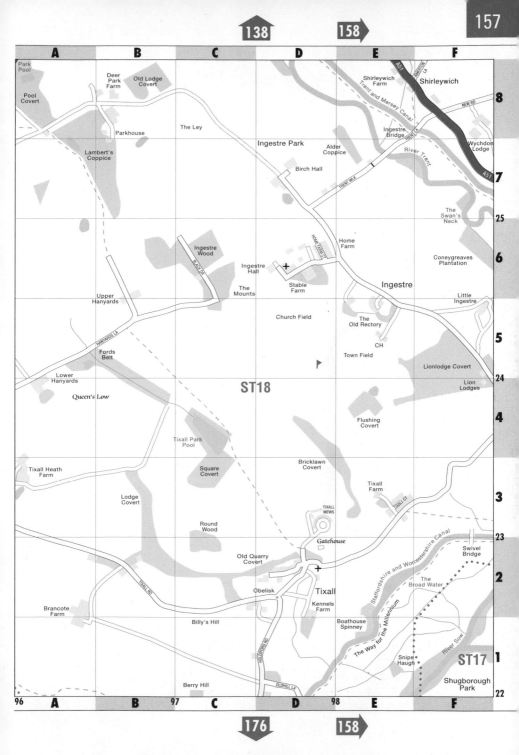

Park Pool
Pool Covert
Deer Park Farm
Old Lodge Covert
Parkhouse
The Ley
Lambert's Coppice
Ingestre Park

Shirleywich Farm
Shirleywich
Trent and Mersey Canal
NEW RD
Ingestre Bridge
Wychdon Lodge
River Trent
The Swan's Neck

Alder Coppice
Birch Hall
Ingestre Wood
Home Farm
Coneygreaves Plantation

Ingestre Hall
The Mounts
Stable Farm
Ingestre
Little Ingestre

Upper Hanyards
Church Field
The Old Rectory
CH
Town Field
Lionlodge Covert

HANYARDS LA
Fords Belt
Lower Hanyards
Queen's Low
ST18
Lion Lodges

Flushing Covert

Tixall Heath Farm
Tixall Park Pool
Square Covert
Bricklawn Covert
Tixall Farm

Lodge Covert
Round Wood
TIXALL MEWS
Old Quarry Covert
Gatehouse
Swivel Bridge
Staffordshire and Worcestershire Canal
The Broad Water

Brancote Farm
TIXALL RD
Obelisk
Tixall
Kennels Farm
Boathouse Spinney
The Way for the Millennium

Billy's Hill
Berry Hill
OLDHILL LA
Snipe Haugh
River Sow
ST17
Shugborough Park

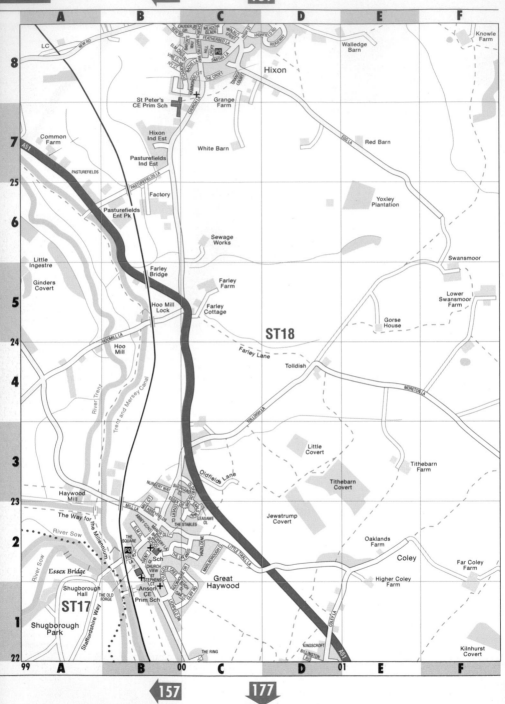

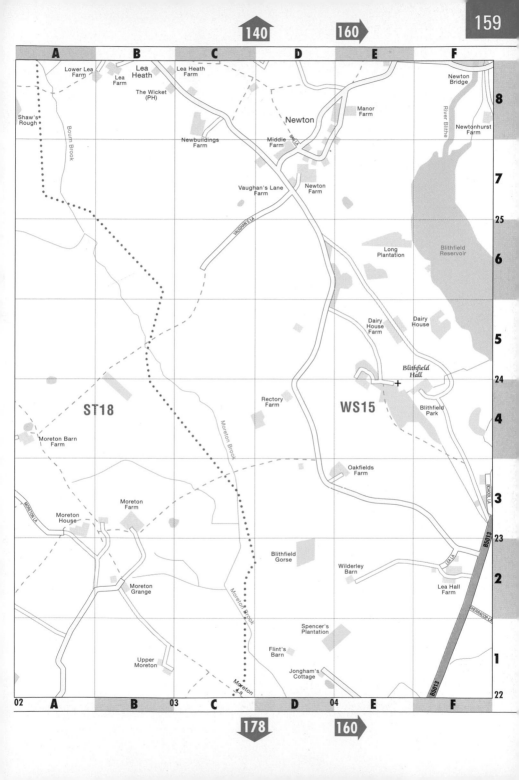

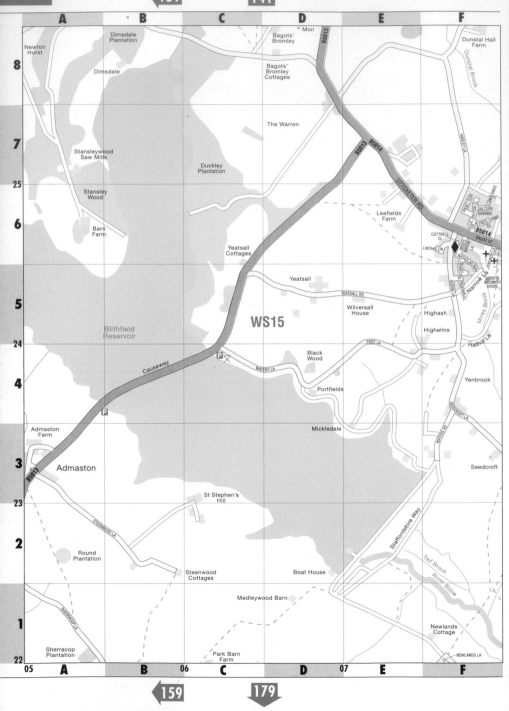

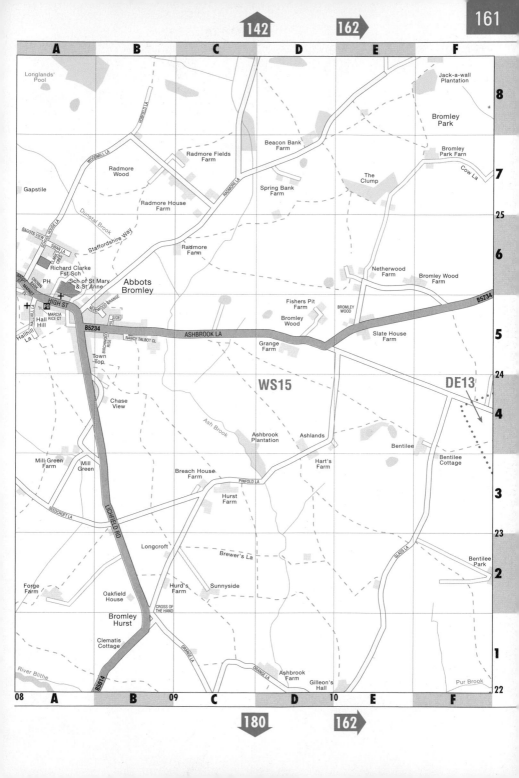

161
143

| | A | B | C | D | E | F |

8

Fieldhouse Farm

Briary Hill Plantation

Briary Hill Farm

Child's Plantation

Pound Farm

Newborough Hall Farm

Newborough

Bromley Park

ELTON LA

HOLLY BUSH RD

MILL ROW

B5234 CHAPEL LA

PO

Newborough House Farm

7

Cow La

Parkgate

Noah's Ark Farm

Needwood CE Prim Sch

The Red Lion (PH)

SQUIRREL RD

YOXALL RD

DUFFIELD LA B5234

Poplars Farm

25

WS15

Eason's Coppice

Newhall Farm

Thorntree Hall Farm

DARK LA

6

B5234

Chantry Wood

THORNEY LANES

River Swarbourn

Moat Hill

MOAT LA

Moat Hall

Birch Wood

Roosthill Wood

5

Roost Hill

Newborough End Farm

Newborough End

Dolefoot Farm

24

Barn Farm

Birch Wood Cottage

Birchwood Farm

Netherwood Farm

Chantry Farm

Locker's Rough

DE13

DOLEFOOT LA

Mare Brook

4

BLUNT'S HOLLOW

ABBOTS BROMLEY RD

Home Farm

Poole's Coppice

Brackenhurst Wood

Pur Brook

3

Paddock Rough

St Michael's House

Hoar Cross

Meynell Ingram Arms (PH)

23

Bath Wood

Hoar Cross Hall

Vicarage

Church Flatts

2

Bentilee Park

Lawnpit Covert

Yew Tree Farm

MAKER LA

Far Hoarcross

Park Hollow

Far Hoar Cross Farm

BECK'S LA

Beck's Bank

1

Ladysmith Farm

Makerlane Farm

Ford

Round Hill

22

| 11 | A | B | 12 | C | D | 13 | E | F |

Cross Hayes Farm

The Deer Park

161
181

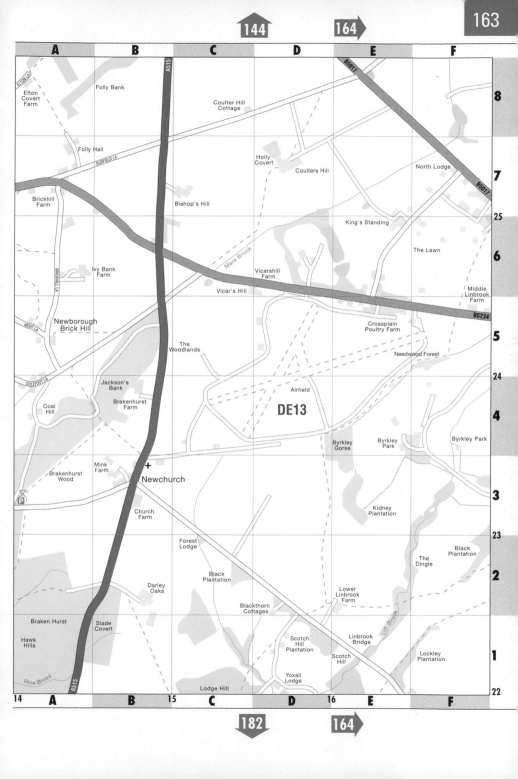

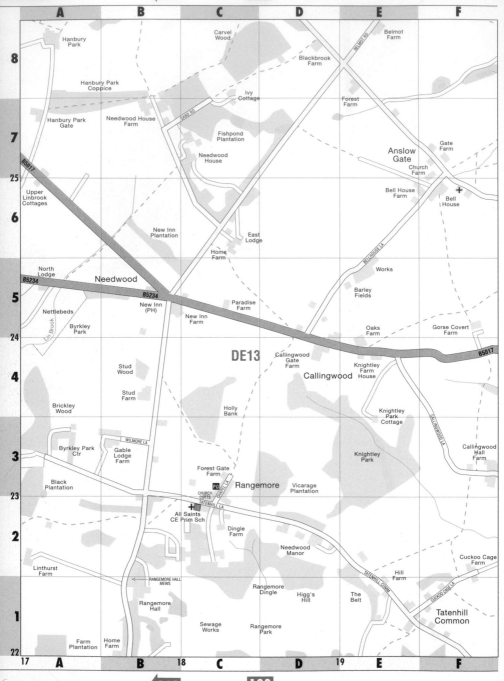

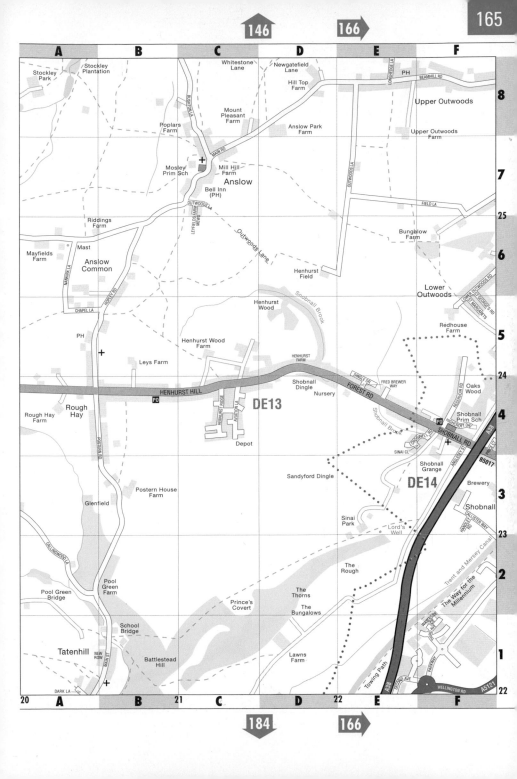

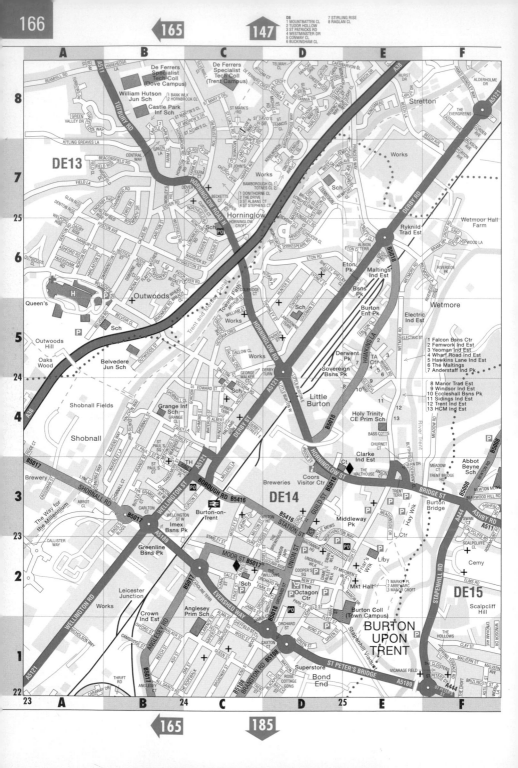

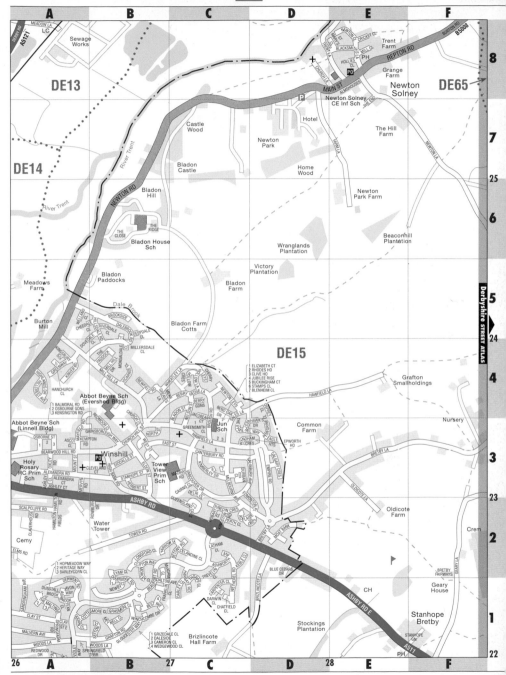

A B C D E F

DE13

DE14

DE65

Newton
Solney

DE15

MEADOW LA
LC

Sewage
Works

Castle
Wood

Newton
Park

Bladon
Castle

Bladon
Hill

THE
RIDGE

THE
CLOSE

Bladon House
Sch

Bladon
Paddocks

Meadows
Farm

Burton
Mill

Dale Brook

BROOKSIDE

Bladon Farm
Cotts

Bladon
Farm

Victory
Plantation

Wranglands
Plantation

Home
Wood

Hotel

The Hill
Farm

Newton
Park Farm

Beaconhill
Plantation

Grafton
Smallholdings

Nursery

Common
Farm

Hanchurch
Cl

Abbot Beyne Sch
(Evershed Bldg)

Abbot Beyne Sch
(Linnell Bldg)

Holy
Rosary
RC Prim
Sch

Winshill

Tower
View
Prim
Sch

1 ELIZABETH CT
2 RHODES HO
3 CLIVE HO
4 JUBILEE RISE
5 BUCKINGHAM CT
6 STAMPS CL
7 BLENHEIM CL

ASHBY RD

Cemy

Water
Tower

Scalpcliffe Rd

1 HOPMEADOW WAY
2 HERITAGE WAY
3 BARLEYCORN CL

Blue Cedars
Dr

ASHBY RD E

Brizlincote
Hall Farm

Stockings
Plantation

Oldicote
Farm

Crem

Bretby
Fairways

Geary
House

Stanhope
Bretby

1 GRIZEDALE CL
2 DALESIDE
3 CAMERON CL
4 WEDGEWOOD CL

Trent
Farm

Grange
Farm

Newton Solney
CE Inf Sch

Newton Solney
CE Inf Sch

Derbyshire STREET ATLAS

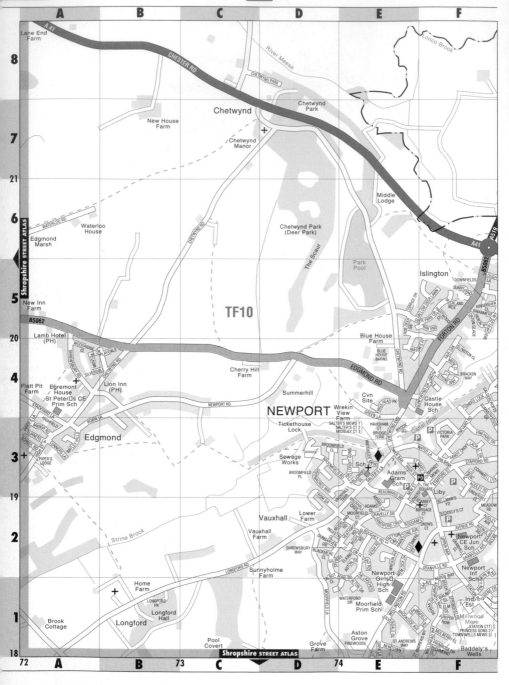

Shropshire STREET ATLAS

TF10

NEWPORT

Chetwynd

Edgmond

Longford

Vauxhall

Islington

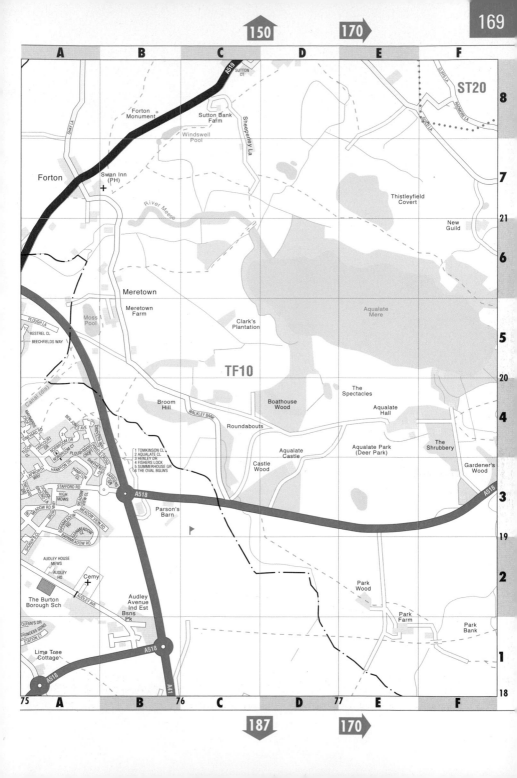

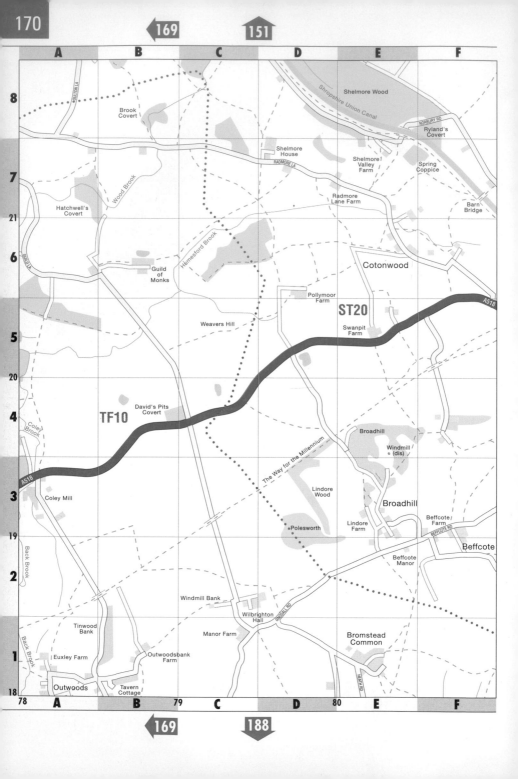

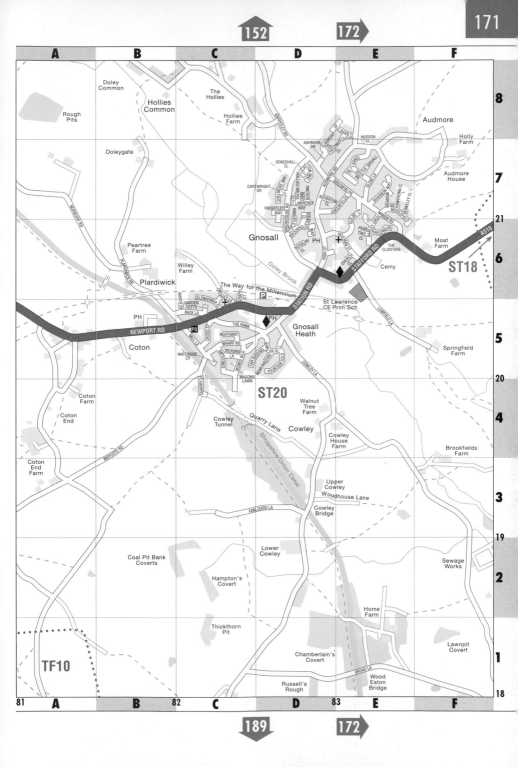

171
153

ST20

A **B** **C** **D** **E** **F**

Whitecross

The Sheppy Farm

Bleak House Farm

8

WOODHOUSE LA

Shutt Heath Farm

Shut Heath

Brazenhill

7

Ivy House Farm

Hurst Farm

Woodhouse Farm

STATION RD

Brazenhill Farm

Leasows Farm

Parkhead House

P

BRAZENHILL LA

21

A518

The Way for the Millennium

Mayo Farm

Pear Tree Bank Farm

Old Park House

HAWTHORN

STEPS GDNS

6

Upper Reule Farm

New Park House

Shropshire Inn (PH)

MOAT HOUSE CL

POPLAR GR

BROOK RD

ST GILES DR

Haughton St Giles CE Prim Sch

The Old Hall

Grassy La

Reule Covert

Haughton Farm

PO

BACK LA

RECTORY LA

PARK VI

5

Middle Covert

ST18

Haughton

A518

WATER CL

20

Ox Leasow Covert

Black Hough

Allimore Brook

Booden Farm

Hanging Pits Farm

4

Lower Reule Farm

Birches Gorse

Hough Farm

The Black Hough Farm

Wheatcroft Covert

3

ST20

Allimore Green

ALSTONE LA

Reulemill Pools

Apeton Bank Covert

19

Alstone Hall Farm

Lower Alstone

Alstone Farm

2

Apeton Slang

Apeton Brook

Church Eaton Brook

Apeton

Alstone Cottages

1

Ford

Upper Barton

18

84 **A** **B** 85 **C** **D** 86 **E** **F**

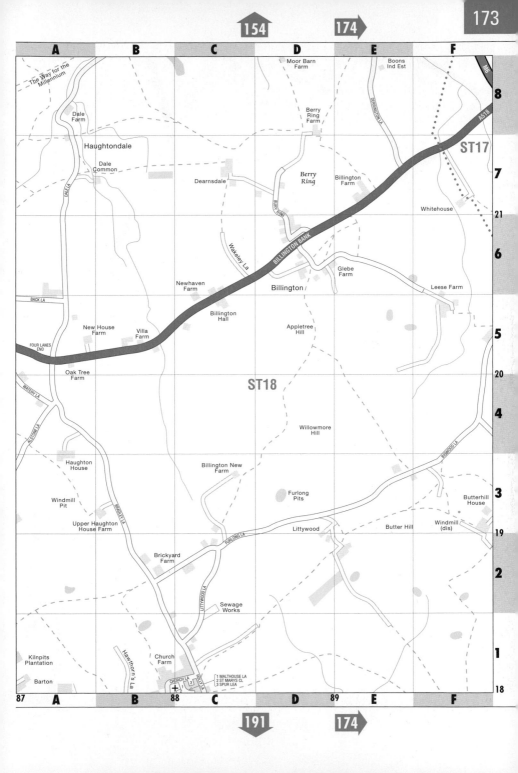

M6
A518
ST17

8

The Way for the Millennium

Dale Farm

Haughtondale

Dale Common

DALE LA

Moor Barn Farm

Boons Ind Est

Berry Ring Farm

7

Dearnsdale

Berry Ring

Billington Farm

Whitehouse

BERRINGTON LA

BURY RING

21

Wakeley La

BILLINGTON BANK

6

Newhaven Farm

Billington

Glebe Farm

Leese Farm

BACK LA

New House Farm

Villa Farm

Billington Hall

Appletree Hill

5

FOUR LANES END

Oak Tree Farm

ST18

20

WATERY LA

Willowmore Hill

4

ALSTONE LA

Haughton House

Billington New Farm

BIRKWOOD LA

Windmill Pit

Furlong Pits

Butterhill House

3

Upper Haughton House Farm

BARKLEY LA

FURLONG LA

Littywood

Butter Hill

Windmill (dis)

19

Brickyard Farm

2

LITTYWOOD LA

Sewage Works

Kilnpits Plantation

Hawthorn's La

Church Farm

1

Barton

CHURCH LA

BURY LA

1 MALTHOUSE LA
2 ST MARYS CL
3 SPUR LEA

18

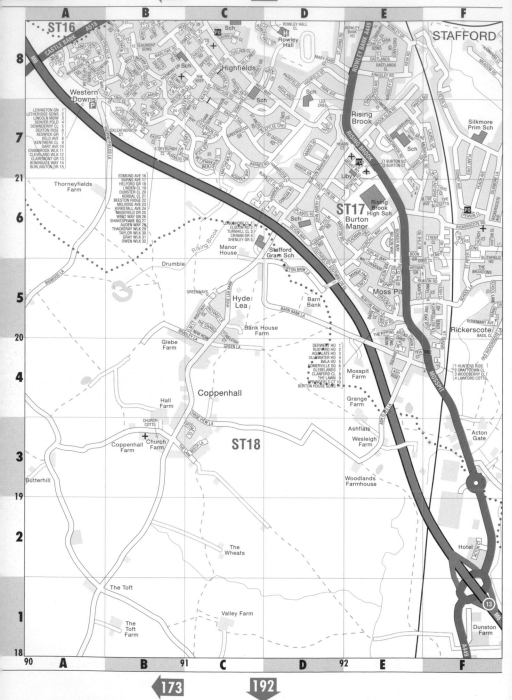

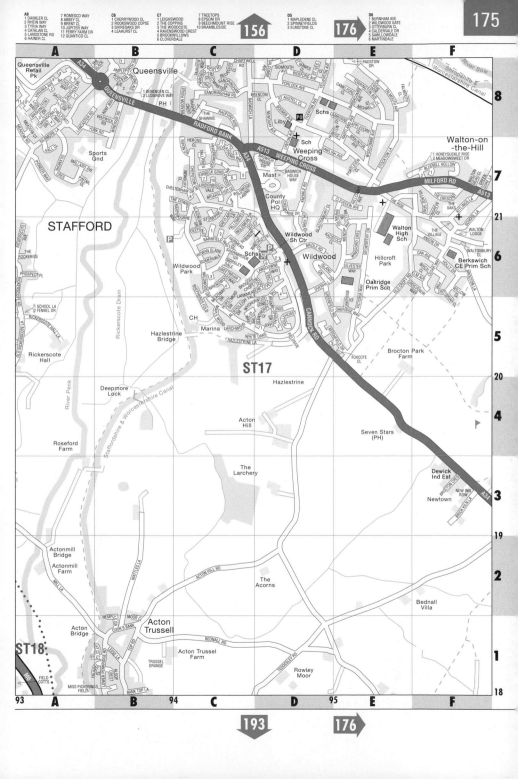

175
157

	A	B	C	D	E	F

8

Walton Bridge

The Swimmings

Black Covert

ST18

Oldhill Bridge

OLDHILL LA

Tixall Bridge

Tixall Lock

The Dark Lantern

Aqueduct Covert

Staffordshire and Worcestershire Canal

River Sow

HOLLYWOOD RD

Shugborough Park

Mon

White Barn Farm

Stafford Plantation

7

Milford Lodge

MAIN RD

PO

PH

RAILWAY TERR

A513

A513

Milford Hall

Milford

THE GREEN

Satnall Hills

Sher Brook

21

Milford Common

Spring Hill

6

Milford Covert

LIZER LA

BROCTON RD

P

The Punch Bowl

Alder Carr

Haywoodpark Covert

Moor Covert

Cressel Wood

Harts Hill

Berry Hill

Cressel Pool

WALTON LA

5

BROCTON LA

The Hole

Oat Hill

Staffordshire Way

20

Brocton Lodge

GREEN LA

Broc Hill

Mere Pits

Mere Valley

Heart of England Way

Brocton Coppice

Devil's Dumble

Sherbrook Valley

4

CH

OLD COACH LA

POST LA

BROOK LA

BROOK LA

ST17

Brocton

Hollywood Slade

Cherrytree Slade

PARK LA

THE GREEN

PO

COPPICE BROOK

COPPICE LA

HEATHER LA

BIRCHWOOD VIEW

BROCTON CP

Coppice Hill

3

BERNROOK CL

OAKPIT LA

OLDACRE LA

Oldacre

Tar Hill

P

P

19

A34

CHASE CRES

CANNOCK RD

Oldacre Brook

CHASE RD

P

Dry Pits

2

The Chetwynd Arms (PH)

Brocton Nature Reserve

Cannock Chase Country Park

Sherbrook Banks

WS15

Brocton Gate Farm

Brocton Field

Oldacre Valley

1

CAMP RD

Sycamore Hill

Belt View Farm

A34

P

18

96	A	B	97	C	D	98	E	F

175
194

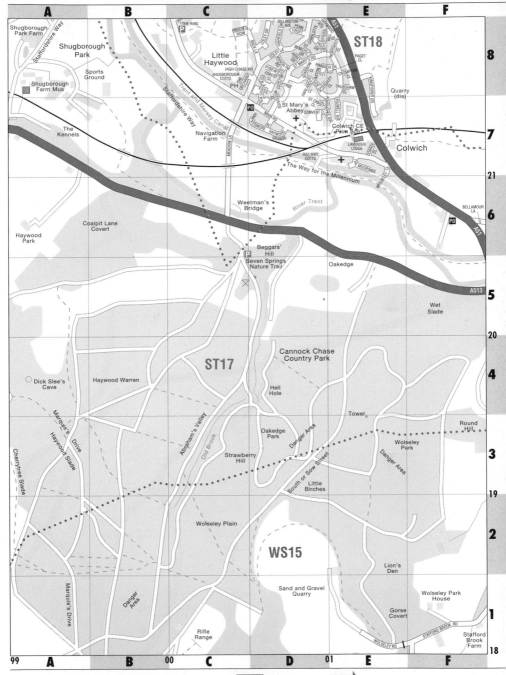

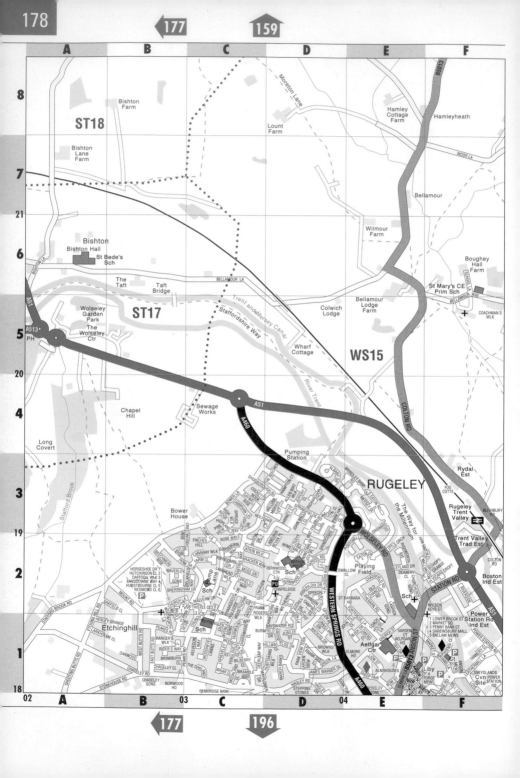

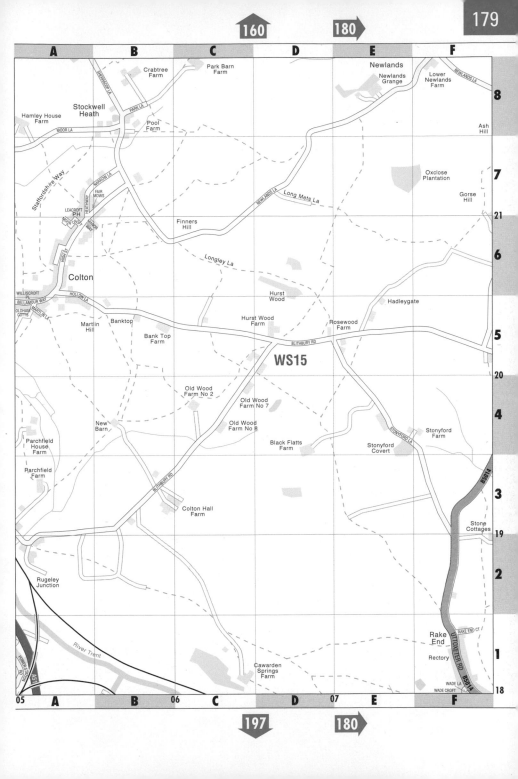

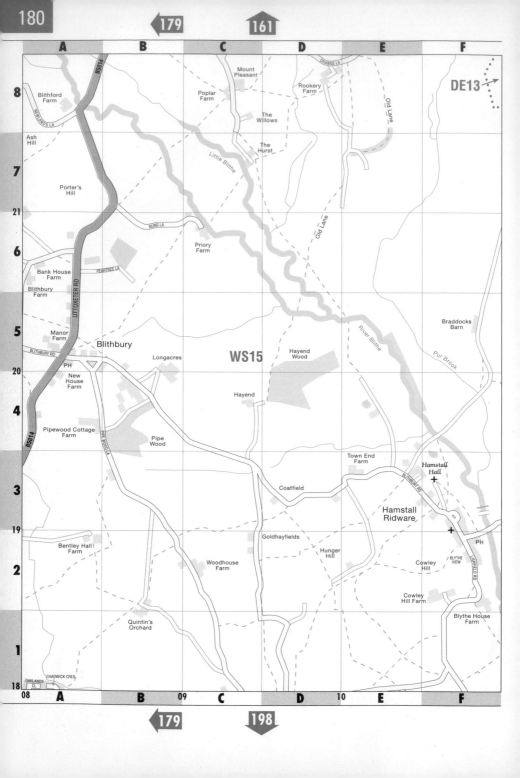

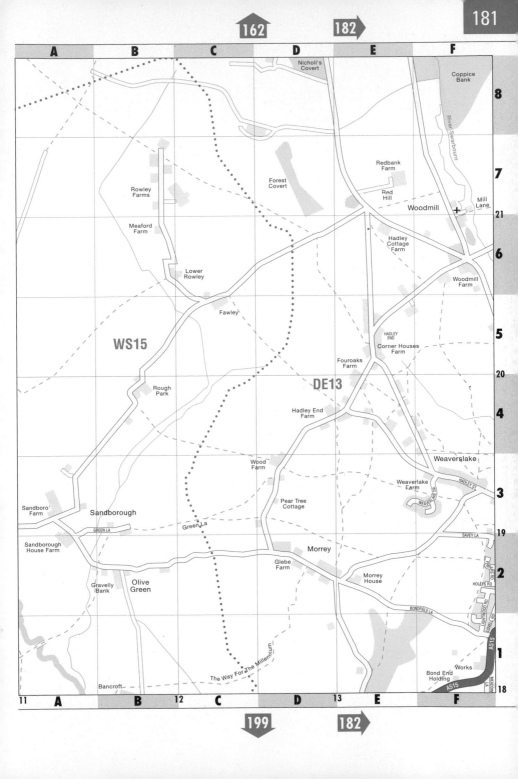

A515

Highfields
Farm

LODGE LA

Woodside
Farm

Whitemere
Farm

Lodgehill
Farm

Foxholes
Covert

Scotch Hill
Plantation

Brankley
Lodge

Forest
Farm

Mill La

Yoxall
Park

Lin Brook

Brankley
Covert

Brankley
House

WOOD LA

PH

Woodlane

Stonyford Brook

Forest Side
Farm

Brankley
Farm

Sherholt
Lodge

White
Wood

Woodlane
Bridge

Sales
Farm

Wood Lane
Bridge
Farm

Whitewood
Farm

Longcroft
Farm

DE13

Sherholt
Plantation

SUDBURY RD

LONGCROFT LA

Wall
House

Lucepool

Thistledown

Hollyhurst
House

Hilltop
Plantation

Holly
Bank
Farm

LUCEPOOL LA

SICH LA

PO

Yoxall
Farm

KING ST

The
Rough

Woodhouses

B5016

St Peter's
CE Prim
Sch

PH

SAVEY LA

Hollybank
Farm

Upper
Blakenhall
Farm

CHURCHFIELDS

Yoxall

TOWN HILL

MAIN ST

FERRERS

B5016

1 SWAINSFIELD RD
2 ROOKERY CL
3 SWARBOURN CL

Bank
House

STRINGER LA

HOLLYS RD

LOVEL RD

A515

ALWYN RD

Bond

BROMLEY LA

River Swarbourn

High-hall-hill
Farm

MEADOW LA

Park Piece
Plantation

Bond End
Farm

The Way For The Millennium

Mason's
Barn

Twichills

Sewage
Works

The
Coppice

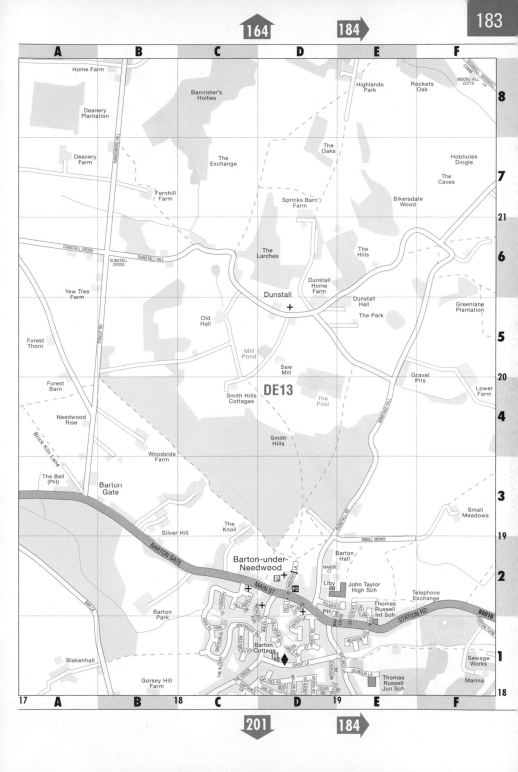

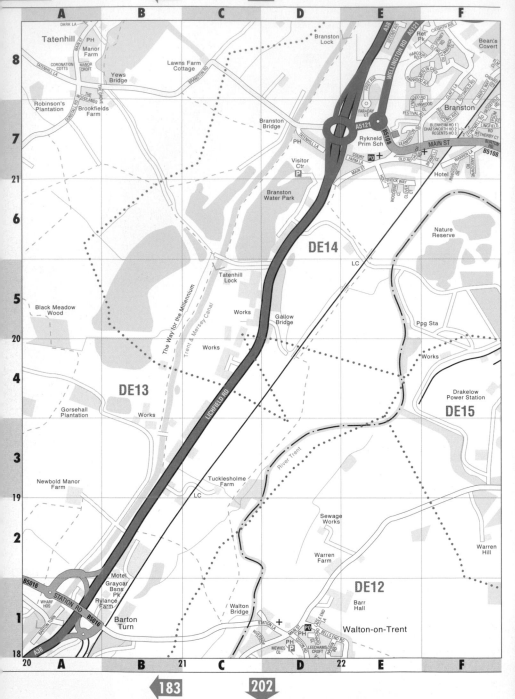

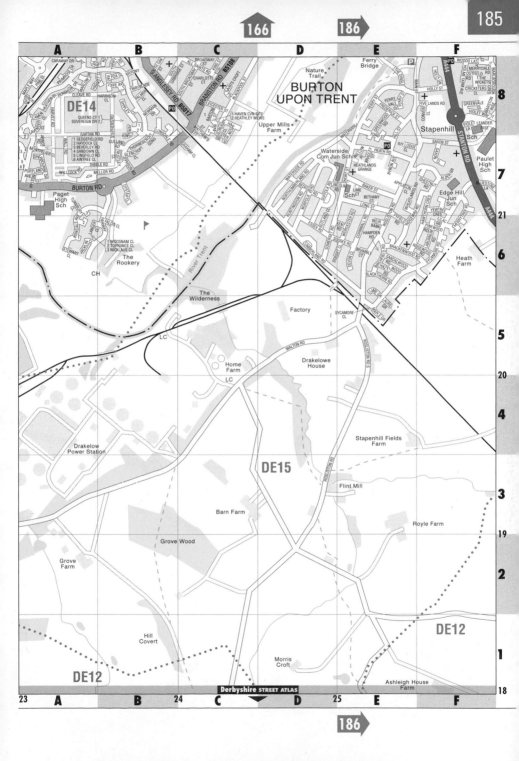

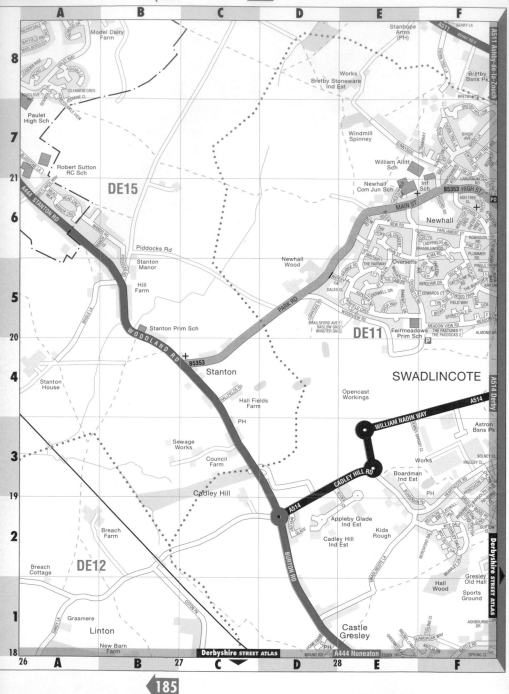

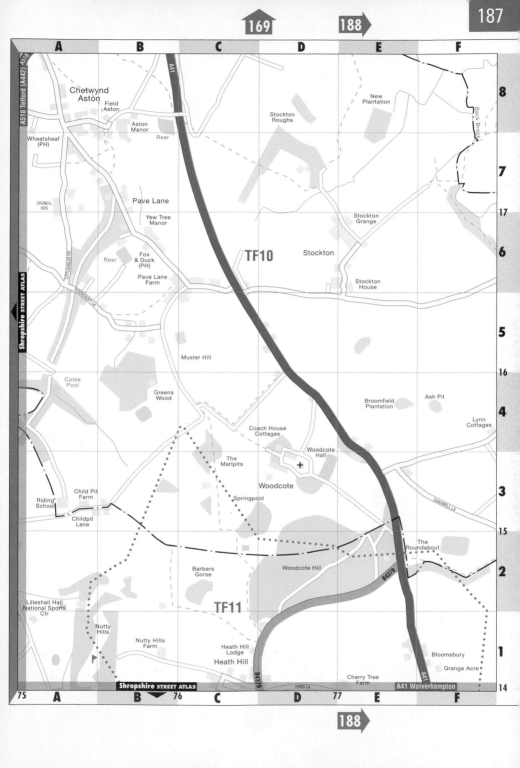

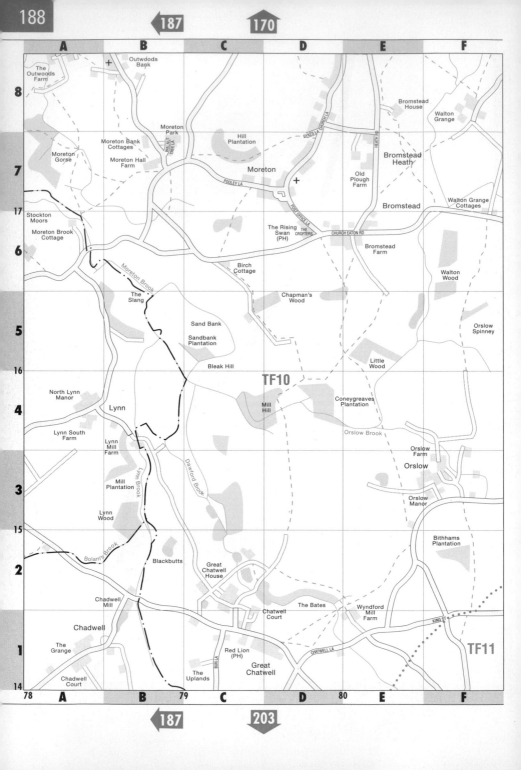

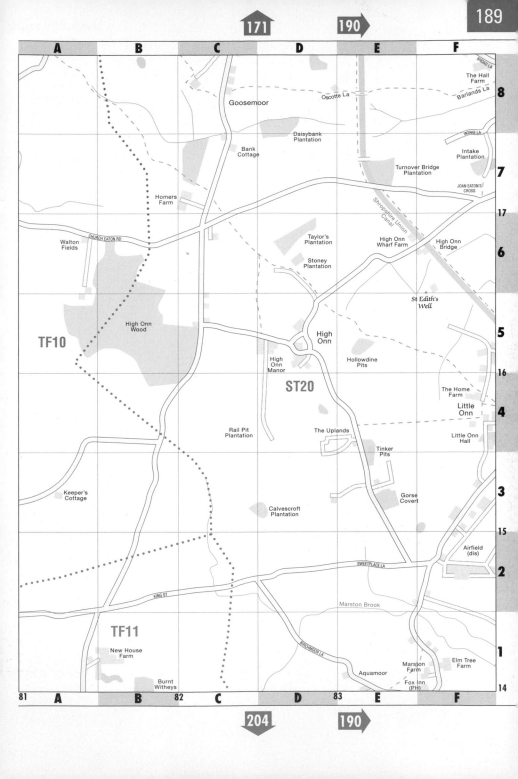

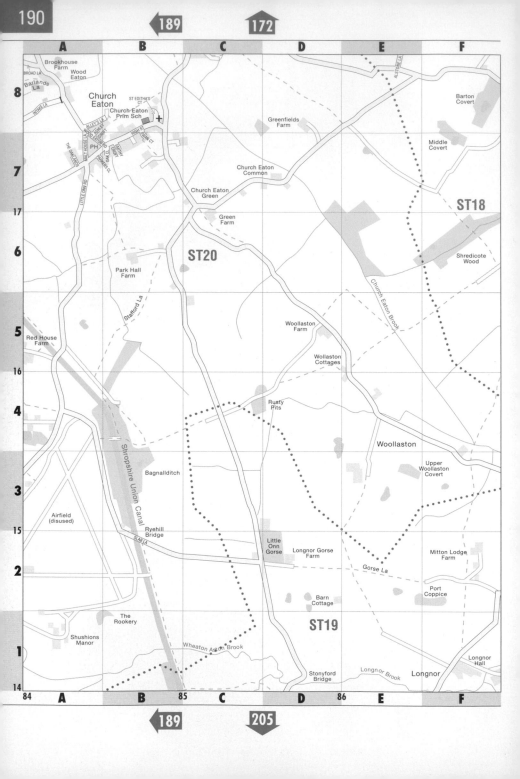

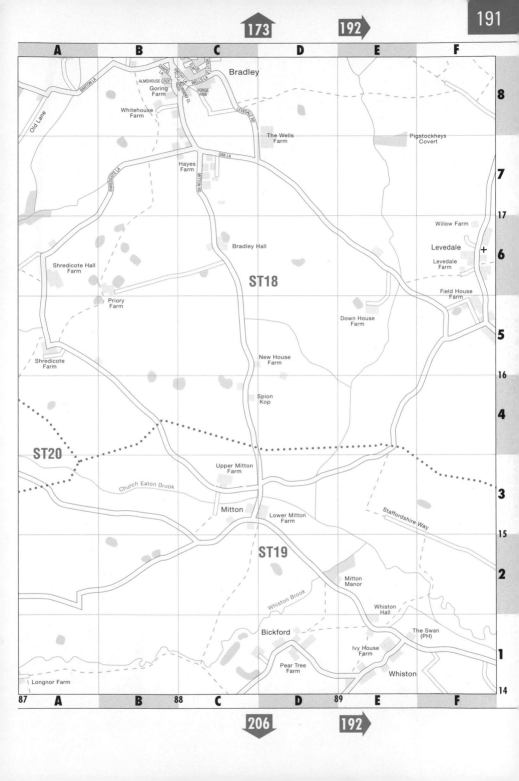

173
192

A B C D E F

Bradley

8

CHAPEL CT
DULEY LA
ELM CT
HOLLY LA
WELLS LA
FORGE RISE
ALMSHOUSE CROFT
Goring Farm
Whitehouse Farm

LEVEDALE RD

The Wells Farm

Pigstockheys Covert

Old Lane

OAK LA

7

Hayes Farm

SHREDICOTE LA

MITTON RD

17

Willow Farm

Bradley Hall

Levedale

ST18

Levedale Farm

6

Shredicote Hall Farm

Field House Farm

Priory Farm

Down House Farm

5

Shredicote Farm

New House Farm

16

Spion Kop

4

ST20

Upper Mitton Farm

Church Eaton Brook

Staffordshire Way

3

Mitton

Lower Mitton Farm

15

ST19

Mitton Manor

2

Whiston Hall

Whiston Brook

The Swan (PH)

Bickford

Ivy House Farm

1

Pear Tree Farm

Whiston

Longnor Farm

14

87 A B 88 C D 89 E F

206
192

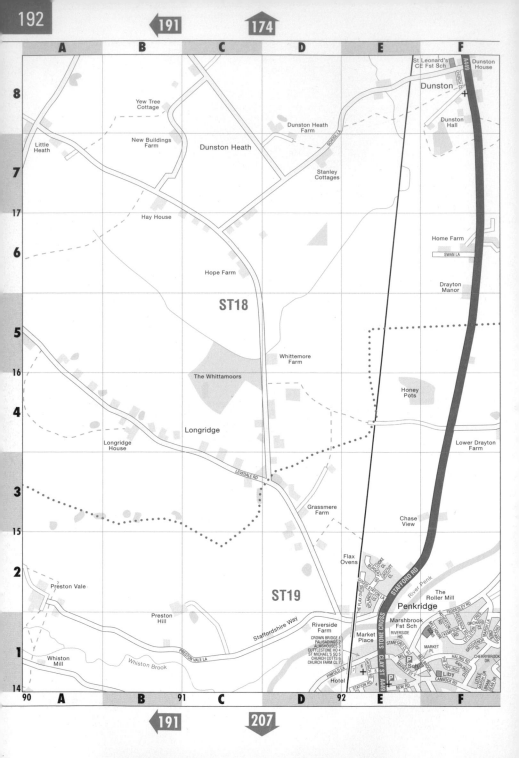

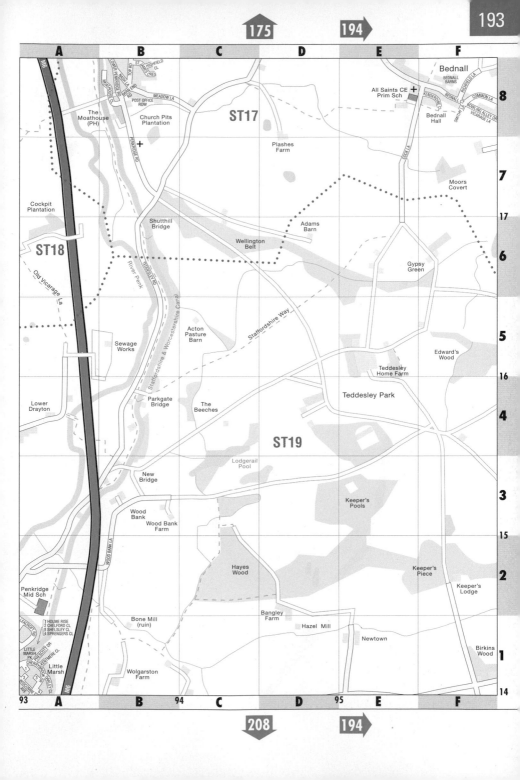

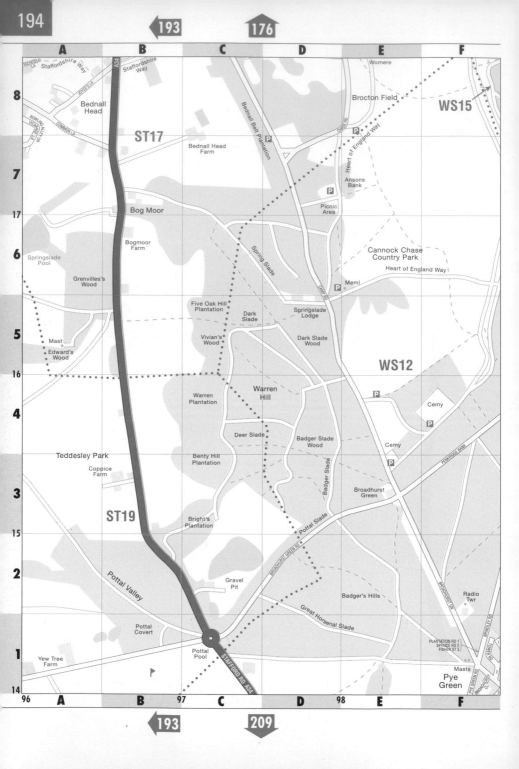

177
196

A B C D E F

8

Danger Area
Rifle Range
Danger Area
Bevin's Birches
Stafford Brook
Little Stafford Brook

Pepper Slade
Kingsley Wood Rd
Shooting Butts Ctr

7
SILVERTREES CVN PK
Birches Valley Forest Ctr
Forest Walk

WS15

17

Parr's Warren
RIFLE RANGE CNR
PENKRIDGE BANK
Birches Valley

6

Birches Valley

White House (PH)
Fairoak Lodge
Stony Brook Pools
Stony Brook

5

Fairoak Pools

16

FLINTS CNR
Heart of England Way
Dimmins Dale

4

Brindley Valley
Marquis Drive Visitor Ctr
MARQUIS DR
Jockey Hill

Cannock Chase Country Park
BRINDLEY RD
WS12
BRINDLEY HEATH RD

3

15

2

Brindley Heath
Furnace Coppice
A460

1 SPRUCE RD
2 BROADHURST GN
3 CEDAR CL
4 HEATHER RD
PLANTATION RD
MERESIDE RD

West Cannock Farm
Cannock Chase Ent Ctr
WEST CANNOCK WAY
WALKERS RISE
Rising Brook
A460
Deercote Slade

1

14

210
196

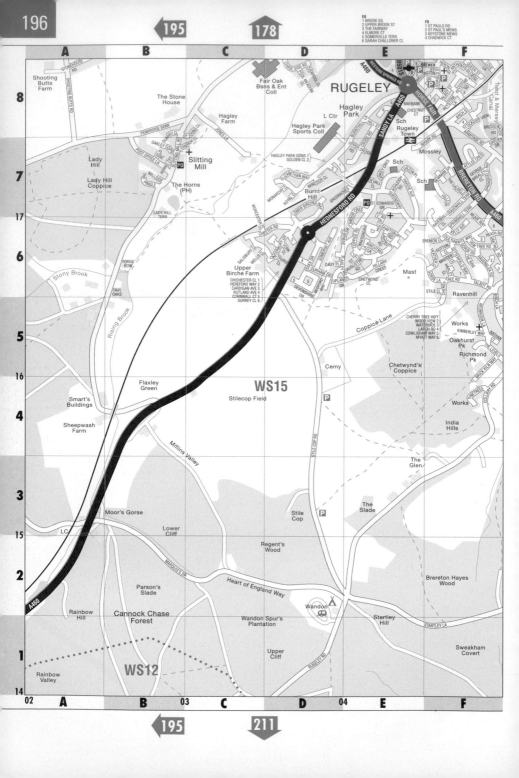

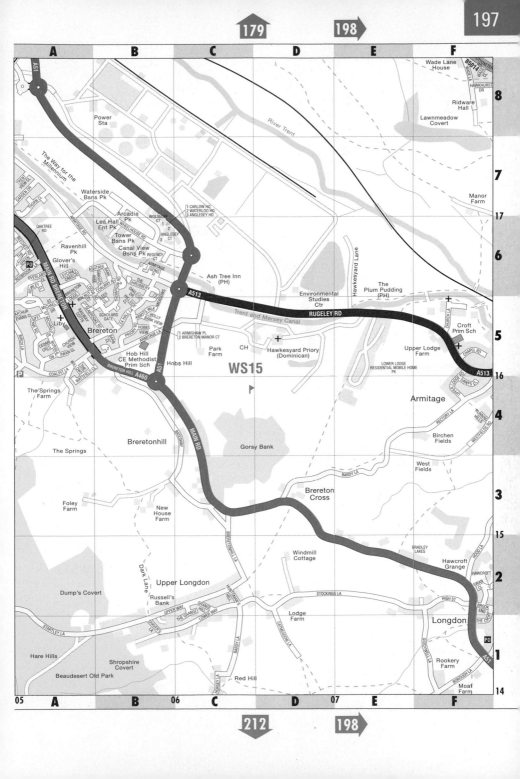

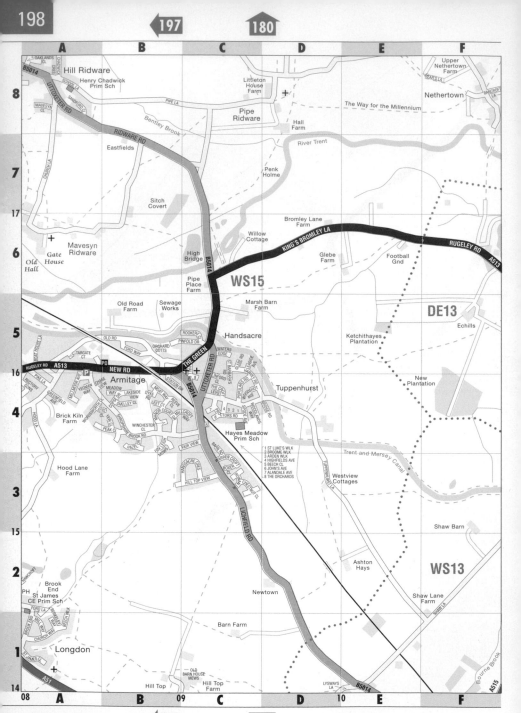

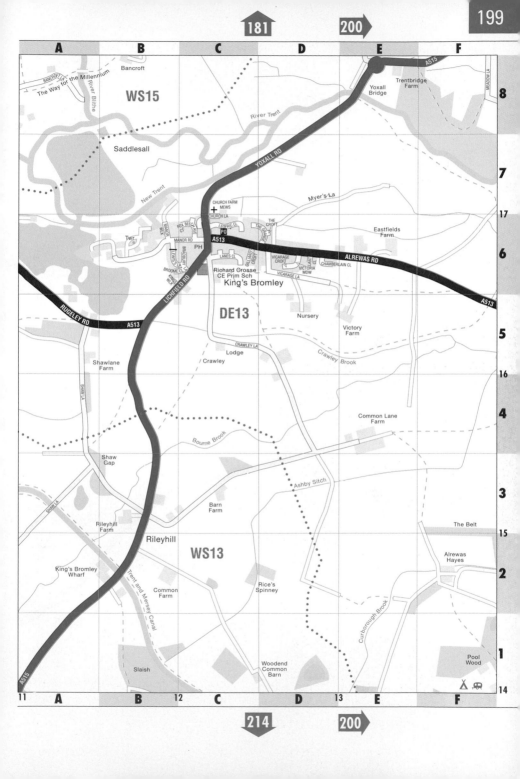

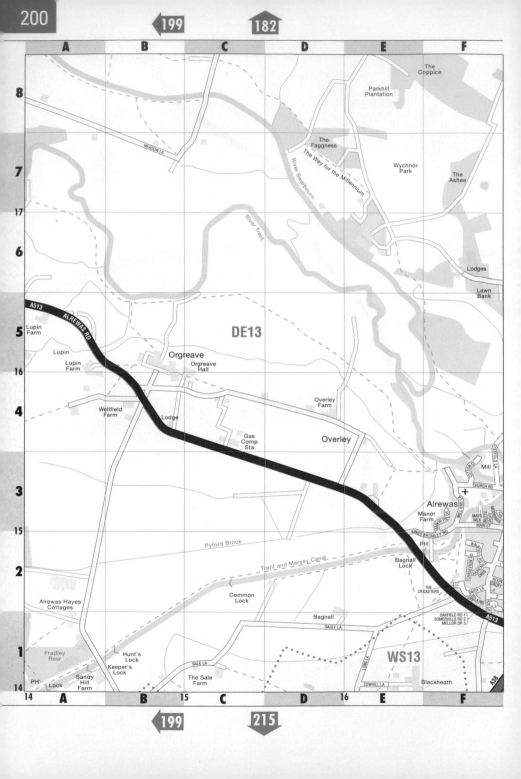

A B C D E F

8

7

17

6

5

16

4

3

15

2

1

14

A 14 B 15 C D 16 E F

The Coppice

Parkhill Plantation

The Faggness

The Way for the Millennium

Wychnor Park

The Ashes

River Swarbourn

River Trent

Lodges

Lawn Bank

A513

ALREWAS RD

Lupin Farm

DE13

Lupin

Lupin Farm

Orgreave

Orgreave Hall

Overley Farm

Wellfield Farm

Lodge

Gas Comp Sta

Overley

Mill

CHURCH RD

Alrewas

Manor Farm

MAYS WLK

MAIN ST

KINGS BROMLEY RD

PH

Pyford Brook

Trent and Mersey Canal

Bagnall Lock

THE CRICKETERS

Alrewas Hayes Cottages

Common Lock

Bagnall

DAISY LA

OAKFIELD RD 1
SOMERVILLE RD 2
MELLOR DR 3

DAISY LA

WS13

Fradley Resr

Hunt's Lock

Keeper's Lock

SALE LA

The Sale Farm

LONG LA

A513

A38

PH

Lock

Sandy Hill Farm

COWHILL LA

Blackheath

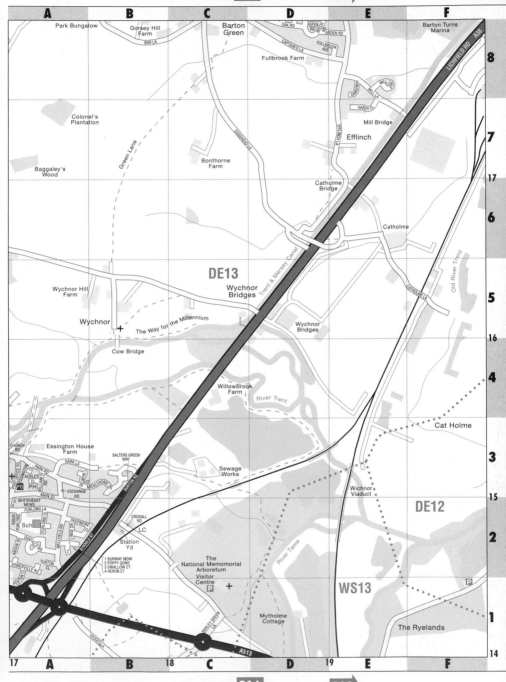

Park Bungalow

Gorsey Hill Farm

BAR LA

Barton Green

Barton Turns Marina

LICHFIELD RD

A38

OAK RD

ASPEN CT

ARDEN RD

CAPTAIN'S LA

FULLBROOK AVE

Fullbrook Farm

8

Colonel's Plantation

Green Lane

Bonthorne Farm

Baggaley's Wood

SPRINGWAY

MILL LA

MILL ORD

HARDY CL

MILL LA

HARVEY CL

Mill Bridge

Efflinch

Catholme Bridge

7

17

DE13

Wychnor Hill Farm

Wychnor Bridges

Trent & Mersey Canal

Catholme

CATHOLME LA

Old River Trent

6

Wychnor

The Way for the Millennium

Wychnor Bridges

5

Cow Bridge

16

Willowbrook Farm

River Trent

4

Cat Holme

CHURCH RD

Essington House Farm

SALTERS GREEN WAY

DARK LA

BURTON RD

Sewage Works

Wichnor Viaduct

DE12

15

PYE OFFICE RD

PARK RD

AUDLEY CL

MICKLEHOAM CL

EXCHANGE RD

MAIN ST

PO

PH

3 WHITEHEART MEWS

FURLONG LA

CROXALL RD

LC

3

GREAT FURLONG LA

FURLONG LA

DEEPMORE

Sch

WELLFIELD RD

LINGE CL

WYNNE ST

Station Yd

2

ARSON RD

OAKLEY RD

TURTON CL

SOMERVILLE RD

FOXTON CL

1 BURWAY MDW
2 POPPY GDNS
3 SWALLOW CT
4 HERON CT

River Tame

WS13

The Ryelands

15

The National Memmorial Arboretum Visitor Centre

P

DE12

P

2

RIDGE LA

BRADLEY GREEN LA

A513

Mytholme Cottage

1

14

17 A B 18 C D 19 E F

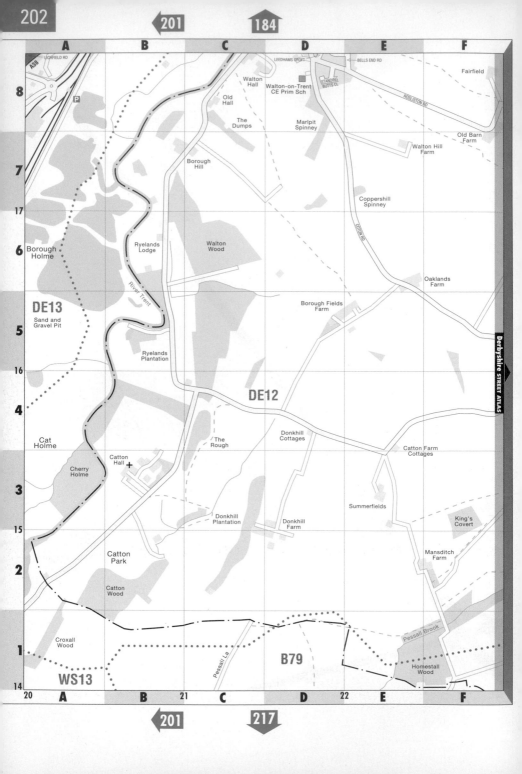

A38 LICHFIELD RD

P

8

Walton Hall

Old Hall

The Dumps

LEEDHAMS CROFT

Walton-on-Trent CE Prim Sch

BELLS END RD

STANDING BUTTS CL

Marlpit Spinney

ROSLISTON RD

Fairfield

Old Barn Farm

Walton Hill Farm

7

Borough Hill

Coppershill Spinney

17

Ryelands Lodge

Walton Wood

6

Borough Holme

Oaklands Farm

River Trent

DE13

Sand and Gravel Pit

Borough Fields Farm

5

Ryelands Plantation

16

DE12

4

Cat Holme

The Rough

Donkhill Cottages

Catton Farm Cottages

Catton Hall +

Cherry Holme

3

Summerfields

Donkhill Plantation

Donkhill Farm

King's Covert

15

Catton Park

Mansditch Farm

2

Catton Wood

Pessall Brook

Croxall Wood

1

Pessall La

B79

Homestall Wood

14

WS13

Derbyshire STREET ATLAS

20 A B 21 C D 22 E F

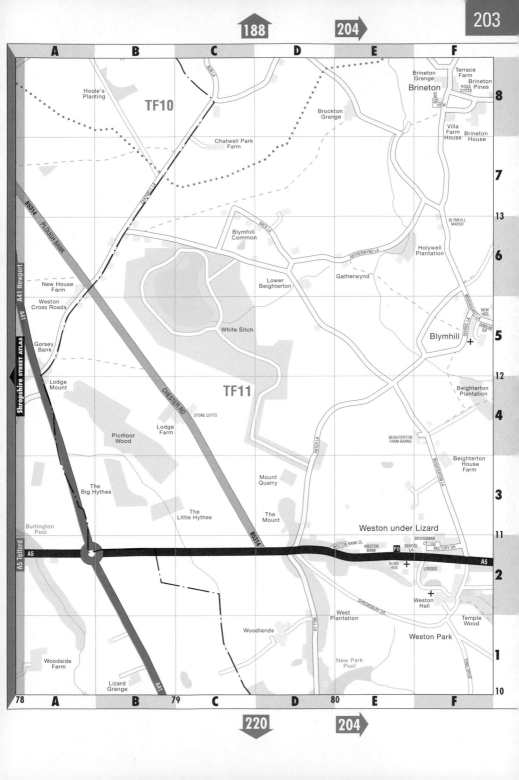

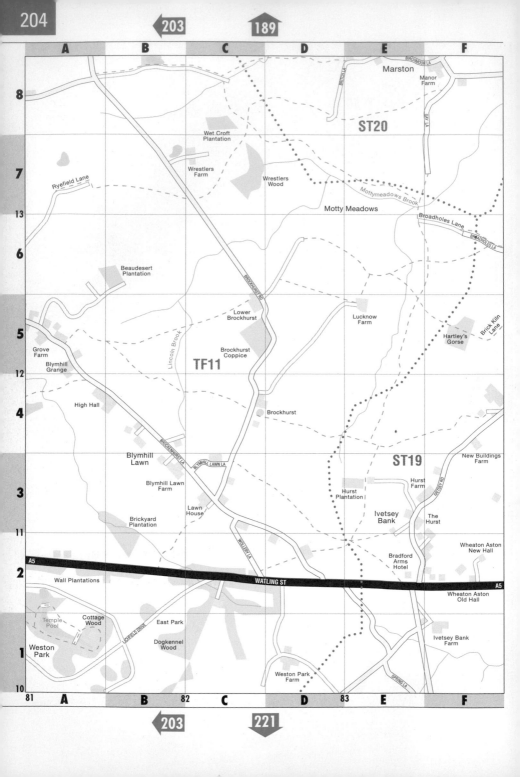

203
189

A B C D E F

8

7

13

6

5

12

4

3

11

2

1

10

BIRCHMOOR LA.

Marston

Manor Farm

ST20

BAY LA.

Wet Croft Plantation

Wrestlers Farm

Wrestlers Wood

Mottymeadows Brook

Motty Meadows

Broadholes Lane

BROADHOLES LA.

Ryefield Lane

Beaudesert Plantation

BROCKHURST RD

Lower Brockhurst

Lucknow Farm

Hartley's Gorse

Brick Kiln Lane

Lincoln Brook

TF11

Brockhurst Coppice

Grove Farm

Blymhill Grange

High Hall

Brockhurst

BROCKHURST LA.

Blymhill Lawn

BLYMHILL LAWN LA.

ST19

New Buildings Farm

Hurst Farm

Blymhill Lawn Farm

Lawn House

Hurst Plantation

Ivetsey Bank

The Hurst

Brickyard Plantation

Wheaton Aston New Hall

Bradford Arms Hotel

A5

WOLLEY LA.

Wall Plantations

WATLING ST

A5

Wheaton Aston Old Hall

LICHFIELD DRIVE

Temple Pool

Cottage Wood

East Park

Dogkennel Wood

Weston Park

Weston Park Farm

IVETSEY RD

Ivetsey Bank Farm

SPRING LA.

81 A 82 B C 82 D 83 E F

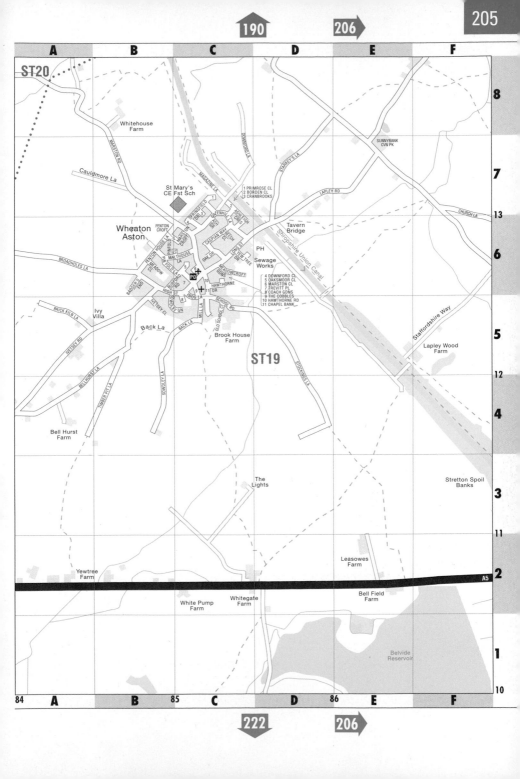

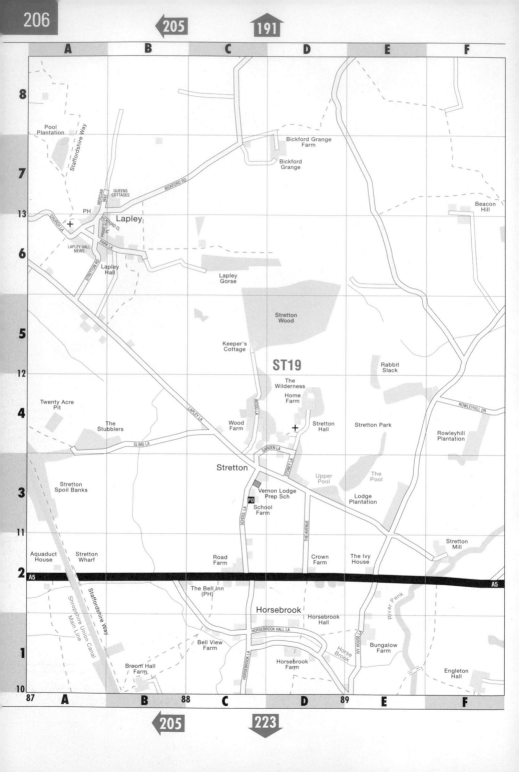

A   B   C   D   E   F

8

Pool
Plantation

7

Bickford Grange
Farm

Bickford
Grange

Staffordshire Way

BICKFORD RD.

QUEENS
COTTAGES

MERIDIAN WAY

Beacon
Hill

13

PH

CHURCH LA.

Lapley

BICKFORD RD.

PRIORS LA.

PARK LA.

6

STRETTON RD.

LAPLEY HALL
MEWS

Lapley
Hall

Lapley
Gorse

Stretton
Wood

5

Keeper's
Cottage

ST19

12

Rabbit
Slack

The
Wilderness

Twenty Acre
Pit

LAPLEY LA.

Home
Farm

ROWLEYHILL DR.

4

The
Stubblers

Wood
Farm

WOOD LA.

Stretton
Hall

Stretton Park

Rowleyhill
Plantation

SLING LA.

GARDEN LA.

Stretton

STONEY LA.

Upper
Pool

The
Pool

3

Stretton
Spoil Banks

Vernon Lodge
Prep Sch

Lodge
Plantation

PO

SCHOOL LA.

School
Farm

11

Aquaduct
House

Stretton
Wharf

Road
Farm

THE AVENUE

Crown
Farm

The Ivy
House

Stretton
Mill

2

Shropshire Union Canal
Main Line

Staffordshire Way

The Bell Inn
(PH)

Horsebrook

Horsebrook
Hall

River Penk

HORSEBROOK HALL LA.

1

Bell View
Farm

HORSEBROOK LA.

Horse
Brook

IVY HOUSE LA.

Bungalow
Farm

Broom Hall
Farm

Horsebrook
Farm

Engleton
Hall

10

87   A   88   C   89   E   F

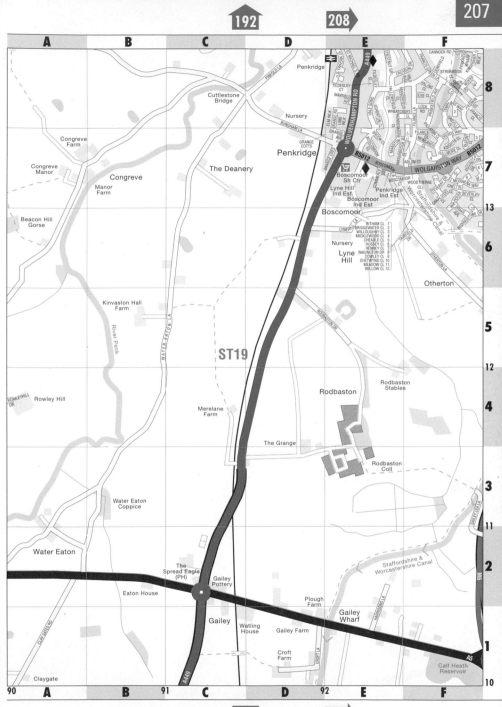

192
208

A   B   C   D   E   F

8

Penkridge

Cuttlestone
Bridge

Nursery

PIMPOLLA

BUNGHAM LA

ELM WLK
GRANGE AVE

Congreve
Farm

Congreve
Manor

Manor
Farm

Congreve

The Deanery

GRANGE
COTTS

Penkridge

WOLVERHAMPTON RD

A449

ST MICHAELS

CHESTNUT GR

CANNOCK RD

CROYDON

HALING

DENE CL

STREAMSIDE
CL

Sch

B5012

WOLGARSTON WAY

B5012

Boscomoor
Sh Ctr

Lyne Hill
Ind Est

Penkridge
Ind Est

Boscomoor
Ind Est

Boscomoor

7

13

Beacon Hill
Gorse

Nursery

Lyne
Hill

LYNEW

BITHAM CL   1
BRIDGEWATER CL 2
WILLOUGHBY CL   3
MICKLEWOOD CL   4
CHEADLE CL   5
HUSSEY CL   6
HENNEY CL   7
NAGINGTON DR   8
COWLEY CL   9
CHETWYND CL   10
MEADOW CL   11
WILLOW CL   12

Otherton

OTHERTON LA

6

Staffordshire & Worcestershire Canal

Kinvaston Hall
Farm

WATER EATON LA

River Penk

ST19

RODBASTON DR

Rodbaston

Rodbaston
Stables

5

12

ROWLEYHILL
DR

Rowley Hill

Merelane
Farm

The Grange

Rodbaston
Coll

4

3

Water Eaton
Coppice

11

GAILEY LA

M6

Water Eaton

The
Spread Eagle
(PH)

Gailey
Pottery

Staffordshire &
Worcestershire Canal

Gailey
Wharf

2

OAK GATES RD

Eaton House

Gailey

Watling
House

Gailey Farm

Plough
Farm

HARDWICK LA

CROFT LA

A5

1

Claygate

Croft
Farm

Calf Heath
Reservoir

10

90   A   B   91   C   D   92   E   F

207
193

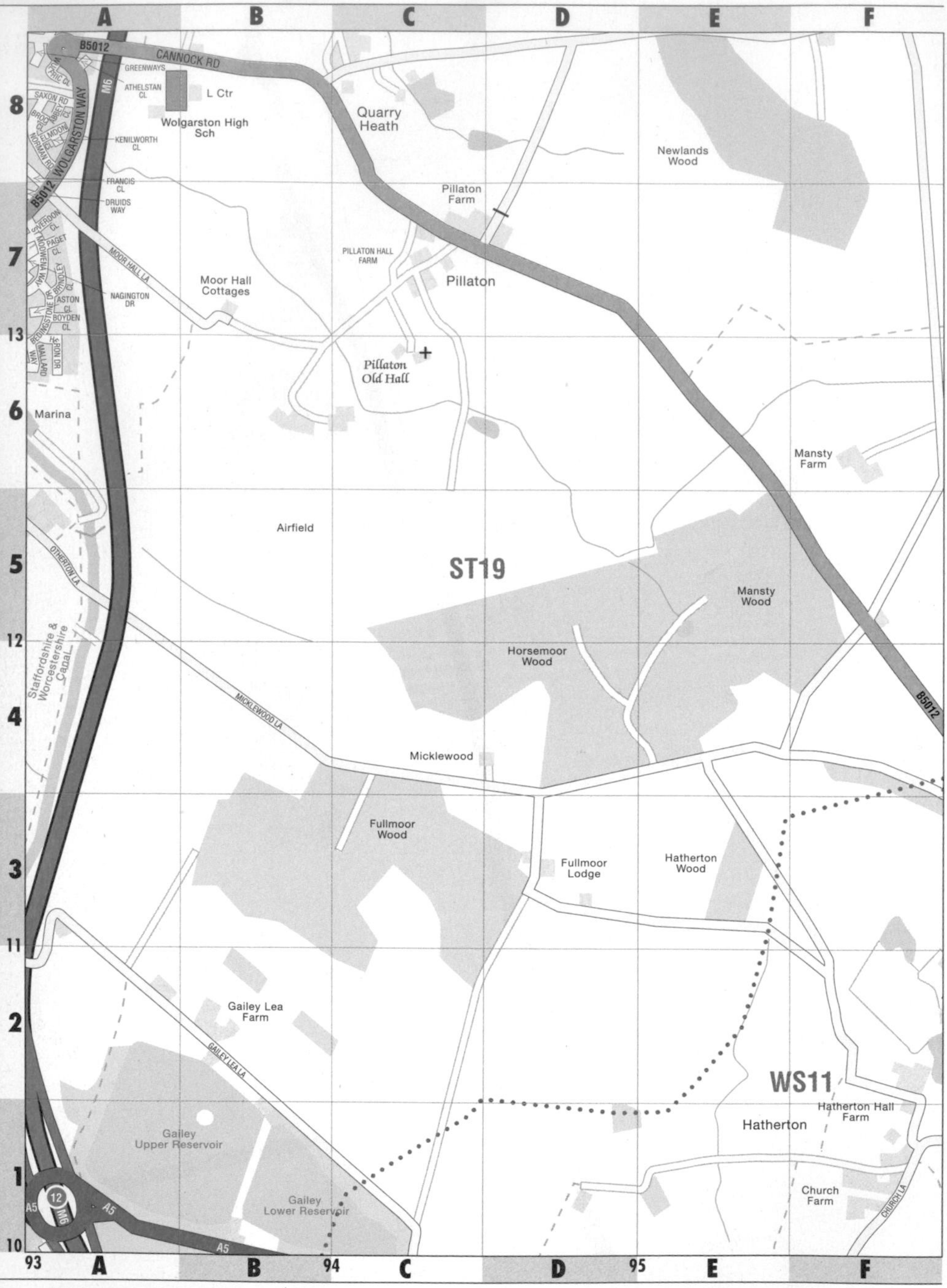

B5012
CANNOCK RD
GREENWAYS
ATHELSTAN CL
L Ctr
Wolgarston High Sch
KENILWORTH CL
FRANCIS CL
DRUIDS WAY
Moor Hall Cottages
NAGINGTON DR
ASTON
BOYDEN CL

M6
WOLGARSTON WAY
B5012
MOOR HALL LA
SAXON RD

Quarry Heath
Newlands Wood
Pillaton Farm
PILLATON HALL FARM
Pillaton
Pillaton Old Hall
Mansty Farm

Marina

Airfield

ST19

Mansty Wood

Staffordshire & Worcestershire Canal
OTHERTON LA

Horsemoor Wood

MICKLEWOOD LA
Micklewood

B5012

Fullmoor Wood
Fullmoor Lodge
Hatherton Wood

Gailey Lea Farm
GAILEY LEA LA

WS11

Gailey Upper Reservoir

Hatherton Hall Farm
Hatherton

A5
M6
12
A5

Gailey Lower Reservoir

A5

Church Farm
CHURCH LA

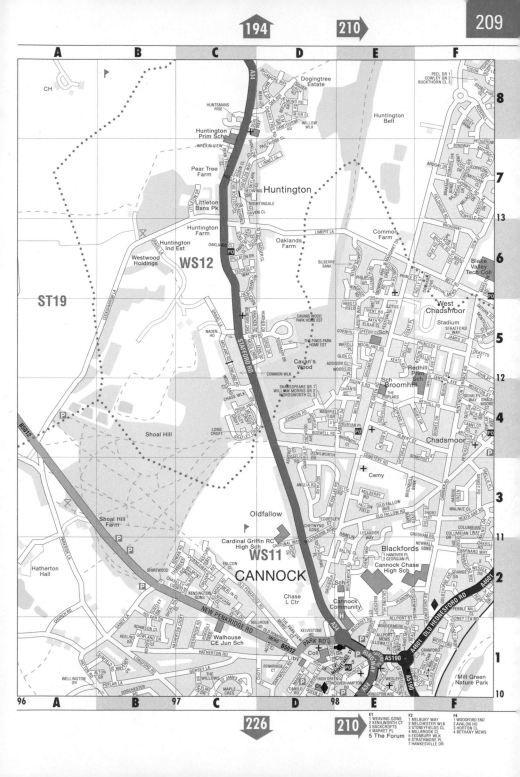

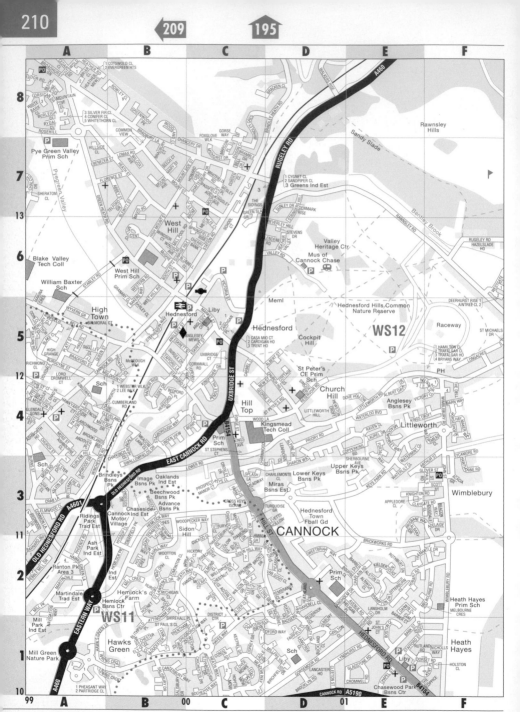

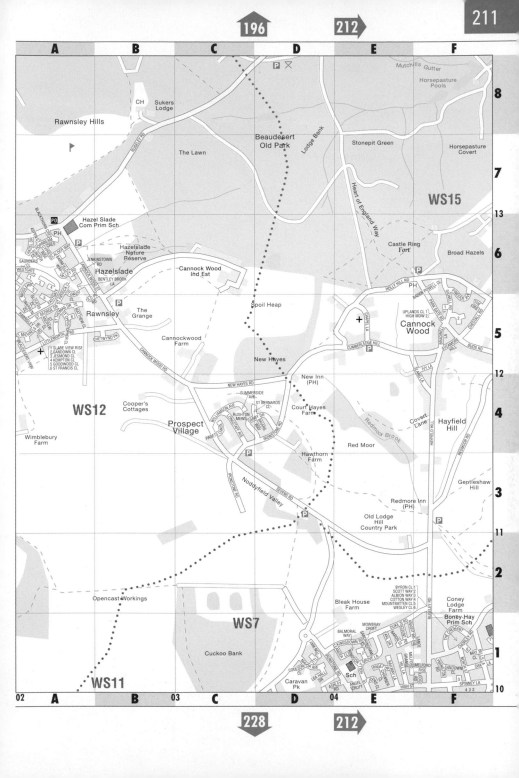

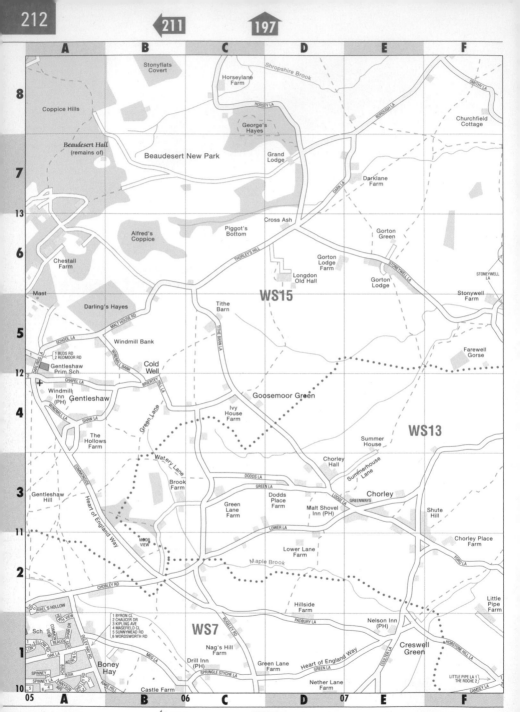

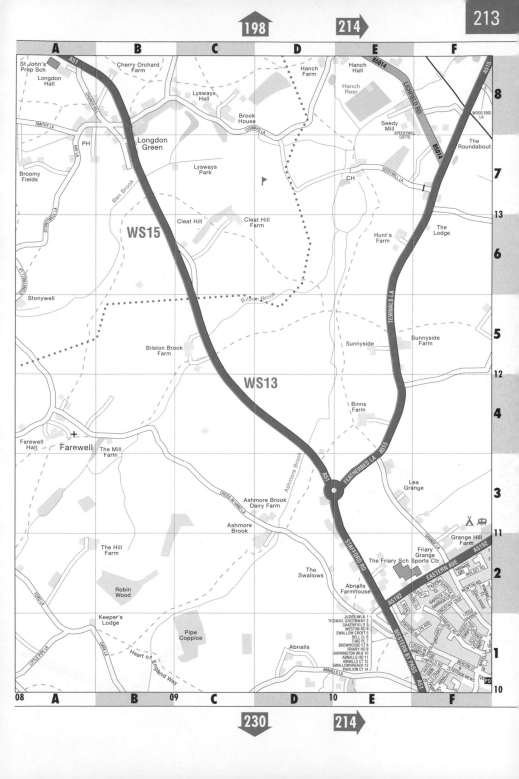

A B C D E F

DE13

Cranberry
Shade House Lock
Middle Lock

Vicar's Coppice

Black Slough

Ravenshaw Wood

Woods Farm

Woodend Lock

WOOD END LA

Black Slough Farm

Fradley Wood

Tomhay Wood

Wood End Farm

Trent and Mersey Canal

Big Lyntus

GORSE LA

New Farm

Full Brook

Fullbrook Farm

Sewage Works

Sprint Course

Little Lyntus

Elmhurst Hall Farm

ASH LA

FOX LA

Corporation Farm

Curborough

Curborough Hall Farm

Curborough Brook

Curborough Farm

Elmhurst

Apsley House

WS13

Curborough House

Ringway Ind Est

SALISBURY CL

WINCHESTER CL

Nether Stowe

Brownfield Cottage

A5192

1 AUGUSTINES WLK
2 PABLS WLK
3 CHRISTOPHER WLK
4 MATTHEWS WLK
5 STEPHENS WLK
6 MARKS WLK
7 PETERS WLK
8 THOMAS GREENWAY
9 JAMES GREENWAY
10 LUKES WLK

Charnwood Prim Sch

Brownsfields Farm

ST MARY'S RD
GILES RD
ST CATHE
ST MARGARETS

DAVID WILLOWS Prim Sch

GARRICK GDNS
HAWKINS

The Mill Pond

LICHFIELD

EDGEWORTH RD
NEEDWOOD HILL
HEWITT CRES
BLOOM

Handel Wlk

PURCELL AVE

SULLIVAN WLK

EASTERN AVE

OAKEN CL
PIPERS CROFT
GREENCROFT

ST PETERS CT
THE GARTH
MILLER

WALKERS CROFT

HAYWORTH RD

WINTER CL

WINDMILL CL
WESTON RD
CHARNWOOD WAY

TECKNAM WAY

Lichfield Bsns Ctr

FRIDAY ACRE

Chadsmead Prim Sch

Sch
DIMBLES HILL

Nether Stowe High Sch

STOWE POOL

Streethay Lodge

WOOD RIDINGS

THE CHAD
GAILAND CRES

ST CHAD'S RD

Stowe

Scotch Orchard Prim Sch

A5127 BURTON RD

1 ARMITAGE HO
2 WHITTINGTON HO
3 SHENSTONE HO
4 RIDWARE HO
5 PENNYS CROFT

ST MICHAEL RD
WISSAGE RD

BRAEBURN
TRENT VALLEY RD

A5192

TRENT VALLEY COTTS 1
BAILYE CL 2

A1
1 LANGTON CT
2 CLEAVELAND MEWS
3 LITTLE BARROW WLK
4 DARWIN CL

DE13

A B C D E F

8

Croxall

CROXALL RD

RIDGET LA

BARLEY GREEN LA

Roddige

Whitemoor Haye

Chetwynd or Salter's Bridge

A513

Dovecote

The Hall

RODDIGE LA

WS13

Brown's Island

Broadfields

Oakley Farm

River Mease

7

13

6

Croxall Mill

River Tame

New Buildings Farm

A513

5

Sittles

Lady Walk

Elford Park

12

4

Sand & Gravel Pit

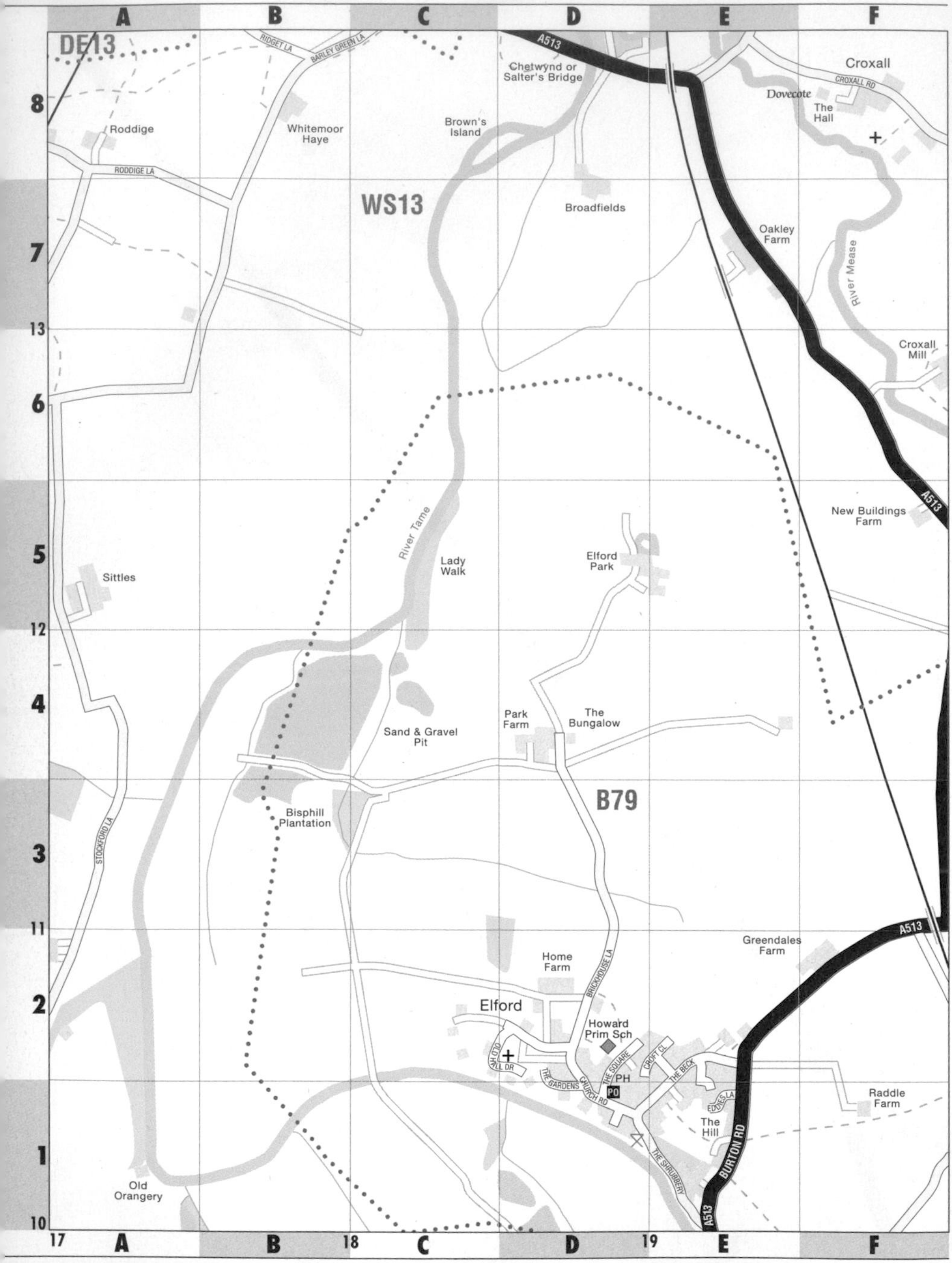

Park Farm

The Bungalow

B79

Bisphill Plantation

STOCKLOW LA

3

11

Home Farm

BROOKSIDE LA

Greendales Farm

A513

2

Elford

Howard Prim Sch

THE GARDENS

COPPIT RD

THE SQUARE

CROFT DR

PH

THE BECK

EAST LA

Raddle Farm

HALL DR

PO

BURTON RD

A513

The Hill

1

THE SHRUBBERY

Old Orangery

10

17 A B 18 C D 19 E F

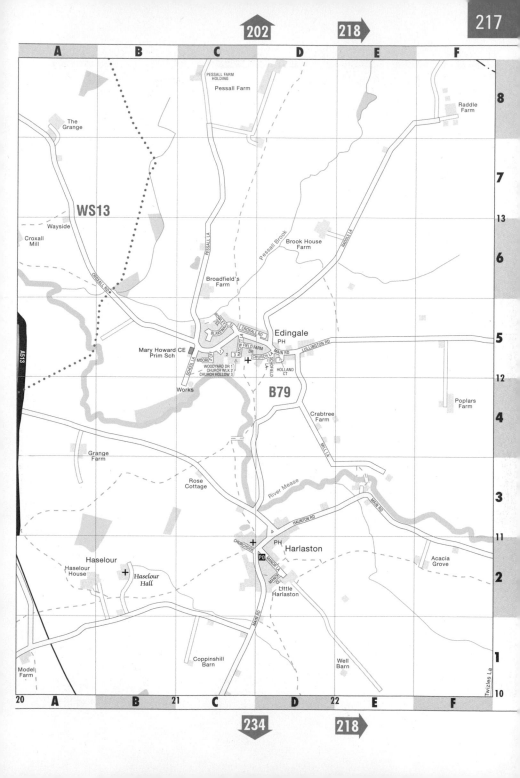

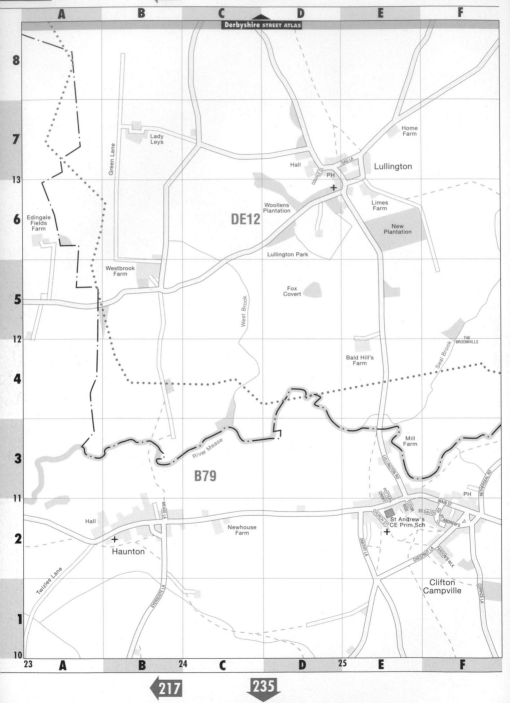

Derbyshire STREET ATLAS

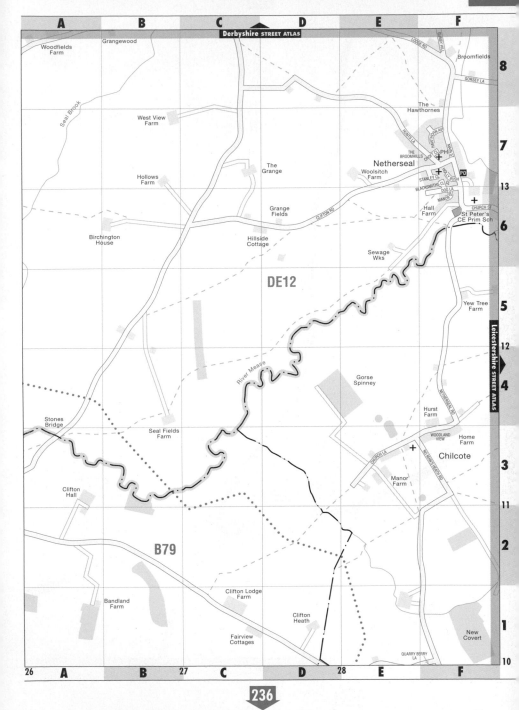

A **B** **C** **D** **E** **F**

8

LODGE RD
BIRDS HILL

Broomfields

GORSEY LA

Woodfields
Farm

Grangewood

The
Hawthornes

Seal Brook

West View
Farm

7

HURTS LA
HATFORD AVE
CHAPEL ST
MAIN ST

THE
BROOMHILLS
PH

Netherseal

Hollows
Farm

The
Grange

Woolsitch
Farm

STANLEY CE
HOLLY BUSH

13

BLACKSMITHS CL
DOG LA
MANOR CT

Birchington
House

Grange
Fields

CLIFTON RD

Hillside
Cottage

Hall
Farm

CHURCH ST

St Peter's
CE Prim Sch

6

DE12

Sewage
Wks

Yew Tree
Farm

5

12

River Mease

Gorse
Spinney

NETHERSEAL RD

Hurst
Farm

4

Stones
Bridge

Seal Fields
Farm

WOODLAND
VIEW

Home
Farm

CHURCH LA

Chilcote

3

Clifton
Hall

Manor
Farm

11

B79

2

Bandland
Farm

Clifton Lodge
Farm

Clifton
Heath

New
Covert

1

Fairview
Cottages

QUARRY BERRY
LA

10

26 **A** 27 **B** **C** 28 **D** **E** **F**

236

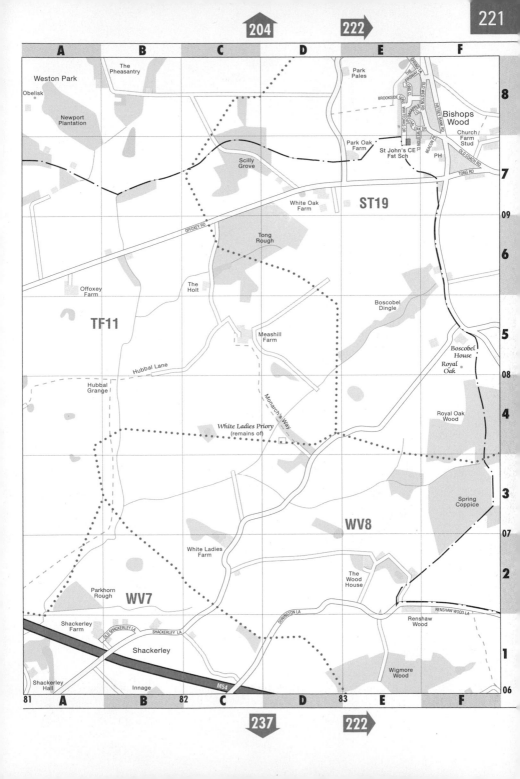

204
222
237
222

A | B | C | D | E | F

Weston Park

Obelisk

The Pheasantry

Park Pales

SPRING LA
THE PRIORY CL
OLD WESTON RD
BROOKSIDE
WHITEOAKS DR
MITRE BANK RD

Bishops Wood

Newport Plantation

Park Oak Farm

OAK DR
WESTON CL

St John's CE Fst Sch

Church Farm Stud

BEACON CT
OLD COACH RD

PH

TONG RD

Scilly Grove

White Oak Farm

ST19

OFFOXEY RD

Tong Rough

Offoxey Farm

The Holt

TF11

Boscobel Dingle

Meashill Farm

Boscobel House

Royal Oak

Hubbal Lane

Hubbal Grange

Monarch's Way

Royal Oak Wood

White Ladies Priory
(remains of)

Spring Coppice

WV8

White Ladies Farm

The Wood House

Parkhorn Rough

WV7

Renshaw Wood

RENSHAW WOOD LA

Shackerley Farm

OLD SHACKERLEY LA

SHACKERLEY LA

DONINGTON LA

Shackerley

Wigmore Wood

Shackerley Hall

Innage

M54

81 | A | B | 82 | C | D | 83 | E | F

8
09
6
5
08
4
3
07
2
1
06

221
205

A **B** **C** **D** **E** **F**

Belvide
Reservoir

8

The
Hawkshutts

Top Barn
Farm

Hag
Wood

Birk's
Barn

SHUTT GREEN LA

Bridleways
Farm

Black
Ladies

7

ST19

Drybrook
Plantation

09

Chambersfield

Paradise

Kiddemore
Green

KIDDEMORE GREEN RD

Oakley

6

New
Inns
(PH)

Wet Hay
Wood

Strangleford
Birch
Farm

FOXES LA

Pearse Hay
Farm

Coldham

Harvington
Birch
Farm

Big Hyde
Rough

5

Cream
Pot

The
Whitemoor

Peckerfield
Wood

08

Hungary Hill
Farm

Old
Coppice

4

Monarch's Way

Wyrley Low
Plantation

Plant's
Hagg

Bath
Farm

Robinson's
Plantation

Chillington
Farm

Horse Paddock
Wood

Langley
Plantation

3

WV8

07

UPPER AVE

Langley Lawn
Farm

Langley Pit

Brick
Kiln
Plantation

Chillington
Hall

CHILLINGTON ST

2

Brick Kiln Lane

RENSHAW WOOD LA

The
Charlemagne

Sham Bridge

The Park

Big Wood

1

The
Pool

The Canal

06

84 **A** **B** **85** **C** **D** **86** **E** **F**

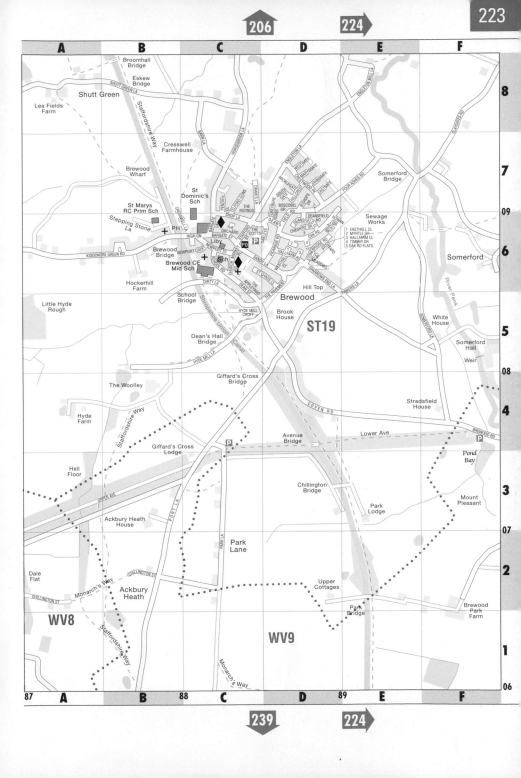

206
224

A B C D E F

8
7
09
6
5
08
4
07
3
2
1
06

Broomhall Bridge
Eskew Bridge
Shutt Green
Lea Fields Farm
Staffordshire Way
Cresswell Farmhouse
Horsebrook La
Engleton Mill La
Oaklands Rd

Brewood Wharf
St Dominic's Sch
St Marys RC Prim Sch
Stepping Stone La
PH
HIGH GN
Brewood Bridge
NEWPORT CRES
Brewood CE Mid Sch
Hockerhill Farm
DIRTY LA
Shropshire Union Canal
School Bridge

Engleton La
Westgate
Market Pl
St Mary & St Chad's
Dean's Hall
Four Ashes Rd
Somerford Bridge
Sewage Works
1 EASTHALL CL
2 MYRTLE GR
3 HALLFARM CL
4 TIMBER GR
5 OAK RD FLATS

Somerford
Somerford Hall
White House
River Penk
Weir

Little Hyde Rough
Kiddemore Green Rd

Dean's Hall Bridge
Hyde Mill Croft
Brook House
Hill Top
Sparrows End La
Tinkers La

Brewood
ST19
Somerford Rd

Giffard's Cross Bridge
Staffordshire Way
The Woolley
Hyde Farm
Hell Floor
Upper Ave
Giffard's Cross Lodge
P
Avenue Bridge
Lower Ave
Coven Rd
Stradsfield House
Brewood Rd
Pond Bay
P
Mount Pleasant

Ackbury Heath House
Port La
Chillington Bridge
Park Lodge
Chillington St
Monarch's Way
Dale Flat
CHILLINGTON ST
Park La
Park Lane
WV8
Ackbury Heath
Staffordshire Way
WV9
Upper Cottages
Park Bridge
Brewood Park Farm
Monarch's Way

87 A B 88 C D 89 E F

239
224

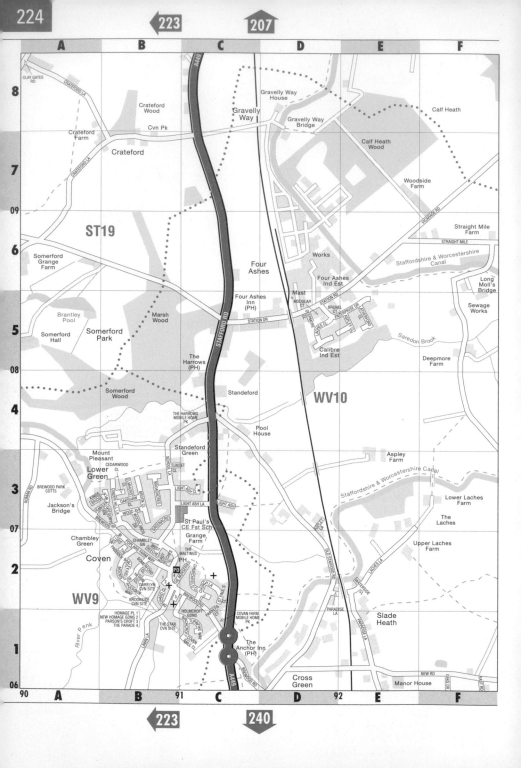

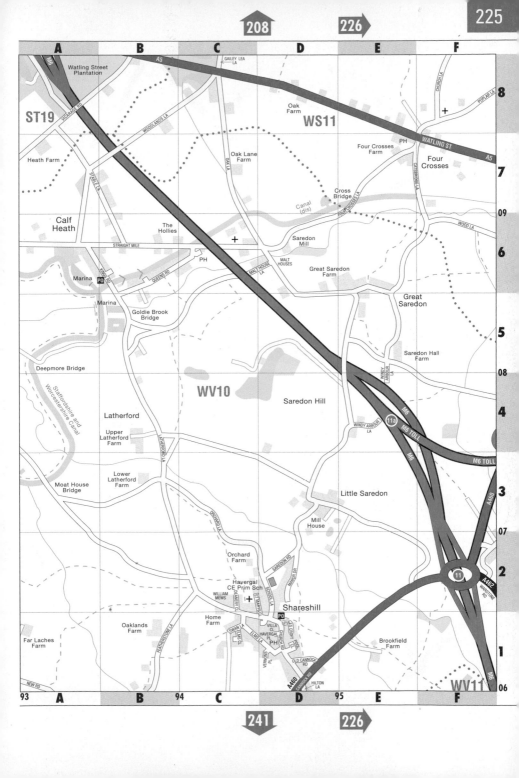

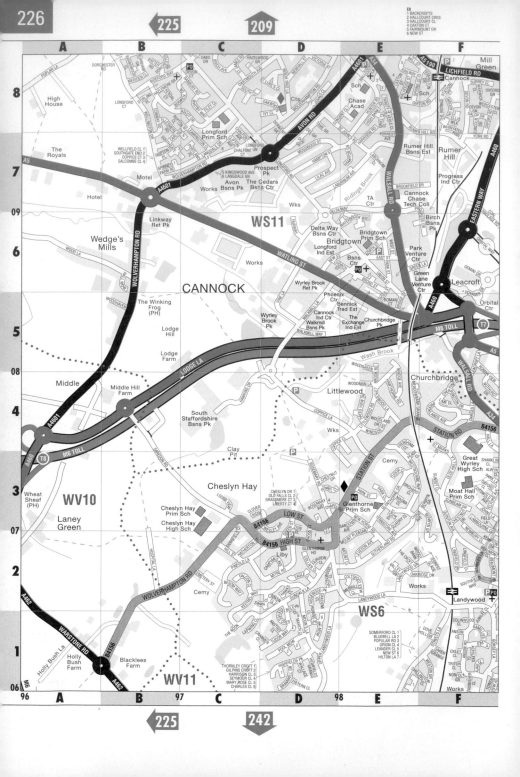

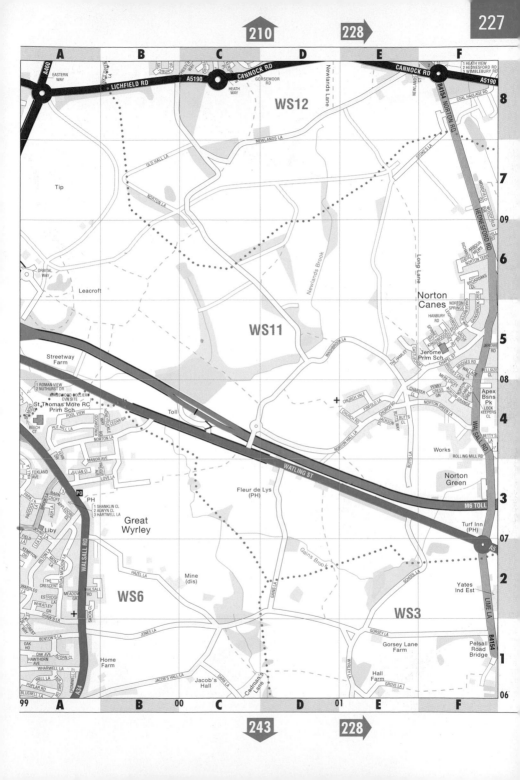

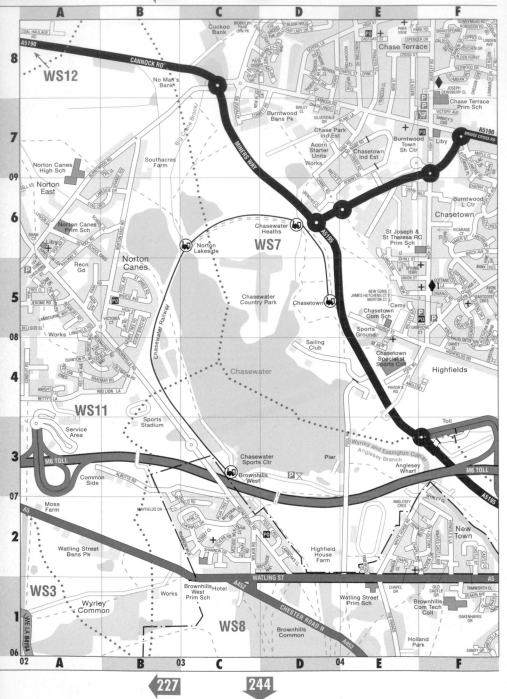

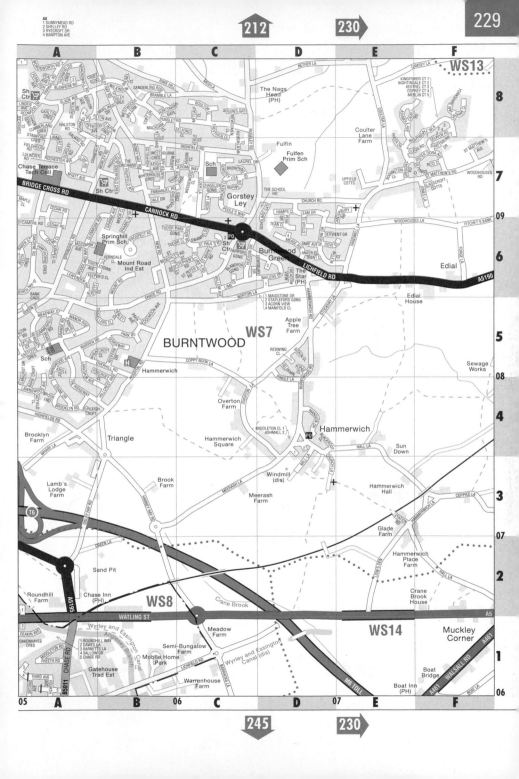

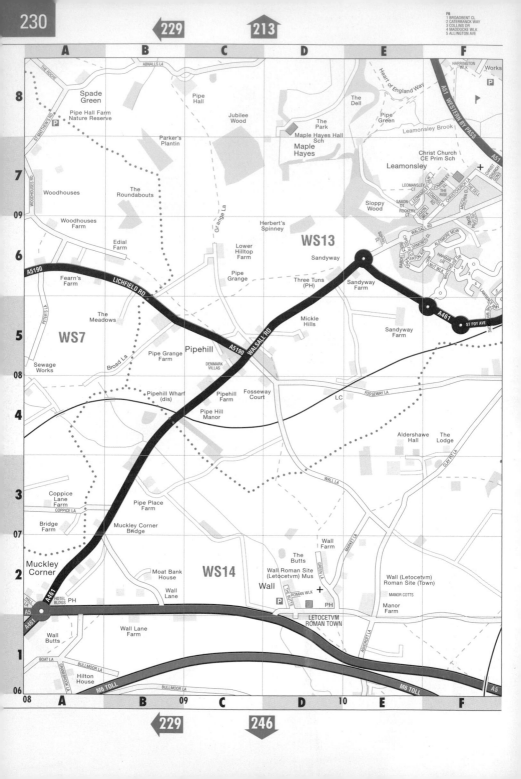

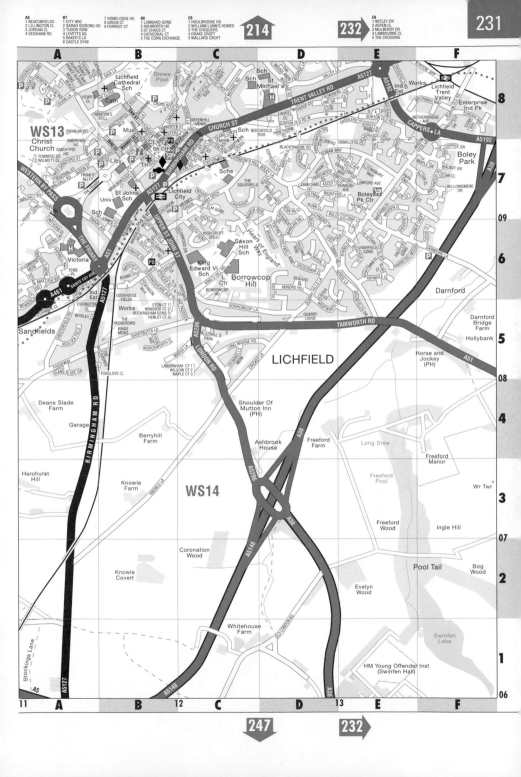

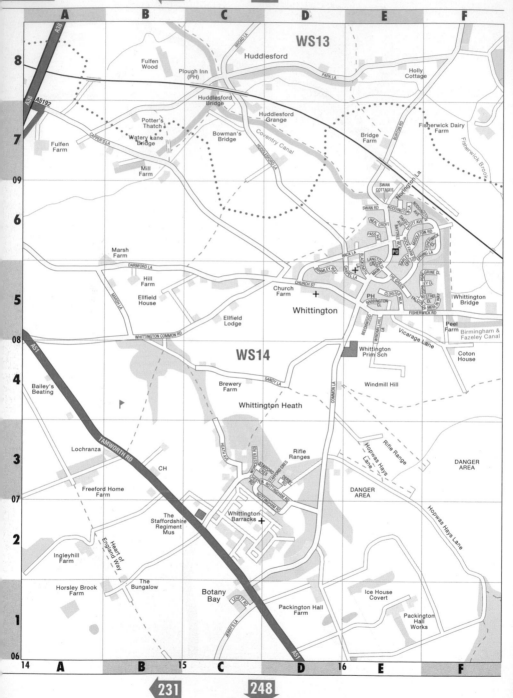

WS13

Huddlesford

Fulfen
Wood

Plough Inn
(PH)

Holly
Cottage

PARK LA

Huddlesford
Bridge

Potter's
Thatch

Huddlesford
Grange

Bridge
Farm

Fisherwick Dairy
Farm

COPPER'S LA

Watery Lane
Bridge

Bowman's
Bridge

Coventry Canal

Fulfen
Farm

Mill
Farm

MOOR LODGE LA

BRIDLE RD

Noxington La

Fisherwick Brook

SWAN
COTTAGES

Marsh
Farm

SWAN RD

NOODINGTON

NOXINGTON

DARNFORD LA

NEAL CROFT

PASS

BAYTREE

DUTT AVE

MOSS LETON RD

FISHERWICK

Hill
Farm

BACK LA

PAMLEY RD

BLACKSMITH

LANGTON
CRES

CHAPEL LA

CROSE CL

BAKEWS

GRINE CL

Whittington
Bridge

Ellfield
House

MASSEY LA

Church
Farm

CHURCH ST

LE GRICE

EY CL

NESTREL
CL

MER

PH

Whittington

BABBINGTON
CL

CLOISTER WAY

FALCON

FISHERWICK RD

Peel
Farm

Ellfield
Lodge

WHITTINGTON COMMON RD

WINDMILL LA

BLACKWOOD

Vicarage Lane

Birmingham &
Fazeley Canal

Coton
House

WS14

Whittington
Prim Sch

Bailey's
Beating

A51

Brewery
Farm

SANDY LA

COMMON LA

Windmill Hill

Whittington Heath

Rifle
Ranges

Lochranza

TAMWORTH RD

CH

HEATH AVE

MANCHESTER RD

CHESTER RD

STAFFORD
CRES

TAFFORD CRES

DEFIEL

NOTTINGHAM RD

Hopwas Hays
Lane

Rifle Range

DANGER
AREA

Freeford Home
Farm

DANGER
AREA

Hopwas Hays Lane

The
Staffordshire
Regiment
Mus

Whittington
Barracks

Ingleyhill
Farm

Heart of
England Way

Horsley Brook
Farm

The
Bungalow

LEYFIELD RD

BERRY LA

Botany
Bay

Ice House
Covert

Packington Hall
Farm

Packington
Hall
Works

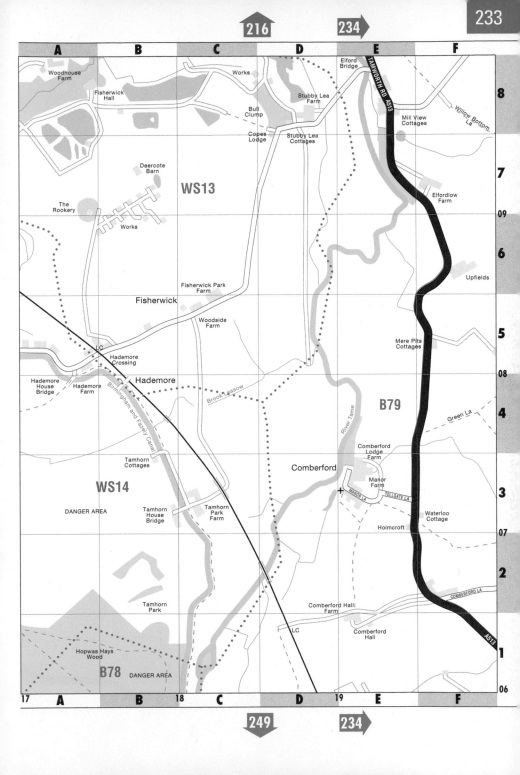

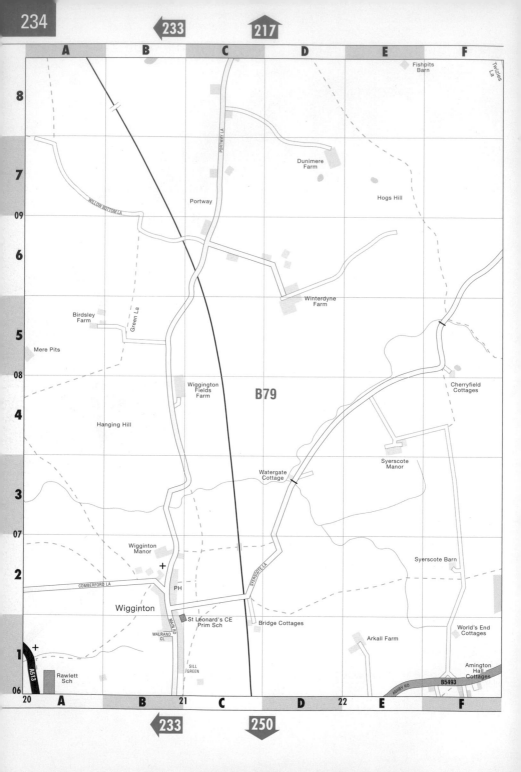

233
217

A B C D E F

8

7

09

6

5

08

4

3

07

2

1

06

Twizles La

Fishpits Barn

Dunimere Farm

PORTWAY LA

Portway

Hogs Hill

WILLOW BOTTOM LA

Green La

Winterdyne Farm

Birdsley Farm

Mere Pits

Wigginton Fields Farm

B79

Cherryfield Cottages

Hanging Hill

Syerscote Manor

Watergate Cottage

Syerscote Barn

SYERSCOTE LA

Wigginton Manor

COMBERFORD LA

PH

Wigginton

World's End Cottages

St Leonard's CE Prim Sch

Bridge Cottages

Arkall Farm

WALRAND CL

MAIN RD

A513

Rawlett Sch

SILL GREEN

ASHBY RD

B5493

Amington Hall Cottages

20 A 21 B C 22 D E F

233
250

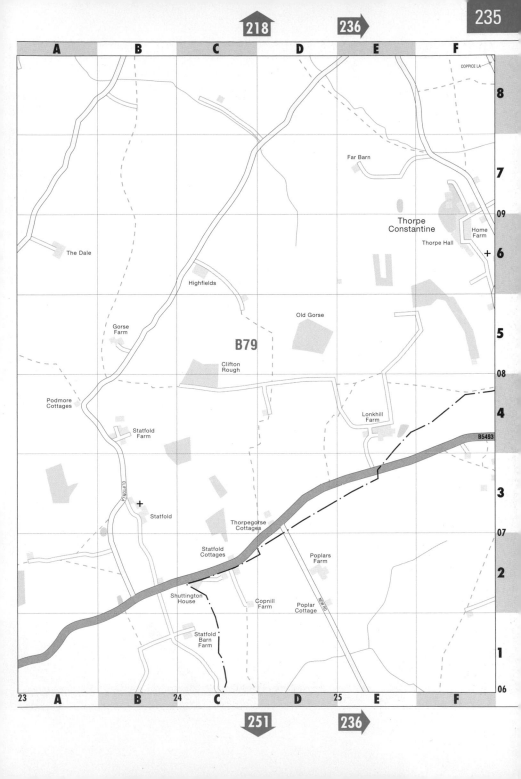

COPPICE LA

A **B** **C** **D** **E** **F**

8

Far Barn

7

09

Thorpe
Constantine

Home
Farm

The Dale

Thorpe Hall

+ 6

Highfields

Old Gorse

Gorse
Farm

B79

5

Clifton
Rough

08

Podmore
Cottages

Lonkhill
Farm

4

Statfold
Farm

B5493

CLIFTON LA

+

Statfold

3

07

Thorpegorse
Cottages

Statfold
Cottages

Poplars
Farm

2

Shuttington
House

Copnill
Farm

Poplar
Cottage

Statfold
Barn
Farm

1

06

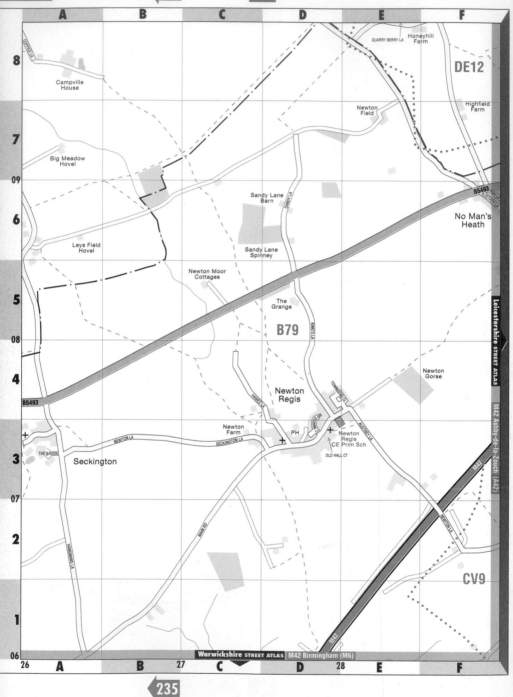

DE12

Honeyhill
Farm

QUARRY BERRY LA

Campville
House

Newton
Field

Highfield
Farm

B5493

No Man's
Heath

Big Meadow
Hovel

Sandy Lane
Barn

SANDY LA

Leys Field
Hovel

Sandy Lane
Spinney

Newton Moor
Cottages

The
Grange

B79

KING ST LA

Newton
Gorse

Newton
Regis

TOWNSEND CFT

HAYES LA

PH

OLD HALL CT

Newton
Farm

Newton
Regis
CE Prim Sch

NEWTON LA

SECKINGTON LA

THE GREEN

Seckington

HANGMANS LA

MAIN RD

AUSTREY LA

NEWTON LA

M42

CV9

B5493

Leitestershire STREET ATLAS

M42 Ashby-de-la-Zouch (A42)

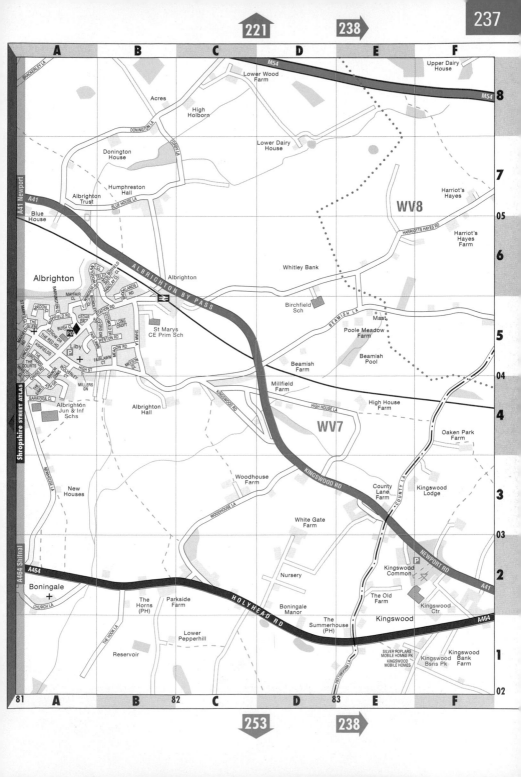

237
222

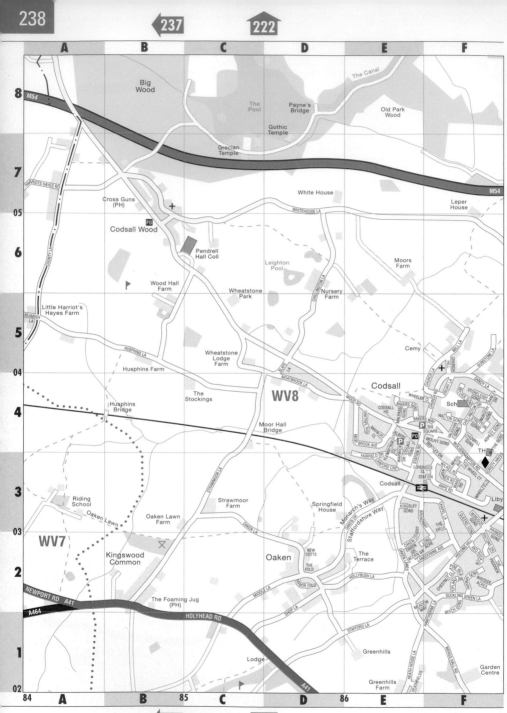

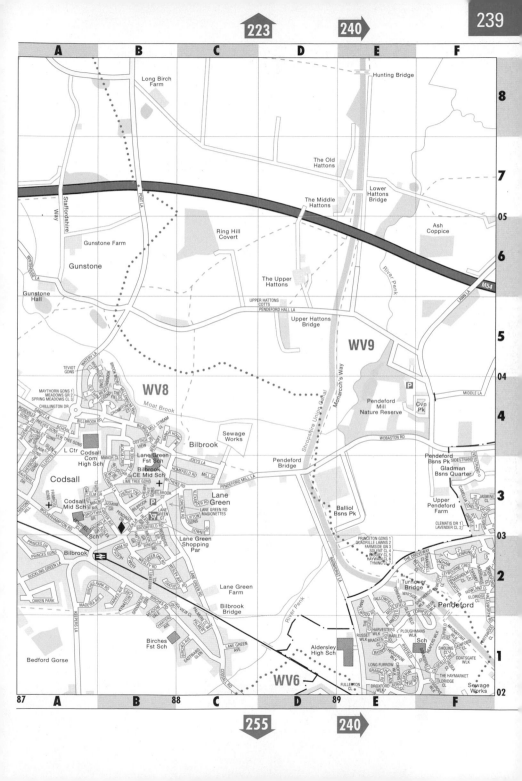

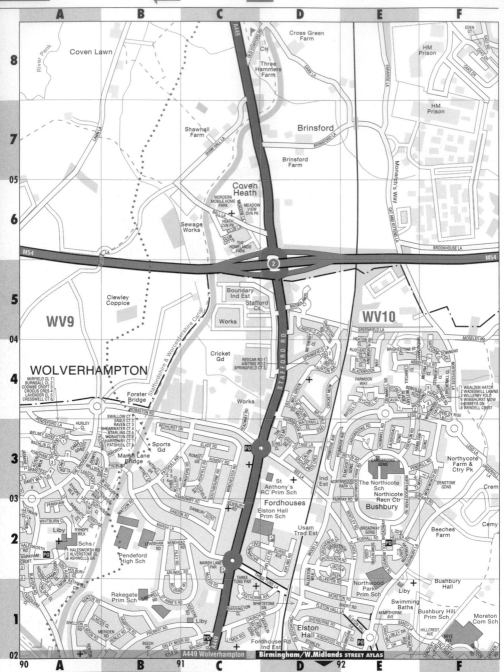

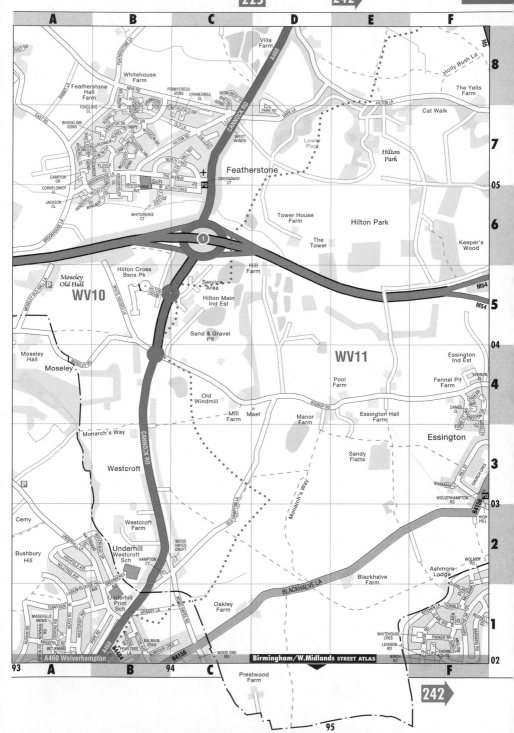

241

226

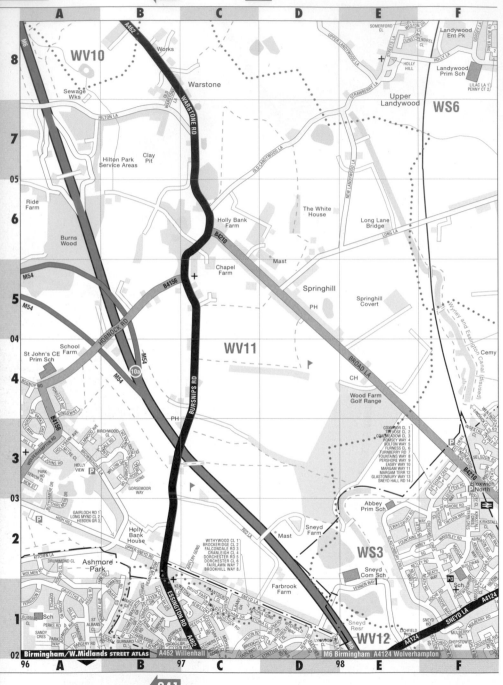

241

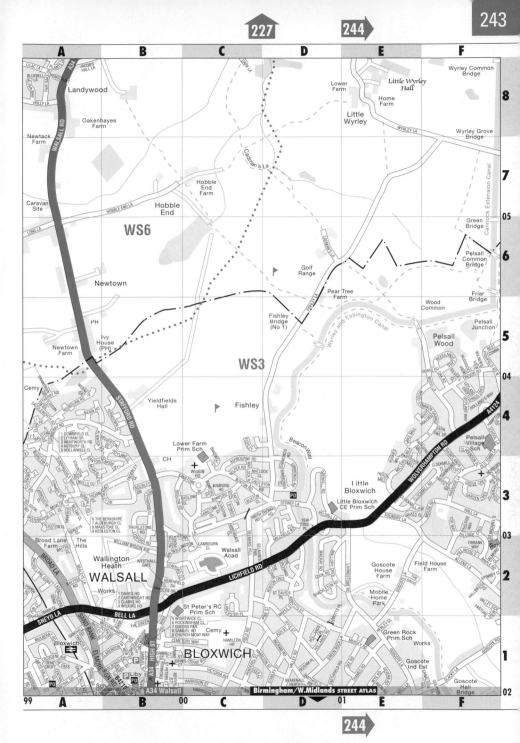

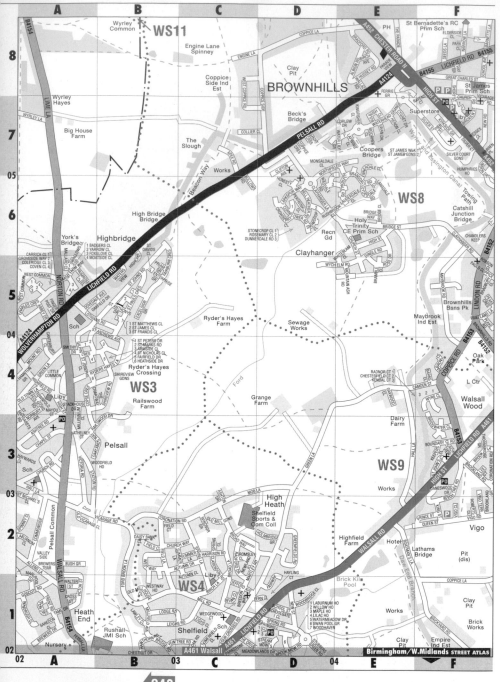

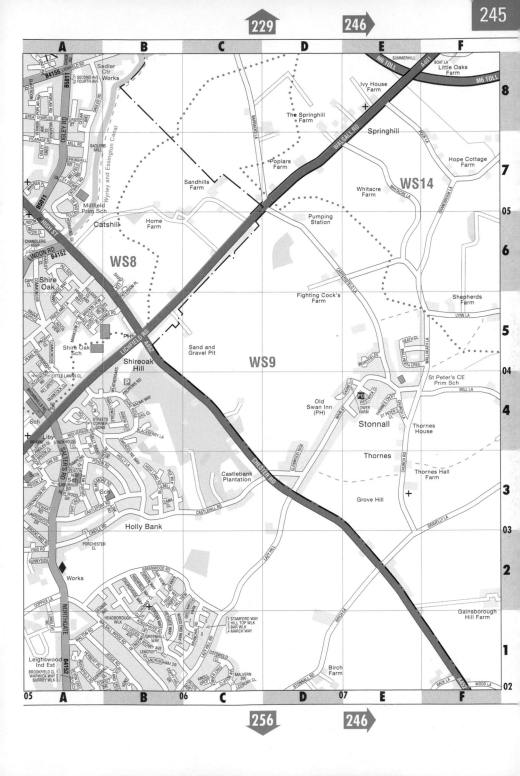

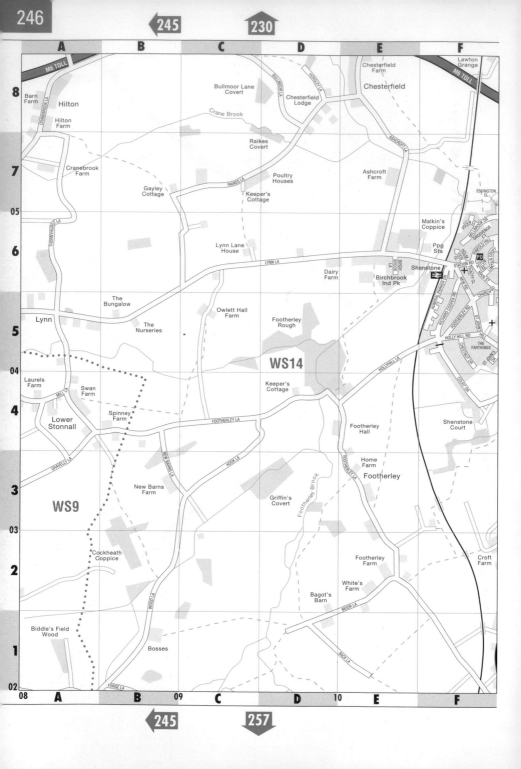

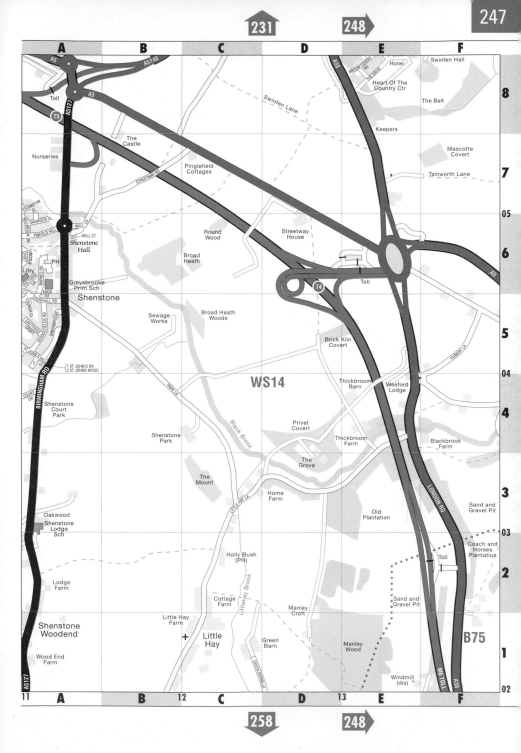

A5

A5148

A5

Toll

T5

A5127

The Castle

STREETWAY RD

Pinglefield Cottages

Nurseries

LESSINGTON CL
OAKWOOD CL
PIMFOLD HILL

MILL LA

MILL CT

Shenstone Hall

PH

Greysbrooke Prim Sch

Shenstone

Liby

BAINES RD
MAIN ST
CHURCHILL RD
GREYSBROOKE
SCHOOL FIELDS RD

ST JOHN'S RD

BIRMINGHAM RD

1 ST JOHN'S DR
2 ST JOHNS WOOD

Round Wood

Broad Heath

Sewage Works

Broad Heath Woods

Swinfen Lane

Streetway House

Brick Kiln Covert

WS14

Thickbroom Barn

Weeford Lodge

HUNGRY LA

A38

BROOM COVERT RD

THE DRIVE

Hotel

Heart Of The Country Ctr

Keepers

Swinfen Hall

The Belt

Mascotte Covert

Tamworth Lane

A5

Toll

T4

Shenstone Court Park

Shenstone Park

PARK LA

Black Brook

Privet Covert

The Mount

LITTLE HAY LA

Home Farm

The Grove

Thickbroom Farm

Old Plantation

Blackbrook Farm

Sand and Gravel Pit

Oakwood
Shenstone Lodge Sch

Lodge Farm

Holly Bush (PH)

Cottage Farm

Littlehay Brook

Little Hay Farm

Shenstone Woodend

Wood End Farm

A5127

Little Hay

Green Barn

GREEN BARNS LA

Manley Croft

Manley Wood

Windmill (dis)

Sand and Gravel Pit

Coach and Horses Plantation

Toll

LONDON RD

M6 TOLL

A38

B75

05

6

5

04

4

3

03

2

1

02

11   A   12   B   C   13   D   E   F

247
232

A B C D E F

8

Broadfields

Packington
Moor

Common
Barn

A51

7

Moor
Covert

05

Tamworth Lane

Knox's Grave La

Riding
School

A51 HOPWAS HILL

6

Hare Park
Wood

A5

ELBELA

Buck's
Head
Cottages

Sand and Gravel
Pit

Packington
Farm

PACKINGTON LA

WS14

Mast

5

Transmitting
Station

The Devil's
Dressing
Room

04

Weeford

Heart of England Way

Buck's Head
Farm

B78

Hanging
Wood

4

Church
Wood

Bourne
House

The
Lodge

Long
Island

Sand and Gravel
Pit

Common
Plantation

HINTS LA

Hints Lane
Farm

A5

Black Brook

ROCK HILL

3

Rough
Leasow

Job's
Hill

Snake's
Hill

Hints

Watling St

Manor
Farm

Hints Hill

03

Gorsey
Hill

ROOKERY LA

SCHOOL LA

Home
Farm

Bangley
Lodge

2

Sand and
Gravel Pit

Crow's
Castle

Rookery

Ford

HINTS CT

Botley
House

Resr

Bourne Brook

B75

New
Plantation

Rookery
Farm

White Owl
Farm

BROOKHURST LA

Roundhill
Wood

1

02

14 A B 15 C D 16 E F

247
259

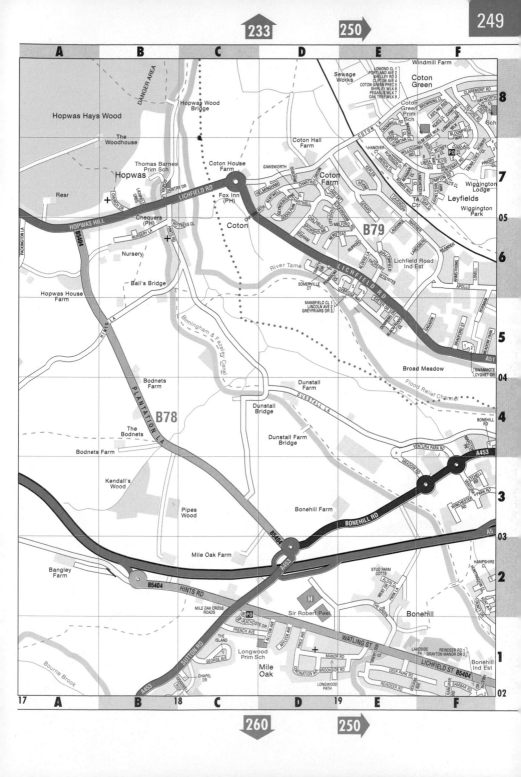

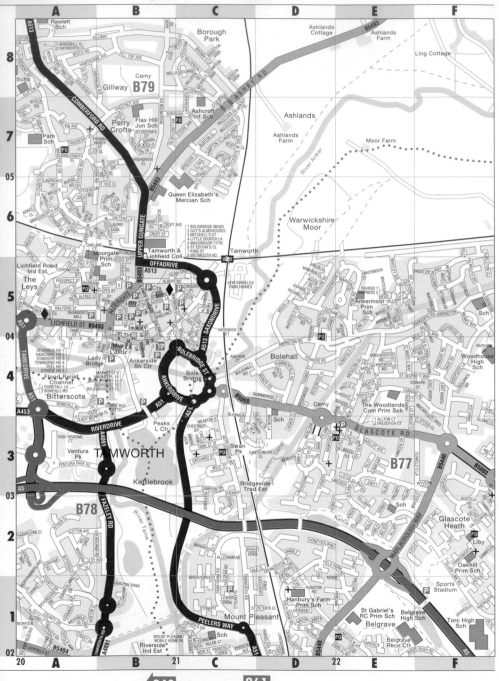

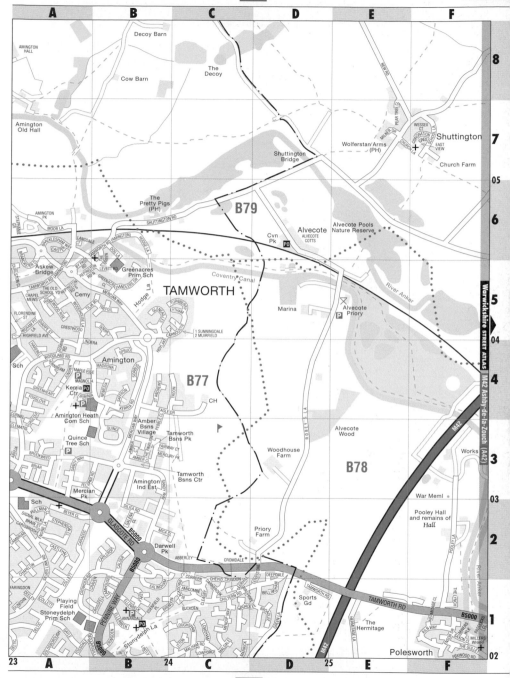

Shropshire STREET ATLAS

TF11

8

7

01

6

5

00

4

3

99

2

1

98

A   B   C   D   E   F

78   79   80

Rous's
Covert

Bishton
Cottages

Bishton
Manor

WV7

Albrighton
Lodge

Wildicote

Shropshire
Lodge

Home
Farm

Patshull
Park

RUSHEY LA

FARM RD

HOME FARM RD

Monkey
Bridge

Wilderness
Hill

Patshull
Hall

Snowdon
Pool

Bennetts
Wood

Monkeybridge
Plantation

Burnhill
Green

Lower
Snowdon

Dartmouth
Arms (PH)

SNOWDON RD

Decoy
Wood

Church
Pool

Old Park

Half Moon
Plantation

Middle
Ley

Shepherds
Buildings

Shepherds
Plantation

Cut
Spinney

The
Great Pool

Old Park
Plantation

WV6

Green's
Coppice

Jubilee
Plantation

Far Ley

Oulton
Garden

Hotel

CH

Plant's
Neck

Mill
Pond

Bridgenorth
Plantation

Stanlow
Farm

Pasford
Farm

Pasford

Kingslow
Cottages

Kingslow

Kingslow
Farm

Kingslow
Hall

Pasford
House

Nun Brook

WV15

Chesterton
Cottage

Birchley
Farm

Shropshire STREET ATLAS

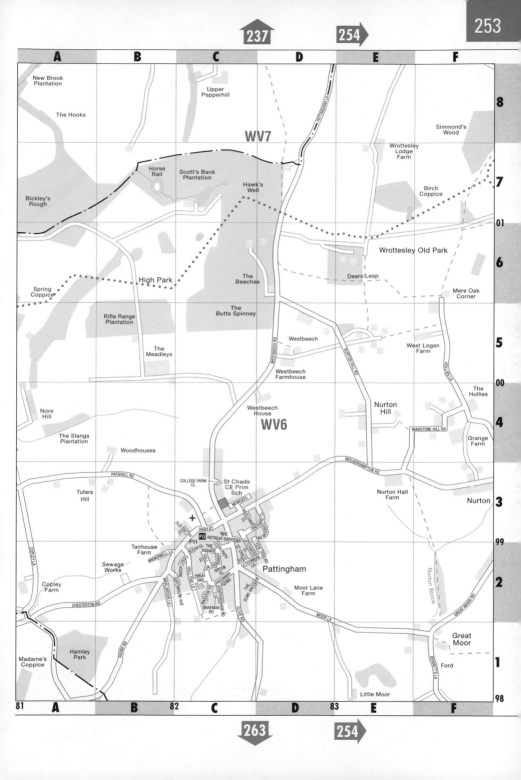

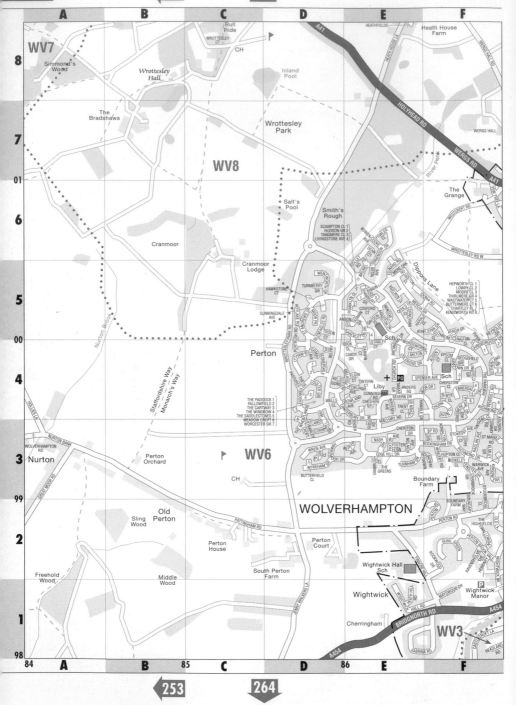

253
238

WV7

Simmond's Wood

8

Bull Ride
WROTTESLEY CT
CH

The Bradshaws

Wrottesley Hall

Inland Pool

Wrottesley Park

7

WV8

01

Salt's Pool

Smith's Rough

SCAMPTON CL 1
HUDSON GR 2
TANGMERE CL 3
LIVINGSTONE AVE 4

6

The Grange

Cranmoor

Cranmoor Lodge

WROTTESLEY RD W

HAWKSTONE CT

TURNBERRY GR

HEPWORTH CL 1
LOWRY CL 2
MOORE CL 3
THIRLMERE GR 4
WASTWATER CT 5
BUTTERMERE CT 6
CHARTLEY CL 7
KENILWORTH RD 8

5

SUNNINGDALE AVE

Dippons Lane

COSFORD CT

00

Perton

Sch

Staffordshire Way
Monarch's Way

Liby

Sch

4

THE PADDOCK 1
FALLOWFIELD 2
THE CARTWAY 3
THE WINDROW 4
THE SADDLESTONES 5
MEADOW CROFT 6
WORCESTER GR 7

PO

SPENSER AVE

CHEPSTOW

EPSOM CL

NURTON BANK
WOLVERHAMPTON RD

3

Nurton

Perton Orchard

WV6

CH

BUTTERFIELD CL

WREN AVE

WYKEHAM CL

THE GREENS

Boundary Farm

99

Old Perton

Sling Wood

PATTINGHAM RD

WOLVERHAMPTON

Boundary Farm

PERTON RD

The Highfields

QUAIL GR

2

Perton House

Perton Court

Wightwick Hall Sch

1

Freehold Wood

Middle Wood

South Perton Farm

Wightwick

Wightwick Manor

98

Cherringham

BRIDGNORTH RD

A454

Sabrina Av

WV3

HEADLAND RD

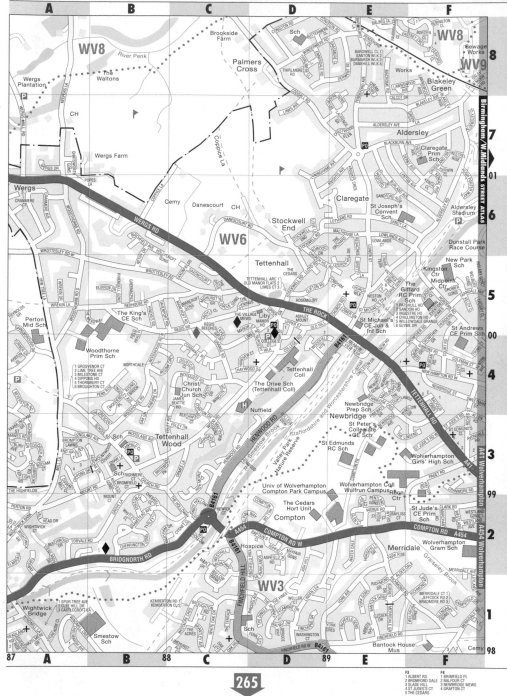

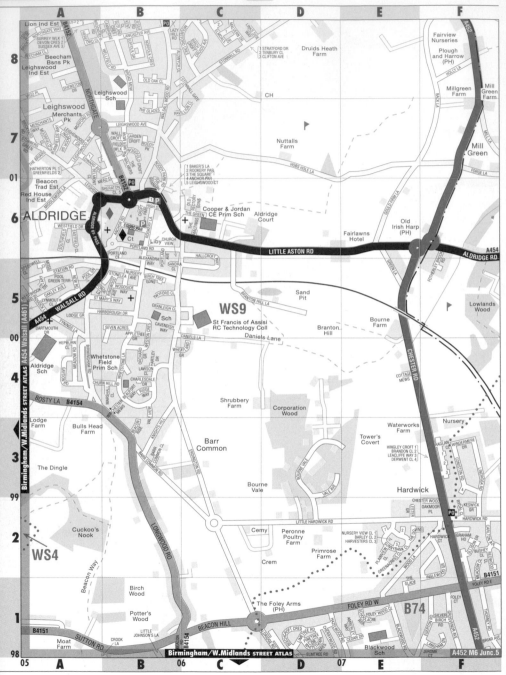

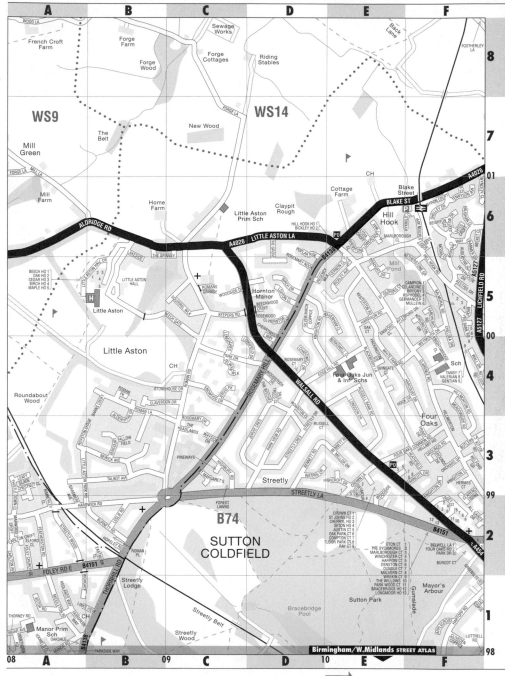

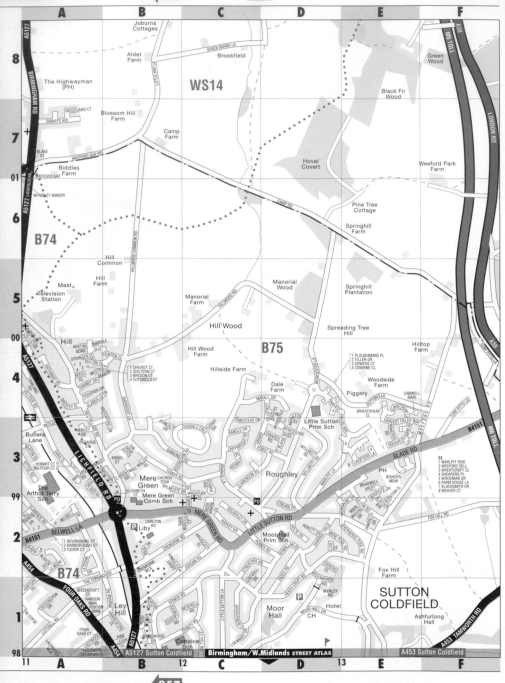

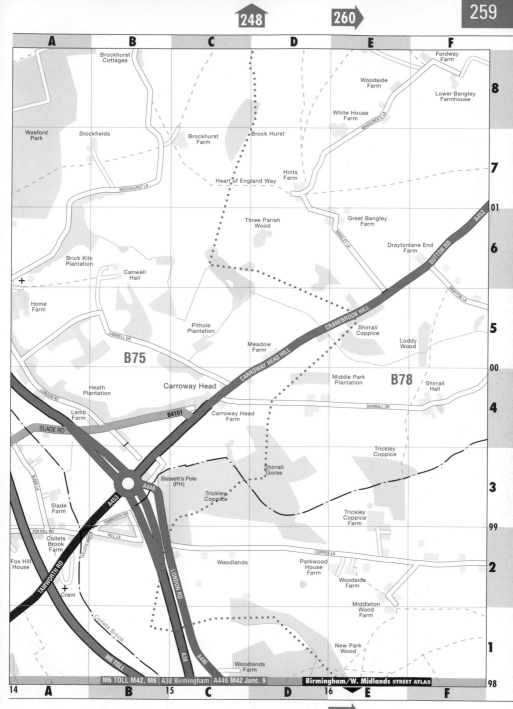

Birmingham/W. Midlands STREET ATLAS

259

249

New House Farm

BANGLEY LA

Fazeley

YORKSAND RD
REINDEER RD
DAMA RD
MAYAMA RD
DRAYTON MANOR DR

Longwood House

CRANWELL RISE

GAINSBOROUGH CR
KIRKLAND AVE
CASTLE DR
PO

A453

Bourne Bridge

Bourne Brook Cut

Seventeen Acre Wood

Works

Alder Wood

Duck Decoy

SUTTON RD

Bourne Brook

DRAYTON MANOR DR

8

Drayton Manor Park

CH

A453

7

Lodge Farm

Hill Farm

Longwood Stables

COLESHILL RD

01

6

A4091

Bullocks End Farm

Heathley Farm

HEATHLEY LA

Edden's Wood

Oak Farm Craft Ctr

Drayton Bassett

SCH CL
OLD BANK CL
MOAT DR
CHURCH CL
PEEL CL
NEW ROW
EDDENS WOOD CL
PO

Manor Prim Sch

5

Stone House

SHIRRAL DR

Heart of England Way

DRAYTON LA

Sewage Works

RECTORY CL

SALTS LA

Drayton Brick Bridge

00

Ashdene Farm

B78

PORTLEYS LA

Brook End Farm

Heart of England Way

4

Brook Farm

Birmingham and Fazeley Canal

Upper House Farm

3

99

Gallows Brook

COPPICE LA

Quarry

Mill Plantation

2

Middleton

CHURCH ROW

SIMMONS CL

Highfields Farm

CHURCH LA

Park-gate Farm

Middleton Park

Newhouse Farm

The Green Man (PH)

VICARAGE HILL

PO

Walker's Spinney

CRANBROOK LA

Middleton Pool

Middleton Hall

1

Langley Brook

Sewage Works

A4091

A4091 Coleshill (A446)

Birmingham/W.Midlands STREET ATLAS

98

17

A

B

18

C

D

19

E

F

259

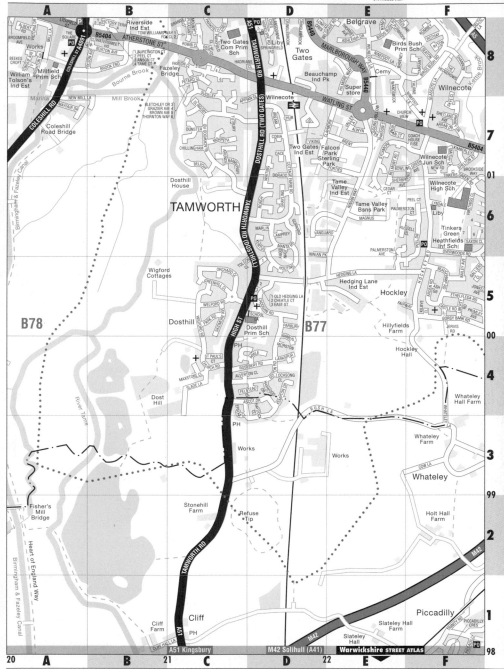

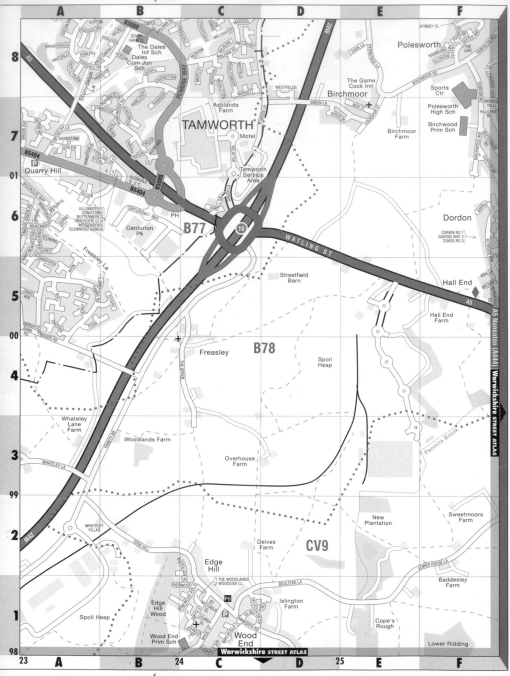

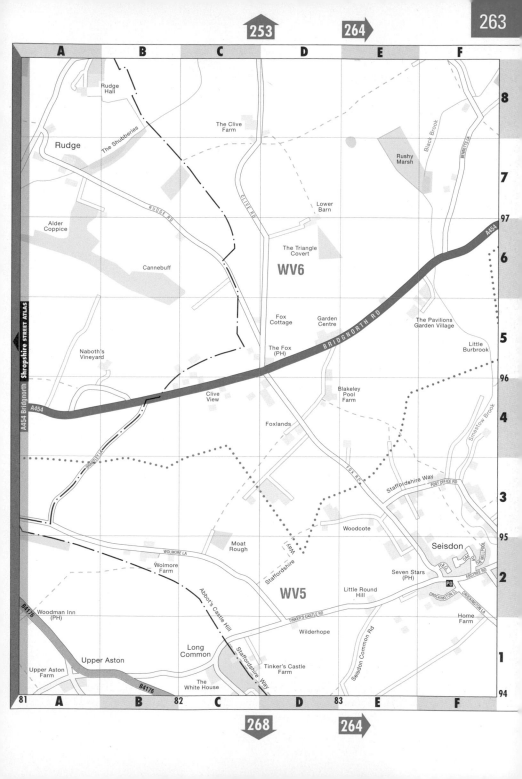

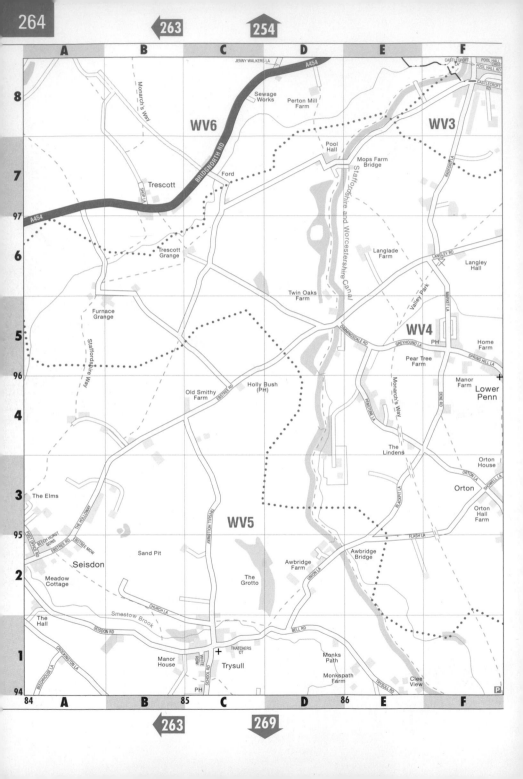

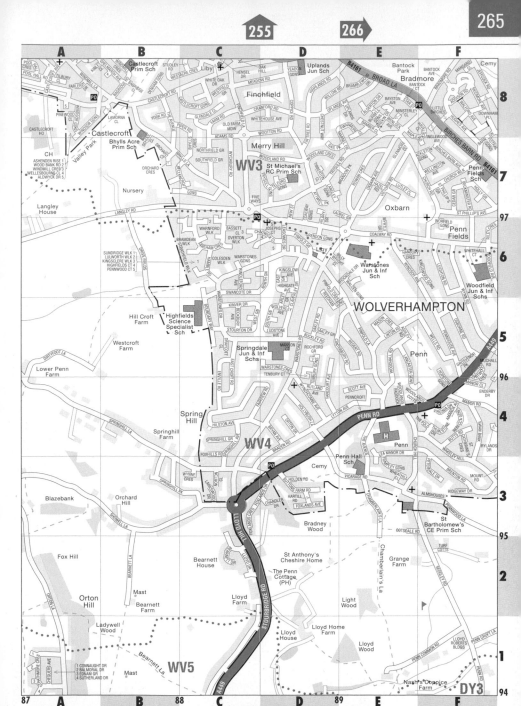

265

C8
1 PAUL ST
2 BLOOMSBURY ST
3 St Johns Ret Pk
4 LITTLE POUNTNY ST
5 KING EDWARDS ROW
6 STEVENS GATE

7 Hollies Ind Est
8 RAINBOW ST

D8
1 DARTMOUTH ST
2 GORDON ST
3 GRANVILLE CL

A449 Wolverhampton A4123 Wolverhampton A41 Wolverhampton

WV3

WOLVERHAMPTON

WV1

WV2

Goldthorn Hill

Goldthorn Park

GOLDTHORN HILL

PARKFIELD RD A4039

Rough Hills

Parkfield

WV4

Colton Hills Com Sch

Park Hill

Park Coppice

Colton Hills

Ashen Coppice

Beacon Ctr for the Blind

Ettingshall Park

Spring Vale Prim Sch

Lanesfield

Greenleighs

Penn Common

Penwood Farm

Alder Coppice

WV14

Alder Coppice Prim Sch

DY3

SEDGLEY

Cinder Hill

Sewage Works

265

271

F4
1 ELLIOT CT
2 HARDIE CT
3 MERIDEN CT
4 MORRIS CT
5 WESLEY CT
6 WARWICK CT
7 RYLCROFT
8 AVONCROFT
9 FIRCROFT
10 HOLMCROFT
11 GENTHORN CL
12 ASHCROFT
13 FLORENCE AVE
14 NORBURY CRES
15 CENTRAL AVE

B'ham / W. Midlands STREET ATLAS A4123 Dudley

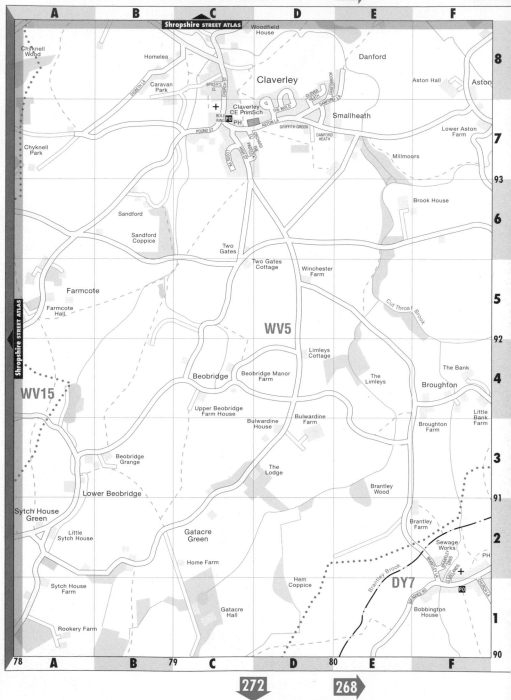

Shropshire STREET ATLAS

Shropshire STREET ATLAS

| A | B | C | D | E | F |

8

Chyknell Wood

Homelea

Woodfield House

Danford

Claverley

Aston Hall

Aston

Caravan Park

SPICER'S CL

Smallheath

Lower Aston Farm

Chyknell Park

Clover Heath

7

Claverley CE PrimSch

BULL RING

PO

PH

ASTON LA

GRIFFITH GREEN

Danford Heath

POUND ST

ORCHARD

HIGH ST

THE PADDOCK

Millmoors

93

Brook House

6

Sandford

Sandford Coppice

Two Gates

Two Gates Cottage

Winchester Farm

Cut Throat Brook

5

Farmcote

Farmcote Hall

WV5

92

Limleys Cottage

The Bank

WV15

Beobridge

Beobridge Manor Farm

The Limleys

Broughton

4

Upper Beobridge Farm House

Bulwardine House

Bulwardine Farm

Broughton Farm

Little Bank Farm

Beobridge Grange

The Lodge

Brantley Wood

91

3

Lower Beobridge

Brantley Farm

Sytch House Green

Little Sytch House

Gatacre Green

Sewage Works

PH

DY7

2

Home Farm

BRANTLEY LA

BEOBRIDGE

SIX ASHES RD

Brantley Brook

PO

CRICK LA

Sytch House Farm

Hem Coppice

Bobbington House

1

Rookery Farm

Gatacre Hall

90

| A | B | C | D | E | F |

78

79

80

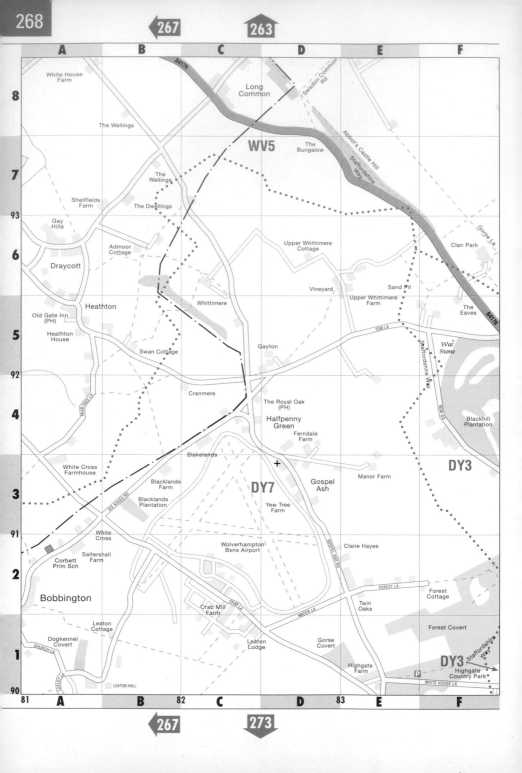

267
263

WV5

White House Farm

The Wellings

Long Common

Seisdon Common Rd

Abbot's Castle Hill

The Bungalow

Staffordshire Way

The Wellings

Shellfields Farm

The Dwellings

Upper Whittimere Cottage

Clan Park

Gorse La

Gay Hills

Admoor Cottage

Vineyard

Sand Pit

Upper Whittimere Farm

The Eaves

B4176

Draycott

Heathton

Whittimere

Old Gate Inn (PH)

TOM LA

War Stone

Heathton House

Gayton

Staffordshire Way

Swan Cottage

NEW LA

Cranmere

The Royal Oak (PH)

Blackhill Plantation

Halfpenny Green

Ferndale Farm

DY3

White Cross Farmhouse

Blakelands

+

Blacklands Farm

DY7

Gospel Ash

Manor Farm

Blacklands Plantation

SIX ASHES RD

Yew Tree Farm

White Cross

Saltershall Farm

Wolverhampton Bsns Airport

Claire Hayes

GOSPEL ASH RD

Corbett Prim Sch

Bobbington

FOREST LA

Forest Cottage

Leaton Cottage

CRAB LA

Crab Mill Farm

WATER LA

Twin Oaks

Forest Covert

Dogkennel Covert

CHURCH LA

Leaton Lodge

Gorse Covert

DY3

Staffordshire Way

Highgate Farm

Highgate Country Park

P

LEATON HALL

WHITE HOUSE LA

81 82 83

267
273

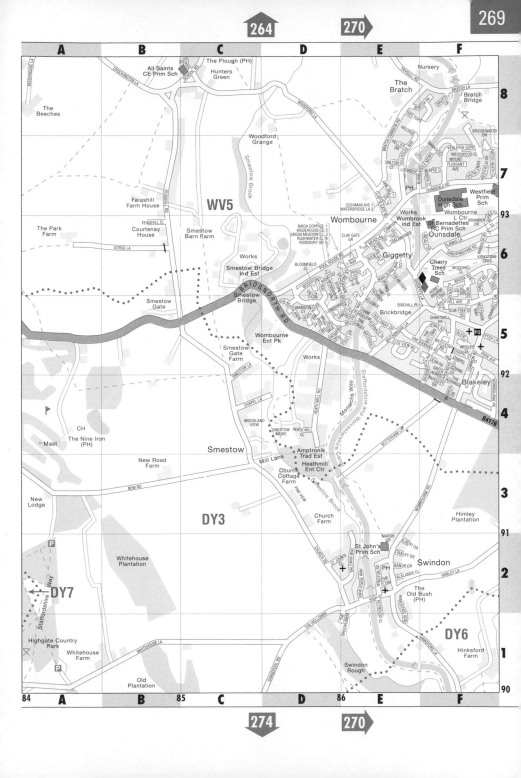

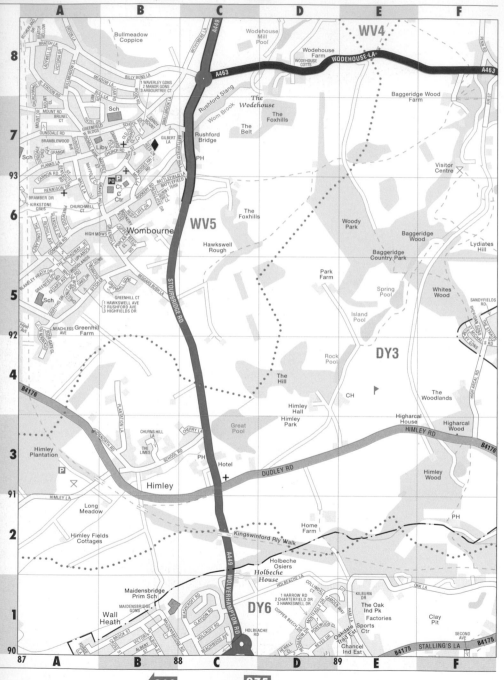

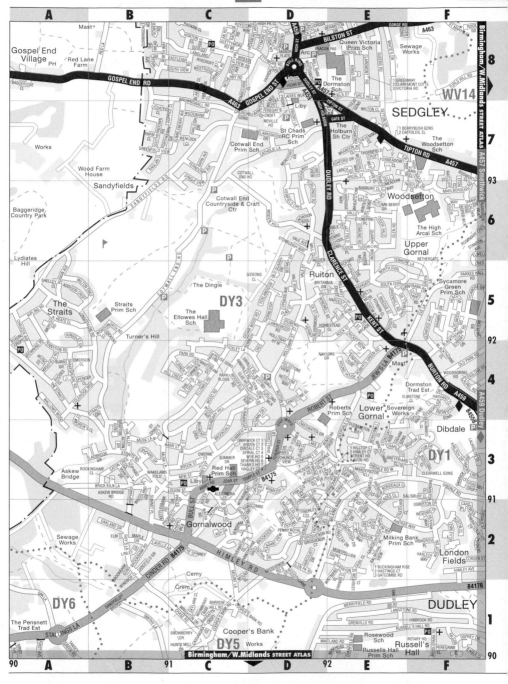

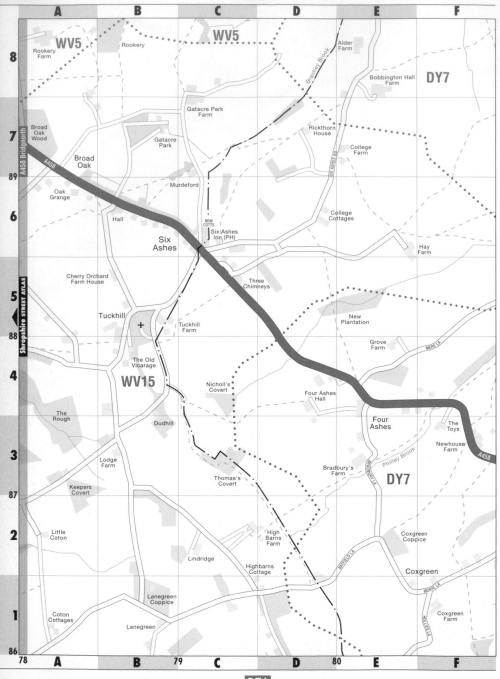

WV5

WV5

DY7

Rookery
Farm

Rookery

Alder
Farm

Branley Brook

Bobbington Hall
Farm

Broad
Oak
Wood

Gatacre Park
Farm

Rickthorn
House

A458 Bridgnorth

A458

Broad
Oak

Gatacre
Park

College
Farm

SIX ASHES RD

Oak
Grange

Murdeford

College
Cottages

Six
Ashes

Hall

NEW
COTTS

Six Ashes
Inn (PH)

College
Cottages

Hay
Farm

Cherry Orchard
Farm House

Three
Chimneys

Shropshire STREET ATLAS

Tuckhill

Tuckhill
Farm

New
Plantation

Grove
Farm

MERE LA

The Old
Vicarage

WV15

Nicholl's
Covert

Four Ashes
Hall

Four
Ashes

The
Rough

Dudhill

The
Toys

Newhouse
Farm

A458

Lodge
Farm

Bradbury's
Farm

Philley Brook

BATTLEFIELD LA

DY7

Keepers
Covert

Thomas's
Covert

Little
Coton

High
Barns
Farm

Coxgreen
Coppice

Lindridge

Highbarns
Cottage

Coxgreen

MORFE LA

Lanegreen
Coppice

MILL LA

Coton
Cottages

Lanegreen

Coxgreen
Farm

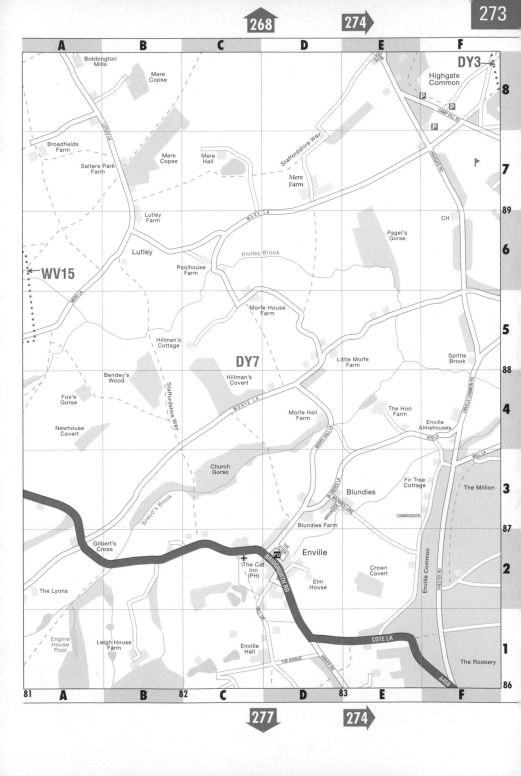

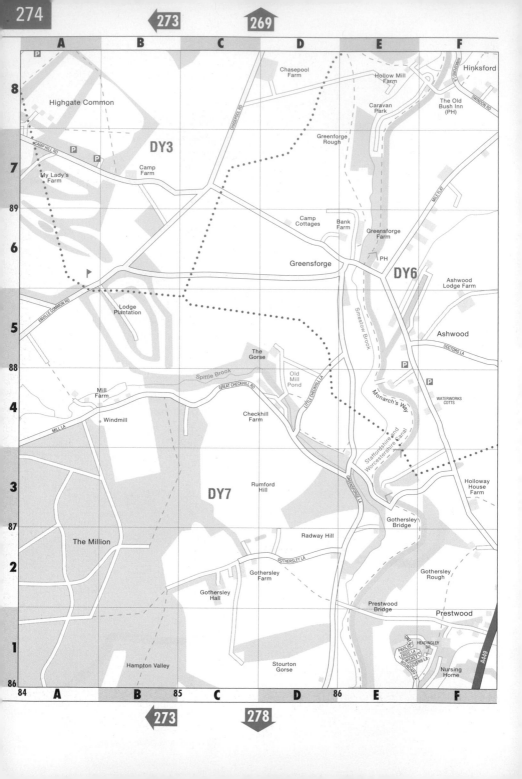

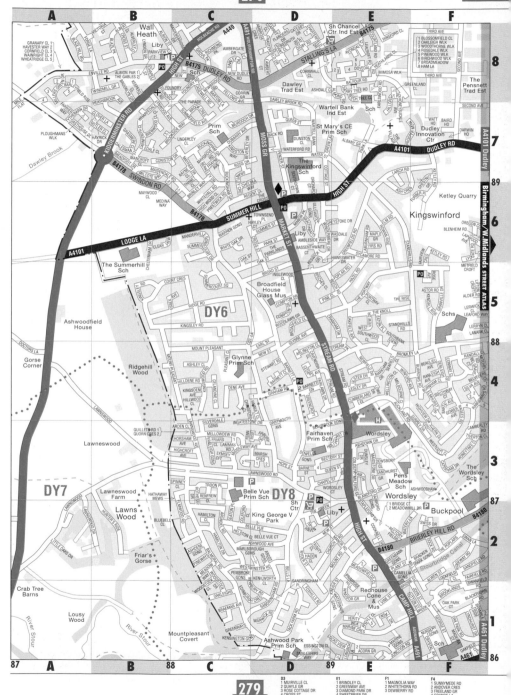

270

D8
1 FRANCIS CL
2 TRESHAM RD
3 GLADSTONE GR
4 HAWKESWELL DR

275

279

D3
1 MUIRVILLE CL
2 QUAYLE GR
3 ROSE COTTAGE DR
4 CROSS ST
D4
1 CYPRESS GDNS
2 The Shops

E1
1 BRINDLEY CL
2 GREENWAY AVE
3 DIAMOND PARK DR
4 SWEETBRIER DR
5 GILBEYS CL

F1
1 MAGNOLIA WAY
2 WHITETHORN RD
3 DEWBERRY RD

F4
1 SUNNYMEDE RD
2 ANDOVER CRES
3 FREELAND GR
4 GRANGE LA
5 MADELEY RD

272

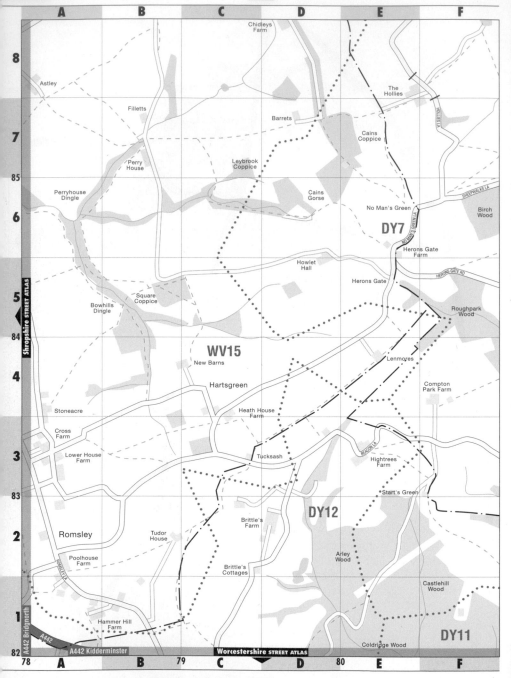

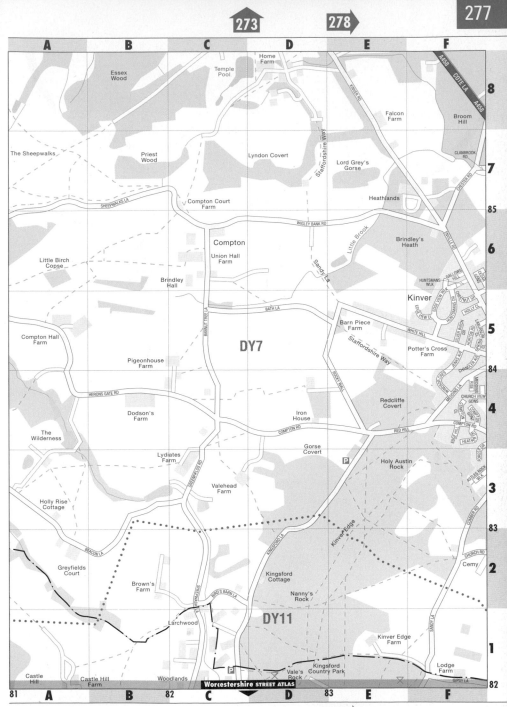

Worcestershire STREET ATLAS

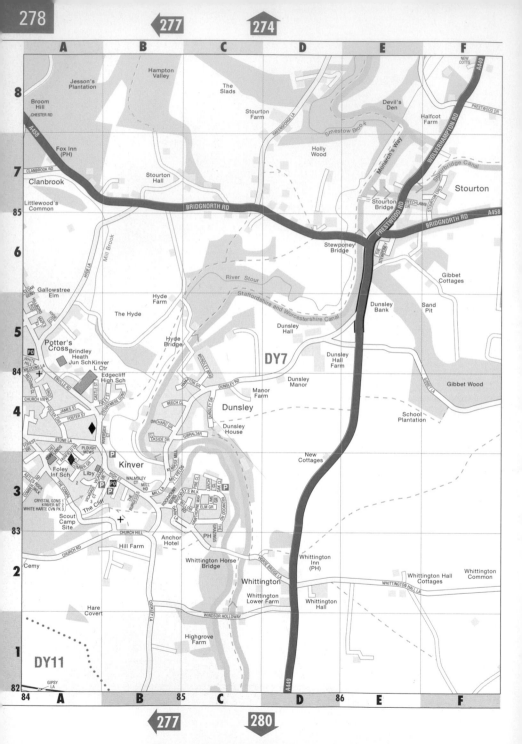

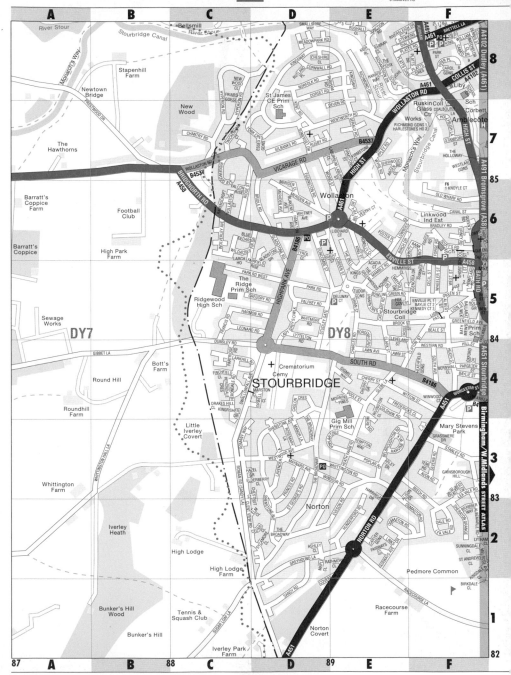

E8
1 THE JUNCTION
2 ALDRIDGE CL
3 LONGBOAT LA
4 STEWKINS CT

F8
1 CRYSTAL AVE
2 SURREY HO
3 WILTSHIRE HO
4 DEVON HO
5 LANCASTER HO
6 HANOVER HO

7 ALLAN CL
8 CORBETT HO
9 DENNIS HALL

STOURBRIDGE

DY7

DY8

Wollaston

Amblecote

Norton

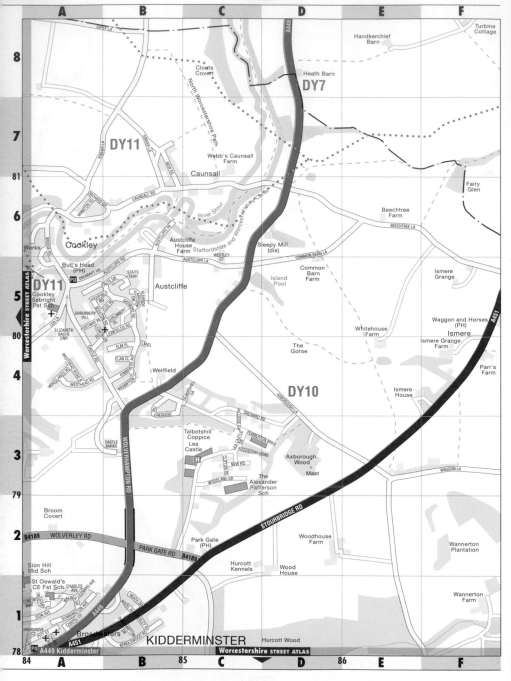

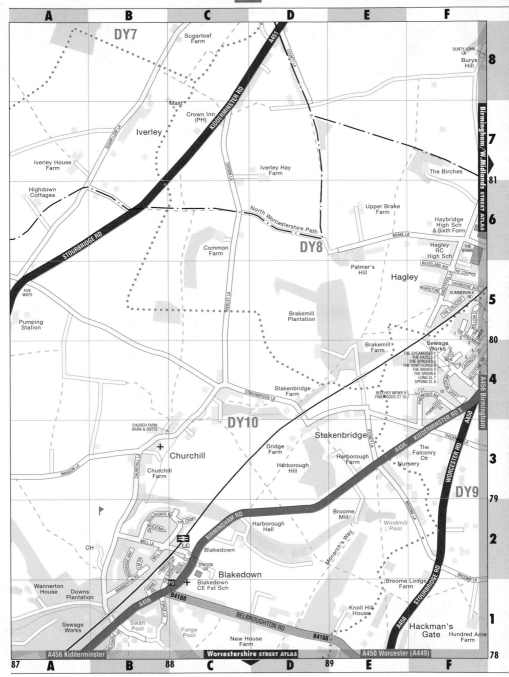

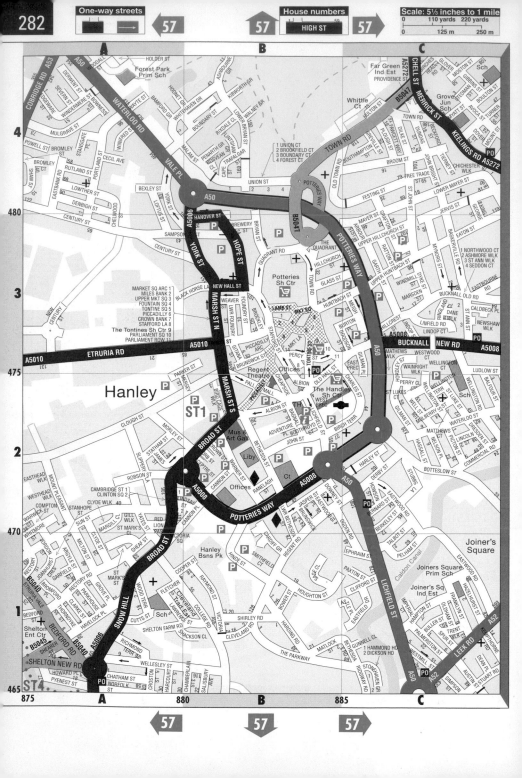

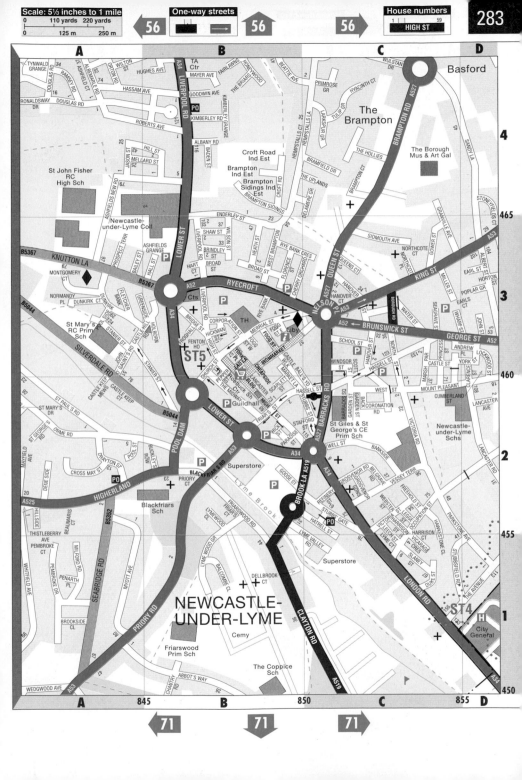

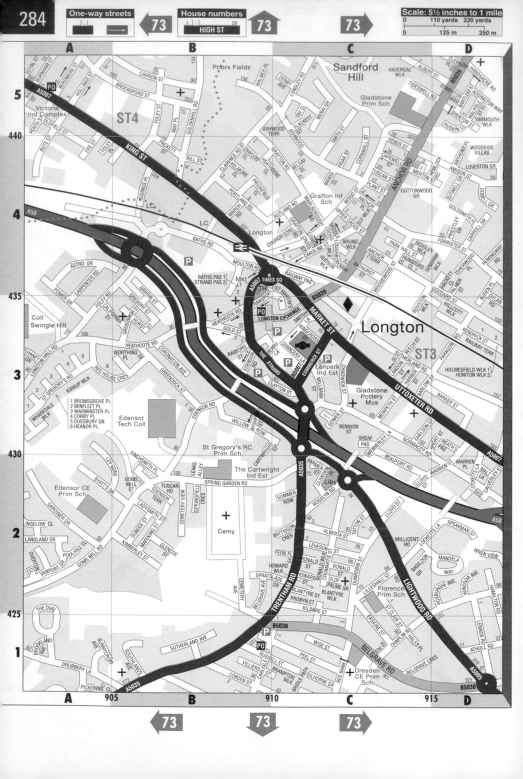

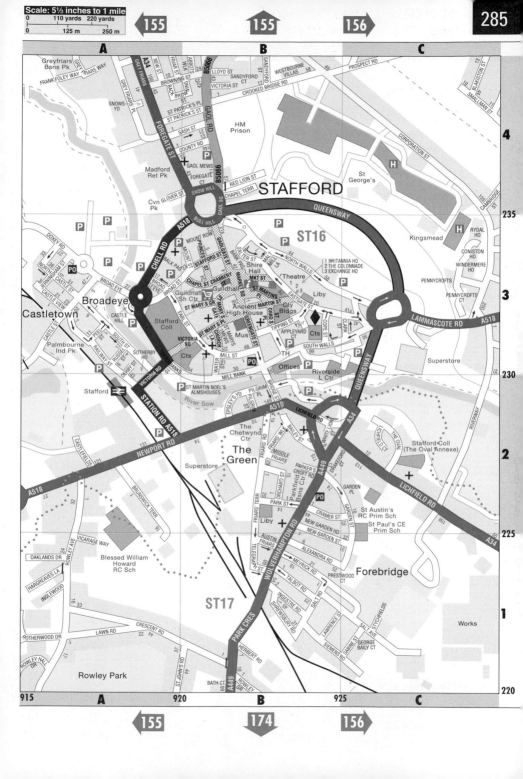

Index

Place name May be abbreviated on the map

Location number Present when a number indicates the place's position in a crowded area of mapping

Locality, town or village Shown when more than one place has the same name

Postcode district District for the indexed place

Page and grid square Page number and grid reference for the standard mapping

Church Rd **6** Beckenham BR2..........**53** C6

Public and commercial buildings are highlighted in magenta   Places of interest are highlighted in blue with a star *

Abbreviations used in the index

Acad	**Academy**	Comm	**Common**	Gd	**Ground**	L	**Leisure**	Prom	**Promenade**
App	**Approach**	Cott	**Cottage**	Gdn	**Garden**	La	**Lane**	Rd	**Road**
Arc	**Arcade**	Cres	**Crescent**	Gn	**Green**	Liby	**Library**	Recn	**Recreation**
Ave	**Avenue**	Cswy	**Causeway**	Gr	**Grove**	Mdw	**Meadow**	Ret	**Retail**
Bglw	**Bungalow**	Ct	**Court**	H	**Hall**	Meml	**Memorial**	Sh	**Shopping**
Bldg	**Building**	Ctr	**Centre**	Ho	**House**	Mkt	**Market**	Sq	**Square**
Bsns, Bus	**Business**	Ctry	**Country**	Hospl	**Hospital**	Mus	**Museum**	St	**Street**
Bvd	**Boulevard**	Cty	**County**	HQ	**Headquarters**	Orch	**Orchard**	Sta	**Station**
Cath	**Cathedral**	Dr	**Drive**	Hts	**Heights**	Pal	**Palace**	Terr	**Terrace**
Cir	**Circus**	Dro	**Drove**	Ind	**Industrial**	Par	**Parade**	TH	**Town Hall**
Cl	**Close**	Ed	**Education**	Inst	**Institute**	Pas	**Passage**	Univ	**University**
Cnr	**Corner**	Emb	**Embankment**	Int	**International**	Pk	**Park**	Wk, Wlk	**Walk**
Coll	**College**	Est	**Estate**	Intc	**Interchange**	Pl	**Place**	Wr	**Water**
Com	**Community**	Ex	**Exhibition**	Junc	**Junction**	Prec	**Precinct**	Yd	**Yard**

Index of localities, towns and villages

A

Abbey Hulton 58 B7
Abbots Bromley 161 B6
Acton 86 C8
Acton Trussell 175 B1
Adbaston 131 D4
Admaston 160 A3
Albrighton 237 A6
Aldersley 255 F7
Aldridge 256 A6
Allgreave 1 C3
Allimore Green 172 D3
Almington 98 C2
Alrewas 200 F3
Alsagers Bank 54 F5
Alsop en le Dale 36 E3
Alstonefield 35 D4
Alton 78 F1
Alvecote 251 D6
Amblecote 279 F7
Amerton 139 A4
Amington 251 B4
Anslow 165 C7
Anslow Gate 164 E7
Apeton 172 C1
Armitage 198 B4
Armsdale 115 D5
Armshead 59 B5
Ash Bank 59 A3
Ashley 100 B5
Ashley Dale 100 B5
Ashmore park 242 A2
Ashwood 274 F5
Aspley 117 B7
Astbury 15 B7
Aston
    Claverley 267 F8
    Newcastle-under-Lyme . .84 A7
    Stafford 154 E4
Aston-By-Stone 120 C4
Aston Heath 129 B6
Audley 39 E2
Audmore 171 F8
Austcliffe 280 B5

B

Back of Ecton 34 F8
Baddeley Edge 43 D1
Baddeley Green 43 B3
Bagnall 43 F2
Balance Hill 126 C5
Baldwins Gate 85 C4
Ball Green 42 D6
Balterley 38 C1
Balterley Green 38 C2

Bank Top
    Draycott in the Clay . . .144 B6
    Stoke-on-Trent 42 B4
Barlaston 88 F2
Barlaston Park 88 F4
Barr Common 256 C3
Barthomley 38 C5
Barton Gate 183 B3
Barton Turn 184 B1
Barton-under-
    Needwood 183 C2
Basford 283 D4
Baswich 156 D1
Bath Vale 6 B3
Beaconside 156 B5
Beamhurst 110 B6
Beamhurst Lane 110 C4
Bearstone 83 A4
Beasley 55 F7
Bednall 193 F8
Bednall Head 194 A8
Beech 87 C1
Beffcote 170 F2
Belgrave 250 E1
Bemersley Green 27 D1
Bentilee 58 D2
Beobridge 267 C4
Berry Hill 57 F1
Betley 53 A6
Betley Common 52 F6
Betton 98 A6
Bickford 191 D1
Biddulph 27 B7
Biddulph Moor 17 B1
Bignall End 39 F3
Bignall Hill 40 B2
Bilbrook 239 C4
Billington 173 D6
Birch Cross 127 C2
Birches Head 57 E6
Birchmoor 262 D8
Bishop's Offley 132 A8
Bishops Wood 221 F8
Bishton 178 A6
Bitterscote 250 A4
Blackbrook
    Baldwin's Gate 84 D2
    Tutbury 145 C1
Blackfords 209 E2
Blackshaw Moor 20 E4
Blackwood Hill 28 F4
Blakedown 281 C2
Blakeley 269 F4
Blakeley Green 255 F8
Blakeley Lane 60 C3
Blakenhall
    Chorlton 52 A4
    Wolverhampton 266 B7
Blithbury 180 A5

Blore
    Loggerheads 99 A2
    Swinscoe 65 F7
Bloreheath 98 E3
Blount's Green 126 A5
Blundies 273 E3
Blurton 72 E1
Blymhill 203 F5
Blymhill Lawn 204 B3
Blythe Bridge 90 E8
Blythe Marsh 91 B7
Bobbington 268 A2
Bog Moor 194 B7
Bolehall 250 D4
Boley Park 231 F7
Bond End 166 D1
Bonehill 249 E2
Boney Hay 212 A1
Boningale 237 A2
Boon Hill 39 F1
Boothen 72 B5
Borough Park 250 C8
Borrowcop Hill 231 C6
Boscomoor 207 E6
Bosley 7 D8
Boundary 75 E2
Bowers 102 B4
Braddocks Hay 27 C8
Bradeley 42 C3
Bradley 191 C8
Bradley in the Moors 94 C7
Bradmore 265 E8
Bradnop 31 E3
Bradshaw 29 D4
Bradwell 56 B8
Bramshall 125 C8
Branston 184 F7
Brazenhill 172 F8
Brereton 197 B5
Brereton Cross 197 D3
Breretonhill 197 B4
Brewood 223 D5
Bridgemere 67 A7
Bridgtown 226 E6
Brindley Ford 27 B1
Brineton 203 F8
Brinsford 240 D7
Broadeye 285 A3
Broadhill 170 E3
Broad Meadow 55 E6
Broad Oak 272 A7
Broadwaters 280 A1
Brockton 117 B4
Brocton 176 C4
Bromley Hurst 161 B1
Bromstead 188 E7
Bromstead Heath 188 E7
Brookhouses 76 A3
Broomhill 209 E4

Broomyshaw 63 C8
Broughton
    Claverley 267 F4
    Loggerheads 115 C8
Brown Edge 43 A8
Brownhills 244 D8
Brown Lees 27 A5
Brund 23 E7
Bucknall 58 A4
Buckpool 275 F2
Buddileigh 52 F7
Buglawton 6 A4
Burnhill Green 252 B6
Burntwood 229 C5
Burntwood Green 229 D6
Burslem 56 F7
Burston 121 B1
Burton Manor 174 E6
Burton upon Trent 166 E1
Burybank 104 C4
Bushbury 240 E2
Butters Green 40 A2
Butterton
    Leek 33 F5
    Newcastle-under-Lyme . .70 D1
Butterton Moor 33 B5
Butt Lane 25 D1
Buxton 4 D8

C

Calf Heath 225 A6
Callingwood 164 D4
Calton 49 E1
Cannock 209 D2
Cannock Wood 211 F5
Carmountside 58 B8
Carroway Head 259 C4
Castlecroft 265 B8
Castle Gresley 186 E1
Castletown 285 A3
Cats Edge 44 D6
Catshill 245 A6
Cat's Hill Cross 117 D2
Cauldon 63 F7
Cauldon Lowe 63 E4
Caunsall 280 C7
Caverswall 74 E2
Cellarhead 59 E4
Chadsmoor 209 F4
Chadwell 188 A1
Chapel Chorlton 102 B8
Chase Terrace 228 E8
Chasetown 228 F6
Chatcull 101 D2
Chatterley 41 B3
Cheadle 76 D4
Chebsey 134 E6

Checkley
    Madeley 52 C1
    Upper Team 109 B8
Checkley Green 67 B8
Cheddleton 45 D5
Cheddleton Heath 45 E7
Chell Heath 42 A5
Chelmorton 5 D8
Cheslyn Hay 226 C3
Chesterfield 246 E8
Chesterton 55 E7
Cheswardine 130 A7
Chetwynd 168 C7
Chetwynd Aston 187 A8
Chilcote 219 F3
Chipnall 114 B3
Chorley 212 E3
Chorlton 37 B1
Christ Church 231 A8
Churchbridge 226 F4
Church Eaton 190 A8
Churchill 281 C7
Church Lawton 25 C3
Church Leigh 109 B4
Church Mayfield 81 D6
Cinder Hill 266 F1
Clanbrook 278 A7
Claregate 255 E6
Claverley 267 D3
Clayhanger 244 D6
Clay Mills 148 A3
Clayton 71 B4
Cliff 261 C1
Cliff Vale 56 F2
Clifton 81 F6
Clifton Campville 219 F1
Cloud Side 7 B3
Clough Hall 40 F8
Coalpit Hill 40 C8
Cobridge 57 B6
Codsall 238 E4
Codsall Wood 238 B6
Coldeaton 36 B6
Coldmeece 118 C5
Cold Well 212 B5
Colshaw 3 E4
Colton 179 A6
Colton Hills 266 B3
Colwich 177 E7
Combridge 111 C8
Compton
    Kinver 277 C6
    Wolverhampton 255 D2
Congleton 6 A4
Congreve 207 B7
Consall 60 D6
Cookley 280 A6
Cookshill 74 C3
Cooper's Bank 271 C1

Compere End 132 E7
Coppenhall 174 C4
Cornhill 42 D5
Cotes 103 A2
Cotes Heath 102 D4
Coton Gnosall 171 B5
  Milwich 122 D5
  Tamworth 127 F6
Coton Clanford 154 A4
Coton Green 249 F8
Coton Hayes 122 F6
Coton Hill 122 F5
Coton in the Clay 144 F7
Cotonwood 170 E6
Cotton 78 D8
Cotvalton 105 F2
Coven 224 A2
Coven Heath 240 C6
Coven Lawn 240 A8
Cowall Moor 28 B4
Cowley 171 D4
Coxgreen 272 E2
Crackley 55 E8
Cracow Moss 53 B3
Craddocks Moss 53 F5
Crakemarsh 111 D5
Cranberry 102 D5
Crateford 224 B7
Craythorne 147 D2
Creighton 111 A5
Cresswell 91 C3
Creswell 155 A7
Creswell Green 212 E1
Crossgate 106 D7
Cross Green 224 D1
Cross Heath 56 A3
Crowborough 28 B7
Crowdecote 13 E7
Croxall 216 F8
Croxden 94 D4
Croxton 116 B5
Croxtonbank 116 B6
Curborough 214 D5

D

Dagdale 110 A1
Dales Green 26 C5
Danebridge 9 B7
Dane in Shaw 16 C8
Danford 267 E8
Dapple Heath 140 F1
Darnford 231 F6
Dayhills 121 F6
Denford 44 F8
Denstone 95 D6
Derrington 154 D1
Dibdale 271 F3
Dilhorne 75 D4
Dimsdale 56 B5
Dods Leigh 108 E2
Doley 130 E8
Dordon 262 F6
Dorrington 83 C7
Dosthill 261 C5
Dove Bank 26 A2
Dove Head 3 D6
Doveridge 127 B7
Doxey 155 B4
Draycott 268 A6
Draycott in the Clay 144 C6
Draycott in the Moors 91 E5
Drayton Bassett 260 D5
Drointon 140 B2
Dudley 271 F1
Duke Bank 42 F4
Dunsley 278 C4
Dunstal 141 F1
Dunstall 183 D6
Dunston 192 F8
Dunston Heath 192 C7
Dunwood 29 D3

E

Earl Sterndale 5 C3
Eaton 6 A8
Eccleshall 133 E6
Ecton 23 D2
Edge Hill 262 C2
Edgmond 168 A3
Edial 229 F6
Edingale 217 D5
Efflinch 201 E7
Egginton 216 C2
Elford 216 E6
Ellastone 80 B3
Ellenhall 134 A1
Elmhurst 214 A5
Endon 43 E7
Endon Bank 43 E8
Englesea-brook 38 A4
Enson 137 C6
Enville 273 D2
Essington 241 F3
Etchinghill 178 B1
Etruria 56 F4
Ettingshall Park 266 D3

F

Fairoak 115 D6
Farewell 213 A4
Far Hoarcross 162 E2
Farley Park 78 D5

Farmcote 267 A5
Fauld 145 C6
Fawfieldhead 12 F3
Fazeley 260 F8
Fenton 35 B6
Fenton Low 241 C7
Fegg Hayes 42 B7
Fenton 72 E5
Festival Park 57 A4
Finchfield 265 D8
Finney Green 54 C1
Fishley 243 C4
Flash 3 A3
Fole 109 E7
Footherley 246 E3
Ford Green 42 E2
Fordhouses 240 D2
Forebridge 285 C1
Forsbrook 91 B7
Forton 169 A7
Foston 129 D4
Four Ashes
  Coven 224 C6
  Enville 272 E3
Four Crosses 225 F7
Four Oaks 257 F3
Foxholes 144 E4
Foxley 39 D7
Foxt 62 C6
Fradley 215 E7
Fradswell 123 A3
Freasley 262 C4
Freehay 93 A7
Froghall 62 A4
Fulford 106 D8

G

Gailey 207 C1
Gailey Wharf 207 E1
Garshall Green 122 C8
Gateham 35 B6
Gayton 138 E6
Gentleshaw 212 A4
Gerrard's Bromley 101 A2
Giggetty 269 E6
Gillow Heath 16 C2
Gillway 250 B8
Glascote Heath 250 F2
Gnosall 171 D6
Gnosall Heath 171 D5
Goldenhill 41 B7
Goldthorn Hill 266 A5
Goldthorn Park 266 C5
Goodleybrook 75 D5
Goosemoor Green 212 C4
Gornalwood 271 C2
Gorstey Ley 229 C7
Gorstyhill 37 E2
Gorsty Hill 142 D7
Gospel Ash 268 D3
Gospel End Village 271 A8
Gradbach 10 A8
Gratton 29 A5
Gratwich 124 C4
Great Bridgeford 135 D3
Great Chatwell 188 C1
Great Chell 42 A6
Great Haywood 158 C2
Great Moor 253 F1
Great Saredon 225 E5
Great Wyrley 227 B3
Green Fields 139 C1
Greenhead 60 F2
Greenleighs 266 C3
Greensforge 274 D6
Grindley 140 D7
Grindon 34 B2
Groundslow Fields 103 F8
Grub Street 151 A7
Gunstone 239 A6

H

Hackman's Gate 281 F1
Hagley 281 E5
Hagley Park 196 D8
Hales 113 F8
Halfpenny Green 268 D4
Hall End 262 F5
Hall Green 25 E5
Halmer End 54 D7
Hammerwich 229 D4
Hamstall Ridware 180 E3
Hanbury 145 A5
Hanbury Woodend 144 E2
Hanchurch 87 B7
Handsacre 198 C8
Hanford 71 E1
Hangingbridge 81 E8
Hanley 282 A2
Hansley Cross 78 C2
Hardings Booth 12 D5
Harding's Wood 25 B3
Hardwick 256 E3
Harlaston 217 D2
Harper's Gate 29 E8
Harriseahead 26 E4
Hartington 24 D5
Hartley Green 138 D8
Hartsgreen 276 C4
Hartshill 71 E7
Hartwell 89 C2
Haselour 217 B2
Hatherton 208 E1
Hatton 146 D8

Haughton 172 F5
Haughtondale 173 B7
Haunton 218 B2
Hawks Green 210 B1
Hazelslade 211 B6
Hazles 61 C5
Heath End 244 A1
Heath Hayes 210 F1
Heath Hill 187 C1
Heathton 268 A5
Heatley 141 D3
Heaton 8 E2
Hednesford 210 D5
Heighley 53 E3
Hem Heath 88 D7
Heron Cross 72 F4
Highbridge 244 B6
High Carr 40 F3
Highfields
  Burntwood 228 F4
  Stafford 174 C8
High Heath 244 D2
Highlanes 116 D6
High Offley 132 B1
High Town 210 A5
Highwood 126 D4
Hilderstone 106 D1
Hill 258 A4
Hill Chorlton 85 D3
Hill Hook 257 E6
Hill Ridware 198 A8
Hill Top 210 C4
Hill Wood 258 C5
Hilton
  Egginton 147 E8
  Shenstone 246 A8
Himley 270 B3
Hinksford 274 F8
Hints 248 D3
Hints Hill 248 F3
Hixon 158 D8
Hixon Heath 139 B1
Hobble End 243 B7
Hockley 261 C5
Hodgefield 28 B2
Hollies Common 171 B8
Hollington 94 B2
Hollins
  Biddulph Moor 28 B8
  Kidsgrove 40 E8
  Kingsley 61 A3
Hollinsclough 11 A4
Holly Bank 245 B3
Hollybush 72 E3
Holly Wall 41 B5
Holmcroft 155 C7
Hookgate 99 F3
Hope 35 D3
Hopedale 35 C2
Hopton 137 D1
Hopton Heath 137 E1
Hopwas 249 B7
Horninglow 166 C2
Horse Bridge 45 A8
Horsebrook 206 D2
Horton 29 C7
Huddlesford 232 C8
Hulme 74 A8
Hulme End 23 F3
Huntington 209 D7
Huntley 92 C7
Hyde Lea 174 C5

I

Ilam 50 E3
Ingestre 157 E6
Ipstones 62 A8
Ireland's Cross 83 C7
Islington 168 F5
Ismere 280 F5
Iverley 281 B7
Ivetsey Bank 204 E3

J

Jack Hayes 58 E8
Joiner's Square 282 C1
Jugbank 100 A4

K

Keele 69 F7
Kerry Hill 58 F7
Kettlebrook 250 B3
Key Green 6 E4
Kiddemore Green 222 D6
Kidderminster 280 B1
Kidsgrove 26 B1
King's Bromley 199 C6
Kingsley 61 E3
Kingsley Holt 62 A1
Kingsley Moor 60 F1
Kingslow 252 C2
Kingstone 141 C8
Kingswinford 275 F6
Kingswood 237 C1
Kingswood Common 238 B2
Kinver 278 B3
Knightley 152 A6
Knightley Dale 152 B3
Knighton
  Adbaston 130 F3
  Loggerheads 83 C5
Knotbury 2 F5

Knowl Bank 53 E7
Knutton 55 F2
Knypersley 27 C5

L

Ladfordfield 134 E1
Landywood 243 A8
Lane Ends 27 A2
Lane Green 239 C3
Lanesfield 266 E4
Laney Green 226 A3
Lapley 206 B6
Lask Edge 28 C7
Latherford 225 B4
Lawnhead 152 E6
Lawns Wood 275 B2
Lawton-gate 25 A4
Leadendale 89 F3
Lea Heath 159 B8
Leamonsley 230 E7
Leek 30 E6
Leekbrook 45 F8
Leighswood 256 A7
Levedale 191 F6
Leycett 54 C2
Leyfields 249 F7
Ley Hill 258 B1
Leys 62 C3
Lichfield 231 D5
Light Oaks 43 E1
Lightwood
  Cheadle 76 F3
  Longton 89 E7
Limepits 85 D8
Linton 186 A1
Lipley 114 E3
Little Aston 257 B4
Little Bloxwich 243 E3
Little Bridgeford 135 B3
Little Burton 166 D4
Little Chell 41 F4
Little Church 112 A8
Little Hay 247 C1
Little Haywood 177 C8
Little Madeley 68 F3
Little Saredon 225 E3
Littleworth 226 E4
Littleworth
  Cannock 210 E4
  Stafford 156 A4
Little Wyrley 243 E8
Loggerheads 99 C5
London Fields 271 F2
Long Common 268 C8
Long Compton 153 D2
Longdon 197 F1
Longdon Green 213 B7
Longford 168 B1
Longnor 13 A6
Longport 56 D8
Longridge 192 C4
Longsdon 29 F2
Longton 284 C3
Lower Beobridge 267 A3
Lower Elkstone 22 D1
Lower Ellastone 80 C2
Lower Gornal 271 E4
Lower Green 224 A3
Lower Hatton 102 D6
Lower Knightley 152 C4
Lower Leigh 108 F4
Lower Nobut 109 F2
Lower Penn 264 F4
Lower Stonnall 246 A4
Lower Tean 92 F2
Loxley Green 125 C2
Loynton 150 F5
Lullington 218 E7
Lynn 188 B4

M

Madeley 68 E6
Madeley Heath 69 B8
Maer 85 C1
Mapleton 66 F4
Marchington 127 C2
Marchington Woodlands 143 A6
Market Drayton 97 B2
Marsh Green 16 D3
Marston
  Stafford 136 E4
  Wheaton Aston 204 E8
Marston on Dove 147 B8
Mavesyn Ridware 198 A6
May Bank 56 C3
Mayfield 81 C8
Meaford 104 D4
Meerbrook 19 F7
Meir 74 A1
Meir Heath 90 A5
Mere Green 258 B3
Meretown 169 B6
Merridale 255 E2
Merry Hill 265 D7
Middle 226 A4
Middle Madeley 68 F7
Middle Mayfield 81 B6
Middleport 56 C8
Middleton 260 A1
Middleton Green 108 B3
Mile Oak 249 D1
Miles Green 54 E8
Milford 176 B7

Milldale 35 F2
Millend 39 C5
Mill Green
  Aldridge 256 F7
  Cannock 226 F8
Millmeece 117 F7
Milton 43 A1
Milwich 122 D5
Mitton 191 C3
Mobberley 92 D7
Moddershall 105 F6
Moneystone 63 A1
Moor Green 91 A8
Moor Hall 258 D1
Moreton
  Drayton in the Clay 144 C8
  Newport 188 D7
Morrey 181 D2
Morrilow Heath 107 E4
Mossgate 106 D7
Mossley
  Congleton 16 A8
  Rugeley 196 F7
Moss Pit 174 E5
Mount Pleasant
  Mow Cop 26 B5
  Stoke-on-Trent 72 D5
  Tamworth 250 C1
  Uttoxeter 126 B7
  Werrington 60 B2
Mow Cop 26 C7
Mucklestone 99 B7
Muckley Corner 230 A2

N

Napley 98 F3
Napley Heath 83 A1
Needwood 164 B5
Netherland Green 126 E2
Netherseal 219 E7
Nether Stowe 214 C3
Netherton 198 F8
Newborough 162 E8
Newborough Brick Hill 163 A5
Newbridge 255 E3
Newcastle-under-Lyme 283 B1
Newchapel 26 E2
Newchurch 163 B3
Newfield 41 D5
Newhall 186 F6
Newpool 27 B6
Newport 168 D4
Newstead 88 E6
Newton 159 D8
Newton Hurst 141 A1
Newton Regis 236 D4
Newton Solney 167 E8
Newtown
  Biddulph 17 B5
  Great Wyrley 243 B6
  Longnor 12 C3
New Town 228 F2
No Man's Heath 236 F6
Norbury
  Gnosall 151 A3
  Roston 80 D1
Norbury Junction 151 D2
Northwood
  Hanley 57 E4
  Newcastle-under-Lyme 71 D2
Norton 279 D2
Norton Bridge 119 A1
Norton Canes 227 F5
Norton East 228 A6
Norton Green 43 A5
Norton in Hales 82 C1
Norton-in-the-Moors 42 F4
Norton 253 F3
Nurton Hill 253 E4

O

Oakamoor 78 B7
Oaken 238 D2
Oak Hill 71 F5
Oakley 98 C6
Oaks Green 128 D7
Offleybrook 132 A8
Offleyhay 132 D7
Offleymarsh 132 A7
Offleyrock 132 B7
Oldfallow 209 D3
Oldfurnace 77 E4
Old Perton 254 B2
Olive Green 181 B2
Onecote 32 F3
Onneley 68 A3
Orgreave 200 B5
Orslow 188 E3
Orton 264 F3
Otherton 207 F6
Oulton
  Newport 151 A1
  Stone 105 C4
Oulton Heath 105 B6
Ounsdale 269 F6
Outlands 115 E1
Outwoods
  Broadhill 170 A1
  Burton upon Trent 166 B6
Overley 200 D4
Overmoor 60 A3
Overton 93 F1
Oxbarn 265 D2
Oxford 42 B8

P

Packmoor ... 26 F1
Palmer Moor ... 127 E7
Palmers Cross ... 255 D8
Park End ... 39 A4
Parkfield ... 266 E5
Parkgate ... 79 F5
Parkside ... 155 D8
Pasford ... 252 E3
Pattingham ... 253 D2
Pave Lane ... 187 B7
Peacock Hay ... 40 F4
Pelsall ... 244 B3
Pelsall Wood ... 243 F5
Pendeford ... 239 F2
Penkhull ... 71 E6
Penkridge ... 192 E2
Penn ... 265 E5
Penn Fields ... 265 F6
Perry Crofts ... 250 B7
Pershall ... 133 B8
Perton ... 254 D4
Piccadilly ... 261 F1
Pillaton ... 208 C7
Pipe Gate ... 83 D6
Pipehill ... 230 C5
Pipe Ridware ... 198 C8
Pitts Hill ... 41 F5
Plardiwick ... 171 B6
Podmore ... 101 A4
Polesworth ... 262 F8
Poolend ... 19 B1
Poolfold ... 16 F4
Porthill ... 56 C6
Potter's Cross ... 278 A5
Prestwood
  Denstone ... 79 E1
  Kinver ... 274 F1
Prospect Village ... 211 C4
Puleston ... 149 C1
Pye Green ... 194 F1

Q

Quarry Hill ... 262 A7
Queensville ... 175 B8
Quixhill ... 95 E7

R

Rake End ... 179 F1
Rakeway ... 93 A8
Ramshorn ... 79 B7
Rangemore ... 164 C3
Ranton ... 153 D5
Ranton Green ... 153 B3
Ravenhill ... 196 F6
Ravenscliffe ... 41 A5
Ravenshall ... 53 A4
Rawnsley ... 211 B5
Red Bull ... 98 D3
Redhill ... 133 F6
Red Street ... 40 E3
Rickerscote ... 174 F5
Ridgeway ... 42 E8
Rileyhill ... 199 B2
Rising Brook ... 174 E7
Robin Hill ... 28 A8
Rocester ... 96 A3
Rock End ... 27 F6
Rodbaston ... 207 E4
Rolleston on Dove ... 147 B4
Romsley ... 276 A2
Rosehill ... 112 A1
Roston ... 96 E7
Rough Close ... 89 F3
Roughcote ... 74 C6
Rough Hills ... 266 F6
Roughley ... 258 D3

Rowley Park ... 285 A1
Rownall ... 59 E8
Rudge ... 263 A7
Rudyard ... 29 E8
Rugeley ... 196 E8
Ruiton ... 271 D5
Rumer Hill ... 226 F7
Rushton Spencer ... 8 B2
Russell's Hall ... 271 F1
Ryecroft Gate ... 18 C8
Rye Hills ... 39 E1

S

Salt ... 137 F4
Salt Heath ... 137 E3
Sandborough ... 181 B3
Sandfields ... 231 A5
Sandon ... 137 D7
Sandonbank ... 137 C5
Sandyfields ... 271 B6
Sandyford
  Stoke-on-Trent ... 41 D6
  Swynnerton ... 103 E6
Saverley Green ... 91 A2
Scholar Green ... 25 E8
Scot Hay ... 54 E4
Scounslow Green ... 142 C8
Scropton ... 129 E1
Seabridge ... 70 F3
Seckington ... 236 A3
Sedgley ... 271 F7
Seighford ... 154 B7
Seisdon ... 263 F2
Shackerley ... 221 B1
Shaffalong ... 45 A5
Shallowford ... 135 B7
Shareshill ... 225 D2
Sharpley Heath ... 107 B3
Shawfield ... 22 C8
Shebdon ... 150 C8
Sheen ... 24 A7
Sheepwash ... 74 E7
Shelfield ... 244 C1
Shelton ... 57 B1
Shelton under Harley ... 86 B3
Shenstone ... 247 A5
Shenstone Woodend ... 247 A1
Shire Oak ... 245 A6
Shirleywich ... 157 F8
Shobnall ... 166 A4
Shraleybrook ... 39 A1
Shut Heath ... 172 E8
Shutlanehead ... 70 B2
Shutt Green ... 223 A8
Shuttington ... 251 F7
Sideway ... 72 B3
Silverdale ... 55 B1
Six Ashes ... 272 B6
Slade Heath ... 224 E1
Slindon ... 117 D5
Slitting Mill ... 196 C7
Smallrice ... 121 E4
Smallthorne ... 42 C2
Smestow ... 269 C4
Smith's Green ... 38 B7
Snelston ... 81 C3
Sneyd Green ... 57 D7
Somerford ... 223 F6
Soudley ... 130 B6
Spade Green ... 230 A8
Sparklow ... 14 C8
Spath ... 111 B3
Springfields ... 71 E5
Springhill ... 245 E8
Spring Hill ... 265 C4
Springwood ... 55 C8
Stableford ... 86 B2
Stafford ... 285 B4
Stakenbridge ... 281 E3
Stallington ... 90 C4
Standon ... 102 A2

Stanfield ... 42 A3
Stanhope Bretby ... 167 F1
Stanley ... 44 A5
Stanley Moor ... 43 F4
Stanshope ... 35 D1
Stanton
  Mayfield ... 65 D1
  Swadlincote ... 186 C4
Stapenhill ... 185 F8
Stockton ... 187 D6
Stockton Brook ... 43 d5
Stockwell End ... 255 D6
Stockwell Heath ... 179 A8
Stoke ... 72 A7
Stoke-on-Trent ... 72 D7
Stone ... 120 B8
Stonefield ... 104 F2
Stone Heath ... 107 C3
Stonehouses ... 91 B6
Stonnall ... 245 E4
Stourbridge ... 279 D4
Stourton ... 278 F7
Stowe ... 214 C1
Stowe-by-Chartley ... 139 C3
Stowford ... 37 C8
Stramshall ... 111 A4
Streethay ... 215 A2
Streetley ... 257 D3
Streetly ... 257 D3
Stretton
  Brewood ... 206 C3
  Burton upon Trent ... 166 E8
Stubwood ... 95 D4
Sturbridge ... 117 E1
Sudbury ... 128 E4
Sugnall ... 116 D2
Sutton ... 150 D1
Sutton Coldfield ... 258 E1
Swadlincote ... 186 F4
Swindon ... 269 F2
Swinscoe ... 65 E5
Swynnerton ... 103 B4
Sytch House Green ... 267 A2

T

Tadgedale ... 99 C5
Talke ... 40 C7
Talke Pits ... 40 E5
Tamworth ... 250 B3
Tatenhill ... 165 A1
Tatenhill Common ... 164 F1
Teanford ... 92 D6
Tettenhall ... 255 D5
Tettenhall Wood ... 255 C3
The Bank ... 26 B7
The Blythe ... 140 F5
The Brampton ... 283 C4
The Bratch ... 269 E8
The Deanery ... 207 C7
The Four Alls ... 112 E4
The Green ... *285 B2
The Handfords ... 154 B1
The Leys ... 250 A5
The Lymes ... 70 C3
The Quarry ... 39 C2
The Rookery ... 26 C3
The Shruggs ... 121 C2
The Straits ... 271 A5
Thorncliffe ... 20 E2
Thornes ... 245 E3
Thorpe ... 51 C1
Thorpe Constantine ... 235 F6
Threapwood ... 77 E2
Thurvaston ... 96 F1
Tillington ... 155 C6
Timbersbrook ... 6 E2
Tittensor ... 88 B1
Tixall ... 157 D2
Tompkin ... 44 C3
Tong ... 220 D3
Tong Forge ... 220 A5

Tong Norton ... 220 D5
Totmonslow ... 92 B4
Townend ... 106 F8
Townhead ... 62 E7
Town Head ... 78 F1
Townsend ... 58 C3
Trentham ... 88 A6
Trent Vale ... 71 F3
Trescott ... 264 B7
Triangle ... 229 B4
Trinity Fields ... 155 B8
Trysull ... 264 C1
Tuckhill ... 272 B5
Tunstall
  Stoke-on-Trent ... 41 C3
  Woodseaves ... 131 E3
Tuppenhurst ... 198 D4
Turnhurst ... 41 F7
Tutbury ... 146 C5
Two Gates ... 261 D8

U

Ubberley ... 58 D1
Underhill ... 241 B2
Upper Aston ... 263 A1
Upper Cotton ... 63 B4
Upper Elkstone ... 22 A3
Upper Ellastone ... 80 B4
Upper Gornal ... 271 F6
Upper Hatton ... 102 D7
Upper Hulme ... 20 E7
Upper Landywood ... 242 E8
Upper Leigh ... 108 E5
Upper Longdon ... 197 C2
Upper Mayfield ... 66 B1
Upper Nobut ... 109 E4
Upper Tean ... 92 D3
Uttoxeter ... 126 D7

V

Vauxhall ... 168 D2
Vigo ... 244 F2

W

Wain Lee ... 26 F4
Walford ... 117 B8
Walk Mill ... 132 D8
Wall ... 230 D2
Wallbridge Park ... 30 C4
Wall Heath ... 275 B8
Wallington Heath ... 243 B2
Walsall ... 243 B2
Walsall Wood ... 244 F4
Walton
  Eccleshall ... 134 E4
  Stone ... 119 E7
Walton Heath ... 119 E5
Walton-on-the-Hill ... 175 F7
Walton-on-Trent ... 184 E1
Warslow ... 23 B1
Warstone ... 242 C8
Warton ... 150 D2
Washerwall ... 59 A4
Water Eaton ... 207 A2
Waterhouses ... 49 A1
Weaverslake ... 181 F3
Wedges Mills ... 226 B6
Weeford ... 248 A4
Weeping Cross ... 175 D7
Wereton ... 39 C1
Wergs ... 255 A6
Werrington ... 59 D4
West Broughton ... 128 A6
West Chadsmoor ... 209 F5
Westcroft ... 241 B3
Western Downs ... 174 A8
West Heath ... 52 E8

West Hill ... 210 B6
Westlands ... 71 A6
Weston
  Crewe ... 37 C5
  Stafford ... 138 D3
Weston Coyney ... 74 A5
Weston Jones ... 150 C5
Weston-under-Lizard ... 203 E3
Westwood ... 30 B6
Wetley Moor ... 58 F5
Wetley Rocks ... 60 B7
Wetmore ... 166 F5
Wetton ... 34 F4
Wetwood ... 115 F7
Whateley ... 261 F3
Wheaton Aston ... 205 B6
Whiston
  Cheadle ... 62 D3
  Penkridge ... 191 E1
Whitecross ... 172 F8
White Hill ... 26 B2
Whitehurst ... 75 D7
Whitemoor ... 16 D6
Whitfield ... 42 C7
Whitgreave ... 135 F5
Whitley Heath ... 133 A1
Whitmore ... 86 A6
Whittington
  Croxton ... 116 D8
  Kinver ... 278 C2
  Lichfield ... 232 D5
Whittington Heath ... 232 C4
Wigginton ... 234 B2
Wightwick ... 254 E1
Wildboarclough ... 1 E6
Wildwood ... 175 D6
Willoughbridge ... 84 A5
Willslock ... 125 F3
Wilnecote ... 261 F8
Wimblebury ... 210 F3
Wincle ... 9 A7
Winnington ... 83 B1
Winnothdale ... 93 C5
Winshill ... 167 B3
Withington ... 109 B3
Withystakes ... 59 E5
Wollaston
  Church Eaton ... 190 E4
  Stourbridge ... 279 D6
Wolstanton ... 56 D5
Wolverhampton ... 266 B7
Wombourne ... 269 E6
Woodcock Heath ... 141 A8
Woodcote ... 187 D3
Woodcroft ... 30 D5
Woodedge ... 144 A6
Woodend ... 145 B1
Wood End ... 262 C1
Woodgate ... 126 E5
Wood Gate ... 144 C5
Woodhouse Green ... 7 D2
Woodhouses ... 182 C3
Woodlane ... 182 D6
Wood Lane ... 40 A1
Woodmill ... 181 F7
Woodseaves
  Eccleshall ... 151 E8
  Market Drayton ... 112 E3
Woodsetton ... 271 E6
Woodshutts ... 25 F1
Woodwall Green ... 116 A4
Woore ... 67 B1
Wootton Eccleshall ... 133 D3
  Ellastone ... 79 E7
Wordsley ... 275 E3
Wrinehill ... 53 B3
Wychnor ... 201 B5

Y

Yarlet ... 136 C6
Yarnfield ... 118 F7

A

Aarons Dr ST7 . . . . .39 F2
Abberley Rd DY3. . . . . 271 D4
Abberley B77 . . . . 251 C2
Abberley Arc DE14 . . . . . . 166 E2
Abbey CI **8** Stafford ST17 175 A8
  Penkridge ST19 . . . . 208 A8
  Rocester ST14. . . . . .96 A3
Abbey Ct Bucknall ST2 . . . . .58 B5
  Newport TF10 . . . . 168 F2
Abbeydale CI CW2 . . . . .37 C2
Abbey Dr Colwich ST18. . . . 177 D8
  Walsall WS3 . . . . 244 A5
Abbeyfield Rd WV10 . . . . . 240 F4
Abbeyfields ST18 . . . . 158 B2
Abbey Gdns ST18 . . . . 158 B2
Abbey Green Rd ST13 . . . . . .30 D7
Abbey Hill Sch & Performing
  Arts Coll ST2. . . . . .58 C5
Abbey Hulton Prim Sch
  ST2. . . . . .58 A5
Abbey La ST2. . . . . .58 A5
Abbey Park Way CW2 . . . . . .37 E3
Abbey Prim Sch WS3 . . . . . 242 E2
Abbey Rd Bucknall ST2 . . . . .58 B5
  Dudley,Goundhaugh DY3 . . 271 C3
  Rocester ST14. . . . . .95 F3
  Tamworth B77 . . . . 250 D3
  Wetley Rocks ST9 . . . . .60 B6
Abbeyside ST18. . . . . 153 D5
Abbey Sq WS3 . . . . 242 E2
Abbey St Bucknall ST2. . . . . .58 A6
  Burton u T DE14. . . . . 166 D2
  Cannock WS12. . . . . 210 B7
  Dudley DY3 . . . . 271 C3
  Newcastle-u-L ST5. . . . . . . .55 C1
  Stone ST15 . . . . 120 A8
Abbey Way TF9 . . . . .97 D2
Abbey Wood CI **1** ST3. . . .30 D6
Abbot Beyne Sch (Evershed
  Bldg) DE15. . . . . 167 B4
Abbot Beyne Sch (Linnell
  Bldg) DE15. . . . . 167 A3
Abbot CI DE14 . . . . 166 A3
Abbots Bromley Hospl
  WS15 . . . . 160 F6
Abbots Bromley Rd
  DE13 . . . . 162 C4
Abbots Ct ST2 . . . . .58 B7
Abbots Field WS11 . . . . . . 209 E5
Abbotsford Rd WS14 . . . . . 231 E7
Abbotsholme Sch ST14. . . .96 B2
Abbots PI ST2 . . . . .58 B6
Abbots Rd ST2 . . . . .58 B6
Abbot's Way ST5 . . . . .71 B6
Abbots Wlk WV3 . . . . 255 E1
Abbots Wlk
  Rugeley WS15 . . . . 197 B5
  Stafford ST16 . . . . 155 E5
Abbott's CI CW12 . . . . .16 B8
Abbott's St ST5 . . . . .57 E8
Abbotts PI WS13 . . . . 243 D1
Abbott's Rd ST13 . . . . .31 A7
Abbotts St WS3. . . . . 243 D2
Abelia B77 . . . . 250 F3
Abercorn St ST4 . . . . .72 F5
Aberford Gr ST1. . . . . .57 F5
Abingdon Rd WS3 . . . . 242 F2
Abingdon Way
  Stoke-on-T ST4 . . . . .88 B7
  Walsall WS3 . . . . 242 F2
Ablon Ct ST19 . . . . 207 F7
Ablow St WV2 . . . . 266 C8
Abnalls Croft WS13 . . . . . . 213 F1
Abnalls Ct WS13 . . . . 213 F1
Abnalls La Lichfield WS13. 213 D1
  Lichfield WS13. . . . . 213 F1
Abney Dr WV14 . . . . 266 F7
Acacia Ave ST5. . . . . .55 E2
Acacia Cres WV8 . . . . 239 B4
Acacia Ct DY8 . . . . 279 E6
Acacia Gdns ST7. . . . . .26 C3
Acacia Gr Cannock WS12 . . 210 F3
  Newcastle-u-L ST5. . . . . . . .55 E2
Achilees CI WS6 . . . . 226 F1
Achilles Way ST2. . . . . .57 F1
Ackleton Gdns WV3 . . . . . 265 F7
Acorn CI Burntwood WS7 . . 212 A1
  Great Wyrley WS6 . . . . 227 A1
  Loggerheads TF9 . . . . .99 D5
Acorn Gr Codsall WV8. . . . 238 E2
  Stourbridge DY8 . . . . 275 E1
Acorn La CW12 . . . . .16 A2
Acorn Rd WV11. . . . . 242 A1
Acorn Rise ST3 . . . . .40 B8
Acorn Starter Units
  WS7. . . . . 228 D7
Acorn View WS7 . . . . 229 C6
Acres Nook CI ST6. . . . . .41 A7
Acres Nook Rd ST6 . . . . .41 A6
Acres The
  Newcastle-u-L ST5. . . . . . . .55 D1
  Wolverhampton WV3 . . . . . 255 C1
Acreswood Rd ST6. . . . . .42 B2
Acton Ct ST18 . . . . 174 F2
Acton Dr DY3 . . . . 271 B3
Acton Hill Rd ST17. . . . . . . 175 C2
Acton St ST1 . . . . .57 D6
Adam Ct WS11. . . . . 209 D1

Adams Ave ST6 . . . . .41 D5
Adams CI TF10. . . . . 168 E2
Adams Cres TF10 . . . . 168 E2
Adams' Gram Sch TF10. . . 168 E3
Adams Gr ST13 . . . . .30 C4
Adamson CI WS11 . . . . 209 B1
Adams Rd Brownhills WS8 245 B5
  Wolverhampton WV3 . . . . . 265 C8
Adams St
  Newcastle-u-L ST5. . . . . . . .56 C4
  Stoke-on-T ST3 . . . . .43 B1
Adamthwaite CI ST11. . . . . .90 D7
Adamthwaite Dr ST11. . . . . .90 D7
Adderley PI ST12 . . . . .88 F3
Adderley Rd
  Market Drayton TF9. . . . . . . .97 B3
  Stoke-on-T ST5 . . . . .42 E3
Adderley Road Ind Est
  TF9. . . . . .97 C2
Addie Rd DE13. . . . . 166 B6
Addington Way ST3 . . . . . . 284 D5
Addison CI WS11 . . . . 209 E5
Addison Croft DY3. . . . . . . 271 A5
Addison Gr WV11 . . . . 241 B1
Addison Rd WV3 . . . . 265 F8
Addison St ST1 . . . . .57 D6
Adelaide Cres DE15. . . . . . 167 C2
Adelaide Dr WS12 . . . . 210 F3
Adelaide St ST6 . . . . .57 A7
Adelaide Wlk WV2 . . . . 266 E8
Adies Alley **7** ST15 . . . . 120 A8
Adkins St ST6 . . . . .55 C7
Admiral Parker Dr WS14 246 F5
Adonis CI B79 . . . . 250 C7
Adrian St ST4 . . . . .72 E6
Advance Bsns Pk WS11 . . 210 B3
Adventure B77 ST1. . . . . . . 282 B2
Adwalton Rd WV6. . . . . 254 F3
Aegean CI ST4 . . . . .88 C8
Aelfgar CI ST15 . . . . 178 E1
Aelfgar Ho WS15 . . . . 178 E1
Affleck Ave B78 . . . . 249 D1
Agenoria Dr DY8 . . . . 279 F5
Agger Hill ST5. . . . . .54 C1
Aiden Ct WS13. . . . . 231 C7
Ainsdale CI **2** Longton ST3 73 D1
  Stourbridge DY8 . . . . 279 F2
Ainsley CI ST2 . . . . .58 B6
Ainsworth Ave ST10. . . . . . .61 D2
Ainsworth Rd WV10 . . . . . 240 E4
Ainsworth St ST4 . . . . .72 C5
Aintree CI
  Burton u T DE14. . . . . 185 A4
  Cannock WS12. . . . . 210 F6
  Stoke-on-T ST4 . . . . .88 B7
Aintree Rd
  Upper Tean ST10 . . . . .92 E4
  Wolverhampton WV10. . . . 240 D4
Aintree Way DY1. . . . . 271 F2
Airdale Gr ST15 . . . . 105 B2
Airdale Rd ST15 . . . . 105 B2
Airdale Spinney ST15 . . . . 105 B2
Airfield Ind Est ST18 . . . . 153 E8
Aitken CI ST18. . . . . 250 A2
Aitken St ST6 . . . . .56 E8
Ajax CI WS6 . . . . 226 F1
Ajax Way ST2 . . . . .57 F1
Akesmoor La Biddulph ST8 .27 A8
  Mow Cop ST7. . . . . .26 F7
Alanbrook Gr ST3. . . . . .89 E8
Alandale Ave WS15 . . . . . . 198 C4
Alan Dale ST9 . . . . .59 B4
Alanley CI ST10. . . . . .88 E8
Alan Rd ST2. . . . . .58 C3
Alastair Rd ST4 . . . . .71 F4
Albany Dr Cannock WS12 . . 210 E3
  Rugeley WS11 . . . . 178 D3
Albany Gr
  Kingswinford DY6 . . . . 275 E7
  Stoke-on-T ST4 . . . . .71 D8
  Willenhall WV11 . . . . 242 C1
Albany Rd
  Newcastle-u-L ST5. . . . . . . 283 B4
  Stoke-on-T ST4 . . . . .71 D8
Albany St ST6 . . . . .41 C7
Albemarle Rd
  Newcastle-u-L ST5. . . . . . . .56 A3
  Stourbridge DY8 . . . . 279 F2
Alberta St ST3 . . . . 284 C2
Albert Ave ST3 . . . . .73 C3
Albert CI WV8. . . . . 238 E4
Albert Davie Dr WS12 . . . . 210 E4
Albert Dr DY3 . . . . 269 E2
Albert PI ST3. . . . . .73 B1
Albert Rd Fazeley B78. . . . 261 A8
  Stoke-on-T ST4 . . . . .88 B6
  Tamworth B79 . . . . 250 B5
Albert St **2** Leek ST13. . . .30 E6
  Audley ST7. . . . . .39 F3
  Biddulph ST8 . . . . .27 B8
  Broomhill WS11 . . . . 209 E4
  Burton u T DE14. . . . . 166 C4
  Cannock WS11 . . . . 210 D5
  Kingswinford DY6 . . . . 275 B8
  Longton ST3 . . . . 284 C5
  Newcastle-u-L,Chesterton
  ST5. . . . . .55 E7
  Newcastle-u-L,Silverdale
  ST5. . . . . .55 C2
  Stone ST15 . . . . 105 A1
  Stourbridge DY8 . . . . 279 F5

Albert Terr
  Newcastle-u-L ST5. . . . . . . .56 C5
  Stafford ST16 . . . . 155 E5
Albion Par DY6 . . . . 275 B8
Albion Rd WS8 . . . . 244 E8
Albion Sq ST1 . . . . 282 B2
Albion St Hanley ST1 . . . . . 282 B2
  Kingswinford DY6 . . . . 275 B8
  Leek ST13 . . . . .30 E5
  Rugeley WS15 . . . . 178 F1
  Tamworth B79 . . . . 250 C5
Albion Terr DE14. . . . . 166 E6
Albion Way WS7 . . . . 211 F1
Albrighton By Pass WV7 237 B6
Albrighton Jun & Inf Schs
  WV7. . . . . 237 A4
Albrighton Sta WV7. . . . . . 237 B5
Albrighton Trust (for the
  disabled)* WV7 . . . . 237 A7
Albutts Rd WS11 . . . . 228 B3
Alcester CI ST6. . . . . .42 B6
Alcove The WS3 . . . . 243 D2
Aldbury CI ST16 . . . . 136 D1
Aldbury PI ST3 . . . . .72 E1
Aldeburgh CI WS3 . . . . 243 A3
Aldeburgh Dr ST5 . . . . .71 B2
Alden Hurst WS7. . . . . 228 F8
Alderbrook CI
  Rolleston on D DE13 . . . . 147 C4
  Sedgley DY3. . . . . 266 B1
Alder CI Aldsgrove ST7 . . . . .41 A8
  Lichfield WS14. . . . . 231 F7
  Loggerheads TF9 . . . . .99 E5
Alder Coppice Prim Sch
  DY3 . . . . 266 C1
Alderdale Ave DY3 . . . . . . 266 C3
Alderdale Ave DY3 . . . . . . 266 C3
Alder Dale WV3 . . . . 255 E2
Alderflat Dr ST4 . . . . .88 D6
Alderford CI WV8 . . . . 255 F8
Aldergate B79 . . . . 250 B5
Alder Gr Burton u T DE14 . 185 F7
  Newcastle-u-L ST5. . . . . . . .55 D8
  Stafford ST17 . . . . 174 B7
Alder La ST17 . . . . 136 C1
Alderlea Ave ST4. . . . . .62 C4
Alderley Ave WS6. . . . . 255 E7
Alderley CI WV6 . . . . 255 E7
Alderley High Sch WV8 239 E1
Alderley Rd WV6. . . . . 255 F6
Alderley Stadium WV6 . . 255 F6
Alderton Dr DE13. . . . . 147 F1
Alders CI ST3. . . . . .73 E8
Alders The DE13 . . . . 183 C1
Alderton Dr WV3 . . . . 265 E8
Alderton Gr ST3 . . . . .90 B6
Alder Way WS12 . . . . 211 A6
Alder Wlk ST4 . . . . .71 E4
Alderwood Prec DY3. . . . . 266 C1
Alderwood Rise DY3 . . . . . 271 D5
Aldin CI B78 . . . . 249 E2
Aldridge By-Pass WS9. . . . 256 A6
Aldridge CI
  2 Stourbridge DY8. . . . . 279 E8
  Polesworth B78 . . . . 262 F8
Aldridge Rd Aldridge B74. . 256 D1
  Little Aston B74,WS9. . . . . 257 B6
Aldridge Sch WS9 . . . . 256 A4
Aldrin CI Meir ST3. . . . . .90 C7
  Stafford ST16 . . . . 156 B5
Aldwych CI WS9 . . . . 256 B8
Aldwyck Dr WV3. . . . . 265 A8
Alesmore Mdw WS13 . . . . 230 F6
Alexander CI WS13. . . . . . . 215 D6
Alexander Patterson Sch The
  DY10. . . . . 280 C3
Alexander Rd WV8 . . . . . . 239 C3
Alexander Trad Est ST4 . . . .57 A2
Alexandra Cres ST14. . . . . 126 B8
Alexandra Ct
  Burton u T DE15. . . . . 167 A3
  Longton ST3 . . . . .73 E2
  Market Drayton TF9. . . . . . . .97 B1
  Newcastle-u-L ST5. . . . . . . .56 C4
  Stafford ST17 . . . . 285 B1
Alexandra St **2** ST5 . . . . 104 F1
  Wolverhampton WV3 . . . . . 266 A6
Alexandra Way WS9. . . . . . 256 B5
Alford Dr ST2 . . . . .59 A3
Alfred Lyons CI WS15 . . . . 160 F6
Alfred St Burton u T DE15 . . .73 E2
  Stone ST15 . . . . .72 E7
  Tamworth B79 . . . . 250 A5
  Walsall WS3 . . . . 243 B1

Alfreton Rd ST4 . . . . .73 A6
Algar Rd ST4 . . . . .71 E6
Alicia Way ST2 . . . . .43 A2
Alison Dr DY8 . . . . 279 E3
Allan CI **7** DY8 . . . . 279 F8
Allard B77 . . . . 250 E2
Allen Birt Wlk WS15 . . . . . 178 D3
Allenby Ct ST5. . . . . .70 F3
Allenby Sq ST4 . . . . .71 E4
Allendale ST16 . . . . 155 B8
Allendale Wlk ST3 . . . . .72 F1
Allen Gdns TF9 . . . . 112 B8
Allens Croft ST14 . . . . 127 E2
Allen's La ST14 . . . . 127 E2
Allens La WS3 . . . . 243 F2
Allensmead B77 . . . . 250 C2
Allensmore Ave ST4 . . . . . . .73 B5
Allen St Cheadle ST10. . . . . .76 E2
  Cheadle ST10. . . . . .76 E3
  Stoke-on-T ST4 . . . . .71 E8
  Tamworth B77 . . . . 250 C1
Allensway ST5. . . . . .70 E4
Allerdale WS8 . . . . 244 E6
Allerton Rd ST4 . . . . .87 F7
Alleston Rd WV10. . . . . 240 D1
Alleston Wlk WV10. . . . . . . 240 D2
Alleyne's High Sch ST15 105 A1
Alley's La ST20 . . . . 190 A8
Alley The DY3. . . . . 271 B3
Alliance St ST16 . . . . 155 D6
Allington Ave **5** WS13 . . 230 F6
Alliss CI ST16 . . . . 156 C4
Allport Mews WS11 . . . . . . 209 E1
Allport Rd WS11 . . . . 209 E1
Allport St WS11. . . . . 209 E2
All Saints CE Fst Sch
  Church Leigh ST10. . . . . . . 109 A4
  Denstone ST14 . . . . .95 E6
  Leek ST13 . . . . .30 F4
  Standon ST21 . . . . 102 C3
All Saints CE Inf Sch
  ST18. . . . . 153 C5
All Saints CE Prim Sch
  Alrewas DE13 . . . . 201 A2
  Bednall ST17 . . . . 193 E8
  Rangemore DE13. . . . . 164 C2
  Trysull WV5. . . . . 269 C8
All Saints Croft DE14. . . . 185 C8
All Saints Dr B74 . . . . 258 A2
All Saints Rd
  Burton u T DE14. . . . . 185 C8
  Stoke-on-T ST4 . . . . .72 A5
  Wolverhampton WV2 . . . . . 266 D8
Allthorpe PI ST5. . . . . .70 F3
Alton Ave B78. . . . . 249 D1
Alton CI B77 . . . . 250 E3
Allways CI ST18. . . . . 122 C5
All Ways St18 . . . . 122 C5
Allways The ST18 . . . . 122 C5
Alma CI ST7 . . . . .25 E7
Alma Rd DE11 . . . . 186 F6
Almar PI ST6 . . . . .42 A5
Alma St Burton u T DE14. . 166 C2
  Leek ST13 . . . . .30 D6
  Stoke-on-T ST4 . . . . .72 D6
  Stone ST15 . . . . 104 F1
Almond CI Cannock WS11 210 C2
  Walsall WS3 . . . . 243 F2
Almond Ct DE13 . . . . 147 E1
Almond Gr Stoke-on-T ST3 . .72 E3
  Swadlincote DE11 . . . . 186 F5
Almond PI ST5 . . . . .40 E1
Almond Rd
  Huntington WS12. . . . . 209 D8
  Kingswinford DY6 . . . . 275 D8
Alms Hos TF11. . . . . 211 A8
Almshouse Croft WS18 . . 191 B8
Almshouses Biddulph ST8 . .16 E3
  Madeley CW5 . . . . .68 E5
  Newton Solney DE15. . . . . 167 E8
  Penkridge ST19 . . . . 192 E1
  Wolverhampton WV4. . . . . 265 F3
Alnwick CI WS12 . . . . 210 E2
Alnwick Rd WS3 . . . . 243 A4
Alpha Way WS6 . . . . 243 A8
Alpine Dr WS12 . . . . 210 D4
Alpine Way WV3 . . . . 255 C2
Alrewas Rd DE13 . . . . 199 E6
Alsager Rd ST7. . . . . .39 D5
Alsop Crest ST17 . . . . .51 C8
Alsop Moor Cotts DE6 . . . . .36 D5
Alsop St ST13 . . . . .30 E5
Alston CI Cannock WS12. . 210 E2
  Sutton Coldfield B74 . . . . . 258 A2
Alstone CI ST16 . . . . 155 B7
Alstone Hostel*
  DE6 . . . . .35 F4
Alstone La ST18 . . . . 172 F2
Althorp Way DE13 . . . . 166 D8
Althrop Gr ST3 . . . . .73 D3
Altona Ct ST15. . . . . 120 B8
Alton CI Newcastle-u-L ST5. .55 B1
  Wolverhampton WV10. . . . 240 E3
Alton Gr Bucknall ST2. . . . . .23 D7
  Cannock WS15. . . . . 197 B1
  Newport TF10 . . . . 168 C1
Alton Towers Theme Pk*
  ST10. . . . . .78 E4
Alvaston CI WS3 . . . . 243 C3

Aar – Ank   289

Alvecote Cotts B79 . . . . . . 251 D6
Alvecote Pools Nature
  Reserve* B79. . . . . 251 E6
Alverley CI DY6 . . . . 275 B8
Alverstoke CI WV9 . . . . . . 240 A2
Alverton CI B77. . . . . 261 C4
Alvis CI B79 . . . . 250 C7
Alwen St DY8 . . . . 275 F2
Alwyn CI WS6 . . . . 227 A3
Alwyn Cres ST6. . . . . .57 D8
Alwyn Rd DE13 . . . . 182 A2
Alwyn B77. . . . . 261 E7
Amanda Ave WV4 . . . . 265 F4
Amber Bsns Village B77. . 251 B3
Amber CI B77 . . . . 251 B3
Amber Ct Stoke-on-T ST9 . . .43 E5
  Tamworth B77 . . . . 251 B3
Amberfield CI ST3 . . . . .73 E4
Ambergate CI WS3. . . . . . . 243 C3
Ambergate Dr DY6. . . . . . . 275 C8
Amber Gn WS11. . . . . 210 C2
Amber Gr WS11. . . . . 210 C2
Amberlands DE13. . . . . . . 147 F1
Amberley Way B74. . . . . . . 256 E1
Amblecote St ST3 . . . . .73 E4
Amblecote Prim Sch
  DY8 . . . . 279 F8
Amblefield Way ST16 . . . . 136 C1
Ambleside CI ST15. . . . . . . 120 D7
Ambleside Gr WV11. . . . . . 242 B1
Ambleside PI ST6. . . . . .42 A3
Ambleside Way DY6. . . . . . 275 C6
Ambrose Cres DY6 . . . . . . 275 D8
Ambrose PI ST6. . . . . .41 F7
Amelia CI ST2 . . . . .43 A2
America St ST6 . . . . .41 D3
Amerton Farm* ST18. . . . . 139 A4
Amerton La
  Amerton ST18 . . . . 139 A3
  Weston ST18. . . . . 138 F1
Amicable St ST6 . . . . .56 F7
Amicombe B77 . . . . 251 C1
Amington CI B75. . . . . 258 D3
Amington Hall B79 . . . . . . 251 A8
Amington Heath Com Sch
  B77. . . . . 251 A4
Amington Ind Est 251 B3
Amington Pk B77 . . . . 251 A6
Amington Rd B77 . . . . 250 D4
Amison St ST3. . . . . .73 D4
Amison CI B75 . . . . 258 D3
Ampleforth Dr ST17. . . . . . 156 B1
Ampthill PY14 . . . . .71 F1
Amptronik Trad Est
  WV5. . . . . 269 C4
Ancaster St ST6 . . . . .41 D7
Anchor CI B77. . . . . 250 E4
Anchor Ct B77 . . . . 250 E4
Anchor Par WS9 . . . . 256 B6
Anchor PI ST3 . . . . 284 C4
Anchor Terr ST3 . . . . 284 C4
Anchor Way ST20. . . . . 171 D7
Ancient High House*
  ST16. . . . . 285 B3
Anderby Gdns DE11. . . . . . 186 F2
Anderson PI ST6. . . . . .42 E3
Anders Sq WV6. . . . . 254 E4
Anderstaff Ind Pk DE14 . . 166 E5
Anders B79. . . . . 250 A6
Anderton View WS15 . . . . 104 E3
Andover CI ST3 . . . . .73 C6
Andover Cres **2** DY6. . . . 275 F4
Andover PI WS11 . . . . 210 A4
Andrew Mulligan CI ST6 . .41 C5
Andrew PI ST5 . . . . 283 D3
Andrews Ho WS13 . . . . 231 A7
Andrews Rd WS9 . . . . 245 B4
Andrews St WS3 . . . . 243 A8
Aneurin Bevan PI WS15 . . 178 D2
Angel Croft WS7 . . . . 211 E1
Angela PI B77 . . . . 250 F4
Angelica CI ST3 . . . . .73 E4
Anglesey Bsns Pk WS12. . 210 E4
Anglesey CI WS7 . . . . 228 F4
Anglesey Cres
  Brownhills WS8 . . . . 228 F2
  Cannock WS12. . . . . 210 C5
Anglesey Ct
  Burton u T DE14. . . . . 166 B1
Anglesey Gr ST13 . . . . .30 D6
Anglesey Ho WS15. . . . . . . 197 B6
Anglesey Mews WS12 . . . . 210 C5
Anglesey Prim Sch DE14 166 C1
Anglesey Rd
  Brownhills WS8 . . . . 228 F2
  Burton u T DE14. . . . . 166 B1
  Lichfield WS13. . . . . 214 B2
Anglesey St
  Burton u T DE14. . . . . 165 F4
  Cannock WS12. . . . . 210 B5
Angle St **6** ST13 . . . . . . .30 D6
Anglia Dr DE11 . . . . 186 F1
Anglia Rd WS11 . . . . 209 D3
Angorfa CI WS13. . . . . 230 F7
Angus CI B79 . . . . 250 A5
Anker CI WS7 . . . . 229 D6
Ankerdrive B79 . . . . 250 B4
Ankermoor CI B77 . . . . 250 E5

Ankermoor Prim Sch
  B77.................................250 E5
Ankerside Sh Ctr B79 .....250 B4
Anker View B77 ....250 C3
Annan Cl 3 CW12 ....6 A1
Annandale B77 ....251 B1
Anna Wlk ST6 ....56 F7
Ann Cres WS11 ....209 E6
Anne Ct ST7........................40 D6
Annefield Cl TF9 ....97 D2
Anne Rd WV4 ....266 B6
Anne St ST6.........................41 C7
Annette Rd ST4...................73 B6
Anslow Gdns WV11 ....241 F1
Anslow La DE13 ....147 A2
Anslow Rd DE13 ....145 A2
Ansmede Gr ST3 ....72 F1
Anson Ave WS13 ....214 A1
Anson CE Prim Sch ST18 158 B2
Anson Cl Burntwood WS7 .229 C7
  Great Wyrley WS6 ....226 F1
  Perton WV6 ....250 A6
Anson Ct Burton u T DE14.166 E3
  Fazeley B78 ....261 B8
  Stafford ST18 ....156 D5
Anson Dr ST17...................175 F6
Anson Mews WS15.............178 F1
Anson Rd Alrewas DE13 ...201 A2
  Great Wyrley WS6 ....226 F1
  Meir ST3 ....90 A8
Anson's Row ST18 ....177 C8
Anson St WS15 ....178 E1
Anstree Cl WS6.................226 D1
Ansty Dr WS12 ....210 D1
Anthony Gr ST3...................89 F4
Anthony Pl ST3 ....284 D4
Antler Dr WS15 ....178 B2
Antom Ct ST16 ....155 F7
Apedale Bsns Pk ST5 ....55 C7
Apedale Com Ctry Pk*
  ST5...................................55 A6
Apedale Rd
  Audley,Wood Lane ST7 ......55 A8
  Newcastle-u-L ST5............55 C6
Apex Rd WS8 ....244 C7
Apley Fl ST4 ....87 F8
Apley Rd DY8 ....279 E7
Apollo Cl WS11 ....210 A5
Apollo Wlk ST6 ....249 F6
Appian Cl B77 ....261 D7
Appleby Gdns WV11 ....242 C2
Appleby Glade Ind Est
  DE11 ....186 E2
Appleby Glade DE11 ....186 D2
Apple Croft CW3.................68 D7
Applecroft ST5 ....40 E1
Applecross B74................257 F1
Appledore Cl
  Cannock WS12................210 E3
  Great Wyrley WS6 ....227 A3
  Stafford ST17 ....175 E8
Appledore Gr ST6...............41 E7
Appleford Pl ST3 ....72 E1
Applegarth Cl ST4 ....73 B6
Apple Gr TF9 ....87 C3
Appleton Cl Biddulph ST8 ...27 E6
  Burton u T DE15.............185 E7
  Congleton CW12 ....15 E8
  Swadlincote DE11 ....186 F6
Appleton Cres WV4 ....266 A5
Appleton Dr ST5..................85 D5
Appletree Gr WS9 ....256 B5
Apple Wlk WS11 ....210 C2
Applewood Cl ST14 ....111 A1
Applewood Cres ST3 ....90 C8
Appleyard Ct ST16 ....285 B3
Appleyard The ST19 ....223 C6
Apse Cl WV5 ....269 F7
Apsley Gr ST12 ....88 A1
Aqualate Cl TF10 ....169 A4
Aqualate Ho ST17.............174 E6
Aquaries Ct ST3 ....73 E1
Aquinas St ST4 ....72 B7
Arbor Cl B77 ....250 D3
Arborfield Rd ST14 ....143 F7
Arbor Gate WS9 ....245 B4
Arbour Cl CW3 ....68 E7
Arbourfield Dr ST2 ....58 A2
Arbour Mews WS11 ....227 F6
Arbour St Hanley ST1 ....282 C3
  Talke Pits ST7 ....40 D5
Arbourtree Ct WV5 ....270 B7
Arbury Dr DY8 ....275 D3
Arcade The DY3................271 E5
Arcadia Pk WS15 ....197 B7
Arcal St ST3 ....271 E7
Arch St WS15 ....196 F8
Arctic Pl ST4 ....88 B8
Arden Cl Leek ST13............31 B5
  Rugeley WS15 ....178 C2
  Stourbridge DY8 ....279 E7
  Stourbridge,West Park DY8 275 C3
  Tamworth B77 ....250 E5
Arden Ct Congleton CW12...16 B7
  Dudley DY3 ....271 D3
Arden Rd Barton-u-N DE13 201 E8
  Tamworth B77 ....261 F5
Arden Wlk WS15 ....198 C4
Argay Dr ST3 ....209 F7
Ardingley Ave ST17 ....156 B1
Argles Rd ST13 ....31 A7
Argosy Cl ST3 ....90 B7

Argyle Ave B77 ....250 D4
Argyle Cl DY8....................275 E1
Argyle Rd WV2 ....266 B6
Argyle St Hanley ST1.........282 A1
  Tamworth B77 ....250 C4
Argyll Cl ST11 ....90 E6
Argyll Rd ST3 ....73 D1
Ariane B79 ....249 E7
Arica Cl ST6 ....41 F6
Arion Cl B77 ....250 D5
Arkall Cl B79 ....250 C7
Arkle Cl ST14 ....126 D7
Arkle B77 ....261 D4
Arkwright Gr ST1 ....57 F8
Arlescote Cl B75...............258 C2
Arley Dr DY8 ....279 E3
Arley Gr WV4 ....265 D5
Arlington Cl DY6...............275 D4
Arlington Way Meir ST3 ......90 A7
  Stoke-on-T ST3 ....89 F7
Armishaw Pl WS15 ....197 B5
Armitage Gdns WS15........197 B6
Armitage Hill DE13 ....183 E4
Armitage Ho WS13 ....214 E1
Armitage La WS15.............197 B5
Armitage Rd WS15............197 A6
Armshead Rd ST9...............59 B5
Armside Cl WS3 ....244 B4
Armstead Rd ST14............240 A3
Armstrong Ave ST16.........156 A4
Armstrong Gn ST6..............57 C7
Armstrong B79 ....249 F6
Arnold Cl B79 ....250 A6
Arnold Gr ST5 ....56 B7
Arnot Rd WS12 ....209 F7
Arnot Rd DE14 ....185 A7
Arps Rd WV8 ....238 F3
Arran Cl WS11 ....210 A3
Arran Dr Stoke-on-T ST3 ....41 F8
  Tamworth B77 ....261 F7
Arrow Dr WV7 ....237 A5
Arthur Cotton Ct ST6 ....42 A1
Arthur Evans Cl WS15 ......197 A5
Arthur Ct DE13 ....147 E2
Arthur St
  1 Stoke-on-T ST6.............41 E3
  Burton u T DE14..............166 C5
  Cannock,Chadsmoor WS11 209 F4
  Cannock WS12 ....210 F3
  Newcastle-u-L ST5..............55 F2
  Stone ST15 ....105 A2
  Wolverhampton WV2........266 D7
Arthur Terry Sch The
  B74...................................258 A3
Arthur Wood Pl WS15.......178 D2
Arundel Dr ST10 ....76 F3
Arundel Gr WV6 ....254 F3
Arundel Rd
  Stourbridge DY8 ....275 C2
  Wolverhampton WV10 ......240 B2
Arundel B77 ....261 D6
Arundel Way ST3 ....73 C6
Ascot Cl Burton u T DE15 .167 A3
  Lichfield WS13 ....231 D7
Ascot Dr Cannock WS11 ...226 C8
  Dudley DY1 ....271 F2
  Tamworth B77 ....261 D4
Ascot Rd ST17...................156 C1
Ascot Gdns DY8 ....275 D2
Ascot Rd ST17...................156 C1
Ash Bank Rd ST2,ST9..........59 B3
Ashbourne Cl WS11 ....210 A4
Ashbourne Gr
  Chorlton CW2 ....37 C1
  Market Drayton TF9...........97 C2
  Newcastle-u-L ST5............55 B1
  Swadlincote DE11 ....186 F1
Ashbourne La DE6..............35 A2
Ashbourne Rd
  Cheadle ST10 ....76 F3
  Leek ST13 ....31 B4
  Mayfield DE6 ....81 C7
  Rocester ST14 ....95 F4
  Uttoxeter,Spath ST14.......111 B3
  Uttoxeter ST14 ....111 B1
  Wetton DE6 ....35 B3
  Wolverhampton,Ettingshall Park
  WV4...............................266 E3
Ashbrook DE15 ....167 A1
Ashbrook Cl Gnosall ST20 171 D7
  Uttoxeter ST14 ....126 C6
Ashbrook La WS15............161 C5
Ashburton St ST6................57 B7
Ashby Cres ST3 ....72 F1
Ashby Rd DE15 ....167 B2
Ashby Rd E DE15 ....167 E1
Ashby Rd B79 ....250 C8
Ashby Cl Cheadle ST10 ....76 F2
  Codsall WV8 ....239 A3
  Uttoxeter ST14 ....126 A8
Ashcombe Gn ST3.............72 F1
Ashcombe Rd ST13 ....45 C4
Ashcombe Way ST3 ....30 F4
Ashcott Wlk ST2..................58 C1
Ash Cres ST6....................275 E6
Ashcroft 12 WS6...............266 F4
Ashcroft Ave ST4 ....71 E2
Ashcroft Cl ST5..................56 A6
Ashcroft Gr ST5 ....56 B6
Ashcroft Inf Sch B79.........250 C7
Ashcroft La
  Lichfield WS14.................230 E1
  Wolverhampton WV10 ......246 E2
Ashcroft Oval ST5 ....56 B6
Ashcroft Pl ST5 ....56 A6
Ashcroft Rd ST5..................56 A6

Ashdale Cl 1 Stone ST15 120 A7
  Burton u T DE15...............186 A8
Ashdale Pk ST15 ....118 F6
Ashdale Rd Leek ST13 ....31 B6
  Stoke-on-T ST4 ....72 C5
  Tamworth B77 ....250 D5
Ashdale Rise ST5 ....71 B3
Ashdene Gdns DY8............275 C2
Ashdown Dr DY8...............275 E3
Ash Dr ST18 ....172 F5
Ashen Cl DY3....................266 C3
Ashendene Gr
  Stoke-on-T ST4 ....71 F1
  Trentham ST14 ....87 F8
Ashenden Rise WV3...........265 A8
Ashenhurst Way ST14..........30 F4
Ashenough Rd ST7...............40 D6
Ashe's La DE6 ....144 D7
Ashfield Ct ST5.................283 A4
Ashfield Gr WV10 ....240 C3
Ashfield Rd
  Wolverhampton,Compton
  WV3..............................255 D2
  Wolverhampton,Fordhouses
  WV10 ....240 C3
Ashfields Gr WV7 ....237 A5
Ashfields Grange ST5........283 B3
Ashfields New Rd ST5.......283 A4
Ashfield Sq ST2 ....58 A2
Ash Flats La ST17,ST18.....174 E4
Ash Gr Audley ST7.............271 E7
Ashford Gr ST15 ....120 C7
Ashford Rd DE13..............166 A6
Ashford St ST4 ....72 C8
Ash Gr Albrighton WV7 .....237 A4
  Barlaston ST12 ....88 D1
  Blythe Bridge ST11 ....90 C8
  Brewood ST19 ⌐..............223 D6
  Cannock WS11.................209 F4
  Penkridge ST19 ⌐............208 A7
  Shenstone WS14..............246 F6
Ash Gr TF10 ....168 E2
Ash Gr Lichfield WS14.......231 E8
  Newcastle-u-L ST5............55 B2
Ashgrove WS7..................228 F5
Ash Grove La DE65...........148 C6
Ash Gr Stoke-on-T ST3........72 E2
  Tamworth B77 ....261 F5
  Whemdon Aston ST19.......205 C6
Ash Hill WV3 ....255 D2
Ash La WS6 ....227 A3
Ashlands Ave ST4 ....71 E8
Ashlands Cl B79 ....250 C7
Ashlands Gr ST4.................71 E7
Ashlands Rd ST4...............139 D1
Ashland St WV3 ....266 B8
Ash La b79 ....236 F6
Ashlar Cl ST6......................42 A8
Ash La ST5 ....118 E5
Ashlea Ct TF9......................97 E2
Ashlea B78 ....262 F5
Ashlea Dr DE6 ....81 D7
Ashleigh Ave DE11 ....186 F5
Ashleigh Cres ST19 ....205 C7
Ashleigh Dr
  Tamworth B77 ....261 E8
  Uttoxeter ST14 ....110 F1
Ashleigh Rd
  Rugeley WS15 ....196 E7
  Upper Tean ST10 ....92 A3
Ashley Cl Burton u T DE15 192 A4
  Kingswinford DY6 ....275 C4
  Stafford ST16 ....155 A4
  Stourbridge DY8 ....279 D2
Ashley Croft ST20.............190 A8
Ashley Ct DE15 ....167 A3
Ashley Gdns WV8 ....238 F4
Ashley Gr ST5 ....56 C4
Ashley Mount WV6...........255 D5
Ashley Rd Burntwood WS7 211 E5
  Kidderminster DY10 ....280 B1
  Walsall WS3 ....242 F1
  Wolverhampton WV4........265 E5
Ashley View TF9 ....97 C1
Ashmall WS7 ....229 D4
Ashman St ST6 ....42 C2
Ashmead Rd WS7 ....229 A8
Ashmole Ave WS11 ....229 E8
Ashmole Cl WS14 ....231 E6
Ashmore Ave WV11 ....242 A1
Ashmore Dr ST20 ....171 D7
Ashmore Wlk ST1..............282 C3
Ashover Cl WS11 ....210 B3
Ashover Rd DE11..............186 E5
Ash Rd ST15 ....120 B7
Ashridge Ave WS15 ....71 B2
Ashridge Gr ST3..................73 D5
Ashridge Wlk ST16...........136 D1
Ash Rise ST17...................174 E4
Ash St Burton u T DE14.....166 B1
  Walsall WS3 ....243 D1
Ashton Ct
  Newcastle-u-L ST5.............71 C2
  Werrington ST9 ....59 A3
Ashton Dr WS4 ....244 C2
Ashtree Bank WS15 ....197 B6
Ashtree Ct ST18 ....177 D8
Ash Tree Cl DE11 ....186 F6
Ash Tree La DE13 ....209 D4
Ash Tree Hill ST10 ....76 C2
Ash Tree La WS13 ....215 A1

Ash Tree Rd DE13..............183 D1
Ashtree Rd WS3................244 A3
Ashurst Gr 2 ST3................90 B7
Ash View
  Huntington WS12 ....209 D8
  Kidsgrove ST7 ....26 B2
Ash Way Newcastle-u-L ST5 .71 A4
  Werrington ST7 ....71 D8
Ashwell Rd ST4 ....71 D8
Ashwells Gr WV9 ....240 A2
Ashwood Ave DY8 ....275 D2
Ashwood Cl TF9 ....97 A1
Ashwood Gr
  Blythe Bridge ST11 ....91 A6
  Wolverhampton WV4........266 A5
Ashwoodhay DY8 ....275 F3
Ashwood ST3 ....284 C4
Ashwood Park Prim Sch
  DY8 ....275 D1
Ashwood Terr ST4.............284 C5
Ashworth Ave DE15 ....167 C2
Ashworth Ho
  2 Lichfield WS13.............231 B8
  Cannock WS11................210 A4
Ashworth St ST4.................72 D6
Ashworth Way TF10..........168 F1
Askerbank La SK11 ....8 A1
Askern Cl ST3 ....73 E1
Askew Bridge Rd DY3.......271 B3
Askew Cl DY3...................271 E5
Aspen Cl
  2 Lichfield WS13.............231 E8
  Harrisehead ST7 ....26 E3
Aspen Croft ST17 ....174 B8
Aspen Ct WV4 ....244 C8
Aspen Gr WS7 ....228 F8
Aspen Rd DE13 ....201 D8
Aspen Way TF10 ....168 F2
Asphodel B74 ....257 F5
Aspley Cl WV10 ....224 E5
Aspley La WV10 ....224 D3
Asquith Cl ST8.....................27 E8
Asquith Dr WS11 ....249 D4
Astbury Cl Kidsgrove ST7 ..26 C3
  Walsall WS3 ....243 A4
Astbury Lane Ends CW12 ..15 F8
Astbury St Mary's CE Prim
  Sch CW12........................15 B8
Aster Cl ST3 ....74 B6
Aster Wlk WV9 ....240 A3
Astil St DE15 ....166 F1
Astle Pl ST11 ....282 C1
Astles Rock Wlk DY7.........278 A3
Aston Chase ST15 ....120 D7
Aston Cl Colwich ST18 .....177 D8
  Penkridge ST19 ..⌐..........208 A7
Aston Dr TF10 ....168 E2
Aston Fields Rd WS13 ......155 E6
Astonfields Ind Est ST16 ..155 E6
Astonfields Road Bsns Pk
  ST16...............................155 E6
Aston Hill ST18 ....154 E4
Aston Ho Aston TF9 ....83 F8
  Claverley WV5 ....267 D7
  Stone ST15 ....120 D3
  Sudbury DE6 ....129 A5
Aston Lodge Parkway
  ST15...............................120 D6
Aston Rd ST5......................40 D1
Aston St WV3 ....266 A8
Aston Terr ST16.................155 E6
Astoria Cl WV12 ....242 D1
Astoria Dr ST17.................174 F6
Astoria Gdns WV12 ....242 D1
Astor Rd Aldridge B74.......257 A1
  Kingswinford DY6 ....275 F5
Astron Bsns Pk DE11........186 F3
Athelney Ct WS3...............244 A3
Athelstan Cl ST19.............208 A8
Athelstan Gr WV6.............254 F5
Athelstan St 1 ST6............41 D3
Athelstan Way B79...........249 F2
Athena Rd ST1 ....57 F5
Atherstone Rd ST4..............88 A7
Atherstone St B77,B78.....261 B8
Athlestan Way DE13.........147 C1
Athlone St ST6....................42 D2
Atholl Rd ST3 ....284 D1
Atkins Way ST14 ....95 F3
Atlam Ct ST2 ....58 A3
Atlantic Gr ST4 ....88 B8
Atlas St ST4 ....72 E5
Attingham Dr WS11 ....210 B2
Attlee Cres Rugeley WS15 196 F7
  Stafford ST17 ....174 D7
Attlee Gr WS11 ....210 C2
Attlee Rd WS11 ....176 D2
Attwell Pk WV3 ....265 D7
Attwood Gdns WV4 ....266 E5
Attwood Rd WS7 ....228 C2
Attwood St ST7 ....26 A2
Aubrey St ST6 ....41 B7
Auchinleck Dr WS13 ....214 C1
Auckland Rd DY6 ....275 E4
Auckland St ST6..................57 A8
Auden Ct WV6 ....254 F4
Auden Pl ST3 ....284 D4
Auden Way ST17...............174 C8
Audlem Rd CW3.................67 B2
Audley Ave TF10 ....169 A4
Audley Avenue Bsns Pk
  TF10...............................169 B2
Audley Avenue Ind Est
  TF10...............................169 B2
Audley Cl DE13 ....201 A3

Audley Ho TF10 ....169 A2
Audley House Mews
  TF10...............................169 A2
Audley Pl ST5 ....71 B5
Audley Rd Audley ST7........39 D8
  Barthomley CW2 ....38 E5
  Newcastle-u-L ST7,ST5......40 B2
  Newport TF10 ....168 F3
  Talke ST7 ....40 B6
Audley St
  Newcastle-u-L ST5..............71 C2
  Stoke-on-T ST6..................41 D3
Audmore Rd ST20 ....171 D7
Audnam DY8 ....275 F1
Augustine Ct ST15 ....120 C7
Augustine Gr B74..............257 F5
Augustines Wlk WS13 ......214 A3
Aulton Rd B75 ....258 E2
Aumbry Cl TF9....................97 A1
Austcliffe La DY10 ....280 C5
Austcliffe Pk DY10 ....280 B6
Austcliffe Rd DY10............280 B5
Austin Cl Cheadle ST10 .....76 C2
  Dudley DY1 ....271 F2
  Stone ST15 ....120 A7
Austin Cote La WS14 ....231 F7
Austin Ct B74 ....257 E3
Austin Friars ST17 ....285 B1
Austin St ST1 ....282 C1
Austrey La
  Newton Regis B79...........236 E3
  No Man's Heath B79 ....236 F6
Austwick Gr ST4 ....71 E5
Autumn Berry Gr DY3 ....271 E6
Autumn Cl WS4................244 C1
Autumn Dr Dudley DY3 ....271 D4
  Lichfield WS13 ....214 D2
  Walsall WS4 ....244 C2
Avalon Ho 2 WS11 ....209 F4
Aveling Gn ST1 ....57 F8
Aveling Rd ST1 ....57 F8
Avenue One CW1 ....37 C8
Avenue Rd Cannock WS12 210 E2
  Newport TF10 ....168 F2
Avenue Rd S TF10.............168 F2
  Wolverhampton WV3........255 C2
Avenue The Bagnall ST9 .....43 F4
  Blakedown DY10 ....281 B2
  Blythe Bridge ST11 ....91 A7
  Cheadle ST10 ....76 D2
  Cheddleton ST13 ....45 C4
  Endon ST9 ....43 E7
  Enville DY7 ....273 D1
  Featherstone WV10 ....241 C7
  Kidsgrove ST7 ....25 F1
  Newcastle-u-L,Basford ST5 .56 D2
  Newcastle-u-L ST5.............71 D8
  Stone ST15 ....105 A1
  Stretton ST19 ....206 D3
  Wolverhampton,Castlecroft
  WV3..............................265 B8
  Wolverhampton,Penn WV4 265 E4
  Wootton DE6 ....79 E5
Avenue Two CW1 ....37 C8
Averill Dr WV15 ....178 D2
Averill Rd ST17 ....174 D8
Aviation La DE13...............165 C4
Avill B77 ....262 A5
Avington Cl DY3 ....271 D7
Avion Cl ST3.......................90 C7
Avoca St ST4 ....282 C4
Avocet Cl ST14 ....126 C6
Avon Bsns Pk WS11 ....226 C2
Avon Cl Kidsgrove ST7........26 B2
  Newcastle-u-L ST5.............71 B4
  Perton WV6 ....254 F4
  Stafford ST16 ....156 B3
Avon Ct WS3 ....244 A1
Avoncroft 3 WV4 ....266 F4
Avondale Cl DY6 ....275 E8
Avon Dale TF10 ....168 F4
Avondale Rd WV6.............255 F3
Avondale St ST6..................56 D8
Avon Gr Cheadle ST10........76 E1
  Loggerheads TF9 ....99 E5
Stone ST15 ....120 B6
Avon Hill WS16 ....156 C3
Avon Ho DY3 ....271 E3
Avonlea Gdns WS15 ....178 C1
Avon Rd Burntwood WS7..228 F5
  Cannock WS11................226 D8
  Stourbridge DY8 ....279 F3
  Walsall WS3 ....243 E1
Avon Rise ST16.................156 B3
Avonside Ave ST6 ....41 F4
Avon B77 ....262 A5
Avon Way
  Burton u T DE15..............167 A1
  Hilton DE65 ....147 D8
Avonwick Gr ST1 ....58 A6
Axborough La DY10 ....280 D4
Axbridge Wlk ST16.............42 C1
Axon Cres ST3....................74 B3
Aylesbury Rd ST2 ....58 C2
Aylesford Cl DY3 ....271 E3
Aylesford Dr B74 ....257 E5
Aynsley Ave ST5.................71 B3
Aynsley Cl ST10..................76 D1
Aynsley Rd ST4...................57 B1
Aynsley's Dr ST11 ....90 E7
Aynsley Specl Sch ST11 .....90 F7
Ayreshire Gr ST3 ....73 D1
Ayr Rd ST10 ....76 E5
Ayrshire Way CW12 ....6 A1
Ayrton Cl WV6 ....255 A4
Ayshford St ST3 ....284 B3
Azalea Cl WV8 ....239 B3

B

Babbacombe Ave ST17 175 E8
Babbington Cl
Tutbury DE13 146 C5
Whittington WS14 232 E5
Babworth Cl WV9 240 A2
Back Browning St ST16 285 A4
Back Bunt's La ST9 43 D4
Backcester La WS13 231 B8
Backcrofts 3 WS11 209 E1
Back Cross La CW12 16 A8
Back Ford Green Rd ST6 42 D2
Back Garden St ST5 283 C2
Back Heathcote St ST7 26 A2
Back La Aldridge WS9 256 F8
Alstonefield DE6 35 E3
Alton ST10 78 F1
Ashley TF9 100 A5
Betley CW3 53 B8
Brown Edge,Hodgefield ST6 28 B1
Brown Edge ST6 43 B7
Colwich ST18 177 D8
Cotes Heath ST21 102 D5
Ellastone DE6 80 A3
Gnosall ST20 171 C5
Haughton ST18 173 A5
Hixon ST18 139 C1
Leek ST13 30 D6
Ranton ST18 153 D4
Shenstone WS14 246 E1
Sutton TF10 150 D1
Uttoxeter ST14 126 C8
Warslow SK17 23 A2
Waterhouses ST10 49 E1
Weston-Under-Lizard TF11 203 D6
Wheaton Aston ST19 205 C5
Whittington WS14 232 E6
Woodseaves ST20 151 D8
Wootton DE6 79 F7
Back Radfords 2 ST15 105 A1
Back Rd DY6 275 D7
Back Westlands Rd ST14 126 B6
Baddeley Green La ST2 43 B1
Baddeley Hall Rd ST2 43 C2
Baddeley Rd ST2 43 B1
Baddeley St Burslem ST6 41 F1
Cheadle ST10 76 E2
Baddely's Ct TF10 168 F2
Baden Powell Cl WS15 211 F6
Baden Rd ST6 42 C1
Baden St ST5 283 B4
Bader Rd WV6 254 E3
Badger Brow Rd TF9 99 D5
Badger Cl WS12 209 D6
Badger Gr ST3 90 C7
Badger La TF9,ST5 84 C3
Badgers Bank Rd B74 257 F5
Badgers Brow ST1 57 E3
Badgers Cl WS3 244 A5
Badgers Croft
Derrington ST18 154 E2
Eccleshall ST21 133 F7
Newcastle-u-L ST5 40 E1
Stafford ST17 175 C6
Badger's End ST19 205 B6
Badgers Hollow ST10 93 B1
Badgers Rise ST13 30 E6
Badgers Sett ST13 30 E6
Badger St DY3 271 E5
Badgers Way WS12 210 D1
Badgery Cl ST14 111 A2
Badminton Cl DY1 271 F3
Badnall Cl ST13 30 E6
Badnall St ST13 30 D6
Baggeridge Cl DY3 271 A8
Baggeridge Ctry Pk* DY3 270 E6
Baggott Pl ST5 70 F8
Baggott St WV2 266 C7
Bag La Marchington ST14 127 E2
Newton WS15 159 D7
Roston DE6 96 E7
Bagnall Rd ST2 43 C1
Bagnall St ST1 282 B2
Bagot Gr ST1 57 F8
Bagots Oak ST17 174 C7
Bagot St WS15 160 F6
Bagots View
Abbots Bromley WS15 161 A6
Church Leigh ST10 109 A4
Bagridge Cl WV3 265 B8
Bagridge Rd WV3 265 B8
Bailey Ave B77 261 F5
Bailey Cl Burntwood WS7 228 D8
Cannock WS11 210 A4
Bailey Cres CW12 6 A4
Bailey Rd ST3 72 E4
Bailey's Bank ST8 16 D3
Bailey St Burton u T DE14 166 D1
Newcastle-u-L ST5 283 A3
Stafford ST17 285 B2
Stoke-on-T ST4 56 F1
Bailye Cl WS13 214 F1
Bainbridge Rd ST4 88 A7
Bains Dr WS13 231 A6
Bains Gr ST5 55 F8
Baird Ho DY6 275 F7
Baker Ave WV14 266 F2
Baker Cl WS7 228 F6
Baker Cres N ST2 43 C3
Baker Cres S ST2 43 B3
Baker Cres ST2 43 C3
Baker Dr WS13 215 C7
Bakers Gdns WV8 238 E4
Baker's La
5 Lichfield WS13 231 B7
Aldridge WS9 256 B6
Weston Jones TF10 150 C4
Baker St Burntwood WS7 228 F6
Burton u T DE15 185 E7
Stoke-on-T ST4 72 E6
Bakers Way
Cannock WS12 210 B5
Codsall WV8 238 F4
Bakers Wlk 1 B77 261 F6
Bakewell Cl
Newcastle-u-L ST5 55 B1
Walsall WS3 243 C3
Bakewell Dr ST15 120 D5
Bakewell Gn DE11 186 E5
Bakewell St ST4 71 F5
Balaam's La ST15 106 D6
Bala Gr ST10 76 F4
Bala Ho ST17 174 E6
Balance Hill ST14 126 C7
Balance St ST14 126 C7
Balcombe Cl ST5 283 B1
Baldwin Gr WS11 210 C2
Baldwin's Gate CE Prim Sch ST5 85 D5
Baldwin Way DY3 269 E2
Balfour Cres WV6 255 F4
Balfour Ct
2 Wolverhampton WV6 255 F4
Sutton Coldfield B74 258 A3
Balfour Gr Biddulph ST8 27 E8
Stafford ST16 155 C8
Balfour Rd DY6 275 E8
Balfour St
Burton u T DE13 166 C6
Hanley ST1 282 C2
Balfour B79 250 A4
Balk Pas ST16 285 A3
Balk The DE13 146 D6
Ballam Mews WS15 178 E1
Ballarat Wlk DY8 279 F5
Ball Green Prim Sch ST6 42 D5
Ball Haye Gn ST13 31 A7
Ball Haye Rd ST13 30 F6
Ball Hayes Rd ST6 42 C5
Ball Haye St ST13 30 F6
Ball Haye Terr ST13 30 F6
Ballington Gdns ST13 30 F5
Ballington View ST13 30 F4
Ballinson Rd ST3 72 F1
Balliol Bsns Pk WV9 239 E3
Balliol St ST4 72 A7
Ball La Coven Heath WV10 240 C6
Leek ST13 30 E6
Stoke-on-T ST6 43 B5
Balloon St ST4 56 D1
Ball's Yd ST5 283 B3
Balmain Cres WV11 241 B1
Balmoral Cl
Lichfield WS14 231 D6
Stoke-on-T ST4 72 A2
Stone ST15 120 B6
Tamworth B79 250 B7
Balmoral Ct WS11 210 A5
Balmoral Dr
Cannock WS12 209 F7
Cheadle ST10 76 B2
Market Drayton TF9 97 E2
Wombourne WV5 265 A1
Balmoral Rd
Burton u T DE15 167 A3
Stafford ST17 156 C1
Stourbridge DY8 275 C2
Sutton Coldfield B74 257 F5
Wolverhampton WV4 266 A5
Balmoral View DY1 271 E2
Balmoral Way WS7 211 E1
Balterley Ct CW2 53 C8
Baltic Cl Cannock WS11 209 E2
Stoke-on-T ST4 88 B7
Balvenie Way DY1 271 F4
Bamber Cl WV3 265 E8
Bamber Pl ST5 55 F6
Bamber St ST4 72 B8
Bamborough Cl DE13 166 D7
Bamburgh B77 261 C7
Bambury St ST3 73 C6
Bamford Cl WS3 243 C3
Bamford Gr Hanley ST1 282 A4
Uttoxeter ST14 110 F2
Bamford Ho WS3 243 C3
Bamford Rd Walsall WS3 243 C3
Wolverhampton WV3 266 A8
Bamford St B77 250 D3
Bampton Ave 4 WS7 229 A8
Bampton Cl ST9 43 F8
Banbery Dr WV5 269 F4
Banbury Cl DY3 271 E6
Banbury Gr ST8 27 C7
Banbury Rd WS11 226 C8
Banbury St ST7 25 D1
Bancroft La
Blythe Bridge ST11 90 F6
Nethertown WS15 199 A8
Bancroft B77 250 F3
Bandridge La SK11 18 A8
Baneberry Dr WV10 241 B7
Bangley La
Drayton Bassett B78 259 E6
Mile Oak B78 260 A8
Bangor Terr ST10 63 E4
Bank Cl ST14 126 C7
Bank Cres WS7 228 F5
Bank Ct 5 ST7 26 A2
Bank End ST6 43 B7
Bankerwall La DE6 80 C7
Bankfield Gr ST5 54 E4
Bankfield Rd ST3 89 F8
Bank Hall Rd ST6 42 B2
Bank Ho ST10 76 D3
Bankhouse Dr CW12 6 A5
Bank House Dr ST5 56 E2
Bankhouse Rd
Forsbrook ST11 91 B8
Stoke-on-T ST4 71 F1
Trentham ST4 87 F8
Bank Pas ST16 285 B3
Bank Rd DY3 271 C2
Bank Side SK17 24 D6
Bankside Meaford ST15 104 D4
Newcastle-u-L ST5 283 C2
Stanton DE6 65 C1
Bank Side ST15 119 F6
Bankside Way WS9 245 B2
Bankside WV5 269 F7
Banks La ST10 61 E4
Banksman Rd ST2 73 D7
Bank St Cannock WS12 210 E1
Cheadle ST10 76 D3
Kidsgrove ST7 26 C4
Stoke-on-T ST6 41 D4
Bank The ST7 26 B7
Bank Top Ave ST6 42 A3
Banktop Ct ST5 56 C6
Bank Top La ST17 175 B1
Banktop Rd DE6 144 B6
Bank Top WS15 178 D1
Bank View ST10 62 A3
Bank Wlk DE13 166 B8
Banky Brook Cl ST6 42 C3
Bannister Cl ST4 72 B4
Bannut Tree La DY7 277 C5
Banstead Cl WV2 266 E7
Bantock Ave WV3 265 F8
Bantock Ct WV3 265 E8
Bantock Gdns WV3 255 E1
Bantock House Mus* WV3 255 F1
Bantock Prim Sch WV3 266 A8
Baonal Way ST15 118 B6
Baptist St 9 ST6 57 A8
Barbara St B79 250 A5
Barber Cl WS12 210 E2
Barber Dr ST7 25 E7
Barber Pl ST6 41 F6
Barber Rd ST6 41 F6
Barber's Sq ST5 56 D4
Barber St ST6 41 F1
Barbridge Rd ST5 40 D1
Barbrook Ave ST3 73 E4
Barclay Cl WV7 237 B6
Barclay St ST3 73 C5
Barcliff Ave B77 250 E3
Bardell Cl WS13 230 E6
Bardolph Cl DE11 186 F3
Bardsey Wlk 1 ST3 73 A3
Bardwell Cl WV8 255 F8
Bardy La Armitage WS15 197 E3
Longdon WS15 197 C1
Barford Rd ST5 70 F3
Barford St ST3 284 B3
Bargate La ST19 223 C6
Bargate St ST19 223 C6
Bargery Rd WV11 242 A1
Bargrave Dr ST5 56 B8
Bargrave St ST2 58 D1
Bar Hill CW3 68 D4
Barker Cl ST16 155 C3
Barker Ho ST3 88 F8
Barker St Longton ST3 284 D3
Newcastle-u-L ST5 55 F6
Barks Dr ST6 42 D4
Bar La DE13 183 A2
Barlaston CE Fst Sch ST12 88 E1
Barlaston Cl ST16 155 C8
Barlaston Hall* ST12 88 E3
Barlaston Old Rd ST4 88 B5
Barlaston Rd Barlaston ST3 89 B5
Stoke-on-T ST3 88 F7
Barlaston Sta ST12 88 D1
Barley Cl Aldridge WS9 256 E2
Burton u T DE14 166 E6
Cannock WS12 210 B5
Dudley DY3 271 F7
Wolverhampton WV8 239 E1
Barleycorn Cl DE15 167 A1
Barleycroft ST10 76 E1
Barley Croft WV6 254 D3
Barleycroft Terr ST7 25 F7
Barley Croft WS14 232 E6
Barley Ct ST16 155 A5
Barley Field WV9 224 B2
Barleyfield Rise DY6 275 A8
Barleyfields Audley ST7 39 D2
Stoke-on-T ST6 42 C3
Barleyford Dr ST3 73 D6
Barley Green La DE13 201 C1
Barley Orch ST20 171 E6
Barley Rd ST10 62 A8
Barlow Cl B77 250 E4
Barlow St ST3 284 C3
Barlstone Ave ST11 90 F6
Barmouth Cl ST8 27 E6
Barmouth Gr ST8 27 B2
Barnaby Sq WV10 240 F4
Barnard Pl WV2 266 E6
Barnard Rd WV11 241 F1
Barnard Way WS11 209 F2
Barn Ave DY3 271 C7
Barn Bank La ST17,ST18 174 D5
Barnbridge Cl ST7 25 E7
Barnbridge B77 250 C2
Barn Cl Dordon B78 262 F6
Lichfield WS13 214 B3
Barn Cl continued
Rugeley WS15 197 B5
Stafford ST17 174 E5
Barn Comm ST20 151 D8
Barn Croft
Burntwood WS7 229 A4
Great Wyrley WS6 227 A3
Barncroft Rd ST6 42 C6
Barn Ct ST5 71 C3
Barn End Rd ST17 193 B8
Barnescroft ST15 106 D2
Barnes Rd
Shenstone WS14 247 A6
Stafford ST17 174 C7
Barnes Way ST3 73 C1
Barnett Cl DY6 275 D4
Barnett Gn DY6 275 D4
Barnett Gr ST6 41 F5
Barnett La DY6,DY8 275 D4
Barnetts La WS8 228 F1
Barnett St DY8 275 D3
Barnfield Cl
Lichfield WS14 231 B6
Stone ST15 119 F7
Barnfield Pl ST13 30 E4
Barnfield Rd Burslem ST6 57 A7
Leek ST13 30 D4
Upper Tean ST10 92 E4
Barnfields Cl ST13 30 D4
Barnfields Ind Est ST13 30 D3
Barnfields La ST10 61 D2
Barnfields Prim Sch ST17 175 C6
Barnfield ST4 71 F6
Barnfield Way
Cannock WS12 211 A6
Stafford ST17 175 C6
Barngate St ST13 30 D5
Barn Gn WV3 265 F7
Barnhurst La WV8 239 E2
Barn La Brewood ST19 223 C7
Standon ST21 101 C5
Barnlea Gr ST3 90 A5
Barnmeadow Cl TF10 169 A3
Barnmeadow Rd TF10 169 A2
Barn Owl Dr WS3 243 F4
Barn Rd WS15 198 C4
Barns Cl WS9 244 F4
Barns Croft B74 257 B4
Barnsdale Cl ST4 88 C5
Barnswood Cl WS11 226 B8
Barnton Edge ST15 104 E3
Barn Way WS12 210 F4
Barnwell Cl ST14 111 A4
Barnwell Gr ST4 72 A1
Barnwood Rd WV8 239 E1
Baron Cl WS7 211 E1
Baron St ST4 284 A5
Baron's Way ST18 158 C8
Barracks La WS9,WS14 245 C8
Barracks Rd ST5 283 C2
Barracks Sq ST5 283 C2
Barracks Way 2 ST13 30 D6
Barrage Rd ST8 28 B7
Barrar Cl DY8 279 E8
Barratt Gdns ST2 58 B8
Barratts Croft DY5 271 C1
Barr Common Cl WS9 256 B3
Barr Common Rd WS9 256 B3
Barrett Cres ST6 57 A6
Barrett Dr ST6 57 A6
Barrie Gdns ST7 40 C8
Barrington Cl
Albrighton WV7 237 A5
Stretton DE13 147 C1
Wolverhampton WV10 240 C1
Barrington Ct ST5 56 E3
Barrow Cl WS9 244 F4
Barrow Hill Rd DY5 271 C1
Barr St DY3 271 C3
Barry Ave ST2 58 A4
Bartholomew Rd ST3 73 F1
Barthomley Rd Audley ST7 39 A2
Balterley ST7 38 F3
Barthomley CW2 38 B7
Hanley ST1 57 D6
Bartic Ave DY6 275 F4
Bartlem St ST3 284 D5
Bartlett Cl ST19 207 F8
Barton Cottage Hospl DE13 183 D1
Barton Cres ST6 41 E1
Barton Gate DE13 183 B2
Barton La Bradley ST18 191 A8
Kingswinford DY6 275 C8
Barton Lodge DE13 183 D1
Barton Rd WV4 266 F4
Barton's La TF9 112 B8
Barton's Rd TF9 112 B8
Barton St DE14 185 C8
Barton Turn DE13 184 A1
Bar Wlk WS9 245 C1
Barwood Ave ST7 25 A5
Basfordbridge La ST13 45 D4
Basfordbridge Terr ST13 45 E5
Basford La ST13 45 F8
Basford Lane Ind Est ST13 45 F8
Basford Park Rd ST5 56 D3
Basford View ST13 45 D6
Basford Villas ST5 56 D2
Basil Cl ST17 174 F5
Basildon Gr ST3 284 C2
Basin La B77 250 D3
Baskerville Rd ST1 282 C3
Baskeyfield Cl WS14 231 D7
Baskeyfield Pl ST6 42 B5
Baslow Cl WS3 243 C3
Baslow Gn DE11 186 E5
Baslow Rd WS3 243 B3
Basnett's Wood ST9 43 E6
Bass Cotts DE14 166 E4
Bassenthwaite Ct DY6 275 D6
Bassett Cl Cheadle ST10 76 D3
Wolverhampton WV4 265 C6
Bassilow Rd ST4 72 F7
Bass's Bldgs DE14 166 B3
Baswich Bsns Pk ST17 156 D2
Baswich Crest ST17 156 D1
Baswich House Dr ST17 175 D7
Baswich House Way ST17 175 D7
Baswich La ST17,ST18 156 D2
Batchelor Cl DY8 279 F8
Batch La DE6 127 B7
Bateman Ave ST8 27 B5
Batesmans Way ST14 126 C8
Batesway WS15 197 C4
Batfield La DY7 272 E2
Bath Ct ST17 285 B1
Bath La DY7 277 D5
Bath Mews DY8 279 F5
Batholdi Way ST17 175 A8
Bath Rd Cannock WS11 209 E5
Newcastle-u-L ST5 54 F2
Stourbridge DY8 279 F5
Baths La ST18 158 C8
Baths Pas ST3 284 B4
Baths Rd ST3 284 B4
Bath St Leek ST13 30 F6
Meir ST3 74 B5
Sedgley DY3 266 E1
Stoke-on-T ST4 72 A7
Bath Terr 9 ST4 72 A7
Bathurst St ST3 284 C4
Bath Vale Cotts CW12 6 A3
Batkin Cl ST6 42 B5
Batten Cl ST3 90 C7
Batten Wlk ST15 118 F6
Battisson Cres ST3 284 C2
Battlefield Hill WV5 270 B7
Battlefield La WV5 270 B6
Battlefield Terr WV5 270 B6
Battle Ridge ST18 156 D8
Battlesteads ST10 78 D1
Baulk La ST11 106 E8
Baxter Gn ST16 155 B4
Bayham Wlk ST2 58 A4
Bayley Hills TF10 168 A3
Baylie Ct DY8 279 F5
Baylie St DY8 279 F4
Bayliss Ct WV3 255 E2
Bayston Ave WV3 265 E8
Bayswater Rd
Dudley DY3 271 D2
Rugeley WS15 178 D1
Baytree Cl
Birches Head ST1 57 F6
Walsall WS3 243 A2
Baytree Rd WS3 243 A2
Baytree Wlk WS14 232 E6
Baywood Cl ST17 156 C1
Beach Ave WV14 266 F3
Beachcroft Rd DY6 270 C1
Beachwood Ave DY6 270 C1
Beacon Ctr for the Blind WV4 266 D4
Beacon Dr DE13 147 B3
Beaconfields 1 WS13 231 A8
Beacon Gdns WS13 214 A1
Beacon Hill WS9 256 C1
Beacon La Kinver DY7 277 B2
Romsley DY11,DY12,WV15 276 E3
Sedgley DY3 266 E1
Beacon Pas DY3 266 D1
Beacon Pk ST19 221 F7
Beacon Rd Aldridge WS9 256 B1
Rolleston on D DE13 147 B3
Stone ST15 120 A5
Beacon Rise
Aldridge WS9 256 B3
Sedgley DY3 266 E1
Stone ST15 120 A5
Beaconsfield Ave WV4 266 D5
Beaconsfield Dr
Stoke-on-T ST3 72 E1
Stoke-on-T ST3 88 E8
Wolverhampton WV4 266 D6
Beaconsfield ST5 56 C7
Beaconsfield Rd DE13 166 B7
Beaconside Cl ST16 156 A5
Beaconside Sports Ctr ST18 156 D4
Beaconside
Stafford,Beaconside ST16 156 B5
Stafford ST16 136 D1
Beacon St Lichfield WS13 231 A8
Wolverhampton WV14 266 F1
Beacon Trad Est WS9 256 A6
Beacon Way
Brownhills WS9 245 A3
Cannock WS12 210 F3
Beadnell Gr ST3 73 C1
Beale St DY8 279 F5
Bealeys Cl WS3 243 A3
Bealeys La WS3 243 A2
Beamhill Rd DE13 165 F8
Beamish La WV7,WV8 237 E5
Beard Gr ST2 58 B7
Bearnett Dr WV4 265 C2
Bearnett La WV4 265 B2

Bearstone Rd
Bearstone TF9 . . . . .83 A4
Knighton TF9 . . . . .83 C4
Norton in H TF9 . . . . .82 E3
Bearwood Hill Rd DE15 . .167 A3
Beasley Ave ST5 . . . . .55 F7
Beasley Pl ST5 . . . . .55 F7
Beata Rd ST5 . . . . .40 F1
Beat La Ryecroft Gate SK11 .18 A8
Woodhouse Green ST8 . . . . .17 E8
Beaton Rd B74 . . . . .258 A3
Beatrice Ct ST4 . . . . .72 A2
Beatrice Ct DE14 . . . . . . .166 B4
Beatrice Wlk ST8 . . . . .27 B2
Beattie Ave ST5 . . . . .283 B4
Beatty Dr CW12 . . . . .6 A4
Beatty Rd ST13 . . . . .31 A6
Beaubrook Gdns DY6 . . . .275 E3
Beauchamp Ind Pk B77 .261 D8
Beauchamp Rd B77 . . . . .261 F5
Beau Ct WS11 . . . . .209 F1
Beaudesert WS7 . . . . .212 A1
Beaudesert View WS12 . .211 A5
Beaufighter Gr ST6 . . . . . .41 C5
Beaufort Ave ST9 . . . . . . .59 A3
Beaufort Ct ST3 . . . . .73 F1
Beaufort Rd
Burton u T DE15. . . . . .167 B1
Longton ST3. . . . . .284 C2
Beaufort Way WS9 . . . . . .256 B4
Beaulieu Ave DY6 . . . . . . .275 F4
Beaulieu Cl ST9 . . . . .59 B3
Beaumaris Cl Dudley DY1 .271 F4
Stoke-on-T ST4 . . . . .71 D8
Beaumaris Ct ST4 . . . . . .283 A2
Beaumaris Rd TF10 . . . . .168 E3
Beaumont Cl Biddulph ST8 .16 D3
Great Wyrley WS6 . . . . . . .226 F2
Beaumont Ct ST5 . . . . . . .70 F3
Beaumont Gdns ST17 . . .174 B8
Beaumont Rd
Great Wyrley WS6 . . . . . . .226 F2
Stoke-on-T ST6 . . . . .41 E3
Beaumont Rise ST11 . . . . .90 D3
Beaumont Way WS11 . . . .228 A4
Beauty Bank Cres DY8 . .279 F6
Beauty Bank Prim Sch
DY8 . . . . .279 F6
Beaver Cl ST4 . . . . .71 E4
Beaver Dr ST10 . . . . .76 B2
Bebington Cl WV8 . . . . . .255 F8
Beckbury Ave WV4 . . . . . .265 C5
Beckdale ST14 . . . . .126 A8
Beckenham Cl ST3 . . . . . . .90 C8
Becket Cl Burton u T DE13 .166 B6
Sutton Coldfield B74 . . . . . .257 F6
Becket Ave ST3 . . . . .74 B1
Becketts Ct DE13 . . . . . . .166 C7
Beckfields Cl ST8 . . . . .17 B1
Beckford St ST1 . . . . .282 C4
Beckminster Rd WV3 . . . .265 F7
Beck's La DE13 . . . . .162 F2
Beck The B79 . . . . .216 E2
Beckton Ave ST6 . . . . .41 E3
Bedale Pl ST3 . . . . .72 A4
Bedcroft ST12 . . . . .88 F2
Beddow Way ST16 . . . . . . .41 F6
Bedford Cres ST5 . . . . .71 C4
Bedford Pl WS12 . . . . .210 B4
Bedford Rd
Burton u T DE15. . . . . .185 D7
Hanley ST1 . . . . .282 A1
Kidsgrove ST7 . . . . .26 A3
Bedford St ST1 . . . . .57 A2
Bedford Way WS15 . . . . . .196 D6
Bedingston Dr ST19 . . . . .208 A7
Bednall Barns ST17 . . . . .193 F8
Bednall Ct ST17 . . . . .193 F8
Bednall Rd ST17 . . . . .175 C1
Beecham Bsns Pk WS9 . .256 A8
Beecham Cl WS9 . . . . . . .256 A8
Beech Ave
Burton u T DE13. . . . . .166 F7
Cheddleton ST13 . . . . .45 C4
King's Bromley DE13 . . . . . .199 C6
Tamworth B77 . . . . .250 E3
Beech Cl Armitage WS15 . .198 C4
Biddulph ST8 . . . . .17 B1
Cheadle ST10. . . . . .76 F2
Dunsley DY7 . . . . .278 B4
Haughton ST18 . . . . .172 F5
Beechcliff La ST4,ST12 . . .87 D2
Beech Cl Leek ST13. . . . . . .30 C2
Newport TF10 . . . . .168 F1
Pattingham WV6 . . . . .253 C2
Sedgley DY3. . . . . .266 E1
Sutton Coldfield B75 . . . . . .258 A4
Tamworth B79 . . . . .250 A8
Uttoxeter ST14 . . . . .126 A8
Weston Aston ST19 . . . . . . .205 C6
Beech Cres WS7 . . . . .11 E3
Beechcroft Ave ST16 . . . .155 C1
Beechcroft ST12 . . . . .88 F2
Beechcroft Cres ST4 . . . .256 D1
Beechcroft B74 . . . . .258 A1
Beechcroft Grange ST16 .155 C1
Beech Croft Madeley CW3 .68 E2
Pattingham WV6 . . . . .253 C2
Beech Ct Cannock WS12 . .210 B7
Great Wyrley WS6 . . . . . . .227 A7
Stone ST15 . . . . .120 B8
Beechdale La
Beech ST4,ST12. . . . . .87 D1

Beechdale La continued
Tittensor ST12. . . . . .103 E8
Beech Dr Burton u T DE13 .166 E8
Talke ST7 . . . . .40 E8
Beechen Gr WS7. . . . . . . .228 F8
Beeches Cl DY6 . . . . .275 D5
Beeches Croft WS13 . . . .215 D7
Beeches Mews DY9 . . . . .281 F4
Beeches Rd WS15. . . . . . .197 A6
Beeches The
Newcastle-u-L ST5. . . . . . . .56 C7
Rugeley WS15 . . . . .178 D3
Sutton Coldfield,Little Aston
B74. . . . . .257 D4
Beechfield Dr ST17 . . . . . .175 D5
Beechfield Rd ST4 . . . . . . .88 B6
Beechfield Rise WS14. . . .231 D8
Beechfields ST12 . . . . .88 F2
Beechfields Way TF10. . . .168 F5
Beech Gate B74 . . . . .257 C5
Beech Gdns Cannock WV8 .238 F2
Lichfield WS14. . . . . .231 C6
Beech Gr
Huntington WS12. . . . . . . .209 D8
Leek ST13. . . . . .30 C6
Loggerheads TF9 . . . . .99 E5
Newcastle-u-L ST5. . . . . . . .56 C4
Stoke-on-T ST4 . . . . .72 C5
Swadlincote DE11 . . . . . . .186 F7
Beech Ho B74 . . . . .257 B5
Beechhouse La WV5 . . . . .264 A1
Beech Hurst Gdns WV5 . .264 A2
Beech La Burton u T DE13 .166 E8
Coppenhall ST18 . . . . .174 C3
Stretton DE13 . . . . .147 E1
Beechlawn Dr DY7 . . . . . .278 E7
Beechmere Rise WS15 . . .178 B2
Beechmount Gr ST1. . . . . .57 F6
Beechmount Rise 🔟
ST17. . . . . .175 C7
Beech Pine Cl WS12 . . . . .210 A8
Beech Rd
Barton-u-N DE13 . . . . .183 D1
Ecclesall ST21. . . . . .133 E6
Kingswinford DY6 . . . . .275 E5
Stoke-on-T ST3 . . . . .72 F1
Stourbridge DY8 . . . . .279 F3
Tamworth B79 . . . . .250 A8
Wolverhampton WV10 . . . . .240 B1
Beech St Burton u T DE14 .166 B1
Longton ST3. . . . . .284 C3
Beech Tree Cl DY6 . . . . . .275 A8
Beech Tree La WS11 . . . .226 D8
Beechtree La DY10. . . . . .280 E6
Beech Tree Rd WS9 . . . . .244 F3
Beechway ST16. . . . . .155 D6
Beech Wlk WS15 . . . . . . .198 A1
Beechwood Bsns Pk
WS11. . . . . .210 B3
Beechwood Cl
Blythe Bridge ST11. . . . . . . .91 A6
Newcastle-u-L ST5. . . . . . . .71 D1
Walsall WS3 . . . . .243 B3
Beechwood Cres ST5 . . . .250 F5
Beechwood Croft B74. . . .257 D5
Beechwood Ct WV6 . . . . .255 C3
Beechwood Dr
Stone ST15 . . . . .120 A6
Wolverhampton WV6. . . . . .255 A2
Beechwood WS14. . . . . . .232 E5
Beecroft Ave WS13. . . . . .214 B1
Beecroft Rd WS11 . . . . . .209 E2
Beecroft Hill Sch WS11 . .209 E2
Beecroft Rd WS11 . . . . . .209 E1
Beekes Croft B78 . . . . . . .261 A8
Bee La WV10 . . . . .240 D3
Beelow La ST10 . . . . .78 D6
Bees La WS15 . . . . .178 D8
Beeston Rd DY10. . . . . . . .280 B5
Beeston Ridge ST17 . . . . .174 B7
Beeston St ST3 . . . . .73 C5
Beeston View ST17. . . . . . .41 A7
Beffcote Rd ST20 . . . . . . .171 B4
Beggars Bush La WV5. . . .270 B5
Beggars La ST13. . . . . .30 C5
Beighterton Farm Barns
TF11. . . . . .203 F4
Beighterton La TF11 . . . . .203 F3
Beighton Cl B74 . . . . .257 F6
Belbroughton Rd
Blakedown DY10 . . . . .281 D1
Stourbridge DY8 . . . . .279 E3
Belfast St ST5 . . . . .42 B2
Belfield Ave ST5 . . . . .56 C4
Belford Rd ST4. . . . . .56 F1
Belfort Way ST17 . . . . . . .175 A8
Belfry Dr ST4 . . . . .284 C3
Belfry Dr DY9 . . . . .279 E6
Belfry The Perton WV6. . . .254 D4
Stretton DE13 . . . . .147 C1
Belgrade Rd WV10 . . . . . .240 B1
Belgrave Ave ST3 . . . . . . .284 B2
Belgrave CE Prim Sch
ST3. . . . . .73 D1
Belgrave Cres ST3 . . . . . .284 C1
Belgrave Ct DY6 . . . . .275 B7
Belgrave High Sch B77 . .250 E1
Belgrave Rd Longton ST3. .284 C1
Newcastle-u-L ST5. . . . . . .283 C2
Tamworth B77 . . . . .261 D8
Belgrove Ho WS11 . . . . . .209 D1
Bellamour La WS15,ST17 .178 C6
Bellamour Way WS15 . . . .178 F5
Bellaport Rd TF9. . . . . .82 A4
Bellassis St ST3 . . . . .73 D2
Bell Ave ST3. . . . . .73 D2
Bellbrook ST19 . . . . .192 F1
Bell Cl Lichfield WS13 . . . .213 F1

Bell Cl continued
Stafford ST16 . . . . .155 F5
Bell Cotts DE6 . . . . .127 D8
Bell Dr WS12 . . . . .210 C7
Bellefield View ST5 . . . . . .56 C3
Bellencroft Gdns WV3. . . .265 C7
Bellerton La ST6. . . . . .42 E2
Belle Vue Ct DY8 . . . . . . .275 D2
Belle Vue ST13. . . . . .30 D6
Belle Vue Prim Sch DY8. .275 C3
Belle Vue ST13 . . . . .30 D6
Belle Vue DY8 . . . . .275 D2
Bellevue St WV14. . . . . . .266 F2
Bellflower Cl WV10 . . . . . .241 A7
Bell Heather Rd WS8. . . . .244 D6
Bell Ho ST3 . . . . .284 B6
Bellhouse La DE13 . . . . . .164 E6
Bellhurst La ST19 . . . . . . .205 A5
Bellingham Gr ST1. . . . . . .57 D6
Bellingham B77 . . . . .251 D1
Bella La Barlaston ST12 . . .88 E4
Barton-u-N DE13 . . . . .183 D2
Doveridge DE6 . . . . .127 C8
Walsall,Wallington Heath
WS3 . . . . .243 B1
Belman's Yd TF10 . . . . . . .168 F2
Bell Orch TF9. . . . . .100 C5
Bell Pl WV2 . . . . .266 C8
Bell Rd WV5 . . . . .264 D1
Bellringer St ST8 . . . . .27 C7
Bellringer Rd ST4. . . . . . . .88 D7
Bells End Rd DE12 . . . . . .184 D1
Bell's Hollow ST5. . . . . . . .40 E3
Bellsize Cl WS11 . . . . .227 F5
Bells La Burntwood WS7 . .211 F1
Stourbridge DY8 . . . . .275 D2
Bell St ST9 . . . . .279 F5
Bellwood Cl ST3 . . . . .90 A5
Belmont Ave WS11. . . . . . .209 C2
Belmont Cl Aldridge WS9 . .256 A7
Great Wyrley WS11 . . . . . . .227 A4
Belmont Rd Hanley ST1. . . .57 A3
Ipstones ST10 . . . . .60 E6
Tamworth B77 . . . . .261 E7
Wolverhampton WV4 . . . . . .266 A5
Belmot Rd DE13 . . . . .145 F1
Belper Rd WS3 . . . . .243 C3
Belsay Cl ST3. . . . . .284 C4
Belsize B77. . . . . .250 E2
Belton Ave WV11 . . . . .241 B1
Belt Rd WS12,WS11. . . . . .210 A5
Belvedere Ave WV4 . . . . . .266 B5
Belvedere Cl
Burntwood WS7. . . . . .228 F5
Kingswinford DY6 . . . . .275 F4
Stafford ST17 . . . . .175 C8
Belvedere Gdns WV6. . . . .255 E7
Belvedere Jun Sch DE14 .166 B5
Belvedere Rd
Burton u T DE14. . . . . .166 A6
Stoke-on-T ST4 . . . . .72 A1
Belvide Gdns WV8 . . . . . .238 F4
Belvoir Ave ST4. . . . . .88 A6
Belvoir Cl Burton u T DE13 .166 B5
Dudley DY1 . . . . .271 E2
Belvoir Rd DE13 . . . . .166 A5
Belvoir B77. . . . . .261 C7
Belwell La B74 . . . . .258 A2
Bemersley Rd
Chell Heath ST6 . . . . .27 C1
Stoke-on-T ST6 . . . . .42 E6
Benches Cl WS7 . . . . .228 D6
Bencroft WS8. . . . . .239 B4
Bend Oak Dr DE15 . . . . . .167 C4
Bend Oak Jun Sch DE15 .167 C3
Benedict Pl ST2 . . . . .56 A3
Benenden Cl ST17 . . . . . .156 B1
Benfleet Pl ST3. . . . . .284 A3
Bengal Gr ST4 . . . . .88 C8
Bengry Rd ST3 . . . . .73 E2
Benion Rd WS11 . . . . .209 F5
Benjamins Way ST7 . . . . . .39 F2
Bennett Pl ST15 . . . . .104 B8
Bennett Rd B74. . . . . .257 F6
Bennetts La Bosley SK11. . . .7 E6
Bramshall ST14 . . . . .125 C6
Bennett's La WS14 . . . . . .253 F1
Bennetts La WV6 . . . . . . .263 F7
Bennett St ST6. . . . . .56 E2
Bennington Way WS14 . . .231 D8
Bennion Rd ST14. . . . . .95 E5
Bennion St ST3 . . . . .284 C3
Benson Ave WV4. . . . . . . .266 D5
Benson Cl Lichfield WS13 .214 F1
Perton WV6. . . . . .254 E5
Benson St ST6 . . . . .41 F5
Benson View B79 . . . . . . .250 C8
Bentilee Prim Sch ST2. . . .73 D8
Bent La Astbury CW12. . . . .15 A8
Whitmore ST5. . . . . .86 A4
Bentley Ave ST5 . . . . .56 B4
Bentley Brook La WS12 . .211 A6
Bentley Cl ST15. . . . . .104 E3
Bentley Rd Stoke-on-T ST6. .42 C5
Uttoxeter ST14 . . . . .110 F1
Wolverhampton WV10 . . . . .240 E2
Bentleys Rd TF9 . . . . .112 A8
Bentley Way B79. . . . . . . .249 F7
Benton Cres WS3 . . . . . . .243 D2
Benton's La ST10 . . . . . . .109 B4
Bentygrange La ST13 . . . .48 D3
Beowulf Covert DE13 . . . .147 B1
Berdmore St ST4 . . . . . . .284 A5

Beresford Cres ST5 . . . . . .71 A6
Beresford Dale
Madeley CW3 . . . . .68 D6
Swadlincote DE11 . . . . . . .186 F2
Beresford La SK17 . . . . . . .24 C2
Beresford Meml CE Fst Sch
ST13. . . . . .31 B7
Beresford St ST4 . . . . .90 A6
Bergamot Dr ST3 . . . . .90 A6
Berkeley Cl Gnosall ST20 .171 E7
Perton WV6. . . . . .254 F3
Berkeley Dr DY6 . . . . .275 C7
Berkeley St Hanley ST1 . . .282 C2
Stone ST15 . . . . .104 F2
Berkeley Way WS15 . . . . .178 A1
Berkshire Gr ST5 . . . . .71 C5
Berkshire The WS5 . . . . . .243 A3
Berkswell Cl Dudley DY1 . .271 E3
Sutton Coldfield B74 . . . . . .257 E4
Berkswich CE Prim Sch
ST17. . . . . .175 C6
Bernard Cheadle Cl
ST15. . . . . .103 C4
Bernard Gr ST3. . . . . .89 F4
Bernard St ST2 . . . . .282 C2
Berne Ave ST5 . . . . .70 E6
Bernwall Cl DY8 . . . . .279 F4
Berrisford Cl TF9 . . . . .97 E1
Berrisford Rd TF9. . . . . . . .97 E1
Berrybush Gdns DY3 . . . . .271 E7
Berryfield Gr ST3 . . . . .73 F4
Berry Ave WS12 . . . . .99 C6
Berry Gdns DE15. . . . . . . .167 B8
Berry Hedge La DE15 . . . .167 C4
Berry Hill W12. . . . . .210 C4
Berry Hill High Sch ST2. . .58 A1
Berry Hill Rd ST4 . . . . .57 E1
Berry Hill Village ST2 . . . .58 A1
Berry La ST3 . . . . .284 B3
Berry St ST6 . . . . .72 B7
Bertelin Rd ST16. . . . . . . .155 F7
Bert Smith Way TF9 . . . . . .97 C2
Berwick Dr WS11 . . . . .226 B8
Berwick Rd ST1 . . . . .57 E8
Berwick Wlks ST5 . . . . . . .70 F7
Berwyn Gr WS6 . . . . .226 F3
Besom Way WS5 . . . . .226 C2
Best Ave DE15 . . . . .167 B1
Best St ST4. . . . . .72 F5
Beswick Cl ST10 . . . . .76 D1
Beswick Rd ST6. . . . . .41 F6
Beswicks La TF9 . . . . .82 C2
Bethany Ct DE15 . . . . .185 E7
Bethany Mews 🔟 WS11 . .209 F4
Bethell Rd ST1 . . . . .57 D7
Bethesda St ST1 . . . . .282 C1
Bethesda St ST1 . . . . .282 B2
Betjeman Pl WV10 . . . . . .241 A1
Betjeman Wlk ST17 . . . . .174 C7
Betley CE Prim Sch CW3. .53 B6
Betley Hall Gdns CW3. . . . .53 A6
Betley Pl ST5 . . . . .71 C6
Betlingspring La DE6 . . . . .81 D3
Beton Rd ST16 . . . . .155 D8
Betony Rd DE15 . . . . .167 C2
Bettany Glade WV10 . . . . .240 E4
Bettany Rd ST6. . . . . .57 A7
Betton Rd TF9 . . . . .97 E7
Betty Hatch La ST16 . . . . .155 C5
Betty's La WS11 . . . . .228 A4
Beulah Dr TF9 . . . . .97 B1
Bevan Ave Talke Pits ST7 . .40 E6
Wolverhampton WV4. . . . . .266 E4
Bevan Cl WS4 . . . . .244 C1
Bevandean Cl ST4 . . . . . . .88 C5
Bevan Lee Rd WS11 . . . . .209 D3
Bevan Pl CW3 . . . . .68 E7
Beveridge Cl ST3 . . . . .74 B2
Beverley Cl ST19 . . . . .207 F7
Beverley Cres
Forsbrook ST11. . . . . .91 A8
Wolverhampton WV4. . . . . .266 F4
Beverley Dr Bucknall ST2. .58 D2
Kingswinford DY6 . . . . .275 C7
Stafford ST16 . . . . .155 C8
Beverley Hill WS12. . . . . . .210 D6
Beverley Rd DE14 . . . . . . .185 A7
Beverston Rd WV6 . . . . . .255 A4
Beville St ST4 . . . . .72 E6
Bevin La ST4 . . . . .58 A3
Bewcastle Gr ST3 . . . . .90 A7
Bewick Ct WV6 . . . . .255 C2
Bew St ST6. . . . . .42 E5
Bexhill Gr ST1 . . . . .57 F6
Bexley St ST1. . . . . .282 A4
Beyer Cl B77 . . . . .251 A2
Bhylls Acre Prim Sch
WV3 . . . . .265 B7
Bhylls Cres WV3 . . . . .265 C7
Bhylls La WV3 . . . . .265 C7
Bibbey's Gn WV10 . . . . . .240 F4
Bickford Cl ST19 . . . . .206 A6
Bickford Rd ST19 . . . . . . .206 B7
Bickley Ho B74 . . . . .257 E5
Bickley Ho ST4 . . . . .72 A1
Bida La CW12. . . . . .16 B8
Biddles La ST12 . . . . .102 D4
Biddulph Common Rd
ST8. . . . . .17 A7
Biddulph Grange Ctry Pk⋆
ST8. . . . . .17 A6
Biddulph Grange Gdn⋆
ST8. . . . . .16 E3
Biddulph High Sch ST8 . . .27 D5
Biddulph Park Rd ST8 . . . .17 A5

Biddulph Rd
Congleton CW12 . . . . .16 B8
Mow Cop ST7 . . . . .26 F6
Stoke-on-T ST8 . . . . .42 B7
Biddulph St CW12 . . . . . . .16 C7
Bideford Ave ST17 . . . . . .175 D8
Bideford Way WS11 . . . . . .226 B8
Bideford Way WS11 . . . . . .254 E5
Bignall End Rd ST7 . . . . . . .40 A4
Bigsbury Wlk 🔟 ST6 . . . . .56 F7
Bigwood La ST18 . . . . .173 F4
Bilberry Bank WS11 . . . . .209 E6
Bilberry Cl WS15. . . . . . . .178 C1
Bilberry Gr WV8 . . . . .239 B3
Bilberry Cres WS12 . . . . . .209 C5
Bilbrook CE Mid Sch
WV8 . . . . .239 B3
Bilbrook Ct WV8 . . . . .239 B3
Bilbrook Gr WV8. . . . . . . .239 B3
Bilbrook Rd WV8 . . . . .239 B4
Bilbrook Sta WV8 . . . . . . .239 A2
Billinge St ST5 . . . . .56 E8
Billington Ave ST18 . . . . . .158 D1
Billington Bank ST18. . . . .173 D6
Billy Buns La WV5 . . . . . . .270 B8
Billy Wright Cl WV4. . . . . .265 D6
Bilston Rd WV2. . . . . .266 F8
Bilston St DY3 . . . . .271 E8
Bilton St ST4 . . . . .72 A6
Bingley Ent Ctr WV3 . . . . .266 A8
Bingley St WV3 . . . . .266 A8
Birchall Ave ST6 . . . . .41 C5
Birchall Cl ST13 . . . . .30 F2
Birchall La ST13 . . . . .30 F2
Birchall Park Ave ST13 . . .30 F3
Bircham Wlk ST5. . . . . . . .71 B2
Birch Ave Biddulph ST8. . . .27 A6
Brownhills WS8 . . . . .244 E8
Burntwood WS7 . . . . .228 F6
Cannock WS11 . . . . .228 C8
Swadlincote DE11 . . . . . . .186 F7
Birchbrook Ind Pk WS14 .246 E6
Birch Brook La WS14. . . . .246 E6
Birch Bsns Pk WS11 . . . . .226 F6
Birch Cl Burton u T DE14. .185 A8
Denstone ST14 . . . . .95 D6
Great Haywood ST18 . . . . . .158 C2
Walton-on-t-H ST17 . . . . . .175 F6
Birch Coppice WV5 . . . . . .269 E6
Birch Croft WV9. . . . . .256 C8
Birchcroft WV9 . . . . .224 C1
Birch Dale CW3. . . . . .68 E6
Birchdown Ave ST6 . . . . . . .42 B3
Birch Dr Little Aston B74. .257 D5
Stourbridge DY8 . . . . .279 E6
Birchendale La ST10 . . . . .92 F2
Birchenfields La ST10. . . .75 F5
Birchenwood Rd ST6. . . . . .26 E1
Birchenwood Way ST7 . . . .26 C1
Birches Ave WV8 . . . . .239 C1
Birches Barn Ave WV3. . . .265 F7
Birches Barn Rd WV3 . . . .265 F7
Birches Cl DE13 . . . . .166 D8
Birches Farm Mews CW3. .68 F5
Birches Head High Sch
ST1. . . . . .57 F7
Birches Head Rd
Bucknall ST2. . . . . .58 A7
Stoke-on-T ST1. . . . . .57 E6
Birches Park Rd WV8 . . . .239 A2
Birches The ST10 . . . . .76 D2
Birches Valley Forest Ctr &
Wlk⋆ WS15. . . . . .195 F7
Birches Valley WS15. . . . . .195 D6
Birches Way ST7 . . . . .26 B2
Birchfield Ave WV8. . . . . . .254 B6
Birchfield Cl DY9 . . . . .262 C1
Birchfield Rd Bucknall ST2 .58 C6
Burton u T DE15. . . . . .185 A6
Birchfield Sch WV7 . . . . . .237 D5
Birchfields Cl WS15 . . . . .119 F6
Birchfields Dr WS12. . . . . .210 D1
Birchgate ST2 . . . . .58 C4
Birchgate Gr ST2 . . . . .58 C4
Birchglade WV3 . . . . .255 D1
Birch Gr B78 . . . . .262 D7
Birch Green Gr ST1 . . . . . . .57 E7
Birch Ho B74 . . . . .257 B5
Birch Hill Ave WV5. . . . . . .269 F5
Birch Ho B74. . . . . .257 B5
Birch House La
Cotes ST15 . . . . .103 A1
Millmeece ST21. . . . . .117 F8
Birch House Rd
Newcastle-u-L ST5. . . . . . . .55 D8
Birch House Way ST15 . . .118 A8
Birchill Pl WV5 . . . . .269 F5
Birch La WS9 . . . . .245 D1
Rugeley WS15 . . . . .197 A5
Walsall WS4 . . . . .244 C1
Birchmoor La ST20 . . . . . .209 E3
Birchmoor Rd B78. . . . . . .262 F8
Birchover Way ST6 . . . . . . .42 A8
Sedgley DY3. . . . . .266 F1
Stone ST15 . . . . .120 B8
Wolverhampton WV11. . . . .241 F1
Birch Rise TF9 . . . . .99 E3
Birch St ST5 . . . . .57 E5
Birch Terr
Burntwood WS7. . . . . .212 A1
Hanley ST1 . . . . .282 B2

Birchtree Dr ST13........45 C8
Birch Tree Gdns WS9...256 B5
Birchtree La WS15....196 E6
Birch Tree La
　The Bank ST7.........26 B8
　Whitmore ST5........85 C7
Birch Valley Rd ST7....26 C1
Birch Wlk ST3.........73 A1
Birchwood Ave B78....262 F7
Birchwood Cl WV11....242 A3
Birchwood Prim Sch
　B78.................262 F7
Birchwood Rd
　Lichfield WS14.......231 F7
　Wolverhampton WV4..266 A4
Birchwood Rise WS15...161 B5
Birchwood Wlk DY6....275 E8
Bird Cage Wlk ST1.....282 B2
Birdhope B77..........251 C1
Bird Rd ST3...........74 B2
Bird's Barn La DY11....277 C2
Birds Bush Prim Sch
　B77.................261 E8
Birds Bush Rd B77.....261 F8
Birdsgrove La DE6.....66 D3
Bird St Dudley DY3.....271 C3
　Lichfield WS14.......231 B7
Birkdale Ave DE14.....185 A6
Birkdale Cl DY8.......279 F2
Birkdale Dr Kidsgrove ST7..26 C3
　Stafford ST16.......156 C3
Birkdale Rd WS3.......243 A3
Birkholme Dr ST3.......90 A5
Birks Dr TF9..........99 E5
Birks St ST4..........72 B5
Birmingham New Rd
　WV4................266 E4
Birmingham Rd
　Aldridge WS9........256 A4
　Blakedown DY10......281 C2
　Lichfield WS14.......231 A4
　Shenstone WS14......247 C4
　Wolverhampton WV2...266 D7
Birrell St ST4.........72 F5
Biscay Gr ST4.........88 C8
Bishop Cl WS11.......209 D2
Bishop Ct ST2.........58 B5
Bishop Rawle CE Prim Sch
　ST10................76 D3
Bishop Rd ST16........42 B5
Bishop's Cl ST17.......48 D8
Bishops Ct ST21......133 E7
Bishops Dr ST19......223 D7
Bishops Grange WS15..178 F2
Bishops La TF9........97 B1
Bishops Mdw B75......258 E3
Bishop Stamer CE Prim Sch
　ST4.................72 B6
Bishops St ST4........73 A5
Bishops Way B74......257 F6
Bishton La ST17,ST18..178 A6
Bitham Cl ST3........207 F8
Bitham Ct DE13.......147 C1
Bitham La ST3........147 D1
Bittell Cl WV10.......240 E4
Bitterne Pl ST2........73 D8
Bittern La TF9.........76 E3
Bitterscote La B78....250 A2
Black Bank Rd ST13....44 D5
Blackbank Rd ST5......55 C4
Blackberry La
　Brownhills WS9......245 B4
　Stafford ST16........155 E4
　Sutton Coldfield B74..257 E4
Blackberry Way S120...151 D8
Blackbird Way
　[1] Packmoor ST7......26 F1
　Biddulph ST8.........27 E8
　Stoke-on-T ST7........41 F8
Blackbrook Ave ST5....55 D8
Blackbrook Way WV10..240 E4
Blackbrook Zoological Pk*
　ST13................48 A4
Blackburn Ave WS6....255 F7
Blackdown B77........251 C1
Black Dr ST18.........157 C6
Blackflats Rd ST15....103 C1
Blackfriars Cl B79....249 E5
Blackfriars F Ed Unit ST2..58 B5
Blackfriar's Rd ST5....283 B2
Blackfriars Sch ST5....283 B2
Blackhalve La WV11....241 D2
Blackheath Cl ST3.....73 D3
Blackheath La ST18....156 E4
Blackhole La ST18.....154 D2
Blackhorse La ST3.....282 B3
Blackie's La Stone ST15..120 D6
　Stone ST15...........120 D7
Blacklake Dr ST3.......90 A4
Black La Sutton TF10...150 E1
　Whiston ST18.........50 A1
Blackmere Cl TF10.....168 D2
Blackpit La
　Doveridge DE6........127 B8
　Orton WV4............264 E3
Blackpool Cl ST4......185 C8
Blackroot Cl WS7......229 D4
Blackshaw Cl ST4......6 B1
Blackshaw Grange Cvn Pk
　ST13................120 C3
Blackshaw Moor CE Prim
　Sch ST13............20 D5
Blacksmith Dr [7] B75..26 E7
Blacksmith La WS14...232 D1
Blacksmiths Cl DE12..219 F7
Blacksmith's La
　Eggington DE65.......148 A6

Blacksmith's La continued
　Newton Solney DE15...167 E8
Blackthorn Ave WS7....22 B8
Blackthorn Cres WS12..211 A6
Blackthorne Cl DY1....271 F4
Blackthorne Rd
　Dudley DY1..........271 F5
　Lichfield WS14.......231 D7
Blackthorn Pl ST5......55 D8
Blackthorn Rd
　Burton u T DE15......185 E6
　Stourbridge DY8......275 F1
Blackwell's Row ST6....57 B6
Blackwood Pl ST3......73 E4
Blackwood Rd
　Aldridge B74.........256 E1
　Tamworth B77........261 C7
Blackwood Sch B74....256 E1
Bladon Ave ST5........71 B3
Bladon Cl ST6.........42 A8
Bladon House Sch DE15..167 B6
Bladon St DE15.......167 C4
Bladon's Yd DE13.....147 B4
Bladon View
　Burton u T DE13......148 A2
　Stretton DE13........147 F2
Blaizefield Cl CW3.....67 C2
Blake Cl WS11........210 A5
Blakedown CE Fst Sch
　DY10................281 C1
Blakedown Sta DY10...281 C2
Blakeley Ave WV6.....255 F7
Blakeley Heath Dr WV5..270 A5
Blakeley Heath Prim Sch
　WV5................270 A5
Blakeley La ST10.......63 A2
Blakeley Rise WV6....255 F7
Blakelow La DE6.......65 B1
Blakelow Rd ST2.......58 B6
Blakemore Rd WS9.....245 A3
Blakenall Heath WS3...243 D1
Blakeney Ave
　Newcastle-u-ST5......71 B3
　Stourbridge DY8......279 D6
Blakeney Cl DY3......271 C8
Blakenhall Gdns WV2...266 D7
Blakenhall Ind Est WV2..266 B7
Blake St ST6..........56 F8
Blake Street Sta B74...257 F6
Blake Valley Tech Coll
　WS12...............209 F6
Blakeways Cl B79......217 C5
Blakiston St ST16.....285 C4
Blanchard Cl ST3......90 C7
Blandford Dr DY8.....275 D5
Blandford Gdns WS7...29 C6
Blanefield WV8........239 E2
Blanford Mere Prim Sch
　DY8................275 E8
Blantyre St ST4.......284 C2
Blantyre Wlk ST3......284 C2
Blatchford Cl ST3......74 B2
Blaydon Ave ST3......73 A6
Blaydon Rd WV9,WV10..240 A1
Blaze Hill Rd DY4.....275 A8
Blaze Pk DY6..........275 B8
Bleak House Dr WS7...258 D8
Bleakridge Ave ST5....56 B8
Bleak St ST5..........56 D3
Bleeding Wolf La ST7...25 E5
Blencarn Gr ST9.......43 C4
Blenheim Cl
　Burton u T DE15......167 C3
　Stafford ST18........156 D3
　Tamworth B77........250 C4
Blenheim Ho DE14.....184 F7
Blenheim Rd
　Burntwood WS7......229 A8
　Kingswinford DY6.....275 D5
　Norton Canes WS11...228 B4
Blenheim St ST4.......72 D5
Blenheim Way
　Dudley DY1..........271 E2
　Fradley WS13........215 C5
Bleriot Cl ST3.........99 C7
Blessed Mother Teresa's RC
　Prim Sch ST17.......174 C8
Blessed William Howard RC
　Sch ST17............285 A1
Bletchley Dr B77......261 C8
Blewitt St WV12.......210 B7
Blithbury Rd Colton WS15..179 B3
　Hamstall Ridware WS15..180 E2
Blithe View ST11.......90 F6
Blithfield Cl ST9.......59 A2
Blithfield Ho ST17....174 F6
Blithfield Pl WS11....210 B1
Bloomfield Cl WV5.....269 D6
Bloomfield Dr WV12....242 D1
Bloomfield Way ST4....242 D8
Bloomsbury St [2] WV2..266 C8
Bloomsbury Way WS11..231 E7
Blore Rd TF9..........98 E1
Blossomfield Cl DY6...275 E8
Blount Cl ST10.......207 F7
Blount's Dr ST14......126 A6
Bloxwich CE Prim Sch
　WS3................243 B1
Bloxwich North Sta WS3..242 F2
Bloxwich Sta WS3.....243 A1
Bluebell Cl Biddulph ST8..27 F7
　Cannock WS12........210 B6
　Stourbridge DY8......275 D1
　Tittensor ST12........103 E8

Bluebell Dr ST5........71 A4
Bluebell Hollow ST17...175 F7
Bluebell La WS4.......227 A1
Bluebell Rd WS9......245 B3
Bluebird Cl WS14......211 A6
Blue Cedars Dr DE15...167 D2
Blue Cedars DY8.......279 C6
Blue House Barns TF10..168 E4
Blue House La WV7....237 B7
Bluestone Ave ST6.....42 B2
Bluestone La DE15.....186 A7
Bluestones Cl ST13....20 E4
Blundies La DY7......273 D3
Blunt's Hollow WS15,
　DE13...............162 A4
Blunt St ST5..........56 D4
Blurton Cotts ST3......72 E1
Blurton High Sch ST3...88 E8
Blurton Prim Sch ST3...72 E2
Blurton Priory ST3.....88 F8
Blurton Rd Barlaston ST12..89 A4
　Stoke-on-T ST3.......72 D1
Blymhill Lawn La TF11..204 C3
Blymhill Marsh TF11...203 F6
Blythe Ave ST3........90 A5
Blythebridge Bank ST14,
　ST18...............141 A7
Blythe Bridge High Sch
　ST11................90 D7
Blythe Bridge Rd
　Burntwood WS7......229 D6
　Stoke-on-T ST11......74 E1
Blythe Bridge Sta ST11..90 F7
Blythe Ct
　Blythe Bridge ST11....90 D7
　Burntwood WS7......229 D6
Blythe Gdns WV8......238 F4
Blythe Lodge ST11.....90 D7
Blythe Mount Pk ST11..91 A7
Blythe Pk ST11........91 D3
Blythe Rd
　Blythe Bridge ST11....91 A7
　Stafford ST17.......174 E6
Blythe St ST7.........250 C4
Blythe View
　Hamstall Ridware WS15..180 F2
　Saverley Green ST11...91 A2
Blythe Way ST11......229 F1
　Weston ST18.........138 C3
Boardman's La WS14...244 E2
Boatyard Cotts ST12...104 D8
Bode Bsns Pk ST13....31 A1
Bodiam Ct WV6.......255 A3
Bodicote Gr B75......258 E3
Bodington Cl WS7.....250 A7
Bodington Rd B75.....258 B3
Bodmin Ave ST17.....175 D8
Bodmin Wlk ST16......42 D1
Bognop Rd WV11......241 D4
Bogs La ST11..........90 F6
Bolberry Cl ST3........72 E1
Bold St ST1...........57 E5
Bolebridge Mews B79...250 B5
Bolebridge St B79.....250 C4
Bolehall Ho B77......250 C4
Boley Cl WS14........231 D7
Boley Cottage La WS14..231 E7
Boley La WS14........231 D7
Boleyn Cl WS6........226 D1
Boley Park Ctr WS14...231 E7
Bolina Gr ST3.........73 B6
Bollin Gr ST8.........16 E1
Bolney Gr ST1.........57 F5
Bolsover Cl ST6........42 A8
Bolton Pl ST3.........89 F8
Bolton Way WS3......242 F3
Boma Rd ST4...........87 F8
Bond End DE13........182 A4
Bondfield La DE13.....181 F2
Bondfield Way ST3....74 B2
Bond St Burton u T DE14..166 D1
Bondway WS12........269 D6
Bonehill Ind Est B78...249 F1
Bonehill Rd B78.......249 F1
Boney Hay Prim Sch
　WS7................211 F1
Boney Hay Rd WS7....229 B7
Boningale Way ST17...174 B8
Bonington Cres ST16...155 C2
Bonnard Cl ST3.......90 C6
Bonner Cl ST4.........71 E4
Bonville Gdns WV10...240 E4
Boon Cl WS14.........231 D7
Boon Gr ST17.........174 A7
Boon Hill Rd ST7.......39 F1
Boons Ind Est ST18....154 E1
Booth St WS14........214 A0
Boothen CE Prim Sch
　ST4.................72 A5
Boothen Green ST4.....72 B5
Boothen Old Rd ST4...72 B5
Boothen Rd ST4.......72 B6
Boothenwood Terr ST4..72 A5
Booth La ST11.........140 E3
Boothroyd St ST4......282 B2

Booth St Audley ST7....39 D1
　Cannock WS12........210 B6
　Newcastle-u-L ST5....55 F6
Boothstone Gdns ST15..118 F6
Booth St ST4..........72 B6
Boothen Ct DY10......280 A1
Bordeaux Cl ST3.......70 F3
Bordeaux Rd ST3......90 F3
Bordeaux Wlk ST5.....70 F3
Borden Cl
　Wheaton Aston ST19..205 C7
　Wolverhampton WV8..255 F8
Border Way ST17......174 E6
Bore St WS13.........231 B7
Borman B79...........282 C4
Borough Cres DY8.....279 E5
Borough La WS15.....212 E8
Borough Mus & Art Gal The*
　ST5.................283 C4
Borough Rd
　Burton u T DE14......166 C3
　Newcastle-u-L ST5....283 C3
Borrowcop Ho WS14...231 C6
Borrowcop La WS14...231 D5
Borrowdale Rd ST6.....42 E3
Boscobel Cl DY1.......271 F3
Boscobel Ho* ST19...221 E5
Boscombe Gr ST4......88 C5
Boscomoor Cl ST19...207 E7
Boscomoor La ST19...207 E7
Boscomoor Ind Est ST19..207 E7
Boscomoor Sh Ctr ST19..207 E7
Bosinney Cl ST4........73 B5
Bosley Brook CW12....16 D5
Bosley Gr ST1.........41 C6
Bosley View CW12......6 A1
Boss Gate Cl WV5......270 A5
Bostock Cl ST15.......120 D6
Boston Cl Cannock WS12..210 E1
　Stoke-on-T ST6.......41 C4
Boston Ind Est WS15...178 F2
Bosty La WS9..........256 A4
Boswell Rd WS11.....209 D4
Boswell St ST4.........56 F1
Bosworth Cl DY3.......271 F7
Bosworth Dr DE13.....166 B7
Botany Bay Rd ST1.....57 E5
Botany Dr DY3.........271 D6
Botesworth Gdns ST16..41 D1
Botfield Cl WV7.......237 B6
Botham Dr ST13........45 D5
Botteslow St ST1......282 C2
Bottom La Ipstones ST10..47 C5
　Market Drayton TF9...112 A7
　Swynnerton ST15....103 B7
Boucher Rd ST13.......45 C4
Boughey Rd Audley ST7..39 E2
　Newport TF10........168 E2
　Stoke-on-T ST4.......72 C8
Boughey St ST4........72 A6
Boulevard The ST6.....41 E3
Boulters La CV9......262 D1
Boulton Cl WS7.......229 C8
Boulton Rd ST6........56 D6
Boundary Cl Leek ST13..30 E3
　Stone ST15...........119 F5
Boundary Cres DY3....271 F3
Boundary Ct ST1......282 B4
Boundary Farm WV4..254 F2
Boundary Hill DY3.....271 F3
Boundary Ind Est WV10..240 C5
Boundary La
　Congleton CW12......16 B8
　Kinver DY7...........274 E1
Boundary Rd
　Brownhills WS9......244 F3
　Eggington DE65......148 D8
Boundary St Hanley ST1..282 B4
　Newcastle-u-L ST5....56 D1
Boundary View ST10....76 B2
Bourne Ave Fazeley B78..249 E1
　Ranton ST18.........135 F6
Bourne Cl Cannock WS12..210 E2
　Tutbury DE13........146 B6
Bourne Pl ST13........30 C6
Bournes Bank ST6.....56 F8
Bournes Bank S [10] ST6..57 A8
Bourne St Mow Cop ST7..72 E4
　Stoke-on-T ST4.......72 E4
Bourne Vale WS9......256 D3
Bouverie Par ST1......57 F7
Bowden St ST6.........42 B1
Bowdler Rd WV2......266 C8
Bowen-cooke Ave WV6..55 B6
Bowen Cl WS11........214 A2
Bowen St WS3........214 D4
Bower End La CW3.....66 B2
Bower Cl WS14........178 C3
Bowers Bent ST21.....102 C4
Bowers Bank ST18.....57 A8
Bowers La Bowers ST21..102 E4
　Stone ST15...........120 D7
Bowfell Gr ST3.........73 B6
Bowhill La Betley CW3...53 E6
　Knowl Bank ST7.......38 B3
Bowland Ave ST5.......55 E2

Bowlers Cl ST6.........57 A6
Bowlingalley La DE6....96 D8
Bowling Alley or Vicarage La
　ST3................193 F8
Bowling Green Ave B77..261 F7
Bowling Green Rd DY8..279 E5
Bowman Gr ST4........42 B7
Bowman Ho ST3........89 F7
Bowmead Cl ST4.......88 C6
Bowmere Cl ST8.......16 C1
Bowness Gr WV11....239 F2
Bowness St ST1.......282 A4
Bowood Dr WV6......255 D6
Bowsey Wood Rd CW3..68 E8
Bowstead St ST4.......72 B7
Bow St WS15.........178 E1
Bowyer Ave ST6.......42 E5
Boxer Cl WS15.........198 C3
Box La ST3............73 C2
Boxwood Pl ST10......55 D8
Boxwood Rd ST10......92 E4
Boyden Cl Cannock WS11..209 B1
Boyles Hall Rd ST7.....39 E2
Brabazon Cl ST3......90 C7
Bracebridge Ho B74...257 F2
Bracken Ave TF9.......99 E5
Brackenberry Cl........56 B3
Bracken Cl
　Burntwood WS7......229 C7
　Cannock WS12........210 D8
　Lichfield WS14.......231 E6
　Stafford ST16.........155 B7
　Stoke-on-T ST3.......89 F5
　Tittensor ST12........88 A1
Bracken Dale ST13.....30 B4
Brackenfield Ave ST2...56 B8
Brackenfield Way ST16..155 D8
Brackenhill Rd WS7....229 A8
Bracken Park Gdns DY8..275 F2
Bracken Rd WS12......209 C5
Brackens The ST5......71 C2
Brackens St ST4........72 E4
Bracken View ST17....176 C3
Bracken Way
　Newport TF10........168 F4
　Stoke-on-T ST4.......72 C8
Brackenwood Mews CW2..37 D2
Brackenwood Rd DE15..185 E6
Bracklesham Way B77..251 A6
Brackley Ave ST6.......42 B1
Bradbury Cl
　Brownhills WS8......244 F5
　Stoke-on-T ST4.......42 B3
Bradbury Ct WS12......42 B3
Bradbury Gdns CW12...15 B7
Bradbury La
　Cannock WS12........210 B8
　Enville DY7..........272 E3
　King's Bromley DE13..199 C6
Bradbury Rise ST16....155 A4
Bradeley Village ST4...42 C3
Braden Rd WV4........265 D4
Bradford Rd WS8......244 E8
Bradford St
　Cannock WS11.......210 A5
　Tamworth B79.......249 F5
Bradgate Dr B74......257 E5
Bradley Dr ST21.......117 F3
Bradley La ST18........173 B3
Bradley Lakes WS15...197 F2
Bradley St DY8.......178 E4
Bradley Rd
　Stourbridge DY8......279 F6
　Wolverhampton WV2..266 C8
Bradley St
　Burton u T DE15......185 E7
　Uttoxeter ST14......126 C8
Bradmore Rd
　Burton u T DE15......166 B5
　Wolverhampton WV3..265 F8
Bradmore Way ST16....155 D8
Bradwall Cl ST4........56 A7
Bradwell Croft B75....258 E3
Bradwell Grange ST5...56 A7
Bradwell Hospl ST5....56 A7
Bradwell La
　Cannock Wood WS15..211 F5
　Newcastle-u-L ST5....56 A7
Bradwell Prim Sch ST5..56 A7
Bradwell St ST6........56 D8
Braemar Ave
　Stourbridge DY8......275 C1
　Sedgley DY3.........266 C1
Braemar Gdns WS12...209 F7
Braemar Rd
　Norton Canes WS11...228 B4
　Pattingham WV6......253 C2
Braemore Rd ST7.......58 B6
Braeside Way WS3.....243 F3
Braham B79...........250 D6
Brailsford Cl DE11....186 E5
Brain St B77..........251 A2
Braithwaite Dr DY6....275 D6
Braithwell Dr ST2......43 A2
Brake La DY8..........281 E6
Brakespeare St ST6.....41 C7
Brake The Hagley DY8...281 B5
　The Bank ST7.........26 E7
Brake Village ST7......26 B7
Bramall Cl ST16......155 C6
Bramall La ST16.......155 C6
Bramber Dr WV5......269 F4

Bramber B77 . . . . 250 D1
Bramble Way DY8 . . . . 279 F2
Bramble Cl WS8 . . . . 244 E5
Bramble Ct DE15 . . . . 185 E6
Bramble Dr WS12 . . . . 210 C7
Bramble Gn DY1 . . . . 271 F5
Bramble La WS7 . . . . 229 B8
Bramble Lea CW3 . . . . 68 E6
Bramble Ct ST8 . . . . 27 D7
Brambleside
16 Stafford ST17 . . . . 175 C7
Stourbridge DY8 . . . . 275 F1
Brambles The
Lichfield WS14 . . . . 231 D6
Newcastle-u-L ST5 . . . . 71 C2
Norton Canes WS11 . . . . . . 228 A5
Bramble Way WS15 . . . . . . 178 C1
Bramblewood Dr WV3 . . . . . 265 E8
Bramblewood
Swadlincote DE11 . . . . 186 F6
Wombourne WV5 . . . . 270 A7
Brambling Cl ST14 . . . . 126 C6
Bramblings The ST17 . . . . . . 175 D5
Brambling B77 . . . . 262 A7
Bramdean Dr ST19 . . . . 192 F1
Bramdean Wlk WV4 . . . . . . 265 C6
Bramell Cl DE14 . . . . 184 F7
Bramfield Dr ST5 . . . . 283 C4
Bramhall Cl ST18 . . . . 154 B7
Bramley Cl ST10 . . . . 76 E2
Bramley Dale DE11 . . . . 186 F2
Bramley Pl ST4 . . . . 71 E2
Bramley Way WS14 . . . . . . 232 D5
Bramling Cross Rd DE14 . . . 166 F6
Brammall Dr ST11 . . . . 90 E7
Brammer St ST6 . . . . 42 C3
Brampton Cl
Cookley DY10 . . . . 280 B4
Gorstyhill CW2 . . . . 37 E3
Stoke-on-T ST9 . . . . 43 F8
Brampton Ct ST5 . . . . 283 C4
Brampton Dr WS12 . . . . 210 E2
Brampton Gdns ST5 . . . . . . 56 C3
Brampton Ind Est ST5. . . . . . 283 B4
Brampton Rd ST5. . . . . 283 C4
Brampton Sidings Ind Est
ST5. . . . . 283 B4
Brampton Sidings ST5. . . . . . 283 B4
Brampton Wlk ST3. . . . . 284 C1
Bramshall Ind Est ST14 . . . . . 125 A7
Bramshall Rd ST14. . . . . . . 125 E8
Bramshaws Acre ST10 . . . . . . 76 E2
Bramstead Ave WV6 . . . . . . 255 B2
Bramwell Dr WS6 . . . . 226 D1
Brancaster Cl B77 . . . . 251 A5
Branchal Rd WS9 . . . . 245 C1
Brandon Cl Aldridge WS9 . . 256 F3
Sedgley DY3 . . . . 271 E7
Brandon Gr ST4 . . . . 87 F8
Brandon Pk WV3 . . . . 265 E2
Brandons The ST17 . . . . 174 F5
Bransdale Rd WS8 . . . . 244 E6
Branson Ave ST3 . . . . 73 E3
Branston Rd
Burton u T DE14. . . . . 185 C8
Tatenhill DE13,DE14 . . . . . . 184 C8
Branston Water Pk★
DE14 . . . . 184 D6
Bransty Gr ST4 . . . . 88 C5
Brant Ave ST5 . . . . 56 A4
Brantley Ave WV3. . . . . 255 C1
Brantley Cres DY7 . . . . 267 F2
Brantley La
Bobbington DY7. . . . . 267 F2
Seisdon WV5, WV6 . . . . 263 A3
Branton Hill La WS9 . . . . . . 256 C5
Brantwood Ave WS7 . . . . . . 229 A5
Brassington St CW3. . . . . . . 53 A6
Brassington Terr CW3 . . . . . 52 F3
Brassington Way ST12 . . . . . 58 C1
Bratch Common Rd
WV5. . . . . 269 E7
Bratch Hollow WV5 . . . . 270 A8
Bratch La WV5. . . . . 269 F8
Bratch Pk WV5 . . . . 269 F8
Brattice Pl ST22 . . . . 73 D7
Brattswood Dr ST7 . . . . 25 A5
Braunton Ave ST17 . . . . 175 E7
Braystones Cl ST6 . . . . 41 E8
Brazenhill La ST18 . . . . 172 F7
Breach La Foston DE6. . . . 129 C5
Upper Tean ST10 . . . . 92 C5
Breach Rd ST6 . . . . 43 C7
Breadmarket St WS13 . . . . . 231 B8
Breamore Cres DY1 . . . . 271 F3
Bream B77 . . . . 261 D7
Bream Way ST6. . . . . 42 B3
Brean Rd ST17. . . . . 175 E6
Brecon Way ST2 . . . . 58 C2
Bredon Cl WV7 . . . . 237 A5
Bredon Ct B75. . . . . 258 B4
Breech Cl ST10 . . . . 48 F2
Bredon Cl ST15 . . . . 55 F3
Bredon Way WS4 . . . . 244 C1
Breeze Ave
Norton Canes WS11 . . . . . . 228 B5
Stoke-on-T ST6 . . . . 41 E5
Brelades Cl DY1 . . . . 271 E3
Brempton Croft ST15 . . . . . . 106 D2
Brendale Cl ST4. . . . . 72 A1
Brendon Cl ST17. . . . . 175 D8
Brendon B77. . . . . 251 B1
Brent Cl **9** ST17. . . . . 175 A8
Brentmill Cl WV10 . . . . 240 F4
Brentnall Dr B75. . . . . 258 B3

Brentnor Cl ST3 . . . . 73 F3
Brenton Rd WV4 . . . . 265 F3
Brent B77 . . . . 261 E7
Brentwood Ct ST9 . . . . 59 B4
Brentwood Dr ST9 . . . . 59 B4
Brentwood Gr
Stoke-on-T 43 C3
Werrington ST9 . . . . 59 B4
Brenwood Cl DY6 . . . . 275 B7
Breretonhill La WS15 . . . . . . 197 C2
Brereton Hill WS15 . . . . 197 B5
Brereton Lodge WS15 . . . . . 197 A6
Brereton Manor Ct
WS15. . . . . 197 B5
Brereton Pl ST6 . . . . 41 E1
Brereton Rd WS15 . . . . 196 F7
Bretby Bsns Pk DE15 . . . . . 186 F8
Bretby Fairways DE15 . . . . . 167 F2
Bretby Hollow DE11 . . . . 186 F7
Bretby Hts DE11 . . . . 186 F7
Bretby La DE15 . . . . 167 E3
Bretby Rd DE11 . . . . 186 F7
Bretby Stoneware Ind Est
DE11 . . . . 186 E8
Bretherton Pl ST6 . . . . 42 A6
Bretlands Way DE15 . . . . . . 186 A6
Brettell La DY8 . . . . 279 F8
Brevitt Rd WV2 . . . . 266 D6
Brewers Dr WS3 . . . . 244 A1
Brewers Terr WS3 . . . . 244 A2
Brewery La ST18. . . . . 158 E2
Brewery St Hanley ST1 . . . 282 B3
Rugeley WS15. . . . . 196 F8
Brewester Rd ST2 . . . . 57 F3
Brewhouse St WS13 . . . . . . 213 F1
Brewhouse The DE14. . . . . . 166 D2
Brewood CE Mid Sch
ST19. . . . . 223 C6
Brewood Park Cotts
WV9 . . . . 224 A3
Brewood Rd
Coven,Cross Green WV9 . . . 224 C1
Coven WV9 . . . . 224 B3
Brewster Cl B78 . . . . 249 E1
Brianson Ave ST6. . . . . 57 C7
Briar Ave B74 . . . . 257 A1
Briarbank Cl ST4 . . . . 71 F1
Briar Cl Cannock WS12 . . . 210 A8
Rugeley WS15. . . . . 178 C1
Swadlincote DE15 . . . . 186 F5
Walton-on-t-H ST17. . . . . . . 175 F6
Briar Gr ST15. . . . . 118 E5
Briarsleigh ST17 . . . . 175 C7
Briars The Aldridge WV5 . . 256 A7
Hagley DY9 . . . . 281 F4
Newcastle-u-L ST5. . . . . . . 283 B4
Briars Way WS12 . . . . 211 D4
Briarswood Biddulph ST8 . . . 16 C1
Kidsgrove ST7 . . . . 26 B1
Briar B77 . . . . 251 A3
Briar Way ST21 . . . . 102 E2
Briarwood Pl ST3 . . . . 74 B2
Brickbridge La WV5 . . . . . 269 E5
Brickfield Cl ST18. . . . . 139 D1
Brickfield Pl ST3 . . . . 73 C6
Brickhill La DE13 . . . . 163 A6
Brick House St ⑧ ST6. . . . 56 F8
Bricklin St WS8. . . . . 244 F7
Brick Kiln La
Brocton ST17. . . . . 175 F3
Codsall Wood ST19 . . . . . . 222 C2
Dudley DY3 . . . . 271 B3
Hopton ST18 . . . . 137 D1
Brick-Kiln La
Newcastle-u-L ST5. . . . . . . 55 E8
Rolleston on D DE13 . . . . . 147 A3
Brick Kiln La
Stoke-on-T ST4 . . . . 56 E1
Weston ST18 . . . . 137 F2
Wheaton Aston ST19 . . . . . . 205 A5
Brick Kiln Way WS15 . . . . . 196 F5
Brick St DY3 . . . . 271 D8
Brickworks Rd WS12 . . . . . 210 E2
Brickyard Rd
Aldridge,Leighswood
WS9 . . . . 256 A7
Aldridge,Leighswood WS9 . . 256 A8
Aldridge,Vigo WS9 . . . . . . 244 F1
Bridestowe Cl ④ ST3 . . . . 90 A7
Bridge Ave WS6 . . . . 226 E4
Brownhills WS8 . . . . 244 E6
Weston ST18 . . . . 138 C3
Bridge Cres ST15 . . . . 120 A7
Bridge Croft ST6. . . . . 42 B6
Bridge Cross Rd WS7 . . . . . 229 A7
Bridge Ct
Blythe Bridge ST11 . . . . . . 90 F6
Stoke-on-T ST4 . . . . 71 E3
Stourbridge DY8 . . . . 275 E2
Uttoxeter ST14 . . . . 126 D7
Woodseaves ST20. . . . . . . 151 D7
Bridge End ST13. . . . . 30 D7
Bridge Farm DE13 . . . . . . 147 E1
Bridgefoot Wlk WV8 . . . . . . 239 F1
Bridge Ho ST5. . . . . 55 C2
Bridge Ind Est ST6. . . . . . . 57 B7
Bridge La ST18 . . . . 139 B3
Bridgeman Ct TF11. . . . . . 203 F7
Bridgemary Cl WV10 . . . . . . 240 F4
Bridgemere Garden World★
CW5 . . . . 67 B4
Bridge Rd Armitage WS15 . . 198 C4
Cookley DY10. . . . . 280 A6
Market Drayton TF9. . . . . . . 97 A1
Stoke-on-T ST4 . . . . 71 E3
Uttoxeter ST14 . . . . 126 D7

Bridge Rd continued
Walsall WS4 . . . . 244 B1
Bridges Cres WS11. . . . . . . 227 F5
Bridgeside DE13. . . . . 147 E1
Bridgeside Trad Est B77 . . . . 250 C3
Bridges Rd WS11 . . . . 227 F5
Bridge St Brindley Ford ST8 . 27 B2
Brownhills WS8 . . . . 244 E6
Burton u T DE14. . . . . 166 F3
Cannock WS11. . . . . 226 E5
Newcastle-u-L,Silverdale
ST5 . . . . 55 C2
Newcastle-u-L ST5. . . . . . . 283 B3
Bridge Street Ind Units
ST14. . . . . 126 D7
Stourbridge DY8 . . . . 275 E1
Stretton DE13 . . . . 147 E1
Tamworth B77 . . . . 250 E5
Tutbury DE13 . . . . 146 C7
Uttoxeter ST14 . . . . 126 D7
Bridge Terr Newport TF10 . 168 E3
Upper Hulme ST13 . . . . . . 20 E6
Bridge The ST10 . . . . 92 D6
Bridgett Cl ST14 . . . . 71 E5
Bridge View DY7 . . . . 81 D8
Bridgewater Cl
Congleton CW12 . . . . 6 B1
Penkridge ST19 . . . . 207 F8
Bridgewater Dr WV5. . . . . . 269 F7
Bridgewater St WS13 . . . . . 196 F8
Bridgewater St
Burslem ST6 . . . . 56 D8
Tamworth B77 . . . . 250 D5
Bridge Way WS8 . . . . 244 E6
Bridgewood St ST3 . . . . . . 284 C4
Bridgford Ave ST14 . . . . . . 184 F7
Bridgnorth Ave WV5 . . . . . . 269 F5
Bridgnorth Gr ST5 . . . . 40 E2
Bridgnorth Rd
Enville DY7. . . . . 273 D2
Himley DY3 . . . . 270 B3
Kinver DY7 . . . . 278 C7
Seisdon WV6 . . . . 263 E5
Stourbridge DY7,DY8. . . . . . 279 C6
Trescott WV6. . . . . 264 C7
Wolverhampton WV6 . . . . . 255 B2
Wombourne WV5. . . . . 269 D5
Bridgtown Bsns Ctr
WS11. . . . . 226 E6
Bridgtown Prim Sch
WS11 . . . . 226 E6
Bridgwater St WV5. . . . . . . 244 F3
Bridgwood Rd ST11. . . . . . . 91 A7
Bridle La Ellenhall ST20 . . . 153 D8
Stanton DE15. . . . . 186 A5
Bridle Path ST3. . . . . 284 C1
Bridle Path The
Madeley CW3 . . . . 68 D7
Newcastle-u-L ST5. . . . . . . 70 F3
Bridle Path ST2. . . . . 59 A3
Bridle Rd Stafford ST17 . . . 175 D6
Stourbridge DY8 . . . . 279 D6
Bridleway The TF9 . . . . 97 B1
Bridle Wlk WS15 . . . . 178 B1
Brierley Hill Rd DY8. . . . . . . 275 F2
Brierley Lodge ST5 . . . . 70 F8
Brierley Rd CW12 . . . . 6 B1
Brierley St ST5 . . . . 42 C1
Brierlow Bar SK17. . . . . 5 B8
Brier Sch The DY6 . . . . 275 F5
Briertey Hill La WS15 . . . . . 212 B4
Brieryhurst Cl ST2 . . . . 58 C5
Brieryhurst Rd ST7. . . . . . . 26 B3
Bright Cres B77 . . . . 250 C2
Brightgreen St ST3 . . . . . . 73 D6
Brighton St ② ST3 . . . . . . 72 A7
Brighton The ST5. . . . . 55 B2
Brights Ave ⑧ ST7. . . . . . . 26 D7
Bright St ST3 . . . . 74 A1
Brightstone Cl WV10 . . . . . 240 F4
Bright St DY9 . . . . 279 D6
Brimfield Pl ❶ WV6 . . . . . . 255 F4
Brindivell Gr ST4. . . . . 88 C6
Brindley Ave WV11. . . . . . . 242 A1
Brindley Bank Rd WS15 . . . 178 C3
Brindley Brae DY7 . . . . . . 278 C5
Brindley Cl
❶ Stourbridge DY8. . . . . . . 275 E1
Albrighton WV7 . . . . 237 A6
Kidsgrove ST7 . . . . 25 E1
Penkridge ST19 . . . . 208 A7
Stafford ST15 . . . . 155 F8
Stone ST15 . . . . 104 E2
Talke ST7 . . . . 40 E8
Wombourne WV5. . . . . 269 D6
Brindley Cres
Cannock WS12 . . . . 210 C8
Cheddleton ST13. . . . . 45 D4
Brindley Heath Jun Sch
DY7 . . . . 278 A5
Brindley Heath Rd WS12 . . . 195 C2
Brindley La ST2,ST9 . . . . . 43 C3
Brindley Mill Mus The★
ST13 . . . . 30 D7
Brindley Pl ST16 . . . . 42 C6
Brindley Rd WS12. . . . . 195 A3
Brindleys Bsns Pk WS11. . . . 210 B3
Brindleys Way ST7 . . . . 39 F2
Brindley Way CW12 . . . . . . 6 B1
Brindon Ct ST13 . . . . 74 B3
Brinkburn Cl WS15. . . . . . . 178 B1
Brinley Way DY6 . . . . 275 C6
Brinscall Gn ST6 . . . . 42 A7
Brinsford La WV10 . . . . 240 D7
Brinsford Rd WV10 . . . . 240 C3
Brinsley Ave ST4 . . . . 88 A6

Brisbane Rd ST16. . . . . 155 B7
Brisbane Way WS12 . . . . . . 210 E3
Brisley Hill ST4 . . . . 71 F6
Bristol Cl WS11 . . . . 210 B1
Bristol St
Newcastle-u-L ST5. . . . . . . 56 D5
Wolverhampton WV3 . . . . . 266 B8
Britannia Dr
Burton u T DE13. . . . . 166 D8
Stretton DE13 . . . . 147 D1
Britannia Gn DY3 . . . . 271 E5
Britannia Ho
Burton u T DE14. . . . . 166 D2
Stafford ST16 . . . . 285 B3
Britannia Park Ind Est
ST6. . . . . 57 B7
Britannia St ⑥ ST13 . . . . . . 30 E6
Britannia Stadium (Stoke City
FC) ST4. . . . . 72 C3
Britannia Way WS13 . . . . . . 231 F8
Britch La ST20. . . . . 204 E8
Brittain Ave ST5 . . . . 56 F7
Brittain Rd WS12 . . . . 45 D5
Brittle Pl DY6 . . . . 42 D2
Britton St ST4 . . . . 56 F1
Brixham Ct ST2 . . . . 57 F1
Brizlincote La DE15 . . . . . . 167 D1
Brizlincote St DE15 . . . . . . 166 F1
Broadacres WV9 . . . . 224 B3
Broadbent Cl ❶ WS13 . . . . . 230 F6
Broad Eye ST16 . . . . 285 A3
Broadfield Cl DY6 . . . . 275 E6
Broadfield House Glass
Mus★ DY6 . . . . 275 D5
Broadfield Rd ST6 . . . . 41 C7
Broadholes La ST19. . . . . . . 205 A6
Broadhurst Cl WS12. . . . . . . 194 F1
Broadhurst Gn ST17. . . . . . 194 F2
Broadhurst Green Rd ST19,
WS12. . . . . 194 D2
Broadhurst St ST6 . . . . 42 B1
Broad La Burntwood WS7. . 230 B5
Church Eaton ST20 . . . . . . 171 E1
Lichfield WS14 . . . . 231 D6
Broadlands DE13 . . . . 166 D8
Broadlands Rise WS14 . . . . 231 D7
Broadlands WV10 . . . . 240 D5
Broad Lane Gdns WS3 . . . . 243 A2
Broad La
Stoke-on-T ST6,ST9 . . . . . 43 C8
Walsall,Essington WV3 . . . . 242 E4
Walsall WS4 . . . . 244 C2
Whittington WS13 . . . . 215 E1
Broadlawns Dr ST3 . . . . 73 B6
Broad La WV3 . . . . 265 E8
Broadlee B77. . . . . 251 C1
Broad Mdw WV9 . . . . 256 B8
Broad Meadow Croft
ST16. . . . . 155 A4
Broad Meadow Ct ST5 . . . . 55 E6
Broad Meadow La WS6 . . . . 227 A2
Broadmine St ST4 . . . . 72 F6
Broadoaks ST11 . . . . 91 D6
Broadoak Way ST3. . . . . . . 72 E1
Broadsmeath B77. . . . . 250 C1
Broad St Cannock WS11 . . . 226 E6
Hanley ST1 . . . . 282 A1
Kingswinford DY6 . . . . 275 D5
Leek ST13 . . . . 30 E5
Newcastle-u-L ST5. . . . . . . 283 B3
Broadstone Cl WV4 . . . . . . 266 D5
Broad St ST16 . . . . 285 A3
Broadway Cannock WS12 . . . 209 F6
Codsall WV8 . . . . 238 E3
Broadway Cl ❶ ST3 . . . . . . 73 E1
Broadway Gdns WV10. . . . . 240 E2
Broadway La ST10 . . . . 49 A4
Broadway Longton ST3. . . . . 73 F2
Newport TF10 . . . . 169 A3
Broadway Pl ❶ ST3. . . . . . 73 F2
Broadway St DE14 . . . . 166 C1
Broadway The
Stourbridge DY8 . . . . 279 D3
Wombourne WV5. . . . . 270 A5
Broad Way WS14 . . . . 244 C2
Broadway
Wolverhampton,Bushbury
WV10 . . . . 240 E2
Wolverhampton,Compton
WV3 . . . . 255 C2
Broadwell La WV6. . . . . 253 B2
Broc Cl ST19 . . . . 208 A8
Brockbank Pl ST6. . . . . 42 B5
Brockeridge Cl WV12 . . . . . 242 C1
Brockhill TF9 . . . . 99 D5
Brockhurst La
Blymhill Lawn TF11. . . . . . . 204 B4
Blymhill TF11. . . . . 203 F5
Weeford B75 . . . . 259 B7
Brockhurst Rd
Blymhill TF11 . . . . 204 C6
Sutton Coldfield B75 . . . . . . 258 D1
Brockhurst Way ST1 . . . . . . 57 E8
Brockley Cl DE6 . . . . 127 F7
Brockley Sq ST11 . . . . 282 B3
Brockley's Wlk DY7 . . . . . . 278 C3
Brocksford Dr DE6 . . . . 127 F7
Brocksford St ST4. . . . . 284 B5
Brockton La ST21. . . . . 117 C3
Brockton Wlk ST3 . . . . 72 E1
Brock Way ST5 . . . . 55 E2
Brocton Cl WS11. . . . . 178 C2
Brocton Hts ST17 . . . . 176 C3
Brocton La ST17 . . . . 175 F6
Brocton Rd ST17 . . . . 176 C6
Brogan St ST4 . . . . 72 F6
Bromfield Ct Stone ST15 . . . 105 A1

Bromfield Ct continued
Wolverhampton WV6 . . . . . 255 B3
Bromford Dale ❷ WV6. . . . . 255 F3
Bromford Pl ST17 . . . . 282 A1
Bromford Rise WV3 . . . . . . 266 B8
Bromley Cl WS12 . . . . 282 A4
Bromley St ST1. . . . . 282 A4
Bromley Gdns WV8 . . . . . . 239 A4
Bromleyhedge La ST13. . . . . 48 D4
Bromley Hills Prim Sch
DY6 . . . . 275 F5
Bromley Hough ST4. . . . . . . 71 F5
Bromley Ho WV4. . . . . 266 A5
Bromley La DY6 . . . . 275 E4
Bromley Lodge WV4 . . . . . . 266 A5
Bromley Pl WV4 . . . . 266 A5
Bromley St Hanley ST1. . . . . 282 A4
Wolverhampton WV2 . . . . . 266 C7
Bromley Wood WS15 . . . . . 161 E5
Brompton Dr ST2 . . . . 43 B3
Brompton Lawns WV6. . . . . 255 A3
Bromsberrow Way ST3 . . . . 90 A7
Bromsgrove Pl ❶ ST3 . . . . . 284 A5
Bromstead Cres ST16 . . . . . 155 B6
Bromwich Dr WS13 . . . . . . 215 D8
Bromwich Rd WV2 . . . . 266 B6
Bromwynd DY7 . . . . 262 A7
Bronant Wlk ❹ ST6. . . . . . . 57 A7
Bronte Cl DE14 . . . . 166 D7
Bronte Ct B79 . . . . 250 A6
Bronte Dr WS11 . . . . 210 C2
Bronte Gr ST2 . . . . 43 A2
Bronte Rd WV2 . . . . 266 B6
Brook Ave B77 . . . . 262 A7
Brookbank Gdns DY3 . . . . . 271 B2
Brookbank Rd DY3. . . . . . . 271 B2
Brook Cl
Blythe Bridge ST11 . . . . . . 91 A7
Brownhills WS9 . . . . 245 A3
Coven WV9 . . . . 224 A3
Doveridge DE6. . . . . 127 C8
Endon ST9 . . . . 44 A8
Lichfield WS13 . . . . 214 A1
Penkridge ST19 . . . . 207 E7
Brook Cres DY6 . . . . 275 C2
Brookdale Dr WV4 . . . . 265 C6
Brookdale DY3 . . . . 271 C3
Brook End
Burntwood WS7. . . . . 229 A4
Fazeley B78. . . . . 261 B8
Haughton ST18 . . . . 172 F6
Longdon WS15. . . . . 198 A1
Brooke Rd WS12 . . . . 209 F6
Brookes St ST4 . . . . 72 E6
Brookfield Cl
Aldridge WS9 . . . . 245 A1
Whiston ST10. . . . . 62 D3
Brookfield Ct Hanley ST1 . . 282 B4
Haughton ST18 . . . . 172 F6
Stone ST15 . . . . 120 C6
Brookfield TF9. . . . . 99 D5
Brookfield Rd
Aldridge WS9 . . . . 245 A1
Codsall WV8 . . . . 239 B3
Stoke-on-T,Baddeley Green
ST2. . . . . 43 C3
Stoke-on-T,Springfields ST4. . 71 E5
Brookfields Rd ST10 . . . . . . 62 A8
Brookgate ST11. . . . . 91 B8
Brook Gdns ST8 . . . . 16 D1
Brook Glen Rd ST17 . . . . . . 174 E7
Brook Gr WV8 . . . . 239 B2
Brookhay La WS13 . . . . 215 E3
Brookhill Cl WV12 . . . . 242 D1
Brookhill Way WV12 . . . . . . 242 D1
Brook Ho TF10 . . . . 168 E3
Brookhouse Cl WV10. . . . . . 241 B6
Brookhouse Ct ST14 . . . . . . 126 F1
Brookhouse Dr ST12 . . . . . . 88 D2
Brookhouse La
Bucknall ST2 . . . . 58 E4
Cheddleton ST13. . . . . 45 A3
Congleton CW12 . . . . 6 C2
Featherstone WV10 . . . . . . 241 B7
Wolverhampton WV10 . . . . 240 F6
Brookhouse Rd
Cheadle ST10. . . . . 76 B3
Gnosall ST20 . . . . 171 D7
Meir ST3 . . . . 74 B2
Newcastle-u-L ST5. . . . . . . 55 B8
Brookhouses Ind Est ST10. . 76 B2
Brookhouse Way
Cheadle ST10. . . . . 76 B2
Gnosall ST20 . . . . 171 D6
Brook La Brocton ST17 . . . . 176 C4
Great Wyrley WS6. . . . . . . 227 A3
Brook Leigh ST10. . . . . . . 108 F6
Church Leigh ST10. . . . . . . 108 F6
Brookland Ave ST3 . . . . . . 284 A1
Brookland Gr WS9 . . . . 244 F3
Brookland Rd
Brownhills WS9 . . . . 244 F3
Stoke-on-T ST6 . . . . 41 F5
Brooklands Ave WS6. . . . . . 226 F4
Brooklands Cl ST14. . . . . . . 126 B6
Brooklands Rd
Albrighton WV7 . . . . 237 B6
Cannock WS11. . . . . 210 A4
Brooklands Sch ST16 . . . . . 155 C6
Brooklands DY8 . . . . 275 F1
Brooklands The DY3 . . . . . 269 E1
Brooklands Way
Cheddleton ST13. . . . . 46 A8
Leek ST13 . . . . 45 F8
Brook La
Newcastle-u-L ST5. . . . . . . 283 B2
Ranton ST18 . . . . 153 C3

Brook La continued
Stoke-on-T ST9 ....43 F8
Brookline Gdns
Featherstone WV10.....241 B7
Stafford ST16 ....155 A5
Brooklyn Gr DY6.......275 B8
Brooklyn Rd
Burntwood WS7.........229 A4
Cannock WS12.........210 D1
Brook Mdws WV8.......239 B4
Brookmead Gr ST3 ......73 B6
Brookmead Ind Est ST16.155 F8
Brook Path ST15.........119 F8
Brook Pl Newcastle-u-L ST5 71 C5
Stoke-on-T ST4 ....56 F1
Brook Prim Sch DY8 ....275 F1
Brook Rd
Cheslyn Hay WS6.......226 E4
Stoke-on-T ST4 ....88 A7
Wombourne WV5.......269 F6
Brookside Ave TF10.....168 E1
Brookside Bsns Ctr ST15 118 B5
Brookside Bsns Pk ST14 126 D7
Brookside Burslem ST6 ..56 D7
Burton u T DE15.........167 B5
Brookside Cl
Newcastle-u-L ST5.....283 A1
Wombourne WV5.......269 E6
Brookside Cotts DE6.....81 C3
Brookside Ct ST10 ......76 B3
Brookside Cvn Site WV9 .224 A8
Brookside Dr Endon ST9 ..44 A8
Stoke-on-T ST3 ....72 E2
Brookside Dudley DY3....271 D2
Enville DY7 ....273 D3
Brookside Gdns ST19 ....221 C8
Brookside Ind Est ST6 ...56 D8
Brookside ST10.........62 A3
Brookside La ST15.......119 F7
Brookside
Marchington ST14.......127 A2
Ranton ST18 ....153 D5
Brookside Rd
Barton-u-N DE13.......183 C1
Tamworth B78 ....249 D1
Uttoxeter ST14 ....126 D7
Brook Side DE13.........147 B4
Brookside Way
Blakedown DY10.......281 B2
Kingswinford DY6.......275 C7
Tamworth B77 ....262 A6
Brook Sq [1] WS15 ......196 E8
Brook St Biddulph ST8 ...27 A5
Burton u T DE14.........166 C3
Dudley,Gornalwood DY3 ..271 C2
Kingswinford DY6.......270 B1
Leek ST13 ....30 E5
Newcastle-u-L ST5.......55 C2
Stoke-on-T ST4 ....72 B7
Stourbridge,Amblecote
DY8................275 F1
Stourbridge DY8 ......279 E5
Swadlincote DE11......186 E6
Brook Vale WS11.......266 E8
Brookview Dr ST3 ......73 F4
Brookweed B77.........250 E2
Brookwillows ST17.....175 C7
Brookwood Cl ST5......71 B3
Brookwood Dr ST3......74 B2
Broom Covert Rd WS14..247 D8
Broome Cl DE13 ....199 C6
Broome Hill 71 C1
Broome La DY9 ....281 F2
Broome Wlk WS15 ......198 C4
Broomfield Ave B78.....261 A4
Broomfield Cl
Newport TF10 ....168 D3
Stone ST15 ....220 B6
Broomfield La ST14......79 F2
Broomfield Pl TF10 ....168 D3
Broomfield Pl N ST1.....57 A3
Broomfield Pl S ST1.....57 A3
Broomfield Rd
Newport TF10 ....168 D3
Stoke-on-T ST6 ....42 E5
Broomhills ST8.........17 B1
Broomhill Bank WS11...209 E3
Broomhill Cl WS11......209 E4
Broomhills The DE12....219 E7
Broomhill St ST6 ......41 D4
Broom Hollow TF9 ......99 F5
Broome La TF9 ....99 D4
Broom's La DE12 ......99 D4
Brooms Park Cvn Pk
ST15 ....120 B5
Brooms Rd ST15 ....120 B5
Broom St ST11.........282 C4
Broomyclose La ST14 ..111 A4
Brough Cl Leek ST13 ....30 E6
Wolverhampton WV4,
WV14 ....266 F3
Brough La ST4.........88 B7
Brough Rd DE15.......167 C3
Broughton Cl ST16.....155 C7
Broughton Cres ST12 ....88 E1
Broughton Dr WV6 .....255 A3
Broughton Rd Bucknall ST2 57 F3
Newcastle-u-L ST5.......56 D7
Wolverhampton WV3.....255 C1
Brow Hill ST13.........30 E6
Brown Ave
Lawton-gate ST7 ....25 A5
Tamworth B77 ....261 C8
Brownfield Rd ST3......74 A2
Brownhill Rd ST6......43 B8
Brownhills Bsns Pk ST1 ..41 D2
Brownhills Com Tech Coll
WS8 ....228 F1

Brownhills High Sch ST6 ..41 E1
Brownhills Rd
Brownhills WS8 ....245 A4
Norton Canes WS11.....228 B4
Brownhills West Prim Sch
WS8 ....228 C2
Brownhills West Sta* .....
WS7 ....228 C3
Browning Cl Cheadle ST10..76 C2
Tamworth B79 ....249 F8
Browning Cres WV10....240 C2
Browning Gr Perton WV6..254 E4
Talke ST7.............40 C8
Browning Rd
Burntwood WS7.........229 C7
Dudley DY3 ....271 A4
Stoke-on-T ST3 ....72 F2
Browning St ST16......285 A4
Brown La SK17 ....3 B3
Brown Lees Ind Est ST8 ..27 B4
Brown Lees Rd
Biddulph ST8..........27 A5
Biddulph ST8..........27 B4
Harrisehead ST7 ......26 F4
Brownley Rd ST6 ....42 D1
Brownsea Pl ST3 ....72 E4
Brownsfield Rd WS13 ....214 F4
Brownshore La WV11 ....242 A3
Brown's La B78.........262 F5
Brown's Lake DY7 ......273 D3
Brown's La Tamworth B79 250 C8
Yoxall DE13 ....182 A2
Brown St Burslem ST6 ....57 A8
Wolverhampton WV2.....266 C7
Brownswall Rd DY3......271 C7
Browns Wlk WS15 ......178 D1
Browsholme TF9 ......249 D6
Broxwood Pk WV6 ......255 B3
Bruford Rd ST4 ....266 A8
Brundall Oval ST12 ......58 D2
Bruna La ST13 ....45 A3
Brundle Ave ST5 ....155 B3
Brunel Cl Burntwood WS7 .229 B8
Stafford ST16 ....155 F8
Tamworth B79 ....250 B6
Brunel Ct
Four Ashes WV10 ......224 D5
Wombourne WV5.......270 A7
Brunel Gr WV6 ....254 E5
Brunel Way DE11.......186 E1
Brunel Wlk ST3.........284 C4
Brunslow Cl WV10 ......240 C1
Brunswick Mill [5] ST13 ..30 E6
Brunswick Pl ST3.......282 B2
Brunswick St ST3.......209 E2
Brunswick St [3] Leek ST13 30 F6
Newcastle-u-L ST5.......55 C3
Brunswick Terr ST16....285 A2
Brunt St ST6 ....55 D6
Brutus Rd ST5 ....55 D6
Bryan Ave WV4 ....265 D4
Bryans La WS15 ....178 F1
Bryan St ST1 ....282 B3
Bryans Way WS12......210 F4
Bryant Rd ST2 ....58 B5
Brymbo Rd ST5 ....55 F5
Brynmawr Rd WV14.....266 F3
Bryony Burton u T DE14...185 B8
Sutton Coldfield B74....257 F5
Buccleuch Rd ST3 ......73 D2
Buckden B77 ....251 C1
Buckingham Cl
[4] Burton u T DE13.....166 D8
Stafford ST17 ....156 C1
Buckingham Cres DE15...167 C3
Buckingham Gdns WS14 .231 B6
Buckingham Gr DY6 ....275 C7
Buckingham Pl [3] WS12 210 C1
Buckingham
Tamworth B79 ....249 E7
Wolverhampton WV4 ....266 A5
Buckingham Rise DY1....271 E2
Buckland Cl WS12 ......210 D1
Buckland Gr ST4.........88 C5
Buckland Wlk TF10 .....168 F5
Buckley Cl ST14 ....125 C7
Buckley Rd Stoke-on-T ST6 42 C5
Wolverhampton WV4.....265 D5
Buckley's Row ST5......283 B2
Buckmaster Ave ST5.....71 C6
Bucknall Hospl ST2......58 C4
Bucknall New Rd ST1....282 C3
Bucknall Old Rd ST1....282 C3
Bucknall Rd Hanley ST1...57 F3
Wolverhampton WV11....242 B1
Buckthorn Cl WS12 .....209 H4
Buckley Ct B75.........258 E2
Bude Dr ST17..........156 C1
Buds Rd
Cannock Wood WS11....211 F5
Gentleshaw WS15......212 A5
Buglawton Hall Specl Sch
CW12...............6 D5
Buglawton Prim Sch CW12 6 A4
Buildwas Cl WV6 ......225 A8
Bulldog La WS13 ....214 B1
Buller St Hanley ST1.....282 C1
Wolverhampton WV4.....266 E6
Bullgap Lane 65 C4
Bull Hill ST16..........285 B3
Bull La Packmoor ST8 ....27 A2
Wombourne WV5.......270 A8

Bullmoor La
Muckley Corner WS14....230 A1
Muckley Corner WS14....230 B1
Bullocks House Rd ST7 ..26 E3
Bullows Rd WS11 ....244 C6
Bull Ring Claverley WV5..267 F7
Sedgley DY3...........271 D8
Bull Ring The ST18......138 D2
Bullrushes Cl
[6] Hanley ST1.........57 F2
Stoke-on-T ST1 ....57 A2
Bull St DY3 ....271 C2
Bulrush Cl WS8.........244 E7
Bulstrode St [8] 56 E8
Bumblehole Mdws WV5 .269 F7
Bungalows The
Adbaston ST20 ....131 D4
Chipnall TF9 ....114 A3
Leek ST13 ....31 A5
Bungham La ST19 ......207 D8
Bun La Blymhill TF10 ....188 C1
Great Chatwell TF10 ....203 C8
Bunny Hill ST5 ....71 C5
Bunting Cl ST14 ....126 B6
Buntingsdale Rd TF9 ....112 A7
Bunting The Kingsley ST10..61 D3
Wetley Rocks ST9.......60 A7
Bunt's La ST3 ....43 D4
Bunyan Pl WS11 ....209 E4
Burcham Cl ST16.......155 B7
Burcot Cl B74 ....257 F2
Burdock Cl WS11 ......210 B3
Burford Ave ST5........40 D1
Burford Rd Stafford ST17..156 D1
Wheaton Aston ST19.....205 B6
Burford Way ST7........58 A1
Burgage Cl TF9........97 D1
Burgage Ct TF10 ......168 F2
Burgage The
Eccleshall ST21........133 F7
Market Drayton TF9......97 D1
Burgesses The DY7 .....278 B3
Burgess St ST6 ....56 E7
Burgis Cl ST13.........45 D4
Burgoyne St WS11 .....210 A5
Burgundy Gr [3] ST3 ....90 A7
Burland Ave ST5........55 D4
Burland Rd ST5.........40 D2
Burleigh Cl WS12 ......210 A8
Burleigh Croft WS7 ....229 A4
Burleigh Gr ST5........56 D3
Burleigh Rd WS3 ......266 A8
Burlidge Rd ST6........42 A6
Burlington Ave ST5.....56 D3
Burlington Cl ST8 ....78 B6
Burlington Dr ST17 .....174 B8
Burmarsh Wlk
[4] Burslem ST6........56 F7
Wolverhampton WV8.....255 F8
Burnaby Rd ST6........41 C6
Burnell Gdns WV3 .....265 E8
Burnet Gr WV10 ....241 B8
Burnett Cl ST16 ....155 A5
Burnett Pl ST6.........42 D4
Burnett Rd B74.........257 B2
Burnfield Dr WS15 .....178 D1
Burnfields Way WS9 ....256 A7
Burnham Ave ST4......175 D6
Burnham Cl DY6........27 D3
Burnham Gn ST5.......226 B8
Burnham St ST4 ....284 A5
Burnhays Rd ST6........41 F2
Burnley St ST7.........57 D6
Burnsall Rd WV9 ......240 A3
Burns Ave Stafford ST17..174 B8
Wolverhampton WV10 ...240 D2
Burns Cl Kidsgrove ST7...41 A8
Lichfield WS14.........231 B6
Burns Dr WS7 ....229 C7
Burns Gr DY3 ....271 A4
Burnside Cl ST3........90 A7
Burnside DE13.........147 B4

Butts Rd
Market Drayton TF9......97 B1
Wolverhampton WV4.....266 A6
Butts The Betley CW3 ...53 A5
Lichfield WS14.........230 D2
Butts Way WS11 ....196 E8
Buxton Ave Fazeley B78 .261 B8
Buxton Cl
Newcastle-u-L ST5.......55 A2
Buxton Old Rd ST13 ....243 C3
Buxton Old Rd [2] 6 A4
Buxton Rd Congleton CW12 ..6 C6
Leek ST13 ....31 B7
Longnor SK17 ....13 B7
Byatt's Gr ST4 ....284 A2
Bycars Farm Croft WS13 .215 E8
Bycars La ST6.........42 A1
Bycars Rd ST6.........41 F1
Byland Cl ST13 ....71 A5
Byland Rd ST6 ....260 D3
Byland Way WS3 ......242 F2
By Pass Rd B77........146 D4
Byrd's Cl ST14 ....125 F8
Byrd's La ST14 ....125 F8
Byrkley Park Ctr* DE13 .164 A3
Byrkley St DE14 ....164 A4
Byrne Rd WV2 ....266 D2
Byrom St [9] ST1.......57 A2
Byron Cl
Burton u T DE15........185 C7
Lichfield WS14.........231 B5
Cheadle ST10.........76 C2
Market Drayton TF9......112 A2
Stafford ST16 ....156 A5

Byron Croft Dudley DY3...271 A5
Sutton Coldfield B74....257 F6
Byron Ct Kidsgrove ST7...41 A8
Sutton Coldfield B74....258 A5
Byron Pl Cannock WS12...178 C2
Rugeley WS15 ....178 C2
Byron Rd Tamworth B79 .250 A7
Wolverhampton WV10 ...241 A1
Byron St ST4 ....56 D1
Bywater Gr [3] ST3......73 D6
Byways WS3 ....243 C3

C

Cable St WV2 ....266 F8
Cabot Gr WV6 ....254 E4
Cacklehill La DE6......81 C2
Cadeby Gr ST2 ....43 B2
Cadley Hill Ind Est DE11.186 D2
Cadley Hill Rd DE11.....186 E3
Cadman Cres ST6......42 E3
Cadman's La WS6,WS3 ..243 D6
Cadogan Rd B77........261 D5
Caernarvon Ave ST15 ...120 C6
Caernarvon Cl
Burton u T DE13.......166 E8
Market Drayton TF9......97 E2
Caernarvon Way DY1....271 E2
Cairn Cl ST2 ....58 D3
Cairns Cl DE15.........167 C3
Cairns Dr ST16 ....156 B5
Caister B77 ....251 A6
Caistor Cl Mile Oak B78 .260 B8
Stoke-on-T ST2 ....43 A1
Calais Rd DE13 ....166 B6
Calcot Dr WV6.........255 E7
Caldback Pl ST1 ....282 C3
Caldercrofts TF10......168 F4
Calder Rise DY3 ....271 F6
Calder B77 ....251 A5
Caldervale Dr [4] ST17..175 D6
Caldew Gr ST4.........88 C5
Caldon Way ST15 ......104 E3
Cale Cl ST7...........250 C2
Caledonian B77 ......251 B6
Caledonia St Hanley ST4..57 B1
Wolverhampton WV2.....266 E8
Calgary Cres DE15 ....167 D3
Calibre Ind Est WV10...224 D5
Californian Gr WS7 ....228 F8
California St ST13 .....283 A3
Callaghan Gr [3] WS11 .210 C2
Callender Pl ST6........57 A8
Callingwood La DE13...164 F3
Callister Way ST4 ......165 F3
Callis Wlk [2] B77 .....261 F6
Callow Hill La ST10.....75 D3
Calrofold Dr ST5........40 D1
Calvary Cres ST2 ......73 D8
Calveley Cl ST13 ......118 F6
Calverley St ST3.......284 C1
Calver St [5] ST4 ....41 D3
Calvert St ST5.........56 B7
Calvin Cl
Wolverhampton WV10 ...240 D3
Wombourne WV5.......269 F5
Calving Hill WS11......209 E2
Camberley Cres WV4....266 E2
Camberley Dr WV4 .....266 A4
Camberley Rd DY8......275 F3
Camberwell Gr ST4......88 C6
Camborne Cl
Congleton CW12 ....15 E8
Stafford ST17 ....175 E8
Camborne Cres ST2......70 F5
Cambrian La WS15 .....178 C3
Cambrian B77 ....251 A2
Cambrian Way ST2 .....58 C4
Cambria St WS11 .....209 D4
Cambridge Cl
Biddulph ST8 ....256 B8
Biddulph ST8..........16 C1
Cambridge Ct ST5......71 D4
Cambridge Dr ST5......71 D4
Cambridge St
Burton u T DE14.......166 B1
Hanley ST1............282 C2
Stafford ST16 ....156 A4
Camden Dr B77 ....250 E3
Camden St
Brownhills WS9 ....244 F4
Stoke-on-T ST4 ....72 E4
Camden Way DY6......270 D1
Camelford St ST4......175 E8
Camellia Cl ST4........56 E1
Camellia Gdns
Stourbridge DY8 ......275 E2
Wolverhampton WV10 ...239 F3
Cameo Ct Cannock WS11 209 F4
Stoke-on-T ST4 ....88 C4
Stretton DE13 ....147 E2
Cameo Dr DY8.........279 F8
Cameo Way ST16.......156 A4
Cameron Cl DE15......167 B1
Cameron Wharf ST15...104 F2
Camhouses B77 ....251 B1
Camoys Ct [8] ST6......57 A7
Camoys Rd ST6 ....57 A7
Campbell Ave ST13 .....30 C4
Campbell Cl
Congleton CW12 ....6 A4
Rugeley WS15 ....178 D2
Tamworth B79 ....249 F8

Campbell PI ST4 . . . . .72 B7
Campbell Rd
  Market Drayton TF9 . . . . . .97 D2
  Stoke-on-T ST4 . . . . .72 B5
Campbell Terr ST1 . . . . . .57 E6
Camp Hill
  Stourbridge DY8 . . . . . . .275 E1
  Whitmore ST5 . . . . .85 A5
Campian's Ave WS6 . . . .226 D2
Campian Way ST6 . . . . . .42 E2
Campion Ave ST5 . . . . . .56 D3
Campion CI
  Eccleshall ST21 . . . . .133 D6
  Wombourne WV5 . . . . . . .269 E6
Campion Dr
  Featherstone WV10 . . . . .241 A7
  Tamworth B77 . . . . .250 C3
Campion B74 . . . . .257 F5
Camp Rd
  Cannock ST17,WS12 . . . .194 D6
  Shenstone B75 . . . . .258 D6
  Stoke-on-T ST6 . . . . .42 C1
Camrose Gdns WV9 . . . .240 A3
Camsey La
  Burntwood WS7 . . . . .229 E8
  Creswell Green WS13 . . .212 F1
Canal Cotts ST20 . . . . . . .151 C2
Canal La ST6 . . . . .41 D2
Canal Mews The ST4 . . . .88 C6
Canal Rd CW12 . . . . .15 F8
Canal Side ST12 . . . . .88 D1
Canalside CI
  Penkridge ST19 . . . . .207 F7
  Walsall WS3 . . . . .243 F1
Canalside Rd ST15 . . . . .104 E2
Canal St Burslem ST6 . . . .56 D8
  Burton u T DE14 . . . . . . .166 C2
  Stourbridge DY8 . . . . . . .279 F6
Canal View Bsns Pk
  WS15 . . . . .197 B6
Canary Rd ST2 . . . . .73 D7
Canaway Wlk WS15 . . . .178 C2
Canberra Cres ST3 . . . . . .90 C6
Canberra Dr ST16 . . . . .156 B4
Candle La CW3 . . . . .62 A7
Canford Cres WV8 . . . .238 E3
Cannel Rd WS7 . . . . .228 D6
Canning Rd B77 . . . . . . .250 F4
Canning St ST4 . . . . .72 F5
Cannock Chase Ctry Pk
  Brocton ST17 . . . . .176 D2
  Cannock WS12 . . . . .195 A3
Cannock Chase Ent Ctr
  WS12 . . . . .195 D1
Cannock Chase High Sch
  WS11 . . . . .209 E2
Cannock Chase Tech Coll
  Cannock,Blackfords
  WS11 . . . . .209 D1
  Cannock,Bridgtown WS11 . .226 E7
Cannock Com Hospl
  WS11 . . . . .209 E2
Cannock Ctr WS11 . . . .226 D5
Cannock Motor Village
  WS11 . . . . .209 F1
Cannock Rd Brocton ST17 . .176 A3
  Burntwood,Chase Terrace
  WS7 . . . . .228 D7
  Burntwood,Gorstey Ley
  WS7 . . . . .229 B7
  Cannock,Heath Hayes
  WS12 . . . . .227 C8
  Cannock,WS12,WS11 . . . .210 A5
  Featherstone WV10 . . . . .241 C7
  Huntington ST19 . . . . . . .208 B8
  Penkridge ST19 . . . . .192 F1
  Stafford ST17 . . . . .175 D5
Cannock Sh Ctr WS11 . .209 E1
Cannock Sta WS11 . . . .226 F8
Cannock Wood Ind Est
  WS12 . . . . .211 C6
Cannock Wood Rd WS11 . .211 B5
Cannock Wood St WS12 . .211 A6
Cannon PI ST1 . . . . .282 B2
Cannon Rd WV5 . . . . . . .270 A6
Cannon St ST1 . . . . .282 B2
Canons CI ST15 . . . . . . .120 A6
Canterbury CI
  Lichfield WS13 . . . . .214 C3
  Tamworth B77 . . . . .250 D3
  Walsall WS3 . . . . .244 A4
Canterbury Dr
  Burntwood WS7 . . . . .229 E7
  Perton WV6 . . . . .254 E4
  Rugeley WS15 . . . . .196 D6
  Stoke-on-T ST6 . . . . .42 C4
Canterbury Rd
  Burton u T DE15 . . . . . . .167 C3
  Wolverhampton WV4 . . . .265 E5
Canterbury Way WS12 . . .210 B3
Canvey Gr ST3 . . . . .90 B7
Canwell Dr B75 . . . . .259 B5
Canwell Gate B75 . . . . . .258 E4
Cape Ave ST17 . . . . .174 B7
Cape St WS8 . . . . .245 A6
Cape St ST1 . . . . .282 B4
Capesthorne CI ST19 . . . .59 B3
Capewell St ST13 . . . . . .284 C2
Capper CI ST17 . . . . .26 A2
Cappers La WS13,WS14 . .231 F8
Capper's La WS14 . . . . . .232 A7
Capper St **5** ST6 . . . . . . .41 E3
Capricorn Way ST6 . . . . . .41 F6
Captain's CI WV3 . . . . . .255 D2

Captain's La DE13 . . . . . .201 D8
Caradoc B77 . . . . .251 A2
Caraway Dr DE14 . . . . . .185 A8
Caraway PI ST3 . . . . .90 A6
Carberry Way ST5 . . . . . . .73 D4
Carder Ave ST16 . . . . . .155 B7
Carder dn SK17 . . . . .13 B6
Cardiff Gr ST1 . . . . .282 B1
Cardiff St WV3 . . . . .266 B8
Cardigan Ave WS15 . . . .196 D6
Cardigan Gr ST4 . . . . .88 C6
Cardigan Ho WS12 . . . . .210 C5
Cardigan PI WS12 . . . . . .210 C5
Cardinal Griffin RC High Sch
  WS11 . . . . .209 D2
Cardinal Way WS11 . . . .209 D2
Cardington CI ST5 . . . . . .71 A4
Cardoness PI DY1 . . . . . .271 F2
Card St ST6 . . . . .57 A7
Cardway ST5 . . . . .56 B7
Cardwell St ST1 . . . . .57 E5
Carey ST7 . . . . .262 A5
Carfax WS11 . . . . .226 E8
Carina Gdns ST6 . . . . .42 D1
Carisbrooke Dr
  2 Stretton DE13 . . . . . .147 E1
  Stafford ST17 . . . . .174 B7
Carisbrooke Gdns WV10 . .240 E3
Carisbrooke Rd
  Perton WV6 . . . . .255 A3
  Wolverhampton WV10 . . .240 E3
Carisbrooke B77 . . . . . . .251 A2
Carisbrooke Way ST4 . . . .88 C5
Carlcroft B77 . . . . .251 B2
Carling CI ST16 . . . . .155 B2
Carling Gr ST4 . . . . .73 A5
Carlisle Rd WS11 . . . . . .226 B7
Carlisle St ST3 . . . . .284 B1
Carlos CI ST10 . . . . .76 D3
Carlos PI ST5 . . . . .140 C3
Carlow Ho WS15 . . . . . . .197 B6
Carlton Ave Aldridge B74 . .257 A2
  Brown Edge ST6 . . . . .43 B6
  Newcastle-u-L ST5 . . . . . .71 B3
  Stoke-on-T ST6 . . . . .42 A4
Carlton CI Brown Edge ST6 . .43 B6
  Cannock WS12 . . . . .210 D1
  Cheadle ST10 . . . . .76 D1
Carlton Cres
  Burntwood WS7 . . . . .229 A8
  Tamworth B79 . . . . .249 F8
Carlton Croft B74 . . . . . .257 A2
Carlton Ct DE14 . . . . . . .166 B3
Carlton Ho B75 . . . . .258 B2
Carlton Rd Stoke-on-T ST4 . .72 C8
  Wolverhampton WV3 . . . .266 A7
Carlton Sq ST17 . . . . . . .174 B8
Carlton St DE13 . . . . . . .166 B5
Carlton Terr ST13 . . . . . . .31 A6
Carlyon PI ST1 . . . . .57 D8
Carmel CI WS12 . . . . . . .210 C5
Carmichael CI WS14 . . . .231 D7
Carmount Rd ST2 . . . . . . .58 B7
Carmountside Prim Sch
  ST2 . . . . .58 B7
Carnation CI ST3 . . . . . . .74 B6
Carnforth CI DY6 . . . . . .275 D7
Carnforth Gr ST4 . . . . . . .41 E8
Carnoustie CI WS3 . . . . .243 A3
Carnoustie B77 . . . . .251 C5
Carol Gdns ST6 . . . . . . .279 F8
Caroline Cres ST6 . . . . . . .43 B6
Caroline St ST3 . . . . .284 C4
Caroline Terr DE14 . . . . .166 C2
Carousels The DE14 . . . .166 C5
Carpenter CI DE15 . . . . .167 C1
Carpenter Rd ST3 . . . . . .284 A4
Carr Bank ST10 . . . . .78 B7
Carriage Dr ST8 . . . . .16 E1
Carrick CI WS3 . . . . .244 A5
Carrick PI ST4 . . . . .72 A1
Carriers Fold WV5 . . . . .270 B7
Carriers Rd DE65 . . . . . .148 D6
Carr La Audley ST7 . . . . .261 F5
  Wetton ST13,DE6 . . . . . . .34 F2
Carroll Dr ST3 . . . . .284 D4
Carron St ST4 . . . . .284 B5
Carraway Head Hill B78 . .259 D4
Carr St ST7 . . . . .26 F1
Carryer ST5 . . . . .70 F8
Carshalton Gr WV2 . . . .266 E7
Carson Rd ST6 . . . . .41 F3
Carson Way ST16 . . . . . .155 C3
Carter Ave WS9 . . . . .258 C8
Carters Croft ST10 . . . . . .92 F3
Cartersfield La WS9 . . . .245 E6
Carter St ST14 . . . . .126 C7
Cartlich St ST6 . . . . .41 D5
Cartlidge St ST4 . . . . . . .56 D1
Cartmel ST16 . . . . .42 B3
Cartway The WV6 . . . . . .254 D4
Cartwright Dr ST20 . . . .171 D7
Cartwright Ho WS3 . . . .243 B1
Cartwright Ind Est The
  ST3 . . . . .284 B2
Cartwright Rd B75 . . . . .258 C3
Cartwright St
  Longton ST3 . . . . .284 B3
  Wolverhampton WV2 . . . .266 D8
Carver Gdns DY8 . . . . . .279 E2
Carver Rd
  Burton u T DE13 . . . . . . .166 C6
  Stafford ST16 . . . . .155 E6
Casa Mia Ct WS12 . . . . .210 C5
Casewell Rd
  Kingswinford DY6 . . . . . .275 D8
  Stoke-on-T ST6 . . . . .57 C7

Casey La Burton u T DE14 . .166 B4
  Weston CW2 . . . . .37 A5
Casey The ST13 . . . . .48 A1
Cash La ST21 . . . . .132 E4
Caslon Cres DY8 . . . . . . .279 D4
Caspian Gr ST4 . . . . .49 A4
Caspian Way ST19 . . . . .205 C6
Cassandra CI DY5 . . . . . .271 C1
Castel CI ST5 . . . . .70 E3
Castle Acre ST4 . . . . . . .174 B7
Castle Bank ST16,ST17 . .174 A8
Castle Barns DY10 . . . . .280 B3
Castlechurch Prim Sch
  ST17 . . . . .174 B8
Castle CI Brownhills WS8 . .228 F2
  Tamworth B77 . . . . .250 E4
Castlecroft Ave WV3 . . .265 A8
Castlecroft Gdns WV3 . . .265 C8
Castlecroft La WV6 . . . .254 F1
Castlecroft St ST5 . . . . .227 E5
Castlecroft Prim Sch
  WV3 . . . . .265 B8
Castlecroft Rd WV3 . . . .265 B8
Castledene Dr ST16 . . . .155 C1
Castle Dr ST3 . . . . .73 E4
Castlefields ST10 . . . . . .285 A2
Castlefield St ST4 . . . . . . .57 A2
Castlefort Jun Mix Inf Sch
  WS9 . . . . .245 A3
Castlefort Rd WS9 . . . . .245 A8
Castle Gr ST2 . . . . .58 B5
Castlehall B77 . . . . .251 A2
Castle Hayes La DE13 . .146 A5
Castle Hill Rd ST10 . . . . .78 E1
Castlehill Rd WS9 . . . . . .245 C3
Castle Hill Rd ST5 . . . . .283 A3
Castle Hill Stafford ST16 . .285 A3
  Tutbury DE13 . . . . .146 B7
Castle Ho ST7 . . . . .26 C3
Castle House Dr ST17 . .155 B1
Castle House Sch TF10 . .168 F4
Castle Inn Rd ST7 . . . . . . .26 F4
Castle Keep Ct ST5 . . . .283 A2
Castle Keep Mews ST5 . .283 A2
Castle La CW3 . . . . .68 F5
Castle Mount ST5 . . . . . .55 E6
Castle Park Inf Sch DE13 . .168 B8
Castle Park Rd DE13 . . .166 B8
Castle Prim Sch ST7 . . . .26 D6
Castle Rd Brownhills WS9 . .245 A3
  Cookley DY10 . . . . .280 A4
  Mow Cop ST7 . . . . .26 D7
  Swadlincote DE11 . . . . . .186 F1
  Tamworth B77 . . . . .261 F5
Castle Ridge ST5 . . . . . . .70 F8
Castle Ring Fort* WS15 . .211 E6
Castle St Brownhills WS8 . .228 F2
  Eccleshall ST21 . . . . .133 E7
  Kinver DY7 . . . . .278 A4
  Newcastle-u-L,Chesterton
  ST5 . . . . .55 E7
  Newcastle-u-L ST5 . . . . .283 C3
  Sedgley DY3 . . . . .271 D8
  Stafford ST16 . . . . .155 E6
  Tutbury DE13 . . . . .146 C6
Castleton Rd
  Stoke-on-T ST3 . . . . .89 E8
  Walsall WS3 . . . . .243 C3
Castle View Biddulph ST8 . .27 C6
  Derrington ST18 . . . . . . .154 E2
Castle View Est ST18 . .154 E1
Castleview Gr ST16 . . . . . .41 E8
Castle View DE65 . . . . . .146 C8
Castleview Rd ST7 . . . . . .26 B3
Castle View Stafford ST16 . .285 A3
  Tamworth B77 . . . . .250 C3
Castle Way ST16 . . . . . .155 C2
Castle Way The DE65 . . .148 F5
Castle Wlk ST5 . . . . .283 B3
Castrum Ct ST14 . . . . .96 A3
Caswell Rd DY3 . . . . . . .271 C8
Catalan CI **4** ST17 . . . . .175 A8
Catalina PI ST3 . . . . .90 C6
Cat And Kittens La
  WV10 . . . . .240 E6
Caterbanck Way **2**
  WS13 . . . . .230 F6
Caterham Dr DY6 . . . . . .275 F3
Caterham PI ST3 . . . . .90 B8
Catesby Dr DY6 . . . . . . .275 D8
Catharine Rd ST6 . . . . . . .42 C6
Cathcart Rd DY8 . . . . . .279 E5
Cathedral Ct **4** WS13 . .231 B8
Cathedral Rise WS13 . . .231 A8
Catherine Ho **1** ST4 . . .71 F8
Catherine St ST6 . . . . . . .56 D4
Catholic La DY3 . . . . . . .271 D7
Catholme La DE13 . . . . .201 F5
Catisfield Cres WV8 . . . .239 F1
Catkin WS15 . . . . .178 C2
Catmeadow La WS15 . . .197 D1
Caton Cres ST6 . . . . .42 F1
Catsbridge La WS11 . . . .225 F2
Catshill Rd WS8 . . . . . . .245 A7
Cauldon Ave
  Cheddleton ST13 . . . . . . .45 D5
  Newcastle-u-L ST5 . . . . . .56 A7
Cauldon CI ST13 . . . . .30 F4
Cauldon CI ST4 . . . . .57 B1
Cauldon Rd ST18 . . . . . . .57 B1
Cauldon Rd ST4 . . . . .57 C1
Caulton St ST6 . . . . .41 F1
Caunsall Rd DY11 . . . . .280 B6
Causeley Gdns ST2 . . . . .58 B3

Causeley Rd ST2 . . . . .58 B3
Causeway PI ST13 . . . . . .33 F6
Cavalier Circus WV10 . . .240 E4
Cavan's CI WS11 . . . . . .209 E4
Cavans Wood Park Home Est
  WS12 . . . . .209 D5
Cavell CI ST11 . . . . .209 E4
Cavell Rd WS7 . . . . .229 E8
Cavendish CI DY6 . . . . .275 D4
Cavendish Dr DY9 . . . . .281 F4
Cavendish Gr ST5 . . . . . . .71 B3
Cavendish Rd ST10 . . . . .92 E5
Cavendish St ST1 . . . . . . .92 E8
Caverswall La ST3 . . . . . .90 C8
Caverswall Old Rd ST11 . .90 F8
Caverswall Rd
  Blythe Bridge ST11 . . . . .90 F8
  Dilhorne ST11 . . . . .75 B3
  Meir ST3 . . . . .79 F3
Caverswall Road Sta*
  ST11 . . . . .74 F1
Cavour St ST1 . . . . .56 F3
Cawdry Bldgs **2** ST13 . . .30 F6
Caxton Ct
  4 Cannock WS11 . . . . . .226 E8
  Burton u T DE14 . . . . . . .166 D1
Caxton St WS11 . . . . . . .226 E8
Cayley PI ST3 . . . . .90 C6
Cecil Ave ST11 . . . . .226 E8
Cecily Gr ST4 . . . . .76 E4
Cecily Terr ST10 . . . . .76 E4
Cecil Payton CI WS15 . .160 F6
Cecil Rd Biddulph ST8 . . .16 C2
  Swadlincote DE11 . . . . . .186 F5
Cecil St Cannock WS11 . .209 F4
  Stourbridge DY8 . . . . . . .279 F5
Cedar Ave
  Blythe Bridge ST11 . . . . .91 A6
  Brownhills WS8 . . . . . . .245 A8
  Kidsgrove ST7 . . . . .25 D1
Cedar CI Burntwood WS7 . .229 A6
  Cannock WS12 . . . . .195 A1
  Cheadle ST10 . . . . .76 F2
  Lichfield WS14 . . . . .231 F7
  Market Drayton TF9 . . . . .97 A1
  Stourbridge DY8 . . . . . . .279 D2
  Uttoxeter ST14 . . . . .110 F1
Cedar Cres Audley ST7 . . .39 F1
  Endon ST9 . . . . .43 E6
  Rugeley WS15 . . . . .197 A5
Cedar Ct Congleton CW12 . .15 F8
  Tamworth B77 . . . . .261 E6
Cedar Dr Albrighton WV7 . .237 A5
  Aldridge B74 . . . . .256 E1
  Stramshall ST14 . . . . . . .110 F4
  Tamworth B79 . . . . .250 E8
Cedar Gdns DY7 . . . . . . .277 F6
Cedar Gr Biddulph ST8 . . .17 B1
  Codsall WV8 . . . . .239 B3
  Great Wyrley WS6 . . . . . .227 B4
  Stoke-on-T ST3 . . . . .72 E3
  Wolverhampton WV3 . . . .265 F7
Cedarhill ST10 . . . . .78 D1
Cedarhill Dr WS11 . . . . .209 F3
Cedar Ho B74 . . . . .257 B5
Cedar Park Rd WV12 . . .242 C8
Cedar Pk ST15 . . . . .120 B8
Cedar Rd
  Barton-u-N DE13 . . . . . .183 D1
  Burntwood WS7 . . . . .229 A7
  Newcastle-u-L ST5 . . . . . .40 D1
Cedars Ave
  Kingswinford DY6 . . . . . .275 D4
  Wombourne WV5 . . . . . .270 A5
Cedars Bsns Ctr The
  WS11 . . . . .226 C7
Cedars Dr ST15 . . . . .120 B5
Cedars Hort Unit The
  WV3 . . . . .255 D2
Cedars The
  5 Wolverhampton,Newbridge
  WV6 . . . . .255 F3
  Wolverhampton,Tettenhall
  WV6 . . . . .255 D5
Cedartree Gr ST1 . . . . . . .57 E8
Cedarwood Dr WV9 . . . .224 B3
Cedar Wood Rd DY3 . . .271 D5
Celandine CI
  Burton u T DE15 . . . . . . .167 C2
  Kingswinford DY6 . . . . . .275 C4
  Stoke-on-T ST2 . . . . .43 B1
Celandines The WV6 . . .269 E6
Celandine
  Sutton Coldfield B74 . . . .257 F5
  Tamworth B77 . . . . .250 C3
Celebration Ct ST6 . . . . .42 C3
Cellarhead Rd ST9 . . . . . .59 E4
Celtic Ave ST7 . . . . .41 F8
Celtic Rd WS11 . . . . .209 E3
Cemetery Ave ST3 . . . . .284 B2
Cemetery Rd
  Cannock WS11 . . . . .209 E4
  Hanley ST4 . . . . .57 B1
  Market Drayton TF9 . . . . .97 B1
  Newcastle-u-L,Knutton ST5 . .55 D5
  Newcastle-u-L,Silverdale
  ST5 . . . . .55 D1
  Weston CW2 . . . . .37 A5
Cemetery St WS6 . . . . . .226 C2
Cemetery View
  Longton ST3 . . . . .284 B2
  Newcastle-u-L ST5 . . . . . .55 E3
Cemetery Way WS3 . . . .243 B1
Cemlyn Ave ST7 . . . . .72 B3

Central Ave
  15 Wolverhampton WV4 . .266 F4
  Bucknall ST2 . . . . .58 B4
  Cannock WS11 . . . . .209 F5
  Coldmeece ST15 . . . . . .118 B8
Central St S ST15 . . . . . .118 B7
Central CI WS3 . . . . .243 A1
Central Dr
  Dudley,Gornalwood DY3 . .271 D2
  Stoke-on-T ST3 . . . . .72 E3
  Walsall WS3 . . . . .243 A1
Central Sq ST10 . . . . .49 A1
Central St ST7 . . . . .26 B6
Central Trad Est WV2 . .266 E8
Central Way DE13 . . . . .166 B7
Centre Rd ST15 . . . . .104 E2
Centrum East Ret Pk
  DE14 . . . . .184 B3
Centurion Pk B77 . . . . . .262 B6
Centurion Way B77 . . . .262 B6
Century Rd ST5 . . . . .40 F2
Century St ST1 . . . . .282 A3
Ceramica* ST6 . . . . .56 F8
Chadsfield Rd WS15 . . . .178 E2
Chadsmead Prim Sch
  WS13 . . . . .214 A1
Chadsmoor CE Jun Sch
  WS11 . . . . .210 A3
Chadsmoor Inf Sch
  WS11 . . . . .210 A3
Chadwell Hls WS13 . . . .214 D2
Chadwell Gdns WV8 . . .238 F4
Chadwell Way ST1 . . . . . .58 D1
Chadwick CI WV4 . . . . .265 D6
Chadwick Cres WS15 . . .198 A8
Chadwick St ST3 . . . . . .284 C3
Chadwick **4** WS15 . . . .196 F8
Chadwyn Dr ST2 . . . . . . .43 B2
Chaffinch CI
  Cannock WS12 . . . . .210 B4
  Stoke-on-T ST3 . . . . .266 C3
Chaffinch Dr Biddulph ST8 . .27 E8
  Uttoxeter ST14 . . . . .126 C6
Chaff La DE6 . . . . .65 D1
Chain La ST17 . . . . .174 E4
Chain St ST6 . . . . .42 C2
Chalcot Dr WS12 . . . . . .210 A7
Chaldon CI WV9 . . . . . .240 A1
Chalfield B79 . . . . .249 D6
Chalford St ST6 . . . . .55 E6
Chalfont Cres WV2 . . . . .37 B2
Chalfont Cres CW2 . . . . .37 B2
Chalfont Ct WS11 . . . . .226 C7
Chalfont Gn ST2 . . . . .58 B2
Challenge CI ST6 . . . . . . .42 C3
Challinor Ave ST11 . . . . .30 E5
Chamberlain Ave ST4 . . .72 A6
Chamberlain CI DE13 . .199 D6
Chamberlain Ct CW3 . . . .3 A6
Chamberlain's La WV4 . .265 E3
Chamberlain St ST11 . .282 B1
Chamberlain Way ST8 . .27 E8
Chambley Gn WV9 . . . .224 B2
Chance Hall La ST7 . . . .25 B8
Chancel Dr TF9 . . . . .97 A1
Chancel Ind Est DY6 . . .270 E1
Chancel Inf Sch WS15 . .178 E2
Chancery Ct WS12 . . . .210 D7
Chancery La ST3 . . . . . .284 C3
Chandler Ave WV7 . . . .277 F5
Chandler Dr WV4 . . . . .265 D3
Chandlers CI WV9 . . . . .240 A1
Chandlers Dr B77 . . . . .251 B5
Chandlers Keep WS8 . . .245 A6
Chanterelle Ct WV4 . . .266 B4
Chanterelle Gdns WV4 . .266 B4
Chantry Rd
  Newcastle-u-L ST5 . . . . .283 B1
  Stourbridge DY7 . . . . . . .279 C2
Chapel Ave WS8 . . . . . . .228 E2
Chapel Bank
  Kidsgrove ST7 . . . . .26 D6
  Wheaton Aston ST19 . . .205 C6
Chapel CI
  Mount Pleasant ST7 . . . . .26 B6
  Wombourne WV5 . . . . . .269 F5
Chapel Ct Barlaston ST12 . .68 C1
  Gnosall ST20 . . . . .171 C6
  Kidderminster DY10 . . . .280 A1
  Newcastle-u-L ST5 . . . . . .55 C2
Chapel Dr Brownhills WS8 . .228 E2
  Mile Oak B78 . . . . .249 C1
Chapel Gn DE6 . . . . .127 C8
Chapel Hill DY10 . . . . . .280 A1
Chapel La Anslow DE13 . .165 A5
  Ashley TF9 . . . . .100 B6
  Audley ST7 . . . . .39 D2
  Biddulph ST8 . . . . .17 A1
  Bradley ST18 . . . . .191 B8
  Brown Edge ST6 . . . . .28 B1
  Burslem ST6 . . . . .57 A8
  Cannock Wood WS15 . . .211 C6
  Cheadle ST10 . . . . .77 D2
  Clifton DE6 . . . . .81 F6
  Codsall WV8 . . . . .238 F3
  Gentleshaw WS15 . . . . .212 A4
  Gratton ST9 . . . . .29 A5
  Hanbury DE13 . . . . .144 F2
  Harriseahead ST7 . . . . . .26 E4
  Kingsley Holt ST10 . . . . .62 A1
  Knighton TF9 . . . . .83 C5
  Lichfield WS14 . . . . .231 B6
  Loggerheads TF9 . . . . . . .99 E3
  Newborough DE13 . . . .148 C1
  Norton in H TF9 . . . . . . .82 C2
  Rangemore DE13 . . . . .164 C3
  Rolleston on D DE13 . . .147 B4
  Smestow DY3 . . . . .269 C4
  Whittington WS14 . . . .232 E5

Chapel Mews B77 . . . . . . 251 A5
Chapel Mus Mow Cop★
ST7 . . . . 26 D7
Chapelon B77 . . . . 251 A2
Chapel Rd WS15 . . . . 197 F5
Chapelside WS15 . . . . . 178 D2
Chapel Sq WS6 . . . . 226 D7
Chapel St Audley ST7 . . . 39 E3
　Brownhills WS8 . . . . 228 E2
　Bucknall ST2 . . . . 58 B4
　Burntwood WS7 . . . . 228 E8
　Cannock WS12 . . . . 210 E1
　Cheadle ST10 . . . . 76 D3
　Forsbrook ST11 . . . . 91 A8
　Kidsgrove ST7 . . . . 25 D2
　Kingsley ST10 . . . . 61 D3
　Kingswinford DY6 . . . . . 275 B8
　Longnor SK17 . . . . 13 B6
　Mount Pleasant ST7 . . . . 26 B6
　Newcastle-u-l,Knutton ST5 . . 55 E3
　Newcastle-u-l,May Bank
ST5 . . . . 56 D4
　Newcastle-u-l,Silverdale
ST5 . . . . 55 C2
　Norton Canes WS11 . . . . 227 F5
　Stafford ST16 . . . . 285 A3
　Stourbridge,Wordsley DY8 . . 275 D3
　Swadlincote DE11 . . . . . . 186 F6
　Walsall WS3 . . . . 244 A3
　Wolverhampton WV2 . . . 266 D7
　Wombourne WV5 . . . . . . 269 F5
Chapel Terr ST16 . . . . . . 285 B4
Chapel Wlk DY3 . . . . 271 C2
Chaplain Rd B35 . . . . . . 210 E2
Chaplin Rd ST3 . . . . 284 C1
Chapter Wlk ST2 . . . . 58 A5
Charlecote Dr DY1 . . . . . 271 E3
Charlemonte Cl WS12 . . 210 F3
Charles Ave
　Essington WV11 . . . . 241 F4
　Kidderminster DY10 . . . . 280 A1
　Wolverhampton WV4 . . . 266 B5
Charles Cl WS6 . . . . 226 D6
Charles Cotton Dr CW3 . . 68 D6
Charles Cotton St ST16 . 155 C6
Charles Cres WS3 . . . . . 244 A5
Charlesdale Dr WS9 . . . 256 B4
Charles Hayward Bglws
WV4 . . . . 266 D3
Charles Rd DY8 . . . . 279 E4
　Cheadle ST10 . . . . 76 D3
　Hanley ST1 . . . . 282 C2
　Newcastle-u-l ST5 . . . . . . 56 D3
Charlestown Gr ST3 . . . . . 90 A7
Charlesway TF9 . . . . 112 B8
Charles Wesley Ct WV3 . 266 A7
Charlock Gr WS11 . . . . . 210 C3
Charlotte Cl ST18 . . . . . . 177 D8
Charlotte St ST16 . . . . . . 41 C7
Charlton St ST4 . . . . 72 B8
Charminster Rd ST3 . . . . . 90 B7
Charmouth Cl ST3 . . . . . . 58 A6
Charnes Rd TF9 . . . . 100 C5
Charnley Dr B75 . . . . 258 E2
Charnley Rd ST16 . . . . . . 155 F6
Charnock Rd ST6 . . . . 42 A7
Charnsford La TF9 . . . . . 100 B4
Charnwood 🄱 ST7 . . . . . . 26 B1
Charnwood Ave DY3 . . . 266 D2
Charnwood Cl
　Cannock WS12 . . . . 210 C3
　Leek ST13 . . . . 30 C4
　Lichfield WS13 . . . . 214 C1
　Rugeley WS15 . . . . 178 C1
Charnwood Ho WS11 . . 214 B2
Charnwood Prim Sch
WS13 . . . . 214 C2
Charnwood Rd
　Burton u T DE13 . . . . 166 B7
　Longton ST3 . . . . 73 D1
Charsley Pl ST13 . . . . 72 F1
Charter Cl WS11 . . . . . . 227 E4
Charter Ct TF9 . . . . 97 D2
Charterfield Dr
　Cannock WS12 . . . . 210 C1
　Kingswinford DY6 . . . . . 275 D8
Charterfields Sh Ctr
DY6 . . . . 275 E8
Charterhouse Dr ST17 . 156 B1
Charter Rd ST5 . . . . 56 A3
Charters Ave WV8 . . . . . 239 B1
Charters The WS13 . . . . 214 B1
Chartley Cl
　Blythe Bridge ST11 . . . . . 90 E6
　Perton WV6 . . . . 254 F4
　Stafford ST16 . . . . 155 C8
Chartley Cotts ST18 . . . 139 D5
Chartley Ct ST14 . . . . . . 126 C7
Chartley Gate ST14 . . . . 126 A6
Chartway The WS3 . . . . . 244 B4
Chartwell Cl ST9 . . . . 59 A3
Chartwell Dr
　Sutton Coldfield B74 . . . 257 D4
　Wolverhampton WV4 . . . 240 A1
　Wombourne WV5 . . . . . . 269 F5
Chartwell Rd ST17 . . . . . 175 C8
Chartwell B79 . . . . 249 D7
Chartwood TF9 . . . . 99 E5
Chase Acad WS11 . . . . . 226 E5
Chase Ave WS6 . . . . 226 E3
Chase Cres ST17 . . . . . . 176 A3
Chaselands WS7 . . . . 228 D7
Chase La ST15 . . . . 103 F6
Chase L Ctr WS11 . . . . . 209 D2
Chaseley Ave WS11 . . . 209 C2

Chaseley Cl WS15 . . . . . 178 B1
Chaseley Croft WS11 . . 209 C2
Chaseley Gdns
　Burntwood WS7 . . . . 229 C7
　Rugeley WS15 . . . . 178 B1
Chaseley Rd WS15 . . . . . 178 B1
Chase Park Ind Est WS7 . 228 D7
Chasepool Rd DY3 . . . . . 274 C8
Chase Rd Brocton ST17 . 176 D2
　Brownhills WS8 . . . . 228 A1
　Burntwood WS7 . . . . 229 B6
　Dudley DY3,DY5 . . . . 271 C1
Chaseside Dr WS11 . . . . 210 B3
Chaseside Ind Est WS7 . 228 D7
Chase Side Rd WS15 . . . 196 D8
Chase Terrace Prim Sch
WS7 . . . . 228 F7
Chase Terrace Tech Coll
WS7 . . . . 229 A7
Chasetown Com Sch
WS7 . . . . 228 E5
Chasetown Ind Est WS7 228 D7
Chasetown Specialist Sports
Coll WS7 . . . . 228 D5
Chase Vale WS7 . . . . 228 D6
Chase View WS15 . . . . . 198 A4
Chase View Com Prim Sch
WS15 . . . . 196 E7
Chase View La ST14 . . . 174 C3
Chaseview Rd DE13 . . . 200 F2
Chase View WV4 . . . . . . 266 E2
Chasewater★ WS7 . . . . . 228 C4
Chasewater Country Pk★
WS7 . . . . 228 C5
Chasewater Gr ST16 . . . . 76 F4
Chasewater Heaths Sta★
WS7 . . . . 228 D6
Chasewater Rly★ WS11 228 B5
Chasewater Way WS11 . 227 F5
Chase Wlk Cannock WS12 209 C4
　Stoke-on-T ST3 . . . . 89 F7
Chasewood Park Bsns Ctr
WS12 . . . . 210 E1
Chatcull La ST15 . . . . . . 101 F1
Chatfield Cl DE15 . . . . . . 167 C1
Chatfield Pl ST3 . . . . 73 D2
Chatham St ST1 . . . . 282 A1
Chatsworth Dr
　Cannock WS11 . . . . 210 A4
　Ford Green ST6 . . . . 42 F5
　Tutbury DE13 . . . . 146 C6
　Werrington ST9 . . . . 59 B3
Chatsworth Gdns WV6 . 255 A7
Chatsworth Ho DE14 . . . 184 F7
Chatsworth Mews ST21 133 E7
Chatsworth Park Ave ST4 72 A1
Chatsworth Pl Longton ST3 73 F1
　Newcastle-u-l ST5 . . . . . . 55 F7
Chatsworth B79 . . . . 249 C7
Chatteris Cl ST1 . . . . 90 B6
Chatterley Cl ST5 . . . . . . 56 B8
Chatterley Dr ST7 . . . . . . 41 B8
Chatterley Rd ST6 . . . . . . 41 C4
Chatterley St ST1 . . . . . . 72 F8
Chatterton Ave WS13 . . 230 E6
Chatterton Pl ST3 . . . . 73 D3
Chatwell La Blymhill TF10 188 D1
　Great Chatwell TF10,TF11 . 203 B3
Chaucer Ave DY3 . . . . . . 271 A5
Chaucer Cl
　Burton u T DE14 . . . . 166 D6
　Lichfield WS14 . . . . 231 B6
　Tamworth B79 . . . . 250 A6
Chaucer Dr WS7 . . . . 212 A1
Chaucer Rd ST17 . . . . . . 174 C8
Chaulden Rd ST16 . . . . . 136 D1
Chawner Cl WS7 . . . . 211 E1
Cheadle Cl ST19 . . . . 200 F7
Cheadle High Sch ST10 . . 76 D2
Cheadle Hospl ST10 . . . . 76 D3
Cheadle Prim Sch ST10 . . 76 D2
Cheadle Rd Alton ST10 . 178 E1
　Blythe Bridge ST11 . . . . . 91 A7
　Cheddleton ST13 . . . . 45 C3
　Draycott in t M ST11 . . . . 91 F6
　Kingsley ST10 . . . . 61 D2
　Leek ST13 . . . . 45 E8
　Upper Tean ST10 . . . . 92 D5
　Uttoxeter ST14 . . . . 111 B1
　Warslow SK17 . . . . 23 B2
　Wetley Rocks ST9 . . . . . . 60 B7
Cheadle Sh Ctr ST10 . . . . 76 D3
Cheam Gdns WV6 . . . . . 255 E8
Cheapside Hanley ST1 . . 282 A2
　Newcastle-u-l ST5 . . . . . . 283 A3
Cheatle Cl B77 . . . . 261 D5
Chebsey Cl ST5 . . . . 58 C4
Chebsey Dr ST16 . . . . . . 155 A6
Checkley Dr ST8 . . . . 16 D1
Checkley Gr 🄱 ST3 . . . . . . 73 D6
Checkley La CW5 . . . . 52 E1
Checkley Rd ST5 . . . . 40 C1
Checkley Row CW5 . . . . . 67 C8
Cheddar Dr ST5 . . . . 54 F2
Cheddleton Flint Mill Mus★
ST13 . . . . 45 C6
Cheddleton Heath Rd
ST13 . . . . 45 E7
Cheddleton Park Ave
ST13 . . . . 45 E6
Cheddleton Rd ST13 . . . . 30 F4
Cheddleton Sta ST13 . . . 45 E5
Cheedale Cl DE15 . . . . . . 167 B5
Chelford Cl ST19 . . . . 193 A1
Chell Cl ST19 . . . . 207 F7
Chell Green Ave ST6 . . . . 42 A6
Chell Green Ct ST6 . . . . . 42 A5

Chell Gr ST5 . . . . 56 A7
Chell Heath Rd
　Stoke-on-T ST6 . . . . 42 B5
　Stoke-on-T ST6 . . . . 42 C4
Chell Rd ST16 . . . . 285 A3
Chell St ST1 . . . . 57 D6
Chelmarsh Ave WV3 . . . 265 B8
Chelmorton Dr ST3 . . . . . 73 E1
Chelmsford Dr ST2 . . . . . . 58 D1
Chelmsford Rd ST5 . . . . . 56 C5
Chelsea Cl ST8 . . . . 16 C1
Chelsea Dr B74 . . . . 257 F4
Chelsea Way
　Kingswinford DY6 . . . . . 275 C6
　Stafford ST16 . . . . 155 C1
Chelson St ST3 . . . . 284 C3
Chelston Dr WV6 . . . . . . 255 E4
Cheltenham Ave ST10 . . 76 E5
Cheltenham Dr
　Kingswinford DY6 . . . . . 275 B6
　Stafford ST17 . . . . 175 C7
Cheltenham Gr
　Birches Head ST1 . . . . 57 F5
　Newcastle-u-l ST5 . . . . . . 54 F2
Chelwood St ST1 . . . . . . 282 A4
Chemical La ST6 . . . . 41 C1
Chenet Way WS11 . . . . . 209 E2
Chepstow Cl Biddulph ST8 16 C1
　Perton WV6 . . . . 254 F4
Chepstow Dr ST17 . . . . . 175 C7
Chepstow Pl ST3 . . . . 73 C6
Chepstow Rd
　Walsall WS3 . . . . 242 F1
　Wolverhampton WV10 . . 240 D5
Chepstow Way WS3 . . . . 242 F1
Chequerfield Dr WV4 . . 266 A6
Chequers Ave WV5 . . . . 265 A1
Chequers Cl WS11 . . . . . 228 A5
Chequers The 🄱 ST15 . . 231 C8
Chequer St WV4 . . . . 266 A6
Cheriton Gr ST2 . . . . 58 D1
Cheriton Gr WV6 . . . . . . 254 C3
Cherrington Dr WS6 . . . 226 F4
Cherrington Gdns WV6 . 255 B2
Cherry Bank ST12 . . . . . 210 C6
Cherrybrook Dr ST19 . . 193 A1
Cherry Cl Burntwood WS7 228 F6
　Fulford ST11 . . . . 106 E8
　Newcastle-u-l ST5 . . . . . . 40 D1
Cherry Ct DE14 . . . . 184 F8
Cherrydale Ct DY1 . . . . . 271 F2
Cherry Gn DY1 . . . . 271 F4
Cherry Gr Stoke-on-T ST3 72 E3
　Stourbridge DY8 . . . . 279 E4
Cherry Hill Dr ST3 . . . . . . 74 A2
Cherry Hill La ST5 . . . . . . 55 E2
Cherry Hill WS11 . . . . 68 E6
Cherry La Cheadle ST10 . 77 A5
　Congleton CW12 . . . . 16 E8
　Gayton ST18 . . . . 138 E5
　Great Bridgeford ST18 . . 135 C2
　Himley DY3 . . . . 270 C3
Cherry Leys ST6 . . . . 167 C4
Cherryl Ho B74 . . . . 257 E3
Cherry Orch
　Lichfield WS14 . . . . 231 C7
　Newcastle-u-l ST5 . . . . . . 283 A3
　Stone ST15 . . . . 120 C7
Cherry St Stourbridge DY8 279 E4
　Tamworth B79 . . . . 250 C3
Cherry Tree Ave ST7 . . . . 25 A5
Cherry Tree Cl
　Eccleshall ST21 . . . . 133 C4
　Stoke-on-T ST4 . . . . 88 A7
　Stone ST15 . . . . 119 F5
　Swadlincote DE11 . . . . . 186 F6
Cherrytree Cres ST18 . . 135 B3
Cherry Tree Gdns WV8 . 239 B3
Cherry Tree Ho WS16 . . 196 F6
Cherry Tree La
　Biddulph ST8 . . . . 17 B1
　Codsall WV8 . . . . 239 B3
　Woore CW3 . . . . 67 C2
Cherry Tree Rd ST7 . . . . . 39 F1
Cherrytree Rd DE15 . . . 185 F6
Cherry Tree Rd
　Huntington WS12 . . . . . . 209 D8
　Kingswinford DY6 . . . . . 275 E8
　Newcastle-u-l ST5 . . . . . . 40 E1
　Norton Canes WS11 . . . . 228 B5
　Rugeley WS15 . . . . 196 F6
　Stone ST15 . . . . 120 C7
Cherry Tree Wlk B79 . . . 250 A8
Cherry Way TF9 . . . . 97 D2
Cherrywood Cl 🄱 ST17 . 175 C6
Cherrywood Dr ST4 . . . . . 89 F6
Cherrywood Rd B74 . . . 256 D1
Cherrywood Way B74 . . 257 D4
Chertsey Pl ST1 . . . . 57 D8
Chervil Cl ST3 . . . . 90 A6
Cherwell Dr WS8 . . . . . . 228 C2
Cherwell B77 . . . . 250 D1
Chesham Gr ST3 . . . . 90 A6
Chesham Rd ST16 . . . . . . 155 F6
Cheshire Cl
　Burntwood WS7 . . . . 229 F8
　Stourbridge DY8 . . . . 279 D8
Cheshire Dr ST19 . . . . . . 223 D6
Cheshire Gdns TF9 . . . . . 97 C2
Cheshire Gr WV6 . . . . . . 254 E4
Cheshire St TF9 . . . . 72 F1
Cheslyn Dr WS6 . . . . 226 D2
Cheslyn Hay High Sch
WS6 . . . . 226 C3
Cheslyn Hay Prim Sch
WS6 . . . . 226 C3
Chessington Cres ST4 . . 88 C7
Chestall Rd WS15 . . . . . . 211 F5

Chester Ave WV6 . . . . . . 255 F7
Chester Cl Cannock WS11 210 B1
　Lichfield WS13 . . . . 214 C3
　Talke ST7 . . . . 25 C7
Chester Cres ST5 . . . . 71 B5
Chesterfield Ave DE11 . 186 E6
Chesterfield Ct WS9 . . . . 244 F4
Chester Rd Aldridge B74 . 256 E4
　Audley ST7 . . . . 39 D2
　Chetwynd TF10 . . . . 168 C8
　Eccleshall ST21 . . . . 133 C7
　Enville DY7 . . . . 273 F2
　Kinver DY7 . . . . 277 F7
　Rugeley WS15 . . . . 196 D6
　Stonnall WS9 . . . . 245 D3
　Talke ST7 . . . . 40 D7
　Weston-Under-Lizard TF11 . 203 B4
　Whittington WS14 . . . . . 232 C3
Chester Road N WS9 . . . 245 D2
Chesterton Com High Sch
ST5 . . . . 55 E7
Chesterton Prim Sch ST5 55 F7
Chesterton Rd
　Burton u T DE14 . . . . 166 D7
　Pattingham WV6 . . . . . . 253 A2
Chesterton Stadium ST5 . 55 D5
Chesterton Way
　Gorstyhill CW2 . . . . 37 C3
　Tamworth B79 . . . . 250 A7
Chester Wood WS9 . . . . 256 F7
Chesterwood Rd ST6 . . . 42 B3
Chestnut Ave B79 . . . . . . 250 B7
Chestnut Cl Aldridge B74 . 257 A3
　Armitage WS15 . . . . 198 C3
　Cannock WS11 . . . . 210 C2
　Codsall WV8 . . . . 238 F2
　Derrington ST18 . . . . 154 E2
　Gnosall ST20 . . . . 171 D7
　Stourbridge DY8 . . . . 279 D3
　Upper Tean ST10 . . . . 92 F3
Chestnut Cres ST11 . . . . 91 A6
Chestnut Ct
　🄱 Stone ST15 . . . . 104 F3
　Burntwood WS7 . . . . 228 F4
　Cotes Heath ST21 . . . . . . 102 D2
　Rugeley WS15 . . . . 196 E8
Chestnut Dr
　Cheslyn Hay WS6 . . . . . . 226 D3
　Great Wyrley WS6 . . . . . 226 F3
　Hagley DY9 . . . . 281 F4
　Shenstone WS14 . . . . . . 246 F5
　Stafford ST17 . . . . 174 E5
　Wombourne WV5 . . . . . . 270 A5
　Yarnfield ST15 . . . . 118 C6
Chestnut Rd
　Brown Edge ST6 . . . . 43 C7
　Burton u T DE15 . . . . 185 F7
　Loggerheads TF9 . . . . 99 E5
　Market Drayton TF9 . . . . 112 A8
Chestnut Way WV3 . . . . 265 D8
Cheswardine Prim Sch
TF9 . . . . 130 A8
Cheswardine Rd ST5 . . . . 56 B8
Cheswell Cl WV6 . . . . . . 255 B2
Chetton Gn WV10 . . . . . 240 B3
Chetwode Cl TF9 . . . . 83 C5
Chetwynd Ave
　Stoke-on-T ST6 . . . . 42 E5
　Werrington ST2 . . . . 59 A3
Chetwynd Cl
　Penkridge ST19 . . . . 207 F7
　Rugeley WS15 . . . . 196 B3
Chetwynd Ctr The ST16 . 285 B2
Chetwynd End TF10 . . . . 168 E3
Chetwynd Gdns WS11 . 209 D3
Chetwynd Gr TF10 . . . . . 168 F4
Chetwynd Pk
　Cannock WS12 . . . . 211 B5
　Chetwynd TF10 . . . . 168 D8
Chetwynd Rd
　Chetwynd TF10 . . . . 168 C6
　Newcastle-u-l ST5 . . . . . . 56 B6
　Newport TF10 . . . . 168 E4
　Wolverhampton WV2 . . . 266 B6
Chetwynd St
　Newcastle-u-l ST5 . . . . . . 56 D5
　Stoke-on-T ST5 . . . . 42 E1
Chevening Cl DY3 . . . . . 271 E7
Chevin The DE13 . . . . . . 147 C1
Cheviot Cl ST5 . . . . 55 E3
Cheviot Dr WS8 . . . . 258 A4
Cheviot Gr ST6 . . . . 42 C2
Cheviot Rd Rugeley WS15 178 C3
　Stoke-on-T ST6 . . . . 42 C2
Cheviot Rd WV2 . . . . 266 F7
Cheviot Rise ST2 . . . . . . 210 C5
Cheviot B77 . . . . 250 D1
Chichester Cl WS15 . . . . 196 D6
Chichester Dr WS12 . . . 210 C1
Chichester Wlk ST1 . . . . 282 C4
Chickerley Pl WS15 . . . . 178 C1
Childerplay Rd ST8 . . . . . 27 C3
Chilgrove Cl ST1 . . . . 57 F5
Chilgrove Gdns WV6 . . . 255 C5
Chillaghem B77 . . . . 261 C7
Chillington Cl WS6 . . . . . 226 F1
Chillington Dr
　Codsall WV8 . . . . 238 F4
　Dudley DY3 . . . . 271 F3

Chillington Hall★ WV8 . 222 E2
Chillington Ho WV6 . . . . 255 E5
Chillington La WV8 . . . . 238 D6
Chillington St
　Codsall Wood WV8 . . . . . 222 F2
　Coven WV9 . . . . 223 E2
Chillington Way ST6 . . . . 42 E1
Chiltern Cl
　Cheslyn Hay WS6 . . . . . . 226 D1
　Chorlton CW2 . . . . 37 B1
　Dudley DY3 . . . . 271 D3
Chiltern Ct B75 . . . . 258 A4
Chiltern La ST21 . . . . 133 F6
Chiltern Pl ST5 . . . . 55 E3
Chiltern Rd
　Swadlincote DE11 . . . . . 186 F3
　Tamworth B77 . . . . 251 C1
Chilton Ct DE13 . . . . 147 E1
Chilton St ST4 . . . . 72 E5
Chilwell Ave ST18 . . . . . 177 E7
Chilworth Gr ST1 . . . . 72 F1
China St ST4 . . . . 72 F5
Chingford Cl DY8 . . . . . . 275 C4
Chivelstone Gr ST14 . . . . 88 C6
Cholerton Cl ST4 . . . . 72 E5
Chorley Ave ST5 . . . . 42 A6
Chorley Rd WS7 . . . . 212 A2
Chorley St ST13 . . . . 30 E5
Chorlton La CW2 . . . . 37 B2
Chorlton Moss ST5 . . . . . 85 D4
Chorlton Rd ST11 . . . . 57 D6
Chorlton Terr ST14 . . . . 111 C3
Christ Church CE Fst Sch
ST15 . . . . 105 A1
Christ Church CE Inf Sch
WV6 . . . . 255 B3
Christ Church CE Jun Sch
WV6 . . . . 255 C4
Christ Church CE Mid Sch
ST15 . . . . 105 A2
Christ Church CE Prim Sch
　Lichfield WS13 . . . . 230 F7
　Stoke-on-T ST4 . . . . 72 E6
Christ Church Gdns
WS13 . . . . 230 F7
Christ Church Inf Sch
DE14 . . . . 166 C2
Christchurch La WS13 . . 230 F7
Christ Church St TF9 . . . 112 A7
Christchurch St ST17 . . . 72 E5
Christchurch Way ST15 . 105 A1
Christie Ave ST16 . . . . . . 155 C3
Christie Pl ST3 . . . . 73 F5
Christie St ST12 . . . . 58 A3
Christopher Rd WV2 . . . 266 E8
Christopher Sq ST4 . . . . . 72 F5
Christopher Terr ST17 . . 156 A2
Christopher Wlk WS13 . . 214 A3
Chubb Way ST4 . . . . 71 B4
Chub B77 . . . . 261 D7
Chumleigh Gr ST6 . . . . . . 42 A2
Church Ave Grindon ST13 . 34 B1
　Hatton DE65 . . . . 146 D8
　Stoke-on-T ST2 . . . . 43 B2
Church Bank Audley ST7 . 39 D2
　Cauldon ST10 . . . . 63 F7
　Keele ST5 . . . . 69 F7
　Oakamoor ST10 . . . . 78 A6
Churchbridge Pk WS11 . 210 B3
Church Cl Biddulph ST8 . . 27 D6
　Burton u T DE15 . . . . 167 B3
　Drayton Bassett B78 . . . 260 E5
　Gnosall ST20 . . . . 171 E6
　Haughton ST18 . . . . 172 E6
　Kingstone ST14 . . . . 141 C8
　Marchington ST14 . . . . . 127 C7
　Ranton ST18 . . . . 153 D5
　Rugeley WS15 . . . . 196 B3
　Shenstone WS14 . . . . . . 247 A5
　Stafford ST17 . . . . 174 F6
　Stoke-on-T ST3 . . . . 89 F5
　Stone ST15 . . . . 120 B8
　Wood End CV9 . . . . 262 C1
Church Cotts
　Biddulph Moor ST8 . . . . . 17 B1
　Coppenhall ST18 . . . . . . 174 B3
　Penkridge ST19 . . . . 192 C1
　Rangemore DE13 . . . . . . 164 C2
Church Cres WS11 . . . . . 241 F3
Church Croft ST14 . . . . . 125 C7
Churchcroft Gdns WS15 178 F2
Church Dr B78 . . . . 249 B7
Church Eaton Prim Sch
ST20 . . . . 190 A8
Church Eaton Rd TF10 . 192 E1
Church Farm TF9 . . . . . . 100 C5
Church Farm Barn & Cotts
DY10 . . . . 281 B3
Church Farm St ST19 . . . 192 E1
Church Farm Mews
DE13 . . . . 199 C7
Churchfield ST14 . . . . . . 110 F4
Churchfield Ave ST4 . . . . 73 C1
Churchfield Cl
　Coven WV9 . . . . 224 C2
　Stafford ST17 . . . . 156 C1
Churchfield Ct ST5 . . . . . . 55 D5
Churchfield Rd ST21 . . . 133 C6
Churchfields CE Jun Sch
WS15 . . . . 196 E8
Church Fields Keele ST5 . . 69 F7
　Norton in H TF9 . . . . 82 C2
Churchfields Prim Sch
ST5 . . . . 55 F6

Churchfields DE13 . . . . **182** A2
Church Gdns ST3 . . . . **284** C4
Church Gr ST21 . . . . **133** D7
Church Hill
Cannock WS12 . . . . **210** D4
Codsall WV8 . . . . **238** F5
Church Hill Dr WV6 . . . . . **255** E5
Church Hill Kinver DY7 . . **278** B2
Longdon WS15 . . . . **213** A8
Church Hill Rd WV6 . . . . **255** D5
Church Hill St DE15 . . . . **167** B3
Church Hill WV4 . . . . **265** E4
Church Hollow B79 . . . . **217** C5
Churchill Ave
Cheddleton ST13 . . . . **45** D5
Trentham ST4 . . . . **87** F7
Churchill Cl
Blythe Bridge ST11 . . . . . . **90** E6
Uttoxeter ST14 . . . . **126** C7
Churchill Cres DE15 . . . . **200** F2
Churchill Gdns DY3 . . . . **271** C7
Churchill La DY10 . . . . . . **281** B3
Churchill Rd Cheadle ST10 . **76** E4
Shenstone WS14 . . . . **247** A5
Stone ST15 . . . . **119** F7
Churchill Way
Stafford ST17 . . . . **174** E6
Trentham ST4 . . . . **87** F7
Church La
Albrighton WV7 . . . . **237** A2
Armitage WS15 . . . . **197** F5
Barton-u-N DE13 . . . . **183** D1
Betley CW3 . . . . **53** C5
Biddulph ST8 . . . . **17** B1
Bobbington DY7 . . . . **268** A1
Bradley ST18 . . . . **173** C1
Bramshall ST14 . . . . **125** C2
Cannock WS11 . . . . **208** F1
Cauldon ST10 . . . . **63** F7
Checkley ST10 . . . . **109** B8
Cheslyn Hay WS11 . . . . . . **225** F8
Chilcote DE12 . . . . **219** E3
Codsall WV8 . . . . **238** F4
Coven WV9 . . . . **224** C2
Croxton ST21 . . . . **116** A6
Derrington ST18 . . . . **154** E2
Draycott in t M ST11 . . . . . . **91** E5
Edingale B79 . . . . **217** D5
Ellastone DE6 . . . . **80** B4
Endon ST9 . . . . **43** F8
Fradley WS13 . . . . **215** E8
Gayton ST18 . . . . **138** D5
Gnosall TF10 . . . . **188** D8
Hammerwich WS7 . . . . . . **229** D3
Hanbury DE13 . . . . **145** A4
Hill Ridware WS15 . . . . . . **198** A7
Hixon ST18 . . . . **158** C8
Ipstones ST10 . . . . **46** E1
King's Bromley DE13 . . . . **199** E6
Kingstone ST14 . . . . **141** C7
Lapley ST19 . . . . **206** A6
Lawton-gate ST7 . . . . **25** C4
Leek ST13 . . . . **30** E6
Marchington ST14 . . . . . . **127** F2
Mayfield DE6 . . . . **81** C6
Middleton B78 . . . . **260** C1
Mow Cop ST7 . . . . **26** E7
Newcastle-u-L,Knutton ST5 . **55** E2
Newcastle-u-L,Wolstanton
ST5 . . . . **56** D4
Newton Solney DE15 . . . . **167** D8
Oulton ST15 . . . . **105** C3
Rocester ST14 . . . . **96** A3
Rugeley WS15 . . . . **178** B2
Scholar Green ST7 . . . . **25** C7
Seisdon WV5 . . . . **264** B2
Shuttington B79 . . . . **151** C7
Stafford ST16 . . . . **285** B3
Standon ST21 . . . . **102** B3
Stoke-on-T ST4 . . . . **71** F2
Stonnall WS9 . . . . **245** E4
Tamworth B79 . . . . **250** B5
Thorpe DE6 . . . . **51** D1
Church Lawton Prim Sch
ST7 . . . . **25** A5
Church Mdw Ipstones ST10 **46** F1
Norton in t TF9 . . . . **32** D2
Church Mews DE5 . . . . . . **146** D8
Church Moat Way WS3 . . **243** B1
Church of the Ascension CE
Prim Sch DY6 . . . . **275** C8
Church Plantation ST5 . . . **70** A7
Church Rd Alrewas ST14 . **200** F3
Ashley TF9 . . . . **100** C6
Biddulph ST8 . . . . **27** D6
Brewood ST19 . . . . **223** C6
Brown Edge ST6 . . . . **43** B8
Brownhills WS8 . . . . **244** F7
Burntwood WS7 . . . . **229** D7
Burton u T DE14 . . . . **184** E7
Codsall WV8 . . . . **238** F4
Egginton DE65 . . . . **148** B4
Elford B79 . . . . **216** D1
Hixon ST18 . . . . **139** C1
Huntington WS12 . . . . **209** A2
Kinver DY7 . . . . **278** A2
Norton Canes WS11 . . . . . **227** E4
Penkridge ST19 . . . . **192** E1
Perton WV6 . . . . **254** E4
Rolleston on D DE13 . . . . **147** A4
Shareshill WV10 . . . . **225** D2
Shenstone WS14 . . . . **246** F5
Snelston DE6 . . . . **81** C3
Stoke-on-T ST3 . . . . **88** F8
Stonnall WS9 . . . . **245** E3

Church Rd continued
Stourbridge DY8 . . . . **275** E2
Stretton DE13 . . . . **147** F2
Swindon DY3 . . . . **269** D2
Tamworth B77 . . . . **261** C4
Walsall WS3 . . . . **244** A3
Wolverhampton,Bradmore
WV3 . . . . **265** F7
Wolverhampton,Oxley
WV10 . . . . **240** C1
Wolverhampton,Tettenhall Wood
WV6 . . . . **255** B3
Wolverhampton,Tettenhall
WV6 . . . . **255** E5
Wombourne WV5 . . . . **270** B7
Church Row B78 . . . . **260** B1
Churchside DE6 . . . . **217** C2
Churchside Way WS9 . . . **245** B2
Church Sq ST6 . . . . **56** B8
Church St Alstonefield DE6 . **35** E3
Audley,Wereton ST7 . . . . **39** D2
Audley,Wood Lane ST7 . . . . . **40** A1
Brownhills WS8 . . . . **244** E6
Burntwood WS7 . . . . **228** E5
Cannock,Bridgtown WS11 . **226** D6
Cannock,Chadsmoor
WS11 . . . . **210** A4
Cannock WS11 . . . . **209** E1
Cheadle ST10 . . . . **76** D3
Claverley WV5 . . . . **267** C7
Clifton Campville B79 . . . . **218** E2
Dudley,Gornalwood DY3 . . **271** D3
Ecclleshall ST21 . . . . **133** D7
Hartington SK17 . . . . **24** D5
Kidsgrove,Butt Lane ST7 . . . . **25** D1
Kidsgrove ST7 . . . . **26** C4
Kingsley ST10 . . . . **61** E2
Leek ST13 . . . . **30** E6
Lichfield WS13,WS14 . . . . **231** C8
Longnor SK17 . . . . **13** B6
Market Drayton TF9 . . . . **97** D1
Mow Cop ST7 . . . . **26** C6
Nethersеal DE12 . . . . **219** F6
Newcastle-u-L,Chesterton
ST5 . . . . **55** E7
Newcastle-u-L,Silverdale
ST5 . . . . **55** B2
Newcastle-u-L ST5 . . . . . . **283** B3
Rugeley WS15 . . . . **178** E1
Stoke-on-T ST4 . . . . **72** B7
Stone ST15 . . . . **120** B8
Tamworth B79 . . . . **250** B5
Tutbury DE13 . . . . **144** C8
Uttoxeter ST14 . . . . **126** C8
Whittington WS14 . . . . **232** D5
Church Terr Burslem ST6 . **57** B6
Sutton Coldfield B75 . . . . . **258** C3
Warslow SK17 . . . . **23** B2
Church Vale WS11 . . . . . . **227** E4
Church View
Adbaston ST20 . . . . **131** C4
Aldridge WS9 . . . . **256** B6
Barton-u-N DE13 . . . . **244** F3
Burton u T DE13 . . . . **166** C7
Clifton DE6 . . . . **81** F6
Cotes Heath ST21 . . . . **102** E2
Dudley DY3 . . . . **271** D3
Church View Gdns DY7 . **278** A4
Church View
Great Haywood ST18 . . . . **158** B2
Newcastle-u-L ST5 . . . . **55** E2
Rugeley WS15 . . . . **197** A5
Scot Hay ST5 . . . . **54** E4
Tamworth B79 . . . . **261** F7
Churchward Dr DE13 . . . **147** F1
Churchward Gr WV5 . . . . **270** A8
Church Way
Longdon WS15 . . . . **198** A1
Walsall WS4 . . . . **244** E4
Churchwell Ct WV5 . . . . . **270** A6
Church Wlk Aldridge WS9 . **217** C5
Newcastle-u-L ST5 . . . . **55** E7
Wombourne WV5 . . . . **82** C2
Church Wlk
Wolverhampton,Penn
WV6 . . . . **265** F7
Wolverhampton,Tettenhall
WV6 . . . . **255** E5
Churnet Cl
Cheddleton ST13 . . . . **45** B4
Mayfield DE6 . . . . **81** C7
Churnet Ct
Burton u T DE14 . . . . **166** E3
Cheddleton ST13 . . . . **45** B4
Churnet Gr WV6 . . . . **254** F4
Churnet Rd
Blythe Bridge ST11 . . . . . . **91** A7
Cheadle ST10 . . . . **76** E1
Hilton DE65 . . . . **147** D8
Churnet Row ST14 . . . . . . **95** F3
Churnetside Bsns Pk
ST13 . . . . **45** D6
Churnet Valley Railway*
Churnet Valley Rd ST10 . . **62** A2
Churnet Valley Rly Ctr*
ST13 . . . . **45** C5
Churnet Valley Wildlife
Sanctuary* ST10 . . . . . . **61** E4
Churnet View ST13 . . . . . . **31** A8
Churnet View Mid Sch
ST13 . . . . **31** A8
Churnet View Rd ST10 . . . . **78** A7
Churn Hill Rd WS9 . . . . . **256** B4
Churns Hill La DY3 . . . . . **270** B3
Churston Cl
Newcastle-u-L ST5 . . . . **71** B2
Walsall WS3 . . . . **243** A3

Churston Pl ST1 . . . . **57** D8
Cicely Haughton Sch
ST13 . . . . **44** F2
Cinderhill Ind Est ST3 . . . . **73** E4
Cinder Hill La WV9 . . . . . **224** B3
Cinderhill La ST3 . . . . **73** D3
Cinder-hill La ST7 . . . . **25** F7
Cinder Rd
Burntwood WS7 . . . . **228** E7
Dudley DY3 . . . . **271** B2
Cinder Rock Way ST7 . . . . **26** C1
Circular Rd WV7 . . . . **220** E1
City Arc 1 WS13 . . . . **231** B7
City Bank ST8 . . . . **16** C2
City La ST9 . . . . **30** A3
City of Stoke-on-Trent Sixth
Form Coll ST4 . . . . **72** D2
City Rd ST4 . . . . **72** D6
Clamgoose La ST10 . . . . . . **76** C7
Clanbrook Rd DY7 . . . . . . **278** A7
Clandon Ave ST6 . . . . **41** E4
Clanford Cl ST17 . . . . **174** F5
Clanford La ST18 . . . . **154** A5
Clanford Rd ST18 . . . . **154** A7
Clanway St ST6 . . . . **41** E5
Clap Gate Gr WV5 . . . . . . **269** E6
Clap Gate Rd WV5 . . . . . . **269** E7
Clare Ave
Newcastle-u-L ST5 . . . . **56** B6
Wolverhampton WV11 . . . . **241** F1
Clare Cres WV14 . . . . **266** F2
Claregate Prim Sch WV6 . **255** F7
Claremont Cl
Newcastle-u-L ST5 . . . . **56** C7
Stone ST15 . . . . **120** B8
Claremont Cotts DY3 . . . . **271** E8
Claremont Gr ST17 . . . . . **174** B8
Claremont Mews WV3 . . . **266** A7
Claremont Rd
Eccleshall ST21 . . . . **133** E6
Sedgley DY3 . . . . **271** E8
Tamworth B79 . . . . **250** A8
Clarence Gdns B74 . . . . . **257** F3
Clarence Rd Longton ST3 . **284** B4
Sutton Coldfield B74 . . . . . **257** F4
Clarence St
Burton u T DE14 . . . . **166** C1
Dudley DY3 . . . . **271** E5
Newcastle-u-L,Porthill ST5 . **56** B5
Stoke-on-T ST4 . . . . **72** E6
Clarendon Dr ST17 . . . . . . **174** B8
Clarendon Pl WS3 . . . . . . **243** F3
Clarendon Rd
Sutton Coldfield B75 . . . . . **258** C3
Walsall WS4 . . . . **244** C2
Clarendon St
Stoke-on-T ST4 . . . . **72** C6
Walsall WS3 . . . . **243** B1
Clare Rd ST16 . . . . **155** C7
Clare St Harriseahead ST7 . **26** E4
Mow Cop ST7 . . . . **26** D1
Stoke-on-T ST4 . . . . **56** D1
Claridge Rd ST4 . . . . **56** E1
Clarion Way WS11 . . . . . . **209** E5
Clarke Ho WS3 . . . . **243** B1
Clarke Ind Est DE14 . . . . **166** E3
Clarke's Ave WS12 . . . . . . **195** A1
Clarkes Cl ST14 . . . . **111** B1
Clarke St ST1 . . . . **282** A1
Clark Rd WV3 . . . . **255** F2
Clark's Cres WS15 . . . . . . **161** A6
Clark St Stafford ST16 . . . . **285** C3
Stourbridge DY8 . . . . **279** E4
Claud St ST14 . . . . **72** D4
Claverdon Cl WS8 . . . . . . **245** A8
Claverdon Dr B74 . . . . . . **257** B4
Claverhouse Rd DE15 . . . **167** A2
Claverley CE Prim Sch
WV5 . . . . **267** C7
Claverley Dr WV4 . . . . . . **265** D5
Clayalders Bank ST21 . . . **101** C6
Claydon Cres ST5 . . . . **71** B2
Claydon Rd DY6 . . . . **270** C1
Clayfield Gr ST3 . . . . **73** C6
Clayfield Gr W ST3 . . . . . . **73** C6
Claygate Rd WS12 . . . . . . **210** E3
Clay Gates Rd ST19 . . . . . **207** A1
Claygates Rd ST19 . . . . . . **223** F8
Clayhanger Cl ST5 . . . . . . **56** B8
Clayhanger La WS8 . . . . . **244** D6
Clayhanger Rd WS8 . . . . . **244** F6
Clayhanger St 5 ST6 . . . . . **56** F8
Clay Hills ST6 . . . . **41** D3
Clay Lake ST9 . . . . **43** E7
Claymills Rd
Burton u T DE13 . . . . **148** A2
Stretton DE13 . . . . **147** F2
Claymore B77 . . . . **261** D7
Clay Pit La WV18 . . . . **230** F3
Clay St DE15 . . . . **167** A1
Clay's La DE14 . . . . **184** F8
Clay St Burton u T DE15 . . **166** F1
Penkridge ST19 . . . . **192** E1
Clayton Ave
Newcastle-u-L ST5 . . . . **71** C4
Stoke-on-T SY4,ST5 . . . . . . **71** D5
Clayton Rd ST5 . . . . **71** C4
Clayton St ST3 . . . . **284** C3
Claytonwood Rd ST4 . . . . . **71** E3
Cleadon Pl ST2 . . . . **58** B6
Clear View DY6 . . . . **275** B6
Clearwater Ind Est WV2 . **266** F7
Clearwell Gdns DY1 . . . . **271** F3

Cleasby B77 . . . . **251** C1
Cleaveland Mews 2
WS13 . . . . **214** A1
Cleave Rd DE14 . . . . **185** A8
Clee Hill Dr WV3 . . . . **255** A1
Clee Hill Rd DY3 . . . . **271** D4
Clee Rd DY10 . . . . **280** B5
Cleeton St WS12 . . . . **210** D4
Clee Dr B74 . . . . **257** F6
Cleeve Rd WS3 . . . . **242** F3
Cleeve B77 . . . . **250** D3
Cleeve Way WS3 . . . . **242** F3
Clee View Mdw DY3 . . . . **266** D2
Clee View Rd WV5 . . . . . . **269** E5
Clegg Rd WS7 . . . . **229** E7
Clematis Ave ST11 . . . . **90** F6
Clematis Cl ST18 . . . . **135** B2
Clematis Cres DE15 . . . . . **186** A8
Clematis Dr WV9 . . . . **239** F3
Clematis B77 . . . . **250** F3
Clement Cl ST16 . . . . **155** F5
Clement Pl ST6 . . . . **42** E3
Clement Rd ST6 . . . . **42** A6
Clent View Rd DY8 . . . . . **279** C2
Clerk Bank ST13 . . . . **30** E6
Clermont Ave ST4 . . . . **72** A2
Clevedon Ave ST17 . . . . . **175** E7
Cleveland Cl WV11 . . . . . **241** F1
Cleveland Ct DE15 . . . . . . **167** B3
Cleveland Dr WS11 . . . . . **210** B4
Cleveland Rd Hanley ST1 . **282** B1
Newcastle-u-L ST5 . . . . **55** E3
Cleveland St
15 Burslem ST6 . . . . **56** F8
Stourbridge DY8 . . . . **279** E4
Cleveland Trad Est ST1 . . **282** A1
Cleveland Wlk ST17 . . . . **174** B8
Cleves Cres WS6 . . . . **226** D1
Clewley Dr WV9 . . . . **240** B3
Clewley Rd DE14 . . . . **184** F8
Clewlow Pl ST3 . . . . **284** D5
Clewlows Bank ST9 . . . . . . **43** F3
Clews St ST6 . . . . **56** E7
Clews Wlk ST5 . . . . **56** E3
Cley Gr ST5 . . . . **71** B2
Cliffdon Ho DE65 . . . . **146** D8
Cliffe Pl ST6 . . . . **42** A3
Cliff Hall La B78 . . . . **261** C1
Clifford Ave ST6 . . . . **42** F5
Clifford Cl B77 . . . . **250** F3
Clifford Rd TF9 . . . . **112** B8
Clifford St Hanley ST1 . . . **282** C1
Tamworth B77 . . . . **250** D5
Cliff Rd ST18 . . . . **158** C1
Cliffs La TF10 . . . . **150** E1
Cliff St ST6 . . . . **42** C1
Cliff Vale Rd ST4 . . . . **56** F1
Clifton Ave Aldridge WS9 . **245** C1
Brownhills WS8 . . . . **244** D7
Cannock WS11 . . . . **226** C2
Tamworth B79 . . . . **250** A7
Clifton Cl Stafford ST16 . . **156** B3
Stoke-on-T ST4 . . . . **72** E5
Swadlincote DE11 . . . . **186** F2
Clifton Dr ST16 . . . . **156** B3
Clifton Gdns WV8 . . . . . . **239** C3
Clifton La B79 . . . . **235** B3
Clifton Rd Clifton DE6 . . . . **81** F7
Kidderminster DY10 . . . . . **280** C3
Nethersеal DE12 . . . . **219** D6
Wolverhampton WV6 . . . . . **255** D5
Clifton St
Newcastle-u-L ST5 . . . . **56** D4
Sedgley WV14 . . . . **266** F1
Stoke-on-T ST4 . . . . **72** E5
Stourbridge DY8 . . . . **279** F4
Clifton Way DE15 . . . . . . **167** B2
Clinton Cres WS7 . . . . . . **229** B8
Clinton La ST17 . . . . **175** D7
Clinton Sq ST17 . . . . **120** A2
Clive Ave ST2 . . . . **43** B3
Clive Cl B75 . . . . **258** D2
Cliveden Ave WS9 . . . . . . **245** B1
Cliveden Coppice B74 . . **257** F1
Cliveden Pl ST3 . . . . **284** C2
Cliveden Rd ST2 . . . . **58** B5
Clive Gdns TF9 . . . . **97** C1
Clive Ho DE15 . . . . **167** C4
Clive Rd Burntwood WS7 . **229** A7
Market Drayton TF9 . . . . **97** C1
Newcastle-u-L ST5 . . . . **56** D6
Pattingham WV6 . . . . **263** C7
Clive St ST6 . . . . **41** E4
Clockmill Ave WS3 . . . . . **243** E3
Clockmill Pl WS3 . . . . **243** F3
Cloister Rd ST4 . . . . **72** A5
Cloisters The
Burton u T DE15 . . . . **166** F1
Gnosall ST20 . . . . **171** E6
Cloister Wlk Bucknall ST2 . **58** A5
Whittington WS14 . . . . **232** E5
Close Bank DE13 . . . . **146** C6
Close La ST7 . . . . **26** D2
Close The Dudley DY3 . . . **271** C4
Enville WV5 . . . . **273** D2
Lichfield WS13 . . . . **231** F6
Madeley CW3 . . . . **68** E7
Meir ST3 . . . . **74** B5
Newton Solney DE15 . . . . **167** B6
Stafford,Moss Pit ST17 . . . **174** E5
Stafford,Rowley Park ST16 . **155** C1
Stoke-on-T ST9 . . . . **43** F7
Swindon DY3 . . . . **269** E2
Tutbury DE13 . . . . **146** B6
Cloud The CW12 . . . . **7** A4
Cloud View CW12 . . . . **6** A2

Clough Hall Dr ST7 . . . . . . **40** E6
Clough Hall Rd ST7 . . . . . . **40** F8
Clough Hall Tech Sch ST7 . **25** F1
Clough La ST7 . . . . **59** A2
Clough St ST1 . . . . **282** A2
Cloughwood Way ST6 . . . . **41** D1
Clovelly Wlk 2 ST6 . . . . . . **56** E7
Clover Ct DE14 . . . . **184** E6
Cloverdale
6 Stafford ST17 . . . . **175** C7
Perton WV6 . . . . **254** D4
Cloverdale Pl ST3 . . . . **73** F3
Cloverdale Rd ST5 . . . . **56** B3
Clover Heath WV5 . . . . . . **267** D7
Clover La DY6 . . . . **275** B7
Clover Mdws WS12 . . . . . **210** C1
Clover Rd ST5 . . . . **56** D6
Clover Ridge WS6 . . . . . . **226** C3
Clowes Rd ST2 . . . . **58** A3
Club Cotts WV10 . . . . **240** C6
Club La WV10 . . . . **240** C6
Club Row DY3 . . . . **271** E5
Club St ST4 . . . . **72** A6
Clumber Ave ST5 . . . . **71** C6
Clumber La DE13 . . . . **146** C6
Clumy Pl ST2 . . . . **58** A5
Clyde Ave ST8 . . . . **16** E1
Clyde Pl ST5 . . . . **71** A4
Clyde Rd ST6 . . . . **57** A7
Clydesdale Rd WS8 . . . . . **244** E6
Clyde St ST1 . . . . **282** A1
Clyde Wlk ST1 . . . . **282** A2
Clynes Way ST3 . . . . **74** B3
Coach La ST5 . . . . **205** C5
Coach Ho The ST7 . . . . **25** C4
Coach House La WS15 . . **178** E1
Coach House Rise B77 . . **261** F7
Coachmans Cl ST16 . . . . . **155** C8
Coachman's Wlk WS15 . . **178** F5
Coalbourn La DY8 . . . . . . **279** F7
Coal Haulage Rd WS12 . **227** F8
Coalmeadow Cl WS3 . . . . **242** F3
Coalpit Hill ST7 . . . . **40** D8
Coalpit La WS15 . . . . **197** A5
Coalport Cl ST10 . . . . **76** D1
Coalport Dr ST15 . . . . **119** F5
Coalville Rd ST3 . . . . **74** B5
Coalway Ave WS3 . . . . . . **266** A6
Coalway Gdns WV3 . . . . . **265** D7
Coalway Rd
Rugeley WS15 . . . . **197** B6
Wolverhampton WV3 . . . . . **265** E6
Coates Pl ST6 . . . . **42** B8
Coatsgate Wlk WV8 . . . . . **239** F1
Cobbett Rd WS7 . . . . **228** D7
Cobbles The ST19 . . . . . . **205** C6
Cobden Cl WS12 . . . . **210** C7
Cobden St Longton ST3 . . **284** B1
Newcastle-u-L ST5 . . . . **56** D6
Stourbridge DY8 . . . . **279** E5
Cobham Cl ST15 . . . . **118** F6
Cobham Pl ST3 . . . . **90** A8
Cobia B77 . . . . **261** D7
Cob Moor Rd ST7 . . . . **26** A4
Cobridge Ind Est ST6 . . . . **57** B7
Cobridge Rd ST1 . . . . **57** A5
Coburn Dr B75 . . . . **258** D2
Cocketts Nook WS15 . . . **178** C3
Cock Hill DE6 . . . . **81** F6
Cock La ST17 . . . . **193** E7
Cocknage Rd Longton ST3 . **73** B1
Meir Heath ST3 . . . . **89** D6
Cockshut Ind Est ST4 . . . . **56** F1
Cockshutts La WV2 . . . . . **266** D7
Cocks La Stoke-on-T ST9 . . . **43** C3
Stoke-on-T ST9 . . . . **43** C4
Cocksparrow La WS12,
WS19 . . . . **209** B5
Cockspur St B78 . . . . **262** E7
Cockster Brook La ST3 . . . **72** F3
Cockster Rd ST3 . . . . **72** F3
Cockstubbles ST14 . . . . . **126** B8
Cocton Cl WV6 . . . . **254** E5
Codsall Com High Sch
WV8 . . . . **239** A4
Codsall Gdns WV8 . . . . . . **238** E4
Codsall Ho WV8 . . . . **238** E4
Codsall Mid Sch WV8 . . . **239** A3
Codsall Rd Codsall WV8 . . **239** C1
Wolverhampton WV6 . . . . . **255** D1
Codsall Sta WV8 . . . . **238** E3
Coghlan Rd ST17 . . . . **174** C8
Colbourne Rd B78 . . . . . . **250** A2
Colbrook B77 . . . . **250** D1
Colclough Ave ST5 . . . . **56** A8
Colclough La ST16 . . . . **41** D7
Colclough St ST3 . . . . **74** B1
Cold Meece Ind Est
ST15 . . . . **118** B6
Cold Norton Cotts ST15 . **119** C5
Coldridge Cl WV8 . . . . . . **239** F1
Coldstream Dr DY8 . . . . . **275** E3
Cole Dr ST16 . . . . **155** C2
Coleford Cl DY8 . . . . **275** C2
Colehill B79 . . . . **250** B5
Coleman St WV6 . . . . **255** F4
Colenso Way ST5 . . . . **56** B8
Coleridge Cl
Market Drayton TF9 . . . . . . **112** A7
Tamworth B79 . . . . **250** A6
Walsall WS3 . . . . **244** A5
Coleridge Ct DE14 . . . . . . **166** C6
Coleridge Dr Cheadle ST10 **76** C2
Perton WV6 . . . . **254** E4
Stafford ST17 . . . . **174** C8
Coleridge Rd ST3 . . . . **73** A2

Coleridge Rise DY3 . . . . . 271 A4
Colesden Wlk WV4 . . . . . . 265 C6
Coleshill Rd B78 . . . . 261 A7
Coleshill St B78 . . . . 261 A8
Cole St ST8 . . . . 27 C7
Coley Gr ST18 . . . . 177 D8
Coley La ST18 . . . . 158 D1
Colin Cres ST3 . . . . 74 B4
Colindene Gr ST4 . . . . 72 A6
Colinwood Cl WS6 . . . . . . 226 F1
Collard Ave ST5 . . . . 56 B3
College Cl CW3 . . . . 68 E8
College Ct WV6 . . . . 255 D4
College Farm Cl WV6 . . . 253 C3
College Fields ST15 . . . . . 118 F6
College La B79 . . . . 250 B5
College Rd Denstone ST14 . . 95 D6
  Hanley ST1, ST4 . . . . 56 C2
  Wolverhampton WV6 . . . . 255 D4
College View WV6 . . . . . . 255 D3
Collet Rd WV6 . . . . 254 E5
Collets Brook B75 . . . . . . 259 A2
Collett B77 . . . . 251 A1
Colley Rd ST6 . . . . 41 F6
Collier Cl
  Cheslyn Hay WS6 . . . . . . 226 D2
  Walsall WS8 . . . . 244 C7
Colliers Way ST8 . . . . 27 C7
Colliery Rd WS3 . . . . 242 F3
Colliery Rd WS15 . . . . . . 196 F4
Collinbourne Cl ST4 . . . . . 88 B6
Collindale Ct DY6 . . . . . . 270 D1
Collingwood Ct ST15 . . . 120 B8
Collingwood Gr ST4 . . . . . 71 E8
Collingwood Rd WV10 . . 240 D2
Collin Rd ST14 . . . . 71 F5
Collins Dr B WS13 . . . . . 230 F6
Collins Hill WS13 . . . . . . 214 A2
Collinson Rd
  Barton-u-N DE13 . . . . . . 183 D1
  Stoke-on-T ST6 . . . . 41 D7
Collis Rd WS8 . . . . 245 A5
Collin St ST14 . . . . 126 B7
Collis St DY8 . . . . 279 F8
Colne Mount ST14 . . . . . 126 B7
Colonnade The ST16 . . . . 285 B3
Colshaw Rd DY4 . . . . 279 E4
Coltman Cl WS14 . . . . . . 231 D7
Colton Hills Com Sch
  WV4 . . . . 266 B4
Colton Rd WS15 . . . . 178 E4
Coltsfoot View WS6 . . . . 226 F2
Columbian Cres WS7 . . . 228 F8
Columbian Dr WS11 . . . . 209 F3
Columbian Way WS13 . . 209 F3
Columbine Wlk E ST6 . . 41 D3
Colville Cl DE12 . . . . 218 D7
Colville St ST14 . . . . 72 F6
Colwall Rd DY3 . . . . 271 D4
Colwich CE Prim Sch
  ST17 . . . . 177 E7
Colwich Cres ST16 . . . . . 156 C3
Colwyn Dr ST8 . . . . 27 D5
Combe Dr ST3 . . . . 90 A5
Comberford La B79 . . . . . 234 A2
Comberford Rd B79 . . . . 250 A7
Comber Gr DY7 . . . . 278 A3
Combermere TF9 . . . . 97 D2
Comber Rd DY7 . . . . 278 A3
Combine Cl B75 . . . . 258 D4
Comfrey Cl ST13 . . . . 90 A6
Commerce Dr ST19 . . . . . 207 E7
Commerce St ST3 . . . . . . 284 C3
Commercial Rd ST1 . . . . 282 C2
Commercial St ST6 . . . . . . 57 A7
Common Barn La DY10 . . 280 D5
Common Rd Bednall ST17 . 194 B4
  Betley ST7 . . . . 52 F6
  Cannock WS11 . . . . 210 A3
  Fradley WS13 . . . . 215 D7
  Gratwich ST14 . . . . 124 C2
  Stoke-on-T ST3 . . . . 89 F4
  Stone ST15 . . . . 119 E6
  Tamworth B79 . . . . 250 E6
  Upper Hatton ST21 . . . . . 102 E7
  Waterhouses ST10 . . . . . . 64 F7
  Whitmore ST5 . . . . 85 D6
  Whittington WS14 . . . . . 232 D4
Common Rd
  Stafford ST16 . . . . 155 E7
  Wombourne WV5 . . . . . . 270 A6
Common The ST10 . . . . . . 75 D3
Common View
  Burntwood WS7 . . . . 212 A1
  Cannock WS11 . . . . 210 B7
Common Wlk WS12 . . . . 209 C5
Community Dr ST6 . . . . . . 42 D1
Como Pl ST5 . . . . 70 E6
Compa The DY7 . . . . 278 A3
Compton Cl Kinver DY7 . . 277 F4
  Stafford ST17 . . . . 156 A1
Compton Ct ST4 . . . . 257 F3
Compton Dr DY6 . . . . 275 D5
Compton Flats ST13 . . . . . 30 E5
Compton Gdns DY7 . . . . 277 F4
Compton Hill Dr WV3 . . . 255 D2
Compton Ho E ST13 . . . . 30 E5
Compton La ST13 . . . . 30 E5

Compton Mews ST13 . . . . 30 F5
Compton Pk WV6 . . . . . . 255 E3
Compton Rd Kinver DY7 . . 277 D4
  Stafford ST17 . . . . 156 D1
  Tamworth B79 . . . . 249 F7
  Wolverhampton WV3 . . . 255 F2
Compton Rd W WV3 . . . . 255 D2
Compton St ST1 . . . . 282 A2
Comptons The TF9 . . . . . 130 A8
Condy ST13 . . . . 30 E4
Condor Gr WS12 . . . . 210 C1
Conduit Rd WS11 . . . . . . 228 A4
Conduit St WS13 . . . . . . 231 B8
Conewood Pl ST3 . . . . 72 E1
Coneybere Gdns ST19 . . 223 D7
Coneygreave Cl ST10 . . . . 76 D1
Coneygreave La ST5 . . . . . 85 D5
Coney Gr ST3 . . . . 74 A3
Conford Cl ST2 . . . . 57 F2
Congleton Edge Rd CW12 . 16 B6
Congleton Rd
  St8 . . . . 27 D8
  Biddulph,Braddocks Hay
  St8 . . . . 27 D8
  Biddulph,Marsh Green St8 . 16 D2
  Kidsgrove ST7 . . . . 25 D1
  Mow Cop ST7 . . . . 26 E8
Congleton Rd N ST7 . . . . . 25 C6
Congleton Rd S ST7 . . . . . 25 D2
Congleton Rd ST7 . . . . 40 D8
Congleton Sta CW12 . . . . . 6 A1
Congreve Cl ST17 . . . . . . 175 F7
Congreve Rd ST3 . . . . 72 F2
Conifer Cl WS12 . . . . 210 A8
Conifer Gr Stafford ST17 . 174 B7
  Stoke-on-T ST3 . . . . 72 F2
Coniston Cl ST4 . . . . 105 B1
Coniston Dr Cheadle ST10 . 76 F4
  Kingswinford DY6 . . . . . . 275 B7
Coniston Gr ST5 . . . . 71 B4
Coniston Ho ST16 . . . . . 285 C3
Coniston Rd ST4 . . . . 87 F7
Coniston Rd Aldridge B74 . 256 F3
  Wolverhampton WV6 . . . 255 D8
Coniston B77 . . . . 262 B7
Coniston Way WS11 . . . . 209 E1
Connaught Dr WV5 . . . . . 265 A1
Connaught Rd ST6 . . . . . . 41 D2
Conners La ST7 . . . . 168 A3
Conrad Cl ST3 . . . . 73 D3
Consall Gr ST4 . . . . 60 D6
Consall La ST9 . . . . 60 D6
Consall Nature Pk* ST9 . . 61 A5
Consall Station ST9 . . . . . 61 B6
Consett Rd ST3 . . . . 88 F8
Consort Pl B79 . . . . 250 C5
Consort St ST4 . . . . 72 B7
Constable Ave ST5 . . . . . . 55 E6
Constable Cl ST3 . . . . 90 B7
Constance Ave ST4 . . . . . . 88 B8
Convent Cl
  Burton u T DE15 . . . . . . 185 F8
  Cannock WS11 . . . . 226 D8
  Colwich ST18 . . . . 177 D7
  Stoke-on-T ST4 . . . . 72 A8
Convent Ct ST4 . . . . 72 A8
Convent La ST15 . . . . . . 105 B4
Conway Cl
  E Burton u T ST13 . . . . . 166 D8
  Kingswinford DY6 . . . . . . 275 F4
Conway Gr ST10 . . . . 76 E1
Conway Rd Biddulph ST8 . . 27 C6
  Cannock WS11 . . . . 226 B8
  Perton WV6 . . . . 254 F3
  Stafford ST15 . . . . 155 A4
Conway St ST4 . . . . 72 C8
Congrese La DE6 . . . . 81 D7
Cook Cl WV6 . . . . 254 E4
Cooke Cl ST19 . . . . 192 E6
Cooke St WV7 . . . . 266 C8
Cookley La DY7 . . . . 278 B1
Cookley Sebright Fst Sch
  DY10 . . . . 280 A5
Cooknell Dr WS7 . . . . . . 228 C7
Cook Rd WS3 . . . . 243 D2
Cook's Bank ST17 . . . . . . 175 B5
Cook's Hollow ST13 . . . . . 47 A8
Cook's La ST3 . . . . 32 A1
Cookson Ave ST3 . . . . 73 C1
Coolidge St E ST6 . . . . . . 41 D3
Coombe Croft WV9 . . . . . 240 A8
Coombe Park Rd ST15 . . . 119 F5
Coombesdale ST5 . . . . 85 F2
Coombes Valley Nature
  Reserve* ST10 . . . . 46 D6
Co-Operative La ST10 . . . . 76 E5
Co-operative St ST16 . . . 155 D6
Cooper Ave ST5 . . . . 56 E2
Cooper Cl ST15 . . . . 120 D7
Cooper & Jordan CE Prim
  Sch WS9 . . . . 256 C6
Cooper Perry Prim Sch
  ST18 . . . . 154 C6
Cooper's Bank Rd DY5 . . 271 C1
Coopers Cl ST13 . . . . 30 C5
Cooper's Sq DE14 . . . . . . 166 D2
Cooper St Hanley ST1 . . . 282 A1
  Newcastle-u-L ST5 . . . . . . 55 C6
Coovers Visitor Ctr* DE14 . 166 D2
Copeland Ave
  Newcastle-u-L ST5 . . . . . . 71 B3
  Tittensor ST12 . . . . 88 A1
Copeland Cl ST10 . . . . 76 D1
Copeland Dr ST10 . . . . . . 120 D5
Copelands The DY7 . . . . . 278 A3
Copeland St ST4 . . . . 72 B7
Cope's Ave ST10 . . . . 41 E8

Cope's Dr B79 . . . . 250 B7
Cope St Stafford ST16 . . . 285 B3
Cope St ST7 . . . . 43 A1
Copes Way ST14 . . . . . . 111 A1
Copley La WV6 . . . . 253 A2
Coplow Ave ST10 . . . . 92 C4
Coplow La DE65 . . . . 129 D5
Copperas Rd DE11 . . . . . 186 D5
Copper Beech Dr
  Kingswinford DY6 . . . . . . 270 D1
  Wombourne WV5 . . . . . . 270 B6
Copperfields WS14 . . . . . 231 D7
Copper Glade ST15 . . . . . 156 B3
Copperhill Rd WV12 . . . . . 16 B7
Copperkins Rd WS12 . . . 210 E4
Coppermill Cl WS12 . . . . 209 F7
Coppice Ave ST15 . . . . 55 A1
Coppice Brook ST14 . . . . 176 C4
Coppice Cl Biddulph St8 . . 27 D7
  Burntwood WS7 . . . . 228 F8
  Cheslyn Hay WS6 . . . . . . 226 D4
  Sedgley DY3 . . . . 271 C7
  Stone ST15 . . . . 105 A1
  Wolverhampton WV11 . . 242 A1
Coppice Cres WS8 . . . . . 244 D7
Coppice Ct WS11 . . . . . . 226 B7
Coppice Dr Newport TF10 . 168 E5
  Polesworth B78 . . . . 262 F7
Coppice Farm Way
  WV11 . . . . 242 B1
Coppice Gdns ST15 . . . . 105 B1
Coppice Gr
  Lichfield WS14 . . . . 231 F7
  Meir ST3 . . . . 74 A3
Coppice Ho ST7 . . . . 40 C8
Coppice La Aldridge WS9 . 244 F1
  Brownhills WS8 . . . . 244 D8
  Cheslyn Hay WS6 . . . . . . 226 D4
  Clifton Campville B79 . . . 218 F1
  Middleton B78 . . . . 259 D2
  Muckley Corner WS7,
  WS14 . . . . 230 A3
  Wolverhampton WV5 . . . 265 B6
Coppice Prim Sch B75 . . 258 B1
Coppice Rd
  Brownhills WS8,WV5 . . . 244 F4
  Rugeley WS15 . . . . 196 E6
  Stone ST15 . . . . 105 B1
  Talke ST7 . . . . 40 C8
  Wolverhampton WV5 . . . 265 D8
Coppice Sch The ST5 . . . 283 E1
Coppice Side WS8 . . . . . 244 D7
Coppice Side Ind Est
  WS8 . . . . 244 C8
Coppice The
  Cannock WS12 . . . . 210 E1
  Hagley DY8 . . . . 281 F5
  Market Drayton TF9 . . . . . 97 B1
  Stoke-on-T ST6 . . . . 42 B1
Coppice View ST5 . . . . 56 A4
Coppice Way ST16 . . . . . 155 C8
Coppins The
  E Stafford ST17 . . . . 175 C7
  Leek ST13 . . . . 30 C5
Copp La ST6 . . . . 41 C2
Copplestone Gr ST3 . . . . . 73 E3
Coppull Pl ST6 . . . . 42 A7
Coppy Hall Gr WS9 . . . . . 245 B1
Coppy Nook La WS7 . . . . 229 C5
Copse Cres WS3 . . . . 244 A4
Copse Dr WS3 . . . . 198 B4
Copse The ST4 . . . . 257 F1
Copsy Dale ST21 . . . . 115 C6
Copthorne Gr WS3 . . . . . 228 F4
Copthorne Rd WV3 . . . . . 266 A7
Coracle Gr ST9 . . . . 27 E6
Coral Gr ST14 . . . . 88 B7
Corbet Ct B TF9 . . . . 97 C1
Corbett Ho B DY8 . . . . . 279 F8
Corbett Rd DY7 . . . . 268 A2
Corbett Wlk E ST6 . . . . . 41 D3
Corbin Rd B78 . . . . 262 F6
Corby Pl ST3 . . . . 284 A3
Corden Ave DE13 . . . . . . 166 F8
Cordy La WV7 . . . . 237 C7
Corfe Cl WV6 . . . . 254 F3
Corfe Gr ST3 . . . . 73 C6
Corfield Pl ST4 . . . . 42 C5
Corfton Dr WV6 . . . . 255 C3
Corina Way ST4 . . . . 73 D4
Cormie Cl ST16 . . . . 42 B5
Corncrake Rd DY1,DY3 . . 271 E3
Cornelious St B ST3 . . . . . 74 A1
Cornel B77 . . . . 250 F4
Corner Ways ST18 . . . . . 154 E2
Cornes St ST1 . . . . 57 D1
Corneville Rd ST2 . . . . 58 B4
Corn Exchange The E
  WS13 . . . . 231 B8
Cornfield Cl DY6 . . . . 275 A8
Cornfield Dr WS14 . . . . . 231 E7
Cornfield Rd ST8 . . . . 27 A2
Cornfield WV8 . . . . 239 F2
Cornflower Rd WV10 . . . 241 A2
Cornflower Way ST4 . . . . 244 D6
Cornhill WS11 . . . . 209 E5
Cornhill Cl ST5 . . . . 40 E1
Cornhill Dr ST5 . . . . 40 E1
Cornhill Rd ST6 . . . . 42 C5
Cornhill E ST13 . . . . 30 E5
Cornmill Lea ST14 . . . . . 168 F3
Cornmill Gr WV6 . . . . . . 254 C3
Corn Mill La ST13 . . . . . . 47 A8
Cornovian CW6 . . . . 254 E5
Corns Gr WV5 . . . . 269 F5

Cornwall Ave
  Newcastle-u-L ST5 . . . . . . 71 D4
  Tamworth B78 . . . . 250 A1
Cornwall Cl
  E Congleton CW12 . . . . . . 6 A1
  Aldridge WS9 . . . . 245 A1
  Kingswinford DY6 . . . . . . 275 D8
Cornwall Ct WS15 . . . . . 196 D6
Cornwall Dr ST17 . . . . . . 156 D1
Cornwallis St ST4 . . . . 72 B6
Cornwall Rd
  Burton u T DE15 . . . . . . 185 E6
  Cannock WS12 . . . . 210 B5
  Stourbridge DY8 . . . . . . 279 D8
  Wolverhampton WV6 . . . 255 C4
Cornwall St ST3 . . . . 284 C4
Cornwood Gr ST3 . . . . 89 E8
Coronation Ave
  Biddulph ST8 . . . . 27 B5
  Longton ST3 . . . . 284 B3
  Mile Oak B78 . . . . 249 D1
Coronation Cotts DE13 . . 184 A8
Coronation Cres
  Kidsgrove ST7 . . . . 25 E1
  Rocester ST14 . . . . 96 A4
  Shuttington ST14 . . . . . . 251 F7
Coronation Rd
  Brownhills WS9 . . . . 245 A3
  Newcastle-u-L ST5 . . . . . 283 C2
  Stafford ST15 . . . . 156 A6
  Stoke-on-T,Hartshill ST4 . . 71 E8
  Walsall WS14 . . . . 244 B2
Coronation St
  Cheadle ST10 . . . . 76 D3
  Stoke-on-T ST6 . . . . 41 E4
  Tamworth B79 . . . . 250 A5
Corporation St
  Newcastle-u-L ST5 . . . . . 283 B3
  Stafford ST16 . . . . 285 C4
  Stoke-on-T ST4 . . . . 72 B6
  Tamworth B79 . . . . 250 B5
Corran Rd ST17 . . . . 174 D6
Correen B77 . . . . 251 C1
Corrie Roy Cotts B78 . . . 250 A4
Corrin Gr DY6 . . . . 275 C8
Corser St DY1 . . . . 271 F2
Corsham Pl ST14 . . . . . . 143 F7
Corsican Cl WS7 . . . . 229 A8
Corsican Dr WS12 . . . . . 210 A8
Cort Dr WS7 . . . . 229 B8
Corve Gdns WV6 . . . . . . 255 C5
Corve View DY3 . . . . 266 C1
Coseley St ST6 . . . . 42 C2
Cosford Ct WV6 . . . . 254 E5
Cosgrove Wlk WV8 . . . . . 239 F1
Cotehill Rd ST9 . . . . 59 B4
Cote La DY7 . . . . 273 E1
Coteshdath St ST1 . . . . . . 57 D1
Cotes La
  Cotes Heath ST21 . . . . . 102 F3
  Swynnerton ST15 . . . . . 103 B2
Cot La DY6,DY8 . . . . 275 C5
Coton Ave ST16 . . . . 156 B3
Coton Green Prec B79 . . 249 F7
Coton Green Prim Sch
  B79 . . . . 249 F8
Coton La
  Coton Clanford ST18 . . . 154 A3
  Ranton ST18 . . . . 153 E4
  Tamworth B79 . . . . 249 E8
Coton Pk DE12 . . . . 186 C1
Coton Rd
  Walton-On-Trent DE12 . . 202 E6
  Wolverhampton WV4 . . . 266 B5
Coton Rise ST12 . . . . 88 E1
Cotsdale Rd WV4 . . . . . . 265 E3
Cotswold Ave
  Great Wyrley WS6 . . . . . 226 F3
  Newcastle-u-L ST5 . . . . . . 55 E3
Cotswold Cl
  Aldridge WS9 . . . . 245 C1
  Cannock WS12 . . . . 210 A8
  Stafford ST22 . . . . 43 A1
Cotswold Ct
  Sutton Coldfield B75 . . . 258 A4
  Wolverhampton WV7 . . . 266 A6
Cotswold Gr WV7 . . . . . . 237 B5
Cotswold Gr WV12 . . . . . 242 B1
Cotswold Rd
  Burton u T DE14 . . . . . . 184 F8
  Cannock WS12 . . . . 210 A8
  Wolverhampton WV4 . . . 266 F7
Cottage Cl
  Burntwood WS7 . . . . 228 F5
  Cannock WS12 . . . . 210 D5
  Longton ST3 . . . . 73 E1
Cottage Ct WS7 . . . . 228 F5
Cottage Dr WS7 . . . . 275 D7
Cottage Farm Rd B77 . . . 261 D7
Cottage La
  Biddulph Moor ST8 . . . . . 28 A8
  Newcastle-u-L ST5 . . . . . 228 F5
  Wolverhampton WV10 . . 240 D3
Cottage Mews ST16 . . . . 156 F4
Cottages The Bagnall ST9 . 43 F2
  Brewood ST19 . . . . 223 D6
Cottage St DY6 . . . . 275 D7
Cottage View WV8 . . . . . 239 B4
Cottage Wlk E B77 . . . . . 261 F6
Cotterill Dr ST5 . . . . 56 B8
Cotterill Rd B77 . . . . 261 B7
Cotters Hill Cl ST18 . . . . 177 D8
Cottesmore Cl DE15 . . . . 167 A1
Cotton Cl DE13 . . . . 200 A7
Cotton Gr WS12 . . . . 195 A1
Cotton La ST10 . . . . 63 B3
Cotton Lane Cotts ST10 . . 63 B3
Cotton Rd ST6 . . . . 41 C6
Cotton Way ST7 . . . . 211 F1

Cottonwood Gr
  Harriseahead ST7 . . . . 26 E4
  Longton ST3 . . . . 284 C4
Cottrell Cl WS15 . . . . . . 160 F6
Cotts The ST4 . . . . 74 A8
Cotwall End Countryside &
  Craft Ctr* DY3 . . . . 271 C6
Cotwall End Ho DY3 . . . . 271 D7
Cotwall End Prim Sch
  DY3 . . . . 271 D7
Cotwall End Rd DY3 . . . . 271 C5
Coulson Cl WS7 . . . . 211 D1
Coulter Gr WV6 . . . . 254 D4
Coulter La WS7 . . . . 229 E8
Coulthwaite Way WS15 . . 196 F6
Council Hos
  Bramshall ST14 . . . . 125 C7
  Chetwynd Aston TF10 . . . 187 A7
  Church Leigh ST10 . . . . . 109 A4
  Kingstone ST14 . . . . 125 C1
  Kingstone,The Blythe ST18 . 140 F6
Council Hos The ST21 . . . 116 B4
Country Park View ST5 . . . 55 A8
County Dr B78 . . . . 250 A2
County La
  Cosall WV7,WV8 . . . . . . 237 E3
  Iverley DY8 . . . . 281 D8
County Rd ST16 . . . . 285 B4
Coupe Dr ST3 . . . . 74 A5
Court Cres DY6 . . . . 275 C5
Court Dr WS14 . . . . 246 F4
Court Farm La DE14 . . . . 184 E7
Courtland Mews ST16 . . . 155 F5
Courtland Rd DY6 . . . . . . 275 C8
Courtlands The WV6 . . . . 255 E4
Court La ST5 . . . . 56 A7
Courtney Pl ST3 . . . . 89 E8
Court No 1 ST3 . . . . 73 E1
Court Par WS7 . . . . 256 B6
Court Rd WV6 . . . . 255 F4
Courts The WV7 . . . . 237 A4
Courtway Dr DY5 . . . . 57 D8
Court Wlk CW3 . . . . 53 A5
Cousins St WV2 . . . . 266 D7
Cowan Farm Mobile Home Pk
  ST4 . . . . 88 B1
Coven Cl WS3 . . . . 244 A5
Coven Mill Cl WV9 . . . . . 224 C1
Coven Rd ST19 . . . . 223 D4
Coventry St ST16 . . . . . . 155 A5
Coverdale Cl ST3 . . . . 90 A7
Coverley Pl ST4 . . . . 71 F6
Covers La DY7 . . . . 274 E1
Covert Cl ST18 . . . . 158 B2
Covert Gdns ST7 . . . . 40 D8
Covert La DY8 . . . . 279 D2
Covert The Keele ST5 . . . . 70 B7
  Newcastle-u-L ST5 . . . . . . 71 C2
  Wolverhampton WV8 . . . 239 C1
Covey Cl WS13 . . . . 214 D1
Cowallmoor La ST13 . . . . 28 B5
Cowan Dr ST16 . . . . 156 A4
Cowen St ST6 . . . . 42 E6
Cowhill La WS13 . . . . . . 200 E1
Cowhouse La ST10 . . . . . 109 B3
Cow La Cauldon ST10 . . . 63 F7
  Whateley B78 . . . . 262 E1
Cowley Cl Penkridge ST19 . 207 F7
  Stafford ST17 . . . . 174 C8
Cowley Dr DY1 . . . . 271 F2
Cowley Gr WS10 . . . . . . 209 F8
Cowley La ST20 . . . . 171 D5
Cowley B77 . . . . 250 E2
Cowley Way ST2 . . . . 73 E7
Cowlishaw Cl ST8 . . . . 27 B5
Cowlishaw Rd ST6 . . . . . . 42 C6
Cowlishaw Way WS15 . . 196 F6
Cowper St ST4 . . . . 72 F6
Coxmoor Cl WS3 . . . . . . 242 F3
Crabbery St ST16 . . . . . . 285 B3
Crab La Bobbington DY7 . 268 C2
  Cannock WS11 . . . . 210 A3
  Stafford ST16 . . . . 155 B8
  Willenhall WV12 . . . . . . 242 D1
Crabtree Ave ST8 . . . . 27 C7
Crabtree Cl ST4 . . . . 72 F8
Crabtree Way WS15 . . . . 178 C2
Crackleldt La
  Stonnall WS14 . . . . 245 F7
  Wall WS14 . . . . 246 A8
Crackley Bank ST5 . . . . . . 81 C3
Crackley Bank Prim Sch
  ST5 . . . . 40 E1
Crackley La ST5 . . . . 54 E3
Cracow Moss CW3 . . . . . . 53 A3
Craddock Rd ST16 . . . . . 155 C7
Craftdown Ct ST17 . . . . . 174 F4
Craigside B ST8 . . . . 27 C8
Cranberry Ct ST17 . . . . . 285 B2
Cranberry Cl ST10 . . . . . . 93 B1
Cranberry Cl ST15 . . . . . 155 A6
Cranberry Dr ST5 . . . . 40 D1
Cranberry Marsh ST21 . . 102 D3
Cranborne Ave ST2 . . . . . 43 B2
Cranbourne Ave WV4 . . . 266 F7
Cranbrook Gr WV6 . . . . . 254 F3
Cranbrook Rd DY6 . . . . . 275 C5
Cranbrook Wlk ST17 . . . 174 B8
Cranbrook Hill B78 . . . . 259 C5
Cranebrook La
  Stonnall WS14 . . . . 245 F7
  Wall WS14 . . . . 246 A8
Crane Dr WS7 . . . . 229 A4
Crane Field WS13 . . . . . 214 B1

Crane Hollow WV5......269 E5
Cranesbill Cl WV10 .....241 C7
Crane St ST1.............57 B6
Crane Terr WV6.........255 E5
Cranfield Pl ST2.........58 B2
Cranfield Rd WS7.......229 A7
Cranford Pl WS11.......209 F1
Cranford Rd WV3.......265 D8
Cranford Way ST4.......58 D3
Cranham Dr DY6.......275 E5
Cranleigh Ave ST1.......57 D8
Cranleigh Cl
 Aldridge WS9..........256 B5
 Willenhall WV12.......242 C1
Cranleigh Way WS14...231 E7
Cranley Dr WV8.........238 F4
Cranmer Cl WS6.........226 D1
Cranmere Ave WV6.....255 A6
Cranmere Ct WV6.......255 A6
Cranmer Gr B74........257 F6
Cranmer St ST4..........72 B7
Cranmore Gr ST15......120 C7
Cranmore Rd WV3......255 F3
Cranswick Gr ST10......71 F5
Crantock Cl WV11.......242 C1
Cranwell Gn WV5.......269 F5
Cranwell Pl ST3..........89 F8
Cranwell Rise B78......249 C1
Cranwood Rd ST12.....88 A1
Cranworth Gr ST3.......89 E8
Crateford La ST19......224 B7
Crathorne Ave WV10...240 C1
Crauford Rd CW12......6 A8
Craven Cl ST4............88 A8
Craven St Burton u T DE13 166 C6
 Wolverhampton WV2....266 F6
Craven B77...............251 B1
Crawford Ave WV4......266 F3
Crawfurd St ST4.........72 D5
Crawley La DE13.......199 C5
Crayford Ave CW12.......6 A5
Craythorne Rd DE13...147 D3
Creamery La ST6.........42 C4
Creighton La ST18......111 A5
Cremorne Dr ST17......175 D7
Cremorne Rd B75.......258 B2
Cremorne Wlk B75.....258 B2
Crescent Gr ST4..........56 E1
Crescent Prim Sch ST3..74 C1
Crescent Rd ST17......285 A1
Crescent The Ashley ST4..100 C5
 Burntwood WS7........211 F1
 Cookley DY10...........280 B4
 Eccleshall ST21.........133 D6
 Great Wyrley WS6.....227 A2
 Hagley DY8.............281 F5
 Leek ST13..............31 A1
 Mayfield DE6...........81 D7
 Newcastle-u-L,Silverdale
   ST5..................55 B2
 Newcastle-u-L ST5....71 A6
 Rudyard ST13..........18 D1
 Stafford,Doxey ST16..155 B4
 Stoke-on-T ST4.........71 E4
 Stone ST15.............105 A1
 Swadlincote DE11.....186 A6
 Walton-on-t-H ST17...175 F7
 Wolverhampton WV6...255 B3
Cressington Dr B74.....258 A1
Cresswell Ave ST5.......40 D1
Cresswell Cres WS3....242 F2
Cresswell Ct WV10.....240 A3
Cresswell La
 Brewood ST19..........223 C6
 Cresswell ST11.........91 D4
Cresswell Old Rd ST11..91 E3
Cresswell Rd Hanley ST1..57 E3
 Wolverhampton WV3...265 A1
Cressy Cl ST15..........106 E3
Crestbrook Rd ST2......58 C6
Crest Cl DE13..........147 E1
Crestfield Rd ST3........89 F8
Crestway Rd ST2.........43 C2
Crestwood Cl DE13....166 D8
Crestwood Dr ST15....119 F6
Crestwood Glen WV6...255 F7
Crestwood Pk ST19....223 D7
Crestwood Rise WS15..178 C3
Crestwood Sch The DY6..275 F5
Crestwood B77..........251 A5
Creswell Dr ST18......154 F8
Creswell Farm Dr ST16..155 B7
Creswell Gr
 Creswell ST18.........154 F8
 Stafford ST18..........155 A8
Crewe Gates Ind Est CW1..37 A8
Crewe Hall Ent Pk CW1..37 D8
Crichton Ave DE13.....166 D7
Crich Way DE11........186 E5
Cricket Cl DE15.........167 E8
Cricketers Cl DE15.....185 F8
Cricketers Mews ST5...56 C5
Cricketers The DE13...200 F2
Cricket La WS14.......231 C5
Cricket Mdw Dudley DY3..271 C5
 Wolverhampton WV6...255 D5
Crick Rd ST1.............57 E2
Crigdon B77............251 C1
Crinan Gr ST17.........174 D6
Cringlebrook B77......250 D1
Crispin Cl ST16........155 C8
Critchlow Gr ST3........73 A1
Critchlows Ct ST3.......72 F1
Crockett The ST11......74 E3
Crockford Dr B75......258 B3

Crockington Cl WV5....263 F2
Crockington La WV5...264 A1
Crocus Cres WV9.......240 A3
Croft Ave Cannock WS12..195 A1
 Newcastle-u-L ST5.....56 B6
 Tamworth B79.........250 B6
Croft Cl Elford B79.....216 E2
 Netherseal DE12.......219 F7
 Rolleston on D DE13...147 B4
Croft Cres
 Brownhills WS8........244 D7
 Stoke-on-T ST4.........72 A6
Croft Cl ST4.............42 C1
Crofter Cl ST8............27 B8
Crofters St ST5...........40 D3
Crofters La B75.........258 E3
Crofters The TF10......188 D6
Crofters Wlk WV8......239 E1
Croftfield St ST12........73 D8
Croft Gdns WS7.........229 A8
Croft Gr ST4............111 C1
Croft La ST19...........207 D1
Croft Leys The WS15...198 C4
Croft Par WS9..........256 B6
Croft Prim Sch ST5.....197 F5
Croft Rd Cheadle ST10...76 D3
 Newcastle-u-L ST5.....71 F5
 Stone ST15.............119 F6
Croft St ST6...............56 F8
Croftstead Ave ST14....95 D6
Croft St B79............250 B6
Croft The
 Blakedown DY10.......281 C2
 Burton u T DE15......166 F1
 Cheadle ST10...........76 D6
 Cheslyn Hay WS6......226 E2
 Hixon ST18............158 C8
 King's Bromley DE13..199 D6
 Longdon WS15.........197 F1
 Maer ST5...............84 C2
 Norton in H TF9........82 B3
 Sedgley DY3...........266 E1
Croft Way TF9............97 B1
Cromartie St ST3.......284 C2
Cromdale B77..........251 C1
Cromer Cres ST1........57 E4
Cromer Gdns WV6.....255 F5
Cromer Rd ST1..........57 F4
Cromer St ST5...........56 D4
Crompton Cl
 Colwich ST18..........177 E8
 Congleton CW12.........6 A6
Crompton Dr WV8......239 B4
Crompton Gr ST4........88 C5
Crompton Rd ST15.....120 B7
Cromwell Cl Hopton ST18 137 D1
 Tutbury DE13..........146 C5
Cromwell Ct WS6.......227 A1
Cromwell Rd
 Cannock WS11.........210 A1
 Tamworth B79.........249 E8
 Wolverhampton WV10..240 E4
Cromwells Mdw WS14..231 C5
Cromwell St Biddulph ST8..27 C8
 Hanley ST1..............57 D6
Cromwell Terr ST13......30 F5
Crony Cl ST13...........217 C5
Crooked Bridge Rd ST16..285 B4
Crook La WV9...........256 B1
Crosby Cl WV6..........255 F5
Crosby Pl ST4............71 E3
Cross Butts ST21.......133 D6
Cross Edge ST6..........43 B7
Crossfell B77...........251 B1
Crossfield Ave
 Biddulph ST8...........27 C6
 Blythe Bridge ST11.....90 F6
Crossfield Rd Ind Est
   ST15................231 E8
Crossfield Rd ST15....231 E8
Crosshill Bank ST18...122 F5
Cross Hill St ST6........56 E7
Cross Ho WV2..........266 C7
Crossing La ST18......154 C2
Crossings The 1 WS14..231 E8
Cross In Hand La
 Lichfield,Farewell WS13..213 C3
 Lichfield WS13.........213 F1
Cross Keys Island WS12..210 C3
Cross Keys ST15.......231 B8
Cross La Audley ST7.....39 C5
 Congleton CW12.........6 A1
 Lichfield WS14........231 D6
Crossland Cres WV6...255 F7
Crossland Pl E ST3......90 A8
Crossland Pl W M ST3...74 A1
Crosslands CW12.........4 A5
Cross La Oulton ST15..105 C6
 Rolleston on D DE13...147 B2
 Sedgley DY3...........266 C1
 Waterhouses ST10......48 D3
Crossley Rd ST6.........42 A3
Crossley Stone WS15...178 E1
Crosslow La DE6.........96 E2
Crossman St ST4........57 B6
Cross May St ST5......283 A2
Crossmead Gr ST1.......57 E4
Cross of the Hand WS15..161 B2
Cross Pl DY3............266 C1
Cross Rd Albrighton WV7..237 A5
Cross St ST5............196 E7
Uttoxeter ST14..........111 B1

Cross St S WV2.........266 C7
Cross Side DE6..........81 F7
Cross St
 4 Stourbridge,Wordsley
   DY6..................275 D3
 7 Leek ST13.............30 F5
 Biddulph ST8............27 C8
 Burntwood WS7.........228 E8
 Burton u T DE14........166 C3
 Cannock,Bridgtown WS11..226 E5
 Cannock WS12.........210 E1
 Cheadle ST10...........76 D3
 Cheslyn Hay WS6......226 D2
 Gnosall ST20..........171 C5
 Kingsley ST10...........61 D3
 Kingswinford DY6......275 D6
 Kingswinford,Wall Heath
   DY6..................275 B8
 Market Drayton TF9....97 D1
 Meir ST3................74 B5
 Newcastle-u-L ST5......55 E8
 Stafford ST16..........155 D5
 Stone ST15.............105 A1
 Stourbridge DY8.......279 E5
 Tamworth B79.........250 B5
 Tamworth,Kettlebrook
   B77..................250 C3
 Tunstall ST6.............56 C8
 Walsall WS3............244 A1
Cross The DY6...........275 D6
Crossway Rd ST6........57 C7
Crossways Biddulph ST8..16 E1
 Pipe Gate TF9...........83 D7
Crossways Rd ST7........25 A4
Crossway ST16.........156 A3
Crossway The ST5........56 C3
Croston St ST3..........282 A1
Crotia Ave CW2...........37 B5
Crouch Ave ST6..........42 A4
Crouch La CW12...........6 D4
Crowberry Cl WS8......244 D6
Crowberry La DE13....183 D2
Crowborough Rd ST8,
   ST13.................28 B6
Crowcrofts Rd ST4......88 E7
Crowden Rd B77.......251 A1
Crowfoot La DE65......129 E8
Crowland Ave WV6.....254 E4
Crown Bank WS15......161 A6
Crown Bank Cres ST7...40 D6
Crown Bank Hanley ST1..282 B3
 Talke Pits ST7...........40 D6
Crown Bridge ST19.....192 E1
Crown Cl DY3............217 C5
Crown Ct B74............257 E3
Crowndale Pl ST6........41 E8
Crown Gdns ST7.........40 D6
Crown Ind Est DE14....166 B1
Crown La Iverley DY8...281 C7
 Stourbridge DY8.......279 F5
 Sutton Coldfield B74...257 E3
Crown Specl Sch DE13..147 D1
Crown St Hanley ST1....282 B2
 Newcastle-u-L ST5.....55 C2
 Stone ST15.............120 A8
Crowther Gr WV6.......255 F4
Crowther Rd WV6......255 F5
Crowther St ST4.........71 E2
Crowtrees Farm Ind Est
   ST10.................48 F2
Croxall Rd Alrewas DE13..201 B2
 Edingale B79...........217 C5
 Edingale B79,WS13....217 B6
Croxden Cl ST10.........92 D8
Croxden Ave WS3......243 A1
Croxden Rd ST2.........58 B6
Croxley Dr WS12.......210 C3
Croxstalls Cl WS3......243 A1
Croyde Pl ST3.............90 B6
Croyde Gr ST19.........207 F8
Cruso St ST13.............64 F4
Crutchley Ave B78......250 A2
Crystal Ave DY8.........271 F1
Crystal Gdns DY7......278 A3
Crystal St ST6...........57 B6
Cubley La DE6............96 E2
Cuckoo Cage La DE13...164 F1
Cuckoo Cl WS11........210 C2
Cullamore La ST14....126 B4
Culland Rd DE14.......185 B7
Cull Ave ST16.............56 A3
Cumberbatch Ave ST6...42 B7
Cumberland Cl
 Kingswinford DY6......275 E4
 Talke ST7...............40 E7
Cumberland Cres WS7..229 A8
Cumberland Dr B78.....250 A1
Cumberland Rd
 Burton u T DE15.......185 D6
 Cannock WS11.........210 A4
Cumberland St
 Newcastle-u-L ST5.....283 C3
 Stoke-on-T ST4.........72 E6
Cumberledge Hill WS15..211 E5
Cumbers The ST18.....154 B6
Cumbria St ST5...........71 C5
Cumming St ST1.........71 E8
Cunningham Rd WV6...254 D4
Curborough Rd WS13..214 B2
Curland Pl ST3...........73 F2
Curlew Cl Lichfield WS14..231 E7
 Uttoxeter ST14........126 C6
Curlew Dr WS8..........244 E7
Curlew Hill WS11......210 A3
Curlew Rd ST7...........26 E1
Curlews Cl B77..........262 A7
Curtis Cl DE13..........166 C7

Curtiss Pl ST3............90 C6
Curtis Way DE14.......166 B4
Curzon Pl WS15........196 E7
Curzon Rd ST6...........42 A2
Curzon Rise ST13........30 B5
Curzon St W DE14......166 B3
Curzon St
 Burton u T DE14.......166 C3
 Newcastle-u-L ST5.....71 D4
 Wolverhampton WV2...266 D7
Cushman Ave WV5.....269 E7
Cuttlestone Ho ST19...192 E1
Cutts St ST1.............282 A1
Cwerne Ct DY3..........271 C3
Cyclamen Cl DE14.....185 A8
Cygnet Cl Cannock WS12..210 C7
 Wolverhampton WV6...255 C2
Cygnet Dr Brownhills WS8 244 E7
 Tamworth B79.........249 F5
Cynthia Gr ST6...........42 A2
Cypress Ave DY3.......271 D5
Cypress Cl
 Market Drayton TF9....97 A1
 Stafford ST17..........156 C1
Cypress Gdns 1 DY6...275 D4
Cypress Gr
 Blythe Bridge ST11.....91 A6
 Newcastle-u-L ST5.....55 D8
Cypress Rise WS12.....211 A6
Cyprus St WV2..........266 C6

D

Dace Gr ST6..............42 B3
Dace B77................261 D7
Daffodil Cl DY3..........271 E7
Daffodil Wlk WS15.....178 C2
Dag La DE22............218 E7
Dahlia Cl ST3............74 B6
Daimler Cl 1 ST17......175 A8
Dain Pl ST5..............56 B6
Dain St ST6...............56 E7
Daintry Cl ST13..........30 D5
Daintry Dr B78..........249 B7
Daintry St Leek ST13....30 E5
 Stoke-on-T ST4.........71 F4
Dairy Cl Leek ST13......31 A6
 Market Drayton TF9....97 D1
Dairyfields Way ST1.....57 D7
Dairyhouse La
 Dilhorne ST10...........60 B2
 Overmoor ST10..........60 E1
Dairylands Rd ST7.......25 A4
Daisy Bank WS12......209 F8
Daisy Bank Cl WS3.....244 B2
Daisy Bank ST13.........30 E6
Daisy La Alrewas DE13..200 D1
 Alrewas DE13..........200 F2
Daisy Pl ST4..............72 E4
Daisy Wlk WV9.........240 A3
Dakota Gr ST6...........41 D4
Dalbeg Cl WV8..........255 E8
Dale Ave ST6............42 E6
Dalebrook Rd DE15....167 B5
Dale Cl Cheadle ST10....76 C3
 Whitmore ST5...........85 C5
Dalecot Gn ST2..........73 D8
Dale Cres DE12...........6 A2
Dale Dr WS7............229 B7
Dalegarth Gr ST3........89 E8
Dalehall Gdns 4 ST6....56 E8
Dalehead Ct ST3.........89 F8
Dalehouse Rd ST13......45 C4
Daleian Ct ST5...........55 C1
Dale La ST18............173 A7
Dalelands Est TF9......112 B8
Dalelands W TF9........112 B7
Dalelow Cl WS14........64 E4
Dale Pk DY8.............279 F2
Dales Cl Biddulph Moor ST8 .28 B7
Dales Com Jun Sch B77..262 B8
Dales Green Rd ST7.....26 C5
Daleside DE15..........167 B1
Dales Inf Sch The B77..262 B8
Dalesman Cl DY6.......275 B7
Dale St Burslem ST6.....56 C8
 Burton u T DE14.......166 C2
Dale The Ashley TF9....100 B5
 Warslow DE6,SK17.....23 C2
Dale View ST11...........90 E1
Daleview Dr ST5..........55 C1
Dale View
 Earl Sterndale SK17......5 B3
 Meir ST3................74 B3
 Mow Cop ST7...........25 D7
Dalewood Rd ST5........55 D5
Dallow Cl DE14.........166 C5
Dallow Cres DE14......166 C5
Dallow St DE14.........166 C5
Dalton Ave DE14........167 B1
Dalton Gr ST2............58 D1
Dalton St WV3..........266 B8
Daltry Way CW3........69 E7
Daly Cres ST5...........64 F4
Dama Rd B78............260 F8
Dame Paulet Wlk D DE6..36 E3
Dam La Alsop en le D DE6..36 E3
 Biddulph ST8............17 E2
Dampier St ST13.........30 C5
Damson Pk WV6.......253 D3
Dams The ST11...........74 D2
Dan St WS3..............231 B8
Danbury Gdns WV10...240 C2

Danby Crest ST17......174 A8
Danby Dr WS12........211 D4
Dandillion Ave ST10.....92 D8
Danebower Rd ST4......88 C6
Danebridge Gr ST17.....57 F5
Dane Dr ST8.............16 E1
Dane Gdns ST7..........26 C2
Dane Gr ST10............76 E1
Dane St ST4..............71 F1
Danehill Wlk WV8......255 F8
Danelagh Cl B79.......249 F7
Danemead Cl ST3.......90 A7
Danesbrook WV5.......267 D8
Danes Cl WV11.........241 F4
Danescourt Rd WV6...255 C6
Danes Croft ST4..........88 B7
Danesmore Park Jun & Inf
 Sch WV11..............242 A1
Daneswood Dr WV9....244 F3
Dane Wlk ST1...........282 C3
Danford Heath WV5....267 D7
Danford La WV5........267 D7
Daniels Cross TF10.....169 B4
Daniels La WS9.........256 C5
Danilo Rd WS11........210 D1
Danta Way ST17........156 C1
Darby Ave WS14.......232 E6
Darelyn Cvn Site WV2...224 B2
Darges La WS6..........226 F4
Darius Ct ST5.............56 B8
Dark La Alrewas DE13...201 A3
 Birchmoor B78.........262 E8
 Brinsford WV10........240 D8
 Featherstone WV10....241 D7
 Great Wyrley WS6.....227 C1
 Kinver DY7.............278 B3
 Lichfield WS13.........213 B1
 Longdon WS15.........212 D7
 Newborough DE13.....162 D7
 Newport TF10..........168 E1
Darley Cl DE15.........167 C1
Darley Dale DE11......186 F3
Darley Gr ST10...........76 E1
Darlings La WS15......212 E1
Darnbrook B77.........251 C1
Darnel Hurst Rd B75...258 D3
Darnford Cl ST16......155 C8
Darnford La
 Lichfield WS14.........231 F6
 Whittington WS14.....232 B5
Darnford Moors WS14..231 E6
Darnford View WS13...214 E1
Darnley St ST4............72 C8
Darrall Gdns ST4........41 E3
Darsham Gdns ST5......71 C2
Dart Ave Stafford ST17..174 B8
 Stoke-on-T ST6..........42 A4
Dart Cl ST8..............16 D1
Dartford Pl ST6..........42 C4
Dartford St3.............242 F1
Dart Gr ST10.............76 E1
Dartmouth Ave
 Cannock WS11.........226 C4
 Newcastle-u-L ST5.....71 A5
 Pattingham WV6.......253 C2
 Stourbridge DY8.......275 D3
Dartmouth Dr WS9....256 A5
Dartmouth Pl ST3........89 F8
Dartmouth Rd WS11...209 D1
Dartmouth St
 1 Wolverhampton WV2..266 D8
 Stafford ST16..........156 A3
 Stoke-on-T ST4.........42 B1
 Wolverhampton WV2...266 E8
Dart Pl ST5...............71 A4
Darwell Pk B77.........251 B2
Darwin Cl Burntwood WS7 229 B7
 Burton u T DE15.......167 C1
 Cannock WS12.........210 C2
 Lichfield WS13.........156 C4
 Stafford ST16..........156 C4
 Stone ST15.............104 E2
Darwin Ct WV6.........254 E4
Darwin Ho DY6.........275 C7
Dash Gr ST6..............42 C1
Datteln Rd WS11.......210 A4
Daurada Dr ST17.......175 A8
Davenport Cl ST13.......30 B4
Davenport Rd WV6....255 B5
Davenport St ST6........56 C7
Daventry Cl ST2.........57 F2
Davey Cl WS7..........228 F4
David Garrick Gdns
   WS13.................214 B2
David Rd ST1............73 F1
Davidson Ave CW12.....6 A4
Davidson Rd WS14.....231 B7
Davies Ave ST4..........110 F1
Davies Ho WS3..........243 B1
Davis Cl ST16...........156 A4
Davison St ST6..........57 A7
Davis Rd B77............250 F4
Davison St ST4...........57 A2
Davy Ct ST2..............58 A3
Davy Pl WS15...........196 D6
Dawes Cl WS11.........210 D1
Dawes La WS8...........229 A1
Dawley Brook Prim Sch
   DY6..................275 D7
Dawley Brook Rd DY6...275 D7
Dawley Cl WS9.........256 C8
Dawley Trad Est DY6...275 D8
Dawlish Ave ST3..........73 D8
Dawlish Dr Bucknall ST2..58 C1
 Bucknall ST2............73 D8
Dawn Ave ST6...........42 A4

Dawney Dr B75 . . . . 258 A4
Dawn View ST3 . . . . 74 B3
Dawson Ave WV14 . . . . . 266 F2
Dayson Pl ST5 . . . . 56 A7
Dayton Dr ST15 . . . . 178 C2
Daywell Rise WS15 . . . . . 178 C3
Deacons Way WS15 . . . . 178 F2
Deadman's Gn ST10 . . . . 109 C8
Deakin Ave WS8 . . . . 228 F1
Deakin Gr ST5 . . . . 71 C5
Deakin Rd ST6 . . . . 42 B5
Deal Ave WS7 . . . . 229 A8
Dean Cl TF9 . . . . 97 A1
Dean Ct WV6 . . . . 254 E6
Deanery Cl Rugeley WS15 .178 F7
  Shareshill WV10 . . . . . . 225 C2
Dean Hollow ST7 . . . . 39 D2
Dean Pl ST1 . . . . 282 C1
Dean Rd WV5 . . . . 269 F5
Deansberry Cl ST4 . . . . . . 88 A8
Deans Croft WS14 . . . . . 231 C8
Deanscroft Way ST3 . . . . . 73 E4
Deansfield ST19 . . . . 223 D6
Deansfield Rd ST19 . . . . . 223 D6
Deansgate **1** ST13 . . . . . . 30 F6
Deanshill Cl ST16 . . . . . . 155 C2
Deans La CW2 . . . . 38 C4
Dean's La ST5 . . . . 40 D2
Deans Slade Dr WS14 . . . 231 A5
Dean St Brewood ST19 . . . 223 D6
  Bucknall ST2 . . . . 58 C4
  Sedgley DY3 . . . . 271 D8
Deansway ST4 . . . . 88 B6
Dean View ST3 . . . . 39 D1
Dearnsdale Cl ST16 . . . . . 155 B7
Deavall Way WS11 . . . . . 210 B2
Deaville Rd ST2 . . . . 58 C3
Debenham Cres ST2 . . . . . 58 A2
Deborah Cl WV4 . . . . 266 C6
Decade Cl ST5 . . . . 40 F2
Deebank Ave ST13 . . . . . . 31 B6
Dee Cl Biddulph ST8 . . . . . 11 E1
  Talke ST7 . . . . 40 E1
Dee Gr WS11 . . . . 226 D8
Dee La ST5 . . . . 71 B4
Deeley B77 . . . . 251 A1
Deep Cut Rd DE6 . . . . . . 144 A7
Deepdale Cl
  Burton u T DE15 . . . . . 167 B5
  Stoke-on-T ST6 . . . . 42 F2
Deepdale La Dudley DY3 .271 E3
  Snelston DE6 . . . . 81 A2
Deepdales Stafford ST17 . 175 C6
  Wombourne WV5 . . . . . 269 E6
Deepdale B77 . . . . 251 D2
Deep Hayes Ctry Pk*
  ST13 . . . . 45 A7
Deepmore Cl
  Alrewas DE13 . . . . 201 A2
  Four Ashes WV10 . . . . . 224 D5
  Norton Canes WS11 . . . 228 B7
  Walsall WS3 . . . . 243 C1
Dee Rd WS3 . . . . 243 E1
Deerfold Cres WS7 . . . . . 229 B7
Deerhill ST17 . . . . 176 C4
Deerhill Rd ST11 . . . . 251 C1
Deerhurst Rise WS12 . . . 210 F6
Deerleap Way WS15 . . . . 178 C1
Deer Park Dr TF10 . . . . . 168 F5
Deer Pk Rd B78 . . . . 249 E1
Deer Pk ST20 . . . . 231 F2
Deer Wlk WV8 . . . . 239 F2
De Ferrers Croft DE13 . . . 166 D8
De Ferrers Specialist Tech
  Coll (Dove Campus)
  DE13 . . . . 166 B8
De Ferrers Specialist Tech
  Coll (Trent Campus)
  DE13 . . . . 166 C8
Defford Ave WS4 . . . . . . 244 C1
Defoe Dr ST3 . . . . 73 E4
De Havilland Dr ST15 . . . 118 F6
Delafield Way WS15 . . . . 178 C2
Delamere Cl CW2 . . . . 37 E4
Delamere Gr
  Newcastle-u-L ST5 . . . . . 283 C4
  Stoke-on-T ST4 . . . . 88 A7
Delamere La ST17 . . . . . . 174 A8
Delaney Dr ST3 . . . . 73 F4
Delhi Cl DE15 . . . . 167 C3
Delhurst Ave WV4 . . . . . 266 E3
Delius Gr ST1 . . . . 57 F5
Dellbrook Cl ST5 . . . . 283 B1
Dell Cl ST16 . . . . 155 B8
Dell The Cannock WS12 . . 210 F4
  Lichfield WS13 . . . . 230 F7
  Newcastle-u-L ST5 . . . . . . 55 C1
  Stourbridge DY8 . . . . . . 279 B6
  Tamworth B79 . . . . 250 B6
Dellway Ct DY8 . . . . 279 B5
Dellwood Gr **2** ST3 . . . . . 73 D6
Delphouse Rd
  Boundary ST10 . . . . 75 F2
  Cheadle ST10 . . . . 76 A2
Delphside ST7 . . . . 39 F2
Delph Wlk ST4 . . . . 72 F2
Delta Way Bsns Ctr
  WS11 . . . . 226 D6
Delta Way WS11 . . . . . . 226 D6
Deltic B77 . . . . 251 A1
Delves Cres CV9 . . . . 262 C1
Delves Pl ST5 . . . . 71 B5
Demontfort Way ST14 . . . 16 C6
Denbigh Cl Biddulph ST8 . 27 C6
  Burton u T DE13 . . . . . . 166 D7
  Dudley DY1 . . . . 271 F2

Denbigh Cl continued
  Newcastle-u-L ST5 . . . . . . 71 D4
Denbigh St ST1 . . . . 282 A4
Denbury Cl WS12 . . . . . . 210 D1
Denby Ave WS3 . . . . 284 C5
Dency Gr ST6 . . . . 42 A3
Dene Ave DY6 . . . . 275 C4
Dene Cl ST19 . . . . 207 F8
Dene Croft WS3 . . . . 243 A1
Denefield ST19 . . . . 207 F8
Denehurst Cl **1** ST8 . . . . . 74 A2
Dene Rd Lower Penn WV4 .264 F4
  Stourbridge DY8 . . . . . . 279 F3
Dene Side ST5 . . . . 283 A2
Denewood Pl ST3 . . . . 74 B1
Denford Rd ST9 . . . . 44 F8
Denham Gdns WV3 . . . . 265 B8
Denham Sq ST3 . . . . 72 E1
Den La CW3 . . . . 52 D4
Denleigh Rd DY6 . . . . . . 275 F4
Denmark Rise WS12 . . . . 210 D7
Denmark Villas WS3 . . . . 230 C5
Dennfield Dr WS6 . . . . . . 226 C2
Dennington Cres ST3 . . . . 72 E1
Dennis Barsby Cl DE11 . . 186 E3
Dennis Hall **9** DY8 . . . . . 277 F8
Dennis St Stoke-on-T ST4 . .72 F5
  Stourbridge DY8 . . . . . . 279 F3
Dennis B77 . . . . 250 E2
Dennis Viollet Ave ST4 . . . 72 C3
Denry Cres ST5 . . . . 56 B8
Denshaw Wlk ST3 . . . . . 284 C4
Denston Ct B74 . . . . 257 F2
Denstone Ave ST4 . . . . . 156 B1
Denstone Coll ST14 . . . . . 95 B5
Denstone Cres ST3 . . . . . 72 F2
Denstone Gdns WV10 . . . 240 F3
Denstone La ST14 . . . . . . 95 C7
Dentdale Cl ST3 . . . . 90 A7
Denton Cl ST5 . . . . 71 C3
Denton Gr ST3 . . . . 73 E3
Denton Rd DE13 . . . . 166 A6
Denton Rise DE13 . . . . . . 166 A7
Dent St B79 . . . . 250 C5
Denver Field ST17 . . . . . . 174 A8
Denver Ct WS13 . . . . 215 C6
Denzil Gn ST17 . . . . 174 A8
Derby Ave WV6 . . . . 255 F7
Derby Mews ST14 . . . . . 110 F1
Derby Pl ST5 . . . . 71 C4
Derby Rd
  Burton u T DE13,DE14 . .166 E7
  Doveridge DE6 . . . . 127 C8
  Eggington DE65 . . . . . . 148 C4
  Stretton DE13 . . . . 148 A1
  Talke ST7 . . . . 40 D7
  Uttoxeter ST14 . . . . . . 111 D1
  Whittington WS14 . . . . . 232 D3
Derby St **8** DE14 . . . . . . 166 C4
  Hanley ST1 . . . . 282 C2
  Leek ST13 . . . . 30 F5
  Stafford ST16 . . . . 285 A3
Derby Turn DE14 . . . . . . 166 D5
Dereham Way ST3 . . . . . . 58 D1
Derek Dr ST1 . . . . 90 B6
Dereton Hill WS15 . . . . . 197 B5
Derrington La
  Bradley ST18 . . . . 173 E8
  Derrington ST18 . . . . . . 154 E1
Derwent Ave ST15 . . . . . . 71 C4
Derwent Cl Aldridge WS9 .256 F3
  Burton u T DE14 . . . . . . 166 E3
Derwent Cres ST7 . . . . . . 26 C2
Derwent Dr
  2 Congleton CW12 . . . . 6 A1
  Biddulph ST8 . . . . 16 E1
  Cheadle ST10 . . . . 76 E1
  Loggerheads TF9 . . . . . . 99 E5
Derwent Gr
  Burntwood WS7 . . . . . . 229 D6
  Cannock WS11 . . . . 226 D8
Derwent Ho ST17 . . . . . . 174 E6
Derwent Pk DE14 . . . . . . 166 E5
Derwent Pl ST5 . . . . 56 A3
Derwent Rd
  Burton u T DE15 . . . . . 167 A1
  Wolverhampton WV6 . . . 255 E8
Derwent St ST1 . . . . 282 A4
Derwent B77 . . . . 250 D1
Devall Cl WS15 . . . . 196 E7
Devana Wlk ST3 . . . . 74 C2
Devereux Ho B79 . . . . . . 250 A4
Devereux Rd B75 . . . . . . 258 C1
Devey Dr WV14 . . . . 147 C1
Devil's La ST9,ST13 . . . . . 29 E5
Devon Cl Burton u T DE15 . .185 E6
  Newcastle-u-L ST5 . . . . . . 71 C4
Devon Cres WS9 . . . . . . 245 A1
Devon Ct WS11 . . . . 226 C8
Devon Gn WS11 . . . . 226 F8
Devon Ho **4** DY8 . . . . . . 279 F8
Devonport Cl **7** ST7 . . . . 26 E4
Devon Rd Cannock WS11 .226 F8
  Stourbridge DY8 . . . . . . 279 E7
Devonshire Ct B74 . . . . . 258 A2
Devonshire Dr
  Rugeley WS15 . . . . 196 D6
  Tamworth B78 . . . . 250 A1
Devonshire Sq ST2 . . . . . . 58 C1
Devon Way ST17 . . . . 174 D6
Dewberry Rd **8** DY8 . . . . 275 F1
Dewick Ind Est ST17 . . . . 175 F3
De-Wint Rd ST5 . . . . 120 B7
Dewsbury Cl DY8 . . . . . . 275 E3

Dewsbury Dr
  Burntwood WS7 . . . . . . 229 C6
  Wolverhampton WV4 . . . 266 A4
Dewsbury Rd ST4 . . . . . . 72 E8
Dexter Way ST8 . . . . 262 F8
Dexton Rise ST17 . . . . . . 174 A8
Deykin Rd WS13 . . . . 231 A6
Dial La Biddulph CW12,SK11 . .7 B1
  Stoke-on-T ST6 . . . . 42 D8
Diamond Ave **3** ST7 . . . . 26 B2
Diamond Cl
  Barlaston ST12 . . . . 104 C8
  Biddulph ST8 . . . . 27 C8
  Meir Heath ST3 . . . . 90 A4
Diamond Gr WS11 . . . . . 210 C3
Diamond Jubilee Cotts
  DE6 . . . . 81 E8
Diamond Park Dr **3**
  DY8 . . . . 275 E1
Diamond Ridge ST12 . . . 104 C8
Diamond Way ST15 . . . . 120 B5
Diana Cl WS9 . . . . 245 A3
Diana Rd ST1 . . . . 57 F6
Diarmid Rd ST4 . . . . 71 F1
Dibble Rd DE14 . . . . 185 A7
Dibdale Cl DY3 . . . . 271 D3
Dibdale Rd W DY1 . . . . . 271 E3
Dibdale St DY1 . . . . 271 F2
Dibden Ct **7** ST4 . . . . 72 A7
Dickens Cl
  Burton u T DE14 . . . . . . 166 D6
  Dudley DY3 . . . . 271 B5
Dickenson Rd E ST6 . . . . . 57 C7
Dickenson Rd W ST6 . . . . 57 C7
Dickens St ST22 . . . . 58 C4
Dickinson Rd WV5 . . . . . 270 A4
Dickson Ho ST11 . . . . . . 282 C1
Dickson Rd ST16 . . . . . . 156 A5
Dicky's La ST20 . . . . 151 E7
Didcot Dr ST14 . . . . 143 F7
Digbeth La WV5 . . . . 267 B8
Digby Rd DY6 . . . . 275 D8
Diglake Cl ST17 . . . . 40 C6
Diglake St ST7 . . . . 39 F3
Digmire La DE6 . . . . 51 D1
Dig St SK17 . . . . 24 D6
Dilhorne Endowed Prim Sch
  ST10 . . . . 75 D5
Dilhorne Gr ST3 . . . . 284 C1
Dilhorne Rd
  Caverswall ST10 . . . . . . 74 F3
  Cheadle ST10 . . . . 76 B3
  Forsbrook ST11 . . . . 75 B2
Dilke St ST1 . . . . 282 C4
Dill Gr ST3 . . . . 90 B6
Dillhorne Park* ST10 . . . 75 C6
Dimble La WV4 . . . . 94 E8
Dimbles Hill WS13 . . . . . 214 B1
Dimbles La WS13 . . . . . . 214 A2
Dimmelow St ST1 . . . . . . 74 B5
Dimmingsdale Rd WV4 . . 264 E5
Dimmingsdale YH* ST10 . .78 A4
Dimmock St WV4 . . . . . . 266 C5
Dimsdale Par E ST5 . . . . . 56 C5
Dimsdale Par W ST5 . . . . 56 A6
Dimsdale St ST6 . . . . 56 E7
Dimsdale View E ST5 . . . . 56 B6
Dimsdale View W ST5 . . . 55 F6
Dingle **2** Cl ST3 . . . . 28 A4
Dingle Dr DE13 . . . . 165 E4
Dingle La Bridgemere CW5 . .67 A5
  Hilderstone ST15 . . . . . . 106 D2
  Woodhouse Green ST8 . . 17 E7
Dingle The Brownhills WS8 .244 E6
  Wombourne WV5 . . . . . 269 F6
Dingle The Brown Edge ST6 43 B7
  Burton u T ST5 . . . . 185 E8
  Wolverhampton WV3 . . . 255 D1
Dingle View DY3 . . . . . . 271 C7
Dinham Gdns WV3 . . . . . 271 E3
Dippons Dr WV6 . . . . . . 255 A3
Dippons Mill Cl WV6 . . . . 255 A3
Dirtyfoot La WV4 . . . . . . 265 A5
Dirty La ST19 . . . . 223 C6
District Ctr WS12 . . . . . . 210 C2
Ditch Cotts SK17 . . . . 5 F8
Ditch The SK17 . . . . 1 F8
Dividy Rd ST2 . . . . 58 B2
Dixon Cl ST15 . . . . 104 E2
Dixon Rd CW12 . . . . 6 A5
Dixon's Row ST5 . . . . 55 D7
Dixon St WV2 . . . . 266 C7
Dobbinthorne La DE6 . . . . 81 F5
Dobbs St WV2 . . . . 266 C8
Dobell Gr ST3 . . . . 284 D4
Dobie Cl ST17 . . . . 177 E7
Dobson St ST6 . . . . 56 C7
Dock Rd DY8 . . . . 275 F2
Doctor's Bank TF9 . . . . . 100 C5
Doctors Cl ST18 . . . . 27 C8
Doctors La
  Kingswinford DY6 . . . . . 275 A4
  Kinver DY7 . . . . 274 F5
  Shenstone WS14 . . . . . . 247 A6
Doddington Pl ST5 . . . . . . 71 B6
Doddespool Barns CW3 . . 52 F7
Dodds La Astbury CW12 . . 15 C6
  Chorley WS13 . . . . 212 C3
Dodslow Ave DE13 . . . . . 148 B3
Dogcroft St6 . . . . 42 C5
Dog Kennel La TF9 . . . . . 112 D8
Dog La Butterton TF13 . . . 33 E7
  Calton ST13 . . . . 30 F3
  Leek ST13 . . . . 30 E5

Doglands Rd ST18 . . . . . . 123 A1
Dog La Nethersea DE12 . . 219 F6
  Ranton ST18 . . . . 153 D4
  Stableford ST4,ST5 . . . . . 86 C3
Tamworth B77 . . . . 251 B6
Weeford WS14 . . . . 248 A4
Dogmoor La ST10 . . . . . . 64 F8
Dogshead La DE13 . . . . . 201 C7
Dolefoot La DE13 . . . . . . 162 F4
Doles La DE6 . . . . 81 F7
Dolespring Cl ST11 . . . . . 91 A8
Doley Cl ST20 . . . . 171 D6
Dolly's La ST6 . . . . 42 A2
Dolphin Cl Stafford ST17 .156 C1
  Walsall WS3 . . . . 243 F1
Dominic St **5** Stone ST15 104 F1
  Stoke-on-T ST4 . . . . 72 A8
Donald Bates Ho ST4 . . . . 71 F6
Donald Rd ST1 . . . . 57 E6
Doncaster La ST4 . . . . . . 71 F7
Don Gr WS11 . . . . 226 D7
Donington La WV7 . . . . . 237 B8
Donithorne Cl DE13 . . . . . 166 C7
Donkey La ST10 . . . . 76 E5
Dorado B77 . . . . 261 D7
Dorcas Dr ST3 . . . . 72 F4
Dorchester Cl ST7 . . . . . . 26 A4
Dorchester Rd
  Cannock WS11 . . . . 209 B1
  Willenhall WV12 . . . . . . 242 C1
Dordon Rd B78 . . . . 262 F8
Doreen Ave CW12 . . . . . . 16 B8
Dorian Way ST9 . . . . 43 F7
Doris Robinson Ct ST3 . . 89 F7
Dorington Cl ST22 . . . . . . 57 F2
Dorlan Cl ST9 . . . . 43 C3
Dormer Ave B77 . . . . . . 250 D5
Dormston Dr ST3 . . . . . . 271 E8
Dormston Trad Est DY1 . . 271 F4
Dorothy Clive Garden The*
  TF9 . . . . 84 A4
Dorridge Gr ST5 . . . . 56 E4
Dorrington Cl ST22 . . . . . 43 A1
Dorrington Dr ST18 . . . . . 155 E6
Dorrington Gr ST5 . . . . . 56 C6
Dorrington Ind Pk ST16 . . 155 E6
Dorrington La CW3 . . . . . 83 B7
Dorset Cl Bucknall ST2 . . . 58 C3
  Burton u T DE15 . . . . . . 185 E6
  Tamworth B78 . . . . 250 A1
Dorset Dr Aldridge WS9 . . 245 A1
  Biddulph ST8 . . . . 27 B8
Dorset Pl Kidsgrove ST7 . . 26 A2
  Newcastle-u-L ST5 . . . . . . 71 D4
Dorset Rd Cannock WS12 .210 E1
  Stourbridge DY8 . . . . . . 279 D8
Dosthill Prim Sch B77 . . 261 D5
Dosthill Rd (Two Gates)
  B77 . . . . 261 D7
Double Gates TF9 . . . . . . 112 B8
Douglas Ave Biddulph ST8 .27 D7
Douglas Ct ST4 . . . . 71 F5
Douglas Pl ST1 . . . . 57 E2
Douglas Rd
  Newcastle-u-L ST5 . . . . . . 56 A3
  Stafford ST16 . . . . 156 A5
Douglas Rd W ST16 . . . . 156 A5
Douglas St ST1 . . . . 57 E2
Doulton Cl Cheadle ST10 . .76 D1
  Stoke-on-T ST5 . . . . 119 E6
Doulton Dr ST5 . . . . 56 B7
Doulton Rd ST18 . . . . . . 156 B8
Doulton St **4** ST6 . . . . . . 57 A8
Douse La ST19 . . . . 32 D4
Doval Gdns ST10 . . . . . . 92 E4
Dovebank Gr ST3 . . . . . . 90 A4
Dove Bank Prim Sch ST7 . .26 A2
Dove Bank ST14 . . . . 126 C8
Dove Cl Burntwood WV5 . .229 D6
  Fradley WS13 . . . . 215 B5
Dovecliff Cres DE13 . . . . . 147 F2
Dovecliff Rd DE13 . . . . . . 147 E3
Dovecote Cl WV6 . . . . . . 255 C4
Dovecote ST17 . . . . 174 F5
Dovecotes Prim Sch
  WV8 . . . . 239 F1
Dovecotes The ST3 . . . . . 258 B3
Dovedale Ave WS3 . . . . . 244 B5
Dovedale WS11 . . . . 210 A5
Dovedale Cl
  Burton u T DE15 . . . . . 167 B5
  Cheadle ST10 . . . . 76 E6
  Congleton CW12 . . . . 6 A4
  Stoke-on-T ST6 . . . . 41 B7
Dovedale Ct WV4 . . . . . . 266 F2
Dovedale Prim Sch ST5 . . 55 A1
Dovedale Rd Kingsley ST10 61 E8
  Kingswinford DY6 . . . . . 275 D6
  Wolverhampton WV4 . . . 266 F2
Dovefields ST14 . . . . 95 F3
Dove Fst Sch ST14 . . . . . 96 A3
Dove Gr Biddulph ST8 . . . 16 D1
  Eggington DE65 . . . . . . 148 A5
Dove Hollow
  Cannock WS12 . . . . 210 E4
  Great Wyrley WS6 . . . . . 226 C2
Dovehouse Fields WS14 . . 231 B6
Dove La ST14 . . . . 96 A4
Dove Lea DE13 . . . . 147 B4
Dove Pl ST15 . . . . 71 B4
Dover Ct DE13 . . . . 166 C7
Dover Rd ST1 . . . . 91 A7
Dover Farm Cl B77 . . . . . 262 B8

Dove Ridge SK17 . . . . 13 C6
Doveridge Prim Sch
  DE6 . . . . 127 C8
Doveridge Rd DE15 . . . . . 167 B1
Dover Rd DE13 . . . . 166 B7
Dover St ST1 . . . . 282 C4
Dover Side DE65 . . . . . . 146 D8
Doveside DE6 . . . . 81 D7
Dove St DE6 . . . . 80 B2
Dovestone B77 . . . . 251 D1
Dove View DE13 . . . . 146 C6
Dove Way The ST14 . . . . 111 C2
Dove Way ST10 . . . . 48 F2
Dove Wlk ST14 . . . . 126 D8
Dowells Gdns DY8 . . . . . 275 D3
Dower Rd B75 . . . . 258 E1
Downderry Cl ST17 . . . . . 174 A8
Downend Cl WV10 . . . . . 240 F4
Downesway WS11 . . . . . 209 C2
Downey St ST1 . . . . 282 B2
Downfield Cl WS3 . . . . . . 243 A4
Downfield Dr DY3 . . . . . . 271 E6
Downfield Gr ST16 . . . . . 155 D8
Downfield Pl ST7 . . . . 42 F1
Downfields TF10 . . . . 168 F5
Downford Cl ST19 . . . . . . 205 C6
Downford La ST19 . . . . . . 205 C6
Downham Pl WV3 . . . . . 265 F8
Downham Rd ST5 . . . . . . 55 E2
Downie Rd WV8 . . . . 239 C3
Downing Ave ST5 . . . . . . 56 E3
Downing Dr B79 . . . . 249 E5
Downing Gdns **3** ST15 . . 120 A7
Downs The Aldridge WS9 .256 E2
  Stafford ST17 . . . . 175 C7
Downsview Gr ST3 . . . . . . 72 F3
Dowty Way WV9 . . . . . . 240 A3
Doxey Fields ST16 . . . . . 154 F4
Doxey Ho ST16 . . . . 155 A4
Doxey Prim Sch ST16 . . . 155 B4
Doxey ST16 . . . . 155 B4
Dragon Sq ST5 . . . . 55 E8
Drake Ave ST19 . . . . 207 F6
Drake Cl Berry Hill ST2 . . . 57 F1
  Walsall WS3 . . . . 243 B1
Drake Croft **4** WS13 . . . . 231 C8
Drake Ct WS3 . . . . 243 B1
Drakeford Ct
  Stafford ST17 . . . . 285 B2
  Stoke-on-T ST6 . . . . 42 E4
Drakeford Gr ST6 . . . . . . 42 E4
Drakes Hill Cl WV8 . . . . . 243 C1
Drakes Hill Cl DY8 . . . . . 279 C4
Draw-Well La ST4 . . . . . . 59 C4
Draycott Manor Prim Sch
  ST11 . . . . 91 D5
Draycott Old Rd ST11 . . . 91 C7
Draycott Rd ST10 . . . . . . 92 C4
Drayton Cl B75 . . . . 258 B3
Drayton Gn ST22 . . . . 58 A2
Drayton Gr ST7 . . . . 97 C1
Drayton La B78 . . . . 260 C5
Drayton Manor Dr
  Drayton Bassett B78 . . . 260 F7
  Fazeley B78 . . . . 260 F8
Drayton Manor Pk B78 . . 260 F2
Drayton Mill Ct TF9 . . . . . 97 C1
Drayton Rd Hanchurch ST4 87 B5
  Longton ST3 . . . . 284 C4
Drayton St
  Newcastle-u-L ST5 . . . . . . 283 A2
  Wolverhampton WV2 . . . 266 C8
Dreiech Cl ST16 . . . . 155 F5
Drenfell Rd ST7 . . . . 25 F7
Dresden CE Prim Sch
  ST3 . . . . 284 C1
Dresden St ST1 . . . . 282 C2
Dreys The ST4 . . . . 88 B7
Driffield Cl ST2 . . . . 58 E1
Drive Fields WV4 . . . . . . 265 B6
Drive Sch (Tettenhall Coll)
  The WV6 . . . . 255 D4
Drive The
  Alsagers Bank ST7 . . . . . 54 F6
  Burton u T DE13 . . . . . . 166 C7
  Codsall WV8 . . . . 238 F3
  Rudyard ST13 . . . . 29 E8
  Shenstone WS14 . . . . . . 247 E8
  Stafford ST16 . . . . 155 B4
  Walsall,Pelsall WS3 . . . . . 243 E2
  Walsall WS4 . . . . 244 C1
  Wolverhampton WV6 . . . 255 C5
Droitron La ST18 . . . . . . 139 D3
Droitwich Cl ST5 . . . . 54 F2
Drovers Way TF10 . . . . . 169 A4
Droveway The WV9 . . . . . 239 F2
Droxford Wlk WV4 . . . . . 239 B1
Drubbery La ST3 . . . . . . 284 A1
Druid Park Rd WV12 . . . . 242 C1
Druids Ave WS9 . . . . 256 C8
Druids Way ST19 . . . . . . 207 F7
Druids Wlk ST4 . . . . 247 E8
Drumart Ho DY10 . . . . . . 280 A5
Drumber La ST7 . . . . 26 B8
Drumburn Cl ST6 . . . . . . 41 F7
Drummond Cl WV11 . . . . 242 A2
Drummond Rd ST16 . . . . 155 E6

Drummond St ST6 . . . . . . .41 D7
Drury La WV8 . . . . .238 F4
Dryburgh Cl ST17 . . . . . . .174 B7
Dryburg Wlk ST2 . . . . .58 A4
Dryden Cres ST17 . . . . . . .155 C1
Dryden Rd Burslem ST6 . . . .57 A6
  Tamworth B79 . . . . .250 A6
  Wolverhampton WV10 . . . .240 F1
Dryden Way ST10 . . . . .76 C2
Dual Way WS12 . . . . .209 D8
Dubarry Ave DY6 . . . . . . .275 C7
Duchy Cl DE13 . . . . .166 E8
Duchy Rd CW1 . . . . .37 A8
Duck La WV8 . . . . .239 B3
Duck St DE65 . . . . .148 B5
Duddell Rd ST6 . . . . .42 C2
Dudding Rd WV4 . . . . . . .266 D5
Dudley Innovation Ctr
  DY6 . . . . .275 F7
Dudley Pl ST3 . . . . .90 A8
Dudley Rd Dudley DY3 . . . .271 E6
  Himley DY3 . . . . .270 D3
  Kingswinford DY6 . . . . . .275 F7
  Kingswinford,Wall Heath
  DY6 . . . . .275 C8
  Wolverhampton WV2 . . . .266 D7
Dudley St DY3 . . . . .271 D8
Dudley Wlk WV4 . . . . . . .266 C5
Dudmaston Way WV11 . . . .271 E3
Duesbury Gn ST3 . . . . . . .284 A3
Duffield Cl WV8 . . . . .239 F1
Duffield La DE13 . . . . .162 F7
Dugdale Cl WS12 . . . . . . .210 F3
Dugdale Cres B75 . . . . . . .258 C3
Duke Bank Terr ST6 . . . . . .42 F4
Duke Pl ST5 . . . . .55 C1
Dukes La ST13,ST10 . . . . . .63 D7
Dukes Rd B78 . . . . .262 F6
Duke St Biddulph ST8 . . . . .27 D7
  Burton u T DE14 . . . . . . .166 C2
  Leek ST13 . . . . .30 F5
  Newcastle-u-L ST5 . . . . . .283 C1
  Stoke-on-T ST4 . . . . .72 E4
  Stoke-on-T ST4 . . . . .72 F5
  Tutbury DE13 . . . . .148 B5
  Wolverhampton,Penn Fields
  WV3 . . . . .266 A7
Dulverton Ave ST5 . . . . . . .71 A5
Dumbill Ho ST7 . . . . .40 C8
Dumbleberry Ave DY3 . . . .271 C7
Dumolo's La B77 . . . . .250 F3
Dumore Hay La WS13 . . . .215 F8
Duncalfe Dr B75 . . . . .258 B3
Duncalf Gr ST5 . . . . .56 B7
Duncalf St ST6 . . . . .56 F8
Duncan St Stoke-on-T ST4 . .72 E6
  Wolverhampton WV2 . . . .266 C7
Duncombe St DY8 . . . . . . .279 D5
Dundalk La WS6 . . . . .226 D2
Dundas St ST1 . . . . .282 C4
Dundee Rd ST1 . . . . .57 A3
Dundee St ST3 . . . . .284 B2
Dunedin Cres DE15 . . . . . .167 C2
Dunedin B77 . . . . .251 A1
Dungarven Dr ST10 . . . . . .168 D2
Dunhampton Dr DY10 . . . .280 B1
Dunkirk ST7 . . . . .40 A6
Dunkirk Ct ST5 . . . . .283 A3
Dunkirk ST5 . . . . .283 A3
Dunlin Dr WV10 . . . . .241 B7
Dunnerdale Rd WS8 . . . . .244 D6
Dunning St ST6 . . . . .41 D3
Dunnington Ave ST10 . . . .280 A1
Dunnock Cl ST14 . . . . . . .126 C6
Dunnock Way ST18 . . . . . .27 E8
Dunrobin St ST3 . . . . .284 C2
Dunsany Gr ST1 . . . . .57 E6
Dunsford Ave ST2 . . . . . . .43 A2
Dunsley Dr Dunsley DY7 . . .278 C8
  Stourbridge DY8 . . . . . . .275 E3
Dunsley Gr WV4 . . . . .266 A4
Dunsley Rd Dunsley DY7 . . .278 C4
  Stourbridge DY8 . . . . . . .279 C4
Dunstall Brook DE15 . . . . .165 E8
Dunstall Cross DE13 . . . . .183 A6
Dunstall Hill DE13 . . . . . . .183 B6
Dunstall La DE13 . . . . . . .249 D4
Dunstall Rd
  Barton-u-N DE13 . . . . . . .183 E3
  Tatenhill DE13 . . . . .184 A7
Dunster Cl ST17 . . . . .174 B7
Dunster Gr WV6 . . . . .254 F3
Dunster Rd ST3 . . . . .73 C5
Dunster B77 . . . . .261 C7
Dunston Cl
  Great Wyrley WS6 . . . . . .242 E8
  Kingswinford DY6 . . . . . .275 D7
Dunston Dr WS7 . . . . .229 A8
Dunton Cl B75 . . . . .258 A4
Dunwood Dr ST6 . . . . .42 A3
Dunwood La ST9,ST13 . . . . .29 D4
Durban Cl DE15 . . . . .167 C3
Durber Cl Audley ST7 . . . . .39 D1
  Stoke-on-T ST4 . . . . .71 E4
D'Urberville Cl WV2 . . . . .266 F6
D'Urberville Wlk
  WS11 . . . . .210 A2
Durfield La DE13 . . . . .163 B7
Durham Cl B78 . . . . .250 A2
Durham Dr Rugeley WS15 . .196 D6
  Stoke-on-T ST3 . . . . .89 C8
Durham Gr ST5 . . . . .71 D4

Durham Rd DY8 . . . . .279 D8
Durlston Cl B77 . . . . .250 F5
Durose Ct ST14 . . . . .125 C7
Dursley Dr WS11 . . . . . . .209 B2
Dursley Rd WS7 . . . . .229 A7
Durston Pl ST3 . . . . .73 E3
Dutton's La B75 . . . . .258 E4
Duttons The ST18 . . . . . . .123 B3
Dutton Way ST15 . . . . . . .119 F5
Dyke Rd WS5 . . . . .198 B4
Dykes La ST10 . . . . .188 D8
Dyke St ST1 . . . . .282 C3
Dylan Rd Biddulph ST8 . . . .27 E6
  Longton ST3 . . . . .73 D3
Dyott Ave WS14 . . . . .232 E6
Dyott Cl WS13 . . . . .215 A1
Dyson Ct ST18 . . . . .156 C5
Dyson St ST18 . . . . .156 C5

E

Eagle Cl Cheslyn Hay WS6 . .226 D2
  Dudley DY1 . . . . .271 F1
  Uttoxeter ST14 . . . . .126 B6
Eagle Cres ST21 . . . . .133 D6
Eagle Ct
  Wolverhampton,Pendeford
  WV10 . . . . .240 B3
  Wolverhampton,Penn Fields
  WV3 . . . . .266 A7
Eagle Dr B77 . . . . .251 C4
Eagle Gr WS12 . . . . .210 C1
Eagle Hts DE15 . . . . .167 D3
Eagle Mill ST1 . . . . .282 A6
Eagle St Hanley ST1 . . . . . .57 E3
  Wolverhampton,Monmore Green
  WV2 . . . . .266 E8
  Wolverhampton,Penn Fields
  WV3 . . . . .266 A7
Ealand St DE13 . . . . .147 D4
Ealingham B77 . . . . .251 B1
Eamont Ave ST6 . . . . .42 A4
Eardleyend Rd ST7 . . . . . . .39 F7
Eardley St ST4 . . . . .71 F6
Earl Dr WS7 . . . . .211 E1
Earlsbrook Dr ST4 . . . . . . .88 C7
Earls Ct Burton u T DE13 . . .166 D8
  Newcastle-u-L ST5 . . . . . .283 D3
Earl's Dr ST5 . . . . .71 B5
Earls Rd ST4 . . . . .88 B7
Earl Sterndale CE Prim Sch
  SK17 . . . . .5 C3
Earl St Kingswinford DY6 . . .275 F4
  Leek ST13 . . . . .30 F6
  Newcastle-u-L,Silverdale
  ST5 . . . . .55 C1
  Newcastle-u-L ST5 . . . . . .283 D3
  Stafford ST16 . . . . .285 B3
Earls Way ST18 . . . . .158 C2
Earlsway ST10 . . . . .64 B8
Earlswood Cres WV9 . . . . .240 A3
Earlswood Rd Bucknall ST1 . .58 A8
  Kingswinford DY6 . . . . . .275 E8
Early La ST15 . . . . .103 C4
Easby Cl ST17 . . . . .174 B7
Easby Way WS3 . . . . .242 F2
Easdale Pl ST5 . . . . .71 B5
Easedale Cl ST2 . . . . .43 A2
Easing La ST13 . . . . .31 E8
East Ave CW2 . . . . .37 C5
Eastbank Rd ST1 . . . . .282 A4
East Bank Ride ST11 . . . . . .91 B8
East Beeches WV9 . . . . . . .224 B2
Eastbourne Cl ST13 . . . . . .30 D6
Eastbourne Rd ST1 . . . . . . .57 E4
Eastbridge Ave ST1 . . . . . . .57 D8
East Butts Rd WS15 . . . . . .178 B1
East Cannock Rd WS12 . . . .210 C4
East Cl ST15 . . . . .119 F7
Eastcote Cres WS7 . . . . . .229 A5
East Cres
  Newcastle-u-L ST5 . . . . . .56 D3
  Stoke-on-T ST7 . . . . .57 E8
East Croft Rd WV4 . . . . . . .265 C6
Eastdean Ave ST2 . . . . . . .58 A2
East Dr Biddulph ST8 . . . . .27 D8
  Cheddleton ST13 . . . . . . .45 D7
Eastern Ave
  Burton u T DE13 . . . . . . .166 F8
  Lichfield WS13 . . . . .214 C2
Eastern Way WS11 . . . . . .210 A2
Easters Gr ST2 . . . . .43 B1
Eastfield Cl Aldridge WS9 . .256 A6
  Stoke-on-T ST3 . . . . .88 E8
Eastfield Dr ST1 . . . . .282 C1
Eastfields Rd ST14 . . . . . .126 D8
Eastgate Brewood ST19 . . .223 D7
Eastgate Ct WS14 . . . . . . .231 C6
Eastgate St
  Burntwood WS7 . . . . . . .228 E8
  Stafford ST16 . . . . .285 B3
East Gn WV4 . . . . .265 D6
East Gr ST5 . . . . .74 A1
Easthall Cl ST19 . . . . .223 D6
Easthead Wlk ST1 . . . . . . .282 A2
Eastholme ST15 . . . . .100 D1
Eastlands B77 . . . . .174 E8
Eastlands Gr ST17 . . . . . . .174 E8
Eastlands ST17 . . . . .174 E8
East Lawns CW3 . . . . .53 A6
Eastleigh DY3 . . . . .271 C8
Eastmoor Cl B74 . . . . .257 B2
Eastney Cres WV8 . . . . . . .255 F8
East Prec ST1 . . . . .282 C3
East Rd
  Featherstone WV10 . . . . . .241 A7

East Rd continued
  Wolverhampton WV4 . . . .266 F4
Eastridge Croft WS14 . . . . .247 A5
East St Burton u T DE15 . . .167 C3
  Cannock WS11 . . . . .209 B2
  Dudley,Gornalwood DY3 . .271 D3
  Leek ST13 . . . . .31 A6
  Meir ST3 . . . . .74 B6
  Tamworth B77 . . . . .261 D5
East Terr ST6 . . . . .42 B6
East View Burslem ST6 . . . .56 F7
  Mayfield DE6 . . . . .81 D7
  Shuttington B79 . . . . . . .251 F7
  Tamworth B77 . . . . .250 E3
Eastward Glen WV8 . . . . . .239 C1
Eastwick Cres ST4 . . . . . . .88 A8
Eastwood Ave
  Burntwood WS7 . . . . . . .229 A8
  Stoke-on-T ST6 . . . . .42 A4
  Stoke-on-T ST4 . . . . .72 E7
  Tamworth B77 . . . . .250 A5
  Wolverhampton WV4 . . . .266 F5
Eastwood Pl ST1 . . . . .282 B2
Eastwood Rd ST1 . . . . .282 C1
Eastwood Rise ST5 . . . . . . .85 A4
Eaton Cres DY3 . . . . .271 B3
Eaton Dr WS15 . . . . .178 E2
Eaton Park Prim Sch ST2 . . .58 A2
Eaton Pl DY6 . . . . .275 E5
Eaton Rd ST14 . . . . .75 F5
Eaton St ST1 . . . . .282 C3
Eaves Court Dr DY3 . . . . . .266 C1
Eaves La Bucknall ST2 . . . . .58 D5
  Cheadle ST10 . . . . .76 E1
  Oakamoor ST10 . . . . .78 A8
  Whiston ST10 . . . . .62 F1
Eaveswood Rd ST2 . . . . . . .58 C6
Ebenezer St WS12 . . . . . . .210 A7
Ebony Cl ST16 . . . . .155 C4
Ebstree Mdw WV5 . . . . . . .264 A2
Ebstree Rd Seisdon WV5 . . .264 A2
  Seisdon WV5 . . . . .264 C4
Ebury Gr ST3 . . . . .73 F1
Eccleshall Bsns Pk DE14 . . .166 F4
Eccleshall Rd
  Great Bridgeford ST18 . . . .135 D2
  Loggerheads,Hookgate TF9 . .99 C3
  Loggerheads,Tadgedale TF9 . .99 B6
  Stafford ST16 . . . . .155 C6
  Stone ST15 . . . . .119 E6
Eccleston St ST6 . . . . .42 A6
Edale Cl Kingswinford DY6 . .275 B7
  Newcastle-u-L ST5 . . . . . .55 B1
  Stoke-on-T ST6 . . . . .41 B7
  Wolverhampton WV4 . . . .266 E3
Eddel B77 . . . . .250 F3
Eddens Wood Cl B78 . . . . .260 E5
Eddies La B79 . . . . .216 E1
Eddisbury Dr ST5 . . . . .40 D2
Edenbridge Cl CW2 . . . . . .37 B2
Edenbridge View DY1 . . . . .271 E3
Eden Cl Biddulph ST8 . . . . .16 E1
  Cannock WS12 . . . . .210 A2
  Hilton DE65 . . . . .147 C8
  Kidsgrove ST7 . . . . .26 B2
Eden St WV10 . . . . .240 F8
Edenfield Pl B77 . . . . .251 B1
Eden Gdns DY3 . . . . .271 E8
Eden Gr Cheadle ST10 . . . . .76 E1
  Loggerheads TF9 . . . . .99 C5
  Longton ST3 . . . . .73 F1
Edenhurst Ave ST3 . . . . . . .90 C8
Edenhurst Prep Sch ST5 . . .71 B4
Edensor CE Prim Sch
  ST3 . . . . .284 A2
Edensor Ct ST5 . . . . .55 E7
Edensor Rd ST3 . . . . .284 B3
Edensor St ST5 . . . . .55 E7
Edensor Tech Coll ST3 . . . .284 B3
Edes Farm Dr ST14 . . . . . . .95 F4
Edgar Cl B79 . . . . .249 F7
Edgar Pl ST3 . . . . .73 C4
Edgbaston Dr ST4 . . . . . . .88 D7
Edge Ave ST6 . . . . .42 B6
Edgecliff High Sch ST7 . . . .278 A4
Edgefield La ST6,ST9 . . . . .43 C5
Edgefield Rd ST3 . . . . .73 C5
Edge Hill Ave WV10 . . . . . .241 B1
Edge Hill Dr Perton WV6 . . .254 E3
  Sedgley DY3 . . . . .266 B1
Edge Hill Jun Sch DE15 . . .185 F7
Edge Hill DY7 . . . . .277 F4
Edgehill Rd ST13 . . . . .30 C5
Edge Hill Rd B74 . . . . .257 E4
Edge La WV5 . . . . .262 B2
Edge La ST9 . . . . .43 D7
Edgeley Rd ST8 . . . . .27 D7
Edgemoor Mdw WV2 . . . . .210 C1
Edge St ST6 . . . . .41 A6
Edge View Cl Kinver DY7 . . .277 F5
  Stoke-on-T ST4 . . . . .43 C2
Edge View Ct ST7 . . . . . . .27 C7
Edgeview Rd CW12 . . . . . . .16 B7
Edge View Rd ST7 . . . . . . .43 C2
Edge View Wlk DY7 . . . . . .277 F5
Edgeware St ST1 . . . . .282 A4
Edgeworth Ho WS13 . . . . .214 A2
Edgmond Rd TF10 . . . . . . .168 E4
Edinburgh Cres ST5 . . . . . .275 C1
Edinburgh Rd WS11 . . . . . .210 A2
Edinburgh Way DE12 . . . . . .56 A2
Edington Way DE15 . . . . . .166 D8
Edison Cl WS12 . . . . .210 C7
Edison St ST4 . . . . .155 F5
Edison St ST4 . . . . .72 D6
Edmonton Cl WS11 . . . . . .210 B2
Edmonton Gr ST2 . . . . . . .42 F1
Edmonton Pl DE15 . . . . . . .167 D2
Edmund Ave ST17 . . . . . . .174 B8
Edmund Rd DY3 . . . . .271 D8
Ednam Gr WV5 . . . . .265 A1

Ednam Pl ST3 . . . . .74 A1
Ednam Rd WV4 . . . . .266 C5
Edwal Rd ST3 . . . . .74 A4
Edward Ave Aldridge WS9 . .256 A4
  Newcastle-u-L ST5 . . . . . .71 B6
  Stoke-on-T ST4 . . . . .88 B7
Edward Ct B77 . . . . .250 F6
Edward Davies Rd ST6 . . . .42 C2
Edward Rd WS6 . . . . .254 C5
Edwards Farm Rd WS13 . . .215 E8
Edwards Rd
  Burntwood WS7 . . . . . . .228 F5
  Sutton Coldfield B75 . . . .258 D3
Edward St 6 Stone ST15 . . .105 A1
  Audley ST7 . . . . .39 F3
  Burton u T DE14 . . . . . . .166 C1
  Cannock WS11 . . . . .209 E4
  Stoke-on-T ST4 . . . . .72 E7
  Tamworth B77 . . . . .250 A5
  Wolverhampton WV4 . . . .266 F5
Edwin Cl Penkridge ST19 . . .207 F8
  Stafford ST17 . . . . .155 B1
Efflinch La DE13 . . . . .201 E7
Egborough Cl WV11 . . . . . .254 E5
Egerton Cl WV6 . . . . .91 A6
Egerton Rd Aldridge B74 . . .256 F1
  Stoke-on-T ST4 . . . . .71 E8
  Wolverhampton WV10 . . .240 E3
Egerton St ST1 . . . . .57 D1
Eggington Dr ST10 . . . . . . .207 F7
Eggington Rd Hilton DE65 . .147 F8
  Stourbridge DY8 . . . . . . .279 C5
Eggington Prim Sch DE65 . .148 B5
Egginton Rd DE65 . . . . . . .148 B8
Egg La ST18 . . . . .158 E7
Eighth Ave DE14 . . . . .184 F8
Eights Croft WS7 . . . . .228 D8
Elaine Ave ST6 . . . . .42 B1
Elan Cl Cookley DY10 . . . . .280 B4
  Dudley DY3 . . . . .271 D3
Elan Rd DY3 . . . . .271 C8
Elburton Rd ST14 . . . . .95 D8
Elderberry Cl DY8 . . . . . . .279 C3
Elder Cl Cannock WS11 . . . .210 C2
  Uttoxeter ST14 . . . . .126 B6
Elder La WS7 . . . . .229 C7
Elder Pl ST6 . . . . .57 B6
Elder Rd ST6 . . . . .57 B6
Elderside Cl WS8 . . . . .244 F8
Eldertree La TF9 . . . . .100 C6
Eldon St Burton u T DE15 . . .167 B3
  Hanley ST1 . . . . .57 D6
Elding Cl WV9 . . . . .239 F2
Eleanor Cres ST5 . . . . .71 A6
Eleanor Harrison Dr
  DY10 . . . . .280 B5
Eleanor Pl ST5 . . . . .71 A6
Eleanor View ST5 . . . . .71 B6
Electric Ind Est DE14 . . . . .166 E5
Electric St ST14 . . . . .166 B8
Elenora St ST4 . . . . .72 B7
Elers Gr ST6 . . . . .56 F7
Elford Cl Armitage WS15 . . .198 B4
  Tamworth B79 . . . . .250 A4
Elford Heath ST21 . . . . . . .133 C6
Elgar Cl Cannock WS11 . . . .209 E5
  Lichfield WS13 . . . . .214 B2
Elgar Cres ST1 . . . . .58 B3
Elgin Cl ST6 . . . . .266 E1
Elgin Ct WV6 . . . . .254 E4
Elgin Rd WS3 . . . . .243 A4
Elgin St ST1 . . . . .57 B1
Elgood La ST6 . . . . .41 C7
Elias Cl WS14 . . . . .231 E6
Eliases La 17 B2
Eliot Cl Armitage WS15 . . . .198 B4
  Tamworth B79 . . . . .250 A6
Eliot Way ST17 . . . . .155 C1
Elisabeth Ct ST4 . . . . .258 B3
Elizabethan Way WS15 . . . .196 F7
Elizabeth Ave
  Rolleston on D DE13 . . . . .147 B3
  Wolverhampton WV4 . . . .266 B5
Elizabeth Bache Cnr
  DY10 . . . . .280 A5
Elizabeth Ct
  Burton u T DE13 . . . . . . .167 C3
  Market Drayton TF9 . . . . .112 C8
  Stoke-on-T ST4 . . . . .71 F8
  Talke Pits ST7 . . . . .40 D5
Elizabeth Dr
  Newcastle-u-L ST5 . . . . . .55 E7
  Stoke-on-T ST4 . . . . .71 F8
Elizabeth St WS11 . . . . . . .209 E6
Elizabeth St ST1 . . . . .57 E4
Elkington Ctr ST14 . . . . . . .110 F2
Elkington St ST6 . . . . .41 E4
Elkington Rise CW3 . . . . . .68 F7
Elkstone Cl ST6 . . . . .41 E4
Ellam's Pl ST5 . . . . .55 E1
Ellastone Gr ST1 . . . . .71 F6
Ellastone Rd ST10 . . . . . . .63 C5
Elldawn Ave ST6 . . . . .42 F2
Ellerbeck B77 . . . . .251 B1
Ellerby Gr ST6 . . . . .42 F6
Ellesmere Ct TF10 . . . . . . .168 E2
Ellesmere Rd ST17 . . . . . . .155 F7
Ellesmere Gr 3 TF9 . . . . . .112 A8
Ellgreave St ST6 . . . . .56 E8
Ellington Ave ST16 . . . . . . .156 F6
Ellington Cl ST4 . . . . .58 A2
Elliot Cl 1 WV4 . . . . .266 A4
Elliot Cl WS11 . . . . .209 F5
Elliot Rd ST4 . . . . .72 F6
Elliott Ave ST3 . . . . .73 F2

Elliotts La WV8 . . . . .239 A3
Elliott St ST5 . . . . .56 D1
Ellison Prim Sch ST5 . . . . .56 D5
Ellison St ST5 . . . . .56 D5
Ellis St ST6 . . . . .57 C7
Ellis Wlk WS11 . . . . .226 F8
Ellowes Hall Sch The
  DY3 . . . . .271 C5
Elm Ave Aldridge WS9 . . . . .256 C8
  Stoke-on-T ST4 . . . . .88 B7
Elsmore Mdw WS13 . . . . . .231 A6
Elm Ave ST17 . . . . .175 F6
Elmbridge Way DY3 . . . . . .271 E6
Elmbrook Cl ST3 . . . . .89 E8
Elm Cl Burton u T DE14 . . . .184 F8
  Cookley DY10 . . . . .280 B4
  Doveridge DE6 . . . . .127 C8
  Dudley DY3 . . . . .271 B2
  Great Haywood ST18 . . . .158 B2
  Kidsgrove ST7 . . . . .41 B8
  Leek ST13 . . . . .30 C5
  Newport TF10 . . . . .168 F1
  Stourbridge DY8 . . . . . . .279 D2
Elm Cres ST18 . . . . .158 C8
Elmcroft Gdns WV10 . . . . .240 E3
Elmcroft Rd ST2 . . . . .58 B6
Elm Ct ST18 . . . . .174 C5
Elmdale Dr WV9 . . . . .256 C8
Elm Dale Rd WV4 . . . . . . .266 A5
Elmdon Cl
  Penkridge ST19 . . . . .208 A8
  Wolverhampton WV10 . . .240 A1
Elmdon Pl ST3 . . . . .90 B7
Elmdon Rd WV10 . . . . . . .240 A1
Elm Dr Blakedown DY10 . . .281 B2
  Bradley ST18 . . . . .191 C8
  Cheadle ST10 . . . . .76 C3
  Market Drayton TF9 . . . . .112 A8
Elm Farm Rd WV2 . . . . . . .266 D7
Elm Gdns WS14 . . . . .231 C7
Elm Gr Codsall WV8 . . . . . .239 A3
  Huntington WS12 . . . . . . .209 D8
  Kinver DY7 . . . . .278 C5
Elmhurst Cl Berry Hill ST2 . .57 F2
  Coven WV9 . . . . .224 B3
  Stoke-on-T ST4 . . . . .155 C8
Elmhurst Dr
  Burntwood WS7 . . . . . . .229 A4
  Kingswinford DY6 . . . . . .275 F4
Elmhurst Eggington DE65 . .148 A5
  Newcastle-u-L ST5 . . . . . .70 F4
Elmley Gr WV6 . . . . .254 F3
Elmore Cl 4 WS5 . . . . .196 E8
Elmore Green Prim Sch
  WS3 . . . . .243 B1
Elmore Green Rd WS3 . . . .243 B1
Elmore Ho WS15 . . . . .178 A1
Elmore La WS15 . . . . .178 A1
Elmore Row WS3 . . . . . . .243 B1
Elm Pl Cookley DY10 . . . . .280 B4
  Stoke-on-T ST3 . . . . .72 F1
Elm Rd Kingswinford DY6 . .275 E6
  Norton Canes WS11 . . . . .120 B8
  Stoke ST15 . . . . .119 B8
Elms Cl WV10 . . . . .225 C1
Elmsdale WV6 . . . . .255 A4
Elms La WS11 . . . . .209 C1
Elms La WV10 . . . . .225 C1
Elmsmere Ave ST5 . . . . . . .73 A1
Elmsmere Rd ST2 . . . . .58 B6
Elms Paddock The WV6 . . . .253 C2
Elm St ST5 . . . . .166 F2
Elm St ST4 . . . . .71 F1
Elms The ST5 . . . . .56 C7
Elm St ST5 . . . . .56 D3
Elmstone Cl
  3 Stafford ST17 . . . . . . .175 D5
  Dudley DY3 . . . . .271 F4
Elms Way ST3 . . . . .74 A2
Elm Tree Cl WV5 . . . . .269 F5
Elm Tree Dr ST7 . . . . .39 F1
Elmtree Rd B74 . . . . .256 D1
Elm Tree Wlk B79 . . . . . . .249 F8
Elm View ST14 . . . . .95 E6
Elm Wlk ST19 . . . . .207 F8
Elmwood Ave WV11 . . . . . .242 A3
Elmwood Cl
  Blythe Bridge ST11 . . . . . .91 A6
  Cannock WS11 . . . . .210 A3
  Gnosall ST20 . . . . .171 D7
  Lawton-gate ST7 . . . . . . .21 A6
Elmwood Gr ST1 . . . . .91 A6
Elmwood Gr ST14 . . . . . . .110 F1
Elmwood Rd DY8 . . . . . . .275 C2
Elmwood Rise DY3 . . . . . .266 B1
Elphinstone Rd ST4 . . . . . .71 F3
Elsby Pl ST6 . . . . .42 A6
Elsdon Rd ST18 . . . . .174 C6
Elton Terr ST6 . . . . .57 A3
Elton Way ST20 . . . . .171 D7
Elston Hall Prim Sch
  WV10 . . . . .240 D2
Elstree Cl ST3 . . . . .73 F2
Elstree Gr ST1 . . . . .58 A6
Elswick Rd ST4 . . . . .72 E8
Eltham Gdns ST5 . . . . .56 C5
Elton Cl Newborough DE13 . .162 F8
  Wolverhampton WV10 . . .240 D4
Elton La DE13 . . . . .162 F8
Elton Terr ST6 . . . . .57 A3
Elton Way ST20 . . . . .171 D7
Elunda Gr WS7 . . . . .228 E5
Elviron Dr WV6 . . . . .255 B5
Elwell Cres DY1 . . . . .271 C6
Elworthy Cl ST16 . . . . .156 A5
Elwyn Cl DE13 . . . . .147 D1
Ely Cl WS11 . . . . .210 B1
Ely Wlk ST3 . . . . .284 C4

Emanuals La SK17 23 B2
Embers Way ST9 44 A8
Emberton St
Newcastle-u-L,Chesterton ST5 55 E6
Newcastle-u-L,Wolstanton ST5 56 C5
Emberton Way B77 250 F5
Embleton Wlk 1 ST6 56 E7
Embry Ave ST16 156 A5
Emerald Way ST15 120 B4
Emerson Cl DY3 271 A4
Emerson Rd Burslem ST6 57 A6
Wolverhampton WV10 240 F1
Emery Ave
Newcastle-u-L ST5 71 A7
Stoke-on-T ST1 57 E8
Emery St ST6 57 B6
Emmanuel Rd WS7 229 B7
Empire Ind Est WS9 244 F1
Empire Pas ST4 72 A6
Empire Rd DE15 167 D3
Empire St ST4 72 A6
Emsworth Cres WV9 240 A2
Emsworth Rd ST3 88 E8
Encounter Pl ST1 57 E5
Enderby Dr WV4 266 A5
Enderby Rise DE13 166 B7
Enderley Cl WS3 243 B3
Enderley Dr WS3 243 B3
Enderley St ST5 283 B4
End Hall Rd WV6 255 A3
Endon Dr ST8 27 B5
Endon Hall Prim Sch ST9 43 F8
Endon High Sch ST9 43 E6
Endon Rd ST6 42 F5
End The DE15 167 E8
Endwood Dr B74 257 C4
Engine La Tamworth B77 251 A2
Walsall WS8 244 C8
Englesea Ave ST3 74 A5
Englesea Brook La CW2 38 A3
Englesea Brook Mus of Primitive Methodism* CW2 38 A3
Engleton La ST19 223 D7
Engleton Mill La ST19 223 E8
English Martyrs RC Prim Sch ST8 27 D7
Ennerdale Cl
1 Burslem ST6 56 E8
Brownhills WS8 244 E7
Ennerdale Dr WV6 254 F4
Ennerdale Rd WV6 255 D8
Enoch St ST6 56 F7
Ensall Dr DY8 275 E1
Ensford Cl B74 257 E5
Enson La Marston ST18 137 B7
Stone ST15 120 D1
Ensor Dr B78 251 F1
Enstone Cl ST3 88 F8
Enstone Ct ST5 71 B3
Enterprise Dr WV10 224 E5
Enterprise Gr WS3 244 B5
Enterprise Ind Pk WS13 231 F8
Enville Cl WS3 243 A3
Enville Common Rd
Enville DY7 273 F5
Kinver DY7 274 A5
Enville Pl DY8 279 E5
Enville Rd Dudley DY3 271 D4
Kingswinford DY6 275 B8
Kinver DY7 278 A5
Wolverhampton WV4 265 C4
Enville St DY8 279 F5
Ephraim St ST1 282 C1
Epping Rd ST4 71 E3
Epsley's Yd ST16 285 B2
Epsom Cl Burton u T DE14 184 F7
Cheadle ST10 76 E5
Lichfield WS14 231 D7
Perton WV6 254 F4
Tamworth B77 261 C4
Epsom Dr 8 ST17 175 C7
Epworth Ho DE15 167 D3
Epworth St ST4 72 A7
Erasmus Way WS13 231 A8
Erdington Rd WS9 256 C3
Eremon Cl WS15 196 F6
Eringden B77 251 B1
Ermington Rd WV4 266 D4
Ernald Gdns 5 ST15 120 A7
Ernest Edgerton Cl ST6 41 C5
Eros Cres ST1 57 E6
Errill Cl ST4 72 D6
Erskine St ST3 284 C1
Eskdale Pl
Newcastle-u-L ST5 71 B5
Stoke-on-T ST4 88 A7
Eskrett St WS12 210 C5
Esk Way ST5 71 B4
Esperanto Way ST6 57 C8
Esselie Ave TF9 100 C5
Essex Ave DY6 275 B5
Essex Dr Biddulph ST8 16 D2
Cannock WS12 210 B4
Castle Gresley DE11 186 E1
Great Haywood ST18 158 B3
Kidsgrove ST7 25 F2
Rugeley WS15 196 D6
Stone ST15 119 F5
Essex Gdns DY8 279 D7
Essex Pl ST5 71 A6
Essex Rd Burton u T DE15 185 D6
Sutton Coldfield B75 258 D2
Essington Cl
Alrewas DE13 201 A3
Lichfield WS14 231 A5
Essington Cl continued
Shenstone WS14 247 A7
Stourbridge DY8 275 E1
Essington Ind Est WV11 241 F4
Essington Rd WV12 242 B1
Estridge La WS6 227 A2
Etchell Rd B78 249 F3
Etching Hill CE Prim Sch WS15 178 C2
Etching Hill Rd WS15 178 A2
Ethelfleda Rd B77 261 F5
Ethelred Cl B74 258 A3
Eton Ave ST5 70 F4
Eton Cl Burton u T DE14 166 E6
Dudley DY3 271 F6
Stafford ST17 156 B1
Eton Ct Lichfield WS14 231 B6
Sutton Coldfield B74 257 F2
Eton Park Jun Sch DE14 166 D7
Eton Pk DE14 166 E6
Eton Rd DE14 166 D6
Etruria Industrial Mus* ST4 57 A2
Etruria Locks ST1 57 A2
Etruria Old Rd ST1 56 F3
Etruria Rd
Hanley,Etruria ST5 56 F3
Hanley ST1 282 A3
Etruria Vale Rd ST1 57 A3
Etruria Way ST5 56 E2
Etruscan Prim Sch ST1 57 A3
Etruscan St ST1 56 F2
Etruscan Wlk ST12 88 F4
Ettingshall Park Farm La WV4 266 E4
Ettymore Cl DY3 271 D8
Ettymore Rd DY3 271 D8
Ettymore Rd W DY3 271 C8
Etwall Rd DE65 148 B7
Europa Way WS13 231 F8
Eva Gr ST5 87 D8
Evans Croft B78 250 A1
Evans St Burslem ST6 41 F1
Wolverhampton,Cinder Hill WV4, WV14 266 F1
Eve La DY1 271 F5
Evelyn St ST4 72 E5
Everest Rd ST7 26 C3
Everglade Rd CV9 262 C1
Evergreen Hts WS12 210 A8
Evergreens The DE13 166 F8
Evershed Way DE14 166 C2
Eversley Ave ST13 30 E5
Eversley Gr DY3 266 C2
Eversley Rd ST3 73 E2
Evesham Cres WS3 242 F3
Evesham Way ST3 73 E3
Eveson Rd DY8 279 E2
Ewe Dale La DE6 35 A3
Exbury Cl WV9 239 F2
Excelsior Gr WS3 244 B5
Exchange Ho ST16 285 B3
Exchange Ind Est The WS11 226 E5
Exchange Rd DE13 201 A3
Exchange The WS3 243 B1
Exeter Dr B79 249 E5
Exeter Gn ST2 58 C2
Exeter Rd WS11 226 B8
Exeter St ST17 174 F8
Exley B77 250 D1
Exmouth Gr ST6 57 A7
Exonbury Wlk 5 WS11 209 F2
Eyam Cl DE15 167 B2
Eynsham Ct WV6 255 E5
Eyre St ST6 56 E7
Eyrie The DE15 167 C3

F

Faber RC Prim Sch The ST10 78 C8
Faceby Gr ST3 90 C7
Fairbank Ave ST4 71 F5
Fairbanks Wlk ST15 103 B4
Fairburn Cres WS3 244 B5
Fairclough Pl ST6 42 A3
Fairfax Rd WV10 240 E3
Fairfax St ST1 57 D6
Fairfield Ave
Brown Edge ST6 43 B7
Newcastle-u-L ST5 56 C4
Rolleston on D DE13 147 D4
Stoke-on-T ST3 89 C8
Fairfield Cl WS12 210 D1
Fairfield Cres DE11 186 E5
Fairfield Ct ST16 155 F6
Fairfield Dr Codsall WV8 238 E4
Kinver DY7 278 A3
Penkridge ST19 207 F6
Walsall WS3 244 B4
Fairfield Rd
Stourbridge DY8 275 F2
Uttoxeter ST14 126 B8
Fairfield Rise DY8 279 D5
Fairfields ST7 39 F2
Fairfields Hill B78 262 F8
Fairfields Rd ST8 17 B1
Fairford Gdns
Burntwood WS7 229 C6
Stourbridge DY8 275 E3
Fairgreen Rd ST5 85 D5
Fairgreen Way B74 257 A1
Fairham Rd DE13 147 F1
Fairhaven CW2 37 B1
Fairhaven Gr ST1 57 E6
Fairhaven Prim Sch DY8 275 D3
Fairhills DY3 271 D8
Fair Lady Dr WS7 228 D8
Fair Lawn WV7 237 A5
Fairlawn Cl Stoke-on-T ST3 89 E8
Willenhall WV12 242 C1
Fairlawn Ct WV7 237 B5
Fairlawn Dr DY6 275 D4
Fairlawns ST5 283 B4
Fairlawn Way WV12 242 C1
Fairlight Gr ST3 90 A7
Fair Mdws WS15 179 A7
Fairmead Cl ST17 175 C6
Fairmeadows Prim Sch DE11 186 E5
Fairmount Dr 5 WS11 226 E8
Fairmount Way WS15 178 C1
Fairoak Ave ST16 155 C8
Fairoak Bank ST21 115 D6
Fairoak Dr WV6 255 B3
Fairoak ST5 70 F4
Fair Oak TF10 168 F4
Fair Oak Rd ST5 40 D1
Fair Oaks Bsn & Ent Coll WS15 196 D8
Fair Oaks Dr WS6 243 A8
Fair Oaks WS15 196 B6
Fair View WS15 198 C4
Fairview Ave CW2 37 B5
Fairview Cl
Cheslyn Hay WS6 226 D2
Tamworth B77 250 F5
Fairview Cres DY6 275 F6
Fair View Rd ST13 31 A4
Fairview Rd WV4 265 C4
Fairview Villas ST5 85 C5
Fairview Way ST17 156 C1
Fairway Burton u T DE14 185 B6
Cannock WS11 226 D6
Fairway Ct B77 251 B3
Fairway Rd ST6 42 A3
Fairways Ave DY8 279 E2
Fairways Cl DY8 279 E2
Fairway ST16,ST17 156 A2
Fairways The DE6 81 F6
Fairway B77 261 F5
Fairway The
3 Rugeley WS15 196 E8
Swadlincote DE11 186 E5
Fairway Trentham ST4 87 E8
Walsall WS4 244 D1
Falcon Bsns Ctr DE14 166 E5
Falcon Cl Burton u T DE14 166 E5
Cannock WS11 209 C2
Cheslyn Hay WS6 226 C2
Falcon Cres WV14 266 F2
Falcondale Rd WV12 242 C1
Falcon Dr WS14 232 E5
Falcon Pk B77 261 E7
Falcon Rd ST3 90 A6
Falcon Rise DY8 279 C6
Falconry Ctr The* DY9 281 F3
Falcon B77 262 A6
Falcon Way DY1 271 F1
Faldo Cl DE14 185 B6
Falkirk Grange ST5 70 F7
Falklands Cl DY3 269 E2
Fallow Deer Lawn TF10 168 F5
Fallow Field WS11 209 E3
Fallowfield Cl
Penkridge ST19 207 E8
Stone ST15 120 C6
Fallowfield Dr DE13 183 C2
Fallow Field
Lichfield WS13 214 C3
Little Aston B74 257 B3
Fallowfield Perton WV6 254 D4
Stafford ST17 175 C6
Stoke-on-T ST3 88 F8
Wolverhampton WV8 239 E2
Fallow Rd B78 249 F1
Falmouth Ave ST17 175 E8
Falmouth Cl ST17 175 E8
Falmouth Ct ST5 71 C5
Falmouth Dr B77 250 F5
Falmouth Rd CW12 15 E8
Falna Cres B79 249 F7
Fancourt Ave WV4 265 D4
Fancy Wlk ST16 155 D5
Fane Rd WV11 242 B2
Fanlizard La ST20 171 D3
Faraday Ave DE13 166 D8
Faraday Ct DE14 184 E7
Faraday Pl ST4 71 E7
Faraday Rd ST16 155 F5
Farcroft Ave ST5 55 F6
Farcroft Dr TF9 97 A1
Fareham Cres WV4 265 C6
Fareham Gr ST3 89 E7
Farewell La WS7 229 E6
Far Green Ind Est ST1 57 D6
Farifields Rd TF9 97 D2
Faringdon B77 250 F1
Farington Pl ST6 42 A6
Farland Gr ST6 42 A6
Far Lane Ind Est ST10 62 A7
Farleigh Dr WV3 265 A8
Farleigh Gr ST2 58 C1
Farleigh Rd WV6 255 A3
Farley La ST10 78 D3
Farley Rd ST10 78 B5
Farmadine ST4 88 B7
Farman Cl ST3 90 C7
Farmbrook Ave WV10 240 D3
Farm Cl Burton u T DE13 166 B7
Cannock WS12 210 C3
Codsall WV8 239 B2
Market Drayton TF9 97 A1
Rugeley WS15 178 C2
Farm Cl continued
Sedgley DY3 271 B7
Tamworth B79 250 C7
Farm Ct DE13 166 C7
Farmdown Rd ST17 156 C1
Farmers Bank ST5 55 C1
Farmer St ST3 284 C2
Farmfields Rise CW3 67 C1
Farm Gr TF10 168 D3
Farm Hollow ST7 40 A2
Farm House La 6 B75 258 E3
Farm La DE15 167 E7
Farm Lea
Hilderstone ST15 106 D2
Stoke-on-T ST6 42 E6
Farmoor Way WV10 240 E4
Farm Rd
Burnhill Green WV6 252 D7
Burton u T DE13 166 C7
Wolverhampton WV3 265 C8
Farmside Gn WV9 239 F2
Farmside La ST8 17 B1
Farm Side DE11 186 F5
Farm View ST15 106 D2
Farm Wood Cl ST3 74 B1
Farnborough Ct B75 258 C2
Farnborough Dr ST3 90 C7
Farncote Dr B74 257 F3
Farndale Ave WV6 255 F5
Farndale St 9 ST6 41 D3
Farne Gr ST3 73 A3
Farnham Dr ST8 27 B5
Farnworth Cl ST8 27 B6
Farnworth Rd ST3 73 E3
Far Ridding ST20 171 C5
Farrier Cl ST15 120 D7
Farriers Gn TF10 169 B3
Farriers Mill WS3 243 E4
Farrier Way DY6 275 A7
Farrington Cl ST6 42 E3
Farrington Rd WV4 266 E3
Farthings The WS14 246 F5
Far View WS9 245 B2
Farwall La ST10 49 E2
Farway Gdns WV8 238 F2
Fasson Cl B77 261 C8
Fauld Ind Pk DE13 145 E6
Fauld La Tutbury DE13 146 A6
Tutbury,Fauld DE13 145 D7
Faulkner Cl DY8 279 F4
Faulkner Pl ST3 73 F4
Faversham Cl WV8 255 E8
Faversham Rd DE13 166 A6
Fawcett Way ST1 282 C4
Fawfield Dr ST6 41 C6
Fawn Cl Huntington WS12 209 C6
Meir ST3 90 A8
Fazeley Rd Tamworth B78 250 A4
Tamworth,Fazeley B78 250 B2
Fearns Ave ST5 41 B1
Fearon Gn ST6 42 E3
Featherbed La
Hixon ST18 158 C8
Lichfield WS13 213 E3
Featherstone Gr ST4 72 A7
Featherstone La
Featherstone WV10 241 B8
Shareshill WV10 225 B1
Featherston Rd B74 257 A2
Fecknam Way WS13 214 C1
Federation Rd ST6 41 F1
Fegg Hayes Rd ST6 42 A6
Feiashill Cl WV5 269 B7
Feiashill Rd WV5 269 B7
Felcourt Gdns ST1 57 E5
Felden Cl ST16 136 D1
Fellbrook Ct ST2 58 A4
Fellbrook La ST2 58 A4
Fellfield Way ST16 155 D8
Fellmeadow Way DY3 271 E7
Fellows Ave DY6 275 C8
Fellows St WV2 266 C8
Fell St ST6 42 C1
Felspar Rd B77 251 B3
Felstead Cl B77 261 C4
Felsted St ST2 43 B3
Felthouse La ST13 45 B2
Femwork Ind Est DE14 166 E5
Fence La CW12 15 D4
Fenlow Ave ST2 57 F2
Fenmere Cl WV4 266 D5
Fennel Cl
Cheslyn Hay WS6 226 D3
Uttoxeter ST14 126 B6
Fennel Dr ST17 174 F5
Fennel Gr ST3 90 B6
Fenners Gr ST4 88 D8
Fenn Rise DY8 275 D3
Fenn St B77 250 E1
Fenpark Ind Est ST4 73 A5
Fenpark Rd ST4 73 A6
Fenton Cl CW12 6 A1
Fenton Croft ST19 205 C6
Fenton Ho ST5 283 B3
Fenton House La ST19 205 B6
Fenton Ind Est ST4 72 E8
Fenton Pk ST4 73 A6
Fenton Rd Berry Hill ST2 57 F2
Bucknall ST2 58 A3
Fereday Rd WS9 245 B3
Fereday's Croft DY3 271 D7
Ferguson St WV11 242 A1
Fermain Cl ST5 70 F3
Fern Cl Mow Cop ST7 26 C6
Walsall WS4 244 D1
Ferncombe Dr WS15 178 C2
Fern Cres CW12 6 A3
Ferncroft Cl ST4 88 B7
Fern Croft WS13 213 F1
Ferndale Cl
Blythe Bridge ST11 90 F6
Burntwood WS7 229 B6
Werrington ST9 59 A4
Weston CW2 37 B5
Ferndale Gdns ST7 26 E3
Ferndale Rd
Essington WV11 242 B3
Lichfield WS13 213 F1
Fern Dell Cl WS11 209 C2
Fern Dene CW3 68 D7
Ferndown Ave DY3 271 C7
Ferndown Cl Longton ST3 73 D1
Walsall WS3 243 B4
Ferndown Dr ST5 71 C2
Ferndown Dr S ST5 71 C1
Ferndown Way CW2 52 C8
Fern Dr Great Wyrley WS6 227 A4
Stafford ST16 155 A5
Ferney Pl ST6 41 C6
Fernhill Rd TF10 150 C1
Fernhurst Cl ST15 120 C7
Fernhurst Gr ST3 89 E8
Fernie Cl ST15 120 C6
Fernlea Cres ST9 43 F8
Fernlea Gr Meir Heath ST3 90 A4
Meir ST3 74 B5
Fernleigh Ave WS7 229 A8
Fernleigh Gdns
Stafford ST16 155 A5
Stourbridge DY8 275 C3
Fern Leys WV3 255 D1
Fern Pl ST3 284 C2
Fern Rd Huntington WS12 209 D5
Wolverhampton WV3 266 A7
Fernwood Croft ST13 30 C4
Fernwood Ctr The WS15 178 D2
Fernwood Dr Leek ST13 30 C4
Rugeley WS15 178 D2
Fernwood Gn ST4 88 C7
Fernwood ST16 155 D7
Ferrand Cl ST4 72 A2
Ferrers Ave DE13 146 B5
Ferrers Cl B75 258 D2
Ferrers Rd Tamworth B77 250 D4
Weston ST18 138 D2
Yoxall DE13 182 A2
Ferrie Gr WS8 244 E8
Ferry Farm Dr 11 ST17 175 A8
Ferry St DE15 185 E8
Ferry Vale Cl DE15 185 E8
Festing St ST1 282 C4
Festival Cl ST6 57 A5
Festival Ct Cannock WS11 209 E5
Lichfield WS13 231 A7
Festival Heights Ret Pk ST1 57 A5
Festival Mews WS12 209 F6
Festival Rd DE14 184 E7
Festival Way ST1 56 F5
Fiddlers Bank ST6 43 B8
Fiddler's La DE13 146 F4
Field Ave Hatton DE65 146 C8
Stoke-on-T ST2 43 B2
Field Cl Blythe Bridge ST11 90 E6
Burton u T DE13 166 A7
Walsall WS4 244 B2
Whitmore ST5 85 C5
Field Cotts ST18 175 A1
Field Cres ST18 154 D2
Field Ct WS4 244 B2
Field Dr DE13 147 B4
Fielden Cl ST6 42 F2
Field End Cl ST4 88 B7
Fieldfare WS7 229 D5
Field Farm Dr B79 217 C5
Field Farm Rd B77 250 D1
Field Head Pl WV6 255 B4
Field House Ct ST15 104 F2
Fieldhouse Rd
Burntwood WS7 229 A7
Cannock WS12 209 F7
Wolverhampton WV4 266 E4
Fielding St ST4 72 B5
Field La Burton u T DE13 166 A7
Church Leigh ST10 109 B1
Great Wyrley WS6 226 F3
Stanton DE6 80 C8
Walsall WS4 244 B2
Field Pl Longton ST3 73 C5
Rugeley WS15 196 B7
Stafford ST16 155 E6
Field Rd Lichfield WS13 214 B3
Walsall WS3 243 C1
Field Rise DE13 166 B7
Field Rise Rd ST12 103 E8
Fieldside Stafford ST17 175 D5
Yarnfield ST15 118 E6
Fields Rd CW12 15 F8
Field St WS11 209 F3
Fields The WV8 239 B4
Field St ST13 30 E5
Fieldstone View DY3 271 D4
Fieldsway ST15 119 E8
Field Terr ST15 105 A1
Field View Biddulph ST8 16 D1
Meir ST3 74 B4
Fieldway
Blythe Bridge ST11 90 D7
Stoke-on-T ST3 72 E3
Field Way DE11 186 F5
Fieldway Trentham ST4 87 E7
Werrington ST2 58 F3
Field Wlk WS9 256 B7

Fife St ST4 . . . . 284 A4
Fifth Ave ST7 . . . . 25 E1
Filance Cl ST19 . . . . 207 F7
Filance La ST19 . . . . 207 F8
Filey Cl Bucknall ST2 . . . . . . 58 D2
  Cannock WS11 . . . . 226 C8
Filey Rd WV10 . . . . 240 A8
Filey B7 . . . . 250 F6
Fillybrooks Cl ST15 . . . . 119 F8
Fillybrooks The ST15 . . . . . . 119 F8
Filton Ave WS7 . . . . 229 A8
Fincham Cl WV9 . . . . 240 A3
Finchdean Cl ST3 . . . . 90 A7
Finchdene Gr WV3 . . . . 255 D1
Finches Hill WS15 . . . . 178 C2
Finchfield Cl DY8 . . . . 279 C4
Finchfield Gdns WV3 . . . . . . 255 E1
Finchfield Hill WV3 . . . . 255 C1
Finchfield La WV3 . . . . 265 C8
Finchfield Rd WV3 . . . . 255 E1
Finchfield Rd W WV3 . . . . . . 255 D1
Finchley Cl DY3 . . . . 271 D2
Finch Pl ST8 . . . . 27 B2
Finchsmith Pl ST3 . . . . 284 B8
Finch St ST8 . . . . 27 B1
Finch Way WS13 . . . . 215 E8
Fine La WS13 . . . . 215 E6
Finger Post Dr WS3 . . . . 244 A5
Finney Gn ST2 . . . . 58 A3
Finstock Ave ST3 . . . . 88 E8
Firbank Pl ST3 . . . . 73 F4
Firbank Way WS3 . . . . 243 F2
Firbeck Gdns ST17 . . . . 175 C7
Firbeck La ST10 . . . . 93 F3
Fir Cl WS12 . . . . 209 D8
Fircroft █ WV4 . . . . 266 F4
Fircroft Cl █ WS11 . . . . 210 A3
Firecrest Cl WV12 . . . . 210 C2
Fir Gr DY8 . . . . 279 D6
Firmstone Ct DY8 . . . . 279 E7
Firmstone St DY8 . . . . 279 E7
Firs Cl The ST17 . . . . 175 D7
Firs Mobile Home Pk The █
  WS11 . . . . 210 A2
Firs Rd DY6 . . . . 275 E6
First Ave Brownhills WS8 . . . 245 A8
  Bucknall ST2 . . . . 58 D3
  Burton u T DE14 . . . . 184 E8
  Kidsgrove ST7 . . . . 25 F1
  Kingswinford DY6 . . . . 271 A1
  Newcastle-u-L ST5 . . . . 56 C7
  Stafford ST16 . . . . 155 C7
Firs The WS15 . . . . 211 F5
Fir St DY3 . . . . 270 F7
Firsway The ST19 . . . . 221 E8
Firsway WV3 . . . . 255 A2
Firtree Cl ST18 . . . . 174 C3
Fir Tree Cl B79 . . . . 249 E2
Fir Tree Cotts CW2 . . . . 38 C5
Fir Tree Dr DY3 . . . . 271 E7
Fir Tree Pl ST5 . . . . 55 E8
Fir Tree Rd Stoke-on-T ST3 . 89 E8
  Wolverhampton WV3 . . . . . 265 D8
Firwood Rd ST8 . . . . 16 F1
Fisher Rd WS3 . . . . 242 F2
Fishers Lock TF10 . . . . 168 F4
Fisher St Brindley Ford ST8 . 27 B2
  Cannock WS12 . . . . 209 F8
  Wolverhampton WV3 . . . . . 266 B8
Fisherwick Cl WS14 . . . . 232 F5
Fisherwick Rd WS14 . . . . . . 232 F5
Fishley Cl WS3 . . . . 243 C4
Fishley La WS3 . . . . 243 D5
Fishpond La
  Egginton DE65 . . . . 148 A5
  Tutbury DE65 . . . . 146 C6
Fishpond Way ST2 . . . . 58 A7
Fistral Cl ST3 . . . . 73 D4
Fistral Gdns WV3 . . . . 265 F7
Fitchet's Bank WS7 . . . . 229 F6
Fithern Cl DY3 . . . . 271 E5
Fitzgerald Cl ST13 . . . . 74 B4
Fitzherbert Cl ST15 . . . . 103 B4
Fitzherbert Rd ST11 . . . . 57 E8
Five Lands Rd DE15 . . . . 185 F8
Five Lanes End ST20 . . . . . . 153 D7
Five Oaks Cl ST5 . . . . 70 E3
Fives Gr WS7 . . . . 228 C8
Five Ways Dudley DY3 . . . . . 271 D3
  Iverley DY10 . . . . 281 A5
Five Ways Prim Sch
  WS12 . . . . 210 D2
Five Ways WV3 . . . . 265 C2
Flackets La DE6 . . . . 128 B7
Flackett St ST13 . . . . 284 C5
Flamborough Gr ST6 . . . . . . 56 E7
Flanders Dr DY6 . . . . 275 D8
Flashbrook Cross Roads
  TF10 . . . . 149 D5
Flash CE Prim Sch SK17 . . . 3 B3
Flashes The ST20 . . . . 171 E7
Flash La Blore TF9 . . . . 98 F1
  Orton WV4 . . . . 264 E2
  Stoke-on-T,Baddeley Edge
  ST2 . . . . 43 C2
Flash Ley Prim Sch ST17 . . . 71 E3
Flash The CW12 . . . . 15 E6
Flather La DE6 . . . . 65 D1
Flats La WS14 . . . . 248 A6
Flatts Cl DE13 . . . . 166 B6
Flatts Rd WS13 . . . . 42 E5
Flavells La DY3 . . . . 271 B2
Flaxcroft Ct ST12 . . . . 88 C2
Flax Croft ST15 . . . . 120 B7

Flax Hill Jun Sch B79 . . . . . . 250 B7
Flaxley Rd WS15 . . . . 196 D6
Flaxman Cl ST12 . . . . 88 F4
Flax Ovens The ST19 . . . . . . 192 E2
Flax St ST4 . . . . 72 B6
Fleckney Ave ST3 . . . . 73 E3
Fleets La ST13 . . . . 49 B8
Fleet St ST4 . . . . 166 D1
Fleming Rd ST4 . . . . 72 B7
Flemmynge Cl WV8 . . . . 238 E4
Fletcher Bank ST5 . . . . 283 A3
Fletcher Cres ST2 . . . . 43 B2
Fletcher Dr WS13 . . . . 215 C6
Fletcher Rd Stoke-on-T ST4 . 72 A5
  Walsall WV12 . . . . 242 D1
Fletcher St ST1 . . . . 282 A1
Fletches The DE13 . . . . 147 B1
Fleur Gr ST4 . . . . 73 B6
Flinn Cl WS14 . . . . 231 D7
Flints Cnr WS12 . . . . 195 B4
Flintsham Gr ST1 . . . . 282 B4
Flint St ST8 . . . . 74 B5
Flora Cl B79 . . . . 250 C7
Florence Ave █ WV4 . . . . . . 266 F4
Florence Dr DE6 . . . . 127 C8
Florence Prim Sch ST3 . . . . 284 C2
Florence Rd Codsall WV8 . . . 239 C3
Florence St
  Cannock WS12 . . . . 210 B7
  Newcastle-u-L ST5 . . . . 283 B3
Florence Terr ST9 . . . . 29 A1
Florendine Com Prim Sch
  B77 . . . . 250 F5
Florendine St B77 . . . . 250 F5
Florida Cl ST6 . . . . 57 B8
Floyd St ST4 . . . . 72 B8
Flynn Row ST4 . . . . 72 F8
Foden Ave ST7 . . . . 25 A3
Foden Cl WS14 . . . . 246 F6
Foden St ST4 . . . . 72 A5
Fog Cotts Rugeley WS15 . . . 178 F3
  Wrinehill CW3 . . . . 52 E4
Fogg St E ST5 . . . . 283 B3
Fogg St W ST5 . . . . 283 B3
Fogg St ST5 . . . . 283 B3
Fold La ST8 . . . . 14 E8
Fold Terr ST13 . . . . 45 C5
Fold The Oaken WV8 . . . . . . 238 D2
  Oulton ST15 . . . . 105 C3
  Wolverhampton WV4 . . . . . 265 F4
Folebank Barns ST14 . . . . . . 109 F8
Fole La ST14 . . . . 109 F8
Foley Ave WV6 . . . . 255 C3
Foley Church Cl B74 . . . . 257 A2
Foley Cl ST4 . . . . 72 B6
Foley Dr WV6 . . . . 255 C3
Foley Gr WV5 . . . . 269 E5
Foley Inf Sch DY7 . . . . 278 A3
Foley Pl ST4 . . . . 284 A4
Foley Rd E B74 . . . . 257 A2
Foley Rd W B74 . . . . 256 E1
Foley St Dunsley DY7 . . . . . . 278 B4
  Longton ST4 . . . . 284 B5
Foley Wood Cl B74 . . . . 256 E1
Folly Fields ST13 . . . . 45 B2
Folly La ST9 . . . . 60 C7
Folly View TF9 . . . . 99 D5
Fontaine Pl ST4 . . . . 72 A5
Fontenaye Rd B79 . . . . 249 F7
Fonthill Wlk ST2 . . . . 58 A4
Fonthill Rd ST16 . . . . 155 F6
Fontwell Rd
  Burton u T DE14 . . . . 184 F7
  Wolverhampton WV10 . . . . 240 D4
Footherley La WS14 . . . . 246 C4
Footherley Rd WS14 . . . . 246 F5
Forber Rd ST4 . . . . 71 F4
Ford Ave ST6 . . . . 42 B5
Ford Brook La WS3 . . . . 244 B2
Ford Cl ST15 . . . . 120 A7
Ford Dr ST15 . . . . 118 E6
Ford Green Hall (Mus)★
  ST6 . . . . 42 D2
Ford Green Rd ST6 . . . . 42 D2
Fordham Gr WV9 . . . . 240 A3
Ford Hayes La
  Bucknall ST2 . . . . 73 D8
  Bucknall ST3 . . . . 58 F1
  Werrington ST3 . . . . 59 A1
Fordhouse Rd Ind Est
  WV10 . . . . 240 D1
Fordhouse Rd WV10 . . . . 240 D1
Ford La
  Creswell Green WS13 . . . . . 212 F2
  Longdon WS15 . . . . 198 A2
Ford Rd TF10 . . . . 168 E1
Fordrough The B74 . . . . 258 A1
Fords La ST7 . . . . 26 D6
Ford St Burton u T DE15 . . . . 185 E7
  Leek ST13 . . . . 30 E6
  Newcastle-u-L ST5 . . . . 55 B2
  Stoke-on-T ST4 . . . . 56 E1
Ford Way WS15 . . . . 198 B5
Foregate St ST16 . . . . 285 B4
Foregate St ST16 . . . . 285 A4
Forest Cl Colwich ST18 . . . . 177 D8
  Newcastle-u-L ST5 . . . . 70 E4
Forest Dr ST17 . . . . 282 B4
Forest Dr DY7 . . . . 278 C2
Forest Edge ST6 . . . . 57 C6
Forest Edge Way DE13 . . . . . 166 A8
Forest Glade WS6 . . . . 226 F2
Forest La DY7 . . . . 268 E2
Forest Lawns DE15 . . . . 184 C3
Forest Park Prim Sch
  ST1 . . . . 282 A4

Forest Rd Burton u T DE13 . 165 E4
  Draycott in t C DE6 . . . . 144 B4
  Dunstall DE13 . . . . 183 B5
  Market Drayton TF9 . . . . . . 112 A8
  Stoke-on-T ST3 . . . . 89 F7
Forest School St DE13 . . . . . 147 C4
Forestside Gr ST4 . . . . 72 A2
Forest Way WS6 . . . . 227 A1
Forge Cl
  Hammerwich WS7 . . . . 229 D5
  Wolverhampton WV8 . . . . . 239 E1
Forge La
  Aldridge,Leighswood
  WS9 . . . . 256 A5
  Aldridge,Mill Green WS9 . . . 256 F7
  Blakedown DY10 . . . . 281 B1
  Burntwood WS7 . . . . 229 F6
  Burton u T DE13 . . . . 148 A2
  Hanley ST1 . . . . 56 F4
  Kingswinford DY6 . . . . 275 A8
  Lichfield WS13 . . . . 214 A1
  Norton in H TF9 . . . . 82 C1
  Shenstone B74,WS14 . . . . 257 C7
  Stretton DE13 . . . . 147 F2
Forge Leys WV5 . . . . 269 E6
Forge Mews WV5 . . . . 178 F1
Forge Rd Rugeley WS15 . . . . 178 F1
  Stourbridge DY8 . . . . 279 A6
  Walsall WS3 . . . . 243 F5
Forge Rise ST18 . . . . 191 C8
Forge Row WS15 . . . . 196 B6
Forge Side ST9 . . . . 44 A8
Forge St ST12 . . . . 210 C4
Forge Valley Way WV5 . . . . . 269 E6
Forge Way ST8 . . . . 27 B4
Formby Ave WV6 . . . . 254 D4
Formby Way WS3 . . . . 243 A3
Forrest Ave
  Cannock WS11 . . . . 226 E8
  Essington WV11 . . . . 242 A4
Forrest Ct █ WS13 . . . . 231 B7
Forrester Cl
  █ Biddulph ST8 . . . . 27 C8
  Fradley WS13 . . . . 215 D6
Forrester Rd ST15 . . . . 120 B7
Forresters Bank ST2,ST9 . . . 43 C3
Forrister St ST3 . . . . 73 D4
Fox Hollow
  Ecclehall ST21 . . . . 133 F6
  Loggerheads TF9 . . . . 99 D5
  Wolverhampton WV6 . . . . . 255 C2
Forsbrook CE Prim Sch
  ST11 . . . . 91 A7
Forster St ST4 . . . . 41 D3
Forsyte Rd ST3 . . . . 73 C6
Forsyth Cl ST4 . . . . 71 E8
Forsythia Gr WV8 . . . . 239 A3
Fort Cres WS9 . . . . 245 A3
Fortescue La WS15 . . . . 178 E2
Fortis B77 . . . . 250 C3
Forton Cl WV6 . . . . 255 B2
Forton Glade TF10 . . . . 168 F5
Forton Rd TF10 . . . . 168 F5
Forty Acre Cl TF9 . . . . 99 E5
Forum Rd ST5 . . . . 55 D5
Forum The █ ST5 . . . . 209 E1
Fosbrooke Pl ST4 . . . . 71 D8
Fossdale Rd B77 . . . . 262 A8
Fosseway La WS13,WS14 . . . 230 E4
Fosseway WS14 . . . . 231 A5
Foster Ave WS12 . . . . 209 F6
Foster Cres DY7 . . . . 278 A4
Foster Ct ST5 . . . . 72 F3
Foster Gn WV6 . . . . 254 E3
Foster Pl DY8 . . . . 279 E6
Foster St DY7 . . . . 278 A4
Foston Ave DE13 . . . . 166 C8
Foston Cl DE65 . . . . 146 C8
Fotherley Brook Rd WS9 . . . 256 F5
Foundry La Bucknall ST2 . . . 58 A3
  Scholar Green ST7 . . . . 25 F7
  Walsall WS3 . . . . 243 E3
Foundry Rd DY6 . . . . 275 C8
Foundry Sq ST5 . . . . 43 A5
Foundry St Hanley ST1 . . . . . 282 B3
  Kingswinford DY6 . . . . 275 C8
Fountain Cl
  █ Burslem ST6 . . . . 56 F8
  Biddulph ST8 . . . . 16 D1
Fountain Fold ST20 . . . . 171 D5
Fountain Pl █ ST6 . . . . 56 F8
Fountain Rd DE6 . . . . 144 D6
Fountains Ave ST5 . . . . 71 B5
Fountain Sq ST1 . . . . 282 B3
Fountains Rd WS3 . . . . 242 E2
Fountain St ST16 . . . . 30 F6
  Stoke-on-T ST4 . . . . 72 E6
Fountains Way WS3 . . . . 242 F2
Four Ashes Ind Est
  WV10 . . . . 224 D6
Four Ashes Rd ST19 . . . . 223 E7
Four Crosses La WS11 . . . . . 225 E7
Four Crosses Rd WS4 . . . . . . 244 C1
Fourlane Ends ST20,ST21 . . . 131 E8
Four Lane Ends
  Ecclechall ST21 . . . . 134 A5
  Milwich ST18 . . . . 122 B8
Four Lanes End
  Gorstyhill CW2 . . . . 37 F2
  Haughton ST18 . . . . 173 A5
  Seighford ST18 . . . . 153 E8
  Uttoxeter ST14 . . . . 126 D4
Four Oaks Common Rd
  B74 . . . . 257 F3
Four Oaks Dr B74 . . . . 258 B1
Four Oaks Inf Sch B74 . . . . . 257 E4
Four Oaks Jun Sch B74 . . . . 257 E4
Four Oaks Rd B74 . . . . 258 A1
Fourth Ave
  Brownhills WS8 . . . . 229 A1
  Bucknall ST2 . . . . 58 E4

Fourth Ave continued
  Kidsgrove ST7 . . . . 25 F1
Fourways CW2 . . . . 37 B5
Fowlchurch Rd ST13 . . . . 30 F7
Fowler Cl WV6 . . . . 254 E6
Fowler's La ST7 . . . . 43 D1
Fowler St WV2 . . . . 266 C6
Fox Cl Burton u T DE14 . . . . . 185 B8
  Seisdon WV5 . . . . 263 F2
  Tamworth B77 . . . . 261 C8
Foxcote Cl ST17 . . . . 175 E5
Fox Covert DY8 . . . . 279 E5
Foxcroft Cl WS7 . . . . 229 B5
Fox Ct DE13 . . . . 199 C6
Foxes La ST19 . . . . 222 C6
Foxes Rake WS11 . . . . 209 E3
Foxfield Cl ST10 . . . . 76 E6
Foxfield Steam Railway★
  ST10,ST11 . . . . 75 B5
Foxfield Steam Rly★
  ST11 . . . . 90 E8
Foxfields Way WS12 . . . . 209 C7
Foxfield Way ST3 . . . . 88 F8
Fox Gdns ST7 . . . . 40 D8
Foxglove Ave
  Burton u T DE15 . . . . 186 A8
  Uttoxeter ST14 . . . . 126 B6
Foxglove Cl
  Featherstone WV10 . . . . . . 241 B7
  Lichfield WS14 . . . . 231 A5
  Meir ST3 . . . . 74 B5
  Rugeley WS15 . . . . 178 C1
  Walsall WS3 . . . . 244 A5
Foxglove La ST5 . . . . 71 C2
Foxglove Rd DY1 . . . . 271 F4
Foxgloves Ave ST18 . . . . 177 E7
Foxglove B77 . . . . 251 A4
Foxglove Wlk WS12 . . . . 210 C7
Fox Gr ST5 . . . . 71 C2
Foxhill Cl WS12 . . . . 210 D2
Fox Hill Rd B75 . . . . 258 F2
Foxhill's Cl WS7 . . . . 229 A5
Foxhills Rd
  Stourbridge DY8 . . . . 275 D1
  Wolverhampton WV4 . . . . . 265 C4
Fox La
  Alrewas DE13 . . . . 200 F2
  Lichfield WS13 . . . . 214 A5
Foxland Ave WS6 . . . . 227 A3
Foxlands Ave WV4 . . . . 265 D3
Foxlands Cl WV4 . . . . 265 C3
Foxlands Dr Dudley DY3 . . . . 271 D5
  Wolverhampton WV4 . . . . . 265 D3
Fox Leigh Mdws WS15 . . . . . 198 B4
Foxley La ST4 . . . . 43 A1
Foxmeadow Cl DY3 . . . . 271 E7
Fox Rd WV5,WV6 . . . . 263 E3
Foxtail Way ST12 . . . . 210 E4
Foxton Cl DE13 . . . . 201 A2
Foxton Man B74 . . . . 258 A1
Fox Wlk WS9 . . . . 245 B3
Foxwood Cl ST15 . . . . 119 E6
Foxwood Rd B78 . . . . 262 F8
Fradgley Ct ST14 . . . . 125 C7
Fradgley Gr ST14 . . . . 110 F2
Fradley La WS13 . . . . 215 E7
Fradswell La ST18 . . . . 123 A2
Framlingham Gr WV6 . . . . . . 255 A3
Frampton Gr ST6 . . . . 41 E6
Frances Dr WS3 . . . . 243 B2
Francis Cl
  █ Kingswinford DY6 . . . . . 275 D8
  Penkridge ST19 . . . . 208 A8
Francis Green La ST19 . . . . . 207 F8
Francis Rd Lichfield WS13 . . . 214 A2
  Stourbridge DY8 . . . . 279 C5
Francis St ST6 . . . . 41 F5
Frank Foley Way ST16 . . . . . 285 A4
Frank Gee Ct ST15 . . . . 178 D1
Franklin Cl DE15 . . . . 167 A8
Franklin Dr WS7 . . . . 229 B7
Franklin Rd ST4 . . . . 71 F7
Franklyn Cl WV6 . . . . 254 E5
Franklyn St ST1 . . . . 282 C1
Frank Rogers Wlk WS15 . . . 178 D2
Frank St ST4 . . . . 72 A6
Frayne Ave DY6 . . . . 275 C7
Frazer Ho █ ST3 . . . . 89 F8
Freckleton Pl ST3 . . . . 90 C7
Fred Brewer Way DE13 . . . . . 165 E4
Frederick Ave ST4 . . . . 72 A7
Frederick Ct B77 . . . . 250 E3
Frederick Rd ST19 . . . . 192 F1
Fredericks Cl DY8 . . . . 279 E4
Frederick St
  Burton u T DE15 . . . . 185 E8
  Stoke-on-T ST4 . . . . 72 E6
  Wolverhampton WV2 . . . . . 266 C8
Freebridge Cl ST3 . . . . 73 E4
Freedom Dr ST7 . . . . 26 E3
Freedom Wlk ST6 . . . . 42 C3
Freeford Gdns WS14 . . . . 231 E6
Freehold St ST5 . . . . 283 C2
Freeland Gr █ DY6 . . . . 275 F4
Freemen St ST16 . . . . 155 E5
Freer Dr WS7 . . . . 229 F2
Freeth Rd WS8 . . . . 229 A1
Free Trade St ST5 . . . . 282 C4
Fremantle Dr WS12 . . . . 210 F2
Fremantle Rd ST4 . . . . 71 F4
Fremont Dr DY1 . . . . 271 E3
French Ave B78 . . . . 249 C1

Frenchmore Gr ST3 . . . . 73 C1
Frensham Cl WS6 . . . . 226 E4
Freshwater Dr
  Chorlton CW2 . . . . 37 B1
  Weston CW2 . . . . 52 C8
Freshwater Gr ST2 . . . . 57 F3
Freville Cl B79 . . . . 250 A5
Frew Cl ST16 . . . . 156 A4
Friar's Alley WS13 . . . . 231 B7
Friars Ave ST5 . . . . 120 A7
Friars Cl Cheadle ST10 . . . . . 76 D4
  Stourbridge DY8 . . . . 279 E5
Friar's Ct ST5 . . . . 283 B2
Friars Gorse DY7 . . . . 279 C8
Friar's La TF11 . . . . 220 D4
Friars Pl ST2 . . . . 58 B7
Friars Rd ST2 . . . . 58 B7
Friars' Rd ST17 . . . . 285 B2
Friar's St ST5 . . . . 283 B2
Friars' Terr ST17 . . . . 285 B2
Friar St Longton ST3 . . . . 284 C4
  Stafford ST16 . . . . 155 D5
Friars' Wlk
  Newcastle-u-L ST5 . . . . 71 B6
  Stafford ST17 . . . . 285 B2
Friars Wlk B77 . . . . 250 C3
Friarswood Prim Sch
  ST5 . . . . 283 B1
Friarswood Rd ST5 . . . . 283 B2
Friary Ave
  Abbots Bromley WS15 . . . . 160 F5
  Lichfield WS13 . . . . 231 A6
Friary Dr B74 . . . . 257 F3
Friary Gdns WS13 . . . . 231 A7
Friary Grange Sports Ctr
  WS13 . . . . 213 F2
Friary Ho WS13 . . . . 213 F1
Friary Rd ST3 . . . . 231 A7
Friary Sch The WS13 . . . . 213 F2
Friary The WS13 . . . . 231 A7
Friday Acre WS13 . . . . 214 A2
Friendly Ave ST5 . . . . 56 B8
Friesian Gdns ST5 . . . . 40 C2
Friezland La WS8 . . . . 245 A5
Friezland Way WS8 . . . . 245 A5
Frinton Cl ST16 . . . . 155 F6
Frith St ST13 . . . . 30 D6
Frobisher Cl WS6 . . . . 226 F1
Frobisher Dr ST16 . . . . 103 B4
Frobisher St ST6 . . . . 43 A5
Frodingham Rd ST2 . . . . 58 E1
Froghall
  Froghall ST10 . . . . 283 B3
Froghall Rd Cheadle ST10 . . . 76 E6
  Ipstones ST10 . . . . 62 A6
Froghall Wharf★ ST10 . . . . . 62 B4
Frog La Lichfield WS13 . . . . . 231 B7
  Market Drayton TF9 . . . . . . 97 C1
  Wheaton Aston ST19 . . . . . 205 C6
Frogmore Ct TF9 . . . . 97 C1
Frogmore Pl TF9 . . . . 97 C1
Frogmore Rd TF9 . . . . 97 C1
Frome Cl DY3 . . . . 271 D2
Frome Wlk ST6 . . . . 42 A4
Froyle Cl WV6 . . . . 255 C5
Fuchsia Dr WV9 . . . . 239 F3
Fulford Prim Sch WS7 . . . . . . 229 D7
Fulford Prim Sch ST11 . . . . . 106 E8
Fulford Rd ST11 . . . . 106 E8
Fullbrook Ave DE13 . . . . 201 E8
Fullelove Rd WS8 . . . . 245 A4
Fuller St ST6 . . . . 41 E4
Fullerton Cl WV8 . . . . 239 E1
Fullmore Cl ST19 . . . . 207 F7
Fullwood Wlk ST5 . . . . 58 C1
Fulmar Pl ST3 . . . . 90 B7
Furber Pl DY6 . . . . 275 F6
Furlong Ave ST10 . . . . 92 F3
Furlong Cl Alrewas DE13 . . . 201 A2
  Upper Tean ST10 . . . . 92 E3
  Weston ST18 . . . . 138 C2
Furlong Dr ST10 . . . . 92 E3
Furlong Ind Est ST6 . . . . 56 E7
Furlong La Alrewas DE13 . . . 201 A2
  Bradley ST18 . . . . 173 C2
  Burslem ST6 . . . . 56 E7
  Hope DE6 . . . . 35 C4
Furlong Par █ ST6 . . . . 56 F8
Furlong Pas █ ST6 . . . . 56 F8
Furlong Rd ST6 . . . . 41 E4
Furlongs Rd DY3 . . . . 271 D6
Furlong The ST15 . . . . 118 F6
Furlong Wlk DY3 . . . . 271 D4
Furmston Pl ST13 . . . . 31 A7
Furnace Cl WV5 . . . . 269 E5
Furnace La CW3 . . . . 68 E7
Furnace Rd ST3 . . . . 73 D2
Furness Cl WS3 . . . . 242 F3
Furness Gr ST17 . . . . 174 B7
Furness B77 . . . . 250 D3
Furnivall Cres WS13 . . . . 214 D1
Furnival St ST6 . . . . 57 B6
Furrows Dr DE13 . . . . 166 A8
Furst St WS8 . . . . 245 A8
Fyfield Rd DE15 . . . . 185 E6
Fynney Fields ST13 . . . . 45 F8
Fynney St ST13 . . . . 30 F5

G

Gable Cotts ST11 . . . . 74 E2
Gable Croft WS14 . . . . 231 F6
Gables The
  Kingswinford DY6 . . . . 275 B8
  Swadlincote DE11 . . . . 186 E5
Gable St ST14 . . . . 72 B6
Gaelic Rd WS11 . . . . 209 D4
Gagarin B79 . . . . 249 F5

Gag La DE6 . . . . .51 D6
Gaiafields Rd WS13 . . . . .214 B1
Gaia La WS13 . . . . .231 B8
Gaialands Cres WS13 . . . . .214 B1
Gaia Stowe WS13 . . . . .214 B1
Gail Cl WS9 . . . . .245 B4
Gailey Lea La ST19 . . . . .208 B2
Gail Pk WV3 . . . . .265 D7
Gainford Cl WV8 . . . . .239 F1
Gainsborough Dr
  Mile Oak B78 . . . . .260 B8
  Perton WV6 . . . . .255 A4
Gainsborough Pl DY8 . . . . .271 E2
Gainsborough Rd
  Newcastle-u-L ST5 . . . . .55 C6
  Stoke-on-T ST3 . . . . .88 E8
Gainsborough Way DE15 .167 B3
Gainsbrook Cres WS11 . . . . . . .227 F5
Gains La WS3,WS11 . . . . .227 D2
Gairloch Rd WV11 . . . . .242 B1
Galahad Dr DE13 . . . . .147 E2
Galena Cl B77 . . . . .251 B2
Galleys Bank ST7 . . . . .26 B3
Galliers Cl B77 . . . . .261 F5
Gallimore Cl ST6 . . . . .41 E1
Gallimore Ho ST7 . . . . .40 D8
Galloway Rd ST2 . . . . .73 E8
Gallows Hill DY7 . . . . .277 F6
Gallowstree La
  Mayfield DE6 . . . . .81 C8
  Newcastle-u-L ST5 . . . . .70 E7
Galsworthy Rd ST3 . . . . .73 B6
Galveston Gr ST4 . . . . .72 F5
Galway Rd WS7 . . . . .229 A7
Gamesfield Gn WV3 . . . . .255 F1
Ganton Rd WS3 . . . . .243 A3
Ganton Wlk WS3 . . . . .255 F8
Gaol Butts ST21 . . . . .133 D6
Gaolgate St ST16 . . . . .285 B3
Gaol Mews ST16 . . . . .285 B4
Gaol Rd ST16 . . . . .285 B4
Gaol Sq ST16 . . . . .285 B4
Garage Cl B77 . . . . .250 D5
Garbett St ST6 . . . . .41 D7
Garden Cotts ST3 . . . . .171 C5
Garden Cres WS3 . . . . .243 F3
Garden Croft WS9 . . . . .256 B7
Garden Dr WS15 . . . . .197 A7
Gardeners Cl ST8 . . . . .27 B5
Gardeners Way WV5 . . . . .269 F5
Gardenholm Cl ST3 . . . . .89 F8
Garden La ST19 . . . . .206 D4
Garden Pl Stafford ST17 . . . . . .285 C2
  Stoke-on-T ST4 . . . . .71 E8
Gardens The Elford B79 . . . . .216 D2
  Lawton-gate ST7 . . . . .25 C4
Garden St Leek ST13 . . . . .16 D6
  Newcastle-u-L ST5 . . . . .283 C2
  Stafford ST17 . . . . .285 C2
  Stoke-on-T ST4 . . . . .71 F6
Garden View WS15 . . . . .178 D1
Garden Village ST10 . . . . .92 D4
Garden Wlk DY3 . . . . .271 C2
Gardiner Dr ST3 . . . . .284 A2
Gardner Pl ST14 . . . . .111 A1
Garfield Ave ST4 . . . . .71 F1
Garfield Cres ST4 . . . . .71 F1
Garfield Ct ST4 . . . . .71 F1
Garfield St ST1 . . . . .282 A1
Garibaldi St ST1 . . . . .56 F3
Garlick St ST6 . . . . .42 B1
Garner St ST4 . . . . .56 E3
Garners Wlk CW3 . . . . .68 E7
Garnet St ST1 . . . . .57 A3
Garnett Rd E ST5 . . . . .56 B5
Garnett Rd W ST5 . . . . .56 B6
Garret Cl DY6 . . . . .275 D8
Garrett Sq ST6 . . . . .147 C4
Garrick Cl Dudley DY1 . . . . . . .271 F3
  Lichfield WS13 . . . . .213 F2
Garrick Ct WS13 . . . . .213 F2
Garrick Rd Cannock WS11 209 D4
  Lichfield WS13 . . . . .213 F2
Garrick Rise
  Burntwood WS7 . . . . .229 B7
  Rugeley WS15 . . . . .197 B6
Garridge Cl WV7 . . . . .237 A4
Garrigill B77 . . . . .251 B1
Garrod Sq ST16 . . . . .156 B5
Garsdale Cres ST3 . . . . .88 F8
Gartan Rd DE14 . . . . .185 A8
Garth Cl ST17 . . . . .174 E5
Garth Rd ST17 . . . . .174 F5
Garth St ST1 . . . . .282 C3
Garth The WS13 . . . . .214 B2
Gaskell Rd ST7 . . . . .58 D3
Gas St ST14 . . . . .111 C1
Gas Works Ind Est ST7 . . . . .25 D2
Gatacre St DY3 . . . . .271 D3
Gatcombe Cl
  Stretton DE13 . . . . .147 D1
  Wolverhampton WV10 . . . .240 F4
Gatcombe Rd DY1 . . . . .271 E2
Gatehouse Trad Est WS8 .229 B1
Gate St Meir ST3 . . . . .74 F6
  Sedgley DY3 . . . . .271 E7
Gateway Ave ST5 . . . . .85 C5
Gateway ST5 . . . . .40 D2
Gatherwynd La TF11 . . . . .203 E6
Gatley Gr ST3 . . . . .90 B6
Gauledge La SK17 . . . . .13 B6
Gaunt St 8 ST13 . . . . .30 D6
Gawain Gr DE13 . . . . .147 E2
Gawbutts The ST10 . . . . .76 C2
Gawsworth Cl ST13 . . . . .73 C6

Gawsworth B79 . . . . .249 D7
Gaydon Cl WV6 . . . . .254 E5
Gaydon Rd WS9 . . . . .256 A4
Gay La ST20 . . . . .204 F8
Gayle B77 . . . . .251 A1
Gaymore Rd DY10 . . . . .280 B5
Gayton Ave ST2 . . . . .43 B2
Geary La DE15 . . . . .167 F7
Geddes Pl ST1 . . . . .71 B2
Geen St ST4 . . . . .72 B7
Gemini Dr WS11 . . . . .226 F6
Gemini Gr ST6 . . . . .41 F6
Geneshall Cl ST20 . . . . .171 D7
Geneva Dr
  Birches Head ST1 . . . . .57 F6
  Newcastle-u-L ST5 . . . . .70 E6
Genge Ave WV4 . . . . .266 E4
Genista Cl ST6 . . . . .186 A8
Genthorn Cl 11 WV4 . . . . .266 F4
Gentian B74 . . . . .257 F4
Gentleshaw Prim Sch
  WS15 . . . . .212 A5
Gentleshaw Wildlife Ctr*
  ST21 . . . . .134 A7
Geoffrey Ave ST13 . . . . .30 D5
Geoffrey Gr ST3 . . . . .74 A4
George Ave Meir ST3 . . . . .74 B1
  Mile Oak B78 . . . . .249 C1
George Baily Ct ST17 . . .285 C1
George Brealey Cl WS15 .196 F7
George Eardley Cl ST6 . . . .41 C5
George Eastham Ave ST4 .72 D3
George Elliott Cl ST14 . . .126 C6
George Hill Ct 3 ST6 . . .155 D5
George La Lichfield WS13 .231 C8
  Stone ST15 . . . . .120 D7
George St Audley ST7 . . . . . .39 D1
  Burton u T DE14 . . . . .166 D3
  Cannock WS12 . . . . .210 C4
  Newcastle-u-L,Chesterton
  ST5 . . . . .55 E7
  Newcastle-u-L,Porthill WS5 .56 D6
  Newcastle-u-L,Silverdale
  ST5 . . . . .55 B1
  Newcastle-u-L ST5 . . . . . . .283 D3
  Stafford ST16 . . . . .155 D5
  Stoke-on-T ST4 . . . . .72 E7
  Stourbridge DY8 . . . . .275 F1
  Tamworth B79 . . . . .250 B4
Georges Way ST17 . . . . .39 F2
George Walker Ct DE14 .166 C5
Georgian Pl WV11 . . . . .209 E2
Gerald Rd DY8 . . . . .279 E7
Gerards Way TF9 . . . . .100 C5
Gerard B79 . . . . .249 E7
Germander B74 . . . . .257 F5
Gerrard St ST4 . . . . .72 A8
Gettings Cl WS7 . . . . .229 F7
Gibbet La Kinver DY7 . . . . . . .278 F4
  Stourbridge DY7 . . . . .279 A4
Gibbins St ST1 . . . . .282 C4
Gibb La DE6 . . . . .128 E5
Gibbons Hill Rd DY3 . . . . .266 D2
Gibbons Rd
  Sutton Coldfield B75 . . . . . .258 B3
  Wolverhampton WV6 . . . . .255 F4
Gibraltar DY7 . . . . .278 C4
Gibson Cl ST16 . . . . .155 F5
Gibson Gr ST5 . . . . .55 D8
Gibson Pl ST3 . . . . .74 A2
Gibson Rd WV6 . . . . .254 E3
Gibson St ST6 . . . . .41 E2
Giddywell La WS15 . . . . .197 F1
Gideons Cl DY3 . . . . .271 D5
Giffard Cl ST19 . . . . .223 D6
Giffard RC Prim Sch The
  WV6 . . . . .255 F5
Giffard Rd WV10 . . . . .240 F3
Giffards Croft WS13 . . . . .214 A1
Giggetty La WV5 . . . . .269 F6
Gig Mill Prim Sch DY8 . .279 E4
Gigmill Way DY8 . . . . .279 D7
Gilbanks Rd DY8 . . . . .279 D7
Gilbert St ST6 . . . . .27 B5
Gilbert Cl 2 Kidsgrove ST7 26 A2
  Newport TF10 . . . . .168 D2
Gilbert La WV5 . . . . .270 B7
Gilbert Rd WS13 . . . . .231 C8
Gilbert St ST6 . . . . .41 C7
Gilbert Wlk WS13 . . . . .214 C2
Gilbeys Cl 5 ST8 . . . . .275 E1
Gilchrist Cl ST6 . . . . .57 B6
Giles Cl ST10 . . . . .76 D3
Giles Ho ST13 . . . . .45 C8
Giles Rd WS13 . . . . .214 A3
Giles Wlk ST1 . . . . .57 E5
Gill Bank Rd Kidsgrove ST7 41 B8
  Stoke-on-T ST6 . . . . .41 B7
Gillespie Cl WS13 . . . . .215 D6
Gillette Cl ST14 . . . . .156 C5
Gilliard's Croft DE13 . . . . .199 C6
Gilliat Wlk ST2 . . . . .58 C1
Gillingham Cres ST16 . . . . . .155 B2
Gillway B79 . . . . .250 B8
Gill Wlk ST1 . . . . .282 A2
Gillyflower Cl ST16 . . . . .156 A5
Gilman Ave ST1 . . . . .43 B2
Gilman Pl ST1 . . . . .282 C3
Gilman St ST1 . . . . .282 C3
Gilmour La DE13 . . . . .183 E1
Gilpin Cres WS3 . . . . .244 A4
Gilpins Croft WS6 . . . . .226 D1
Gilwell Rd WS15 . . . . .211 F5
Gimson St ST4 . . . . .72 E6
Ginger Hill ST20 . . . . .171 D5
Ginger La ST21 . . . . .116 B3

Gipsy La Alstonefield DE6 . . . .35 F4
  Cookley DY7,DY11 . . . . . . .280 A8
Girsby Cl ST4 . . . . .88 C5
Girton Rd WS11 . . . . .226 F8
Gisborne Cl DE13 . . . . .182 A3
Gitana St ST1 . . . . .282 B3
Glades The WS9 . . . . .256 B7
Glade The Aldridge B74 . . . . .256 C5
  Cannock WS11 . . . . .209 C2
  Newcastle-u-L ST5 . . . . .71 B2
Stafford ST17 . . . . .175 B8
  Wolverhampton WV8 . . . . .239 E1
Gladman Bsns Quarter
  WV9 . . . . .239 F3
Gladstone Dr DY8 . . . . .279 D6
Gladstone Gr
  8 Kingswinford DY6 . . . . .275 D8
  Biddulph ST8 . . . . .27 D8
Gladstone Pl ST4 . . . . .71 F5
Gladstone Pottery Mus*
  ST3 . . . . .284 C3
Gladstone Prim Sch
  Longton ST3 . . . . .284 C3
  Longton ST3 . . . . .73 D5
Gladstone Rd
  Cannock WS12 . . . . .210 E1
  Stourbridge DY8 . . . . .279 D6
Gladstone St Leek ST13 . . . .30 C5
  Stoke-on-T ST4 . . . . .56 E1
Gladstone Terr ST10 . . . . .94 E8
Gladstone Way ST18 . . . . .156 C5
Gladwyn St ST1 . . . . .57 A3
Glaisher Dr ST3 . . . . .90 C7
Glamis Cl DE13 . . . . .166 D8
Glamis Dr ST15 . . . . .120 C5
Glamorgan Way DE11 . . . . . . .186 F1
Glandore Rd ST2 . . . . .73 F4
Glanville Dr B75 . . . . .258 A4
Glascote Ct ST7 . . . . .250 E4
Glascote Heath Prim Sch
  B77 . . . . .251 A2
Glascote La B77 . . . . .261 F8
Glascote Rd
  Tamworth B77 . . . . .251 B2
  Tamworth,Glascote Heath
  B77 . . . . .250 E3
Glasscroft Cotts WS7 . . . . . .229 F7
Glassford Dr WV6 . . . . .255 E6
Glasshouse Coll DY8 . . . . . . .279 F7
Glass La WS15 . . . . .161 E2
Glass St ST1 . . . . .282 B3
Glastonbury Cl
  Stafford ST17 . . . . .175 D6
  Stoke-on-T ST19 . . . . .43 D3
Glastonbury Cres WS3 . .242 E2
Glastonbury Way WS3 . . .242 E1
Glebe Ave ST5 . . . . .155 D6
Glebe Cl Blythe Bridge ST11 91 A6
  Cheswardine TF9 . . . . .130 A8
  Doveridge DE6 . . . . .127 B8
  Rolleston on D DE13 . . . . . .147 A4
Glebe Ct Cheadle ST10 . . . . . .76 C2
  Stone ST15 . . . . .72 C7
Glebedale Ct ST4 . . . . .72 E5
Glebedale Rd ST4 . . . . .72 E5
Glebefields ST20 . . . . .151 D7
Glebe Gdns ST10 . . . . .76 C2
Glebe La ST20 . . . . .171 E7
Glebelands
  Bobbington DY7 . . . . .267 F2
  Stafford ST17 . . . . .174 F6
Glebe La DY8 . . . . .279 E4
Glebe Prim Sch ST14 . . . . .72 F6
Glebe Rd Armitage WS15 .198 C5
  Cheadle ST10 . . . . .76 C2
  Kingsley ST10 . . . . .61 E2
Glebe St Kidsgrove ST7 . . . .25 D2
  Stoke-on-T ST4 . . . . .72 B7
Glebe The
  Albrighton WV7 . . . . .237 A5
  Norton Bridge ST15 . . . . . .135 A8
Glebeville ST13 . . . . .30 E4
Gledhill Pk WS14 . . . . .231 C5
Glencastle Way ST4 . . . . .88 C5
Glen Cl WS11 . . . . .209 E5
Glencoe Dr WS11 . . . . .210 A4
Glencoe St ST3 . . . . .284 B2
Glencroft Cl DE14 . . . . .185 B7
Glen Ct Codsall WV8 . . . . .239 A4
  Wolverhampton WV6 . . . . .255 C8
Glendale Cl WV3 . . . . .265 C8
Glendale Ct
  Newcastle-u-L ST5 . . . . .71 C2
  Tamworth B77 . . . . .262 B6
Glendale Dr WV5 . . . . .270 A6
Glendale Gdns WS11 . . . . . . .210 A4
Glendale St ST6 . . . . .57 A7
Glendawn Cl 3 WS11 . . .210 A3
Glendene Rd WS12 . . . . .210 D6
Glendon Cl 2 TF9 . . . . .112 A8
Glendower Cl ST20 . . . . .171 C6
Glendower Rd WS9 . . . . .245 B1
Glen Dr ST10 . . . . .94 E8
Glendue Gr ST4 . . . . .88 C6
Gleneagles Cres ST1 . . . . . . .57 E6
Gleneagles Dr
  Stafford ST16 . . . . .156 C3
  Stretton DE13 . . . . .147 C1
Gleneagles Rd
  Perton WV6 . . . . .254 D5
  Walsall WS3 . . . . .242 F3
Gleneagles B77 . . . . .251 B5
Glenfield Rise DE13 . . . . .166 B7
Glenfield Cl ST17 . . . . .250 C1
Glenfield Dr ST3 . . . . .89 E1
Glenfield WV8 . . . . .239 E2
Glengarry Gdns WV3 . . . . . . .255 F1
Glenhaven WS15 . . . . .178 C2

Glenmore Ave WS7 . . . . .229 A6
Glenmore Cl WV3 . . . . .265 E7
Glen Park Rd DY3 . . . . .271 D2
Glen Rd Dudley DY3 . . . . .271 E6
  Stourbridge DY8 . . . . .279 F3
Glen Rise DE13 . . . . .166 A7
Glenroyd Ave ST2 . . . . .58 A1
Glenroyd Wlk ST2 . . . . .58 C1
Glensyl Way DE14 . . . . .166 E4
Glen The 2 ST15 . . . . .120 A7
Glenthorne Cl ST17 . . . . .175 D5
Glenthorne Dr WS6 . . . . .226 D3
Glenthorne Ho WS6 . . . . .226 D2
Glenthorne Prim Sch
  WS6 . . . . .226 E3
Glenwood Cl CV9 . . . . .262 C1
Glenwood Cl Longton ST3 .284 B4
  Newcastle-u-L ST5 . . . . .55 C1
Glenwood Gdns B77 . . . . .262 B6
Glenwood Rise WV9 . . . . .245 D3
Globe Ave ST17 . . . . .174 F6
Globe St ST6 . . . . .56 E8
Gloucester Cl WS13 . . . . .214 B3
Gloucester Gr ST5 . . . . .71 C5
Gloucester Rd ST7 . . . . .26 A3
Gloucester Way
  Burton u T DE15 . . . . .167 B1
  Cannock WS11 . . . . .210 B1
Glovers Cl WS12 . . . . .211 A5
Glover St Cannock WS12. .210 F2
  Hanley ST1 . . . . .282 C4
  Stafford ST16 . . . . .285 A4
Glyme Dr WV6 . . . . .255 E5
Glyndebourne B79 . . . . .249 D7
Glyne Ave DY6 . . . . .275 D5
Glynne Prim Sch DY6 . . . . . .275 C4
Glyn Pl ST6 . . . . .41 F3
Gnosall Rd
  Gnosall,Knightley Dale
  ST20 . . . . .152 B3
  Gnosall TF10 . . . . .170 D2
Goddard St ST3 . . . . .284 D2
Godfrey Rd ST3 . . . . .58 B3
Godleybarn La ST10 . . . . .75 E6
Godley La ST10 . . . . .75 D5
Godolphin B79 . . . . .249 D7
Gofton B77 . . . . .262 A8
Golborn Ave WS3 . . . . .90 A4
Golborn Cl ST3 . . . . .90 B4
Goldcrest B77 . . . . .262 A6
Goldcrest Way ST4 . . . . .27 E8
Golden Cl WS15 . . . . .196 D7
Golden Hill CW2* 2 E7
Goldenhill Prim Sch ST6 .41 C7
Goldenhill Rd DE14 . . . . .284 B5
Goldenhill St Joseph's RC
  Prim Sch ST6 . . . . .41 D7
Goldfinch 5 ST7 . . . . .26 F1
Goldfinch View TF9 . . . . .99 C3
Goldhurst Dr ST10 . . . . .92 F2
Golding Cres DE14 . . . . .166 F6
Goldsborough B77 . . . . .251 A1
Goldsmith Pl
  Longton ST3 . . . . .284 D4
  Tamworth B79 . . . . .250 A7
Gold St ST3 . . . . .284 D4
Goldthorn Ave WV4 . . . . .266 B6
Goldthorn Cres WV4 . . . . .266 A6
Goldthorne Ave WS11 . . . . . .209 F2
Goldthorn Hill WV2,WV4. .266 C6
Goldthorn Park Prim Sch
  WV4 . . . . .266 D5
Goldthorn Rd WV2,WV3. .266 B6
Golf Links Cl ST6 . . . . .41 C7
Goms Mill La ST3 . . . . .284 B2
Goms Mill Rd ST3 . . . . .284 A2
Goodfellow St ST6 . . . . .41 D4
Goodill Cl ST15 . . . . .119 F5
Goodman St DE14 . . . . .166 D5
Goodrich Ave WV6 . . . . .255 A3
Goodson St ST1 . . . . .282 C3
Goods Station La ST19 . . . . .192 E2
Goodwick Cl ST4 . . . . .88 C5
Goodwin Ave ST5 . . . . .283 B4
Goodwin Rd ST3 . . . . .74 B2
Goodwood Ave ST10 . . . . .76 F3
Goodwood Cl
  Cannock WS12 . . . . .211 A5
  Lichfield WS14 . . . . .231 D7
  Stretton DE13 . . . . .147 C1
Goodwood Rd ST4 . . . . .88 B7
Goosefield Cl TF9* 97 B1
Goose La WS15 . . . . .160 F5
Goosemoor Gr 10 ST3 . . . . . .90 A7
Goose St ST5 . . . . .283 B2
Goostry Cl B77 . . . . .250 D5
Goostry Rd B77 . . . . .250 D5
Gordale Cl CW12 . . . . .6 A3
Gordon Ave Cheadle ST10 .76 B3
  Stafford ST15 . . . . .155 C7
  Stoke-on-T ST6 . . . . .57 C7
  Wolverhampton WV4 . . . . .266 F3
Gordon Banks Dr ST4 . . . . . .72 D3
Gordon Cl ST13 . . . . .30 C4
Gordon Cres ST1 . . . . .57 E7
Gordon Ct ST5 . . . . .56 D2
Gordon Rd ST6 . . . . .41 C6
Gordon St
  2 Wolverhampton WV2 . .266 D8
  Burton u T DE14 . . . . .166 B3
  Newcastle-u-L ST5 . . . . .55 E3
  Stoke-on-T ST6 . . . . .42 B1
Gorge Rd Sedgley DY3 . . . . . .271 E8
  Wolverhampton WV4,DY3 .266 F1
Gorsebrook Leys ST16 . . . . .155 A5
Gorseburn Way WS3 . . . . .178 C2
Gorse Cres TF9 . . . . .99 E5
Gorse Dr WS12 . . . . .209 D5

Gorse La Astbury CW12 . . . . .15 D5
Church Eaton ST19 . . . . .190 E2
Fradley WS13 . . . . .215 A7
Gnosall ST20,ST21 . . . . . . .152 A7
Rocester WS15 . . . . .231 E6
Rugeley WS15 . . . . .196 F6
Wombourne WV5 . . . . .269 B6
Gorsemoor Prim Sch
  WS12 . . . . .210 D1
Gorsemoor Rd WS12 . . . . . . .210 D1
Gorsemoor Way WV11 . .242 B3
Gorse Rd WS11 . . . . .196 F6
Gorse St ST4 . . . . .72 E5
Gorseway WS7 . . . . .229 B5
Gorse Way WS12 . . . . .210 C8
Gorsey Bank ST6 . . . . .42 E6
Gorsey La Cannock WS11 .209 C3
  Great Wyrley WS6 . . . . .226 F1
  Nethersoal DE12 . . . . .219 F8
  Norton Canes WS3 . . . . . . .227 E1
Gorsley Dale WS7 . . . . .175 C6
Gorsty Bank WS14 . . . . .231 E8
Gorsty Hayes WV8 . . . . .238 F3
Gorsty Hill Cl CW2 . . . . .37 F2
Gorsty Hill Rd ST10 . . . . .92 E5
Gorsty La ST18 . . . . .154 B3
Gorsy Bank Rd B77 . . . . .261 F5
Gorsy La
  Cotes Heath ST21 . . . . .102 A5
  Weston Jones TF10 . . . . . . .150 A3
Gort Rd ST5 . . . . .55 F4
Gosberryhole La CW12. . . . .7 A2
Goscote Ind Est WS3 . . . . . . .243 E1
Goscote La WS3 . . . . .243 F1
Goscote Rd WS3 . . . . .244 A1
Gosforth Gr ST3 . . . . .90 C7
Gospel Ash Rd DY7 . . . . .268 D2
Gospel End Rd DY3 . . . . .271 B8
Gospel End St DY3 . . . . .271 D8
Gothersley La DY7 . . . . .274 D2
Gough Cl ST16 . . . . .155 C8
Gough Side DE14 . . . . .166 D2
Gould Firm La ST9 . . . . .256 E6
Govan Rd ST4 . . . . .72 F8
Gowan Ave ST6 . . . . .42 A4
Gower Ave DY6 . . . . .275 F4
Gower St Sedgley DY3 . . . . . .271 B8
  Stone ST15 . . . . .120 B7
Gower St Longton ST3 . . . . . .284 C3
  Newcastle-u-L ST5 . . . . . . .283 C3
  Wolverhampton WV2 . . . . .266 E8
Gowland Dr WS11 . . . . .209 B1
Goya Cl WS11 . . . . .210 D2
Grace Moore Ct WS11 . .209 F4
Grace St ST13 . . . . .30 C6
Gradbach Mill* SK17 . . . . .2 A1
Grafton Ave ST6 . . . . .42 B1
Grafton Cl 4 WV6 . . . . .255 A3
Grafton Gdns DY3 . . . . .271 B3
Grafton Ho WV4 . . . . .266 E5
Grafton Inf Sch ST3 . . . . .284 C4
Grafton Rd
  Burton u T DE15 . . . . .167 B1
  Longton ST3 . . . . .284 C4
Graham Cl DE14 . . . . .185 C7
Graham Ho B74 . . . . .256 F2
Graham Rd DY6,DY8 . . . . .275 D4
Graham St ST2 . . . . .58 A3
Grainger Ct WS11 . . . . .209 D2
Graiseley Hill WV2 . . . . .266 C8
Graiseley Prim Sch WV2 266 C8
Graiseley Row WV2 . . . . .266 C8
Granary Cl Cannock WS12 .210 B5
  Kingswinford DY6 . . . . .275 A8
Granary Rd WV8 . . . . .239 E1
Granary The WS9 . . . . .256 B6
Granchester Cl ST13 . . . . .71 F6
Grange Ave Aldridge WS9 245 A1
  Burntwood WS7 . . . . .229 B7
  Penkridge ST19 . . . . .207 E7
  Sutton Coldfield B75 . . . . . .258 C3
Grange Cl
  Burton u T DE14 . . . . .166 B4
  Ellenhall ST21 . . . . .134 A1
  Gorstyhill CW2 . . . . .37 A4
  Tamworth B77 . . . . .261 C8
Grange Cotts ST19 . . . . .207 D7
Grange Court ST18 . . . . .158 C8
Grange Cres ST19 . . . . .207 E7
Grange Ct Biddulph ST8 . . . . .16 D2
  Burslem ST6 . . . . .57 A7
  Eggington DE65 . . . . .148 B5
  Newcastle-u-L ST5 . . . . .56 D5
Grange Dr WS11 . . . . .209 F2
Grangefield Cl
  Cheddleton ST13 . . . . .45 D4
  Wolverhampton WV8 . . . . .239 F1
Grangefields ST8 . . . . .16 E3
Grange Hill WS13 . . . . .30 D4
Grange Hill WS15 . . . . .197 C2
Grange Inf Sch ST4 . . . . .166 B4
Grange La
  4 Kingswinford DY6 . . . . .275 F4
  Lichfield WS13 . . . . .213 F2
  Newcastle-u-L ST5 . . . . .56 D4
  Sutton Coldfield B75 . . . . . .258 C3
Grange Park Dr ST8 . . . . .16 E3
Grange Prim Sch WV8 . .239 F1
Grange Rd Biddulph ST8. . . .16 E4
  Burntwood WS7 . . . . .229 A5
  Cheddleton ST13 . . . . .45 C4

Grange Rd *continued*
Meir ST3 . . . . 90 A6
Norton Canes WS11 . . . . 228 B6
Penkridge ST19 . . . . 207 E8
Stone ST15 . . . . 120 C7
Swadlincote DE11 . . . . 186 E5
Uttoxeter ST14 . . . . 111 A1
Wolverhampton,Blakenhall WV2 . . . . 266 B6
Wolverhampton,Tettenhall WV6 . . . . 255 C4
Woodseaves ST20 . . . . 151 F5
Grange St Burslem ST6 . . . . 57 B6
Burton u T DE14 . . . . 166 B3
Grange The
Burton u T DE14 . . . . 166 B3
King's Bromley DE13 . . . . 199 D6
Longdon WS15 . . . . 197 C2
Meir ST3 . . . . 74 A2
Stafford ST18 . . . . 174 C5
Wombourne WV5 . . . . 270 A7
Grangewood Ave ST3 . . . . 89 F6
Grangewood Rd ST3 . . . . 74 A1
Granstone Cl ST6 . . . . 42 A7
Grant Cl DY6 . . . . 275 D8
Grantham Pl ST2 . . . . 58 A6
Grantley Cl ST3 . . . . 73 A1
Grantley Cres DY6 . . . . 275 C7
Grantown Gr WS3 . . . . 243 A4
Grant St ST4 . . . . 72 C7
Grants Yd DE14 . . . . 166 C3
Granville Ave
Newcastle-u-L ST5 . . . . 283 C3
Newport TF10 . . . . 168 F2
Stoke-on-T ST1 . . . . 57 D7
Granville Cl
3 Wolverhampton WV2 . . . . 266 D8
Newport TF10 . . . . 168 F2
Granville Dr DY6 . . . . 275 F5
Granville Rd Bucknall ST2 . . . . 58 B5
Newport TF10 . . . . 168 F2
Granville Sq 3 ST15 . . . . 105 A1
Granville St WV2 . . . . 266 D8
Granville B77 . . . . 250 F1
Granville Terr ST15 . . . . 105 A1
Granville Villas TF10 . . . . 168 F2
Grasmere Ave
Aldridge B74 . . . . 257 A2
Newcastle-u-L ST5 . . . . 71 B4
Perton WV6 . . . . 254 F4
Grasmere Cl
Burton u T DE15 . . . . 167 B1
Kingswinford DY6 . . . . 275 B7
Wolverhampton,Tettenhall WV6 . . . . 255 E8
Grasmere Pl WS11 . . . . 209 E5
Grasmere Terr ST6 . . . . 42 A3
Grassholme B77 . . . . 262 A8
Grassmere Ct WS6 . . . . 226 D3
Grassmere Dr DY8 . . . . 279 F3
Grassmere Hollow ST16 . . . . 154 F5
Grassygreen La ST7 . . . . 39 E1
Grassy La WV10,WV11 . . . . 241 B1
Gratley Croft WS12 . . . . 209 C4
Gratton La ST9 . . . . 29 A3
Gratton Rd ST2 . . . . 58 D3
Gravel Hill WV5 . . . . 270 B6
Gravel La
Huntington WS12 . . . . 209 C5
Stafford ST17 . . . . 174 F4
Gravelly Bank ST3 . . . . 89 F7
Gravelly Dr TF10 . . . . 168 E2
Gravelly Hill TF9 . . . . 100 A5
Gravelly La WS9 . . . . 245 F3
Gravenhunger La CW3 . . . . 83 D8
Graycar Bsns Pk DE13 . . . . 184 B1
Grayling Gr ST6 . . . . 42 B3
Grayling B77 . . . . 261 D6
Grayling Willows CW3 . . . . 68 E6
Gray Rd WS12 . . . . 209 F6
Gray's Cl ST7 . . . . 26 B7
Grayshott Rd ST6 . . . . 41 E5
Grayston Ave B77 . . . . 250 E4
Gray Wlk ST17 . . . . 174 C7
Grazier Ave B77 . . . . 261 C8
Grazings The DY7 . . . . 278 C3
Greasley Rd ST2 . . . . 58 B6
Greatbatch Ave ST4 . . . . 71 F7
Great Charles St WS8 . . . . 244 F8
Great Checkhill Rd DY7 . . . . 274 C4
Great Fenton Bsns Pk ST4 . . . . 72 D4
Great Furlong DE13 . . . . 201 A2
Great Hales St TF9 . . . . 97 D1
Greatmead B77 . . . . 250 C1
Great Moor Rd
Nurton WV6 . . . . 254 A3
Pattingham WV6 . . . . 253 F2
Greatoak Rd ST7 . . . . 39 F4
Great Wood Com Prim Sch ST10 . . . . 92 E3
Great Wood Rd ST10 . . . . 92 E4
Great Wyrley High Sch WS6 . . . . 226 F3
Greaves La DE6,DE13 . . . . 144 E4
Greenacre Cl B77 . . . . 251 B5
Greenacre Dr WV8 . . . . 239 B2
Greenacre ST18 . . . . 139 D1
Greenacres Ave
Blythe Bridge ST11 . . . . 90 C8
Wolverhampton WV10 . . . . 241 B2
Greenacres Cl WS9 . . . . 256 E2
Greenacres WV9 . . . . 224 B3
Greenacres Dr ST14 . . . . 111 A2
Greenacres Prim Sch B77 . . . . 251 B5
Greenacres
Rugeley WS15 . . . . 196 E7
Sedgley DY3 . . . . 266 B1
Greenacres Way TF10 . . . . 168 D3
Greenacres WV6 . . . . 255 B5
Green Acres WV5 . . . . 269 F5
Greenacre The DE6 . . . . 81 F7
Greenaway Ct WV10 . . . . 241 C7
Greenbank Gdns DY8 . . . . 275 E2
Greenbank Rd
Newcastle-u-L ST5 . . . . 56 C3
Stoke-on-T ST6 . . . . 42 A3
Green Barn Ct ST18 . . . . 138 D2
Green Barns La WS14 . . . . 258 C8
Greenbirches Ind Est ST6 . . 41 D4
Green Brook Ct ST5 . . . . 56 B3
Green Cl Barlaston ST12 . . . . 88 D1
Blythe Bridge ST11 . . . . 90 D7
Pattingham WV6 . . . . 253 C2
Stone ST15 . . . . 119 F7
Greencroft
Kingswinford DY6 . . . . 275 D4
Lichfield WS13 . . . . 214 A2
Green Croft ST15 . . . . 118 F6
Green Ct 8 WS13 . . . . 231 B7
Greendale Cotts ST10 . . . . 77 E4
Greendale Dr ST5 . . . . 40 D1
Greendale La ST10 . . . . 77 D4
Greendock St ST3 . . . . 284 B3
Greenfield Ave
Armitage WS15 . . . . 198 A4
Brown Edge ST6 . . . . 43 C7
Stourbridge DY8 . . . . 279 F5
Greenfield ST8 . . . . 27 D6
Greenfield Bldgs WV5 . . . . 270 A7
Greenfield Cl ST6 . . . . 43 C7
Greenfield Cres ST10 . . . . 76 E4
Greenfield Dr ST14 . . . . 126 A8
Greenfield La WV10 . . . . 240 E5
Greenfield Pl ST6 . . . . 43 C7
Greenfield Prim Sch DY8 . . . . 279 F5
Greenfield Rd Endon ST9 . . . . 43 E8
Stafford ST17 . . . . 175 D5
Stoke-on-T ST6 . . . . 41 E5
Greenfields Aldridge WS9 . . . . 256 B7
Cannock WS11 . . . . 209 E2
Denstone ST14 . . . . 95 D6
Greenfields Dr WS15 . . . . 178 D1
Greenfields ST20 . . . . 171 E7
Greenfields La TF9 . . . . 97 B2
Greenfields Rd
Hixon ST18 . . . . 139 C1
Kingswinford DY6 . . . . 275 E6
Kinver DY7 . . . . 277 C3
Walsall WS4 . . . . 244 D2
Wombourne WV5 . . . . 270 A5
Greenfield View DY3 . . . . 271 B7
Greenfinch Cl ST14 . . . . 126 C6
Greengates St ST6 . . . . 41 E4
Greengate St ST16 . . . . 285 B3
Green Gore La ST17 . . . . 175 F7
Greenhall Com Specl Sch ST16 . . . . 155 B7
Greenhead St ST6 . . . . 56 F8
Greenheart B77 . . . . 251 A4
Green Heath Rd WS12 . . . . 210 A7
Greenhill Cl B77 . . . . 261 C5
Greenhill Ct WV5 . . . . 270 B5
Greenhill Gdns WV5 . . . . 270 B5
Greenhill La ST19 . . . . 205 C7
Greenhill WS13 . . . . 231 C8
Greenhill Mews WS13 . . . . 231 C8
Greenhill Rd Dudley DY3 . . . . 271 E5
Stoke-on-T ST6 . . . . 42 E6
Greenhill Way WS9 . . . . 245 B1
Greenhill WV5 . . . . 270 B6
Greenhough Rd WS13 . . . . 231 A8
Green La Aldridge WS9 . . . . 256 E5
Alsop en le D DE6 . . . . 36 C2
Ashley TF9 . . . . 100 D5
Birchmoor B77,B78 . . . . 262 D7
Blythe Bridge ST11 . . . . 91 A6
Brownhills WS8 . . . . 229 B2
Burntwood WS7 . . . . 212 D1
Burton u T DE13 . . . . 166 B7
Cannock WS11 . . . . 226 E6
Chorley WS13 . . . . 212 C3
Clifton Campville DE12 . . . . 218 B7
Clifton DE6 . . . . 81 E7
Dudley DY3 . . . . 271 F5
Eccleshall ST21 . . . . 133 E6
Hamstall Ridware WS15 . . . . 181 B3
Kingswinford DY6 . . . . 275 D7
Lichfield WS14 . . . . 230 D2
Marchington ST14 . . . . 128 A2
Greenland Cl DY6 . . . . 275 E8
Greenlands WV5 . . . . 269 F7
Green Lane Venture Ctr WS11 . . . . 226 E6
Green La Newport TF10 . . . . 168 E4
Roston DE6 . . . . 96 F8
Rudyard ST13 . . . . 18 F2
Rugeley WS15 . . . . 178 D1
Stafford ST18 . . . . 174 C4
Sutton TF10 . . . . 150 E1
Tamworth B77 . . . . 262 C6
Tutbury DE13 . . . . 146 C5
Walsall,High Heath WS4, WS9 . . . . 244 D3
Walsall,Pelsall WS3 . . . . 244 A4
Waterhouses DE6 . . . . 65 A7
Whitgreave ST18 . . . . 135 F7
Wolverhampton WV6 . . . . 255 F7
Greenlea Cl ST4 . . . . 88 C5
Green Lea Fst Sch ST18 . . . . 122 D4
Greenlea B77 . . . . 262 A8
Greenleighs DY3 . . . . 266 D3
Greenline Bsns Pk DE14 . . . . 166 B3
Greenly Rd WV4 . . . . 266 D5
Green Mdws 2 WS12 . . . . 210 C1
Green Meadow Cl WV5 . . . . 269 E5
Greenmeadow Gr ST9 . . . . 43 E6
Greenmeadows Rd CW3 . . . . 68 E7
Greenmoor Ave ST6 . . . . 42 A8
Green Oak Rd WV8 . . . . 239 B2
Greenock Cl ST5 . . . . 70 F7
Green Pk Checkley ST10 . . . . 109 C8
Eccleshall ST21 . . . . 133 F6
Fulford ST11 . . . . 90 E1
Green Rd Stoke-on-T ST4 . . . . 71 E3
Weston ST18 . . . . 138 D2
Green Rock La WS3 . . . . 243 D1
Green Rock Prim Sch WS3 . . . . 243 E1
Greensforge La
Kinver DY7 . . . . 274 E3
Stourton DY7 . . . . 278 D8
Greenside Ave ST9 . . . . 43 C3
Greenside Cl ST7 . . . . 41 A7
Greenside
Newcastle-u-L ST5 . . . . 283 A3
Yarnfield ST15 . . . . 118 F6
Greens Ind Est WS12 . . . . 210 C7
Green Slade Gr WS12 . . . . 210 C7
Greenslade Rd DY3 . . . . 266 B2
Green's La ST2 . . . . 58 E3
Greensleeves B74 . . . . 257 F1
Greensmith Cl DE15 . . . . 167 C3
Greensome Cl ST16 . . . . 155 A4
Greensome Cres ST16 . . . . 155 A5
Greensome Ct ST16 . . . . 155 A4
Greensome La ST16 . . . . 155 A5
Green St DE14 . . . . 166 D1
Greens The WV6 . . . . 254 E3
Green St DY8 . . . . 279 F5
Green The Aldridge WS9 . . . . 256 C6
Armitage WS15 . . . . 198 C5
Barton-u-N DE13 . . . . 183 C1
Brocton,Milford ST17 . . . . 176 C7
Brocton ST17 . . . . 176 B3
Brown Edge ST6 . . . . 43 B7
Caverswall ST11 . . . . 74 D3
Cheadle ST10 . . . . 76 B2
Chebsey ST21 . . . . 134 E6
Fazeley B78 . . . . 249 E2
Fulford ST11 . . . . 90 E1
Hagley DY9 . . . . 281 F4
Kingsley ST10 . . . . 61 D2
Lawton-gate ST7 . . . . 25 A4
Newcastle-u-L ST5 . . . . 71 C3
Rugeley WS15 . . . . 197 A6
Seckington B79 . . . . 236 A3
Stourbridge DY8 . . . . 275 D2
Stretton DE13 . . . . 147 E1
Tamworth B77 . . . . 251 B5
Walsall WS3 . . . . 243 B1
Weston ST18 . . . . 138 D2
Whittington WS14 . . . . 232 E5
Wood End B78 . . . . 262 C4
Woodseaves ST20 . . . . 151 C8
Greenvale Cl DE15 . . . . 185 F8
Green Valley Dr DE13 . . . . 166 A8
Green View TF11 . . . . 203 F8
Green Way WS9 . . . . 245 B2
Greenway Ave
2 Stourbridge DY8 . . . . 275 E1
Stoke-on-T ST6 . . . . 42 B2
Stone ST15 . . . . 120 B6
Greenway Bank ST8 . . . . 27 D3
Greenway Bank Ctry Pk* ST8 . . . . 27 E3
Greenway Bank ST2 . . . . 43 C2
Greenway
Burton u T DE15 . . . . 167 A4
Eccleshall ST21 . . . . 133 E6
Greenway Gdns
Pattingham WV6 . . . . 253 C2
Sedgley DY3 . . . . 266 E1
Greenway Hall Rd ST2, ST9 . . . . 43 D3
Greenway Pl ST2 . . . . 58 B7
Greenway Rd ST8 . . . . 16 E2
Greenways Audley ST7 . . . . 39 F2
Chorley WS13 . . . . 212 E3
Greenways Dr ST10 . . . . 76 D4
Greenway DY3 . . . . 266 E1
Greenways ST19 . . . . 208 A8
Greenways Prim Sch ST9 . . . . 43 C4
Greenways Stafford ST18 . . . . 174 C5
Stourbridge DY8 . . . . 275 C1
Greenway ST16 . . . . 156 A3
Greenways The 1 ST2 . . . . 43 C3
Greenway ST3 . . . . 72 E3
Greenway The
Hagley DY9 . . . . 281 F5
Newcastle-u-L ST5 . . . . 56 C3
Pattingham WV6 . . . . 253 C2
Greenway ST4 . . . . 87 E7
Green Way ST14 . . . . 126 B8
Greenwich Ave DE11 . . . . 186 E1
Greenwood Ave ST4 . . . . 71 E2
Greenwood Dr WS14 . . . . 231 B6
Greenwood Gr ST17 . . . . 174 C7
Greenwood Pk
Aldridge WS9 . . . . 245 C2
Cannock WS12 . . . . 210 B8
Greenwood Rd
Aldridge WS9 . . . . 245 B2
Burton u T DE15 . . . . 185 E8
Forsbrook ST11 . . . . 91 A8
Greenwoods The DY8 . . . . 279 E5
Gregory La ST20 . . . . 150 D6
Gregory Rd
Burntwood WS7 . . . . 229 E7
Stourbridge DY8 . . . . 279 D5
Gregorys Gn WV9 . . . . 224 B3
Gregory St ST3 . . . . 284 B3
Gregson Cl 5 ST3 . . . . 73 A3
Greig Ct WS11 . . . . 210 C2
Grenadier Cl ST4 . . . . 88 C4
Grendon Gdns WV3 . . . . 265 D6
Grendon Gn ST2 . . . . 58 C2
Grenfell Rd WS3 . . . . 243 D3
Grenville Cl ST14 . . . . 110 F1
Grenville Rd DY1 . . . . 271 E1
Gresham Rd WS11 . . . . 209 F3
Gresley Cl B74 . . . . 258 A4
Gresley Row WS13 . . . . 231 C8
Gresley B77 . . . . 250 F1
Gresley Way ST7 . . . . 39 F2
Gresley Wood Rd DE11 . . . . 186 F2
Gresty St ST4 . . . . 72 A7
Gretton Ave DE13 . . . . 147 E1
Greville Cl ST19 . . . . 207 F8
Greville St ST1 . . . . 282 C4
Greyfriars Bsns Pk ST16 . . . . 285 A4
Greyfriars Cl DY1 . . . . 271 E3
Greyfriars Ct 2 ST16 . . . . 155 D5
Greyfriars Dr B79 . . . . 249 E6
Grey Friars' Pl ST16 . . . . 285 A4
Greyfriars Rd ST2 . . . . 58 A5
Grey Friars ST16 . . . . 155 D5
Grey Friars Way ST16 . . . . 155 D5
Greyhound Ct CW3 . . . . 68 E6
Greyhound La
Lower Penn WV4 . . . . 264 E5
Stourbridge DY8 . . . . 279 D2
Greyhound Way ST1,ST6 . . . . 57 A5
Greylarch La ST17 . . . . 175 C7
Greysan Ave ST7 . . . . 41 F8
Greysbrooke Prim Sch WS14 . . . . 247 A6
Greysbrooke WS14 . . . . 247 A5
Greystoke Dr DY6 . . . . 275 D6
Greyswood Rd ST4 . . . . 71 E3
Grice Rd ST4 . . . . 71 E8
Griffin Cl Burntwood WS7 . . . . 228 E8
Norton in H TF9 . . . . 82 C2
Griffin St ST3 . . . . 284 B3
Griffithgreen WV5 . . . . 267 D7
Griffiths Dr
Wolverhampton WV11 . . . . 242 A1
Wombourne WV5 . . . . 270 A5
Griffiths Way ST15 . . . . 120 D6
Grimley Way WS11 . . . . 209 F4
Grindcobbe Gr WS15 . . . . 178 D3
Grindley Hill Ct ST4 . . . . 71 E6
Grindley La
Kingstone ST18 . . . . 140 E6
Meir ST3,ST11 . . . . 90 B6
Grindley Pl ST4 . . . . 71 F6
Grindsbrook B77 . . . . 262 A8
Grisedale Cl 5 ST3 . . . . 90 A7
Grissom Cl ST16 . . . . 156 A5
Gristhorpe Way ST2 . . . . 58 D1
Gritton St ST6 . . . . 41 D2
Grizedale Cl DE15 . . . . 167 B1
Grocott Cl ST19 . . . . 192 E2
Grosvenor Ave
Aldridge B74 . . . . 256 F1
Stoke-on-T ST4 . . . . 71 F4
Grosvenor Cl
Lichfield WS14 . . . . 231 D6
Penkridge ST19 . . . . 192 F1
Stoke-on-T ST9 . . . . 43 F8
Sutton Coldfield B75 . . . . 258 C1
Wolverhampton WV10 . . . . 240 D2
Grosvenor Cres WV10 . . . . 240 D2
Grosvenor Ct Dudley DY3 . . . . 271 D2
Shenstone WS14 . . . . 246 F6
Wolverhampton,Tettenhall WV6 . . . . 255 A3
Grosvenor Gdns ST5 . . . . 283 C2
Grosvenor Pk WV4 . . . . 265 F5
Grosvenor Pl
Newcastle-u-L ST5 . . . . 56 C5
Stoke-on-T ST6 . . . . 41 D4
Grosvenor Rd
Dudley DY3 . . . . 271 D2
Longton ST3 . . . . 73 F1
Market Drayton TF9 . . . . 97 D2
Newcastle-u-L ST5 . . . . 283 C2
Wolverhampton,Bushbury WV10 . . . . 240 D2
Wolverhampton,Ettingshall Park WV4 . . . . 266 E3
Grosvenor Road S DY3 . . . . 271 D2
Grosvenor St Leek ST13 . . . . 30 F5
Longton ST3 . . . . 284 B3
Grosvenor Way ST17 . . . . 175 F6
Grotto La WV6 . . . . 255 E5
Grotto Rd TF9 . . . . 112 B8
Groundhollow ST10 . . . . 94 A3
Grounds Dr B74 . . . . 257 F3
Grounds Rd B74 . . . . 257 F3
Grove Ave Kidsgrove ST7 . . . . 25 E1
Lawton-gate ST7 . . . . 25 A4
Stoke-on-T ST3 . . . . 72 E4
Talke ST7 . . . . 40 E8
Grovebank Rd ST4 . . . . 71 E3
Grove Cl WS11 . . . . 227 F5
Grove Cres Walsall WS3 . . . . 243 F3
Woore CW3 . . . . 83 C8
Grove Gdns TF9 . . . . 97 D1
Grove Jun Sch ST1 . . . . 282 C4
Grove La DE6 . . . . 127 E8
Grovelands Cres WV10 . . . . 240 D3
Grove La
Norton Canes WS3 . . . . 227 E1
Wolverhampton WV6 . . . . 255 B2
Grovenor Ct TF9 . . . . 97 D2
Grove Park Ave ST7 . . . . 25 A4
Grove Pk DY6 . . . . 275 C8
Grove Pl ST1 . . . . 282 A1
Grove Prim Sch The ST17 . . . . 174 D8
Grove Prim Sch WV2 . . . . 266 E8
Grove Rd Stoke-on-T ST4 . . . . 72 D4
Stone ST15 . . . . 119 F8
Grove Road Ind Est ST4 . . . . 72 D4
Grove Sch The TF9 . . . . 97 D1
Groveside Way WS3 . . . . 244 A5
Grove St Burslem ST6 . . . . 57 A6
Leek ST13 . . . . 30 D6
Newcastle-u-L ST5 . . . . 55 E3
Wolverhampton WV2 . . . . 266 D8
Grove Terr 11 ST13 . . . . 30 D6
Grove The
Blythe Bridge ST11 . . . . 90 E6
Burntwood WS7 . . . . 228 D8
Lawton-gate ST7 . . . . 25 A4
Little Aston B74 . . . . 257 D6
Newcastle-u-L ST5 . . . . 71 B6
Stoke-on-T ST6 . . . . 42 B2
Stone ST15 . . . . 120 C3
Tatenhill DE13 . . . . 184 A8
Wolverhampton,Lanesfield WV4 . . . . 266 E5
Grub St ST20 . . . . 151 A6
Grunmore Dr DE13 . . . . 147 E2
Guernsey Cl CW12 . . . . 6 A1
Guernsey Dr ST5 . . . . 70 E3
Guernsey Wlk 2 ST3 . . . . 73 A3
Guildford St ST4 . . . . 72 C8
Guildhall Sh Ctr ST16 . . . . 285 B3
Guild La TF10 . . . . 169 F8
Guild St DE14 . . . . 166 D3
Guinevere Ave DE13 . . . . 147 E2
Gullet The B78 . . . . 251 F1
Gullick Way WS7 . . . . 228 D8
Gun Battery La ST8 . . . . 28 A8
Gunby Hill DE12 . . . . 219 F8
Gunnell Cl Hanley ST1 . . . . 282 C1
Stafford ST16 . . . . 155 C2
Gunn St ST8 . . . . 27 C8
Gunstone La WV8 . . . . 238 F5
Gurnard Cl WV12 . . . . 242 B1
Gurnard B77 . . . . 261 D6
Guthrum Cl WV6 . . . . 254 F5
Guy's Almshouses B79 . . . . 250 B5
Guys Cl B79 . . . . 249 F7
Guy's La DY3 . . . . 271 B2
Guy St ST2 . . . . 58 B4
Gwendoline Way WS9 . . . . 245 B4
Gwenys Cres ST3 . . . . 72 E4
Gwyn Ave ST8 . . . . 27 D5
Gypsum Way DE6 . . . . 144 D6

H

Hackett Cl Longton ST3 . . . . 284 D4
Wolverhampton WV14 . . . . 266 F1
Hackford Rd WV4 . . . . 266 F4
Hackwood Cl ST12 . . . . 88 F4
Hadden Cl ST9 . . . . 59 B2
Haddon Gr ST5 . . . . 55 F6
Haddon La ST5 . . . . 85 E1
Haddon Pl Bucknall ST2 . . . . 58 C5
Stone ST15 . . . . 120 D7
Haden Cl DY8 . . . . 275 D2
Hadfield Gn ST6 . . . . 42 D2
Hadleigh Cl ST5 . . . . 71 B2
Hadleigh Rd ST2 . . . . 58 B6
Hadley Dr CW2 . . . . 37 E4
Hadley End DE13 . . . . 181 E5
Hadley Park Sports Coll WS15 . . . . 196 D8
Hadley St DE13 . . . . 181 F3
Hadrians Cl B77 . . . . 261 D8
Hadrian Way ST5 . . . . 55 D5
Haggar St WV2 . . . . 266 C6
Hagley Ct DY3 . . . . 271 D3
Hagley Dr WS15 . . . . 178 D1
Hagley Park Gdns WS15 . . . . 196 D7
Hagley RC High Sch DY8 . . . . 281 F6
Hagley Rd WS15 . . . . 178 D1
Haig Cl WS11 . . . . 210 A5
Haigh Cl ST13 . . . . 45 D5
Haig Rd ST13 . . . . 31 A7
Haig St ST3 . . . . 73 D2
Hailes Park Cl WV2 . . . . 266 E6
Hailsham Cl ST6 . . . . 41 F5
Hainer Cl 6 ST17 . . . . 175 A8
Hainult Cl DY8 . . . . 275 D4
Halcyon Way DE14 . . . . 166 B4
Hales Hall Rd ST10 . . . . 76 F4
Hales Pl ST3 . . . . 284 C1
Halesworth Cres ST5 . . . . 71 B2
Halesworth Rd WV9 . . . . 239 F2
Halford St B79 . . . . 250 A5
Halfpenny Green Vineyard* DY7 . . . . 268 D6
Halfshire La DY10 . . . . 281 B1
Halfway Pl ST5 . . . . 55 E1
Halifax Cl ST3 . . . . 90 C7
Halifax Rd WV7 . . . . 220 F1
Haliford Ave ST1 . . . . 57 D7
Haling Cl ST19 . . . . 207 F8
Haling Rd ST19 . . . . 192 F1
Hallahan Cl ST15 . . . . 120 C6
Hallahan Gr ST4 . . . . 72 A8
Hallam Rd ST14 . . . . 110 F1
Hallams Row DE14 . . . . 166 C4
Hallam St ST4 . . . . 72 E6
Hall Ave ST13 . . . . 31 A7
Hall Bank SK17 . . . . 24 E5
Hallbridge Cl WS3 . . . . 243 F2

Hall Cl Pattingham WV6 253 C2
Stafford ST17 175 A7
Hallcourt Cl 3 WS11 226 E8
Hallcourt Cres 2 WS11 226 E8
Hallcourt La WS11 226 E8
Hallcroft Cl TF10 168 E3
Hallcroft Gdns TF10 168 E3
Hallcroft Way WS9 256 C5
Halldearn Ave ST11 74 D3
Hall Dr Enville DY7 273 C1
Hanbury DE13 145 A4
Meir ST3 74 B4
Hall End Cl WV6 253 C2
Hall End La WV6 253 C2
Hallfarm Cl ST19 223 D6
Hall Farm Cl ST18 139 C1
Hall Farm Cres ST18 137 F4
Hallfarm Rd ST19 223 D6
Hallfield Gr ST6 41 E5
Hallfields Rd DE15 186 C4
Hall Gdns ST14 127 E2
Hall Green Ave DE13 147 F2
Hall Grounds DE13 147 A4
Hall Hill Dr ST2 73 D8
Hallhill La WS15 161 A5
Hall La Brownhills WS9 244 E3
Cotes Heath ST21 102 D3
Doveridge DE6 127 B8
Great Wyrley WS6 227 A3
Hammerwich WS7 229 E4
Hilderstone ST15 106 F3
Muckley Corner WS7, WS14 229 F2
Stanton DE6 80 A7
Swynnerton ST15 103 D3
Walsall WS3 243 F3
Wolverhampton WV14 266 F1
Wootton DE6 79 F7
Hall Mdw WS11 226 B6
Hall Orch Bramshall ST14 125 C7
Cheadle ST10 76 D3
Hall Pl ST5 56 D5
Hall Rd Armitage WS15 198 C5
Marchington ST14 127 E2
Rolleston on D DE13 146 F4
Rolleston on D DE13 147 A4
Uttoxeter ST14 126 A8
Halls Rd Biddulph ST8 16 C1
Mow Cop ST7 26 C7
Hall St Audley ST7 39 D2
Burslem ST6 56 F8
Newcastle-u-L ST5 283 B3
Sedgley DY3 271 D8
Hall Yd ST10 92 E4
Halston Rd WS7 229 B8
Halton Gn ST3 88 E8
Haltonlea B77 262 A8
Hambledon Cl WV9 240 A2
Hamble Gr WV6 254 E4
Hamble Rd WV4 265 C6
Hamble B77 250 D2
Hambleton Pl ST8 27 B5
Hamble Way ST2 58 D1
Hambridge Cl ST17 174 D7
Hambro Pl ST6 42 B7
Hamelin St WS11 209 E3
Hames La B79 236 D3
Hamil Dr ST13 30 D6
Hamil Rd ST6 42 A1
Hamilton Ave DY8 279 D6
Hamilton Cl
Cannock WS12 210 F4
Sedgley DY3 271 C8
Stourbridge DY8 275 C2
Hamilton Ct ST5 71 C2
Hamilton Dr DY8 275 C2
Hamilton Fields DE15 167 A2
Hamilton Gdns WV10 240 F3
Hamilton Ho WS3 243 C1
Hamilton Inf Sch ST1 57 D6
Hamilton Lea WS11 228 A6
Hamilton Rd
Burton u T DE15 167 A2
Longton ST3 284 D2
Hamilton Rise ST2 43 B2
Hamilton St
Stoke-on-T ST4 72 C5
Walsall WS3 243 D1
Ham La DY6 270 E1
Hamlet The WS11 227 E5
Hamlett Pl ST6 42 E3
Hammersley Hayes Rd ST10 76 E6
Hammersley St ST1 57 E6
Hammerton Ave ST2 57 F2
Hammerwich Hospl WS7 229 B5
Hammerwich La WS7 229 F3
Hammerwich Rd WS7 229 D5
Hammond Ave ST6 43 B7
Hammond Ho ST1 282 C1
Hammond Rd ST5 55 E8
Hammonds Croft ST18 158 C8
Hammoon Gr ST2 58 B2
Hamner Gn ST2 73 D8
Hampden Ho DE15 185 E6
Hamps Cl WS7 229 D7
Hampshire Cl
Stoke-on-T ST9 43 F7
Tamworth B78 249 F2
Hampshire Cres ST3 89 C8
Hampson Ct ST15 120 B8
Hampstead Gr ST4 88 C7
Hamps Valley Rd ST10 48 F2
Hampton Cl
Newport TF10 169 A3
Tamworth B79 250 C7
Hampton Ct Leek ST13 30 D5
Hampton Ct *continued*
Rugeley WS15 178 D3
Wolverhampton WV10 241 B2
Hampton Dr
Market Drayton TF9 97 B2
Newport TF10 169 A3
Hampton Gdns ST18 156 D3
Hampton Gn WS11 226 E7
Hampton Gr Dunsley DY7 278 C4
Walsall WS3 244 A4
Hampton Rd WV10 240 B1
Hampton St
Cannock WS11 226 D7
Hanley ST1 282 C1
Hams Cl ST8 27 C7
Hanbridge Ave ST5 56 A7
Hanbury Cres WV4 265 E6
Hanbury Hill DE13 145 A5
Hanbury Rd
Brownhills WS8 228 F2
Norton Canes WS11 227 F5
Tamworth B77 250 F4
Hanbury's Farm Com Prim Sch B77 250 D1
Hanchurch Cl DE15 167 A4
Hanchurch Crossroad ST5 87 C8
Hanchurch Hills Circular Wlks* ST4 86 F4
Hanchurch La ST4 87 B7
Hancock St ST4 72 C7
Handel Ct WS11 210 C2
Handel Gr ST1 58 A6
Handel Wlk WS13 214 C2
Hand La TF11 187 D1
Handley Banks ST11 74 E4
Handley Dr ST8 27 B2
Handley Rd DE14 165 F3
Handley Sh Ctr The ST1 282 B2
Handley St ST7 27 A2
Handsacre Cl DE11 186 F3
Handsacre Cres WS15 198 C3
Handsacre Rd ST3 284 D5
Hand St ST6 41 E2
Hangmans La B79 236 A2
Hankins Heys La CW3 82 B8
Hanley Bsns Pk ST1 282 B1
Hanley Rd ST6,ST1 57 D8
Hanlith B77 262 A8
Hannaford Way WS11 209 F2
Hanney Hay Rd WS7,WS8 229 B3
Hanover Ct
Newcastle-u-L ST5 283 C3
Tamworth B79 249 E7
Wolverhampton WV6 255 C4
Hanover Ho
6 Stourbridge DY8 279 F8
Longton ST4 73 B5
Hanover Pl WS11 209 E2
Hanover St Hanley ST1 282 B3
Newcastle-u-L ST5 283 C3
Hanson Man B74 258 A1
Hanyards La ST18 156 F4
Harald Cl WV6 254 E5
Harber St ST3 284 C3
Harbin Rd DE12 184 D1
Harborne Cres ST10 76 E4
Harborne Rd ST10 76 E4
Harborough Ct B74 258 A2
Harborough Dr WS9 256 B5
Harbourne Ct ST10 76 E4
Harbury St DE13 166 A6
Harcourt Ave ST3 73 F1
Harcourt Dr Dudley DY3 271 D2
Newport TF10 169 A4
Sutton Coldfield B74 257 F4
Harcourt Ho B79 250 A4
Harcourt Rd DE14 184 F8
Harcourt St ST1 282 A1
Harcourt Way ST16 155 B7
Hardewick Cl ST9 59 B3
Hardie Ave WS15 196 E7
Hardie Ct 2 WV4 266 F4
Hardie Gn WS11 209 F3
Hardinge St ST4 72 D6
Harding Rd ST1 282 B1
Hardings Mdw ST7 25 F2
Hardingswood Rd ST7 25 E2
Harding Terr ST4 72 A6
Hardman St ST2 43 A1
Hardon Rd WV4 266 F5
Hardwick Cl ST4 88 C4
Hardwick Ct Aldridge B74 256 F2
Tamworth B79 250 C5
Hardwick Rd B74 257 A2
Hardy Cl Barton-u-N DE13 201 E7
Cheadle ST10 76 C2
Hardy Rd ST17 174 B8
Hardy Sq WV2 266 F6
Hardy St ST6 41 D4
Harebell Cl
Cannock WS12 210 D2
Featherstone WV10 241 A7
Harebell Gr ST7 26 F1
Harebell B77 251 A4
Harecastle Ave ST7 25 E1
Harecastle Bank ST15 104 E3
Harecastle Ct ST7 40 E6
Haregate Rd ST13 31 A8
Haregate Terr ST13 31 A7
Harehedge La
Burton u T DE13 166 B8
Stretton DE13 147 B1
Hareshaw Gr ST6 42 A8
Hares La ST10 77 C3
Harewell Dr B75 258 C1
Harewood Cl ST10 76 D4
Harewood Est ST10 76 B5
Harewood St ST6 41 D2
Hargate Rd DE15 167 C1
Hargreave Cl ST3 90 C7
Hargreaves Ct 5 ST13 30 E5
Hargreaves La ST17 285 A1
Harington Dr ST3 73 E5
Harland Cl ST18 177 D8
Harland Rd B74 258 A3
Harlaxton St DE13 166 A6
Harlech Ave ST3 73 E1
Harlech Dr ST8 27 C6
Harlech Way
Burton u T DE13 166 D8
Dudley DY1 271 F2
Harlequin Dr ST6 42 C2
Harlestones Ho DY8 279 F7
Harley Cl Brownhills WS8 245 A6
Rugeley WS15 196 F6
Harley La
Abbots Bromley WS15 160 F7
Beech ST4 87 C1
Harley St ST1 282 C2
Harley Thorn La ST4 87 B3
Harman Dr WS13 230 F6
Harmon Rd DY8 279 C5
Harmony Gn ST17 174 B8
Harney Ct WS15 178 D3
Harold St ST6 42 C1
Harper Ave
Burton u T DE13 166 C7
Newcastle-u-L ST5 56 B4
Harper Ct DE13 166 C7
Harper St ST6 56 E7
Harpfield Prim Sch ST4 71 D8
Harpfield Rd ST4 71 E5
Harplands Hospl ST4 71 D6
Harplow La ST10 76 B1
Harptree Wlk ST4 71 F2
Harpur-Crewe Cotts DE6 35 D3
Harrier Cl ST3 90 A6
Harringay Dr DY8 279 E3
Harrington Cl ST13 30 E3
Harrington Wlk WS13 213 F1
Harriotts Hayes Rd WV7 237 F6
Harriseahead La ST7 26 D4
Harrison Cl
Burton u T DE14 185 B8
Cheslyn Hay WS6 226 D1
Halmer End ST7 54 D7
Walsall WS3 243 C1
Harrison Ct ST5 283 C1
Harrison Rd
Cannock WS11 226 E7
Stoke-on-T ST6 42 E3
Sutton Coldfield B74 257 E5
Walsall WS4 244 C2
Harrisons La ST19 207 E1
Harrison St
Newcastle-u-L ST5 283 C2
Walsall WS3 243 C1
Harrison Way ST13 45 D5
Harrison & Woodburn Cotts ST5 54 C3
Harris Rd ST16 156 B4
Harris St ST4 72 A8
Harrogate Gr ST5 54 F2
Harrop St ST1 57 D6
Harrop Way DY8 279 E8
Harrots La SK17 24 D6
Harrowby Ct WV10 240 B3
Harrowby Dr ST5 70 F4
Harrowby Rd Meir ST3 90 A8
Wolverhampton WV10 240 C2
Harrowby St ST16 156 A3
Harrow Ct B74 257 F2
Harrow Dr DE14 185 C8
Harrow Pl ST15 120 D7
Harrow Rd DY6 270 D1
Harrows Mobile Home Pk The WV9 224 C4
Hart Ct ST5 283 B3
Hartill Rd WV4 265 D3
Hartill St ST4 72 C8
Hartington CE Prim Sch SK17 24 D5
Hartington Hall Youth Hostel* SK17 24 E5
Hartington St Leek ST13 30 E5
Newcastle-u-L ST5 56 B5
Hartland Ave
Stafford ST17 175 E8
Stoke-on-T ST6 42 C3
Hartlands Rd ST21 133 E7
Hartlebury Cl WS11 210 C2
Hartleyburn B77 262 A8
Hartley Dr Aldridge WS9 256 B4
Stone ST15 104 F1
Hartley Gdns CW12 16 B8
Hartsbourne Way ST17 175 C7
Hartshill Rd ST4 71 F8
Hartslade WS14 231 E6
Hartwell Gr ST16 155 A7
Hartwell La
Great Wyrley WS6 227 A3
Hartwell ST15 89 C2
Hartwell ST5 70 F4
Hartwell Rd ST3 90 A8
Hartwood Cl TF10 168 F5
Hartwood Cres WV3 265 F5
Harvard Cl DY1 271 F4
Harvest Cl DY3 271 E5
Harvesters Cl WS9 256 E2
Harvesters Wlk WV8 239 E1
Harvester Way DY6 275 A8
Harvest Fields Way
Sutton Coldfield B75 258 D4
Sutton Coldfield B75 258 E3
Harvey Dr B75 258 C2
Harvey Pl ST14 111 B1
Harvey Rd Armitage WS15 198 C4
Burton u T DE14 185 A8
Congleton CW12 6 A5
Meir ST3 74 B2
Harvine Wlk DY8 279 E3
Harwell Cl B79 250 C7
Harwin Cl WV6 255 F7
Harwood Ave DE14 184 F8
Harwood Dr B77 261 D4
Harwood Rd WS13 214 B3
Haslemere Ave ST2 43 B1
Haslington Cl ST5 40 D1
Hassall St ST1 282 C2
Hassam Ave ST5 283 A4
Hassam Par ST5 56 B5
Hassell St ST5 283 C3
Haste Hill Ave ST10 61 F2
Hastings Cl B77 261 F6
Hastings Ct DY1 271 E2
Hatchett La B79 217 C5
Hatch Heath Cl WV5 269 F7
Hatch La TF11 203 D4
Hateley Dr WV4 266 E4
Hatfield Cres ST3 88 E8
Hathaway Mews DY8 275 C3
Hathaway Rd B74 258 A4
Hathersage Cl ST3 73 C5
Hatherton Cl ST5 40 D2
Hatherton Croft WS11 209 C1
Hatherton Gdns WV10 240 E2
Hatherton Pl WS9 256 A7
Hatherton Rd
Cannock WS11 209 C1
Penkridge ST19 192 F1
Hatherton St
Cheslyn Hay WS6 226 C2
Stafford ST16 156 A3
Hatrell St ST5 283 C2
Hatton Rd Cannock WS11 209 A1
Wolverhampton WV6 255 F3
Hattons Gr WV8 239 B2
Hatton Waterworks Cotts ST21 102 D7
Haughton St Giles CE Prim Sch ST18 172 F5
Haunton Rd B79 217 D3
Havannah La CW12 6 A5
Havannah Prim Sch CW12 6 A5
Havefield Ave WS14 231 E7
Havelet Dr ST5 70 F3
Havelock Cl WV3 265 F8
Havelock Gr ST8 27 C7
Havelock Pl ST1 282 A1
Haven Ave ST6 57 D8
Haven Cres ST9 59 B4
Haven Cvn Site DE14 185 C8
Haven Gr ST5 56 C7
Havensfield Dr ST10 92 E5
Haven The
Stourbridge DY8 275 D2
Wolverhampton WV2 266 C8
Havergal CE Prim Sch WV10 225 D2
Havergal Pl WV10 225 D1
Havergal Wlk ST3 73 C5
Haverhill Cl Chorlton CW2 37 B3
Walsall WS3 243 A3
Havisham Ct TF10 168 E3
Hawcroft WS15 197 F2
Hawes St ST6 41 D4
Haweswater Dr DY6 275 D6
Hawfield La
Burton u T DE15 167 C3
Burton u T DE15 167 D4
Hawfinch Rd ST10 76 E3
Hawfinch B77 262 A6
Hawk Cl ST3 90 A7
Hawke Rd ST16 155 C7
Hawkesford Cl B74 258 B1
Hawkesmoor Dr WS14 231 D8
Hawkesmore Dr ST18 177 D7
Hawkestone Cl ST5 283 C2
Hawkesville Dr 7 WS11 209 F2
Hawkeswell Dr 4 DY6 275 D8
Hawkhurst Dr WS15 197 F8
Hawkins Cl WS13 214 B2
Hawkins Dr WS11 226 C4
Hawkins La
Burton u T DE14 166 E5
Fradswell ST18 122 F2
Hawkins Lane Ind Est DE14 166 E5
Hawkins St ST4 72 D6
Hawks Cl WS6 226 D2
Hawksdale Cl ST3 90 A7
Hawk's Dr DE15 167 D3
Hawks Green La WS11 210 A1
Hawkside B77 262 B8
Hawksley Dr DE13 147 B4
Hawksmoor Cl ST3 89 E7
Hawksmoor Dr WV6 254 D3
Hawksmoor Rd ST17 174 E7
Hawkstone Ave TF10 168 E2
Hawkstone Ct WV6 254 D5
Hawkswell Ave WV5 270 A5
Hawksworth Ave ST13 30 D4
Hawksworth Cl ST13 30 D4
Hawksworth B77 250 F2
Hawkyard Ct WS11 210 A4
Hawley Cl ST15 120 D5
Haworth Ave CW12 6 A5
Hawthorn Ave
Great Wyrley WS6 227 A1
Netherseal DE12 219 F7
Stone ST15 119 F5
Hawthorn Cl
Denstone ST14 95 E6
Hawthorn Cl *continued*
Gnosall ST20 171 E7
Great Bridgeford ST18 135 B2
Haughton ST18 172 E6
Lichfield WS14 231 D8
Hawthorn Cres DE15 185 F7
Hawthornden Ave ST14 126 A8
Hawthornden Cl ST14 126 A8
Hawthornden Gdns ST14 125 F8
Hawthornden Manor Mews ST14 126 A8
Hawthornden Manor ST14 126 A8
Hawthorne Ave Audley ST7 39 F1
Stoke-on-T ST4 71 E5
Tamworth B79 250 B8
Hawthorne Cl ST10 92 F3
Hawthorne Cres WS7 229 A6
Hawthorne Dr ST19 205 C6
Hawthorne Gr DY3 271 D2
Hawthorne La WV8 238 F2
Hawthorne Rd
Cannock WS12 210 F3
Cheslyn Hay WS6 226 E4
Essington WV11 242 A3
Huntington WS12 209 D8
Wheaton Aston ST19 205 C6
Wolverhampton WV2 266 D6
Hawthorne Terr ST13 30 F6
Hawthorne Way DY7 278 C3
Hawthorn Gdns ST7 40 D8
Hawthorn Gr ST8 27 E7
Hawthorn Mews ST14 126 C8
Hawthorn Pl 2 ST3 89 F8
Hawthorn Rd
Aldridge B74 257 A1
Newcastle-u-L ST5 40 E1
Walsall WS4 244 B1
Hawthorn Rise DE11 186 F7
Hawthorn St ST6 57 B6
Hawthorns The
Hagley DY9 281 F4
Keele ST5 69 F7
Hawthorn Way
Market Drayton TF9 97 D2
Rugeley WS15 178 D2
Stafford ST17 156 A1
Haybank La ST10 78 E5
Hay Barns The ST15 103 B4
Haybarn The ST16 155 F7
Haybridge Ave DY8 281 F5
Haybridge High Sch & Sixth Form DY8 281 F6
Haycroft Dr B74 258 A4
Haydock Cl
Burton u T DE14 185 A7
Cheadle ST10 76 E5
Tamworth B77 261 D4
Haydock Ct ST5 55 C1
Haydon Ct ST4 56 E2
Haydon St ST4 56 E1
Hay End La WS13 215 C8
Hayes Cl ST13 30 F7
Hayes Meadow Prim Sch WS15 198 C4
Hayes St ST6 42 C2
Hayes The TF9 112 A7
Hayes View Dr WS6 226 E4
Hayes View WS13 213 F1
Hayes Way WS12 210 C1
Hayeswood La ST7 54 E6
Hayfield Cres ST4 72 E7
Hayfield Hill WS15 211 F4
Hayfield Rd ST5 55 B1
Hay Gr WS8 244 F8
Hayhead Cl ST7 26 B2
Hay La Ellastone DE6 79 E4
Foston DE65 129 E5
Longdon WS15 213 A7
Hayle Cl ST17 156 E1
Hayle B77 250 D2
Hayley Ct DY6 275 D6
Hayling Ct WS4 244 D1
Hayling Gr WV2 266 B6
Hayling Pl ST3 72 F3
Haymaker Way WS12 210 F4
Haymarket 3 ST6 41 D3
Haymarket The WV8 239 E1
Haymoor WS14 231 E7
Hayner Gr ST3 74 B4
Hayrick Dr DY6 275 B7
Hays La ST10 48 F4
Haywain Cl WV9 239 F2
Haywards Cl WS3 243 F3
Haywood Ct CW3 68 E5
Haywood Dr WV6 255 D4
Haywood Grange ST18 177 D7
Haywood High Sch ST6 42 A2
Haywood Hospl ST6 42 A3
Haywood Hts ST18 177 D8
Haywood La TF9 113 C1
Haywood Rd ST6 42 A2
Haywood St Leek ST13 30 F5
Stoke-on-T ST4 57 B1
Hayworth Cl B79 249 F8
Hayworth Rd WS13 214 C2
Hazel Cl Kidsgrove ST7 26 B3
Stoke-on-T ST4 71 F5
Uttoxeter ST14 126 B6
Hazeldene ST18 158 C2
Hazeldene Rd ST4 88 C7
Hazel Dr Armitage WS15 198 B4
Cannock WS12 211 A6
Hazelgarth B77 262 B8
Hazel Gdns WV8 239 A4

Hazel Gr **2** Longton ST3 ....73 F2
Biddulph ST8 ....17 B1
Lawton-gate ST7 ....25 A2
Leek ST13 ....30 C5
Lichfield WS14 ....231 C7
Stafford ST16 ....155 C8
Stourbridge DY8 ....279 C3
Wombourne WV5 ....270 A7
Hazelhurst Dr ST13 ......45 D4
Hazelhurst Rd ST6 ....41 F6
Hazelhurst St ST1 ....282 C1
Hazel La WS6 ....227 B2
Hazelmere Dr
Burntwood WS7 ....228 F4
Wolverhampton WV3 ......255 A1
Hazel Rd
Kingswinford DY6 ....275 E5
Newcastle-u-L ST5 ....55 D8
Wolverhampton WV3 ......265 E7
Hazel Slade Com Prim Sch
WS12 ....211 A6
Hazelslade Rd ST10 ......210 F6
Hazelslade Nature Reserve*
WS12 ....211 B6
Hazels The DY3 ....281 F5
Hazelwood Cl
Cheslyn Hay WS6 ....226 D2
Hanley ST6 ....57 C6
Hazelwood Gr WS11 ....226 C8
Hazelwood Rd
Aldridge B74 ....256 D1
Burton u T DE15 ....185 E6
Dudley DY1 ....271 F5
Endon ST9 ....43 E6
Hazlemere Dr B74 ....258 B1
Hazlemere Gr WS11 ....226 B8
Hazlescross Rd ST10 .....61 D3
Hazlestrine La ST17 .....175 C5
Hazleton Gn ST17 ....174 D6
Hazlitt Way ST3 ....73 E5
HCM Ind Est DE14 ....166 E4
Headborough Wlk WS9 .....245 B1
Headingley Dr DY7 ....274 F1
Headingley Gr ST4 ....88 D7
Headland Rd WV3 ....255 A1
Headlands The B74 ....257 C3
Headland Way ST10 ....78 F1
Headway Rd WV10 ....240 C3
Heakley Ave ST6 ....42 F4
Healey Ave ST8 ....27 B5
Healey B77 ....250 E2
Heanor Pl ST3 ....284 A3
Heantun Row WV11 ....242 B2
Hearn Ct ST17 ....174 D7
Hearthcote Rd DE11 ......186 F3
Heart Of The Country Ctr*
WS14 ....247 E8
Heath Ave
Newcastle-u-L ST5 ....56 C3
Werrington ST9 ....59 E4
Whittington WS14 ....232 C3
Heathbank Dr WS12 ....209 C6
Heathbrook Ave DY6 ......275 B7
Heath Cl WS14 ....245 E5
Heathcote Ave TF9 ....99 F3
Heathcote Ct **1** ST3 ..73 D5
Heathcote Dr B78 ....249 C1
Heathcote Rd
Halmer End ST7 ....54 E7
Longton ST3 ....284 B3
Heathcote Rise ST3 ......74 B5
Heathcote St
Kidsgrove ST7 ....26 A2
Longton ST3 ....73 C5
Newcastle-u-L ST5 ....55 E8
Heath Croft Rd B75 ......258 D1
Heath Cross ST14 ....126 A8
Heath Cvn Pk WV10 ....240 C6
Heathdene Cl ST3 ....284 B4
Heath Dr
Kidderminster DY10 ......280 B1
Stafford ST16 ....155 B7
Heather Cl Brocton ST17 .176 C4
Burton u T DE14 ....185 A8
Great Bridgeford ST18 ...135 C2
Lichfield WS13 ....214 D1
Rugeley WS15 ....196 F6
Werrington ST9 ....59 A4
Heather Cres ST3 ....90 A4
Heather Dr
Huntington WS12 ....209 D5
Kinver DY7 ....277 F4
Heather Glade CW3 ....68 D7
Heather Hill ST17 ....176 C4
Heather Hills ST9 ....43 D5
Heatherlands Cl ST3 .....89 F5
Heatherleigh Gr ST1 .....57 F6
Heather Mews WS12 ....210 A8
Heather Rd WS12 ....210 A8
Heatherside ST7 ....26 C6
Heather Valley WS12 .....210 D6
Heather View ST6 ....42 E6
Heath Farm Rd
Codsall WV8 ....239 B2
Stourbridge DY8 ....279 E3
Heathfield Ave ST15 .....120 A7
Heathfield Ct ST6 ....41 C7
Heathfield Dr
Newcastle-u-L ST5 ....40 D1
Walsall WS3 ....243 B2
Heathfield Gdns DY8 .....279 H4
Heathfield Gr ST13 ......89 F6
Heathfield Rd
Stoke-on-T ST6 ....42 C5

Heathfield Rd continued
Sutton Coldfield B74 ....257 F3
Uttoxeter ST14 ....126 B8
Heathfields WV8 ....238 E1
Heathfields Inf Sch B77 .261 F6
Heathfield Specl Sch ST6 .42 C5
Heath Gap WS13 ....215 D7
Heath Gap Rd WS11 ....209 F3
Heath Gdns ST15 ....119 F6
Heath Gn DY1 ....271 F5
Heath Gr Codsall WV8 ....239 B3
Loggerheads TF9 ....99 D4
Meir Heath ST3 ....90 A5
Heath Hayes Prim Sch
WS12 ....210 F2
Heath Hill Rd WV6 ....254 E1
Heath House Dr WV5 ......269 D5
Heath House La
Bucknall ST2 ....58 A4
Codsall WV8 ....238 E1
Lower Tean ST10 ....93 A3
Rudyard ST13 ....18 C1
Heathland Cl ST12 ....210 D2
Heathlands Cl DY6 ....275 E8
Heathlands Dr ST14 ......111 B1
Heathlands Grange
DE15 ....185 E7
Heathlands The WS5 ......269 D5
Heath La Newton WS15 ....140 D1
Stourbridge DY8 ....279 F4
Heathley La B78 ....260 E5
Heathley Mews DE14 ......185 C8
Heath Mill Cl WV5 ....269 D4
Heathmill Ent Ctr WV5 ..269 D3
Heath Mill Rd WV5 ....269 D4
Heath Pl ST5 ....56 C3
Heath Rd Burton u T DE15 .185 E7
Gnosall TF10 ....188 E7
Rugeley WS15 ....196 F6
Uttoxeter ST14 ....111 B1
Heath Row ST14 ....111 B1
Heath Row CW5 ....69 B8
Heathside Dr WS3 ....244 A4
Heathside La ST6 ....41 C7
Heath's Pas ST3 ....284 D3
Heath St Biddulph ST8 ...27 C7
Cannock WS12 ....210 B7
Newcastle-u-L,Broad Meadow
ST5 ....55 F6
Newcastle-u-L ST5 ....283 B3
Stoke-on-T ST6 ....41 C7
Tamworth B79 ....250 C5
Heath Top TF9 ....99 F4
Heath View
Burntwood WS7 ....212 A1
Cannock WS12 ....227 E8
Heathview ST13 ....45 E7
Heath View CW2 ....37 B5
Heath Way WS11 ....210 B2
Heathway Colton WS15 ...179 A7
Gnosall ST20 ....171 C5
Heath Way D65 ....146 C8
Heathwood Rd TF10 ......168 E2
Heatley Back La WS15 ...141 C3
Heatley La WS15 ....141 C2
Heaton Cl WV10 ....240 E5
Heaton Terr
Endon Bank ST9 ....29 A1
Newcastle-u-L ST5 ....56 B6
Heaton Villas ST6 ....43 C7
Heaton Way CW2 ....37 E4
Hebden Gr WV11 ....242 B1
Hebden B77 ....262 B8
Heber St ST3 ....284 C4
Hedgerow Cl WS12 ....209 F7
Hedgerow Dr DY6 ....270 D1
Hedgerows The
Lichfield WS14 ....231 B5
Tamworth B77 ....261 F8
Hedgerow Wlk WV8 ....239 E1
Hedges The WS5 ....269 E6
Hedging Lane Ind Est
B77 ....261 E5
Hedging La B77 ....261 E5
Hedley Pl ST5 ....70 F8
Hednesford Hills Common
Nature Reserve*
WS12 ....210 E5
Hednesford Rd
Brownhills WS8 ....228 C2
Cannock,Blackfords WS11 .209 F2
Cannock WS12 ....210 E1
Norton Canes WS11 ......227 F6
Rugeley WS15 ....196 D7
Hednesford Sta WS12 ....210 B5
Hednesford St WS11 .....209 E1
Heenan Gr Lichfield WS13 .214 E2
Stafford ST17 ....174 E5
Heighley Castle Way CW3 .68 E8
Heighley Ct CW3 ....53 A6
Heighley La CW3 ....53 F3
Heights The ST13 ....30 B2
Helen Sharman Dr ST16 ..156 B5
Helford B77 ....174 B8
Heligan Pl WS12 ....210 E2
Hellaby Ho B74 ....257 F3
Hexham Way D65 ....146 C8
Hellier Dr WV5 ....269 E7
Hellier Rd WV10 ....240 E2
Helmingham B79 ....249 D7
Helston Ave ST3 ....73 E3
Helston Cl Stafford ST17 .156 E1
Stourbridge DY8 ....275 C2
Tamworth B79 ....250 C8
Helston Rd WS5 ....284 C4
Hemingway Rd ST3 ......73 D4
Hemlock Bsns Ctr WS11 .210 B2
Hemlock Pk WS11 ....210 B2

Hemlock Rd ST3 ....284 D4
Hemlock Way WS11 ....210 B3
Hemmings Cl DY8 ....279 F5
Hempbutts The ST15 ....120 B8
Hempits Gr ST17 ....175 B1
Hemplands Rd DY8 ......279 F5
Hempstalls Ct ST5 .....283 B4
Hempstalls La ST5 .....56 C3
Hempstalls La ST5 .....283 C4
Hempstalls Prim Sch ST5 .56 B3
Hemsby Way ST5 ....71 B2
Hencroft ST13 ....30 E6
Henderson Cl WS14 .....231 D7
Henderson Gr ST3 .....74 B2
Hendon Cl DY3 ....271 D7
Henhurst Farm DE13 ....165 D5
Henhurst Hill DE13 ....165 C4
Henhurst Ridge DE13 ...165 C4
Hen La ST10 ....108 D6
Henley Ave ST8 ....27 A6
Henley Cl Barlaston ST12 .88 E4
Burntwood WS7 ....229 B5
Henley Cres DE13 ......165 D5
Henley Dr Newport TF10 .169 A4
Sutton Coldfield B74 ....258 A3
Henley Grange WS15 ....178 A1
Henley Rd Chorlton CW2 .37 B1
Wolverhampton WV10 ....240 B1
Henney Cl ST19 ....207 F7
Henry Chadwick Prim Sch
WS15 ....198 A8
Henry Prince CE Fst Sch The
DE6 ....81 D7
Henry St Stafford ST16 ..155 F5
Stoke-on-T ST6 ....41 D4
Hensel Dr WV3 ....265 C8
Henshall Hall Dr CW12 ..6 B1
Henshall Pl ST6 ....41 D6
Henshall Rd ST5 ....55 E8
Henshaw Way ST15 ......119 A6
Henson Rd B77 ....72 D6
Henwood Rd WV6 ....255 D3
Hepburn Cl WS9 ....256 A4
Hepworth Cl WV6 ......254 F4
Herbert Rd **2** Longton ST3 .73 D2
Aldridge WS9 ....245 A1
Stafford ST17 ....285 B1
Herbert St
Burton u T DE15 ....167 B3
Stoke-on-T ST4 ....72 D6
Herbhill Cl WV4 ......266 D4
Herd St ST6 ....41 F1
Hereford Ave ST5 .....71 C4
Hereford Cl WS9 ......256 A8
Hereford Gr ST2 ......58 D2
Hereford Rd WS12 .....210 B4
Hereford Way
Rugeley WS15 ....196 D6
Tamworth B78 ....250 A2
Heritage Ct WS14 .....231 D6
Heritage Way DE15 ....167 A1
Herm Cl ST5 ....70 E4
Hermes Cl ST3 ....90 C7
Hermes Ct B74 ....257 F3
Hermes Rd WS13 ......214 D1
Hermitage Cl DE15 ....251 F1
Hermitage Gdns **1** ST14 .111 A1
Hermitage La Mayfield DE6 .81 B6
Polesworth B78 ....251 E1
Hermit St DY3 ....271 D5
Heron Cl Brownhills WS8 .244 E7
Coven WV9 ....224 B2
Madeley CW3 ....68 F7
Heron St Rugeley WS15 ..196 F8
Herons Cl ST17 ....175 C7
Herons Gate Rd DY7 ...277 B4
Heron St Rugeley WS15 ..196 F8
Heronswood ST17 ......175 C7
Heron Way TF10 ......168 F5
Hertford St ST4 ......71 D4
Hertford St ST4 ......72 E4
Hesketh Ave ST6 .....42 D6
Hesketh Rd DE15 .....174 E6
Heskin Way ST6 ......42 A6
Hesleden B77 ....262 B8
Hester Cl ST3 ....73 C6
Hethersett Wlk ST2 ..58 D2
Hever Cl DY1 ....271 E3
Hewell Cl DY6 ....270 D1
Hewitt Cl WS13 .....214 A2
Hewitt Cres ST9 .....59 B3
Hewitt St ST6 ....41 F6
Hewston Croft WS12 .210 D4
Hexham Way D65 .....146 C8
Hextall La ST18 .....153 D6
Heybridge Cl ST10 ..92 F2
Heyburn Cres ST6 ...56 E8
Heyfields Cotts ST12 .104 B8
Heygate Way WS9 ....245 B1
Heysham St ST3 .....74 B4
Hickman St ST3 .....58 A3
Hickmerelands La DY3 .266 C1
Hickory Ct WS11 ....210 C2
Hick St ST5 ....283 B2

Hidden Hills CW3 ....68 E8
Hide La Hartington SK17 .24 E7
Sparklow SK17 ....14 F1
Hide Pl ST4 ....72 B7
Hide St ST4 ....72 B7
Higginson Cl CW12 .....16 C8
Higgins Rd DE11 ....186 F6
Higgott Cl DE14 ....185 B8
Higgs Rd WV11 ....242 A1
High Arcal Dr DY3 .....271 F7
High Arcal Rd DY3 .....270 F4
High Arcal Sch The DY3 .271 F6
High Bank WS11 ....226 E8
High Bank Pl ST6 .....42 B1
High Bank Rd DE15 ....167 B3
Highbrook Cl WV9 .....240 A2
High Broome Ct B78 ...250 A3
Highbury Rd
Sutton Coldfield B74 ...257 C3
Werrington ST9 ....59 C4
High Carr Bsns Pk ST5 .40 C2
High Carr Network Ctr
ST5 ....40 F2
High Chase Ho ST18 ...177 D8
High Chase Rise ST18 ..177 D8
Highcliffe Rd B77 ....261 D8
High Croft WS9 ....245 B2
Highcroft Ave DY8 ....275 C3
High Croft Cres WS14 ..231 C7
Highcroft Dr
Burton u T DE14 ......165 F4
Sutton Coldfield B74 ..257 E3
Highcroft Wlk ST6 ....42 B2
High Cross SK17 ......24 F5
Higher Ash Rd ST7 ....40 D8
Highland Ct **6** ST7 ..26 A2
Highland St ST5 ......283 A2
Higher Woodcroft ST13 .30 D4
Higher Works Cotts SK11 .7 C6
Highfield Ave
Burntwood WS7 ....229 B7
Cheadle ST10 ....76 D4
Kidsgrove ST7 ....26 B2
Longton ST3 ....73 F1
Newcastle-u-L ST5 ....56 D4
Tamworth B77 ....251 A5
Wolverhampton WV10 ..241 A2
Highfield Cl
Acton Trussell ST17 ..193 B8
Blythe Bridge ST11 ...90 D7
Burntwood WS7 ....229 B7
Burton u T DE13 ......166 B7
Highfield Cres ST10 ..76 D4
Highfield Ct
Cannock WS11 ....210 B5
Newcastle-u-L ST5 ...71 C6
Highfield Dr
Burton u T ST15 .....166 F3
Colwich ST18 ....177 D8
Stoke-on-T ST3 ......73 F2
Highfield Gdns WS14 ..231 E6
Highfield Grange ST5 .56 E4
Highfield Gr ST17 ...174 D8
Highfield La SK17 ...24 F5
Highfield Rd
Burntwood WS7 ......229 C7
Cannock WS12 ....210 E1
Kidsgrove ST7 ......26 A3
Highfield Rd E ST18 ..27 D8
Highfield Rd N WS3 ..243 F5
Highfield Rd Sedgley WV3 .266 D1
Walsall WS3 ....244 A4
Highfield Rd W ST8 ...27 D8
Highfield Rise ST4 ...87 F8
Highfields Ave WS15 ..198 C4
Highfields Cl WS12 ...210 D4
Highfields Ct WW4 ...265 D6
Highfields Dr WV5 ...270 A5
Highfields Grange WS6 .226 D1
Highfields TF9 ......112 B8
Highfields Pk WS6 ...226 D1
Highfields Prim Sch
WS7 ....229 C7
Highfields Rd WS7 ...228 F4
Highfields Science Specialist
Sch WV4 ....265 C5
Highfields The
Croxton ST21 ....116 B5
Wolverhampton WV6 ..255 A3
Highfield Way WS9 ...245 B2
Highgate B74 ....257 A1
Highgate Ave WV4 ...265 D6
Highgate Cl ST6 ....42 E4
Highgate Country Pk*
DY3 ....269 A1
Highgate Rd DY7 ....273 F7
High Gn Brewood ST19 .223 C6
Cannock WS11 ....209 D1
High Grange
Cannock WS11 ....210 A5
Lichfield WS13 ......213 F1
High Green Ct WS11 ..209 E1
Highgrove Cl
Stretton DE13 ......147 D1
Tamworth B79 ......250 B7
Highgrove Ct DY10 ...280 A1
Highgrove Pl WV1 ...271 F2
Highgrove Rd ST4 ...71 F3
Highgrove Stone ST15 .120 C5
Wolverhampton WV6 ..255 C3
High Hill WV11 .....242 A2
High Holborn DY3 ...271 D7
High House La WV7 ...237 D4
High La Alsagers Bank ST7 .55 A5

High La continued
Brown Edge ST6 ....43 B6
Leek ST13 ....45 E7
Highland Cl
Biddulph Moor ST8 ...28 B8
Blythe Bridge ST11 ..90 E7
Highland Dr Longton ST3 .73 D1
Stoke-on-T ST3 ......89 D8
High Land Rd WS9 ...245 B3
Highland Rd
Cannock WS12 ....209 C6
Newport TF10 ....168 E2
Highlands Dr DE15 ..167 A4
Highlands Rd WV3 ...265 D8
Highlands Stafford ST17 .174 D8
Stone ST15 ....119 F5
Highland Way WS15 ..178 C3
Highlanes ST21 .....116 E5
High La ST5 ....42 A3
High Lows La ST15 ..118 F6
High Mdw
Cannock Wood WS15 ..211 F5
Norbury ST20 ....151 B3
High Mdws Newport TF10 .169 A3
Wolverhampton WV6 ..255 C3
Wombourne WV5 .....270 B6
High Mount St WS12 ..210 B6
High Offley Rd ST20 .151 D8
Highover Dr B75 ....258 F4
Highpark Ave DY8 ...279 D5
High Park Cl DY3 ...271 D8
High Park Cres DY3 .266 D1
High Path WV6 .....253 C2
High Pk WS16 ......155 C1
High Ridge WS15 ...178 C3
High St (May Bank) ST5 .56 D4
High St (Sandyford) ST6 .41 D5
High St
Abbots Bromley WS15 .161 A5
Albrighton WV7 ....237 A5
Aldridge WS9 ......256 B6
Alsagers Bank ST7 .54 E6
Alton ST10 ....78 E1
Audley ST7 ....40 A1
Biddulph ST8 ....27 C8
Brownhills,Clayhanger
WS8 ....244 E6
Brownhills,Vigo WS9 .244 F3
Brownhills WS8 ....244 F8
Burntwood,Chasetown
WS7 ....228 F6
Burntwood WS7 ....211 E1
Burton u T DE14 ...166 E2
Caverswall ST11 ...74 E3
Cheadle ST10 ......76 D3
Cheslyn Hay WS6 ..226 D2
Cheswardine TF9 ..130 A8
Church Eaton ST20 .190 B8
Claverley WV5 .....267 C7
Colton WS15 ....179 A6
Dilhorne ST10 .....75 C4
Ecclesshall ST21 ..133 E7
Edgmond TF10 .....168 A3
Gnosall ST20 ......171 D6
Hixon ST18 ....158 C8
Ipstones ST10 .....47 A1
Kidsgrove,The Rookery ST7 .26 C4
Kingsley ST10 .....61 E2
Kingswinford DY6 .275 E6
Kingswinford,Wall Heath
DY6 ....275 C8
Kinver DY7 ....278 B3
Leek ST13 ....30 E6
Longdon WS15 .....197 F2
Longnor SK17 .....13 C6
Marchington ST14 .122 E2
Market Drayton TF9 .97 D1
Mow Cop ST7 .....26 D7
Newcastle-u-L,Chesterton
ST5 ....55 B1
Newcastle-u-L,Knutton ST5 .55 B3
Newcastle-u-L,Silverdale
ST5 ....55 B1
Newcastle-u-L ST5 .283 B2
Newcastle-u-L,Wolstanton
ST5 ....56 C5
Newchapel ST7 ...26 E2
Newport TF10 .....168 E3
Norton Canes WS11 .228 B5
Pattingham WV6 ..253 C3
Rocester ST14 ....95 F3
Sedgley DY3 ......271 D8
Stoke-on-T,Golden Hill ST6 .41 D7
Stoke-on-T,Newfield ST6 .41 D4
Stoke-on-T,Tunstall ST6 .41 D3
Stone ST15 ....120 A8
Stourbridge,Amblecote
DY8 ....279 F7
Stourbridge,Wollaston
DY8 ....279 F2
Stourbridge,Wordsley DY8 .275 E2
Swadlincote DE11 .186 F6
Swindon DY3 ......269 E2
Talke Pits ST7 ...40 D6
Tamworth B77 ....261 C5
Tutbury DE13 .....146 C6
Upper Tean ST10 .92 D4
Uttoxeter ST14 ..126 C8
Walsall,Wallington Heath
WS3 ....243 B1
Walsall WS3 ......244 A4
Wheaton Aston ST19 .205 B6
Wolverhampton WV6 ..255 D4
Wombourne WV5 .....270 B7
Highton Ct ST2 ...43 C1
Highton St ST2 ...43 C1

Highup Rd ST13 . . . . .19 C1
Highview Dr DY6 . . . . . . .275 F4
High View Meir Heath ST3 . .90 A5
  Mount Pleasant ST7 . . . . .26 B5
Highview Rd ST11 . . . . . . .106 E8
High View Rd Leek ST13 . .31 B5
  Stoke-on-T ST5 . . . . .43 F8
High View WV14 . . . . .266 F1
Highway La ST5 . . . . .69 E7
High Wood Cl DY6 . . . . . .275 C6
Highwood Ct ST14 . . . . . .126 C6
Highwood Rd ST14. . . . . .126 C6
Higson Ave ST4. . . . . .72 A8
Hilary Dr Aldridge WS9 . . .256 A5
  Wolverhampton WV3 . . . . . .265 D7
Hilcote Gdns ST21. . . . . . .134 B8
Hilcote Hollow ST16. . . . .155 B6
Hilderstone Rd
  Hilderstone ST15 . . . . .106 D5
  Meir Heath ST3,ST15. . . . . .90 A2
Hillary Ave ST12 . . . . .6 A2
Hillary Crest Dudley DY3 . .271 E5
  Rugeley WS15. . . . . .196 E6
Hillary Rd ST7 . . . . .26 B3
Hillary St ST7 . . . . .57 B6
Hill Avenue Prim Sch
  WV4 . . . . .266 F3
Hill Ave WV4 . . . . .266 F3
Hillberry Cl ST2 . . . . .58 A2
Hillboro Rise DY7 . . . . . . .278 A5
Hillchurch St ST1. . . . . . . .282 B3
Hill Cl Sedgley DY3 . . . . . .266 E1
  Uttoxeter ST14 . . . . .110 F1
Hillcott Wlk ST3 . . . . .284 D3
Hill Cres Alsagers Bank ST7 .54 F6
  Stone ST15 . . . . .120 A6
Hillcrest Ave
  Burton u T DE15. . . . . .167 A4
  Kingsley Holt ST10 . . . . . . .62 A2
  Wolverhampton WV10. . . . .240 E1
Hillcrest Cl
  Kingsley Holt ST10 . . . . . . .62 A2
  Tamworth B79 . . . . .250 B6
Hill Crest Dr WS13 . . . . . .214 A1
Hill Crest DY3 . . . . .271 C4
Hillcrest Hixon WS15 . . . .140 E3
  Leek ST13 . . . . .30 D6
Hillcrest Rd B78 . . . . .262 F7
Hillcrest Rise WS7 . . . . . .229 B4
Hill Crest ST17 . . . . .174 C8
Hillcrest St ST1. . . . . .282 C3
Hillcrest DE13 . . . . .146 B5
Hillcroft Ave ST17 . . . . . .175 E7
Hill Croft ST18 . . . . .158 C8
Hilldene Rd DY6 . . . . .275 C4
Hill Dr ST15 . . . . .120 A6
Hill End ST15 . . . . .105 E5
Hillfarm Cl ST17 . . . . .174 F5
Hillfield Ave ST4 . . . . .71 E4
Hillfield La DE13 . . . . .147 F1
Hillgreen Rd ST3 . . . . .73 D5
Hill Hook Ho B74 . . . . . . .257 E5
Hill Hook Rd B74 . . . . . . .257 F5
Hill La Burntwood WS7 . . .211 E1
  Church Leigh ST10. . . . . . .108 B3
  Middleton B75 . . . . .259 B2
Hillman St ST2 . . . . .43 B1
Hillman B77 . . . . .250 E2
Hillmorton Rd WS14. . . . .257 F4
Hillmorton B74. . . . . .257 F3
Hill Pk WS9 . . . . .245 A4
Hillport Ave ST5 . . . . .56 B7
Hillrise ST10 . . . . .94 E8
Hill Rise ST18 . . . . .137 F4
Hillsdale La ST13 . . . . .33 F3
Hillsdale Rd DE15 . . . . . . .167 B5
Hillside WS15. . . . . .161 B5
Hillside Ave
  Forsbrook ST11 . . . . .91 A8
  Kidsgrove ST7 . . . . .41 A8
  Longton ST3 . . . . .73 F1
  Stoke-on-T ST9 . . . . .43 F8
Hillside WS8 . . . . .245 A6
Hillside Cl Biddulph ST8 . . .17 B1
  Brownhills WS8 . . . . .245 A6
  Burntwood WS7 . . . . .228 C5
  Cannock WS12. . . . . .210 A7
  Fulford ST11. . . . . .106 E8
  Gorstyhill CW2. . . . . .37 E3
  Kidsgrove ST7 . . . . .26 D7
  Rugeley WS15. . . . . .197 B5
Hillside Cres WS3 . . . . . . .243 F3
Hillside Dr Colwich ST18 . .177 D8
  Leek ST13 . . . . .30 C4
Hillside ST21 . . . . .133 E6
Hillside Gdns DE11 . . . . . .186 F2
Hillside Gr DY10 . . . . .280 C3
Hillside Lichfield WS14. . . .231 D6
  Market Drayton TF9. . . . . .112 E4
  Newcastle-u-L ST5. . . . . . .283 A2
Hillside Prim Sch ST2. . . . .43 C2
Hillside Rd
  Cheddleton ST13 . . . . .45 C4
  Stoke-on-T ST2 . . . . .43 C3
  Sutton Coldfield B74 . . . . .258 A4
  Werrington ST9 . . . . .59 B4
Hillside DE13 . . . . .45 C4
Hill Side DY3 . . . . .271 C4
Hillside ST21 . . . . .133 E6
Hillside Gdns DE11 . . . . . .186 F2
Hillside Wlk ST14 . . . . .71 D8
Hillside WS15. . . . . .269 E8
Hill St Burntwood WS7 . . .228 E5
  Burton u T DE15. . . . . .185 E8
  Cannock WS12. . . . . .210 C3
  Cheslyn Hay WS6. . . . . . . .226 C2

Hill St continued
  Dudley,Upper Gornal DY3 . 271 D5
  Essington WV11. . . . . .241 F3
  Newcastle-u-L ST5. . . . . . .283 B4
  Norton Canes WS11 . . . . . .227 F6
  Rugeley WS15. . . . . .196 E8
  Stoke-on-T ST4 . . . . .72 B7
Stourbridge,Amblecote
  DY8 . . . . .279 F8
  Stourbridge DY8 . . . . .279 F4
  Swadlincote DE11 . . . . . . .186 F6
Hillswood Ave ST13. . . . . . .30 D6
Hillswood Cl ST9 . . . . .43 E7
Hillswood Dr ST9 . . . . .43 E7
Hill Terr ST7 . . . . .39 D2
Hilltop Ave ST5. . . . . .56 E2
Hill Top B79 . . . . .250 B8
Hill Top ST6 . . . . .28 B2
Hill Top ST16. . . . . .28 B1
Hilltop Com Prim Sch
  ST7 . . . . .40 D7
Hill Top Cres ST3 . . . . .90 A5
Hill Top Ct DY3 . . . . .271 E3
Hilltop WS15. . . . . .196 F7
Hill Top View WS15. . . . . .198 C3
Hill Top Wlk WS9 . . . . . . .245 C1
Hill View ST4 . . . . .245 B2
Hillview Cres ST5. . . . . .85 C5
Hill View Leek ST13. . . . . . .31 A5
  Stoke-on-T ST2 . . . . .43 B2
Hill Village Rd
  Sutton Coldfield B75 . . . . .258 A4
  Werrington ST9 . . . . .59 C4
Hillway Cl WS13 . . . . .178 D1
Hill West Prim Sch B74 . .257 F4
Hillwood Cl DY6 . . . . .275 C4
Hillwood Common Rd
  B75. . . . . .258 B6
Hillwood Rd
  Madeley Heath CW3 . . . . . .69 A8
  Sutton Coldfield B75 . . . . .258 C5
Hill Wood WS3 . . . . .243 F2
Hilmore Way B77 . . . . . . .261 E8
Hilsea Cl WV8 . . . . .239 F1
Hilsea Cres ST14. . . . . . . .143 F7
Hilston Ave WV4 . . . . .265 C4
Hilton Cl ST3 . . . . .243 A2
Hilton Cross Bsns Pk
  WV10. . . . . .241 B5
Hilton Cross WV10 . . . . . .241 B5
Hilton Dr ST21. . . . . .117 F3
Hilton La
  Featherstone WV10,
  WV11 . . . . .241 E8
  Great Wyrley,Warstone
  WV11 . . . . .242 B7
  Great Wyrley WS6 . . . . . . .227 A2
Hilton Main Ind Est
  WV11 . . . . .241 C5
Hilton Park Service Area
  WV11. . . . . .242 B7
Hilton Rd Burntwood WS7 .228 C8
  Egginton DE65. . . . . .148 B7
  Featherstone WV10. . . . . .241 E7
  Stoke-on-T ST4 . . . . .71 E7
  Willenhall WV12 . . . . .242 C1
  Wolverhampton WV4. . . . .266 F4
Hilton Trad Est WV4 . . . . .266 F4
Himley Ave DY1. . . . . .271 F2
Himley Cres WV4 . . . . . . .266 B5
Himley Ct DY3 . . . . .271 E3
Himley Gdns DY3 . . . . . . .270 F4
Himley La DY3 . . . . .269 F2
Himley Rd DY1,DY3 . . . . . .271 C2
Hinbrook Rd DY1 . . . . . . .271 E1
Hinchco PI ST4 . . . . .42 E4
Hinckes Rd WV6. . . . . .255 B5
Hinckley Gr ST4 . . . . .88 B5
Hinde St ST4 . . . . .282 B1
Hines St ST4 . . . . .72 E5
Hingley Croft WS9 . . . . . .256 F3
Hinksford Gdns DY3 . . . . .269 E1
Hinksford La DY3,DY6 . . . .269 F1
Hinsford Cl DY6 . . . . .275 D4
Hinsley Mill La TF9 . . . . . . .97 E2
Hinstock Cl WV4. . . . . . . .266 A4
Hinton Cl Stafford ST17 . . .174 F6
  Stoke-on-T ST3 . . . . .88 F8
Hints Ct B78. . . . . .248 D2
Hints La Hopwas B78. . . . .249 B5
  Weeford B78 . . . . .248 F4
Hints Rd Hopwas B78 . . . .249 B6
  Mile Oak B78. . . . . .249 C2
Hislop Rd WS15. . . . . .196 E6
Histons Dr WV8. . . . . .238 F2
Histons Hill WV8. . . . . . . .238 F2
Hitchman St ST4 . . . . .72 E6
Hixon Airfield Est (Ind Est)
  ST18. . . . . .139 B1
Hixon Ind Est ST18. . . . . .158 B7
HM Young Offender Inst
  (Swinfen Hall) WS14. . . . .231 E1
Hoarstone DY8 . . . . .281 F5
Hobart Cl DE15 . . . . .167 C2
Hobart Ct ST4. . . . . .258 A3
Hobart Rd WS12 . . . . .210 E2
Hobart St ST6 . . . . .57 A7
Hobb La ST14 . . . . .142 A7
Hobble End La WS6. . . . . .243 F1
Hobbs Way WS15. . . . . . . .197 B5
Hobby Cl ST3 . . . . .90 A1
Hobfield La WS15. . . . . . . .161 B5
Hob Hill CE Methodist Prim
  Sch WS15 . . . . .197 B5
Hobnock Rd WV11. . . . . . .242 B5
Hobs Hole La WS9 . . . . . .256 D7
Hobson St ST6. . . . . .57 A8

Hob's Rd WS13 . . . . .214 E1
Hobstone Hill La WS13 . . .212 F1
Hockley Rd
  Tamworth B77 . . . . .261 F5
  Uttoxeter ST14 . . . . .126 B7
Hodge La
  Marchington ST14 . . . . . . .127 A1
  Tamworth B77 . . . . .251 B6
Hodgkins Cl WS8 . . . . .245 A6
Hodgkinson St ST5 . . . . . . .55 F6
Hodnet Rd ST1 . . . . .282 A4
Hodnet Pl WS11 . . . . .210 B2
Hodson Way WS11. . . . . . .210 B2
Hogan Way ST16. . . . . . . .156 C4
Hogarth Pl ST5 . . . . .55 E6
Holbeach Ave ST12 . . . . . . .58 A2
Holbeache La DY6. . . . . . .270 D1
Holbeache Rd DY6 . . . . . .275 C8
Holbeach Way ST16. . . . . .155 B6
Holborn ST5 . . . . .283 B3
Holborn Row ST10 . . . . . . .92 E4
Holborn Sh Ctr The DY3. .271 D7
Holborn The CW3. . . . . . . .16 A2
Holbrook Wlk ST2 . . . . . . .58 C1
Holbury Cl WV9. . . . . .240 A2
Holcroft Rd DY6 . . . . .270 C1
Holdcroft Rd ST2 . . . . .58 C5
Holden Ave ST5 . . . . .56 D3
Holden Ave N ST6 . . . . .57 D8
Holden Ave S ST6 . . . . .57 D8
Holden Lane High Sch
  ST1. . . . . .57 F8
Holden Lane Prim Sch
  ST1. . . . . .57 F7
Holden Rd WV4. . . . . .265 D3
Holder Dr WS11 . . . . .209 B2
Holder St ST1 . . . . .57 B6
Holdiford Rd
  Brocton ST18 . . . . .176 C8
  Tixall ST18. . . . . .157 D1
Holding Cres ST7 . . . . .54 D7
Holdings La CW3 . . . . .67 F4
Holditch Ind Est ST5 . . . . . .56 A4
Holditch Rd ST5 . . . . .55 F5
Holecroft St ST6 . . . . .57 A8
Holehouse La
  Endon ST6,ST9. . . . . .28 D2
  Scholar Green ST7. . . . . . . .25 D8
Holehouse Rd ST2. . . . . . . .58 C6
Holendene Way WV5. . . . .269 E7
Holland Cl WS13 . . . . .215 A1
Holland Ct B79 . . . . .217 D5
Holland Pk DE13 . . . . .183 E2
Hollands Pl WS3 . . . . .243 D1
Holland St 2 ST6 . . . . .41 D3
Hollands The ST8 . . . . .17 C3
Holland's Way ST3 . . . . . .243 D4
Hollies Ave WS11. . . . . . . .209 F1
Hollies Brook CT20. . . . . .171 D7
Hollies Cl Clifton DE6. . . . .167 E8
  Newton Solney DE15 . . . . .167 E8
Hollies Ct WS11 . . . . .209 F1
Hollies Dr ST3 . . . . .90 A4
Hollies Ind Est 7 WV2 . . .266 C8
Hollies La Enville DY7 . . . .276 A8
  Nurton WV6. . . . . .254 A4
  Pattingham WV6 . . . . .253 F5
Hollies Park Rd WS11 . . . .209 F1
Hollies The
  Newcastle-u-L ST5. . . . . . .283 C4
  Wolverhampton WV2. . . . .266 C8
Hollings St ST4 . . . . .284 A5
Hollington Dr ST6 . . . . .42 B8
Hollington La ST14 . . . . . .110 F5
Hollington Rd ST10 . . . . . . .93 B4
Hollins Bsns Ctr 4 ST16 .155 D5
Hollinsclough CE Prim Sch
  SK17. . . . . .4 D2
Hollinsclough Rake SK17 . .4 B2
Hollins Cres ST7 . . . . .25 E1
Hollinscroft Ct ST10 . . . . . .92 E3
Hollins Grange ST7. . . . . . .40 D8
Hollinshead Ave ST5. . . . . .56 B4
Hollinshead Cl ST7 . . . . . . .25 F7
Hollins La ST10 . . . . .61 B4
Hollinwell WS3 . . . . .243 A3
Hollinwood Cl ST7 . . . . . . .40 E8
Hollinwood Rd ST7 . . . . . . .40 E8
Hollis La ST14 . . . . .95 B6
Holloway Dr WV5. . . . . . . .269 D7
Holloway La ST5. . . . . .84 C6
Holloway St DY3 . . . . .271 D4
Holloway St W DY3 . . . . . .271 D4
Holloway B79. . . . . .250 B4
Holloway The
  Seisdon WV5. . . . . .264 A3
  Stourbridge DY8 . . . . .279 F7
  Swindon DY3 . . . . .269 D1
  Wolverhampton WV4. . . . .255 C2
Hollow Cres DE15. . . . . . .167 C4
Hollow La
  Burton u T DE15. . . . . .167 C4
  Cheddleton ST13 . . . . .45 C5
  Colton WS15 . . . . .179 A5
  Draycott in t L DE6 . . . . . .144 D6
  Mayfield DE6. . . . . .66 C1
Hollowood Pl ST6 . . . . .42 E5
Hollowood Wlk ST6 . . . . . .42 E5
Hollows The DE15. . . . . . .166 F1
Hollow The
  Caverswall ST11 . . . . .74 E3
  Mount Pleasant ST7 . . . . . .26 B5
  Roston DE6 . . . . .56 E7
Holly Ave ST13 . . . . .31 A6
Hollybank Ave WV11 . . . . .242 A3
Hollybank Cl WS3 . . . . . . .243 A4

Hollybank Cres ST4. . . . . . .72 A5
Holly Bank ST4 . . . . .87 E7
Holly Bank WS3 . . . . .197 B5
Holly Bush Cl DE12 . . . . . .219 F7
Holly Bush Cotts ST13 . . . .44 F8
Hollybush Cres ST3 . . . . . . .72 E3
Hollybush La WV8 . . . . . . .238 E2
Holly Bush La ST5 . . . . .85 B4
Hollybush La
  Stourbridge DY8 . . . . .279 F7
  Wolverhampton WV4. . . . .265 D4
Holly Bush Rd DE13. . . . . .143 F2
Hollybush Rd ST3. . . . . . . .72 E3
Holly Cl Kinver DY7. . . . . .277 E5
  Market Drayton TF9. . . . . .112 A8
  Wolverhampton WV10. . . .240 B7
Hollycroft Gdns WV6. . . . .255 B6
Holly Ct ST2. . . . . .73 E7
Holly Dr Fradley WS13 . . . .215 D8
  Walton-on-t-H ST17. . . . . .175 F6
  Werrington ST9 . . . . .59 A3
Holly Fields WS15. . . . . . .118 E6
Holly Gn DE15 . . . . .185 F8
Holly Grove La WS7. . . . . .211 E1
Holly Grove Prim Sch
  WS7. . . . . .211 E1
Holly Gr Stone ST15 . . . . .120 B7
  Stourbridge DY8 . . . . .279 F5
  Wolverhampton WV10. . . .265 F7
Holly Hill WS6 . . . . .242 E8
Hollyhill La WS14 . . . . . . .246 E5
Holly Hill Rd
  Cannock Wood WS15. . . . .211 E6
  Shenstone WS14 . . . . .246 F5
Hollyhock Way DE14 . . . . .184 E6
Hollyhurst ST7 . . . . .235 E3
Hollyhurst La ST18. . . . . . .140 F6
Hollyhurst ST17. . . . . .175 D5
Holly La Aldridge WS9 . . . .256 F8
  Bradley ST18 . . . . .173 C1
  Brownhills WS9 . . . . .245 A4
  Great Wyrley WS6 . . . . . . .242 F8
  Harrisehead ST7 . . . . .27 F5
  Huntington WS12 . . . . . . .209 F7
  Ranton ST18 . . . . .153 E1
  Sutton Coldfield B74 . . . . .258 A3
  Uttoxeter ST14 . . . . .125 D1
Holly Mdw ST10 . . . . .109 C3
Holly Mews ST5 . . . . .69 F7
Hollyoak Way WS11 . . . . . .209 F1
Holly Pl ST4. . . . . .72 E4
Holly Rd Barton-u-N DE13 .183 E1
  Newcastle-u-L ST5. . . . . . . .40 E1
  Uttoxeter ST14 . . . . .111 B1
Hollys Rd DE13 . . . . .182 A2
Holly St Burton u T DE15. .185 F8
  Cannock WS12. . . . . .209 F6
Holly Tree Dr ST8 . . . . .16 C2
Holly View WV11 . . . . .242 A3
Hollywall La ST6. . . . . .41 C5
Hollywall Prim Sch ST6 . . .41 C6
Hollywood La ST5 . . . . .54 D1
Holmbridge Gr WS4. . . . . .244 D2
Holm Cl ST4. . . . . .72 B5
Holmcroft Rd WV4 . . . . . .266 F4
Holmcroft Rd ST16 . . . . . .155 C6
Holme Bank DE6. . . . . .81 D7
Holme Farm Ave DE15 . . .185 F8
Holme Mill WV10 . . . . . . .240 D4
Holme Rise ST19 . . . . .193 A1
Holmes Cl ST16. . . . . .155 B2
Holmesfield Wlk ST3 . . . . .284 D3
Holmes The WV10. . . . . . .240 D3
Holmes Way ST16. . . . . . . .42 B8
Holm Oak Dr CW3 . . . . . . .68 C7
Holmroyd Rd ST10 . . . . . . .78 C2
Holmroft Gdns WV9. . . . . .224 C2
Holm View Cl WS14 . . . . .246 F6
Holmewood Rd ST3 . . . . . .58 A6
Holston Cl ST12. . . . . .210 F1
Holsworth St B77 . . . . . . .250 D1
Holt Cres WS11 . . . . .210 B2
Holte Dr B75 . . . . .258 D2
Holt La ST10. . . . . .61 F2
Holt's La DE13 . . . . .146 B6
Holwick B77 . . . . .250 E2
Holy Austin Rock* DY7 . . .277 E3
Holyhead Cres ST3 . . . . . . .74 C4
Holyhead Rd
  Albrighton WV7 . . . . .237 C2
  Codsall WV8 . . . . .238 C1
Holyoake Pl WS15 . . . . . . .178 D3
Holyrood Cl
  Stafford ST18 . . . . .156 C3
  Stoke-on-T ST6 . . . . .120 C6
Holy Rosary RC Prim Sch
  ST5. . . . . .167 A3
Holy Trinity CE Prim Sch
  Brownhills WS8 . . . . .244 E6
  Burton u T DE14. . . . . .166 E4
Holywell Cl ST8. . . . . .27 E6
Holywell Rise WS14 . . . . . .231 D6
Home Farm Cotts SK17 . . . .5 C2
Home Farm Ct
  Castle Gresley DE11 . . . . . .186 D1
  Stoke-on-T ST15. . . . . .157 D6
Home Farm Rd WV6 . . . . .252 C7
Home Farm ST21 . . . . . . .116 D2
Homefield Rd WV8 . . . . . .239 C3
Homelands Park The
  WV10. . . . . .240 C6
Homelodge Ho 7 WS13 . .231 B7
Homer Pl ST16 . . . . .42 B5
Homer Rd B75. . . . . .258 D2
Homestead Cl DY3 . . . . . .271 E5
Homestead Cotts ST18. . . . .53 E4
Homestead Ct WS16. . . . . .155 E7

Hig – Hor 309

Homestead Dr B75. . . . . . .258 C3
Homestead St ST7 . . . . .73 D8
Homestead The ST9. . . . . . .43 C3
Honesty Cl WS8 . . . . .244 D6
Honeybourne Cres WV5 . .269 F5
Honeybourne B77 . . . . . . .250 D2
Honeysuckle Ave
  Blythe Bridge ST11. . . . . . . .90 F6
  Kingswinford DY6 . . . . . . .275 E7
Honeysuckle Cl ST10. . . . . .92 F3
Honeysuckle Dr WV10. . . . .72 A5
Honeysuckle La ST9 . . . . . .29 E2
Honeysuckle Rise ST17 . . .175 F7
Honeysuckle Way WS6 . . .227 B4
Honeytree Cl DY6. . . . . . .275 E7
Honeywall Ho 4 ST4 . . . . .72 A7
Honeywall La
  Madeley Heath CW3 . . . . . .69 B7
  Stanton DE6. . . . . .80 E8
Honeywall ST4 . . . . .283 B4
Honeywood ST5 . . . . .283 B4
Honiton Cl ST17 . . . . .175 D8
Honiton Wlk ST3 . . . . .284 D3
Honor Ave WV4. . . . . .266 C5
Hood La Armitage WS15. . .198 A4
  Longdon WS15. . . . . .197 F2
Hook Dr B74. . . . . .257 F4
Hook La Shenstone WS14 . .246 C2
  Stramshall ST14 . . . . .111 B6
Hook La The WV7. . . . . . . .237 B1
Hoo La DY7 . . . . .273 F4
Hoomill La ST18 . . . . .158 B5
Hoon Ave DE65. . . . . .146 D8
Hoon Rd DE65 . . . . .146 D8
Hoover St ST6 . . . . .41 D3
Hopedale Cl Longton ST4. . .73 B6
  Newcastle-u-L ST5. . . . . . . .71 B3
Hope St Audley ST7 . . . . . . .39 F3
  Hanley ST1 . . . . .282 B3
  Stourbridge DY8 . . . . .279 D3
Hopley Rd DE13 . . . . .165 B5
Hopleys Cl ST21 . . . . .153 F6
Hopmeadow Way DE15. . .167 A1
Hopshort TF9 . . . . .130 B5
Hopstone Gdns ST4 . . . . .265 C9
Hopton Bank ST8 . . . . . . .137 C1
Hopton Cl WV6 . . . . .254 F3
Hopton Ct ST16. . . . . .155 D5
Hoptonhall La ST18 . . . . . .137 D1
Hopton La ST18 . . . . .137 C1
Hopton Mdw WS12. . . . . .210 C1
Hopton St ST16. . . . . .155 F6
Hopton Way ST16. . . . . . . .42 A8
Hopwas Hill B78 . . . . .249 A6
Hopwood La ST14. . . . . . .166 F6
Hopwood Pl ST2. . . . . .58 B3
Hopyard Ct DY3 . . . . .271 B3
Hopyard La DY3 . . . . .271 B3
Horatius Rd ST5 . . . . .55 D6
Hordern Cl WV6. . . . . .255 F5
Hordern Gr WV6. . . . . . . .255 F5
Hordern Rd WV6 . . . . .255 F5
Hordley St ST1 . . . . .282 C3
Hornbeam Cres ST21 . . . .211 A6
Hornbeams The 2 ST14 . .111 A4
Hornbeam B77 . . . . .251 A4
Hornbrook Cl DE13 . . . . . .166 B8
Hornbrook Rd DE13. . . . . .166 B7
Hornby Rd WV4. . . . . .266 C5
Hornby Row ST4. . . . . .72 A7
Horncr Ave WS13 . . . . . . .223 C8
Horninglow Croft DE13. . .166 C6
Horninglow Inf Sch
  DE13 . . . . .166 C6
Horninglow Rd DE14 . . . . .166 D3
Horninglow Road N
  DE13 . . . . .166 C7
Horninglow St DE14 . . . . .166 D3
Horns Croft WS15. . . . . . .196 B3
Hornton Cl B74. . . . . .257 D5
Hornton Rd DE13 . . . . . . .166 B7
Horse Bridge La DY7. . . . .278 D2
Horsebrook Hall La
  ST19 . . . . .206 D1
Horsebrook La ST19 . . . . .223 C8
Horsecroft Cres ST13 . . . . .31 A7
Horsecroft Gr ST13 . . . . . . .31 B7
Horse Fair
  Eccleshall ST21 . . . . .133 E2
  Rugeley WS15. . . . . .196 E8
Horsehills Dr WV3 . . . . . . .255 E2
Horse Rd ST10. . . . . .78 C1
Horseshoe Dr
  Cannock WS12. . . . . .210 F4
  Rugeley WS15. . . . . .178 B2
Horsey La WS15 . . . . .212 C8
Horsham Ave DY8. . . . . . .275 C3
Horsley Gr ST3 . . . . .88 E8
Horsley La
  Eccleshall ST21 . . . . .132 C5
  Shenstone WS14 . . . . .246 D8
Horsley Rd
  Coldmeece ST15 . . . . .118 C8
  Little Aston B74 . . . . .257 B2
Horsley Way ST15 . . . . . . .118 C2
Horton Ave DE13. . . . . . . .166 F7
Horton Cl
  3 Cannock WS11 . . . . . . .209 F4
  Sedgley DY3 . . . . .271 C8
Horton Dr ST3. . . . . .74 A5
Horton Lodge Com Specl Sch
  ST13. . . . . .18 D2
Horton Rd DY7 . . . . .277 F5
Horton St Leek ST13. . . . . .30 F6

Horton St continued
Newcastle-u-L ST4. . . . . .56 D1
Horwood Gdns ST6 . . . . .42 C1
Horwood ST5 . . . . .70 C6
Hose St ST6 . . . . .41 D3
Hoskings Cl ST15 . . . . .120 C7
Hoskins Rd ST6 . . . . .41 E5
Hospital La
Cheslyn Hay WS6. . . . . .226 B2
Market Drayton TF9 . . . . . . .112 A8
Hospital Rd WS7. . . . . .229 B5
Hospital St B79 . . . . .250 B5
Hotel Bldgs WS14 . . . . .230 A2
Hot La LST10 . . . . .109 C1
Hot La Biddulph ST8. . . . . . .17 C2
Burslem ST6 . . . . .57 B8
Hot Lane Ind Est ST6 . . . . .57 B8
Hougher Wall Rd ST7 . . . . .39 D1
Hough Hill ST6 . . . . .43 B8
Houghton St ST1 . . . . .282 B1
Houghwood La ST9 . . . . . . .43 D4
Houldsworth Dr WS14 . . . .231 C6
Houldsworth Dr ST6. . . . . . .42 B7
Housefield Rd ST2 . . . . .73 D8
Houseman Dr ST3 . . . . .73 F4
Houston Ave ST9 . . . . .43 E8
Houting B77. . . . . .261 D5
Houx The DY8 . . . . .279 E8
Hoveringham Dr
Berry Hill ST2 . . . . .57 F1
Bucknall ST2 . . . . .58 A1
Howard Cl Leek ST13 . . . . . .30 C4
Werrington ST9 . . . . .59 B4
Howard Cres
Cannock WS12. . . . . .210 C2
Hanley ST1 . . . . .57 E2
Howard Gr ST5 . . . . .71 A6
Howard Pl Hanley ST1 . . . .282 A1
Newcastle-u-L ST5. . . . . .71 A6
Howard Prim Sch B79 . . . .216 D2
Howard St ST17 . . . . .174 E7
Howard St Longton ST3 . . .284 C2
Wolverhampton WV2 . . . . . .266 D8
Howard Wlk ST3. . . . . .284 C2
Howdle's La WS8 . . . . .228 F2
Howe Gr ST5 . . . . .55 E2
Howell Rd WV2 . . . . .266 E7
Howitt Cres ST14 . . . . .111 B2
Howitt House Sch DE13 . .144 E3
Howland Cl WV9. . . . . .239 F2
Howson St ST1 . . . . .282 C2
Hoylake Cl WS3. . . . . .243 B4
Hoylake Rd WV6 . . . . .254 D5
Hoylake B77. . . . . .251 B4
Hubbal La TF11 . . . . .220 D3
Huddlesford La WS14 . . . .232 D7
Huddlestone Cl WV10 . . . .241 B6
Huddocks View WS3 . . . . . .243 F5
Hudson Cl Cannock WS11. .210 B2
Gnosall ST20 . . . . .171 E8
Hudson Dr WS7 . . . . .229 C6
Hudson Gr WV6. . . . . .254 E5
Hudson Wlk ST3 . . . . .284 C4
Hugh Bourne Pl ST8 . . . . . .27 B2
Hughes Ave
Newcastle-u-L ST5. . . . . . . .283 B4
Wolverhampton WV3 . . . . . .265 F8
Hughes St ST6 . . . . .57 A7
Hugh Porter Way WV6 . . .255 F6
Hughson Gr ST6 . . . . .42 E3
Hugo Meynell CE Prim Sch
TF9. .99 E4
Hugo St ST13 . . . . .30 E5
Hugo Way TF9 . . . . .99 E4
Hulland Cl ST5 . . . . .55 B1
Hullock's Pool Rd ST7 . . . .39 E5
Hulme Cl ST5 . . . . .55 B1
Hulme La ST3,ST9 . . . . .59 A2
Hulme Rd ST3 . . . . .73 F6
Hulme St ST4 . . . . .71 E8
Hulse St ST4 . . . . .73 B6
Hulton Cl CW12. . . . . .6 B1
Hulton Rd ST2 . . . . .58 B6
Hulton St ST1 . . . . .282 C4
Humber Dr ST8 . . . . .27 E8
Humbert Rd ST1 . . . . .56 F7
Humber Way ST5 . . . . .71 B3
Humphrey St DY3 . . . . .271 D3
Humphries Ho WS8 . . . . . . .244 F7
Hungerford La CW2. . . . . . .68 F5
Hungerford Pl CW2 . . . . . . .38 D5
Hungerford Rd DY8 . . . . . .279 E2
Hungry La WS14 . . . . .247 F5
Hunsford Cl ST3 . . . . .284 C4
Hunslet Rd WS7 . . . . .229 B8
Huntbach St ST1 . . . . .282 B3
Hunter Ave WS7 . . . . .229 B7
Hunter Cl WS14 . . . . .231 D6
Hunter Rd WS11 . . . . .226 E8
Hunters Cl ST18 . . . . .27 C8
Hunters Ct ST18 . . . . .137 F4
Hunters Dr ST4. . . . . .71 F6
Hunter's Point TF9 . . . . . . .99 D5
Hunter's Ride ST17 . . . . . .174 E4
Hunter's Ride DY7 . . . . . . .275 B2
Hunter St DE14 . . . . .166 D6
Hunters Way
Stoke-on-T ST4 . . . . .72 A6
Talke ST7. . . . . .40 D8
Huntilee Rd ST6 . . . . .41 F3
Huntington Cl B78 . . . . . . .249 F2
Huntington Pl ST1 . . . . .57 F6
Huntington Rd DE15. . . . . .185 D7
Huntington Ind Est
WS12. . . . . .209 B6

Huntington Prim Sch
WS12 . . . . .209 C8
Huntington Terrace Rd
WS11 . . . . .209 F4
Huntley Ave ST4 . . . . .72 A6
Huntley Cl ST10 . . . . .76 D1
Huntley La ST10 . . . . .92 C8
Huntley Rd ST13. . . . . .44 E7
Huntsbank Dr ST5 . . . . .40 D1
Hunts La DE12 . . . . .219 E2
Huntsman Dr DY7. . . . . . . .277 F5
Huntsmans Gate WS7 . . . .229 B8
Huntsman's Hill WS15 . . . .197 C2
Huntsmans Rise WS12 . . . .209 C8
Huntsmans Wlk
Kinver DY7. . . . . .277 F6
Rugeley WS15 . . . . .178 D1
Hunts Mill Dr DY5 . . . . . . .271 C1
Hunt St ST6 . . . . .41 E3
Hurlingham Rd ST16. . . . . .155 C7
Huron Cl WS11 . . . . .210 B2
Huron Gr ST4. . . . . .88 A8
Hurricane Cl ST16 . . . . . . .136 B1
Hurricane Gr ST6 . . . . .41 C4
Hurstbourne Cl WS15 . . . .178 C2
Hurst Cl ST7 . . . . .40 D6
Hurst Dr DE13 . . . . .147 E1
Hurstmead Dr ST17 . . . . . .175 C5
Hurstons La ST10 . . . . .78 E1
Hurstons The ST10 . . . . .78 E1
Hurst Rd Biddulph ST8 . . . . .17 A3
Sedgley WV14 . . . . .266 F1
Hurst St ST3 . . . . .58 A3
Hurst Yd ST10 . . . . .76 D3
Husphins La WV8 . . . . .238 B5
Hussey Cl ST19 . . . . .207 F7
Hussey Rd
Brownhills WS8 . . . . .244 E8
Norton Canes WS11 . . . . . . .227 F5
Hutchinson Cl WS15 . . . . . .178 B2
Hutchinson Meml CE Fst Sch
ST10. . . . . .109 B8
Hutchinson Wlk 6 ST3 . . . .73 A3
Hut Hill La WS6. . . . . .227 A4
Hutton Dr CW12 . . . . .6 A2
Hutton Way ST2 . . . . .58 D2
Huxley Cl WV9 . . . . .240 A3
Huxley Pl ST3 . . . . .73 D4
Hyacinth Ct ST15 . . . . .283 C4
Hyacinth Rd ST4. . . . . .56 E1
Hyde Cl DY7 . . . . .174 A7
Hyde La ST17 . . . . .178 A7
Hyde La DY7 . . . . .278 A6
Hyde Lea Bank ST18 . . . . . .174 C5
Hyde Mill Croft ST19 . . . . .223 C5
Hyde Mill La ST19 . . . . .223 C5
Hylton Cl DE14 . . . . .185 A7
Hyndley Cl ST2 . . . . .58 A3
Hyperion Dr WV4 . . . . .266 A3
Hyperion Rd DY7 . . . . .279 C7
Hyssop Cl WS11 . . . . .210 B3
Hyssop Pl ST6 . . . . .42 D2

I

Ian Rd ST7 . . . . .26 D3
Ibsen Rd ST3 . . . . .74 A4
Ibstock Cl ST13 . . . . .166 B6
Icknield Cl B74 . . . . .257 A1
Idonia Rd WV6. . . . . .254 F5
Ikins Dr ST7 . . . . .39 F2
Ilam CE Prim Sch DE6 . . . . .50 E2
Ilam Cl ST5 . . . . .55 B1
Ilam Ctry Pk* DE6. . . . . . . .50 E2
Ilam-Moor La DE6 . . . . .50 E6
Ilford Side ST3 . . . . .88 E8
Ilkley Rd ST3 . . . . .54 F3
Illshaw WV9 . . . . .240 A3
Image Bsns Pk WS11. . . . . .210 B3
Imandra Cl ST4. . . . . .88 A8
Imex Bsns Pk DE14 . . . . . .166 B3
I-Mex Bsns Pk ST4 . . . . . . .72 F5
Imex Bsns Pk WV2 . . . . . . .266 C7
Imex Ho WV2 . . . . .266 B7
Imex Tech Pk ST4. . . . . .88 D7
Imogen Cl ST4 . . . . .73 B6
Imperial Cl ST1. . . . . .282 C1
Impstones ST20. . . . . .171 C5
Ingatestone Dr DY8 . . . . . .275 C3
Inge Dr DE13 . . . . .201 A2
Ingelow Cl ST3 . . . . .73 A2
Ingelow Rd ST3 . . . . .73 A2
Ingestre Cl Cannock WS11 .210 B1
Newport TF10 . . . . .168 D2
Walsall WS3 . . . . .242 F3
Ingestre Ho WV6. . . . . .255 E5
Ingestre Rd Stafford ST17 .285 A1
Wolverhampton WV10 . . . . .240 C1
Ingestre Sq ST3 . . . . .88 F8
Inglebrough Pl ST17 . . . . . .43 D1
Ingleby Cl DE11. . . . . .186 F3
Ingleby Rd ST3 . . . . .88 E8
Inglefield Ave ST6 . . . . .42 B1
Inglemere Dr ST17. . . . . . . .175 C6
Ingleside WS15 . . . . .178 C1
Ingleton Gr ST3 . . . . .90 A7
Inglewood Ave WV3 . . . . . .265 F8
Inglewood Cl WV6. . . . . . . .275 D5
Inglewood Dr ST5 . . . . .56 D6
Inglewood Gr
Aldridge B74. . . . . .256 F2
Newcastle-u-L ST5. . . . . .56 C6
Inglewood ST17 . . . . .285 A1
Inglis St ST4. . . . . .72 C8
Ingram Pit La B77 . . . . . . .251 A5
Ingram Pl WS3 . . . . .243 D1
Ingram Rd WS3 . . . . .243 D1
Inhedge St DY3. . . . . .271 E5

Intake La ST20. . . . . .190 A8
Intake Rd ST6 . . . . .42 E4
Intakes La ST10. . . . . .108 E4
Inworth WV9 . . . . .240 B3
Iona Pl ST3 . . . . .72 F3
Irene Ave
Newcastle-u-L ST5. . . . . .56 D2
Stoke-on-T ST6 . . . . .41 F4
Ireton Rd WV10 . . . . .240 E3
Iris Cl Meir ST11 . . . . .74 C5
Tamworth B79 . . . . .250 C6
Irnham Rd B74 . . . . .258 B1
Ironbridge Dr ST5 . . . . .55 F1
Ironmarket ST5 . . . . .283 B3
Ironstone La WS13. . . . . . . .215 E5
Ironstone Rd
Burntwood WS7 . . . . .228 E8
Prospect Village WS12 . . . . .211 D4
Ironwalls La DE13. . . . . . . .146 C5
Irvine Rd ST9. . . . . .59 C4
Irving Cl Dudley DY3 . . . . . .271 A4
Lichfield WS13 . . . . .213 E2
Irwell B77 . . . . .261 D5
Isabel Cl ST17 . . . . .174 B8
Isherwood Pl ST3 . . . . .284 D4
Island Gn ST17 . . . . .175 D6
Island The Mile Oak B78. . .249 C1
Oakamoor ST10. . . . . .78 A6
Upper Tean ST10 . . . . .92 D4
Islay Wlk 3 ST3 . . . . .73 A3
Islington Cl TF10. . . . . .168 F4
Islington Cres CV9. . . . . . . .262 C1
Ismere Way DY10 . . . . .280 A1
Itchen Gr WV6. . . . . .254 E4
Ivanhoe Rd WS14. . . . . .231 B6
Ivatt B77 . . . . .250 F2
Iverley La DY10,DY8 . . . . . .281 C5
Ivetsey Bank Rd ST19 . . . .221 F8
Ivetsey Cl ST19 . . . . .205 B5
Ivetsey Rd
Ivetsey Bank ST19. . . . . . . .204 F3
Wheaton Aston ST19. . . . . . .205 A5
Ivy Cl Acton Trussell ST17 .175 B1
Blythe Bridge ST11. . . . . . . .90 F6
Cannock WS11 . . . . .226 D8
Uttoxeter ST14 . . . . .126 A8
Ivy Cottage Mobile Home Pk
ST18. . . . . .137 D2
Ivy Cotts ST13 . . . . .20 A6
Ivycourt ST17 . . . . .175 B1
Ivy Croft WV9. . . . . .239 F3
Ivy Ct Acton Trussell ST17 .175 B1
Eggington DE65 . . . . .148 A5
Hixon ST18 . . . . .158 B8
Ivy Gdns WS11 . . . . .228 A5
Ivy Gr Brownhills WS8 . . . . .245 A4
Burton u T DE13. . . . . .166 C7
Trentham ST4 . . . . .87 F8
Ivy Ho WS9 . . . . .245 A4
Ivyhouse Dr ST12 . . . . .88 E4
Ivy House La ST19 . . . . .206 E1
Ivy House Rd Biddulph ST8 . .16 C2
Hanley ST1 . . . . .57 E3
Ivyhouse Wlk 6 B77. . . . . .261 F6
Ivy La WS15 . . . . .211 F5
Ivy Lodge Cl ST5 . . . . .185 E7
Izaac Walton Way CW3. . . . .68 E5
Izaak Walton ST16 . . . . . . .155 D6
Izaak Walton's Cottage &
Mus* ST15 . . . . .135 B7
Izaak Walton ST16 . . . . . . .155 D5

J

Jack Ashley Ct ST4 . . . . . . .72 D6
Jackdaw Cl DY3 . . . . .266 C2
Jackfield Inf Sch ST6 . . . . . .42 B1
Jackfield St ST6 . . . . .42 B1
Jack Haye La Bagnall ST9 . . .58 E8
Stoke-on-T ST2 . . . . .43 D1
Jack La CW2 . . . . .37 D6
Jacklin Cl DE14 . . . . .185 A6
Jackman Cl WS13. . . . . .215 D6
Jackman Rd WS13 . . . . .215 D6
Jacks La ST14 . . . . .127 E2
Jackson Ave DE13 . . . . .166 F7
Jackson Cl
Featherstone WV10 . . . . . . .241 A6
Norton Canes WS11 . . . . . . .227 E4
Jackson Rd WS13 . . . . .214 B3
Jackson St 2 ST6 . . . . .57 A8
Jacobean Ct DE15 . . . . .167 C4
Jacobs Croft ST16 . . . . .155 C7
Jacob's Hall La WS6 . . . . . .227 B1
Jacqueline St ST6 . . . . .41 D4
Jade Ct ST3 . . . . .73 D4
Jade Gr WS11 . . . . .210 C2
Jaguar B77 . . . . .250 E2
Jamage Rd
Newcastle-u-L ST7. . . . . .40 D4
Talke Pits ST7 . . . . .40 D5
James Beattie Ho WV6. . . .255 C4
James Brindley ST17 . . . . . .174 D6
James Brindley High Sch
ST6 .41 F6
James Brindley Way
DE13 . . . . .166 F8
James Cres ST9 . . . . .59 C4
James Ct DE14 . . . . .166 C1
James Greenway WS13 . . . .214 A2
James Hutchens Ct ST7 . . .228 F5
James St Burton u T DE14. .166 C2
Cannock WS11. . . . . .209 F5
Cheadle ST10 . . . . .78 A4
Leek ST13 . . . . .30 D6
Newcastle-u-L ST5. . . . . .56 D6
Stoke-on-T ST4 . . . . .72 A5

James St continued
Uttoxeter ST14 . . . . .126 B8
James Warner Cl WS15 . . .178 D1
James Way ST8. . . . . .27 A6
Janet Pl ST1 . . . . .57 E4
Janson St ST4. . . . . .71 F1
Jardine La ST14 . . . . .95 D4
Jasmine Cl
Blythe Bridge ST11. . . . . . . .90 F6
Burton u T DE15. . . . . .186 A7
Wolverhampton WV9 . . . . . .240 A3
Jasmine Cres ST7 . . . . .26 D2
Jasmine Gr WV8 . . . . .239 B3
Jasmine Rd
Great Bridgeford ST18 . . . . .135 C2
Tamworth B77 . . . . .251 A4
Jasmin Way ST7 . . . . .27 A2
Jason Cl B77 . . . . .250 D5
Jason St ST5 . . . . .283 A4
Jasper Cl Barlaston ST12 . . .88 F4
Newcastle-u-L ST5. . . . . .56 B7
Jasper St ST1 . . . . .282 C4
Java Cres ST4 . . . . .88 B7
Jaycean Ave ST6. . . . . .41 E4
Jay Rd DY6 . . . . .275 D8
Jean Cl ST6 . . . . .42 A2
Jedburgh Ave WV6. . . . . . .254 E4
Jeddo St WV2 . . . . .266 C8
Jeffcock Rd WV3 . . . . .266 A7
Jefferson St ST6. . . . . .41 D4
Jeffery Cl WS13 . . . . .213 E2
Jeffrey Ave WV4. . . . . .266 F5
Jeffs Ave WV2 . . . . .266 D8
Jenkinson Cl ST5 . . . . .70 F8
Jenkins St 2 ST6. . . . . .56 F8
Jenkinstown Rd WS12 . . . .211 A6
Jenks Ave DY7 . . . . .277 F5
Jenks Rd WV5 . . . . .269 F5
Jennings Way DE14 . . . . . .166 A3
Jenny Walkers La WV6. . . .254 D1
Jensen B77 . . . . .250 E2
Jephson Rd DE14 . . . . .185 B7
Jerbourg Cl ST5 . . . . .70 E4
Jeremy Cl ST4. . . . . .71 F6
Jeremy Rd WV4 . . . . .266 C5
Jerningham St ST16 . . . . . .285 A3
Jerome Ct B74 . . . . .256 F1
Jerome Dr WS11 . . . . .228 A5
Jerome Rd WS11 . . . . .228 A5
Jerome Way WS7 . . . . .229 C7
Jerry's La WS14 . . . . .248 B8
Jersey Cl Congleton CW12. . .6 A1
Newcastle-u-L ST5. . . . . .70 E4
Jersey Cres ST3 . . . . .73 D1
Jervis Cres B74. . . . . .257 D3
Jervis La ST15 . . . . .104 C3
Jervison St ST3 . . . . .73 D6
Jervis Pk B74 . . . . .257 C4
Jervis Rd Stone ST15 . . . . . .120 B7
Tamworth B77 . . . . .261 F5
Jervis St ST1 . . . . .282 C4
Jesmond Cl WS12. . . . . .211 A6
Jesmond Gr ST3 . . . . .88 E8
Jessie Rd WS9. . . . . .245 B1
Jessop Dr B77 . . . . .250 E5
Jew's La DY3 . . . . .271 E4
Jinny Cl DE65 . . . . .146 C8
Joan Eaton's Cross ST20 . .189 E7
Joanhurst Cres ST21 . . . . .282 A1
Joan St WV2 . . . . .266 E6
Jockey Field DY3 . . . . .271 E6
Jodrell View ST17. . . . . .41 B8
Joe Jones Ct DY3. . . . . . . .266 D1
Joeys La WV8 . . . . .239 C3
John Amery Dr ST17. . . . . .174 D6
John Ball Cl WS15 . . . . . . .178 D3
John Bamford Prim Sch
WS15 . . . . .178 C1
**John Baskeyfield CE Prim
Sch**
Burslem ST6 . . . . .41 E1
Burslem ST6 . . . . .56 F8
John Bright St ST1 . . . . . . .282 C4
John Donne St ST16 . . . . . .155 D6
Johndory B77 . . . . .261 D6
John Offley Rd CW3. . . . . . .68 E5
John of Rolleston Prim Sch
DE13 . . . . .147 C3
John O' Gaunt's Rd ST5. . .283 A3
John Pershall Ct ST21 . . . .133 D7
John Rhodes Way ST6 . . . . .41 D5
Johns Ave WS15 . . . . .198 C4
Johnsgate ST19 . . . . .223 D7
Johns La WS6 . . . . .227 B3
Johnson Ave ST5 . . . . .56 A4
Johnson Cl Congleton CW12 . .6 B1
Lichfield WS13 . . . . .214 C1
Ranton ST18 . . . . .153 C5
Rugeley WS15 . . . . .178 D2
Johnson Cres ST10 . . . . .61 D2
Johnson Gr ST15 . . . . .120 D7
Johnson Pl ST6. . . . . .42 B6
Johnson Rd
Burntwood WS7 . . . . .228 F8
Cannock WS11. . . . . .209 D4
Uttoxeter ST14 . . . . .111 B1
Johnson St
Newcastle-u-L ST5. . . . . .55 D7
Wolverhampton,Cinder Hill
WV14 . . . . .266 F1
Wolverhampton WV2 . . . . . .266 D7
Wood End DY9 . . . . .262 C1
John St Biddulph ST8 . . . . . .27 C8
Cannock,Chadsmoor
WS11 . . . . .210 A4
Cannock,Wimbleberry
WS12 . . . . .210 F3

John St continued
Hanley ST1 . . . . .282 B2
Leek ST13 . . . . .30 E5
Newcastle-u-L,Knutton St5 . .55 E2
Newcastle-u-L ST5. . . . . . . .283 D3
Johnstone Ave ST9 . . . . .59 C4
John St Stafford ST16 . . . . .156 A4
Stourbridge DY8 . . . . .275 F1
Swadlincote DE11 . . . . .186 E6
Tamworth B77 . . . . .250 E4
Uttoxeter ST14 . . . . .126 B8
John Taylor High Sch
DE13 . . . . .183 E2
John Till Cl WS15 . . . . .178 E1
John Wheeldon Prim Sch
ST16. . . . . .155 E5
Joiner's Square Ind Est
ST1. . . . . .282 C1
Joiner's Square Prim Sch
ST1. . . . . .282 C1
Jolley St ST6 . . . . .42 C1
Jolliffe St 3 ST13 . . . . .30 E5
Jolpool La ST18 . . . . .121 C4
Jolt La ST18 . . . . .172 E5
Jolyon Cl ST4 . . . . .73 B6
Jonathan Rd ST4 . . . . .88 C5
Jones Cl Fradley WS13 . . . . .215 E8
Stafford ST17 . . . . .174 D7
Jones La Burntwood WS7 . .229 F7
Great Wyrley WS6 . . . . .227 B1
Rugeley WS15 . . . . .178 D3
Jonkel Ave B77 . . . . .262 A5
Jordan Ave DE13 . . . . .147 F2
Jordan Cl
3 Lichfield WS13 . . . . .231 A8
Fradley WS13 . . . . .215 D6
Sutton Coldfield B75 . . . . . .258 B1
Jordan Croft WS13. . . . . . . .215 D7
Jordan Rd B75 . . . . .258 C2
Jordan Way Aldridge WS9 .245 B1
Stone ST15 . . . . .120 B7
Jordon St ST1 . . . . .282 A1
Joseph Dewsbury Cl
WS7 . . . . .228 F8
Joseph Dix Dr WS15 . . . . . .178 D2
Joseph St 6 ST6 . . . . .56 E8
Josiah Wedgwood St ST1 . .57 A3
Joules Dr ST15 . . . . .104 E3
Jowett B77 . . . . .250 E2
Joyce Ave ST6 . . . . .42 B2
Joyce's La ST17 . . . . .194 A8
Jubilee Ave ST1 . . . . .57 A3
Jubilee Cl Biddulph ST8 . . . .27 D8
Great Wyrley WS6 . . . . .226 F2
Jubilee Ct Stafford ST16 . . .155 F5
Uttoxeter ST14 . . . . .126 B7
Jubilee Dr ST10 . . . . .62 D3
Jubilee Gr Of TF11. . . . . . . .203 F5
Jubilee Rd
Newcastle-u-L ST5. . . . . .56 D3
Trentham ST4 . . . . .87 F8
Jubilee Rise DE15 . . . . .167 C3
Jubilee Sq DE6 . . . . .81 D7
Jubilee St WS15 . . . . .178 D1
Jubilee Terr 12 ST13 . . . . . .30 D6
Judes Wlk ST3 . . . . .213 F2
Judgefield La ST16 . . . . .28 F8
Judith Gr ST4 . . . . .72 C5
Jug Bank Ashley TF9. . . . . .100 B4
Burslem ST6 . . . . .57 B6
Julian Cl WS6 . . . . .227 A3
Junction Rd Leek ST13 . . . . .30 E4
Stourbridge,Amblecote
DY8 . . . . .275 E1
Junction The 1 DY8 . . . . . .279 E8
June Cres B77 . . . . .250 E5
June Rd ST4. . . . . .73 B6
Juniper Cl
Burntwood WS7 . . . . .229 A6
Cannock WS12. . . . . .211 A6
Meir ST3 . . . . .90 A6
Newcastle-u-L ST5. . . . . .40 E1
Juniper Row TF10 . . . . .168 F1
Juniper B77 . . . . .250 E6
Jupiter Bsns Pk ST18 . . . . .139 B2
Jupiter Cl ST3 . . . . .42 C1
Jupiter Way 10 ST17 . . . . .175 A8
Justin Cl ST5 . . . . .55 C5

K

Kamienna Cl ST17 . . . . .174 F8
Kara Pl ST4 . . . . .88 B8
Kaydor Cl ST19 . . . . .59 B4
Kay Dr DE11. . . . . .186 F5
Kayne Cl DY6 . . . . .275 C7
Kean Cl WS13 . . . . .213 E2
Kearsley Way ST3 . . . . .88 E8
Keary St ST4 . . . . .72 B6
Keates St 7 ST6 . . . . .56 F8
Keating Gdns B75. . . . . . . .258 A4
Keats Ave Cannock WS11 . .209 E5
Stafford ST17 . . . . .174 C8
Keats Cl Dudley DY3 . . . . . .215 A5
Sutton Coldfield B74 . . . . . .257 F6
Tamworth B79 . . . . .249 E8
Keats Gdns ST7 . . . . .41 A8
Keats Rd WV10 . . . . .241 A6
Keble Cl Burntwood WS7 . .229 C2
Burton u T DE15. . . . . .167 C2
Cannock WS11. . . . . .226 E8
Keble Way ST3 . . . . .73 A2
Keble Wlk B79 . . . . .250 A6
Kedleston Cl
Stretton DE13 . . . . .147 C1
Walsall WS3 . . . . .243 A3

Kedleston Rd ST6 42 A2
Keele Rd Keele ST5 70 A7
Madeley Heath CW3 69 B8
Newcastle-u-L ST5 70 D8
Keele Science Pk ST5 70 B7
Keele Service Area ST5 69 F4
Keele St ST6 41 D4
Keele Univ ST5 70 B7
Keeling Dr WS11 209 B1
Keeling Rd ST10 76 E3
Keelings Dr ST4 71 F4
Keelings Rd ST1 57 E5
Keeling St ST5 56 C6
Keene Cl ST6 42 E3
Keepers Cl WS9 244 F3
Keeper's Cl WS7 229 A6
Keepers Cl
Kingswinford DY6 275 B8
Lichfield WS14 231 E7
Keepers La Codsall WV8 239 A1
Wolverhampton WV6,WV8 255 A7
Keepers Rd B74 257 C5
Keep The ST17 174 C8
Keir Pl DY8 279 E8
Keld Ave ST17 174 A8
Keldy Cl WV6 255 F5
Kelham Rd ST4 73 A6
Kelly Ave WS15 196 F6
Kelly Gn ST6 42 B6
Kelmore Cl ST3 284 B4
Kelsall St ST6 42 B1
Kelsall Way ST7 39 D1
Kelso Gdns WV6 254 D4
Kelvedon Way WS15 178 C1
Kelvestone Ho WS11 209 D1
Kelvin Ave ST1 57 D7
Kelvin Dr WS11 210 A3
Kelvin St ST5 56 D4
Kemball Ave ST4 72 D4
Kemball Specl Sch ST4 72 F5
Kemberton Cl WV3 255 C1
Kemberton Rd WV3 255 C1
Kemnay Ave ST6 42 B8
Kempson Rd ST19 192 F1
Kempthorne Ave WV10 240 E1
Kempthorne Gdns WS3 243 A2
Kempthorne Rd ST1 282 C1
Kempton Cl WS12 211 A6
Kempton Dr
Great Wyrley WS6 226 F2
Tamworth B77 261 D4
Kempton Gr ST10 76 E5
Kempton Rd DE15 167 A3
Kempton Way DY8 279 E3
Kendal Cl Stafford ST17 174 B7
Wolverhampton WV6 255 F6
Kendal Ct Brownhills WS9 244 F4
Cannock WS11 226 B8
Kendal Gr ST2 58 D2
Kendall Rise DY6 275 F5
Kendal Pl ST5 71 B6
Kendal Rise WV6 255 F6
Kendal Way CW2 37 C1
Kenderdine Cl ST17 193 F8
Kendlewood Rd DY10 280 B1
Kendrick St ST3 73 D3
Kenelyn Cres ST3 72 E4
Kenilworth Ave DE13 166 D7
Kenilworth Cl
Market Drayton TF9 97 E2
Penkridge ST19 208 A8
Stourbridge DY8 275 D2
Kenilworth Cres WV4 266 F4
Kenilworth Ct 2 WS11 209 E1
Kenilworth Dr WS11 209 D4
Kenilworth Gr
2 Longton ST3 73 F1
Newcastle-u-L ST5 56 E3
Kenilworth Rd
Lichfield WS14 231 B6
Perton WV6 254 F4
Tamworth B77 250 E4
Kenilworth Wlk ST10 76 B2
Kenley Ave ST9 43 F8
Kenmore Ave WS12 209 F7
Kennedy Cl B77 250 C1
Kennedy Cres DY3 271 D4
Kennedy Ct DY8 279 F5
Kennedy Pl ST21 133 D6
Kennedy Rd ST4 88 B6
Kennedy Way ST16 155 B8
Kennedy Wlk ST9 59 B4
Kennermont Rd ST2 58 C6
Kennet Cl Brownhills WS8 228 C2
Newcastle-u-L ST5 71 B3
Kennet B77 250 D1
Kennington Oval ST4 88 D8
Kenrick Cl CW3 67 C1
Kenrose Mill DY7 278 B3
Kensington Cl ST15 120 C5
Kensington Ct
Stoke-on-T,Trent Vale ST4 71 E3
Stoke-on-T,Tunstall ST6 41 E4
Kensington Dr
Stafford ST18 156 C3
Sutton Coldfield B74 257 F5
Tamworth B79 250 B7
Kensington Gdns
Cannock WS11 209 C2
Stourbridge DY8 275 C1
Kensington Pl WS12 227 C8
Kensington Rd
Burton u T DE15 167 A3
Stoke-on-T ST4 72 A4
Kensworth Cl ST5 71 A3
Kent Ave B78 249 F2
Kent Cl WS9 245 B1
Kent Dr ST9 43 E6
Kent Gr Newcastle-u-L ST5 55 E8
Stone ST15 104 F2
Kent Ho ST7 40 D6
Kentish Cl ST17 174 A8
Kentmere Cl Longton ST4 73 B5
Penkridge ST19 193 A1
Stafford ST17 174 A8
Kentmere Pl ST5 71 B6
Kenton Ave WV6 255 F4
Kent Pl Cannock WS12 210 F1
Stoke-on-T ST4 72 E6
Kent Rd Burton u T DE15 185 E6
Stourbridge DY8 279 D7
Wolverhampton WV2 266 E7
Kents Row ST12 88 E2
Kent St DY3 271 E5
Kent Way ST17 175 B8
Kentwell B79 249 D7
Kenworthy Rd ST16 155 E6
Kenworthy St ST6 41 E4
Kepler B79 249 E7
Kerria Ctr B77 251 A4
Kerria Rd B77 251 B4
Kerridge Cl WV9 240 A2
Kerry La ST21 133 C6
Kersbrook Cl ST4 88 C6
Kervis Gr ST3 90 B6
Kesterton Rd B74 257 E5
Kesteven Wlk ST2 58 B3
Kestrel Ave ST3 90 C7
Kestrel Cl Biddulph ST8 27 B6
Newport TF10 169 A5
Stafford ST17 156 C1
Uttoxeter ST14 126 B6
Whittington WS14 232 F5
Kestrel Ct WS7 229 F8
Kestrel Dr
Loggerheads TF9 99 D4
Sutton Coldfield B74 257 F5
Kestrel Gr WS12 210 C1
Kestrel La ST10 76 E3
Kestrel Rise WV6 255 F7
Kestrel B77 262 A6
Kestrel Way
Burton u T DE15 167 D3
Cheslyn Hay WS6 226 C2
Keswick Dr DY6 275 D6
Keswick Gr Aldridge B74 256 F2
Stafford ST17 174 A8
Keswick Pl ST5 71 B6
Ketley Rd
Kingswinford DY6 275 F6
Kingswinford DY6 275 F7
Kettering Dr Berry Hill ST2 57 F1
Bucknall ST2 58 A1
Kettlebrook Rd B77 250 C3
Kettlesbank Rd DY3 271 B2
Ketton Cl ST6 42 B8
Kewstoke Cl WV12 242 B1
Kewstoke Rd WV12 242 C1
Keyes Dr DY6 270 D1
Keynsham Wlk ST6 42 D2
Keys Cl WS12 210 C3
Keys Park Rd WS12 210 E3
Keystone La WS15 196 F8
Keystone Mews 3 WS15 196 F8
Keystone Rd WS15 196 F8
Keyworth Wlk ST2 58 A2
Kibblestone Rd ST15 105 C5
Kibworth Gr ST1 282 B4
Kidbrooke Pl ST3 88 E8
Kiddemore Green Rd
Brewood ST19 223 A6
Kiddemore Green ST19 222 D6
Kidderminster Rd
Iverley DY8 281 C7
Kingswinford DY6 275 B7
Kidderminster Rd S DY9 281 F3
Kidsgrove Bank ST7 41 B8
Kidsgrove Rd ST6 41 C8
Kidsgrove Sta ST7 25 F1
Kidson Eventide Homes
WV6 255 F5
Kielder Cl WS12 210 E2
Kilburn Dr DY6 270 E1
Kilburn Pl ST2 57 F2
Kilburn Way DE11 186 F5
Kilbye Cl B77 261 F5
Kildare St ST3 284 C2
Kilmorie Rd WS11 209 C2
Kiln Bank Cres TF9 112 C8
Kiln Bank Rd TF9 112 C8
Kiln Croft ST10 92 D4
Kilndown Cl ST1 57 A2
Kiln La ST13 30 C6
Kiln Way B78 251 F1
Kilsby Gr ST2 43 B2
Kimberlee Ave DY10 280 B4
Kimberley Cl B74 257 A2
Kimberley Dr
Burton u T DE15 167 C3
Uttoxeter ST14 110 F1
Kimberley Grange ST5 283 B4
Kimberley Rd Hanley ST1 57 A3
Newcastle-u-L ST5 283 B4
Kimberley St Longton ST3 284 B2
Wolverhampton WV3 266 A8
Kimberley B77 261 F7
Kimberley Way
Rugeley WS15 196 F5
Stafford ST17 174 A8
Kinder Pl ST5 55 B1
Kineton Rise DY3 266 C2
Kinfare Dr WV6 255 B4
Kinfare Rise DY3 271 E4
King Charles Cl ST3 90 A7
Kingcross St ST3 284 C3
Kingcup Rd ST17 174 E5
King Edward Pl DE14 166 B3
King Edward's Row 5
WV2 266 C8
King Edward St ST10 76 E4
King Edward VI High Sch
ST17 155 C1
King Edward VI Sch
WS14 231 C6
Kingfisher Cl
Brownhills WS8 244 E7
Madeley CW3 68 F7
Newport TF10 168 F5
Sedgley DY3 266 C2
Kingfisher Cres
Cheadle ST10 76 F3
Fulford ST11 106 E8
Kingfisher Ct WS7 229 F8
Kingfisher Dr
Cannock WS12 210 C5
Colwich ST18 177 E8
Stourbridge DY8 279 C4
Kingfisher Gr ST6 42 C3
Kingfisher B77 262 A6
Kingfisher Way ST14 126 C6
Kingfisher Wlk ST19 207 F8
King George St ST1 282 C4
Kingham Cl DY3 271 C2
King Ho ST7 40 D5
Kings Ave Cannock WS12 210 C4
Market Drayton TF9 112 A8
King's Ave
Newcastle-u-L ST5 56 C5
Stone ST15 105 A1
Kingsbridge Ave ST5 71 B5
Kings Bridge WV9 224 A3
King's Bromley La WS15 198 D6
Kings Bromley Rd DE13 200 F2
Kingsbury Cl DE15 167 A4
Kingsbury Gr ST1 57 F6
King's CE Sch The WV6 255 B5
Kingsclere Gr ST1 57 E7
Kingsclere Wlk WV4 265 C6
Kings Croft WS12 210 E4
Kingscroft ST18 158 D1
King's Croft ST4 56 D1
Kings Ct Stourbridge DY8 279 E5
Sutton Coldfield B75 258 B3
Kingsdale Cl ST3 90 A7
Kingsdale Croft DE13 166 D8
Kingsdene Ave DY6 275 C4
Kingsdown Cl CW2 37 C1
Kingsdown Mews ST5 71 C4
Kingsdown Rd WS7 211 E1
Kings Dr ST18 156 D8
Kingsfield Cres ST8 27 D8
Kingsfield Fst Sch ST8 27 C8
Kingsfield Oval ST4 56 D1
Kingsfield Rd Biddulph ST8 27 D8
Stoke-on-T ST4 56 D1
Kingsford Country Park*
DY11 277 D1
Kingsford La DY7,DY11 277 D2
Kingsford Pl ST3 90 A8
Kingshayes Rd WS9 245 B1
Kings Head Pk TF10 168 E4
King's Hill Rd WS14 231 C6
Kingside Gr ST4 88 C5
Kingsland Ave ST4 71 F4
Kingsland CE Prim Sch
ST2 58 C4
Kingsland Cl ST15 120 C7
Kingsland Ct ST15 120 C7
Kingsland Rd ST15 120 C7
King's La B79 236 C5
Kingsleigh Croft B75 258 B2
Kingsley Ave
Cannock WS12 210 C7
Wolverhampton WV6 255 B4
Kingsley Cl Stafford ST17 174 E8
Talke Pits ST7 40 D6
Tamworth B79 250 A6
Kingsley & Froghall Sta*
ST10 62 B3
Kingsley Gdns WV8 238 E3
Kingsley Gr DY3 271 A5
Kingsley Rd
Burton u T DE14 166 D6
Congleton CW12 6 A3
Kingswinford DY6 275 C5
Overmoor ST9 60 B3
Stafford ST17 174 E8
Talke Pits ST7 40 D6
Werrington ST9 59 F3
Kingsley St ST3 74 A1
Kingsley View ST13 45 D5
Kingsley Wood Rd WS15 195 D7
Kingslow Ave WV4 265 D6
Kingsmead DE13 166 E8
Kingsmead Hospl ST16 285 C3
Kingsmead Rd ST3 89 F7
Kingsmead Tech Coll
WS12 210 C4
Kings Mews WS14 231 B5
Kingsnorth Pl ST3 90 B6
Kings Pl ST4 56 D2
Kings Rd Sedgley DY3 271 E8
Shareshill WV10 225 A6
Stoke-on-T ST4 72 A1
King St Audley ST7 39 D1
Biddulph ST8 27 C8
Blymhill TF10,TF11 189 A1
Brownhills WS9 244 F2
Burntwood WS7 228 F5
Burton u T DE14 166 C1
Kings Terr ST4 56 D1
King St Kidsgrove ST7 26 A2
Leek ST13 30 E5
Longton ST3,ST4 284 B4
King St *continued*
Newcastle-u-L,Chesterton
ST5 55 E7
Newcastle-u-L,Cross Heath
ST5 56 A3
Newcastle-u-L ST5 283 C3
Kingston Arc WS11 209 E1
Kingston Ave
Stafford ST16 156 B4
Stoke-on-T ST1 57 E7
Kingston Cl B79 250 C7
Kingston Ctr WV6 255 F5
Kingston Dr ST15 120 B6
Kingston Hill Ct ST16 156 C3
Kingston Pl Biddulph ST8 16 E2
Stoke-on-T ST6 42 E3
Kingston Rd DE15 167 C2
Kingston Row ST16 156 A3
Kingston Way DY6 275 C7
King St Rugeley WS15 196 F8
Stourbridge DY8 279 E6
Talke Pits ST7 40 D5
Tamworth B79 250 B5
Yoxall DE13 182 A3
Kingsway Burton u T DE14 185 B8
Cannock WS11 210 A4
Kingsway E ST5 71 B6
Kingsway Essington WV11 242 A4
Stafford ST16 155 C2
Stoke-on-T ST4 72 B7
Stourbridge DY8 279 E8
Kingsway W ST5 71 A6
Kingswear Ave WV6 254 F3
Kingswell Rd ST4 56 D1
Kingswinford Pl ST4 57 D7
Kingswinford Sch The
DY6 275 D7
Kings Wlk DE13 199 B6
Kingswood Ave
Cannock WS11 226 C7
Chorlton CW2 37 B3
Kingswood Bsns Pk WV7 237 F1
Kingswood Colliery Cvn Site
WS6 227 A4
Kingswood Ctr WV7 237 F2
Kingswood Dr
Great Wyrley WS6 227 A4
Norton Canes WS11 227 F5
Kingswood Gdns WV4 265 F6
Kingswood ST7 26 B1
Kingswood Mobile Homes
WV7 237 E1
Kingswood Rd
Albrighton WV7 237 C4
Albrighton WV7 237 D3
Kingswinford DY6 275 C4
King William St
Stoke-on-T ST6 41 E3
Stourbridge DY8 279 F8
Kinlet Cl WV3 265 A8
Kinloch Dr DY1 271 F3
Kinnersley Ave ST7 40 F8
Kinnersley St 1 ST7 26 A2
Kinross Ave WS12 209 F7
Kinsall Gn B77 262 C6
Kinsey St ST5 55 B2
Kinver Cl DE6 81 C8
Kinver Cres WS9 245 C1
Kinver Dr WV4 265 C5
Kinver Edge* DY7 277 E2
Kinver La DY11 280 B7
Kinver Mt DY7 278 A3
Kinver Rd
Burton u T DE15 167 A4
Kinver DY7 277 E8
Kinver St Stoke-on-T ST6 42 C1
Stourbridge DY8 275 E1
Kiplass La ST18 121 C4
Kipling Ave WS7 212 A1
Kipling Rd Dudley DY3 271 A5
Wolverhampton WV10 240 D2
Kipling Rise B79 249 F8
Kipling Way ST2 58 D1
Kirby Dr DY1 271 E3
Kirby St ST6 57 A6
Kirkbride Cl ST3 73 D4
Kirkham St ST4 72 A6
Kirkland La ST4 72 A6
Kirkland Way B78 260 B8
Kirkside Gr WS8 244 F7
Kirkstall Ave ST17 174 B7
Kirkstall Cl WS3 242 F2
Kirkstall Cres WS3 242 F2
Kirkstall Pl ST5 71 B5
Kirkstone Cres WV5 269 F6
Kirk St ST6 42 C1
Kirkup Wlk ST3 284 A3
Kirkwall Gr ST2 43 B2
Kirstead Gdns WV6 255 B3
Kirtley B77 250 E2
Kirton Gr WV6 255 C4
Kitchen La WV11 241 F1
Kite Gr Kidsgrove ST7 26 D3
Meir ST3 90 A6
Kitling Greaves La DE13 166 A7
Kitlings La ST17 175 F7
Kittoe Rd B74 258 A3
Kitwood Ave B78 262 F6
Knarsdale Cl 2 ST3 73 D5
Knaves Castle Ave WS8 228 F2
Knebworth Ct CW12 16 B8
Knenhall La
Moddershall ST3,ST15 89 F1
Stone ST15 89 F1
Knenhall ST15 105 E7
Knight Ave ST16 156 A4
Knight La ST10 78 E1
Knightley Cl ST20 171 D6
Knightley CW3 68 F5
Knightley Rd ST20 171 D8
Knightley Way ST20 171 D7
Knighton Cl B74 257 F3
Knighton Dr B74 257 F3
Knighton Rd
Cannock WS12 210 E3
Sutton Coldfield B74 257 D5
Knight Rd WS7 211 E1
Knights Ave WV6 255 E6
Knightsbridge Cl B74 257 F4
Knightsbridge Way
12 Stoke-on-T ST6 41 D3
Burton u T DE13 166 D7
Knights Cl ST19 207 F7
Knights Cres WV6 255 E7
Knights Croft ST5 69 F7
Knights Ct
Norton Canes WS11 228 A4
Stretton DE13 147 E2
Knightsfield Rd DE13 144 E2
Knights Hill WS9 256 B3
Knight St ST6 41 D4
Kniveden La ST13 31 B5
Knoll Cl WS7 229 A5
Knoll Croft WS9 245 C1
Knoll The DY6 275 E5
Knotty La CW12 17 A8
Knowlbank Rd ST7 53 F7
Knowle La WS14 231 B3
Knowle Rd Biddulph ST8 27 C7
Stafford ST17 175 D7
Knowles Hill DE13 147 B3
Knowle St ST4 72 A8
Knowle Wood View ST3 72 F3
Knowsley La Kidsgrove ST7 26 A4
Lawton-gate ST7 25 F4
Knowsley Rd ST9 44 D3
Knox Rd WV2 266 D6
Knox's Grave La WS14,
B78 248 D7
Knoyle Ct 1 DY8 279 F6
Knutsford Rd ST7 25 A6
Knutton La ST5 55 F2
Knutton Rd ST5 56 C5
Knutton St Mary's Prim Sch
ST5 55 E2
Knype Cl ST5 56 A7
Knypersley Fst Sch ST8 27 B6
Knypersley Rd ST6 42 E4
Knype Way Biddulph ST8 27 B6
Newcastle-u-L ST5 56 A7
Kohima Dr DY8 279 E5
Kurtus B77 261 D6
Kyffin Rd ST2 58 B6
Kyle Cl WV10 240 B1
Kyle Rd DE65 147 D8
Kynaston Cres WV8 239 B2
Kynnersley Croft ST14 111 B1

L

Laburnam Cl ST7 40 E7
Laburnham Ct WS14 231 C5
Laburnham Rd DY6 275 E6
Laburnum Ave
Cannock WS11 226 E7
Tamworth B79 250 B8
Laburnum Cl
Blythe Bridge ST11 91 A6
Cannock WS11 226 E7
Great Bridgeford ST18 135 B2
Kinver DY7 277 F5
Market Drayton TF9 97 D2
Stourbridge DY8 279 E7
Walsall WS3 244 A2
Laburnum Gr
Burntwood WS7 228 F6
Stoke-on-T ST3 72 E3
Laburnum Ho WS4 244 D1
Laburnum Pl
1 Stoke-on-T ST3 89 F8
Newcastle-u-L ST5 40 D1
Laburnum Rd
Brownhills WS9 245 A3
Burton u T DE15 185 F6
Swadlincote DE11 186 F6
Wolverhampton WV4 266 F3
Laburnum St DY8 279 E7
Laches Cl WV10 224 D5
Laches La WV10 224 E2
Ladbrook Gr DY3 271 B3
Ladderedge Ctry Pk*
ST13 30 B4
Ladderedge ST13 30 C2
Ladford Covert Ind Pk
ST18 134 E1
Ladfordfields Ind Est
ST18 134 D1
Ladfordfields Ind Pk
ST18 153 D8
Ladford Trad Pk ST18 134 E1
Ladies Wlk DY3 271 D8
Lad La ST5 283 B3
Ladle End La DE12 184 D1
Ladybank Gr ST3 88 E8
Lady Bank B79 250 B4
Ladydale Cl ST13 30 F4
Ladyfields Way DE11 186 F6
Ladygates CW3 53 B6
Lady Grey's Wlk DY8 279 D5
Lady Hill Terr WS15 196 B7
Lady Meadow Cl
Denstone ST14 95 E5

Lady Meadow Cl continued
  Tamworth B78........250 A3
Ladymoor La ST6.........28 B3
Ladysmith Rd ST11......57 A3
Ladysmith St ST3......284 B2
Ladywell Cl Stretton DE13 147 E1
  Wombourne WV5......270 A8
Ladywell Rd ST6.........41 D3
Lagonda Cl ST8..........27 B6
Lagonda B77...........250 E3
Lagrange B79.........249 B8
Lair The B78............262 F8
Lakeland Dr B77.......262 B7
Lakenheath B79.......250 C7
Lake Rd ST13...........18 E1
Lakesedge ST15......119 B5
Lakeside Betley CW3.....53 A6
  Bosley SK11...............7 D8
Lakeside Cl [1] Hanley ST1..56 F2
  Whitmore ST5...........80 C6
Lakeside Dr WS11......228 B6
Lakeside B74..........257 B5
Lakeside Pk B78......249 F1
Lakeside Prim Sch B77 .256 D2
Lakeside View WS15 .198 B4
Lake St DY3...........271 D3
Lakewood Dr ST12......88 E4
Lakewood Gr ST1........57 A3
Lally Pl ST8............27 B2
Lamb Cres WS15......269 F6
Lambert Cl DY6.......275 D8
Lambert Dr WS7......229 A8
Lambert Rd ST14......110 F1
Lambert's La CW12.....15 F3
Lambert St ST6.........41 E3
Lamb La ST15.........119 F7
Lambourn Cl WS13....243 C2
Lambourne Cl
  [4] Lichfield WS14....231 E8
  Great Wyrley WS6....226 F3
Lambourne Dr ST1......43 C1
Lambourne Way WS11..228 A5
Lambourn Pl ST3........88 E8
Lamb Shutt Flats TF9..97 D1
Lamb St Hanley ST1...282 B3
  Kidsgrove ST7..........26 A2
Lamerton Gr ST3........73 F2
Lammascote Rd ST16..285 C3
Lammas Rd DY8.......275 C3
Lamorna Cl WV3.......265 B8
Lamotte Cl ST4..........73 B5
Lamprey B77..........261 D6
Lanark Cl DY6........275 F5
Lanark Wlks ST5........70 F7
Lancaster Ave
  [2] Packmoor ST7.......26 F1
  Brownhills WS8.......244 E7
  Cheslyn Hay WS6.....226 C1
Lancaster Bldg ST5...283 B2
Lancaster Cres ST4.....71 D8
Lancaster Dr
  Stoke-on-T ST6........42 F4
  Tutbury DE13........146 B5
Lancaster Gdns WV4..265 E5
Lancaster Ho
  [5] Stourbridge DY8...279 F8
  Cannock WS12........210 D1
Lancaster Pl WS3......243 C2
Lancaster Rd
  Fradley WS13........215 C5
  Newcastle-u-L ST5...283 D2
  Stafford ST17.........175 A8
Lance Dr WS7..........211 F1
Lancelot Dr DE13.....147 E2
Lanchester Cl Biddulph ST8 27 B6
  Tamworth B79.......249 E7
Lancia Cl ST8............27 B5
Lancing Ave ST17.....175 B8
Lander Cl ST15.........120 D7
Lander Pl ST6...........42 B6
Landon St ST3.........284 C3
Landor Cres WS15.....196 E7
Landor Way ST17.......42 A3
Landport Rd WV2.....266 F8
Landrake Gr ST6........41 F7
Landsberg B79........249 F6
Landseer Pl ST5.........55 E6
Landstone Rd [5] WS15.242 E8
Landywood Ent Pk WS6.242 F8
Landywood Gn WS6...226 C2
Landywood La WS6....226 C2
Landywood Prim Sch
  WS6.................242 F8
Landywood Sta WS6..226 F2
Lane End SK17..........23 D7
Lane Farm Gr ST1......57 E7
Lane Green Ave WV8..239 C1
Lane Green Dr WV8...239 B3
Lane Green Fst Sch WV8 239 B4
Lane Green Rd WV8...239 C2
Lane Green Sh Par WV8.239 B3
Lane Head SK17.........13 B7
Lanehead Rd ST1.......56 F3
Lanehead Wlk WS11..178 C2
Lanes Cl
  King's Bromley DE13..199 C6
  Wombourne WV5....269 E5
Lane The ST18........174 C3
Langdale Cl WS8......244 E6
Langdale Cres ST11....57 D7
Langdale Dr [1] ST4..251 A6
Langdale Dr WS11....226 C7

Langdale Gn WS11....226 C7
Langdale Jun & Inf Schs
  ST5....................71 B5
Langdale Rd ST5.......71 B5
Langer Cl DE14......185 B6
Langford Rd Bucknall ST2 .58 C3
  Newcastle-u-L ST5....71 A4
Langford St ST13.......30 D5
Langham Rd B74......256 F1
Langham St ST2.........42 A1
Langholm Gr WS12...210 E2
Langland Dr Longton ST3..73 A2
  Sedgley DY3..........271 C8
Langley Cl
  Brownhills WS9......245 A3
  Newcastle-u-L ST5....40 D2
Langley Gdns WV3...265 D2
Langley Rd WV3,WV4..265 B7
Langley St ST4..........56 D1
Langot La ST21.......115 D4
Langstone Rd DY1....271 F1
Langton Cres ST14.....232 E6
Langton Ct
  [5] Lichfield WS13...214 A1
  Werrington ST9........59 A4
Langtree Cl WS12....210 D1
Lanrick Gdns WS15...178 E2
Lansbury Cl ST17.....174 E8
Lansbury Dr WS11....209 E4
Lansbury Gr ST3........74 B3
Lansbury Rd WS15....196 E6
Lansdell Ave ST5.......56 B6
Lansdowne Ave WV8 .238 F2
Lansdowne Cl Leek ST13..30 C5
  Stone ST15...........119 F5
Lansdowne Cres
  Tamworth B77.......261 D8
  Werrington ST9........59 A4
Lansdowne Inf Sch
  DE14.................166 D5
Lansdowne Rd
  Burton u T DE14.....184 F7
  Stoke-on-T ST3........56 E1
Lansdowne St ST3......73 B1
Lansdowne Terr DE14..166 D5
Lansdowne Way
  Rugeley WS15........178 C2
  Stafford ST17........175 D6
Lant Cl DE13...........199 D6
Lanthorn Cl WS13....231 A7
Lapley Ave ST16.......155 A7
Lapley Dr DE13.......166 E8
Lapley Hall Mews ST19 .206 A6
Lapley La ST19........206 C4
Lapley St ST19........205 D7
Lapper Ave WS4.......266 F2
Lapwing Cl
  [2] Packmoor ST7.......26 F1
  Brownhills WS8.......244 E7
Lapwing Rd ST7........26 D3
Lapwing B77..........262 A6
Lapworth Way TF10..169 A3
Lara Cl ST16...........155 B3
Larch Cl Kidsgrove ST7..41 A8
  Kinver DY7..........278 C3
  Lichfield WS14.......231 C7
Larch Ct [3] ST6........57 A7
Larches The TF10.....168 E2
Larchfields ST15......120 B6
Larch Gr Sedgley DY3 ..271 F7
Larch Ho DY8.........279 C6
Larchmere Dr WV11..242 B3
Larchmount Cl ST4.....88 B7
Larch Pl ST5............55 E8
Larch Rd
  Kingswinford DY6...275 E7
  Rugeley WS15........196 F6
  Swadlincote DE11...186 F6
Larchwood Dr WS11..210 A4
Larchwood Keele ST5...70 A6
  Stafford ST17........175 C5
Larcombe Dr WV4....266 D5
Lark Ave ST7...........26 D3
Lark Ho DY8..........279 C6
Lark Hall Com Inf Sch
  B79..................250 A8
Larkhill La TF9........100 A4
Larkhill Rd DY8......279 C4
Larkholme Cl WS15..178 A1
Larkin Ave ST3.........73 D4
Larkin Cl Stafford ST17..174 C7
  Wolverhampton WV10..241 A1
Lark Rise ST14.........126 B6
Larksfield Rd ST6.......42 D1
Larksmeadow Vale WS15 .175 D6
Larks Mill WS3........243 E4
Larkspur Ave WS7....229 A5
Larkspur Dr WV10...241 B7
Larkspur Gr ST5......283 C4
Larkspur B77..........261 D4
Larkspur Way WS8...244 D6
Larkstone La ST13,DE6 ..34 F1
Larkswood Dr
  Sedgley DY3..........271 D7
  Wolverhampton WV4..265 C3
Lascelles Cl ST5.........41 D2
Lask Edge Rd ST9,ST13..28 F7
Laski Cres ST4..........74 B2
Latebrook Cl ST6.......41 C7
Latham Gr DE11.......167 C2
Latham St ST6.........162 B2
Latherford Cl WV10..224 E5
Latherford La WV10..225 B4
Lathkill Dale DE11...186 F2
Latimer Way ST2........58 C2

Lauder Cl DY3........266 C1
Lauderdale St ST4....244 E6
Lauderdale Gdns WV10..240 E3
Lauder Gr ST18.......158 C8
Lauder Pl N ST2........73 E8
Lauder Pl S ST1........73 E8
Launceston Cl DY7...250 D2
Laureates Wlk B74...258 A1
Laurel Bank B79......250 B6
Laurel Cl WS14.......231 D8
Laurel Cres ST9........59 A3
Laurel Dr Burntwood WS7 229 C7
  Cannock WS12........210 E4
  Harrisehead ST7......26 E3
  Newport TF10........168 F3
Laurel Gr Burton u T DE15 .185 E5
  Stafford ST17........174 F7
  Stoke-on-T ST3.........72 D2
  Wolverhampton WV4..265 E6
Laurel Rd DY1.........271 F4
Laurels The WS15....196 F7
Laurence Gr WV6....255 E7
Lauren Cl ST4...........72 E6
Lauriston Cl DY1.....271 F3
Lavender Ave WS11....90 F5
Lavender Cl
  Burton u T DE14.....185 A8
  Great Bridgeford ST18 .135 C2
  Meir ST3...............74 C5
  Wolverhampton WV9..239 F3
Lavender La DY8......279 D3
Lavender Lodge ST17..127 E7
Lavender Rd B77......250 F4
Laverock Gr CW3.......68 E6
Lawford Ave WS14...231 E7
Lawford Cotts ST17..174 F4
Lawley Cl WS4........244 B1
Lawley St ST3...........73 D3
Lawn Ave DY8........279 E4
Lawn Farm Cres ST21...24 E6
Lawn La Cheswardine TF9.113 F1
  Coven Heath WV9....240 A7
Lawnhoaks Cl WS8...228 D2
Lawn Rd Stafford ST17..285 A1
  Wolverhampton WV2..266 F6
Lawnsfield Wlk ST16..136 C1
Lawns The
  Market Drayton TF9...97 D1
  Rolleston on D DE13 ..147 A4
  Uttoxeter ST14.......111 A2
Lawn St DY8..........279 E4
Lawnswood Ave
  Burntwood WS7......228 F5
  Stourbridge DY8.....279 C3
  Wolverhampton,Parkfield
  WV4...............266 C4
  Wolverhampton,Tettenhall
  WV6...............255 E8
Lawnswood Dr [2] WS12 .210 D1
Lawnswood Dr
  Brownhills WS9......245 A3
  Stourbridge DY7.....275 A2
Lawnswood Rd
  Dudley DY3..........271 D5
  Stourbridge DY8.....275 D3
Lawnswood Rise WV6.255 F8
Lawnswood DY7.......275 A2
Lawn The ST17........174 C5
Lawrence Ct B79......250 A6
Lawrence Dr ST15....103 B4
Lawrence St Hanley ST1 .282 A1
  Stafford ST17........285 B1
Lawrence Way WS13..230 F5
Lawson Cl WS9........245 A3
Lawson Terr
  Newcastle-u-L,Knutton
  ST5...................55 E2
  Newcastle-u-L,Porthill ST5 .56 C6
Lawton Ave ST7.........25 D3
Lawton Coppice ST7....25 E4
Lawton Cres ST8........27 D8
Lawton Est ST17........25 A5
Lawton Hall ST7........25 C4
Lawton St Biddulph ST8 ..27 D8
  Kidsgrove ST7..........26 C4
  Stoke-on-T ST6........42 A2
Laxey Rd ST5...........56 A3
Laxton Gr ST4..........88 C4
Lazar La ST17.........176 B6
Lazy Hill Rd WS9.....245 C1
Lazy Hill WS9.........245 D2
Lea Castle Dr DY10....280 C3
Lea Castle Hospl DY10..280 C3
Leacliffe Way WS9...256 F3
Lea Cl ST5...............85 D5
Leacote Dr WV6......255 C4
Lea Cres ST17.........174 D7
Leacroft Ave WV10...240 F1
Leacroft Cl WS9......245 B1
Leacroft La WS11......179 A7
Leacroft La WS11.....226 F5
Leacroft Rd
  Kingswinford DY6...275 E8
  Meir ST3..............90 A8
  Penkridge ST19.......193 A1
Leadbeater Ave ST4....71 F5
Leadendale La ST3......89 F3
Leadendale Mews ST3..89 F8
Leafdown Cl WS12...210 D3
Leafenden Ave WS7..229 A6
Leaford Way DY6.....275 F6
Leaford Wlk ST2........57 F2
Leafy Glade B74......257 A3
Leafy Rise DY3........271 D4
Lea Gdns WV3........266 B8
Lea Gn ST16..........155 C8
Lea Hall Dr WS7......211 D1

Lea Hall Ent Pk WS15 ..197 B6
Lea Hall La WS15.....197 B5
Leahurst Cl [4] ST17...175 C6
Leaks Alley ST3.......284 B2
Lea La Admaston WS15..159 F2
  Cookley DY10........280 A5
  Great Wyrley WS6...227 A3
Lea Manor Dr WV4...265 E4
Leam Dr WS7..........229 D7
Leamington Cl WS11..226 C7
Leamington Gdns ST5...56 E3
Leamington Rd DE14..184 E7
Leander Cl
  Burntwood WS7......211 E1
  Great Wyrley WS6...226 F1
Leander Rise DE15...186 A8
Lea Pl ST3...............74 B2
Lea Rd Hixon ST18...139 C1
  Stone ST15..........119 F6
  Wolverhampton WV3..266 B8
Lear Rd WV5..........270 B8
Leasowe Ave WS15..198 C5
Leaside Rd ST4.........75 E6
Leason Rd ST3..........74 B2
Leason St ST4...........72 B7
Leasowe Rd WS15....197 B5
Leasowes Dr Perton WV6 254 D4
  Wolverhampton WV4..265 E6
Leasowes Jun & Inf Schs
  ST17.................175 D8
Leasowe The WS13...214 A1
Lea Vale Rd DY8......279 E3
Leawood Rd ST4.......71 F3
Lebanon Gr WS7......228 F8
Ledbury Cl WS9......245 C1
Ledbury Cres ST5......57 F5
Ledstone Way ST3.....73 E4
Leech Ave ST5..........55 F6
Leech St ST5..........283 C1
Lee Ct WS9............244 F3
Leedham Ave B77.....250 D5
Leedhams Croft DE12..202 D8
Leeds St ST4............72 F5
Lee Gr ST5..............71 B4
Leekbrook Ind Est ST13..45 E8
Leekbrook Way ST13....30 F1
Leek Coll of F Ed & Sch of
  Art ST13..............30 F6
Leek Fst Sch ST13......31 A5
Leek High Sch ST13....31 A6
Leek La ST9.............28 B8
Leek Morlands Hospl
  ST13.................31 A5
Leek New Rd ST1,ST2,ST6 .42 F1
Leek Old Rd ST9........29 E1
Leek Rd Brown Edge ST6 ..43 C7
  Bucknall ST2...........58 A6
  Cheadle ST10........280 A5
  Cheddleton,Cheddleton Heath
  ST13.................45 D7
  Cheddleton ST9,ST10...60 C3
  Congleton CW12........16 A8
  Endon ST9.............43 E6
  Hanley ST1............57 E2
  Longnor SK17.........13 B6
  Longsdon ST12.........43 B1
  Stoke-on-T ST6.........42 F4
  Warslow SK17..........23 A2
  Werrington ST9.........59 F3
  Wetley Rocks ST9......60 A6
  Wetton DE6............34 D3
Leek Road Ind Est SK17..23 A2
Lees La WS15..........197 B5
Leese La
  Acton Trussell ST17..175 B1
  Moddershall ST15....105 F6
Leese St ST4..........108 E2
Lees La ST10..........108 E2
Leet Ct WS15.........198 B4
Lee Wlk WS11.........210 B4
Legge La ST18........139 D1
Legge St
  Newcastle-u-L ST5...283 C2
  Wolverhampton WV2..266 E6
Legion Cl WS11.......228 A6
Legs La WV10.........240 F3
Leicester Cl ST5........71 C5
Leicester Ct ST14....110 F1
Leicester Pl ST2........58 C2
Leicester St DE14....185 C8
Leigh Ave WS7........229 B7
Leigh Bank ST10.....108 F8
Leigh Cl ST17.........174 F5
Leigh La Bramshall ST14..125 B8
  Church Leigh ST10...108 D5
  Lower Team ST10......92 F1
Leigh Rd
  Leigh Rd Congleton CW12 ..6 B7
  Newport TF10........168 E2
Leighs Cl WS4........244 C1
Leighs Rd WS4.......244 C1
Leigh St ST6............42 B2
Leighswood [1] ST7..175 C7
Leighswood Ave WS9..256 B7
Leighswood Cl WS11..227 F5
Leighswood Gr WS9..256 B6
Leighswood Gr WS9..256 A7
Leighswood Ind Est
  WS9..................256 A8

Leighswood Rd WS9 ..256 A6
Leighswood Sch WS9 ..256 B8
Leighton Cl Dudley DY1 .271 C2
  Stoke-on-T ST9.........43 C4
  Uttoxeter ST14.......126 C6
Leighton Rd
  Uttoxeter ST14.......126 C6
  Wolverhampton WV4..265 F6
Leisure La SK17.........24 E5
Leisure Wlk [7] ST7 ..261 F6
Lema Way ST16........156 C3
Le More B74...........258 A2
Lennox Gdns WV3...266 A8
Lennox Ind Est ST3 ..284 C3
Lenpark Ind Est ST3 ..284 C3
Lenthall Ave CW12.....15 F8
Leofric Cl DE13......199 C6
Leomansley Cl WS13..230 F7
Leomansley Ct WS13..230 F7
Leomansley Rd WS13 ..230 F7
Leomansley View WS13..230 E7
Leonard Ave
  Kidderminster DY10 ..280 A1
  Stoke-on-T ST2........43 B7
Leonard Dr ST6..........43 B7
Leonard Rd DY8......279 C5
Leonard St Leek ST13....30 F5
  Stoke-on-T ST6.........42 B1
Leonora St ST6..........56 F7
Leopold St ST4..........72 E7
Lerridge La ST20.....131 E6
Lerryn Cl DY6.........275 F5
Lerwick Cl DY6.......275 F5
Lesley Dr DY6........275 E4
Leslie Rd B74.........257 B2
Lesscroft Cl WV9.....240 A3
Lessways Cl ST5........56 A8
Lessways Wlk [1] ST6 ..56 F7
Lester Gr WS9........256 C2
Letchmere Cl WV6...253 C2
Letchmere La WV6...253 C2
Letheridge Gdns ST17..174 A8
Levedale Cl ST16.....155 A7
Levedale Rd Bradley ST18 191 C8
  Penkridge ST18,ST19 ..192 C3
Levels The WS15......196 F5
Leven Dr WV11.......242 B1
Lever St WV2..........266 D4
Leveson Ave WS6.....226 E2
Leveson Rd Trentham ST4 .71 F1
  Wolverhampton WV11..241 F1
Leveson St ST3.........284 C2
Levett Rd Tamworth B77..251 B5
  Whittington WS14....232 C1
Levetts Fields WS14....231 C7
Levetts Hollow WS12..210 D3
Levetts Sq [4] WS13 ..231 B7
Levington Cl WV6....254 F5
Levita Rd ST4...........71 D8
Lewis Cl WS14.........231 E7
Lewis Dr ST6..........166 B7
Lewisham Rd WV10..240 B2
Lewisham St ST6........41 C7
Lewis's La DE13......199 B6
Lewis St ST4.............72 B8
Lewthorn Rise WV4..266 D4
Lexan Pl ST3...........73 E2
Lexington Gn ST17...174 A8
Leybourne Cres WV9..239 F2
Leycett La ST5..........54 C2
Leycett Rd ST5.........54 E4
Leyfield Rd ST4.........84 B6
Leyfields Farm Mews
  DE13.................165 C7
Leyfields WS13.......214 B2
Ley Gdns ST3.........284 A2
Ley Hill Rd B75.......258 C1
Leyland Ave WS3.....255 F1
Leyland Croft WS3...243 F4
Leyland Dr WS15.....178 C2
Leyland Gn ST6.........42 A6
Leyland Rd B77.......250 E3
Ley Rise DY3..........266 C1
Leys Dr ST5..............70 F4
Leys La ST2.............43 C3
Leys The DE11........186 E6
Liberty Ct WS6........226 D3
Liberty La ST6..........42 C3
Liberty Pk ST17.......174 A8
Liberty Rd B77........261 F5
Libra Cl B79..........249 F7
Libra Pl ST6............41 F6
Lichen Cl WS12.......209 C6
Lichfield Bsns Ctr WS13..214 D1
Lichfield Cathedral Sch
  WS13.................231 B8
Lichfield City Sta WS13..231 B7
Lichfield Cl ST5.........55 D2
Lichfield Cres B78....249 B7
Lichfield Ct ST17.....285 C2
Lichfield Dr
  Blymhill Lawn TF11..204 B1
  Great Haywood ST18..158 B1
Lichfield Dr
  Abbots Bromley WS15..161 B3
  Armitage WS15......198 C3
  Brownhills,Shireoak Hill WS8,
  WS9.................245 B5
  Brownhills WS8,WS14..245 A8
  Burntwood WS7......229 D6
  Burton u T DE13,DE14..184 C4
  Cannock WS11.......227 B8
  Hamstall Ridware DE13 ..162 B7
  King's Bromley DE13..199 C6
  Lichfield SW7,SW13..230 B6
  Sandon ST18.........137 D8
  Stafford ST17........285 B2

Lichfield Rd continued
Stafford ST17 . . . . 285 C2
Stone ST15 . . . . 120 C7
Sutton Coldfield B74 . . . . . 258 A3
Talke ST7 . . . . .40 D7
Tamworth B78,B79 . . . . . . 249 E6
Walsall,Highbridge WS3 . . 244 B6
Walsall,New Invention WS3,WS4,
  WS8,WS9 . . . . 242 E1
Walsall,Shelfield WS4 . . . . 244 C1
Walsall,Wallington Heath
  WS3 . . . . 243 D2
Lichfield Road Ind Est
B79 . . . . 249 E6
Lichfield St
Burton u T DE14 . . . . 166 D2
Fazeley B78 . . . . 249 F1
Hanley ST1 . . . . 282 C1
Rugeley WS15 . . . . 196 F8
Stone ST15 . . . . 120 A8
Tamworth B79 . . . . 250 A5
Lichfield Trent Valley Sta
WS13 . . . . 231 F8
Liddiard Ct DY8 . . . . 279 E6
Liddle St ST4 . . . . .72 A6
Lidgate Gr ST3 . . . . .72 F2
Lidgate Wlk ST5 . . . . .71 B2
Lid La Cheadle ST10 . . . . . .76 C3
Roston DE6 . . . . .96 E7
Liffs Rd DE6,SK17 . . . . .36 C7
Lifton Croft DY6 . . . . 275 F5
Light Ash Cl WV9 . . . . 224 C3
Light Ash WV9 . . . . 224 C3
Light Ash La WV9 . . . . 224 C3
Lightfoot St ST4 . . . . 110 F1
Light Oaks Ave ST2 . . . . . . .43 D1
Light Oaks Cl DE14 . . . . . . 166 E6
Lightoaks Cl ST2 . . . . .77 F5
Lightwater Gr ST2 . . . . .42 F1
Lightwood Rd
Longton ST3 . . . . 284 C2
Newcastle-u-L ST5 . . . . . . .40 D1
Stoke-on-T ST4 . . . . .89 F6
Yoxall DE13 . . . . 181 F2
Lilac Ave WS11 . . . . 226 D7
Lilac Cl
Great Bridgeford ST18 . . . 135 C2
Meir ST3 . . . . .74 C5
Newcastle-u-L ST5 . . . . . . .40 D1
Uttoxeter ST14 . . . . 126 B6
Lilac Dr WV5 . . . . 266 F6
Lilac Gr Burntwood WS7 . . 228 F7
Burton u T DE15 . . . . 185 F6
Stafford ST17 . . . . 174 F7
Stoke-on-T ST3 . . . . .72 E3
Lilac Ho WS4 . . . . 244 D1
Lilac La WS6 . . . . 243 A8
Lilac Rd B79 . . . . 250 A8
Lilleshall Cres WV2 . . . . . 266 D7
**Lilleshall Hall National
  Sports Ctr** TF10 . . . . . . 187 A2
Lilleshall Rd ST5 . . . . .71 D5
Lilleshall St ST3 . . . . 284 C2
Lilleshall Way ST17 . . . . . 174 B7
Lillington Cl [2] WS13 . . . . 231 A8
Lillydale Rd ST2 . . . . .58 B3
Lily St ST5 . . . . .56 D5
Limbrick Rd ST7 . . . . .39 A1
Lime Ct Burton u T DE15 . . 185 C8
Doveridge DE6 . . . . 127 B8
Great Wyrley WS6 . . . . . . 226 F4
Meir ST3 . . . . .74 C5
Lime Ct B[2] ST5 . . . . 104 F1
Lime Gr Barlaston ST12 . . . .88 F4
Burntwood WS7 . . . . 229 C6
Burton u T DE15 . . . . 185 E5
Kinver DY7 . . . . 278 C3
Lichfield WS14 . . . . 231 D8
Waterhouses ST10 . . . . . . .48 F3
Limeheath Pl ST16 . . . . . . .41 E5
Limehurst Ave WV3 . . . . . 255 C1
Lime Kiln La Alton ST10 . . .78 E1
Kingstone ST14 . . . . .25 E2
Lime La
Norton Canes WS3 . . . . . . 228 A1
Walsall WS3 . . . . 244 A7
Limepit La WS11,WS12 . . . 226 D6
Lime Rd Huntington WS12 . 209 D8
Sedgley DY3 . . . . 266 F1
Limes Ave ST9 . . . . .30 A1
Limes Ct Stoke-on-T ST4 . . .71 E8
Wolverhampton WV6 . . . . 255 D5
Limes Rd WV6 . . . . 255 D4
Limes The
Albrighton WV7 . . . . 237 A4
Himley DY3 . . . . 270 B3
Newcastle-u-L ST5 . . . . . . .56 C7
Lime St Stoke-on-T ST4 . . . .72 B6
Wolverhampton WV10 . . . 266 B8
Limes View DY3 . . . . 271 D7
Limetree Ave ST16 . . . . . . 155 D5
Lime Tree Ave WV6 . . . . . 255 A3
Lime Trees Gdns WR8 . . . 239 B3
Limetree Rd B74 . . . . 256 D1
Lime Tree Rd WV4 . . . . . . 239 B4
Lime Wlk ST19 . . . . 207 E8
Limewood Cl ST11 . . . . . . .91 A6
Linacre Rd ST21 . . . . 133 E6
Linacre Way ST3 . . . . .73 E5
Lincoln Ave
Newcastle-u-L ST5 . . . . . . .71 C5
Tamworth B79 . . . . 249 E6
Lincoln Cl WS13 . . . . 214 C3
Lincoln Croft ST14 . . . . . . 246 F6
Lincoln Ct ST14 . . . . 110 F1
Lincoln Dr WS11 . . . . . . 226 F7

Lincoln Gn WV10 . . . . 240 D2
Lincoln Gr ST5 . . . . .71 C5
Lincoln Mdw WS17 . . . . . . 174 A8
Lincoln Rd Burslem ST6 . . .57 A7
Burton u T DE15 . . . . 185 D7
Kidsgrove ST7 . . . . .25 F2
Lincoln St ST1 . . . . 282 C2
Lindale Cl CW12 . . . . .6 A5
Lindale Dr WV5 . . . . 269 F6
Lindale Gr [3] ST3 . . . . .90 B7
Linda Rd ST6 . . . . .41 E5
Linden Ave WS7 . . . . 229 A8
Lindenbrook Vale ST17 . . 175 C7
Linden Cl Congleton CW12 . .16 A8
Newcastle-u-L ST5 . . . . . . .56 B3
Stafford ST17 . . . . 174 B8
Tamworth B77 . . . . 250 F4
Linden Dr ST8 . . . . .16 C1
Linden Gr Biddulph ST8 . . .16 C1
Newcastle-u-L ST5 . . . . . . .56 B3
Linden Lea WV3 . . . . 255 D1
Linden Pl ST3 . . . . .72 F1
Linden Rd DE13 . . . . 183 D1
Lindens The Stone ST15 . . 120 B5
Wolverhampton WV6 . . . . 255 E3
Linden View WS13 . . . . . . 210 B4
Linden Way TF9 . . . . .97 D2
Lindera B77 . . . . 251 A4
Lindisfarne B77 . . . . 250 D3
Lindley Pl ST3 . . . . .90 A4
Lindley St ST5 . . . . .57 B7
Lindon Cl WS8 . . . . 245 A6
Lindon Dr WS8 . . . . 244 F7
Lindon Rd WS8 . . . . 244 F5
Lindon View WS8 . . . . 245 A5
Lindop Ct ST1 . . . . 282 C3
Lindops La CW3 . . . . .68 F7
Lindrick St ST1 . . . . 282 C3
Lindrick Cl WS3 . . . . 242 F3
Lindrosa Rd B74 . . . . 256 F3
Lindsay St ST1 . . . . 282 A2
Lindum Ave ST4 . . . . .88 C7
Line Houses Cvn Site ST6 .41 A6
Lineker Cl ST16 . . . . 155 B3
Liner Gr ST1 . . . . .26 E1
Linfield Gdns DY3 . . . . . . 266 C1
Linfield St ST1 . . . . 282 C3
Linford Cl WS15 . . . . 198 C4
Lingard St ST6 . . . . .57 A8
Lingfield Ave
Stoke-on-T ST4 . . . . .43 A8
Wolverhampton WV10 . . . 240 D5
Lingfield Cl WS6 . . . . 226 F2
Lingfield Dr WS6 . . . . 226 F2
Lingfield Gr WV6 . . . . 254 F4
Lingfield Rd
Burton u T DE14 . . . . 184 F7
Norton Canes WS11 . . . . . 228 A5
Lingmoor Gr WS9 . . . . 256 A7
Ling Rd WS12 . . . . 209 C5
Linhope Gr [1] ST3 . . . . .90 B7
Linkend Cl ST1 . . . . .57 F5
Link Rd Brownhills WS9 . . 245 B3
Wombourne WV5 . . . . 270 A7
Links Ave
Newcastle-u-L ST5 . . . . . . .56 B4
Wolverhampton WV6 . . . . 255 D7
Links Dr DY8 . . . . 279 E2
Links Rd WV4 . . . . 266 A3
Links Side Way WS9 . . . . 256 C8
Links View B74 . . . . 257 B1
Linksway Cl CW12 . . . . . . .15 F8
Linksway Ret Pk WS11 . . . 226 B6
Linkwood Ind Est DY8 . . . 279 F6
Linley Dr WV10 . . . . 240 E1
Linley Gr Dudley DY3 . . . . 271 B2
Lawton-gate ST7 . . . . .25 A3
Linley Rd Lawton-gate ST7 . .25 A2
Stoke-on-T ST4 . . . . .71 E8
Talke ST7 . . . . .40 C8
Linley Trad Est
Kidsgrove ST7 . . . . .25 C1
Talke ST7 . . . . .40 C8
Linnburn Rd ST3 . . . . .73 E4
Linnet Cl WS12 . . . . 209 D7
Linnet Way ST18 . . . . .27 E8
Linslade Cl WV4 . . . . 266 D4
Lintake Dr ST1 . . . . 160 F6
Linthouse Wlk [3] B77 . . . 261 F6
Lintly B77 . . . . 251 B1
Linton Rd WV4 . . . . 265 E5
Linwood Dr WS12 . . . . . . 209 F7
Linwood Way WS6 . . . . . . .41 C5
Lionel Gr ST4 . . . . .71 E6
Lionfields Cl DY10 . . . . . . 280 A5
Lionfields Rd DY10 . . . . . 280 B5
Lion Gr ST5 . . . . .55 E8
Lion Ind Est WS9 . . . . 256 A8
Lion Pas DY8 . . . . 279 F5
Lion's Den WS7,WS14 . . . 229 E2
Lion St Rugeley WS15 . . . 178 E1
Stourbridge DY8 . . . . 279 F5
Lion Way ST17 . . . . 175 A8
Lisbon Pl ST5 . . . . .70 F7
Liskeard Cl ST17 . . . . 222 E4
Lister Gr ST11 . . . . .90 D3
Lister Rd ST16 . . . . 155 F5
Litley Dr ST10 . . . . .92 D8
Little Aston Hall Dr B74 . . 257 B5
Little Aston Hall B74 . . . . 257 B5
Little Aston Hospl B74 . . . 257 B5
Little Aston La B74 . . . . . 257 A5
Little Aston Park Rd B74 . 257 A3

Little Aston Prim Sch
B74 . . . . 257 C6
Little Aston Rd WS9 . . . . . 256 D6
Little Barrow Wlk [3]
WS13 . . . . 214 A1
Little Birches WV3 . . . . . . 265 F8
Little Bloxwich CE Prim Sch
WS3 . . . . 243 D3
Little Burton E DE14 . . . . 166 D4
Little Burton W DE14 . . . . 166 D4
Little Checkhill La DY7 . . . 274 D4
Little Chell La ST6 . . . . . . .41 F5
Little Church La B79 . . . . . 250 B5
Little Cliffe Rd ST3 . . . . . . .72 E4
Little Comm WS3 . . . . 244 A4
Little Cornbow WS13 . . . . 249 D7
Little Eaves La ST2 . . . . . . .58 C6
Littlefield La Ellastone DE6 .80 A2
Snelston DE6 . . . . .81 B4
Little-Field ST4 . . . . .72 A8
Little Grange WS13 . . . . . 213 F1
Littlehales Rd TF10 . . . . . 187 A6
Little Hardwick Rd WS9 . . 256 D2
Little Hay La WS14 . . . . . . 231 D8
Little Johnson's La WS9 . . 256 B1
Little Lakes CW2 . . . . .37 D2
Little La ST3 . . . . .89 F4
Little Lawns Cl WS9 . . . . . 245 A4
Little Marsh Gr ST19 . . . . 192 F1
Little Marsh Pk ST19 . . . . 193 A1
Little Moss Cl ST7 . . . . . . .25 E5
Little Moss La ST7 . . . . . . .25 E5
Little Oaks Dr DY7 . . . . . . 275 A2
Little Onn Rd ST20 . . . . . . 190 A7
Little Orch WS15 . . . . 178 E2
Little Pipe La
Creswell Green WS13 . . . . 212 F1
Lichfield WS13 . . . . 213 A1
Little Pountney St [4]
WV2 . . . . 266 C8
Little Rd ST10 . . . . .76 A4
Little Row
[5] Kidsgrove ST7 . . . . . . .26 B2
Stoke-on-T ST7 . . . . .72 F8
Little Sutton La B75 . . . . . 258 C1
Little Sutton Prim Sch
B75 . . . . 258 D3
Little Sutton Rd B75 . . . . . 258 D2
Little Tixall La ST18 . . . . . 158 C2
Littleton Bsns Pk WS12 . . 209 C7
Littleton Cl ST16 . . . . 156 A3
Littleton Cres ST19 . . . . . 192 F1
Littleton Dr WV10 . . . . . . 209 C2
Littleton Way WS7 . . . . . . 211 D1
Littlewood La WS6 . . . . . . 226 E4
Littlewood Rd WS6 . . . . . . 226 E4
Littlewood Rd WS6 . . . . . . 226 E4
Littleworth Hill WS12 . . . . 210 D4
Littleworth Rd WS12 . . . . 210 E4
Littondale Cl CW12 . . . . . . .6 A5
Litton B77 . . . . 251 C1
Littywood La ST18 . . . . . . 173 C2
Liverpool Rd E ST7 . . . . . . .25 E2
Liverpool Rd
Kidsgrove ST7 . . . . .26 A1
Newcastle-u-L,Cross Heath
  ST5 . . . . .56 A3
Newcastle-u-L,Red Street
  ST5 . . . . .40 D2
Newcastle-u-L ST4 . . . . . . .72 B7
Liverpool Rd W ST7 . . . . . .25 B4
Livingstone Ave WV6 . . . . 254 E5
Livingstone Rd WS3 . . . . . 243 E2
Livingstone St Leek ST13 . .30 F5
Stoke-on-T ST6 . . . . .56 F3
Lizard La TF11 . . . . 220 A6
Llewellyn Roberts Way
TF9 . . . . .97 D2
Lloyd Dr WV4 . . . . 265 C2
Lloyd George Gr WS11 . . . 210 C2
Lloyd Hill WV4 . . . . 265 C3
Lloyd Rd WV6 . . . . 255 D5
Lloyd Roberts Bldgs
WV4 . . . . 265 F1
Lloyd St Cannock WS11 . . 209 D1
Longton ST3 . . . . 284 C2
Stafford ST16 . . . . 285 B4
Wolverhampton WV6 . . . . 255 F4
Lloyd The TF9 . . . . 113 F7
Lochalsh Gr WV11 . . . . . . 242 B1
Lochsong Cl B77 . . . . 261 D4
Lockerbie Cl ST13 . . . . . . .31 B5
Locketts Cl WS11 . . . . 209 F5
Locketts La ST3 . . . . .73 E5
Lockett St ST1 . . . . .57 D6
Locke Way ST16 . . . . 156 B3
Lockfield Cl DY8 . . . . 275 F4
Lockhart Dr B75 . . . . 258 C1
Lockington Ave ST1 . . . . . .58 D1
Locklands Dr WS11 . . . . . 209 F6
Lockley St WS11 . . . . .26 C5
Lock Rd ST14 . . . . 207 F8
Lockside Dr DY7 . . . . 278 B4
Lockside View WS15 . . . . 196 F8
Locks View WV5 . . . . 269 E7
Locks View DY8 . . . . 275 E7
Lockwood Cl ST10 . . . . . . .62 A1
Lockwood Rd ST10 . . . . . . .77 B6
Lockwood St
Newcastle-u-L ST5 . . . . . . 283 D3
Stoke-on-T ST4 . . . . .43 B3
Lode La DE6 . . . . .35 F4
Lodge Barn Rd ST17 . . . . . .27 F6
Lodgefield Mobile Home Pk
ST17 . . . . 156 D2
Lodge Gr Aldridge WS9 . . 256 A8
Newcastle-u-L ST5 . . . . . . .56 C6
Lodge Hill DE13 . . . . 146 E3

Lodge La
Cheslyn Hay WS11 . . . . . . 226 C5
Chorley WS15 . . . . 212 D3
Fairoak ST21 . . . . 115 F5
Ilam DE6 . . . . .55 B3
Ilam DE6 . . . . .50 D3
Kingswinford DY6 . . . . . . 275 B6
Woodseaves ST20 . . . . . . 151 E6
Yoxall DE13 . . . . 182 B8
Lodge Pk WV5 . . . . 267 C7
Lodge Rd Burntwood WS7 .211 F1
Nethersea DE12 . . . . 219 E8
Rugeley WS15 . . . . 197 A6
Stoke-on-T ST4 . . . . .71 E7
Talke Pits ST7 . . . . .40 D6
Walsall WS4 . . . . 244 B1
Lodges ST11 . . . . 203 F2
Lodge View WS6 . . . . 226 C3
Loftus Ct WS7 . . . . 229 A5
Loftus St ST1 . . . . 282 A4
Logan Gr ST3 . . . . .73 E5
Lohengrin Ct DE13 . . . . . 147 E2
Lomas St ST4 . . . . .57 A2
Lomax Cl WS13 . . . . 214 A1
Lomax Rd WS12 . . . . 210 B7
Lombard Gdns [1] WS13 . . 231 B8
Lombard St WS13 . . . . . . 231 B8
Lombardy Gr
Burntwood WS7 . . . . 228 F8
Stoke-on-T ST4 . . . . .74 A2
Lomita Cres B77 . . . . 261 D8
Lomond Cl B79 . . . . 249 F8
Lomond Gr ST10 . . . . .76 F5
Lomond Rd DY3 . . . . 266 C1
Lomond Wlk ST17 . . . . . . .88 F7
London Rd
Bridgemere CW5 . . . . .67 A5
Knighton CW3,TF9 . . . . . . .83 C6
Lichfield WS14 . . . . 231 C5
Newcastle-u-L,Chesterton
  ST5 . . . . .55 E7
Newcastle-u-L,City General Hospl
  ST5 . . . . 283 C1
Shenstone B75,WS14 . . . 258 F7
Stoke-on-T ST4 . . . . .72 A6
Sutton Coldfield B75 . . . . 259 A4
Weeford WS14 . . . . 247 F3
Weston ST18 . . . . 138 D2
London St ST13 . . . . .30 F5
Long Acre WV8 . . . . 238 F2
Longacres Cannock WS12 .210 F5
Little Aston B74 . . . . 257 C4
Longboat La DY8 . . . . 275 E1
Longbow Cl DE13 . . . . . . 147 C1
Longbow Gr DE13 . . . . . . 147 C1
Longbridge Hayes Rd ST5 56 C8
Longbrook La WS14 . . . . . 231 C5
Longbrook Ave ST3 . . . . . .72 F2
Longclough Rd ST3 . . . . . .40 D2
Long Croft
Albrighton WV7 . . . . 237 B5
Cannock WS12 . . . . 209 C4
Longcroft La DE13 . . . . . . 182 B4
Long Eaton WV8 . . . . .73 F3
Longdales Ct ST3 . . . . .73 F3
Longdon Ave Dr B74 . . . . 257 F3
Longfellow Cl WS14 . . . . . 166 D7
Longfellow Pl WS11 . . . . . 209 E4
Longfellow Rd
Burntwood WS7 . . . . 212 A1
Dudley DY3 . . . . 271 B5
Longfellow Wlk B79 . . . . . 249 F8
Longfield Ave WS15 . . . . . 119 F7
Longfield Cl B77 . . . . 250 E4
Longfield Dr B74 . . . . 257 D4
Longfield Rd St14 . . . . . . .71 E8
Longford Cl
Burton u T DE15 . . . . 167 B2
Wombourne WV5 . . . . 269 D5
Longford Ct WS11 . . . . . . 226 B8
Longford Gn WS11 . . . . . . 226 C7
Longford Ind Est WS11 . . 226 D6
Longford Pk TF10 . . . . . . 168 B1
Longford Prim Sch
WS11 . . . . 226 C8
Longford Rd
Cannock WS11 . . . . 226 D7
Newport TF10 . . . . 168 C2
Longford Wlk ST2 . . . . . . .58 A2
Longhedge La DE13 . . . . . 146 F1
Longhope Dr ST11 . . . . . . 119 F6
Longhurst Dr ST16 . . . . . 156 C4
Longhurst La Airewas WS13 200 E1
Longland Gdns ST3 . . . . . .73 D5
Longlake Ave WV6 . . . . . . 255 B3
Longlands Dr B77 . . . . . . 250 F4
Longlands La TF9 . . . . .97 D1
Longlands Pl WS15 . . . . . 160 F8
Longlands Prim Sch TF9 .97 D2
Longlands The WV5 . . . . . 270 A6
Long La De6 . . . . .35 B5
Longleat Dr DY1 . . . . 271 E2
Longleat Rd WS9 . . . . 245 A1
Longleat B79 . . . . 249 D7
Longley Rd ST3 . . . . .73 C5
Long Mdw
Newcastle-u-L ST5 . . . . . . .71 C3
Stafford ST17 . . . . 174 E5
Long Meadow Dr DY3 . . . 266 B2
Long Mynd Cl WV11 . . . . . 242 B1
Longmoor Ho B74 . . . . . . 257 F2
Longnor Craft Ctr* SK17 . .13 B8
Longnor B79 . . . . 258 A2
Longport Rd ST6 . . . . .56 D7

Longport Sta ST6 . . . . .56 D7
Long Row Caversall ST11 . .74 D3
Longport St7 . . . . .26 A1
Kidsgrove ST7 . . . . .26 A1
Longsdon Cl ST5 . . . . .40 C1
Longsdon Gr ST3 . . . . .73 E4
Longshaw Ave ST5 . . . . . . .56 F7
Longshaw La Alton ST10 . .78 E3
Oakamoor ST10 . . . . .78 E7
Longshaw St ST6 . . . . .56 D8
Longshore Cl ST18 . . . . . 174 C6
Longslow Cl TF9 . . . . .97 B1
Longslow Rd TF9 . . . . .97 A1
Longstaff Ave WS12 . . . . . 211 C4
Longstaff Croft WS13 . . . 213 F2
Long St Burton u T DE15 . .185 E2
Wheaton Aston ST19 . . . . 205 C6
Longton Exchange ST3 . . 284 C3
Longton Hall Rd ST3 . . . . .72 F2
Longton High Sch ST3 . . . .73 F2
Longton Hospl ST3 . . . . . .73 D1
Longton Rd Barlaston ST12 88 F2
Oulton ST15 . . . . 105 D4
Stoke-on-T ST4 . . . . .88 B6
Longton Sta ST3 . . . . 284 B6
Longus Ind Est ST6 . . . . . .41 D4
Long Valley Rd ST8 . . . . . .16 C2
Longview Cl ST3 . . . . .73 D5
Longwood Path B78 . . . . . 249 D1
Longwood Prim Sch
B78 . . . . 249 D1
Longwood Rd WS9 . . . . . . 256 D6
Lonsdale CE Prim Sch
ST21 . . . . 133 D6
Lonsdale Ct
Ecclesshall ST21 . . . . 133 D7
Market Drayton TF9 . . . . . .97 D1
Lonsdale Rd
Burton u T DE14 . . . . 185 B8
Wolverhampton WV3 . . . . 266 B7
Lonsdale St ST4 . . . . .72 B6
Loomer Rd ST5 . . . . .55 E5
Loomer Road Ind Est ST5 .55 E5
Loop Rd ST15 . . . . 118 C7
Lord Cromwell Ct WS11 . . 210 A5
Lords Cl ST4 . . . . .88 D7
Lordship La ST4 . . . . .72 D7
Lordshire Pl ST7 . . . . .26 F2
Lords La DY7 . . . . 274 E1
Lordsley La TF9 . . . . 100 A7
Lord St Biddulph ST8 . . . . .27 D7
Stoke-on-T ST6 . . . . .42 C1
Lordswell Rd DE14 . . . . . 165 F4
Lordswood Rd ST4 . . . . . . .88 D7
Lorien Cl ST13 . . . . .30 C4
Lorien St ST4 . . . . .72 A8
Loring Rd ST5 . . . . .56 B6
Lorne Terr S ST5 . . . . .56 C6
Lorne St Burntwood WS7 . 228 E8
Stoke-on-T ST6 . . . . .42 A1
Lorraine St ST7 . . . . .26 F1
Lorton B79 . . . . 249 D7
Lothersdale B77 . . . . 262 C8
Lothians Rd Walsall WS3 . 244 A5
Wolverhampton WV6 . . . . 255 E6
Lotus Ave ST18 . . . . .27 B6
Lotus Ct WS11 . . . . 209 E5
Lotus Dr WS11 . . . . 105 A2
Lotus B77 . . . . 250 E3
Lotus Way ST16 . . . . 155 F5
Loughborough Wlk ST3 . . 284 C4
Loughshaw B77 . . . . 251 C1
Louise Dr ST3 . . . . .72 F3
Louise St Dudley DY3 . . . 271 C3
Stoke-on-T ST3 . . . . .42 A2
Lount La DE13 . . . . 146 E1
Louvain Gr ST1 . . . . .57 D7
Lovage Gr ST2 . . . . .58 A3
Lovatt Ave ST5 . . . . .56 A4
Lovatt Cl DE13 . . . . 147 F2
Lovatt Dr ST16 . . . . 209 E5
Lovatt Pl WS11 . . . . 209 E4
Lovatt St Stafford ST16 . . 155 D5
Stoke-on-T ST4 . . . . .72 A2
Lovelace Cl ST17 . . . . . . 174 C8
Love La Great Wyrley WS6 227 B3
Rugeley WS15 . . . . 178 F1
Wolverhampton WV6 . . . . 255 D6
Lovell Dr ST16 . . . . 156 B5
Lovell Rd DE13 . . . . 182 A2
Lovell B79 . . . . 249 F6
Loveridge Cl WV8 . . . . . . 238 F3
Lovers La TF9 . . . . .99 F4
Loveston Gr ST3 . . . . 284 D4
Lovett Cl WS15 . . . . 178 D2
Lowdham B77 . . . . 251 C1
Lowe Dr WV6 . . . . 275 E4
Lowell Dr ST3 . . . . .73 F4
Lower Ash Rd ST7 . . . . . . .25 E5
Lower Bar TF10 . . . . 168 C3
Lower Bethesda St ST1 . . 282 B2
Lower Birches Way
WS15 . . . . 196 D7
Lower Brook St WS13 . . . 178 E1
Lower Bryan St ST1 . . . . . 282 B4
Lower Cres ST4 . . . . .71 E8
Lowercroft Way ST4 . . . . . 257 C6
Lower Cross St ST3 . . . . . 284 C4
Lower Farm Prim Sch
WS3 . . . . 243 C3
Lower Farm WS9 . . . . 245 E4
Lower Foundry St ST3 . . . 284 B5
Lower Gn WV6 . . . . 255 C5
Lower Gungate B79 . . . . . 250 B5
Lower Hadderidge [13] ST6 56 F8

Lower High St
Mow Cop ST7 26 D7
Stourbridge DY8 279 F6
Tutbury DE13 146 C7
Lower House La CV9 262 F2
Lower Keys Bsns Pk
WS12 210 D3
Lower La Chorley WS13 212 D3
Hopton ST18 156 D8
Lower Lodge Residential Mobile Home Pk WS15 197 E5
Lower Mayer St ST1 282 C4
Lower Milehouse La ST5 55 F3
Lower Outwoods Rd
DE13 165 F6
Lower Oxford Rd ST5 56 E2
Lowerpark B77 250 C1
Lower Penkridge Rd
ST17 175 B1
Lower Rd Ashley TF9 100 B4
Cannock WS12 210 C3
Gnosall ST20 152 B5
Lower Rookery Rd ST15 118 C6
Lower Sandford St
WS13 231 A7
Lower Spring Rd 3 ST3 73 D2
Lower St 1 Burslem ST6 57 A7
Doveridge DE6 127 B8
Newcastle-u-L ST5 283 B3
Wolverhampton WV6 255 E5
Lower Villiers St WV2 266 C7
Lower Way WS15 197 C1
Lowe St ST4 72 B7
Loweswater Dr DY3 271 D3
Lowfield Dr ST5 56 E5
Lowfield La ST20 171 E5
Lowforce B77 251 C1
Lowhurst Dr ST6 42 A7
Lowland Rd WS12 209 C5
Lowlands Ave WV6 255 E6
Lowlands Ct WV6 255 E6
Lowlands Rd ST6 41 B4
Lowndes Cl ST4 71 F6
Lowndes Rd DY8 279 E6
Lowry Cl WV6 254 F4
Low St WS6 226 D3
Lowther Pl ST13 31 A5
Lowther St ST1 282 A4
Lowthorpe Way ST2 58 E1
Loxley Hall Sch ST14 125 C5
Loxley La ST14 125 C5
Loxley Pl ST3 89 F7
Loxley Rd B75 258 D3
Loxton Cl B74 257 D5
Loynton Cl ST16 155 B7
Loynton Sands ST20 151 A5
Lucas St ST6 56 E8
Lucepool La DE13 182 D3
Lucerne Pl ST5 70 E7
Ludbrook Rd ST4 73 B5
Ludford Cl ST5 40 D2
Ludgate St DE13 146 C6
Ludgate B79 250 A5
Ludgrove Way ST17 175 B8
Lud La B79 250 A5
Ludlow Cl WS11 210 C2
Ludlow St ST1 282 C3
Ludlow Way DY1 271 E2
Ludstone Ave WV4 265 D5
Ludwall Rd ST3 73 E1
Lugano Cl ST5 70 F6
Lukesland Ave ST4 71 E6
Luke St ST6 56 E7
Lukes Wlk WS13 214 A2
Lullington Rd
Clifton Campville B79 218 E3
Edingale B79 217 D5
Lulworth Gr ST6 41 E6
Lulworth Rd WS7 229 A7
Lulworth Wlk WV4 265 C6
Lundy Rd ST3 72 F3
Lune Cl 1 CW12 6 A1
Lunns Croft WS13 231 C8
Lunts Moss ST7 25 C7
Lutley Cl WV3 265 E7
Lutley La DY7 273 B8
Luttrell Rd B74 258 A1
Lychgate Cl ST4 72 A5
Lydford Pl ST3 73 F3
Lydford Rd WS3 243 B3
Lydgate Rd DY6 275 F6
Lydia Croft B74 257 E6
Lydia Dr ST1 57 F6
Lydiates Cl DY3 271 B7
Lyme Brook Pl ST4 71 E3
Lyme Ct ST5 283 C1
Lymedale Small Firms Ctr
ST5 55 F5
Lyme Dr ST4 71 D5
Lyme Gr ST5 56 C3
Lyme Rd ST3 74 B1
Lymer Rd WV10 240 C1
Lymer's La ST18 123 A1
Lymes Rd ST5 70 B4
Lymevale Rd ST4 71 E4
Lyme Valley Rd ST5 283 C1
Lymewood Cl ST5 283 B2
Lyme Wood Gr ST5 283 B1
Lymington Rd
Burntwood WS7 211 F1
Stafford ST16 156 C4
Lyminster Gr ST2 43 B1
Lymsey Croft DY8 275 C3
Lynam St ST4 72 A7
Lynam Way CW3 68 E7
Lyn Ave WS13 213 F1
Lynch The B78 251 F1
Lyncroft WV7 237 A5
Lyndale Rd DY3 266 B2
Lyndale B77 261 F6
Lyndham Ave DE15 166 F1
Lyndhurst Dr Biddulph ST8 27 A6
Stourbridge DY8 275 F1
Lyndhurst Gr ST15 120 D6
Lyndhurst Rd
Cannock WS12 210 E1
Wolverhampton WV3 266 A7
Lyndhurst St ST6 56 E8
Lyndon Cl DY3 266 E1
Lyndon Gr DY6 275 B8
Lyne Ct DE14 166 A3
Lyneham Cl B79 250 C8
Lyne Hill Ind Est ST19 207 E7
Lynehill La ST19 207 E6
Lyneside Rd ST8 27 B5
Lynfield Rd WS13 213 F1
Lynmouth Cl
Aldridge WS9 256 A5
Biddulph ST8 27 C6
Lynmouth Gr ST6 41 F7
Lynn Ave ST7 40 C8
Lynn La WS14 246 D6
Lynn St ST3 74 B5
Lynsey Cl ST7 54 E7
Lynton Ave Stafford ST17 175 D8
Wolverhampton WV6 255 F6
Lynton Gr ST3 89 E8
Lynton Rd ST5 70 F5
Lynwood Ave DY6 275 B7
Lynwood Cl
Burton u T DE14 184 F7
Walsall WV12 242 E1
Lynwood Dr DY10 281 C2
Lynwood Rd DE14 184 E8
Lyric Cl ST17 174 F6
Lysander Rd ST3 90 B7
Lysander Way WS11 209 E3
Lysways La WS13,WS15 213 C8
Lytham Cl DY8 279 F2
Lytham Dr ST16 156 C3
Lytham Gr WS3 243 A4
Lytham Rd WV6 254 D4
Lytham B77 251 C5
Lyttelton Rd DY8 279 D5
Lytton Ave WV4 265 E4
Lytton St ST4 72 C7

M

Macadam Cl WS7 229 B8
McAdam Cl DE15 167 B2
McBean Rd WV6 255 F4
Macbeth Ho ST7 40 C8
Macclesfield Rd
Congleton CW12 6 A8
Leek ST13 30 C7
Macclesfield St ST6 42 B1
Macdonald Cres ST3 74 A3
Mace St ST4 71 F4
McGeough Wlk WS11 210 B5
McGhie St WS12 210 B6
McGough St 8 ST6 41 D3
McGowan Ho ST7 40 D8
Macgregor Cres B77 250 F3
Macgregor Tithe B79 250 B5
Machin Cres ST5 56 B7
Machin St ST6 41 E4
Macintyre St ST6 57 A7
Mackay Rd WS3 243 D2
McKellin Cl ST7 39 E2
Mackenzie Cres ST10 76 E1
McKie Way WS15 196 F6
McKinley St ST6 41 D3
Maclagan St ST4 72 B6
McLean Rd WV10 240 C1
Macrome Rd WV6 255 E8
Madden Cl WS15 196 F6
Maddocke Wlk 4 WS13 230 F6
Maddock St Audley ST7 39 D1
Burslem ST6 56 E7
Madeira Ave WV8 239 A2
Madeira Ct DY8 275 F1
Madeira Pl ST6 41 D3
Madeley High Sch CW3 68 E6
Madeley Rd 5 DY6 275 F4
Madeley St N ST5 55 B2
Madeley St
Newcastle-u-L ST5 55 B1
Stoke-on-T ST6 41 D4
Madford Ret Pk ST16 285 A4
Madison St ST6 41 D4
Madox Cl B79 249 E8
Madras Rd DE15 167 C3
Madrona B77 251 B4
Maer La TF9 97 D2
Maer Lane Ind Est TF9 97 D2
Maer La ST21 101 E5
Maerway La ST5 84 C5
Mafeking St ST3 284 B2
Magazine La ST19 205 C7
Magdalen Rd ST3 88 E8
Magdalen Wlk ST3 88 E7
Magenta Dr ST5 55 E2
Magna Cl WS6 226 E3
Magnolia Cl ST18 135 B2
Magnolia Dr ST6 42 F2
Magnolia Gr WV8 239 B3
Magnolia B77 251 A4
Magnolia Way 1 DY8 275 F1
Magnus St ST6 56 F7
Magnus B77 261 E6
Magpie Cres 9 ST7 26 B2
Mahogany Dr ST16 155 C4
Maidendale Rd DY6 275 B7
Maidensbridge Dr DY6 275 C8
Maidensbridge Gdns
DY6 270 B1
Maidensbridge Prim Sch
DY6 270 B1
Maidensbridge Rd DY6 270 B1
Maidstone Dr
Burntwood WS7 229 D6
Stourbridge DY8 275 E3
Maidstone Gr ST2 58 C2
Main Rd Adbaston ST21 131 D6
Anslow DE13 165 C7
Armitage WS15 197 C4
Betley CW3 53 A5
Main Rd Brereton WS15 197 A6
Main Rd Cauldon Lowe ST10 63 E4
Coldmeece ST15 118 B7
Colwich ST18 177 D7
Draycott in t C DE6 144 D7
Edingale B79 217 D5
Harlaston B79 217 D1
Harlaston B79 217 E3
Mayfield DE6 81 D8
Newton Regis B79 236 C2
Norton in H TF9 82 C1
Stafford ST17 176 B7
Sudbury,Aston Heath DE6 129 A4
Sudbury DE6 128 E5
Tamworth B79 250 B8
Weston CW2 37 C6
Wetley Rocks ST9 60 B7
Wigginton B79 234 B2
Main Road Brereton
WS15 197 A6
Main St Alrewas DE13 201 A3
Barton-u-N DE13 183 C2
Burton u T DE14 184 F7
Burton u T,Stapenhill DE15 185 E8
Clifton Campville B79 218 F2
Egginton DE65 148 B5
Meir ST3 74 B5
Netherseal DE12 219 F7
Newton Solney DE15 167 E8
Shenstone WS14 246 F6
Stonnall WS9 245 D4
Stretton DE13 147 E1
Swadlincote DE12 186 E6
Tatenhill DE13 165 B1
Walton-on-T DE12 184 D1
Whittington WS14 232 E5
Yoxall DE13 182 A2
Mainwaring Dr B75 258 E2
Maitland Gr ST4 88 B6
Maitland Rd DY1 271 E1
Maitland B77 250 F2
Majors Barn ST10 76 C2
Major St WV2 266 E7
Maker La DE13 162 D2
Malam St ST1 282 B4
Malcolm Cl ST2 43 B2
Malcolm Ct ST2 58 C5
Malcolm Dr ST2 58 C5
Malcolm Rd ST17 174 D6
Maldale B77 251 C1
Malhamdale Rd CW12 6 A5
Malham Rd
Newcastle-u-L ST5 55 E2
Tamworth B77 262 C8
Malins Rd WV4 266 E5
Malkin Way ST6 56 E6
Mallard Ave ST17 175 A7
Mallard Cl Uttoxeter ST14 126 C6
Walsall WS3 244 A5
Mallard Croft 5 WS13 231 C8
Mallard Way
Penkridge ST19 208 A6
Stoke-on-T ST6 42 D3
Mallens Croft ST14 125 C7
Mallicot Cl WS13 214 D1
Mallorie Rd ST6 42 D4
Mallory Cl ST15 120 B6
Mallory Cres WS3 243 D2
Mallory Rd WV6 254 E3
Mallory Way ST10 76 F3
Mallow Cl ST21 133 E5
Mallowdale Cl ST4 88 C6
Malloy Ho ST13 45 D7
Malpass Gdns WV8 238 E4
Malpas Wlk ST6 41 C7
Malstone Ave ST2 43 C2
Malthouse La
Barlaston ST12 88 F2
Bradley ST18 173 C1
Caverswall ST3 74 C8
Malt House La
Church Eaton ST20 190 A7
Shareshill WV10 225 C6
Malthouse La
Wheaton Aston ST19 205 C6
Wolverhampton WV6 255 E6
Malthouse Rd Alton ST10 78 E1
Bucknall ST2 58 B3
Malt House Rd WS15 212 B5
Malt Houses WV10 225 D6
Malthouse The DE14 166 E3
Maltings Ind Est DE14 166 E6
Maltings The
Aldridge WS9 256 C6
Burton u T,Stapenhill DE15 167 A1
Burton u T,Wetmore DE14 166 E5
Coven WV9 224 B2
Uttoxeter ST14 126 C8
Malt La ST3 284 D2
Malt Mill La ST16 285 B3
Malton Gr ST6 41 D5
Malvern Ave
Burton u T DE15 167 A1
Newcastle-u-L ST5 54 F2
Malvern Cl Stafford ST17 156 B1
Stoke-on-T ST4 88 A7
Malvern Ct B74 257 F2
Malvern Dr Aldridge WS9 256 C8
Rugeley WS15 178 C2
Malvern St DE15 166 F1
Malvern View Rd DY3 271 D4
Mamble Rd DY8 279 E5
Manchester Ct ST14 110 F1
Mancroft Cl DY6 275 B7
Mancroft Gdns WV6 255 C5
Mancroft Rd WV6 255 C5
Mandela Way ST3 284 D2
Manderley Cl DY3 266 C2
Manderston Cl DY1 271 E3
Mander St WV3 266 B8
Manderville Gdns DY6 275 C6
Mandeville Cl ST6 42 C3
Manifold CE Prim Sch
SK17 23 A2
Manifold Cl
Burntwood WS7 229 D6
Newcastle-u-L ST5 55 B1
Waterhouses ST10 48 F2
Manifold Dr ST10 76 E1
Manifold Rd ST11 90 F8
Manifold Valley Visitor Ctr
SK17 23 E3
Manifold Wlk ST2 58 C1
Manley Rd WS13 214 D1
Manlove St WV3 266 A8
Mannin Cl ST3 74 A4
Mann St ST3 74 C3
Manor Ave
Cannock WS11 209 D1
Great Wyrley WS6 227 A4
Manor Cl Codsall WV8 239 B4
Congleton CW12 6 A1
Draycott in t M ST11 91 C6
Great Haywood ST18 158 B2
Harlaston B79 217 D2
Market Drayton TF9 97 C1
Stanton DE15 186 A6
Uttoxeter ST14 126 B8
Weston ST18 138 D2
Wolverhampton WV4 265 F4
Manor Cotts WS14 230 E2
Manor Court Dr WS15 198 B4
Manor Cres DE15 186 A6
Manor Croft
Burton u T DE14 166 D2
Tatenhill DE13 184 A8
Uttoxeter ST14 126 C8
Manor Ct
Barton-u-N DE13 183 D2
Stone ST15 119 F6
Manor Ct St ST4 71 F6
Manor Dr Burton u T DE14 166 E2
Dudley DY3 271 B3
Netherseal DE12 219 F6
Shareshill WV10 225 D2
Swindon DY3 269 E2
Manor Farm Cres ST17 174 E5
Manor Farm Rd ST18 177 D8
Manorfield Cl ST19 207 E8
Manor Fields DE13 200 F3
Manor Flats DY3 271 D8
Manor Fold WV8 238 D2
Manor Gdns
Albrighton WV7 237 A5
Market Drayton TF9 97 C1
Wombourne WV5 270 B7
Manor Glade ST5 85 A7
Manor Gn ST17 174 D7
Manor Hill Fst Sch ST15 119 E7
Manor House Pk WV8 239 B4
Manor Ho WV6 255 D5
Manorial Rd B75 258 E3
Manor La Harlaston B79 217 D2
Stourbridge DY8 279 D3
Wigginton B79 233 E3
Manor Pk DY6 275 D6
Manor Prim Sch
Aldridge B74 257 A1
Drayton Bassett B78 260 E5
Manor Rd Aldridge B74 257 A1
Edgmond TF10 168 A3
Gnosall ST20 171 E7
King's Bromley DE13 199 C6
Madeley CW3 68 E3
Mile Oak B78 249 D1
Mow Cop ST7 26 D7
Stanton DE15 186 A6
Stourbridge DY8 275 E2
Tamworth B77 250 D4
Uttoxeter ST14 126 B8
Whitmore ST5 85 A7
Wolverhampton,Penn WV4 265 F4
Manor Rise
Burntwood WS7 229 A5
Lichfield WS14 231 C7
Stone ST15 119 F7
Manor Sq ST17 174 D7
Manor St Stoke-on-T ST4 72 E7
Wolverhampton WV6 255 D5
Manor Trad Est DE14 166 E4
Manor Way WS15 179 A6
Manor Wlk DE13 199 B6
Mansard Cl WV3 265 F8
Manse Cl ST3 284 C4
Mansell Cl ST16 155 C2
Mansfield Cl
Newcastle-u-L ST5 71 C2
Tamworth B79 249 E6
Mansfield Dr ST8 27 A5
Mansion Cl ST10 76 E2
Mansion Ct WV5 269 D5
Mansion Dr WS7 229 D4
Manson Ct WV4 265 D5
Manston Dr WV6 254 E5
Manston Hill ST19 207 E7
Manston View B79 250 C8
Manta Rd B77 261 D6
Manton Cl
2 Stretton DE13 147 F1
Swadlincote DE11 186 F6
Maple Ave
Newcastle-u-L ST5 40 E1
Talke ST7 40 D8
Maple Cl Burntwood WS7 228 F7
Cheadle ST10 76 F2
Kinver DY7 278 A5
Stoke-on-T ST6 43 A5
Stourbridge DY8 279 D2
Yarnfield ST15 118 F5
Maple Cres
Blythe Bridge ST11 91 A6
Cannock WS11 209 C1
Maple Ct Lichfield WS14 231 C5
Stafford ST17 155 C1
Mapledene Cl 1 ST17 175 D5
Maple Dr Derrington ST18 154 D1
Dudley DY3 271 B2
Huntington WS12 209 D8
Loggerheads TF9 99 D5
Maple Gdns ST15 120 A6
Maple Gr Burton u T DE15 185 E5
Cheddleton ST13 45 C7
Kingswinford DY6 275 E6
Lichfield WS14 231 F7
Stafford ST17 174 E7
Wolverhampton WV3 255 C2
Maple Hayes Hall Sch
WS13 230 D8
Maple Ho Little Aston B74 257 B5
Walsall WS3 244 D1
Maplehurst Cl ST6 57 B8
Maple Pl ST3 74 B2
Maple Rd Walsall WS3 243 F2
Wolverhampton WV3 265 E8
Maple Rise B77 251 A4
Maple St WS3 243 D2
Maple Way DE14 184 F8
Maple Wood ST17 175 C5
Marcel Cl ST4 72 A2
Marchant Rd WV6 255 F2
March Banks WS15 178 D1
March Cl WS6 226 D1
Marchington Ind Est
ST14 143 F8
March La Overmoor ST9 60 A3
Whitgreave ST18 135 E5
March Rd ST3 284 B4
March Way WS9 245 C1
Marchwood Ct ST4 71 E6
Marcia Rice Ct WS15 161 A5
Marconi Gate ST18 156 C5
Marconi Pl WS12 210 C7
Marcus Ind Est ST1 57 F3
Mardale Cl CW12 6 A5
Maree Gr WV11 242 B1
Margam Cres WS3 242 F2
Margam Terr WS3 242 F2
Margam Way WS3 242 F2
Margaret Ave ST4 87 F8
Margaret Dr WS11 209 E6
Margaret St
6 Stone ST15 104 F1
Hanley ST1 57 E4
Margery Ave ST7 25 E7
Margill Cl ST1 282 A2
Marholm Cl WV9 239 F2
Maries Way ST5 55 D1
Marigold Cl WS11 210 C3
Marina Cres WS12 210 A5
Marina Dr ST5 56 C3
Marina Rd ST4 71 F3
Marina Way ST1 57 A4
Marine Cres DY8 275 E1
Marine Gdns DY8 275 E1
Mariner B79 249 E6
Market Drayton Cottage Hospl TF9 112 C8
Market Drayton Inf Sch
TF9 97 C1
Market Drayton Jun Sch
TF9 112 B8
Market Drayton Rd TF9 99 D4
Marketfields ST21 133 E7
Market Hall St WS11 209 E1
Market La Hanley ST1 282 B3
Lichfield WS14 230 E2
Lower Penn WV4 264 F5
Newcastle-u-L ST5 283 B3
Market Mews TF10 168 F3
Market Pl 10 Leek ST13 30 E6
4 Cannock WS11 209 E1
4 Stone ST15 120 A8
Abbots Bromley WS15 161 A6
Brewood ST19 223 C6
Burslem ST6 56 F8
Burton u T DE14 166 E2
Cheadle ST10 76 D3
Hartington SK17 24 D5
Longnor SK17 13 B6
Penkridge ST19 192 E1
Tamworth B79 250 B4
Uttoxeter ST14 126 C7
Walsall WS3 243 B1
Market Sq Arc ST1 282 B3
Market Sq Hanley ST1 282 B3
Rugeley WS15 178 E1
Stafford ST16 285 B3

Market St Cannock WS12 . 210 C5
Kidsgrove ST7 . 26 A1
Kingswinford DY6 . 275 D6
Leek ST13 . 30 F6
Lichfield WS13 . 231 B8
Longton ST3 . 284 C3
Penkridge ST19 . 192 E1
Rugeley WS15 . 178 F1
Stafford ST16 . 285 B3
Tamworth B79 . 250 B4
Uttoxeter ST14 . 126 C7
Markham Croft WV9 . 240 A2
Markham Dr DY6 . 275 E4
Marklew Cl WS8 . 245 A5
Marklin Ave WV10 . 240 D1
Marks Wlk WS13 . 214 A2
Marlborough Ave ST16 . 156 C4
Marlborough Cl
Great Haywood ST18 . 158 C2
Sutton Coldfield B74 . 257 E6
Marlborough Cres
Burton u T DE15 . 186 A8
Endon ST9 . 43 E8
Marlborough Ct
Lichfield WS13 . 231 B7
Sutton Coldfield,Four Oaks B74 . 257 F2
Marlborough Gdns
Stourbridge DY8 . 275 D2
Wolverhampton WV6 . 255 E4
Marlborough Ind Est
WV2 . 266 D7
Marlborough Rd
Dudley DY3 . 271 F6
Longton ST3 . 284 C4
Stone ST15 . 119 F5
Marlborough St
Stoke-on-T ST4 . 72 D5
Walsall WS3 . 243 B1
Marlborough Way
Stoke-on-T ST6 . 41 C5
Tamworth B77 . 250 F2
Uttoxeter ST14 . 110 F1
Marlbrook Dr WV4 . 266 B6
Marlbrook La WV6 . 253 B2
Marlburn Way WV5 . 269 E6
Marldon Pl ST6 . 41 D6
Marley Mount Cres TF9 . 97 C2
Marlin B77 . 261 D6
Marlow Cl ST3 . 73 D5
Marlow Dr DE14 . 185 A8
Marlowe Rd ST17 . 174 B8
Marlow Rd Longton ST3 . 73 D5
Tamworth B77 . 250 D5
Marlpit La Denstone ST14 . 95 D6
Ellastone DE6 . 80 A3
Moddershall ST15 . 105 F5
Sutton Coldfield B75 . 258 D3
Marlpit Rise [1] B75 . 258 E3
Marlpool Dr WS3 . 244 A1
Marmion Pk B79 . 250 B6
Marmion St B79 . 250 B5
Marnel Dr WV3 . 265 E7
Marney Wlk ST6 . 42 B2
Marquis Dr WS12,WS15 . 195 D3
Marquis Drive Visitor Ctr*
WS15 . 195 C3
Marquis's Dr WS15 . 196 B2
Marrick B77 . 251 C1
Marriott St ST4 . 73 A5
Marsden St ST1 . 282 C3
Marsett B77 . 262 C8
Marshall Ave ST6 . 43 B7
Marshall Cl WS9 . 256 B4
Marshall Gr ST8 . 16 B8
Marshalls Ind Est WV2 . 266 C7
Marshall St Burslem ST6 . 41 F1
Tamworth B77 . 250 E5
Marsh Ave
Newcastle-u-L ST5 . 56 C5
Newchapel ST7 . 26 E2
Stoke-on-T ST6 . 42 B2
Marshbrook Fst Sch
ST19 . 192 F1
Marsh Cl ST9 . 59 A4
Marsh Cres DY8 . 275 D3
Marsh Ct ST16 . 155 D5
Marshfield La ST8 . 16 C2
Marsh Gr ST8 . 16 C3
Marsh Green Cl ST8 . 16 D2
Marshgreen Rd ST8 . 16 D3
Marsh Gr DY3 . 269 E2
Marsh La
Cheswardine TF9 . 130 A8
Ellenhall ST21 . 134 B1
Lichfield WS14 . 231 C5
Marshland Gr ST6 . 42 A8
Marshlands Sch ST17 . 175 C6
Marsh Lane Par WV10 . 240 C2
Marsh La Penkridge ST19 . 192 F1
Stanton DE6 . 80 D8
Whittington WS14 . 232 B5
Wolverhampton WV10 . 240 B2
Marsh Mdws ST20 . 131 C4
Marsh Par ST5 . 283 C3
Marsh Prim Sch ST11 . 91 A6
Marsh St N ST1 . 282 B3
Marsh St S ST1 . 282 B2
Marsh St ST16 . 155 D5
Marsh View ST3 . 90 A5
Marsh Way ST5 . 56 C5
Marshwood Cl [2] WS11 . 210 A2
Marsland Cl ST16 . 155 A4
Marsland Rd ST16 . 155 A4
Mars St ST6 . 42 C1
Marston Cl
Stourbridge DY8 . 279 D4
Wheaton Aston ST19 . 205 C6
Marston Croft ST19 . 205 C6
Marston Ct ST16 . 155 D5
Marston Dr ST16 . 155 E5
Marston Gr Stafford ST16 . 155 E5
Stoke-on-T ST1 . 57 D8
Marston Ind Est WV2 . 266 C7
Marston La Hatton DE65 . 146 D8
Marston ST18 . 136 E3
Rolleston on D DE13 . 147 A4
Marston Old La DE65 . 146 D8
Marston Pk B78 . 249 F4
Marston Rd
Cannock WS12 . 209 F6
Marston-On-Dove DE65 . 147 B8
Stafford ST16 . 155 E5
Wheaton Aston ST19 . 205 B7
Wolverhampton WV2 . 266 C7
Marston Rise DE15 . 185 F8
Marston Road Trad Pk
ST16 . 155 E5
Marsworth Way ST16 . 136 D1
Martham Dr WV6 . 255 B2
Martin Croft WS13 . 214 A1
Martindale
[6] Stafford ST17 . 175 D6
Cannock WS11 . 210 A2
Martindale Cl ST3 . 89 F8
Martin Dale TF9 . 99 D5
Martindale Trad Est
WS11 . 210 A2
Martin Dr ST16 . 155 C3
Martin's La DE13 . 145 A4
Martinslow La ST10,ST13 . 48 E4
Martins Mill CW12 . 16 C8
Martin St Burslem ST6 . 57 B7
Stafford ST16 . 285 B3
Wolverhampton WV4 . 266 F5
Martins Way ST18 . 158 C8
Martley Rd WS4 . 244 C2
Martlin La WS15 . 179 A5
Marton Ave WS7 . 229 A8
Marwood Croft B74 . 257 A2
Marychurch Rd ST2 . 58 B3
Maryfield Wlk ST4 . 71 E7
Maryhill Cl ST7 . 26 A3
Maryhill High Sch ST7 . 26 A3
Maryhill Prim Sch ST7 . 26 A3
Mary Howard CE Prim Sch
B79 . 217 C5
Mary Rand Cl ST17 . 174 D8
Mary Rose Cl Bucknall ST2 . 58 B3
Cheslyn Hay WS6 . 226 D1
Marysgate ST19 . 223 D7
Mary St WS12 . 210 B7
Maryvale Ct WS14 . 231 D7
Masefield Cl
Burntwood WS7 . 212 A1
Cheadle ST10 . 76 D5
Lichfield WS14 . 231 B6
Market Drayton TF9 . 112 A7
Masefield Cres DE14 . 166 D7
Masefield Dr
Stafford ST17 . 155 C1
Tamworth B79 . 250 A7
Masefield Gr WS11 . 209 E4
Masefield Mews WV10 . 241 A1
Masefield Rd Dudley DY3 . 271 A4
Longton ST3 . 73 A2
Wolverhampton WV10 . 241 A1
Mason Cres WV4 . 265 E5
Mason Dr ST8 . 27 B8
Masons Lawn ST20 . 171 C5
Masons Pl TF10 . 168 E4
Mason's Pl TF10 . 168 E5
Mason St Stoke-on-T ST4 . 72 F5
Wolverhampton WV2 . 266 C7
Masterson St ST4 . 72 D6
Mathews Wlk ST1 . 282 C3
Matlock Cl WS3 . 243 C3
Matlock Dr WS11 . 210 A4
Matlock Pl ST5 . 55 A2
Matlock Rd WS3 . 243 C3
Matlock St ST1 . 282 B1
Matthews Ct ST1 . 282 C2
Matthews Pl CW12 . 6 A2
Matthews Rd ST17 . 174 C7
Matthews Wlk WS13 . 214 A2
Maud St ST4 . 72 E7
Maunders Rd ST2 . 43 A1
Maureen Ave ST6 . 41 D6
Maureen Gr ST5 . 56 C3
Mavesyn Cl WS15 . 198 A8
Mavis Rd WS12 . 210 B7
Mavor Ave WS7 . 211 D1
Mawdesley St ST6 . 57 B6
Mawgan Dr WS14 . 231 D6
Mawson Gr ST4 . 57 D1
Maxstoke Cl
Tamworth B77 . 261 C4
Walsall WS3 . 243 A3
Maxtock Ave WS13 . 231 A6
Maxton Way ST3 . 74 B2
Maxwell Cl WS14 . 231 C7
Maxwell Pl ST4 . 71 E7
Maxwell Rd
Congleton CW12 . 16 A8
Wolverhampton WV2 . 266 D8
Mayall Dr B75 . 258 D4
Mayama Rd B78 . 260 F8
May Ave Newcastle-u-L ST5 . 56 D3
Stoke-on-T ST6 . 41 F3
Maybank Cl WS14 . 231 E8
May Bank Inf Sch ST5 . 56 D3
Maybank WS15 . 196 E7
Maybrook Ind Est WS8 . 244 F5
Maybrook Rd WS8 . 244 F5
Maybury Cl WV8 . 238 E4
Maybury Way ST2 . 43 A1
Maybush Gdns WV10 . 240 C1
May Cl WS7 . 211 F1
Maycroft Cl WS12 . 209 F7
Mayer Ave ST5 . 283 B4
Mayer Bank [6] ST6 . 57 A8
Mayers Ct [3] ST13 . 30 E5
Mayer St ST1 . 282 C3
Mayfair Ave ST10 . 62 A8
Mayfair Cl WV7 . 237 A5
Mayfair Dr Fazeley B78 . 261 A7
Kingswinford DY6 . 275 C7
Mayfair Gdns
[14] Stoke-on-T ST6 . 41 D3
Wolverhampton WV3 . 255 D2
Mayfair Gr ST9 . 43 E8
Mayfair DE11 . 186 E6
Mayfield Ave Hanley ST1 . 57 E5
Mayfield DE6 . 81 C7
Newcastle-u-L ST5 . 283 A2
Penkridge ST19 . 207 E8
Mayfield Cl ST13 . 30 B5
Mayfield Cres ST1 . 57 E4
Mayfield Dr
Blythe Bridge ST11 . 90 D8
Burton u T DE15 . 186 A8
Mayfield Pl E ST4 . 71 E5
Mayfield Pl ST5 . 56 C4
Mayfield Pl W ST4 . 71 E5
Mayfield Rd
Albrighton WV7 . 237 A5
Biddulph ST8 . 27 D6
Burton u T DE15 . 167 A3
Hangingbridge DE6 . 81 F8
Stafford ST17 . 156 C1
Mayfields Dr WS8 . 228 B2
Mayfield B77 . 262 C8
Mayfield Terr DE6 . 81 D6
Mayflower Dr WS15 . 178 C1
Maygrove Rd DY6 . 275 C7
Maylea Cres ST6 . 57 C7
Maynard Ave DY8 . 279 D3
Maynards Croft TF10 . 169 A4
Mayneford Pl ST4 . 71 F1
Mayne St ST4 . 71 F1
Mayock Cres ST16 . 155 B2
Mayou Ct WS3 . 244 A4
May Pl Longton ST4 . 284 B5
Newcastle-u-L ST5 . 56 C3
Maypole Ct WV5 . 270 A6
Maypole Dr DY8 . 279 E5
Maypole St WV5 . 270 B7
May St Newcastle-u-L ST5 . 55 C1
Stoke-on-T ST6 . 42 B1
Mays Wlk DE13 . 200 F3
Mayswood Dr WV6 . 254 F1
Maythorne Rd ST3 . 73 A1
Maythorn Gdns
Codsall WV8 . 239 A4
Wolverhampton WV6 . 255 C3
Maywood Cl DY6 . 275 B6
Mead Ave ST7 . 25 E7
Mead Cl WS9 . 256 B6
Mead Cres DE15 . 186 A6
Meadfoot Dr DY6 . 275 B7
Meadlands The WV5 . 269 E6
Meadow Ave Longton ST3 . 73 C1
Newcastle-u-L ST5 . 56 A4
Weston CW2 . 37 B5
Wetley Rocks ST9 . 60 B6
Meadowbank Ave ST18 . 138 C2
Meadowbank Grange
WS6 . 226 E4
Meadow Bank B78 . 250 B1
Meadow Bank Wlk ST16 . 155 C8
Meadowbrook Ct ST15 . 120 D6
Meadowbrook Gdns
WV8 . 239 B4
Meadowbrook Rd WS13 . 214 B3
Meadow Cl Aldridge B74 . 256 F2
Blythe Bridge ST11 . 90 E6
Eccleshall ST21 . 133 E7
Forsbrook ST11 . 91 B8
Gnosall ST20 . 171 E7
Leek ST13 . 31 A5
Market Drayton TF9 . 97 A1
Penkridge ST19 . 207 F7
Wheaton Aston ST19 . 205 B6
Meadowcroft Ave ST3 . 90 C8
Meadow Croft WS12 . 209 C4
Meadowcroft Gdns ST19 205 C6
Meadow Croft
Hagley DY9 . 281 F4
Perton WV6 . 254 D3
Streethay WS13 . 215 A1
Meadow Ct Barlaston ST12 . 88 C2
Burton u T DE14 . 166 F3
Newchapel ST7 . 26 E2
Norton Bridge ST15 . 135 A8
Stafford ST17 . 175 A8
Meadow Dr Cheadle ST10 . 76 D3
Haughton ST18 . 172 E6
Stoke-on-T ST3 . 89 A8
Meadowfields Cl DY8 . 275 E2
Meadow Glade ST18 . 158 C8
Meadow Gr WS6 . 227 A2
Meadow Hill Dr [5]
WS11 . 210 A3
Meadowhill Dr DY8 . 275 E2
Meadow La
Acton Trussell ST17 . 193 B8
Burton u T DE13 . 167 A8
Colwich ST18 . 177 C7
Coven Heath WV10 . 240 C6
Derrington ST18 . 154 E2
Fulford ST11 . 106 E8
Millmeece ST21 . 117 E7
Meadowlands Dr WS4 . 244 D1
Meadow La ST5 . 56 A4
Meadow Lark Cl WS12 . 210 B4
Meadow La Roston DE6 . 96 C7
Stoke-on-T ST4 . 88 C7
Swadlincote DE11 . 186 F5
Wombourne WV5 . 270 B8
Yoxall DE13 . 200 B7
Meadowpark Rd DY8 . 279 D8
Meadow Pk B79 . 249 F5
Meadow Pl ST3 . 74 B1
Meadow Rd
Albrighton WV7 . 237 B5
Aldridge WS9 . 256 A4
Barlaston ST12 . 88 D1
Brown Edge ST6 . 43 B6
Burton u T DE14 . 166 F4
Coldmeece ST15 . 118 A6
Newport TF10 . 169 A3
Stafford ST17 . 174 F8
Stoke-on-T ST6 . 42 C5
Tamworth B78 . 249 E3
Wolverhampton WV3 . 265 D8
Meadow Ridge ST17 . 175 C8
Meadow Rise DE13 . 183 E1
Meadows Gr WV8 . 239 A4
Meadowside Ave ST7 . 39 D2
Meadow Side ST8 . 27 B6
Meadowside Dr DE14 . 166 E3
Meadowside La ST7 . 26 B7
Meadowside
Loggerheads TF9 . 99 E5
Mayfield DE6 . 81 D6
Meadowside Rd B74 . 257 F3
Meadowside
Saverley Green ST11 . 91 B2
Stoke-on-T ST4 . 88 B7
Meadows Prim Sch CW3 . 69 A8
Meadows Rd ST7 . 25 F1
Meadows The
Brewood ST19 . 223 D6
Hilderstone ST15 . 106 D2
Kingstone ST14 . 141 C8
Rugeley WS15 . 197 B6
Salt ST18 . 137 F4
Stoke-on-T ST9 . 43 F7
Uttoxeter ST14 . 111 A2
Wrinehill CW3 . 53 A3
Meadow Stile Home Park
Cvn Site ST8 . 27 A6
Meadow St
Newcastle-u-L ST5 . 55 F6
Stoke-on-T ST2 . 43 B1
Tamworth B77 . 250 C3
Meadow Sweet Cl ST6 . 42 E2
Meadowsweet Dr ST17 . 175 F7
Meadowsweet Way
WS12 . 210 E4
Meadow Vale WV8 . 239 B2
Meadow View WS7 . 229 D6
Meadow View Cl TF10 . 169 A3
Meadow View Cvn Pk
WV10 . 240 C6
Meadow View DE6 . 127 C8
Meadow View Rd
Newport TF10 . 169 A3
Swadlincote DE11 . 186 F5
Meadow View
Rolleston on D DE13 . 147 C4
Sedgley DY3 . 266 C1
Meadowview ST6 . 42 E3
Meadow View Terr WV6 . 255 E4
Meadowview ST15 . 118 E6
Meadow Way
Armitage WS15 . 198 B4
Cannock WS12 . 210 C1
Codsall WV8 . 238 E2
Lawton-gate ST7 . 25 A5
Stone ST15 . 119 F6
Stourbridge DY8 . 275 C2
Upper Tean ST10 . 92 D3
Whitmore ST5 . 85 D5
Mead The Sedgley DY3 . 271 B8
Stoke-on-T ST4 . 88 B7
Meadway Cl WS12 . 210 C3
Meadway Dr ST17 . 175 C6
Meadway St WS7 . 229 A5
Meadway The WV6 . 255 A5
Mead Wlk DE15 . 186 A6
Meaford Ave ST15 . 104 F2
Meaford Dr ST3 . 72 E3
Meaford Rd ST12,ST15 . 104 D6
Meakin Ave ST5 . 71 B3
Meakin Cl Cheadle ST10 . 76 C1
Congleton CW12 . 6 B1
Stone ST15 . 120 C6
Meakin Gr ST16 . 155 B6
Meakin Ho ST15 . 104 F1
Mear Greaves La DE15 . 167 B4
Mear's La WS15 . 198 F8
Mease Ave WS7 . 229 D6
Mease La B79 . 218 B2
Mease The DE65 . 147 E8
Meddins Cl DY7 . 278 A4
Meddins La DY7 . 277 F4
Meddins Rise DY7 . 277 F4
Media Way ST1 . 56 F4
Medina Cl WV10 . 240 F4
Medina B77 . 250 E1
Medina Way Kidsgrove ST7 . 26 B2
Kingswinford DY6 . 275 C6
Medway Dr ST8 . 16 D1
Medway Pl ST5 . 71 B4
Medway Rd WS8 . 228 C2
Medway B77 . 250 E1
Medway Wlk
Brownhills WS8 . 228 C2
Stoke-on-T ST6 . 42 A4
Meece Ave ST15 . 118 D7
Meece Rd ST15 . 118 D6
Meerash La WS7 . 229 C3
Meerbrook Cl ST4 . 88 B5
Meerbrook Rd ST13 . 19 D1
Meerbrook Youth Hostel*
ST13 . 19 F6
Meere Cl ST6 . 42 E3
Meeson Cl WV7 . 237 B5
Megacre ST7 . 40 A1
Meg La WS7 . 212 B1
Meigh Rd ST2,ST9 . 59 A4
Meigh St ST1 . 282 C3
Meiklejohn Pl ST6 . 42 A6
Meirhay Rd ST3 . 73 D2
Meir Heath Prim Sch ST3 . 90 A4
Meir Prim Sch ST3 . 74 B1
Meir Rd ST3 . 73 E1
Meir St ST6 . 41 E4
Meir View ST3 . 74 A1
Melbourne Ave DE15 . 167 C3
Melbourne Cl DY6 . 275 E4
Melbourne Cres
Cannock WS12 . 210 F2
Stafford ST16 . 156 B5
Melbourne Rd WS12 . 210 F2
Melbourne St ST3 . 73 D5
Melbury Way [1] WS11 . 209 F2
Melchester Gr ST3 . 73 E1
Melchester Wlk [2] WS11 209 F2
Melfont St ST6 . 41 E3
Melford Cl DY3 . 266 C2
Melford Grange WS7 . 211 E1
Melford Rise WS7 . 211 F1
Melford B79 . 249 E6
Meliden Way ST4 . 71 F6
Mellard St Audley ST7 . 39 D1
Newcastle-u-L ST5 . 283 A4
Mellor Dr Alrewas DE13 . 200 F2
Sutton Coldfield B74 . 257 E3
Uttoxeter ST14 . 111 B1
Mellor Rd DE14 . 185 B7
Mellors Bank ST7 . 26 D6
Mellor St ST7 . 26 F2
Mellowdew Rd DY8 . 275 C3
Mellow La ST10,ST13 . 47 E3
Mellwaters B77 . 262 C8
Melmerby B77 . 262 C8
Melrose Ave
Meir Heath ST3 . 90 A4
Newcastle-u-L ST5 . 71 A5
Stafford ST17 . 174 C8
Stoke-on-T ST1 . 57 D7
Stone ST15 . 120 C5
Stourbridge DY8 . 279 F2
Melrose Cres TF9 . 112 B8
Melrose Dr
Cannock WS12 . 209 F7
Perton WV6 . 254 E4
Melrose Pl ST13 . 30 B5
Melstone Ave ST6 . 41 F3
Melville Ct ST5 . 71 C1
Melville Rd ST3 . 73 E2
Melville St ST1 . 57 E3
Melvyn Cres ST6 . 56 C7
Menai Dr ST8 . 27 D6
Menai Gr ST3 . 284 C5
Mendip Ave ST17 . 175 E6
Mendip Cl Dudley DY3 . 271 D3
Wolverhampton WV2 . 266 F7
Mendip Gn ST2 . 43 A1
Mendip Pl ST5 . 55 E3
Mendip Rd WS12 . 195 A1
Mendip Way B77 . 251 C1
Mentone Cres TF10 . 168 B4
Menzies Ho
[4] Stoke-on-T ST3 . 89 F8
Cheddleton ST13 . 45 C7
Meon Gr WV6 . 254 F4
Mercer Ave ST15 . 120 C7
Mercer St ST3 . 73 B1
Merchant Cl WV6 . 253 C3
Merchants Pk WS9 . 256 A7
Merchants Way WS9 . 256 A7
Mercia Cl Hatton DE65 . 146 D8
Tamworth B79 . 249 E7
Mercia Cres ST6 . 57 A6
Mercia Dr WV6 . 254 E5
Mercian Ct
Lichfield WS14 . 231 C7
Market Drayton TF9 . 97 C1
Mercian Pk B77 . 251 A3
Mercian Way Lapley ST19 206 A7
Tamworth B77 . 251 B3
Mercury Pk B77 . 251 B3
Mercury Pl ST6 . 42 C1
Mercury Rd WS11 . 210 A5
Mere Cl TF10 . 168 F4
Mere Croft WS11 . 227 F4
Mere Ct CW2 . 37 B5
Meredith Cl DE14 . 166 D6
Meredith Rd DY3 . 271 A5
Mere Dr B75 . 258 B2
Mere Green Cl B75 . 258 C2
Mere Green Comb Sch
B75 . 258 B2
Mere Green Rd B75 . 258 C2
Mere La DY7 . 273 C6
Merelake Rd ST7 . 40 B8
Meremore Dr ST5 . 40 D2
Mere Oak Rd WV6 . 254 E5
Mere Pool Rd B75 . 258 E2
Mere Rd Stourbridge DY8 . 279 E3
Weston CW2 . 37 B5
Mere Rise ST21 . 132 D7
Mere Side Cl [5] ST1 . 56 F2
Merevale Ave ST2 . 58 A2

Merganser B77 .... 262 A6
Meriden Ave DY8 ...... 279 D6
Meriden Cl
  Cannock WS11 .... 226 B8
  Stourbridge DY8 ...... 279 D6
Meriden Gn 3 WV4 .... 266 F4
Meriden Rd
  Newcastle-u-L ST5 .... 71 C2
  Wolverhampton WV10 ... 240 B1
Merino Cl ST3 .... 89 C8
Merlin Cl Cannock WS1 .. 209 C2
  Stoke-on-T ST6 ...... 42 A8
  Tamworth B77 .... 262 A6
  Uttoxeter ST14 ...... 126 C6
Merlin Cres DE14 .... 184 F8
Merlin Ct WS7 .... 229 F8
Merlin Gn CW3 .... 68 E6
Merlin Way Kidsgrove ST7 .. 26 D3
  Whittington WS14 .... 232 F5
Merrial St ST5 ...... 283 B3
Merrick St ST1 ...... 282 C4
Merridale Ave WV3 ... 255 F1
Merridale Ct WV3 .... 255 F1
Merridale Gr WV3 .... 255 E1
Merridale St W WV3 .. 266 A8
Merrill Cl WS3 ...... 226 E2
Merrion Dr ST6 ...... 42 B3
Merrivale Rd ST17 ... 174 E7
Merrydale Rd DE15 ... 186 A8
Merryfield Rd DY1 ... 271 E1
Merryfields Sch ST5 . 56 B4
Merry Rd ST17 ...... 174 E7
Mersey Cl WS13 ..... 178 E3
Mersey Rd
  Newcastle-u-L ST5 .. 71 A3
  Walsall WS3 .... 243 E1
Mersey St ST1 ...... 282 A2
Merthyr Gr ST8 ..... 27 E6
Merton Cl WS7 ..... 228 F5
Merton St ST3 ..... 284 C4
Mervyn Rd DE15 ... 167 A3
Mesnes Gn WS14 .. 231 C7
Metcalf Cl WS7 ... 229 C8
Metcalfe Cl WS12 . 210 C6
Metcalfe Rd ST6 .. 42 A3
Metfield Cl B79 ... 250 C8
Metfield Croft DY6 . 275 F6
Mewies Cl DE12 ... 184 D1
Mews Cl ST2 ...... 58 A2
Mews The Cannock WS11 .. 209 C1
  Newcastle-u-L ST5 .. 56 D4
Meynell Cl DE15 ... 167 B1
Meynell Field TF9 . 99 E4
Meyrick Rd ST17 .. 285 B1
Mica Cl B77 ...... 251 B2
Michael Cl ST3 ... 74 B3
Michaels Cl ST5 .. 56 C7
Michael's La DE6 . 80 C5
Michigan Cl WS11 . 210 B2
Michigan Gr ST4 .. 288 B8
Micklea La ST9 ... 29 F1
Mickleby Way ST3 . 90 C7
Micklegate ST19 .. 223 D7
Micklehome Dr DE13 .. 201 B3
Mickleton B77 .... 262 C8
Micklewood Cl ST19 .. 207 F7
Micklewood La ST19 .. 208 B4
Middle Cross St ST3 . 284 C4
Middle Entry B79 .. 250 B4
Middlefield ST20 .. 171 E7
Middlefield Rd ST .. 73 D8
Middlefield WM ... 239 E2
Middle Friars ST17 . 285 B2
Middlehurst Specl Sch
  ST7 .... 41 F7
Middle La Codsall WV8 .. 238 C2
  Congleton CW12 .... 6 D4
  Wolverhampton WV9 . 240 A5
Middlemore La WS9 . 256 A6
Middlepark Rd DY1 . 271 F1
Middlesmoor B77 .. 262 C8
Middleton Cl
  Hammerwich WS7 .. 229 D4
  Stoke-on-T ST6 ... 42 E3
Middleton Hall* B78 . 260 E1
Middleton Rd
  Aldridge B74 ..... 257 A1
  Brownhills WS8 ... 229 A1
  Whittington WS14 . 232 E6
Middleway Ave DY8 . 275 C3
Middleway WS12 ... 211 A6
Middleway Pk DE14 . 166 E3
Midfield Cl ST8 ... 16 C2
Midgley Cl TF10 .. 168 E3
Midgley Dr ST4 ... 258 A2
Midhurst Cl ST7 .. 41 F8
Midhurst Dr WS12 . 210 C7
Midhurst Gr WV6 .. 255 C5
Midland Rd WS12 . 209 C5
Midpoint Ctr WV6 . 255 F5
Midway Dr ST11 .. 90 E6
Midway The ST5 .. 283 B2
Midwinter Ct ST6 . 56 E6
Milan Dr ST5 .... 70 E6
Milan Gr ST3 .... 73 E4
Milborne Dr ST5 . 71 C5
Milburn Rd ST6 .. 57 B6
Milburn B77 .... 262 C8
Milcote Way DY6 . 275 B7
Mildenhall B79 .. 250 C8
Mile Cl ST5 ..... 55 F3
Mile Flat
  Kingswinford DY6 . 275 A7
  Kinver DY6 ...... 274 F7
Milehouse La ST5 . 56 B4

Mile Oak Cross Rds B78 .. 249 C2
Miles Bank ST1 ...... 282 B3
Miles Green Rd ST7 .. 54 E8
Milestone Ct WV6 ... 255 A3
Milestone Dr DY9 ... 281 F4
Milford Ave ST9 .... 59 B4
Milford Cl DY8 ..... 275 E3
Milford Rd
  Newcastle-u-L ST5 . 283 A1
  Walton-on-t-H ST17 . 175 F7
  Wolverhampton WV2 . 266 C7
Milford St ST4 .... 72 F5
Milgreen Ave ST1 .. 57 D7
Milking Bank DY1 .. 271 E2
Milking Bank Prim Sch
  DY1 .... 271 E2
Milk St ST13 ..... 30 F7
Mill Bank Dr ST14 . 96 A3
Mill Bank Pl ST15 . 55 F1
Mill Bank Sedgley DY3 . 271 D8
  Stafford ST16 ... 285 B3
Millbank St Longton ST3 . 284 C3
  Wolverhampton WV11 . 241 F1
Millbeck Cl CW2 .. 37 B5
Millbridge Cl ST3 . 90 B6
Millbrook Cl 4 WS11 . 209 F2
Millbrook Dr WS14 . 246 F6
Millbrook Gdns ST11 . 90 F7
Millbrook Gr ST2 . 43 A1
Millbrook Way ST10 . 76 F2
Mill Cl Blakedown DY10 . 281 B2
  Caverswall ST3 .. 74 C3
  Dudley DY3 ..... 271 D6
  Newton Solney DE15 . 167 E8
Mill Cotts Sandon ST18 . 137 D7
  Stowe-by-Chartley ST18 . 139 C5
Millcourt ST4 .... 87 F7
Mill Cres Barton-u-N DE13 . 201 E8
  Cannock WS11 ... 210 B2
Millcroft Way WS15 . 198 C4
Mill Ct
  Great Haywood ST18 . 158 B2
  Shenstone WS14 .. 247 A6
  Walsall,Lile Cres WV10 . 240 D4
  Walsall,End La DE13 . 200 F3
Millend La ST7 ... 39 C5
Millenium Way ST5 . 40 F2
Millennium Cl WS3 . 244 A4
Millennium Way
  Codsall WV8 ..... 239 B4
  Stone ST15 ...... 104 E2
Miller Cl WS13 ... 232 B1
Millersdale Cl DE15 . 167 B5
Millers Gate 2 ST15 . 120 A8
Millers Gn WV7 .. 237 A5
Millers Green Dr DY6 . 275 A8
Millers La
  Burton u T DE14 .. 166 C3
  Stoke-on-T ST2 .. 43 A1
Miller St ST5 .... 283 C3
Millers Vale
  Cannock WS12 ... 210 D1
  Wombourne WV5 .. 269 D5
Millers View Cheadle ST10 . 76 F2
  Kidsgrove ST7 ... 26 A1
Millers Wharf B78 . 251 F1
Millers Wlk WS3 .. 243 E3
Millett Rd ST2 ... 58 A3
Mill Farm Ct ST21 . 134 D6
Millfield Ave
  Walsall,Little Bloxwich
    WS3 .... 243 D3
  Walsall WS4 ..... 244 B1
Millfield Cres ST2 . 43 A1
Millfield Dr WS7 .. 97 F2
Millfield Prim Sch
  Brownhills WS8 .. 245 A7
  Fazeley B78 ..... 261 A8
Millfield Rd WS8 .. 245 A7
Mill Fields DY7 ... 278 B3
Millfields Way WV5 . 269 E5
Mill Gn WV10 .... 240 D4
Mill Gr Cheadle ST10 . 76 E2
  Codsall WV8 ..... 239 C3
Mill Green Nature Pk*
  WS11 .... 209 F1
Mill Gr ST7 ..... 25 D1
Mill Hayes Rd
  Biddulph ST8 .... 27 C4
  Burslem ST6 ..... 41 E1
Mill Hill Cres ST6 . 42 A4
Mill Hill Dr DE15 . 167 B4
Mill Hill La DE15 . 167 B4
Mill Hill Prim Sch ST6 . 41 F4
Mill Ho DE14 .... 278 B3
Millhouse Dr ST10 . 76 E1
Millhouse Gdns ST19 . 192 F1
Millicent Ho ST3 . 284 C2
Millicent St ST4 . 72 E6
Millington St WS15 . 178 F2
Mill La
  Acton Trussell ST17 . 175 A2
  Albrighton WV7 ... 220 F1
  Aldridge WS9 .... 256 F7
  Barthomley CW2 .. 38 C7
  Barton-u-N DE13 .. 201 E8
  Blakedown DY10 .. 281 B2
  Blakenhall CW5 .. 52 B4
  Codsall WV8 ..... 238 F5
  Congleton CW12 .. 16 C8
  Doveridge DE6 ... 127 A8
  Edingale B79 .... 217 D4
  Ellastone DE6 ... 80 B2
  Fazeley B78 ..... 261 A8
  Foston DE65 ..... 129 D7
  Gnosall ST20 .... 171 C5

Mill La continued
  Gratwich ST14 ...... 124 E3
  Great Haywood ST18 . 158 B2
  Hammerwich WS7 ... 229 D3
  Hartington SK17 ... 24 D5
  Kinver,Blundies DY7 . 274 A4
  Kinver DY7 .... 278 B3
  Little Aston WS9 .. 257 A7
  Madeley CW3 ..... 68 F7
  Milwich ST18 ..... 122 D4
  Moddershall ST15 .. 105 E6
  Roston DE6 .... 96 D7
  Rugeley WS15 .... 178 F1
  Scropton DE65 ... 129 F1
  Shenstone WS14 .. 247 A6
  Standon ST21 .... 102 C3
  Stonnall WS9,WS14 . 246 A4
  Sudbury DE6 ..... 128 E1
  Tamworth B79 .... 250 C5
  Tettenhall Wood WV6 . 255 A3
  The Bank ST7 .... 26 A7
  Weston CW2 ..... 37 B6
  Weston-u-L TF11 .. 220 D7
  Weston-Under-Lizard
    TF11 .... 203 D1
  Wetley Rocks ST9 . 59 F7
  Wheaton Aston ST19 . 205 C5
  Wombourne WV5 .. 270 B6
Mill Mdw DE13 ... 162 F8
Mill Meece Marsh ST21 . 102 D1
Mill Meece Pumping
  Station* ST21 .... 117 E8
Millmoor Ave WS15 . 198 A4
Mill Park Ind Est WS11 . 210 A1
Mill Pk WS15 .... 210 A2
Mill Pond The WS13 . 214 C2
Mill Pool Cl WV5 . 269 D5
Mill Pool Rd ST10 . 210 B6
Millpool The WV5 . 263 F2
Mill Rd Brownhills WS8 . 245 A7
  Cheadle ST10 .... 76 E2
  Coldmeece ST15 .. 118 B6
  Oakamoor ST10 ... 78 A6
  Walsall WS4 ..... 244 C1
Mill Rise ST7 .... 26 A1
Millrise Rd ST2 .. 43 A1
Mills Cres WV2 .. 266 E8
Millside Rugeley WS15 . 196 B7
  Wombourne WV5 .. 269 E5
Mills Rd WV2 .... 266 E8
Mill St Cannock WS11 . 209 E1
  Leek ST13 .... 30 D6
  Newcastle-u-L ST5 . 55 D1
  Stone ST15 ...... 25 E1
Millstone Ave ST7 . 25 E1
Millstone Edge ST13 . 45 B1
Mill St ST19 ..... 192 E1
Millstream Cl ST10 . 76 E2
Mill Stream Cl WV8 . 239 B4
Mill St Rocester ST14 . 96 A3
  Stafford ST16 ... 285 B3
  Stone ST15 ...... 120 A8
  Stourbridge DY8 .. 275 F2
Mill The ST7 .... 26 C5
Milltown Way ST13 . 31 A4
Mill View ST6 ... 42 D6
Millwalk Ave ST15 . 120 C7
Millwalk Dr WV9 . 240 A3
Millward Rd ST2 . 58 C3
Mill Waters ST10 . 76 E1
Millway La DE6 .. 95 A8
Mill Way WS15 ... 198 A1
Mill Way The ST15 . 103 B4
Milne Ave WS13 .. 215 D6
Milner Dr B79 ... 251 E7
Milner Terr ST1 . 31 A7
Milnes Cl ST3 ... 73 A2
Milo Cres B78 ... 250 A2
Milton Ave B79 .. 250 A7
Milton Cres Dudley DY3 . 271 A5
  Talke ST7 .... 40 C8
Milton Ct WV6 ... 254 E4
Milton Dr TF9 ... 97 C2
Milton Gr ST17 .. 174 B8
Milton Ho DE14 .. 166 D3
Milton Prim Sch ST2 . 43 B1
Milton Rd Cannock WS11 . 209 E4
  Stoke-on-T ST1 .. 42 F1
  Stoke-on-T ST1 .. 57 E8
Milton St Burton u T DE14 . 166 C3
  Hanley ST1 ...... 282 A1
Milvale St ST6 ... 56 E7
Milverton Dr ST14 . 110 F1
Milverton Pl 4 ST13 . 73 A3
Milward Gr ST3 .. 89 F6
Mimosa Wlk DY6 . 275 E8
Minard Gr ST3 ... 74 A4
Minden Gr ST6 .. 57 D8
Mineal Rd ST2 ... 57 B8
Minehead Rd Dudley DY1 . 271 A1
  Wolverhampton WV10 . 240 B2
Miners Way WS7 .. 228 C7
Miners Wlk B78 .. 251 F1
Minerva Cl Biddulph ST8 . 27 B5
  Tamworth B77 ... 250 D5
Minerva Rd ST4 .. 72 F6
Minewood Cl WS3 . 242 F3
Minion Cl ST17 .. 41 A8
Minn-End-La SK11 . 4 B6
Minnie Cl ST7 ... 54 E7
Minors Hill WS14 . 231 D6
Minshall St ST4 . 72 C5
Minshall St ST4 . 72 C5
Minsterley Cl WV3 . 265 E8
Minsterpool Wlk WS13 . 231 B8
Minster St ST6 ... 42 B1
Minster The WV3 . 266 A7
Minstrel Ct ST8 . 27 D7

Minton Cl Cheadle ST10 . 76 D1
  Congleton CW12 ... 6 B1
Minton Pl ST5 ... 56 D5
Minton St
  Newcastle-u-L ST5 . 56 D5
  Stoke-on-T ST4 .. 71 E8
Miranda Gr ST6 .. 42 D1
Miras Bsns Est WS12 . 210 D3
Mires Brook La WS15 . 160 F6
Mires The DE6 ... 35 A3
Mirfield Cl WV9 . 240 A3
Miss Pickerings Field
  ST17 .... 175 B1
Mistley Wlk ST6 . 41 C7
Mitcham Cl WS12 . 209 F7
Mitchell Ave ST7 . 25 D1
Mitchell Cl WS13 . 215 C6
Mitchell Dr ST7 . 25 D1
Mitchell High Sch ST2 . 58 C3
Mitchell Rise ST15 . 118 F6
Mitchell's Ct B79 . 250 B5
Mitchell St ST6 . 41 F1
Mitchel Rd DY6 . 275 F4
Mitre Cl WV11 ... 242 A3
Mitre Fold WS6 . 256 B8
Mitton Rd ST18 . 191 C7
Moat Bank DE15 . 167 D2
Moat Brook Ave WV8 . 238 E4
Moatbrook La WV8 . 238 D4
Moat Dr B78 .... 260 E5
Moat Farm Way WS3 . 244 A5
Moat Hall Prim Sch WS6 . 226 F3
Moathouse Cl ST17 . 193 B8
Moat House Dr ST18 . 133 E6
Moat La Audley ST7 . 39 B3
  Great Wyrley WS6 . 227 A2
  Newborough DE13 . 162 F6
Moatside Cl WS3 . 244 A5
Moat The ST3 ... 74 B4
Moat Way WS15 .. 198 B4
Mobberley Rd ST6 . 41 C7
Mob La WS4 ..... 244 C3
Moccasin Way ST16 . 155 F5
Moddershall Oaks ST1,
  ST15 .... 90 A1
Moden Cl DY3 ... 271 D6
Moden Hill DY3 . 271 D6
Modular Ct WV10 . 224 D5
Moffat Gr ST2 .. 73 E7
Moffatt Way ST5 . 55 A2
Moises Hall Rd WV5 . 270 B7
Moisty La
  Marchington ST14 . 127 C3
  Uttoxeter ST14 .. 126 F4
Mollatts Cl ST13 . 30 B1
Mollatts Wood Rd ST13 . 30 B1
Mollison Rd ST3 . 90 A8
Monaco Pl ST5 .. 70 E7
Monarch Cl DE13 . 166 D8
Monarchy WV WS15 . 196 D7
Mona Rd DE13 .. 166 B6
Moncreiff Dr ST13 . 148 A1
Moneystone Cotts ST10 . 63 A1
Monkhouse ST10 . 76 D3
Monkleigh Cl ST4 . 88 B5
Monks Cl
  Newcastle-u-L ST5 . 71 C6
  Wombourne WV5 .. 269 E6
Monksfield TF9 .. 97 A1
Monk St DE13 ... 146 C7
Monks Way
  Swynnerton ST15 . 103 B4
  Tamworth B77 ... 250 F5
Monks Wlk ST20 . 171 C5
Monkton Cl ST3 . 73 A3
Monmore Bsns Pk WV2 . 266 F7
Monmouth Pl ST5 . 71 D4
Monsaldale Cl
  Brownhills WS8 .. 244 D7
  Burton u T DE15 . 167 B4
Monsal Gr ST1 .. 57 F5
Monteagle Dr DY6 . 270 D1
Montford Gr DY3 . 271 D7
Montfort Pl ST5 . 71 B6
Montgomery Ct ST5 . 283 A1
Montgomery Pl ST3 . 74 B2
Montley B77 .... 262 C8
Montpelier Cl DE14 . 185 A7
Montpellier Gdns DY1 . 271 F1
Montrose Cl WS12 . 209 F5
Montrose St ST4 . 72 F5
Montville Dr ST17 . 155 B1
Monty Pl ST14 .. 73 B6
Monument Cl ST12 . 88 A2
Monument Dr WV10 . 241 C8
Monument La
  Sedgley DY3 .... 266 E1
  Tittensor ST12 .. 88 A2
Monument Rd ST17 . 40 D6
Monument View ST7 . 39 F2
Monyash Ct ST3 . 90 C7
Monyash Dr ST13 . 31 A5
Moon's La WS6 .. 226 D1
Moor Cl
  Acton Trussell ST17 . 175 B1
  Biddulph ST8 .... 16 E1
  Burntwood WS7 .. 229 D7
Moorcroft Ave WS13 . 231 B8
Moorcroft Cl ST17 . 76 C1
Moor Croft WS15 . 179 A6
Moorcroft Mus* ST6 . 57 B7
Moore Cl Perton WV6 . 254 F4
  Sutton Coldfield B74 . 257 F6
Moores Cl DE13 . 166 B6
Moores Croft B79 . 217 C5
Moore St Burslem ST6 . 57 A7
  Wolverhampton WV2 . 266 C7
Moorfield Ave ST8 . 27 C8

Moorfield Ct TF10 .. 168 E2
Moorfield La TF10 .. 168 D1
Moorfield Prim Sch
  TF10 .... 168 E1
Moorfield Rd WV2 . 266 C7
Moorfields Cl
  Aldridge WS9 .... 256 A7
  Cauldon Lowe ST10 . 63 E4
Moorfields Ind Est ST12 . 82 E3
Moorfields Leek ST13 . 30 F5
  Stafford ST16 ... 155 D7
Moor Fst Sch ST8 . 17 B1
Moor Furlong DE13 . 147 F1
Moorgate Com Prim Sch
  B79 .... 250 A5
Moorgate B79 ... 250 A5
Moor Gr ST14 ... 126 A8
Moor Hall Dr B75 . 258 D1
Moor Hall Dr B75 . 258 D1
Moor Hall Prim Sch B75 . 258 D2
Moorhead Dr ST9 . 43 F4
Moorhen Cl WS8 . 244 E7
Moorhen Way ST6 . 41 E8
Moorhill Prim Sch
  Cannock WS11 ... 209 E4
  Cannock WS11 ... 209 E5
Moorhouse Ct ST15 . 119 A6
Moorhouse La ST13 . 30 F5
Moorings The
  3 Stone ST15 ... 120 A8
  Alrewas DE13 ... 200 F3
  Colwich ST17 ... 177 E7
  Wolverhampton WV9 . 239 F2
Moor La Cheadle ST10 . 76 F5
  Church Leigh ST10 . 108 E5
  Colton WS15 .... 179 A8
  Gayton ST18 .... 138 F6
Moorland Ave ST9 . 59 C4
Moorland Cl
  Rugeley WS15 ... 178 C1
  Werrington ST9 .. 59 B4
Moorland Rd Biddulph ST8 . 27 D8
  Burslem ST6 .... 57 A8
  Cannock WS11 .. 209 E4
  Cheddleton ST13 . 45 C5
  Leek ST13 ...... 31 B5
  Mow Cop ST7 ... 26 D7
  Newport TF10 ... 168 E2
  Stoke-on-T ST6 . 42 B1
Moorlands Dr DE6 . 81 C7
Moorlands Sixth Form Ctr
  ST10 .... 76 D1
Moorland View ST6 . 42 C3
Moorland Wlk ST10 . 76 D1
Moor La Pattingham WV6 . 253 D2
  Seighford ST18 .. 154 D7
  Shenstone WS14 . 246 E2
  Tamworth,Amington B79 . 251 A6
  Tamworth,Bolehall B77 . 250 D5
Moorleys La ST18 . 139 A5
Moorpark Jun Sch ST6 . 42 A1
Moor Pk Perton WV6 . 254 D5
  Walsall WS3 .... 243 B3
Moor St S WV2 .. 266 C7
Moors Dr WV9 ... 224 B2
Moors Hill Cotts DE13 . 183 F8
Moorside High Sch ST9 . 59 E4
Moorside Rd ST4 . 71 E5
Moorson Ave ST7 . 25 F8
Moor St Burton u T DE14 . 166 C2
  Tamworth B77 ... 250 A5
Moorsyde Rd ST4 . 71 E5
Moor The WS13 .. 215 D8
Moorthorne Cres ST6 . 56 A6
Moor View WS7 .. 212 B2
Moorview Gdns ST7 . 26 E6
Moran Gr ST6 ... 56 F6
Moran Rd ST5 ... 55 F2
Mordaunt Dr B75 . 258 E2
Mordern Mobile Home Pk
  WV10 .... 240 C6
Moresby Cl ST2 . 43 B1
Moreton Ave
  Hanchurch ST5 .. 87 D8
  Kingsley ST10 ... 61 D2
  Wolverhampton WV4 . 266 E4
Moreton Cl Kidsgrove ST7 . 41 B8
  Werrington ST9 .. 59 B2
Moreton Com Sch WV10 . 240 F1
Moreton Ho ST5 . 56 D4
Moreton La
  Draycott in t C DE6 . 144 C8
  Great Haywood ST18 . 158 C4
Moreton Par ST5 . 56 D4
Moreton Pl ST7 . 25 E6
Moreton Rd WV10 . 240 D1
Moreton St WS11 . 209 F4
Morfe Hall La DY7 . 273 D4
Morfe La DY7 .... 273 C4
Morford Rd WS9 . 256 A7
Morgan Rd B78 . 250 A4
Morgan Way ST6 . 42 B6
Morland Cl ST15 . 120 B5
Morley Cl DE15 . 167 B2
Morley Dr WV12 . 6 A1
Morley Rd WS7 .. 229 B7
Morley Road Sch WS7 . 229 B7
Morley's Hill DE13 . 166 B7
Morley St Hanley ST1 . 282 A2
  Leek ST13 ...... 30 D5
Morlings Dr WS7 . 229 B8
Morning Pines DY8 . 279 C4
Morningside CW3 . 68 E6
Mornington Rd ST1 . 57 E8
Morpeth St ST13 . 284 C3
Morpeth B77 .... 261 C2

Morridge Side ST13 ....32 A1
Morridge View ST13 ....45 C4
Morris Ct 4 WV4 ....266 F4
Morris Dr ST16 ....156 C3
Morris Hill B78 ....262 F7
Morris Sq ST5 ....56 D5
Morston Dr ST5 ....71 B2
Morston B77 ....261 D4
Mortimer Pl ST3 ....73 F4
Morton Rd ST17 ....174 D6
Morton St ST6 ....56 E7
Morville Cl ST4 ....72 E7
Moscow La ST20 ....151 D7
Mosedale Ave ST3 ....89 E8
Moseley Ct WV11 ....241 F3
Moseley Old Hall* WV10 ....241 A5
Moseley Old Hall La WV10 ....241 A5
Moseley Rd WV10 ....241 A4
Moseley Row ST18 ....137 C1
Mosley Dr ST14 ....111 A1
Mosley Mews DE13 ....147 A4
Mosley Prim Sch DE13 ....165 C7
Mosley St DE14 ....166 C3
Mossbank Ave WS7 ....229 A6
Moss Cl Aldridge WS9 ....256 A5
Werrington ST9 ....59 B4
Moss Cres WS12 ....209 C5
Mossdale B77 ....262 C8
Mossdale Way DY3 ....271 E7
Mossfield TF9 ....130 A6
Mossfield Cres 4 ST7 ....26 B2
Mossfield Dr ST8 ....27 E7
Mossfield Rd ST3 ....73 C6
Moss Gn WS15 ....178 C2
Moss Green Rd ST2 ....73 D7
Moss Gr Kingswinford DY6 ....275 D7
Newcastle-u-L ST5 ....40 D3
Moss Hill ST9 ....43 D5
Moss La Betton TF9 ....97 F6
Cheadle ST10 ....77 A2
Chipnall TF9 ....114 C3
Hilderstone ST15 ....106 E6
Lawton-gate ST7 ....25 F4
Madeley CW3 ....68 D6
Maer ST5 ....84 F1
Mossland Rd ST3 ....73 C5
Moss La Whitmore ST5 ....85 C5
Woodseaves ST20,ST21 ....151 F8
Yarnfield ST15 ....119 A7
Mossley CE Prim Sch CW12 ....16 B8
Mossley Cl WS3 ....242 F1
Mossley Ct CW12 ....15 F8
Mossley Garth Cl 5 CW12 ....6 A1
Mossley La WS3 ....242 F2
Mossley Prim Sch WS3 ....242 F2
Moss Park Ave ST9 ....59 B4
Mosspit ST17 ....174 F4
Moss Pl ST7 ....26 B3
Moss Rd Cannock WS11 ....210 A3
Congleton CW12 ....15 E7
Moss Rise ST5 ....71 C1
Moss Side ST1 ....57 E8
Moss St Cannock WS11 ....210 A4
Stoke-on-T ST6 ....42 E5
Mossvale Gr ST16 ....155 A5
Mosswood St WS11 ....226 D7
Moston St ST1 ....57 D6
Mostyn Cl ST8 ....27 E6
Mott Pl ST6 ....56 D8
Moulton Rd ST3 ....284 B4
Mounfield Pl ST4 ....72 D6
Mountain Ash Rd WS8 ....244 E5
Mountain Pine Cl WS12 ....210 A8
Mount Ave Cannock WS12 ....210 B7
Stoke-on-T ST4 ....71 F7
Stone ST15 ....104 F2
Mountbatten Cl
1 Burton u T DE13 ....166 D8
Burntwood WS7 ....211 F1
Mount Cl
Cheslyn Hay WS6 ....226 E2
Dudley DY3 ....271 C2
Stone ST15 ....120 D6
Werrington ST9 ....59 C4
Wombourne WV5 ....270 A7
Mount Cotts ST20 ....131 B4
Mount Cres ST15 ....104 F2
Mount Ct WV6 ....255 B2
Mount Dr WV5 ....270 A7
Mount Edge ST18 ....137 B1
Mount Fields ST10 ....94 B2
Mountford Cres WS9 ....256 C8
Mountford St ST6 ....41 F1
Mount Gdns WV8 ....238 F4
Mount Ind Est ST15 ....104 F2
Mount La Dudley DY3 ....271 C2
Market Drayton TF9 ....112 C8
Mount Pleasant Ave WV5 ....269 F7
Mount Pleasant WS6 ....226 E2
Mount Pleasant Cl ST15 ....120 D6
Mount Pleasant
Derrington ST18 ....154 E2
Hanley ST1 ....282 A2
Ipstones ST10 ....62 A8
Kidsgrove ST7 ....26 A1
Kingswinford DY6 ....275 C4
Leek ST13 ....30 E6
Loggerheads TF9 ....99 F5
Mount Pleasant Mobile Home Pk B77 ....250 C1
Mount Pleasant
Newcastle-u-L,Chesterton ST5 ....55 E6
Newcastle-u-L ST5 ....283 C2
Mount Pleasant Rd ST7 ....26 B7
Mount Pleasant B77 ....261 C8
Mount Pl ST11 ....91 A7
Mount Rd
Blythe Bridge ST11 ....91 A7
Burntwood WS7 ....229 B6
Castle Gresley DE11 ....186 D1
Kidsgrove ST7 ....26 B1
Leek ST13 ....31 B5
Rugeley WS15 ....178 B2
Stone ST15 ....104 F2
Stourbridge,Wordsley DY8 ....275 E2
Walsall WS3 ....244 A4
Wolverhampton,Goldthorn Hill WV4 ....266 A4
Wolverhampton,Lanesfield WV4 ....266 F2
Wolverhampton,Tettenhall Wood WV6 ....255 A3
Wombourne WV5 ....270 A7
Mount Road Ind Est WS7 ....229 B6
Mount Row ST16 ....285 B3
Mount St Georges The ST5 ....56 C6
Mountside Gdns ST13 ....31 B6
Mount Side St WS12 ....210 C7
Mountsorrel Cl ST4 ....88 C6
Mount St Burton u T DE15 ....167 A3
Cannock WS12 ....210 B7
Hanley ST1 ....57 E5
Newcastle-u-L ST5 ....55 E6
Stafford ST16 ....285 B3
Stone ST15 ....105 A2
Mount The Creswell ST18 ....154 F7
Kidsgrove ST7 ....26 A1
Newcastle-u-L ST5 ....55 E6
Scholar Green ST7 ....25 E7
Mountwood Covert WV6 ....255 B3
Mouse Hill WS3 ....243 F3
Mousley St ST6 ....56 E8
Mowbray Croft WS7 ....211 E1
Mowbray Wlk ST1 ....57 F8
Mow Cop Rd ST7 ....26 D6
Mow La Biddulph ST7,ST8 ....16 B2
Mount Pleasant ST7 ....26 B5
Mow Cop CW12 ....15 F4
Moxhull Cl WV12 ....242 C1
Moxhull Gdns WV12 ....242 C1
Moxley Ave ST1 ....57 D7
Mozart Ct WS11 ....210 C2
Muchall Rd WV4 ....266 A5
Mucklestone Rd
Loggerheads TF9 ....99 D5
Norton in H TF9 ....82 D2
Mucklestone Wood La TF9 ....99 E6
Muirfield Cl WS3 ....243 A3
Muirfield B77 ....251 C5
Muirville Cl 1 DY8 ....275 D3
Mulberry Cl TF10 ....168 F1
Mulberry Dr 3 WS13 ....231 E8
Mulberry Gn DY1 ....271 F5
Mulberry Pl
Newcastle-u-L ST5 ....55 E8
Walsall WS3 ....242 F1
Mulberry Rd
Cannock WS11 ....209 E3
Walsall WS3 ....243 A1
Mulberry St ST1 ....282 C2
Mulberry Way ST13 ....31 A4
Muldoon Cl WS11 ....210 B4
Mulgrave St ST1 ....282 A4
Mullein B74 ....257 F5
Mulliner Cl ST2 ....58 D3
Munro St ST4 ....72 A5
Munster Terr ST4 ....71 F5
Murdoch Dr DY6 ....275 C7
Murhall St ST6 ....56 E8
Murray St ST6 ....41 C7
Murton B77 ....262 C8
Muse La DE6 ....129 B7
Musk La DY3 ....271 B3
Musk La W DY3 ....271 B3
Mus of Cannock Chase* WS12 ....210 D6
Mustang Cl ST6 ....41 C4
Mustang Dr ST16 ....155 B8
Muxloe Cl WS3 ....243 A3
Myatt Ave
Burntwood WS7 ....229 A7
Wolverhampton WV2 ....266 E6
Myatt Cl WV2 ....266 E6
Myatt St ST1 ....282 C4
Myatt Way WS15 ....196 D6
Mynors St Hanley ST1 ....282 C3
Stafford ST16 ....156 A3
Myott Ave ST5 ....283 A1
Myrtle Ave ST3 ....74 B3
Myrtle Gr Brewood ST19 ....223 D6
Wolverhampton WV3 ....265 E6
Myrtle St WV2 ....266 F6

N

Nabb La Alton ST10 ....94 F7
Denstone ST14 ....95 A4
Nabbs Cl ST7 ....26 B2
Nabbswood Rd ST7 ....26 B2
Nab Hill Ave ST13 ....30 D6
Nab Hill Ct ST13 ....30 C6
Naden Ho WS12 ....209 C5
Naesby Rd WV6 ....254 F3
Nagington Dr ST19 ....207 F7
Nailers Dr WS7 ....229 D6
Nairn Rd WS3 ....243 A4
Nancy Talbot Cl WS15 ....161 B5
Nankirk La DE13 ....165 A6
Nanny Goat La ST15 ....105 A1
Nantwich Rd Audley ST7 ....39 B1
Balterley ST7 ....38 F1
Woore CW3 ....67 B1
Naomi Way WS9 ....245 B4
Napier Gdns 3 ST7 ....26 A2
Napier Rd WV2 ....266 D7
Napier St Burton u T DE14 ....166 C1
Stoke-on-T ST4 ....72 D6
Napier B77 ....250 E3
Naples Cl ST3 ....73 E4
Naples Dr ST5 ....70 F6
Napley Dr TF9 ....82 C2
Napley Rd TF9 ....82 D1
Narlow La DE6 ....51 F2
Narrow La
Brownhills WS8 ....244 F8
Colton WS15 ....179 B7
Denstone ST14 ....95 D6
Milwich ST15 ....121 F7
Narvik Cres ST6 ....42 C2
Nash Ave Perton WV6 ....254 E3
Stafford ST16 ....155 B6
Nashe Dr ST3 ....73 A2
Nash La
Acton Trussell ST17 ....193 B8
Lichfield WS13 ....214 A5
Nash Peake St ST6 ....41 D3
Nash St ST5 ....55 E2
Natham Cl ST11 ....74 D3
Nathan Ct WS15 ....196 F5
Nathans Mdw CW12 ....16 C7
National Meml Arboretum The* DE13 ....201 C2
Nave Rd ST4 ....72 A5
Navigation Loop ST15 ....104 E2
Navigation Rd ST6 ....56 F7
Navigation St ST6 ....56 E7
Navigation Way WS11 ....210 A2
Naylors Gr DY3 ....271 E4
Naylor St ST6 ....41 F5
Naylor Yd 1 ST13 ....30 E6
Neachless Ave WV5 ....270 A5
Neachley La TF11 ....220 A2
Neal Croft WS14 ....232 E6
Neale Ho WV2 ....266 C7
Neale Pl ST2 ....58 B5
Neander B79 ....249 F6
Near Ridding ST20 ....171 D5
Neath Cl ST3 ....73 D3
Neath Pl 2 ST3 ....73 C6
Neath Rd WS3 ....242 F2
Neath Way WS3 ....242 F2
Needwood Ave DE13 ....147 C4
Needwood CE Prim Sch DE13 ....162 F7
Needwood Cl WV2 ....266 B6
Needwood Ct DE13 ....146 C6
Needwood Dr WV4 ....266 F4
Needwood Grange WS15 ....161 A5
Needwood Hill WS13 ....214 A2
Needwood Pk DE13 ....183 D1
Needwood St DE14 ....166 B4
Nellan Cres ST6 ....42 D1
Nelson Bank ST6,ST7 ....41 A7
Nelson Bldgs ST7 ....26 A1
Nelson Cres ST21 ....102 E2
Nelson Dr WS12 ....210 F4
Nelson Ind Est ST7 ....25 C1
Nelson Pl Hanley ST1 ....282 C2
Newcastle-u-L ST5 ....283 C3
Nelson Rd ST4 ....71 E8
Nelson St Burton u T DE15 ....167 C4
Leek ST13 ....30 F7
Newcastle-u-L ST5 ....56 C5
Stoke-on-T ST4 ....72 D6
Nelson Way ST17 ....174 E6
Nemesia B77 ....251 B4
Nene Cl DE13 ....147 C1
Nene Way DE65 ....147 D8
Nephew St ST6 ....56 E8
Neptune Gr ST1 ....57 F6
Ness Gr ST10 ....76 E5
Nest Comm WS3 ....243 F5
Nether Beacon WS13 ....214 A1
Netherbridge Ave WS14 ....231 E7
Netherby Rd DY3 ....271 C8
Nethercote Pl ST2 ....73 D8
Nethergate DY3 ....271 F5
Nether La WS7 ....229 D8
Netherseal Rd
Chilcote DE12 ....219 F4
Clifton Campville B79 ....218 F2
Netherset Hey La CW3 ....68 F4
Netherstone Gr B74 ....257 F5
Nether Stowe High Sch WS13 ....214 B1
Netherstowe La WS13 ....214 D2
Netherstowe WS13 ....214 C2
Netherton Gr ST2 ....43 C2
Nethy Dr WV6 ....255 B5
Netley Pl ST3 ....88 E7
Netley Rd WS3 ....242 E2
Netley Way WS3 ....242 E2
Nevada La ST6 ....57 B8
Neve Ave WV10 ....240 F1
Neville Ave WV4 ....266 D5
Neville Cl DE13 ....147 B3
Neville Ho DY3 ....271 D7
Neville St Stoke-on-T ST4 ....71 F4
Tamworth B77 ....250 E3
Nevill St B79 ....250 A5
Nevin Ave ST8 ....27 D5
Nevis Ct WV6 ....255 E2
Nevis Gr WV12 ....242 B1
Newall Ave ST16 ....156 B5
Newark Gr ST6 ....41 C7
New Ave ST11 ....91 C6
New Barns La WS14 ....246 B3
New Bldgs Barlaston ST12 ....88 D1
Biddulph ST8 ....27 C3
Newbold Cl WS13 ....231 A5
Newborough Cl ST1 ....57 F6
Newbridge Ave WV6 ....255 E3
Newbridge Cres WV6 ....255 E4
Newbridge Dr WV6 ....255 E4
Newbridge Gdns WV6 ....255 E4
Newbridge Mews 3 WV6 ....255 F4
Newbridge Prep Sch WV6 ....255 E4
Newbridge Rd DY6 ....275 C8
Newbridge St WV6 ....255 F4
Newburn Gr ST4 ....88 B8
Newbury Cl
Great Wyrley WS6 ....226 F2
Stafford ST17 ....175 C7
Newbury Dr DE13 ....147 C1
Newbury Gr ST3 ....88 E7
Newbury Rd
Norton Canes WS11 ....228 A5
Stourbridge DY8 ....275 D1
Wolverhampton WV10 ....240 C2
Newby Cl DE15 ....167 B1
Newcastle Com High Sch ST5 ....70 F7
Newcastle Ent Ctr ST5 ....55 E2
Newcastle La ST4 ....71 E6
Newcastle Rd Ashley TF9 ....100 B7
Astbury CW12 ....15 A7
Cotes Heath ST21 ....102 F3
Eccleshall ST21 ....133 E8
Leek ST13 ....30 D4
Loggerheads TF9 ....99 E5
Madeley CW3 ....68 F7
Market Drayton TF9 ....97 F2
Newcastle-u-L ST5 ....71 C1
Stoke-on-T ST4 ....71 E5
Stone ST15 ....104 E1
Talke ST7 ....40 E7
Woore CW3 ....67 E1
Newcastle St Burslem ST6 ....56 E8
Newcastle-u-L ST5 ....55 D2
Stone ST15 ....104 F1
Newcastle-under-Lyme Coll ST5 ....283 A3
Newcastle-under-Lyme Schs ST5 ....283 C2
New Century St ST1 ....282 A3
New Chapel Ct ST6 ....41 D4
Newchapel Observatory* ST7 ....26 E2
Newchapel Rd ST7 ....26 C3
New Close Ave ST11 ....91 B8
Newcomen Cl WS7 ....229 C8
Newcomen Gr ST2 ....73 D7
New Cott DE6 ....36 E3
Newcott Cl WV9 ....239 F2
New Cotts Foxt ST10 ....62 C5
Oaken WV8 ....238 D2
Six Ashes WV15 ....272 C6
Stourton DY7 ....278 F8
New Council Hos TF9 ....98 C2
Newcroft Ct ST5 ....56 C5
Newcrofts Wlk ST6 ....42 D6
New Dudley Rd DY6 ....275 C8
Newfield Dr DY6 ....275 E4
Newfield Rd DE15 ....167 B4
Newfield St ST6 ....41 D4
Newfold Cres ST6 ....43 B8
Newford Cres ST2 ....42 F1
New Ford Prim Sch ST6 ....42 D1
New Garden Ho ST17 ....285 B2
New Garden St ST17 ....285 B1
Newgate WV6 ....253 C3
Newgate St WS7 ....229 A5
New Gdns WS7 ....228 F5
New Haden Rd ST10 ....76 B1
Newhall Com Jun Sch DE11 ....186 E6
Newhall Cres WS11 ....210 B3
Newhall Gdns WS11 ....209 F2
Newhall Inf Sch DE11 ....186 F7
New Hall Rd ST3 ....73 E2
Newhall St WS11 ....209 D1
New Hall St ST1 ....282 B3
Newhall St ST10 ....61 D3
New Hampton Rd W WV6 ....255 F4
Newhaven Gr ST4 ....88 B5
New Hayes Rd
Prospect Village WS12 ....211 C4
Stoke-on-T ST6 ....41 E4
Newhay DE13 ....147 F1
New Homage Gdns WV9 ....224 B2
New Horse Rd WS6 ....226 E3
New Hos TF11 ....203 F5
Newhouse Ct ST2 ....58 B5
Newhouse La WV7 ....237 A3
Newhouse Rd ST2 ....58 B5
Newick Ave B74 ....257 B3
Newington Gr ST4 ....88 C5
New Inn Bank ST21 ....131 D8
New Inn La ST4 ....88 A7
New Inn Row ST17 ....175 F3
New King St ST7 ....39 C1
New Kingsway ST3 ....74 A4
New La ST6 ....28 B1
Newland Ave ST16 ....155 D7
Newland Cl WS4 ....244 C2
Newlands Cl
Newcastle-u-L ST5 ....71 B5
Penkridge ST19 ....207 F7
Stone ST15 ....119 F6
Newlands Ct WS12 ....227 E8
Newlands La
Colton WS15 ....179 D7
Norton Canes WS12 ....227 D8
Newlands St ST4 ....57 B1
New Landywood La WS6 ....242 E7
Newleigh St ST2 ....43 B1
Newlyn Ave CW12 ....15 F8
Newlyn Cl WS14 ....231 D7
Newman Ave WV4 ....266 F4
Newman Cl ST15 ....120 C7
Newman Dr DE14 ....185 B8
Newman Gr WS15 ....196 F7
Newman Rd WV10 ....241 A1
Newmarket Rd WS11 ....228 B4
Newmarket Way ST10 ....76 E5
New Mill La B78 ....261 A7
Newmill St ST2 ....43 B1
Newmount Rd ST4 ....73 B5
New Park Gdns ST4 ....88 C5
New Park Sch WV6 ....255 F5
New Penkridge Rd WS11 ....209 C1
New Plant La WS7 ....228 C8
Newpool Cotts ST8 ....27 B5
Newpool Rd ST8 ....27 B6
Newpool Terr ST8 ....27 B5
Newport CE Jun Sch TF10 ....168 F2
Newport Cl DE14 ....166 E7
Newport Croft ST19 ....223 C6
Newport Girls' High Sch TF10 ....168 E1
Newport Gr ST5 ....40 E2
Newport Inf Sch TF10 ....168 F2
Newport La ST6 ....56 E7
Newport Rd
Albrighton TF11,WV7 ....220 D1
Codsall WV7 ....237 F2
Eccleshall ST21 ....133 E6
Edgmond TF10 ....168 C4
Gnosall ST20 ....171 B5
Great Bridgeford ST18 ....135 C2
Market Drayton TF9 ....112 E6
Stafford ST16 ....285 A2
Tong TF11 ....220 D3
Woodseaves ST20 ....151 D7
Newport St
Brewood ST19 ....223 C6
Burslem ST6 ....56 E8
Newport B77 ....250 F5
Newquay Ave ST17 ....175 D8
Newquay Cl CW12 ....15 E8
New Rd Aldridge WS9 ....256 A5
Alton ST10 ....78 E1
Armitage WS15 ....198 B5
Astbury CW12 ....15 B4
Audley ST7 ....39 E3
Brownhills WS8 ....244 F7
Burntwood WS7 ....229 B6
Checkley ST10 ....109 B8
Cookley DY11 ....280 B7
Dilhorne ST10 ....75 C4
New Rd Est (Ind Est) ST18 ....139 B1
New Rd Flash SK17 ....3 A3
Hales TF9 ....113 F8
Halfpenny Green DY3 ....268 F4
Hixon ST18 ....158 A8
Kidderminster DY10 ....280 C3
Madeley CW3 ....68 E7
Penkridge ST19 ....192 E1
Shenstone WS14 ....246 F6
Shuttington B79 ....251 E8
Slade Heath WV10 ....224 F1
Smestow DY3 ....269 B3
Swadlincote DE11 ....186 E6
Tamworth B77 ....261 F7
Upper Tean ST10 ....92 D4
Uttoxeter ST14 ....111 A1
Werrington ST2 ....58 F3
Wolverhampton,Newbridge WV6 ....255 E4
New Row
Drayton Bassett B78 ....260 E5
Madeley Heath CW3 ....69 A8
Stafford ST18 ....174 C5
Tatenhill DE13 ....165 A1
Newshaw Wlk ST1 ....282 C3
New Sreet Cotts CW12 ....6 A6
New St
6 Cannock,Mill Green WS11 ....226 E8
Biddulph Moor ST8 ....28 A8
Biddulph ST8 ....27 F7
Birchmoor B78 ....262 E7
Burntwood,Chase Terrace WS7 ....228 E8
Burntwood,Chasetown WS7 ....228 E5
Burslem ST6 ....56 F8
Burton u T DE14 ....166 D2
Cannock,Bridgtown WS11 ....226 D6
Cannock WS12 ....210 C4
Dudley,Gornalwood DY3 ....271 C3
Newstead Prim Sch ST3 ....88 F6
Newstead Rd ST2 ....58 B5
Newstead B79 ....249 D6
Newstead Trad Est ST4 ....88 D7
New St Essington WV11 ....242 A3
Fazeley B78 ....261 B8
Great Wyrley WS6 ....227 A1
Kingswinford DY6 ....275 D4
Kingswinford,Wall Heath DY6 ....275 C8

New St continued
Leek ST13 . . . . .30 F6
Newcastle-u-L ST5 . . . . .56 D5
Newport TF10 . . . . .168 E3
Norton Bridge ST15 . . . . . .135 A8
Stafford ST16 . . . . .155 D5
Stourbridge DY8 . . . . .279 F5
Stourbridge,Wordsley DY8 275 D2
Tamworth,Bolehall B77 . . . .250 E4
Tamworth,Mount Pleasant
B77 . . . . .250 C1
Uttoxeter ST14 . . . . .126 B7
Walsall,Wallington Heath
WS3 . . . . .243 B1
Walsall WS4 . . . . .244 D1
Wolverhampton,Merry Hill
WV3 . . . . .265 D7
Wolverhampton,Parkfield
WV4 . . . . .266 E6
Newton Cl DE15 . . . . .167 E8
Newton Ct ST9 . . . . .59 A4
Newton La
Newton Regis CV9 . . . . . . .236 F2
Newton Solney ST15 . . . . . .167 F7
Seckington B79 . . . . .236 B3
Newton Leys DE15 . . . . . .167 C4
Newton Mews DE15 . . . . .166 F3
Newton ST10 . . . . .77 E2
Newton Rd Lichfield WS13 213 F2
Newcastle-u-L ST5 . . . . . . .56 B5
Newton Solney DE15 . . . . .167 B6
Stafford ST16 . . . . .155 D5
Newton Regis CE Prim Sch
B79 . . . . .236 C3
Newton's Coll WS13 . . . . .231 B8
Newton Solney CE Inf Sch
DE15 . . . . .167 E8
Newton St ST4 . . . . .56 E2
Newtown
Market Drayton TF9 . . . . . .112 D8
Newchapel ST7 . . . . .26 E2
Newport TF10 . . . . .168 E1
New Wood Cl DY7 . . . . . . .279 C8
New Wood Way WS9 . . . . .245 A3
Niall Rd ST4 . . . . .71 F1
Nicholas Gr ST13 . . . . .30 B5
Nicholas St ■ ST6 . . . . . . .56 F8
Nicholl's La ST15 . . . . . . .105 B3
Nicholls St ST4 . . . . .72 B5
Nicholls Way WS12 . . . . . .210 F1
Nicholson Way
Burton u T DE14 . . . . .166 A1
Leek ST13 . . . . .30 D6
Nicklaus Cl DE14 . . . . .185 A7
Nidderdale Cl CW12 . . . . . . .6 A5
Nightingale Cl
Huntington WS12 . . . . .209 C7
Lower Tean ST10 . . . . .92 F1
Nightingale Ct WS7 . . . . . .229 F8
Nightingale B77 . . . . .262 A6
Nightingale Wlk WS7 . . . .229 F8
Nile St ST6 . . . . .57 A8
Nimbus B77 . . . . .261 D4
Ninefoot La
Tamworth,Belgrave B77 . . .261 E8
Tamworth,Wilnecote B77 . .261 F7
Ninian Pk B77 . . . . .261 D6
Ninian Way B77 . . . . .261 E6
Nirvana Cl WS11 . . . . .209 C2
Noblett Rd ST1 . . . . .57 E7
Nocke Rd WV11 . . . . .241 F1
Noddington Ave WV4 . . . .232 E6
Noddington La WS14 . . . .232 E6
Noddy Park Rd WS9 . . . . .256 B7
Noddy Pk WS9 . . . . .256 B7
No Man's Green La DY7 . .276 E6
No Man's Heath Rd DE12 219 F3
No Name Rd WS7 . . . . . . .228 E7
Nook The WS6 . . . . .226 C1
Noon Croft DE13 . . . . .200 F2
Norbroom Ct TF10 . . . . . .169 A4
Norbroom Dr TF10 . . . . . .169 A4
Norbury Ave
Stoke-on-T ST2 . . . . .43 B1
Walsall WS3 . . . . .244 A3
Norbury CE Prim Sch DE6 96 E7
Norbury Cres ■ WV4 . . . .266 E4
Norbury Ct WS15 . . . . . . .120 A8
Norbury Hollow DE6 . . . . .80 D1
Norbury Rd ST20 . . . . .171 A7
Norfolk Cl ST1 . . . . .71 B2
Norfolk Cres WS9 . . . . . . .256 B8
Norfolk Dr B78 . . . . .250 A1
Norfolk Gr Biddulph ST8 . . .16 C1
Great Wyrley WS6 . . . . . . .226 F1
Norfolk Ho ST7 . . . . .40 D6
Norfolk Rd
Burton u T DE15 . . . . .185 D7
Kidsgrove ST7 . . . . .25 D2
Stourbridge DY8 . . . . .279 D8
Wolverhampton WV3 . . . . .266 A8
Norfolk St ST1 . . . . .282 A1
Norfolk Way ST17 . . . . . . .174 C7
Normacot Grange Rd ST3 .90 A7
Normacot Rd ST3 . . . . . . .284 C3
Norman Ave ST6 . . . . .41 F3
Normanbrook Ct TF9 . . . . .97 C1
Norman Cl B78 . . . . .249 E2
Normandy Gr ST2 . . . . .43 A2
Normandy Pl ST5 . . . . . . .283 A3
Norman Gr ST5 . . . . .56 D2
Norman Keep DE13 . . . . . .146 C6
Norman Rd
Penkridge ST19 . . . . .208 A8

Norman Rd continued
Tutbury DE13 . . . . .146 C6
Normanton Gr ST3 . . . . . . .73 D6
Norris Cl TF9 . . . . .100 C5
Norris Rd ST6 . . . . .41 F3
Northam Rd ST1 . . . . .57 D6
North Ave Leek ST13 . . . . . .30 D5
Stafford ST16 . . . . .155 D7
North Castle St ST16 . . . .285 A3
Northcliffe ■ ST13 . . . . . . .30 D6
Northcote Ave ST4 . . . . . . .72 A8
Northcote Ct ST8 . . . . . . .177 E8
Northcote Cl ST5 . . . . . . .283 C3
Northcote St ST5 . . . . . . .283 C3
Northcote St ST4 . . . . .57 B5
North Cres WV10 . . . . .241 C7
Northdale WV6 . . . . .255 B4
North Dr ST20 . . . . .171 C5
Northesk Pl ST5 . . . . .71 A5
Northesk St ■ ST15 . . . . .105 A1
Northfield Ave ST4 . . . . . . .96 A4
Northfield Cl ST14 . . . . . .111 A2
Northfield Dr ST8 . . . . .16 E2
Northfield Gr WV3 . . . . . .265 C7
Northfield Rd DE13 . . . . . .166 C7
Northfields Way WS8 . . . .244 D7
Northfleet St ST2 . . . . .58 A3
Northgate WS9 . . . . .256 A7
Northgate Way WS9 . . . . .256 A8
North Gn WV4 . . . . .265 D6
Northicote Recn Ctr
WV10 . . . . .240 E3
Northicote Sch The
WV10 . . . . .240 E3
Northlands CW3 . . . . .67 C1
North Oval DY3 . . . . .271 E5
Northover WV9 . . . . .240 A2
North Pl Bucknall ST2 . . . . .58 B6
Stafford ST16 . . . . .155 D5
North Prim Sch ST6 . . . . . .57 B7
North Rd Burslem ST6 . . . . .57 B7
Wolverhampton,Parkfield
WV4 . . . . .71 E8
North Springfield DY3 . . . .266 E1
North Staffordshire Hospl
Ctr (Outpatients Dept)
ST4 . . . . .71 E8
North Staffordshire Medical
Inst ST4 . . . . .71 F7
North Staffordshire Nuffield
Hospl The ST5 . . . . .71 C3
North Staffordshire Royal
Infmy ST4 . . . . .71 F7
North St Burntwood WS7 . .211 F1
Burton u T DE15 . . . . .167 B3
Cannock WS11 . . . . .226 E6
Leek ST13 . . . . .30 D6
Mount Pleasant ST7 . . . . . .26 B6
Newcastle-u-L ST5 . . . . . .283 C3
North Street ST4 . . . . .72 A8
North St ST4 . . . . .72 A8
North Terr ST5 . . . . .56 B5
Northumberland Cl B78 . .250 A1
Northumberland Rd
DE15 . . . . .185 D7
North Walls ST16 . . . . . . .285 B3
Northway DY3 . . . . .266 C2
North West Terr ST6 . . . . . .42 C1
North Wlk ST3 . . . . .74 B1
Northwood Cl ST5 . . . . .71 D2
Northwood Ct ST1 . . . . . .282 C3
Northwood Gn ST1 . . . . . . .57 E4
Northwood Inf Sch ST1 . . .57 E4
Northwood La
Ellastone DE6 . . . . .80 C5
Newcastle-u-L ST5 . . . . . . .71 D2
Northwood Park Cl
WV10 . . . . .240 E3
Northwood Park Prim Sch
WV10 . . . . .240 E1
Northwood Park Rd
Hanley ST1 . . . . .57 E4
Wolverhampton WV10 . . . .240 E3
Northycote Farm & Ctry Pk*
WV10 . . . . .240 F3
Northycote La WV10 . . . . .240 F4
North Ave ST6 . . . . .42 A3
Norton Bridge Sta ST15 . .135 A8
Norton Canes High Sch
WS11 . . . . .228 A7
Norton Canes Prim Sch
WS11 . . . . .227 F7
Norton Cl Tamworth B79 . .250 C7
Wolverhampton WV4 . . . . .265 C3
Norton Cres ST6 . . . . .57 D8
Norton Dr ST6 . . . . .57 D8
Norton East Rd WS11 . . . .228 B6
Norton Grange Cres
WS11 . . . . .227 F4
Norton Grange WS11 . . . .227 F4
Norton Green La WS11 . . .227 F4
Norton Hall Cl ST6 . . . . . . .42 E3
Norton Hall La WS11 . . . .227 D4
Norton Ind Est WS11 . . . . .42 E2
Norton in Hales CE Prim Sch
TF9 . . . . .82 C2
Norton La
Burntwood WS7 . . . . .229 C6
Great Wyrley WS6 . . . . . . .227 A4
Norton Lakeside Sta*
WS11 . . . . .228 C2
Norton La
Norton Canes WS12 . . . . .227 B7
Stoke-on-T ST6 . . . . .42 F3
Norton Prim Sch ST6 . . . . .42 F3
Norton Rd
Burton u T DE13 . . . . .166 A6

Norton Rd continued
Norton Canes WS11,WS12 .227 F8
Stourbridge DY8 . . . . .279 E2
Walsall WS3 . . . . .244 A5
Norton Springs WS11 . . . .227 F5
Norton St ST2 . . . . .43 B1
Norton Terr WS11 . . . . . . .227 F6
Norwich Cl WS13 . . . . .214 C3
Norwich Pl ST5 . . . . .71 C5
Norwich Rd ST7 . . . . .58 D2
Norwood Ho WS15 . . . . . .178 B1
Nottingham Ct ST14 . . . . .110 F1
Nottingham Rd WS14 . . . .232 D3
Novi La ST11 . . . . .31 A7
Nuffield Hospl WV6 . . . . . .255 C4
Nunn's Cl ST13 . . . . .74 C5
Nunn St ST13 . . . . .30 D6
Nuns La WS15 . . . . .180 B6
Nurseries The WV9 . . . . . .224 B2
Nursery Ave
Aldridge WS9 . . . . .256 B5
Stoke-on-T ST9 . . . . .43 C4
Nursery Cl Bradley ST18 . .191 C8
Brown Edge ST6 . . . . .43 A7
Cheadle ST10 . . . . .76 C3
Kidsgrove ST7 . . . . .25 D1
Nursery Croft WS13 . . . . .213 F1
Nursery Dr Biddulph ST8 . .16 C2
Penkridge ST19 . . . . .192 E2
Wombourne WV5 . . . . .269 F4
Nursery Gdns
Codsall WV8 . . . . .238 F4
Stourbridge DY8 . . . . .279 F1
Nursery La Hopwas B78 . .249 B6
Stafford ST16 . . . . .155 D5
Stoke-on-T ST9 . . . . .43 C3
Sutton Coldfield B74 . . . . .258 A2
Nursery Rd Rugeley WS15 197 A5
Scholar Green ST7 . . . . .25 E5
Nursery St ST4 . . . . .72 A5
Nursery View WV6 . . . . . .256 C2
Nursery Way ST18 . . . . . . .158 B3
Nursery Wlk WV6 . . . . . . .255 D4
Nurton Bank WV6 . . . . . . .254 A3
Nurton Hill Rd WV6 . . . . .253 E6
Nutbrook Ave ST4 . . . . . . .72 C4
Nuthurst Dr WS11 . . . . . . .226 F4
Nyewood Ave ST3 . . . . .73 D5
Nymet B77 . . . . .261 E8

O

Oadby Rise DE13 . . . . .166 A6
Oakamoor Rd ST10 . . . . . . .77 C4
Oakapple Cl ST19 . . . . . . .221 E8
Oak Ave Cheddleton ST13 . .45 C4
Great Wyrley WS6 . . . . . . .227 A1
Huntington WS12 . . . . . . .209 D8
Newport TF10 . . . . .168 F1
Walton-on-t-H ST17 . . . . . .175 F6
Oak Cl Church Eaton ST20 .190 B7
Great Haywood ST18 . . . . .158 C1
Kinver DY7 . . . . .278 C3
Uttoxeter ST14 . . . . .110 F1
Oak Ct ST4 . . . . .257 E5
Oakdale B74 . . . . .257 A1
Oakdale Cl CW2 . . . . .37 B3
Oakdale Ct ST5 . . . . .71 C3
Oakdale Trad Est DY6 . . . .270 E1
Oakden Cl ST14 . . . . .125 C7
Oakdene Ave ST5 . . . . .56 A6
Oakdene Cl
Cheslyn Hay WV6 . . . . . . .226 D2
Forsbrook ST11 . . . . .91 B6
Newcastle-u-L ST5 . . . . . . .56 A6
Oakdene Rd WS7 . . . . .229 A6
Oakdene Way ST8 . . . . .27 D7
Oak Dr Mile Oak B78 . . . . .249 C1
Scholar Green ST7 . . . . .25 E6
Seisdon WV5 . . . . .263 F2
Wheaton Aston ST19 . . . . .205 C6
Oaken Covert WV8 . . . . . .238 E2
Oaken Dr WV8 . . . . .238 E3
Oakenfield WS13 . . . . .214 A2
Oaken Gdns WS7 . . . . .229 A8
Oaken Grange WS6 . . . . . .226 F1
Oaken Gr WV8 . . . . .238 E2
Oakenhayes Cres WS8 . . .228 F1
Oakenhayes Dr WS8 . . . . .228 F1
Oaken La WS8 . . . . .238 C3
Oaken Lanes WV8 . . . . . . .238 E2
Oaken Pk WV8 . . . . .239 A2
Oak Farm Craft Ctr*
B78 . . . . .260 B5
Oakfield Ave DY6 . . . . .270 E5
Oakfield Cl Rugeley WS15 178 A2
Stourbridge DY8 . . . . .275 F1
Oakfield Dr WS3 . . . . .244 B5
Oakfield Gr ST5 . . . . .27 E7
Oakfield Rd
Alrewas DE13 . . . . .201 A2
Codsall WV8 . . . . .239 C2
Market Drayton TF9 . . . . . . .97 B1
Stoke-on-T ST3 . . . . .73 F2
Oak Gn WV6 . . . . .255 B3
Oakham Way ST2 . . . . .58 C2
Oakhill Ave ST4 . . . . .71 F4
Oakhill Cl ST10 . . . . .92 C4
Oakhill Prim Sch
Stoke-on-T ST4 . . . . .71 F3
Tamworth B77 . . . . .250 F2
Oakhill Rd WS11 . . . . .209 F2
Oak Hill WV3 . . . . .255 C1
Oak Ho Great Wyrley WS6 .227 A1
Little Aston B74 . . . . .257 B5

Oakhurst Cres ST3 . . . . . . .90 A6
Oakhurst WS14 . . . . .231 C7
Oakhurst Pk WS15 . . . . . .196 F5
Oak Ind Pk The DY6 . . . . .270 E1
Oak La Astbury CW12 . . . . .15 B4
Bradley ST18 . . . . .191 C7
Burntwood WS7 . . . . .212 A1
Cheslyn Hay WV10 . . . . . .225 C7
Kingswinford DY6 . . . . . . .271 A1
Oakland Ct B79 . . . . .250 A5
Oakland Dr DY3 . . . . .271 B2
Oakland Ho B74 . . . . .258 A4
Oaklands Ave ST5 . . . . .56 C6
Oaklands Cl
Fradley WS13 . . . . .215 D6
Hill Ridware WS15 . . . . . . .198 A8
Huntington WS12 . . . . . . .209 C6
Wetley Rocks ST9 . . . . .60 A6
Oaklands Dr ST17 . . . . . . .285 A1
Oaklands Ind Est WS12 . .210 B3
Oaklands Rd WV3 . . . . . . .266 B8
Oaklands The
Church Eaton ST20 . . . . . .190 A7
Rugeley WS15 . . . . .178 C1
Oaklands Way WS3 . . . . . .244 B3
Oaklands WS9 . . . . .266 B8
Oak Lea ST13 . . . . .30 B4
Oakleigh Ave DE11 . . . . . .186 F5
Oakleigh Ct ST15 . . . . . . .120 D6
Oakleigh Dr Codsall WV8 .239 A3
Rugeley WS15 . . . . .178 C1
Oakleighs DY8 . . . . .275 C1
Oakleigh Wlk DY6 . . . . . . .275 E8
Oakley Ave WS9 . . . . .256 A5
Oakley Cl Lichfield WS13 . .214 B2
Penkridge ST19 . . . . .193 A1
Oakley Copse WS15 . . . . .196 B7
Oakley Folly TF9 . . . . .99 A4
Oakley Gr WV4 . . . . .265 D5
Oakley Rd WS7 . . . . .98 A6
Oakley Way WS11 . . . . . . .209 F2
Oakley Pl ST6 . . . . .42 A7
Oakley Rd WV4 . . . . .265 D5
Oakleys ST19 . . . . .223 D6
Oak Leys WS3 . . . . .255 C1
Oakmoor Pl WS9 . . . . .256 F2
Oakmount Cl WS3 . . . . . . .243 F3
Oak Mount Rd ST9 . . . . . . .59 C4
Oakover Cl ST14 . . . . .126 C6
Oak Park Ct
Stourbridge DY8 . . . . .275 F1
Sutton Coldfield B74 . . . . .257 E3
Oak Park Rd DY8 . . . . .275 F1
Oak Rd Barton-u-N DE11 . .201 D8
Brewood ST19 . . . . .223 D6
Brownhills WS9 . . . . .245 A3
Denstone ST14 . . . . .95 D5
Ecclesshall ST21 . . . . .133 D6
Featherstone WV10 . . . . . .212 A4
Oak Flats ST19 . . . . .223 D6
Stone ST15 . . . . .120 B8
Walsall,Pelsall Wood WS3 .243 F5
Walsall WS4 . . . . .244 C1
Oakridge Cl ST17 . . . . . . .175 E5
Oakridge Dr WS6 . . . . .226 E2
Oakridge Prim Sch ST17 .175 E5
Oakridge Way ST17 . . . . . .175 E5
Oaks Dr Cannock WS11 . . .209 C3
Featherstone WV10 . . . . . .240 F8
Wombourne WV5 . . . . .270 A5
Oakshaw Cl WV9 . . . . .224 B3
Oakshaw Gr ST4 . . . . .88 B8
Oaksmoor Cl ST19 . . . . . . .205 C6
Oak Sq DE11 . . . . .186 F2
Oak St Burton u T DE14 . . .166 C1
Newcastle-u-L ST5 . . . . . . .56 D3
Oak Tree Cl ST17 . . . . .174 B8
Oaktree La ST7 . . . . .40 D5
Oaktree Rd Rugeley WS15 .196 F6
Stoke-on-T ST4 . . . . .88 B6
Oaktree Rise WV8 . . . . . . .238 E4
Oak Tree Wlk B79 . . . . . . .249 F7
Oakville Ave ST6 . . . . .42 B2
Oakwell Cl ST3 . . . . .73 C1
Oakwell Gr ST3 . . . . .73 C1
Oakwood Cl
Brownhills WS9 . . . . .244 E4
Essington WV11 . . . . .242 B3
Hatton DE65 . . . . .146 C8
Shenstone WS14 . . . . .247 A6
Oakwood Pl ST5 . . . . .55 E8
Oakwood Rd Leek ST13 . . .30 C6
Stoke-on-T ST3 . . . . .72 F2
Oakwood WS15 . . . . .178 B1
Oakwoods WS11 . . . . .226 D8
Oakwood Sch WS9 . . . . . .245 A3
Oasis The DY9 . . . . .281 A5
Oatlands Cl DY6 . . . . .275 A7
Oatfield CW12 . . . . .15 C3
Oatlands Way WV6 . . . . . .254 D3
Oban Cl ST5 . . . . .70 F8
Oberon Cl WS11 . . . . .42 D1
Occupation Rd WS8 . . . . .245 A4
Occupation St ST5 . . . . . .283 C2
Octagon Ctr The DE14 . . .166 D2
Octagon Sh Pk The ST1 . .57 A4
Odell Gr ST6 . . . . .41 A5
Odger Cl ST3 . . . . .74 B2
Odiham Cl B79 . . . . .250 C7
Odin Cl WS11 . . . . .210 A5
Offadrive B79 . . . . .250 B5

Offa's Dr WV6 . . . . .254 E5
Offa St B79 . . . . .250 B5
Offoxey Rd TF11,ST19 . . . .221 C6
Ogden Rd ST1 . . . . .282 C2
Ogley Cres WS8 . . . . .245 A7
Ogley Hay Rd
Burntwood,Boney Hay
WS7 . . . . .229 B8
Burntwood,Triangle WS7,
WS8 . . . . .229 A3
Ogley Rd WS8 . . . . .245 A4
Ogley Vale WS7 . . . . .229 B8
Ogmore Gr ST3 . . . . .90 A8
O'Hare Pl ST13 . . . . .31 B7
Ohio Gr ST6 . . . . .57 B8
Oldacre La ST17 . . . . .176 B3
Oldacres Rd ST14 . . . . .88 C5
Old Armoury The TF9 . . . .112 C8
Old Barn Cl ST20 . . . . .171 E8
Old Barn DE6 . . . . .81 D8
Old Barn House Mews
WS15 . . . . .198 C1
Oldbury Ct B79 . . . . .250 B5
Old Butt La ST7 . . . . .25 D2
Old Cannock Rd WV10 . . .225 D1
Oldcastle Ave ST5 . . . . .56 A6
Old Castle Gr WS8 . . . . . . .228 F2
Old Chancel Rd WS15 . . . .178 C2
Old Chapel Cl ST5 . . . . .69 E8
Old Coach La ST17 . . . . . . .176 B4
Old Coach Rd ST19 . . . . . .221 F7
Old Coalpit La SK17 . . . . . . .5 E8
Old Colehurst Manor*
TF9 . . . . .112 A3
Old Cottage Hospl The ■
ST13 . . . . .30 F6
Oldcott Cres ST7 . . . . .41 C8
Oldcott Dr ST7 . . . . .41 C8
Oldcourt St ST6 . . . . .41 D3
Old Croft Rd ST17 . . . . . . .175 E6
Old Dalelands TF9 . . . . . . .112 B8
Old Eaton Rd WS15 . . . . . .178 E3
Olde Hall La WS6 . . . . .226 F3
Olde Hall Rd WV10 . . . . . .241 C7
Oldershaws La ST20 . . . . .150 F7
Old Fallings La WV10 . . . .240 F1
Old Fallow Ave WS11 . . . .209 E3
Old Fallow Rd WS11 . . . . .209 E3
Old Falls Cl WS6 . . . . .226 D2
Old Farm Dr WV8 . . . . .238 E7
Old Farm Mdw WV3 . . . . .265 C3
Old Fdns ST6 . . . . .42 D7
Oldfield Ave ST6 . . . . .42 D7
Oldfield Cl ST5 . . . . .120 C6
Oldfield Dr ST15 . . . . .120 C6
Oldfield Ind Est ST4 . . . . . .72 F7
Oldfield La Egginton DE65 148 A1
Snelston DE6 . . . . .81 B3
Oldfields Cres ST18 . . . . .158 C2
Oldfields Hall Mid Sch
ST14 . . . . .126 A4
Oldfields Rd ST14 . . . . . . .126 B7
Oldfield St ST4 . . . . .73 A5
Oldford La ST18 . . . . .154 B4
Old Forge Cl DE65 . . . . . . .148 A3
Old Forge The ST18 . . . . . .158 B2
Old Hall Cl B79 . . . . .236 D3
Old Hall Dr Elford B79 . . . .216 C2
Newcastle-u-L ST5 . . . . . . .56 A8
Old Hall La Fradley WS13 .215 D8
Millmeece ST21 . . . . .117 F7
Norton Canes WS11,WS12 .227 E7
Old Hall St ST1 . . . . .282 B3
Oldham Cotts WS15 . . . . .179 A5
Oldham St ST1 . . . . .282 C1
Old Hedging La B77 . . . . .261 D5
Old Hednesford Rd
WS11 . . . . .210 A3
Oldhill Cl ST17 . . . . .40 E5
Oldhill La ST18 . . . . .157 D1
Old Hill WV6 . . . . .255 D5
Oldicote La DE15 . . . . .167 A3
Old Knotty Way ST14 . . . .126 C7
Old La Beech ST4 . . . . .87 B1
Brown Edge ST6 . . . . .28 A1
Checkley ST10 . . . . .110 F6
Featherstone WV10 . . . . . .242 C7
Old Landywood La WS6 . .242 D7
Old La WV6 . . . . .254 F2
Old Lodge Hill Ctry Pk*
WS15 . . . . .211 E3
Old London Rd WS14 . . . .231 D1
Old Man of Mow* ST7 . . . .26 D8
Old Manor Cl B78 . . . . . . .260 E5
Old Manor Flats WV6 . . . .255 D5
Old Mill Gdns WS4 . . . . . .244 C2
Old Mill House Cl WS4 . . .244 B1
Old Mill La Bagnall ST9 . . . .44 A3
Bagnall,Tompkin ST9 . . . . .44 C3
Oldmill St ST4 . . . . .72 C7
Old Mill The ■ ST13 . . . . . .30 E6
Old Oak Cl WS15 . . . . .256 B8
Old Park Rd
Cannock WS12 . . . . .211 A5
Dudley DY1 . . . . .271 F4
Stowford CW1 . . . . .37 C7
Stowford CW1 . . . . .37 D8
Old Penkridge Mews
WS11 . . . . .209 D1
Old Penkridge Rd WS11 . .209 C2
Old Quarry Dr DY3 . . . . . .271 D5
Old Rd Armitage WS15 . . . .198 B5
Oldroyd St 39 E3
Old Rd Cellarhead ST9 . . . . .60 C1
Old Rd Cl ST15 . . . . .105 A1
Old Rd Oulton ST15 . . . . . .105 B5
Stoke-on-T ST4,ST10 . . . . . .88 C3
Upper Tean ST10 . . . . .92 F4
Weston ST18 . . . . .138 D2

Old Rd continued
Wrinehill CW3 . . . . .53 A3
Old Rectory La Stone WS9 . .256 C6
Old Rectory Rd ST15. . . . .120 B8
Old Rickercote La ST17 175 A5
Old Saddler's Yd ST14 . .126 C7
Old School Cl
Kidsgrove ST7 . . . . .26 A1
Weston ST18. . . . . .138 D3
Old School Ct ST19 . . . .205 C5
Old School Dr ST16. . . . .155 C8
Old School Pl 8 ST13 . . .30 B5
Old School Wlk B77 . . . .250 B6
Old School Yd The B77. .251 A5
Old Shackerley La WV7 .221 B1
Old Smithy Cl WV6. . . . .253 C3
Old Stafford Rd
Brinsford WV10 . . . . .240 C8
Slade Heath WV10. . . . . .224 D2
Old Town La WS3 . . . . . .243 F3
Old Town Rd ST11 . . . . .282 B4
Old Tramway ST4 . . . . . . .72 F5
Old Vicarage Cl
Walsall WS3 . . . . .244 A2
Wombourne WV5. . . . . . .270 B7
Oldway Pl ST3. . . . . .73 C5
Old Weston Rd ST19 . . . .221 F8
Old Wharf Pl ST1. . . . . . .57 E2
Old Wharf Rd DY8 . . . . .279 F6
Old Whieldon Rd ST4 . . .72 C6
Olive Ave WV4. . . . . .266 E5
Olive Gr ST5. . . . . .40 C1
Oliver Lodge Ho 8 ST4. .72 A7
Oliver Rd ST4. . . . . .71 E7
Ollison Dr B74. . . . . .256 F7
Olof Palme Gr ST3 . . . . .284 C2
Omega Way ST4. . . . . . . .88 A8
One Oak Rise ST17 . . . . .174 F5
Onsetter Rd ST2. . . . . . . .73 D7
Onslow Dr ST5 . . . . .56 B8
Ontario Cl ST4. . . . . .88 A8
Opal Bsns Ctr ST15 . . . .120 A5
Opal Rd ST4. . . . . .72 E5
Opal Way ST15 . . . . .120 A5
Oram's La ST19 . . . . .223 C7
Orange La WS15 . . . . . . .161 C1
Orbital Way WS11. . . . . .226 F6
Orb St ST1. . . . . .282 B2
Orchard Ave ST15 . . . . . .209 C2
Orchard Cl Ashley TF9 . .100 C5
Cheslyn Hay WS6. . . . . . .226 C2
Claverley WV5. . . . . .267 C7
Coven WV9 . . . . .224 B2
Lichfield WS13. . . . . .213 F1
Oulton ST15. . . . . .105 C4
Pattingham WV6 . . . . . . .253 D3
Penkridge ST19 . . . . .192 F1
Rugeley WS15 . . . . .178 E3
Stone ST15 . . . . .119 F7
Sudbury DE6. . . . . .128 E5
Tamworth B77 . . . . .261 C5
Uttoxeter ST14 . . . . .111 B1
Walton-on-T DE12. . . . . .184 D1
Orchard Cotts WS15. . . .198 B5
Orchard Cres
Kidsgrove ST7 . . . . .25 D1
Penkridge ST19 . . . . .192 F1
Wolverhampton WV3 . . . .265 B7
Orchard Ct
Kingswinford DY6 . . . . . .275 D6
Leek ST13 . . . . .30 C6
Wolverhampton WV3 . . . .265 B7
Orchard Gdns
Cannock WS12. . . . . .209 F6
Leek ST13 . . . . .30 C6
Orchard Gr Aldridge WS9. .256 B4
Cookley DY11. . . . . .280 A6
Dudley DY3 . . . . .271 B3
Dunsley DY7 . . . . .278 B4
Sutton Coldfield B74 . . . .257 F3
Wolverhampton WV6. . . .266 A4
Orchard La Codsall WV8. .239 D3
Shareshill WV10 . . . . . . .225 C3
Stafford ST18 . . . . .174 C5
Orchard Mobile Home Pk
ST18. . . . . .137 C2
Orchard Pk DE14 . . . . . .166 D2
Orchard Pl ST12 . . . . .88 D1
Orchard Rd DY10 . . . . . .280 C3
Orchard Rise
Blythe Bridge ST11. . . . . .90 E7
Market Drayton TF9 . . . . .112 A8
Orchard St DE14 . . . . . . .166 D2
Orchards The
Armitage WS15 . . . . .198 C4
Stafford ST19 . . . . .72 E4
Orchard St
Newcastle-u-L ST5. . . . . . .56 D5
Stafford ST17 . . . . .285 B2
Swadlincote DE11 . . . . . .186 F6
Tamworth,Kettlebrook
B77. . . . . .250 C3
Tamworth,The Leys B79 . .250 B5
Orchard The
Albrighton WV7 . . . . .237 A5
Brewood ST19 . . . . .223 C6
Burntwood WS7. . . . . . . .229 B7
Colwich ST18 . . . . .177 D8
Newcastle-u-L ST5. . . . . . .55 D8
Newcastle-on-T ST6 . . . . .43 A8
Stramshall ST14 . . . . .111 A4
Swynnerton ST15. . . . . . .103 B4
Walsall WS3 . . . . .243 D2
Wolverhampton WV6 . . . .255 E6
Orchid Cl DE15 . . . . .186 A8
Orchid Gr ST4 . . . . .56 E1
Ordish Ct DE14 . . . . .166 D2

Ordish St DE14 . . . . .166 D2
Ordley La DE6. . . . . .65 F1
Oregon Cl DY6. . . . . .275 F6
Oregon Gdns WS7 . . . . .228 F8
Orford St ST9 . . . . .43 F7
Orford St ST5. . . . . .56 D7
Orford Way ST3. . . . . .88 E8
Orgreaves Cl ST5. . . . . . .56 B8
Orgreave St ST6. . . . . . . .57 A7
Oriel Cl Cannock WS11. . .226 E8
Dudley DY1 . . . . .271 E2
Oriel Dr WV10 . . . . .240 D3
Oriel St ST14 . . . . .72 A7
Orion Cl ST14 . . . . .126 C6
Orion Cl WS6 . . . . .226 F1
Orion Ct ST5 . . . . .70 F8
Orion St ST6 . . . . .42 C1
Orkney Ave ST7 . . . . .41 F8
Orkney Dr B77. . . . . .261 F7
Orlestone Pl ST6 . . . . .42 B7
Orme Rd Biddulph ST8 . . . .27 D5
Newcastle-u-L ST5. . . . . .283 A2
Newcastle-u-L ST5. . . . . . .55 F1
Ormes La WV6. . . . . .255 C3
Orme St ST6. . . . . .56 F8
Ormonde St ST4. . . . . . . .72 F5
Ormonds Cl WS13. . . . . .230 E6
Orpheus Gr ST1 . . . . .57 F6
Orton Gr WV4 . . . . .265 D4
Orton La WV4,WV5 . . . . .265 A2
Orton St ST6 . . . . .283 A4
Orwell Cl ST4 . . . . .279 D4
Orwell Dr Longton ST3 . . .73 F5
Stafford ST17 . . . . .174 B8
Orwell Pl ST5. . . . . .71 B4
Osberton Dr WV10 . . . . . .271 F2
Osborne Cres ST17 . . . . .175 C8
Osborne Ct DE13 . . . . . .166 B6
Osborne Ho ST10 . . . . . . .76 D4
Osborne Rd Stoke-on-T ST4 71 E8
Wolverhampton WV4 . . . .265 F5
Osborne St
Burton u T DE15. . . . . . . .167 A3
Leek ST13 . . . . .31 A6
Osborne B79 . . . . .249 D7
Osbourne Gdns DE15 . . .167 A3
Oslo Gr ST1 . . . . .57 F6
Osmaston Rd DY8. . . . . .279 F2
Osprey Ave ST3. . . . . .90 A7
Osprey Cl
Burton u T DE15. . . . . . . .167 D4
Whittington WS14 . . . . . .232 E5
Osprey Dr ST4. . . . . .229 F8
Osprey Dr DY1 . . . . .271 F1
Osprey Gr WS12 . . . . . . .210 C1
Osprey B77. . . . . .262 A6
Osprey View ST7. . . . . . . .26 D3
Ostler Cl DY6 . . . . .275 B7
Ostlers La ST13. . . . . .45 B4
Oswald Ave ST7 . . . . .74 B5
Otherton Cl ST19 . . . . . . .207 F8
Otherton La ST19 . . . . . . .207 F6
Otterburn Cl
8 Stafford ST17. . . . . . . .175 D6
Cannock WS12. . . . . .210 A2
Otterstone Cl DY3 . . . . . .266 C2
Ottery B77 . . . . .262 B5
Oulton Cl ST5,ST15 . . . . .105 C4
Oulton La TF10,ST10. . . .170 A8
Oulton Mews ST15 . . . . .105 A1
Oulton Rd Cheadle ST10. . .76 F3
Stoke-on-T ST6. . . . . .42 B7
Stone ST15 . . . . .105 B2
Oulton Way ST16 . . . . . . .155 B6
Oundle St ST5 . . . . .283 F2
Ounsdale Cres WV5. . . . .270 A7
Ounsdale High Sch WV5 .269 F7
Our Lady & St Benedict RC
Prim Sch ST2. . . . . .58 A5
Our Lady & St Werburgh's RC
Prim Sch ST5 . . . . .71 B4
Our Lady's RC Prim Sch
ST4. . . . . .72 D6
Our Lady's RC Prim Sch
ST5. . . . . .103 B3
Ousley La DE6. . . . . .80 C5
Outclough Rd ST8 . . . . . . .27 B1
Outfield Rd DE15 . . . . . . .185 F8
Outlook The ST6. . . . . . . .42 C3
Outwoods Cl
Burton u T DE13. . . . . . . .166 A6
Weston ST18. . . . . .138 D2
Outwoods Gn ST18. . . . . .138 D2
Outwoods La
Anslow DE13 . . . . .165 C7
Burton u T DE13. . . . . . . .165 E7
Outwoods Rd DE13 . . . . .166 B5
Oval Bglws The TF10. . . .169 A3
Ovaldene Way ST4. . . . . .88 D7
Oval The Longton ST3 . . .284 A2
Market Drayton TF9 . . . . .112 C8
Stafford ST17 . . . . .285 C2
Werrington ST9 . . . . .59 E4
Overbrook Cl DY3. . . . . . .271 C2
Overcroft ST14 . . . . .125 C7
Overdale Pl ST13 . . . . . . .30 B5
Overfield Rd DY1 . . . . . . .271 A1
Overhill Rd
Burntwood WS7. . . . . . . .229 B5
Stafford ST17 . . . . .175 D6
Overhouse St ST4 . . . . . . .42 B7
Overland Cl WV15. . . . . . .197 A6
Overland Dr ST4. . . . . .43 A8
Overpool Cl WV15. . . . . . .196 D8
Oversetts Ct DE11 . . . . . .186 F6

Oversetts Rd DE11 . . . . .186 E5
Oversley Rd ST6 . . . . .42 B7
Overstrand WV9 . . . . .239 F3
Over The Hill ST8. . . . . . . .17 A2
Overton Bank 8 ST13. . . .30 B5
Overton Cl ST3 . . . . .284 A2
Overton La WS7 . . . . .229 C4
Overton Rd ST6. . . . . .16 F6
Overton Wlk WV4 . . . . . .265 C6
Overwood Pl ST6 . . . . . . .41 F7
Overwoods Rd B77 . . . . .262 A4
Owen Gr ST3 . . . . .57 A8
Owen Rd WV3 . . . . .265 C7
Owen's Bank DE13 . . . . .146 B6
Owens Cl WS15 . . . . .178 E1
Owen Wlk ST17. . . . . .174 C7
Oxbarn Ave WV3 . . . . . . .265 E7
Oxbarn Rd ST17 . . . . .174 D6
Oxbridge Way B79 . . . . .249 E6
Oxclose La DE6. . . . . .36 C2
Oxford Ave ST1 . . . . .57 D7
Oxford Cl WS6. . . . . .226 F3
Oxford Cres ST4. . . . . .72 A7
Oxford Dr DY8. . . . . .279 F4
Oxford Gdns ST16. . . . . .155 F5
Oxford Gn WS11. . . . . . . .226 F8
Oxford Rd Cannock WS11. .226 F8
Newcastle-u-L ST5. . . . . . .56 F5
Stoke-on-T ST6 . . . . .42 B7
Oxford St Burton u T DE14 .166 B1
Stoke-on-T ST4 . . . . .72 A7
Stoke-on-T ST8 . . . . .16 D1
Oxhay Ct ST5. . . . . .56 C3
Oxhay View ST5. . . . . .56 C3
Ox-Hey Cres ST8 . . . . .16 D1
Ox-Hey Dr ST8 . . . . .16 D1
Oxhey Fst Sch ST8. . . . . . .16 E1
Oxleathers Ct ST17 . . . . .174 B7
Oxley Cl WS6 . . . . .226 A3
Oxley Moor Rd
Wolverhampton,Blakeley Green
WV9 . . . . .255 F8
Wolverhampton,Oxley WV9
WV10 . . . . .240 B1
Oxley Rd DE15 . . . . .167 A3
Oxmead DE6. . . . . .81 D7
Ox Pasture ST13 . . . . .45 C5
Ox St DY3 . . . . .271 D5
Oyster Cl DE14 . . . . .185 B7

P

Pacific Rd ST4. . . . . .88 B7
Packett St ST4. . . . . .284 B4
Pack Horse La ST6. . . . . . .56 F8
Packington Cl B74. . . . . . .257 E4
Packington La B78. . . . . . .248 F5
Packmoor Prim Sch ST7 .42 A2
Padarn Cl DY3 . . . . .266 C1
Padbury La WS7 . . . . .212 D1
Padbury WV9. . . . . .240 B3
Paddock Cl ST16. . . . . . . .155 C8
Paddock Cotts ST4 . . . . . .88 A6
Paddock La Aldridge WS9 .256 A5
Great Wyrley WS6. . . . . .227 A3
Paddock Rise ST4 . . . . . . .88 A6
Paddocks Cl B78 . . . . . . .251 F1
Paddocks Gn CW12 . . . . . .1 F8
Paddocks The
Market Drayton TF9. . . . . .97 B1
Swadlincote DF11 . . . . . .186 F5
Yarnfield ST15 . . . . .118 F6
Paddock The
Burton u T DE15. . . . . . . .167 B4
Cheadle ST10. . . . . .76 D2
Claverley WV5 . . . . .267 C7
Codsall WV8 . . . . .238 F2
Coven WV9 . . . . .224 B2
Dudley DY3 . . . . .271 E5
Lichfield WS14 . . . . .231 C5
Perton WV6 . . . . .254 D4
Seighford ST18 . . . . .154 C6
Wombourne WV5. . . . . . .269 E6
Padstow Dr ST17 . . . . . . .156 E1
Padstow Rd B77 . . . . .250 F5
Padstow Way ST4. . . . . . . .88 C5
Padworth St ST3. . . . . .74 A3
Paget Cl Colwich ST18 . . .177 E8
Lichfield WS13. . . . . .214 B2
Penkridge ST19 . . . . .208 A3
Paget Dr WS7 . . . . .211 E1
Paget High Sch DE14 . . .185 A7
Paget Rd WV3,WV6. . . . . .255 F3
Paget Rise WS15. . . . . . . .160 F6
Pagets Chase WS12 . . . . .211 C4
Paget St DE14 . . . . .166 C2
Pagham Cl WV9 . . . . .239 F2
Painsley RC High Sch
ST10. . . . . .76 D2
Paisley Cl ST2 . . . . .73 E8
Paladin Ave ST3 . . . . .74 B4
Palatine Cl ST5. . . . . .55 D6
Palermo Dr ST3 . . . . .74 A5
Pale St DY3 . . . . .271 E5
Palfrey Rd DY8 . . . . .279 D5
Palisadings ST19 . . . . . . .192 E1
Pall Mall ST1. . . . . .282 B2
Palmbourne Ind Pk
ST16. . . . . .285 A3
Palmer Cl
Barton-u-N DE13 . . . . . . .183 D2
Burton u T DE14. . . . . . . .185 B8
Stafford ST16 . . . . .154 B4
Wolverhampton WV11. . . .241 F1
Palmers Cl WV8 . . . . .239 C1
Palmers Cross Prim Sch
WV6 . . . . .255 D8

Palmers Gn ST4 . . . . .71 D8
Palmer St ST3. . . . . .284 D4
Palmerston Ave B77 . . . . .261 E6
Palmerston Ct B77. . . . . . .261 F6
Palmerston St
2 Newcastle-u-L ST5. . . . .56 C5
Hanley ST1 . . . . .282 C1
Palmerston Way ST8. . . . . .16 D1
Palmers Way
Codsall WV8 . . . . .239 C1
Newcastle-u-L ST5. . . . . . .71 D8
Palomino Cl ST3. . . . . .89 C8
Pandora Gr ST1 . . . . .57 F6
Panton Cl ST16. . . . . .156 B4
Pantuff Cl ST17 . . . . .155 B1
Panturner Rd ST2. . . . . . . .73 D7
Parade The
Brownhills WS8 . . . . .228 E1
Coven WV9 . . . . .224 B2
Kingswinford DY6 . . . . . .275 B7
Newcastle-u-L ST5. . . . . . .55 C1
Parade View WS8 . . . . . .244 E8
Paradise Gr WS3 . . . . . . .243 F3
Paradise La
Slade Heath WV10. . . . . .224 D2
Walsall WS3 . . . . .243 F3
Wolverhampton WV10 . . .240 D8
Paradise St
6 Stoke-on-T ST6. . . . . . .41 D3
Newcastle-u-L ST5. . . . . .283 B2
Paragon Ave ST5 . . . . .71 B3
Paragon Cl ST6 . . . . .76 C1
Paragon Rd ST3 . . . . .284 D3
Paramount Bsns Pk ST6 .57 A8
Parbury B77 . . . . .261 D5
Parchments The WS13 . . .214 B1
Pargeter St DY8 . . . . .279 F4
Paris Ave ST5 . . . . .70 E6
Park Ave Burntwood WS7 .229 B5
Cheadle ST10. . . . . .76 E2
Meir ST3 . . . . .74 A5
Newcastle-u-L ST5. . . . . . .56 C5
Norton Canes WS11 . . . . .228 A5
Stafford ST17 . . . . .174 D8
Stone ST15 . . . . .119 E8
Talke ST7 . . . . .40 E8
Uttoxeter ST14 . . . . .111 B2
Werrington ST9 . . . . .59 D4
Park Ave W ST5 . . . . .56 B5
Park Ave
Wolverhampton,Goldthorn Park
WV4 . . . . .266 D6
Wombourne WV5. . . . . . .269 F5
Park Bldgs DY3 . . . . .271 C4
Park Cl Barton-u-N DE13. .183 C1
Brownhills WS8 . . . . .244 E8
Cheslyn Hay WS6. . . . . . .226 E3
Madeley CW3 . . . . .68 E8
Park Cres ST17 . . . . .285 B1
Park Croft WS7. . . . . .228 F8
Park Ct ST5 . . . . .55 E7
Parkdale DY3 . . . . .271 D8
Park Dr Barlaston ST12. . .104 D8
Cheadle ST10. . . . . .76 D4
Little Aston B74. . . . . . . .257 C4
Sutton Coldfield B74 . . . .257 F2
Trentham ST4 . . . . .72 F7
Wolverhampton WV4 . . . .266 C5
Parkend ST11. . . . . .91 B8
Park End Lichfield WS14. .231 E7
Newport TF10 . . . . .168 F5
Parker Bowles Dr 1
TF9. . . . . .112 A8
Parker-Jervis Rd ST3 . . . .73 F4
Parker Paul Ind Est WV2 .264 D7
Parker Rd WV11 . . . . .241 F1
Parkers Cl ST20 . . . . .190 A7
Parker's Croft Rd ST3 . . .285 B2
Parkers Ct WV9. . . . . .224 C1
Parker St Burton u T DE14 .166 D1
Hanley ST1 . . . . .282 A3
Leek ST13 . . . . .31 A5
Walsall WS3 . . . . .243 A1
Parkes Ave WV8 . . . . .239 B2
Parkes Hall Rd DY1 . . . . .271 F5
Parkfield Bsns Ctr ST17 .285 C2
Parkfield Chalet Pk
WV2 . . . . .266 D6
Parkfield Cl B77 . . . . .261 C8
Parkfield Colliery WV4 . .266 F5
Parkfield Cres
Tamworth B77 . . . . .261 C8
Wolverhampton WV2. . . .266 E6
Parkfield Gr WV2 . . . . . . .266 E6
Parkfield High Sch WV4 .266 E5
Parkfield La DE6. . . . . .81 D4
Parkfield Prim Sch WV4 .266 E5
Parkfield Rd Longton ST3 .73 C1
Wolverhampton WV2,WV4.266 E6
Parkfields Cl
Barlaston ST12 . . . . .88 C1
Newcastle-u-L ST5. . . . . . .55 A2
Parkfields Farm ST12 . . . .88 C1
Parkfields Stafford ST17 .174 D8
Stoke-on-T ST5 . . . . .43 F7
Parkgate La DE6. . . . . .79 F5
Park Gate Rd
Cannock Wood WS15 . . . .161 F5
Wednesfield DY10 . . . . . .280 B2
Park Hall Ave ST3 . . . . . . .74 A4
Park Hall Cl WS15 . . . . . .178 D3
Park Hall Cres ST3. . . . . . .74 A4

Parkhall Cty Pk* ST3. . . . .74 A6
Parkhall Cty Pk* ST3 . . . .73 F6
Park Hall Ind Est ST6 . . . .41 E2
Park Hall Prim Sch ST3 . .73 E5
Park Hall Rd Longton ST3 .73 E5
Meir ST3 . . . . .74 A4
Wolverhampton WV4 . . . .266 D5
Park Hall St ST3 . . . . .284 C4
Parkhead Cres ST3 . . . . . .74 A3
Parkhead Dr ST3 . . . . .74 A3
Parkhead Rd ST3 . . . . .74 A4
Park House Dr ST15 . . . . .120 C7
Parkhouse Dr ST5 . . . . . . .56 A8
Parkhouse Ind Est E ST5 .56 A8
Parkhouse Ind Est W ST5 .55 F8
Parkhouse Rd E ST5 . . . . .40 F1
Parkhouse Rd W ST5. . . . .40 E1
Parkhouse St ST1. . . . . . .282 A1
Park La Ashley TF9 . . . . . .100 B8
Audley ST7 . . . . .39 B4
Biddulph ST8 . . . . .27 D6
Blore TF9 . . . . .99 B1
Brewood WV9 . . . . .223 C2
Brocton ST17 . . . . .176 B4
Cheadle ST10 . . . . .76 D2
Cheddleton ST13 . . . . . . .45 B6
Colton WS15 . . . . .179 B8
Congleton CW12 . . . . .6 A1
Endon ST9 . . . . .44 B7
Fazeley B78 . . . . .249 E2
Great Wyrley WS6 . . . . . .227 A3
Haughton ST18 . . . . .172 E5
High Offley ST20 . . . . . . .132 B1
Huntington WS12 . . . . . . .47 B1
Kingswinford DY6 . . . . . .275 E7
Parklands ST8 . . . . .17 B1
Parklands Dr CW2 . . . . . . .37 E3
Parklands ST7 . . . . .26 B1
Parklands Rd ST10. . . . . . .92 E4
Parklands The
Congleton CW12 . . . . .6 A2
Kingswinford DY6 . . . . . .275 D6
Wolverhampton WV10 . . .255 D1
Park Lane Cl ST10 . . . . . . .76 C3
Park La Shenstone WS14 .247 B4
Stoke-on-T ST4 . . . . .72 F5
Stretton ST19 . . . . .206 A6
Tutbury DE13 . . . . .146 B6
Whittington WS13 . . . . . .232 D8
Park Mid Sch ST18 . . . . . .27 C6
Park Pale The DE13 . . . . .146 C5
Park Rd Alrewas DE13 . . .201 A3
Barton-u-N DE13 . . . . . . .183 C2
Burntwood,Chase Terrace
WS7 . . . . .228 F8
Burntwood,Triangle WS7. .229 B5
Cannock WS11 . . . . .209 D1
Dudley,Lower Gornal DY3. .271 D4
Dudley,Upper Gornal DY3 .271 C8
Leek ST13 . . . . .30 E7
Newcastle-u-L,Butterton
ST5. . . . . .70 E2
Newcastle-u-L,Silverdale
ST5. . . . . .55 D8
Norton Canes WS11 . . . . .228 A5
Stoke-on-T ST4 . . . . .42 B1
Stourbridge DY8 . . . . . . .279 D5
Swadlincote DE15,DE11 . .186 D5
Tamworth B77 . . . . .261 C5
Walsall,Wallington Heath
WS3 . . . . .243 B1
Werrington ST9 . . . . .59 C4
Park Rd W DY8 . . . . .279 D5
Park Rise WV3. . . . . .255 E2
Park S ST5 . . . . .56 C6
Park Sch B79. . . . . .250 A7
Parks Cres WV11 . . . . . . .242 A3
Parkside Ave ST16 . . . . . .155 D8
Parkside Cres ST9 . . . . . . .43 F8
Parkside Dr ST5 . . . . .56 B5
Parkside Ind Est WV1 . . .266 E8
Parkside La Gayton ST18 .139 A7
Huntington WS11 . . . . . .209 A2
Parkside Prim Sch ST16. .155 D8
Parkside Stoke-on-T ST4 . . .88 B7
Tamworth B77 . . . . .250 C1
Parkside Way ST4 . . . . . . .56 B3
Park St Burton u T DE14 . .166 C2
Cannock WS11. . . . . .226 E6
Cheslyn Hay WS6. . . . . . .226 E3
Parks The ST7 . . . . .88 D7
Parkstone Ave ST5 . . . . . .283 C2
Parkstone Cl WS4 . . . . . . .244 C1
Park St Stafford ST17 . . . .285 B2
Stoke-on-T ST4 . . . . .72 F5
Stourbridge DY8 . . . . . . .279 D5
Tamworth B79 . . . . .250 A5
Uttoxeter ST14 . . . . .111 C1
Park Terr ST6 . . . . .41 E3
Park The DE6. . . . . .81 C8
Park Venture Ctr WS11. . .226 C6
Parkview
Blythe Bridge ST11. . . . . .90 E6
Burntwood WS7. . . . . . . .228 E8
Parkview Cl ST3 . . . . .72 E2
Park View Ct WS11. . . . . .209 D1

Parkview Ct DY6..........**275** B8
Park View Ct ST3.........73 B1
Parkview Dr WS8..........**228** F2
Park View Gr ST2..........43 C2
Park View Rd
  Kidsgrove ST7 ....26 B3
  Sutton Coldfield B74 ....**257** D3
Park View ST15..........**103** B3
Park View Terr WS15....**178** D1
Parkway DE14 ....**165** F1
Park Way ST11 ....91 A8
Parkway ST15 ....**120** C7
Parkway The Hanley ST1. **282** B1
  Perton WV6 ....**254** F4
Parkway ST4 ....87 E7
Park Way WV11 ....**242** A1
Parkwood Ave ST4 ....87 A7
Parkwood Cl WS8.........**245** A5
Park Wood Ct B74.......**257** F2
Park Wood Dr ST5........85 A7
Parkyn St WV2 ....**266** E8
Parliament Row ST1......**282** B3
Parliament Sq ST1........**282** B3
Parliament St DE11......**186** F6
Parma Gr ST3 ....73 E4
Parnell Ave WS13 ....**231** A6
Parnell Sq CW12..........6 A2
Parsonage St ST6.........41 D4
Parsons Cl SK17 ....24 D5
Parson's Croft WV9 ....**224** B2
Parsons Dr ST20.........**171** E6
Parsons Hollow B77 .....**261** E7
Parsons La ST13..........33 D3
Parson St ST7...........**261** E7
Parson's Wlk B79.......**218** F2
Parton Gr ST3.............74 A3
Partridge Cl 7 Meir ST3..90 A7
  Cannock WS11............**210** A1
  Huntington WS12.........**209** D7
Partridge Croft WS13....**231** C8
Partridge Dr ST14 ....**126** C6
Partridge Mill WS3 ......**243** E3
Partridge Rd DY9 ....**279** C4
Partridge Ride TF9.......99 D4
Parva Cl ST13 ....**110** F1
Parville Ho ST6...........57 A6
Paskin Cl WS13 ....**215** D8
Pass Ave WS14 ....**232** E6
Passfield Ave WS12 .....**210** C7
Pastoral Cl CW3 ....68 F5
Pasture Cl ST5 ....85 D5
Pasturefields Ent Pk
  ST18......................**158** B6
Pasturefields La ST18....**158** A7
Pasturefields Ind Est
  ST18......................**158** B7
Pasturefields La ST18....**158** B7
Pasture Gate WS11 ......**209** C2
Pasture La DE6 ....35 E1
Pastures Dr CW2 ....37 D3
Pastures The
  Perton WV6 ....**254** D4
  Swadlincote DE11.........**186** F5
Pasture View WS3 ....**243** F2
Patch Cl DE13 ....**166** B6
Patch Meadow Rd ST10...76 B3
Paterson Ave ST21.......**117** F3
Paterson Pl WS8.........**245** B5
Patricia Ave WV4 ....**266** D5
Patrick Ave 2 WS11....**210** A3
Patrick Mews WS13......**213** F1
Patrick Pl ST8 ....27 B2
Patshull Ave WV10.......**240** B3
Patshull Ct WV10 ....**240** B3
Patshull Gr WV10 ....**240** B3
Patshull Ho WV6.........**255** C6
Patshull Rd WV6..........**253** B3
Patterdale Rd WS11.....**210** A4
Patterdale St ST6.........**142** A8
Pattingham La WV7.....**253** D8
Pattingham Rd WV6......**254** C2
Paulet High Sch DE15...**185** F7
Pauls Coppice WS8 ......**245** A5
Paul St 1 WV2 ....**266** C8
Pauls Wlk WS13 ....**214** A3
Paynter St ST19 ....**223** D6
Peace Cl WS6.............**226** E3
Peacehaven Gr ST4.......88 C5
Peach Ave ST17 ....**174** F7
Peacock Hay Rd ST7.....40 F4
Peacock La ST4,ST5......87 A8
Peacock Rd ST5 ....55 F5
Peacock View ST4 ....57 F1
Peak Cl WS15.............**198** B4
Peak Dale Ave ST6.......41 C7
Peak Dr DY3...............**271** E3
Peake Cres WS8 ....**244** F5
Peake Rd WS8 ....**245** A5
Peakes Rd WS15..........**178** B1
Peake St ST5 ....55 E3
Peaks L Ctr B79 ....**250** B3
Peak View ST13...........31 A5
Pearis Dr ST10 ....94 E8
Pearl Gr ST3 ....90 A8

Pear Pl ST2 ....73 D7
Pearson Dr ST15.........**120** C7
Pearson St WV2 ....**266** C8
Pear Tree Ave DE11.....**186** F7
Peartree Cl ST12..........88 D1
Pear Tree Cl
  Gnosall ST20.............**171** E6
  Huntington WS12........**209** C7
  Shuttington B79..........**251** E7
Pear Tree Dr CW3.........68 D7
Peartree La WS15.........**180** B6
Pear Tree La
  Bobbington WV5 ....**268** A4
  Brownhills WS8 ....**228** C2
  Newcastle-u-L ST5.........55 D8
  Wolverhampton WV11....**241** B1
Pear Tree Rd ST17........39 F1
Peascroft Rd ST6.........42 D4
Pebble Cl B77 ....**235** F3
Pebble Mill Cl WS11.....**209** F2
Pebble Mill Dr WS11....**210** A2
Pebble Mill ST11..........56 F4
Peckforton View ST7......41 A7
Peck Mill La ST8 ....27 C1
Pedley Cl ST3 ....88 F8
Pedley Gr ST6.............42 D1
Pedley La CW12...........58 C2
Peebles Gn ST2..........58 C4
Peebles Rd ST5...........54 F2
Peel Cl B78 ....**260** E5
Peel Ct 4 Kidsgrove ST7 ..26 A7
  Fazeley B78 ....**261** B8
  Tamworth B77 ....**261** F6
Peel Dr Astbury CW12......15 B7
  Cannock WS12............**209** F8
  Tamworth B77 ....**261** F6
Peelers Way B77 ....**250** C1
Peel Hollow ST7 ....**218** A2
Peel Ho B79 ....**250** A4
Peel La CW12..............15 D7
Peel St Burton u T DE14 ..**166** C1
  Longton ST3...............**284** C1
  Newcastle-u-L ST5.........56 C5
  Stafford ST16 ....**285** A3
  Tunstall ST6................56 C8
Peel Terr ST16...........**155** E5
Pegasus Ct B74..........**258** A3
Pegasus Gr ST6...........42 D1
Pegasus Wlk B79........**249** F7
Peggs La ST20...........**150** E8
Peggy's Bank ST7 ....54 F8
Pegroy Gr ST5.............42 D2
Pelham St ST1...........**282** C1
Pellfield Ct ST18.........**138** D2
Pelsall La
  Walsall,Little Bloxwich
  WS3 ....**243** D3
  Walsall WS3,WS4 ....**244** A1
Pelsall Rd WS8 ....**244** D7
Pelsall Village Sch WS3..**243** F4
Pemberton Cres DY10....**280** C3
Pemberton Dr ST3.........90 A5
Pembridge Rd ST3.........88 E7
Pembroke Cl B79.........**249** D6
Pembroke Ct ST5.........**283** A1
Pembroke Dr
  Newcastle-u-L ST5........**283** A2
  Stone ST15 ....**120** C7
Pembroke Gdns DY8.....**275** C2
Pembroke Rd ST2 ....43 B1
Penarth Gr ST1...........**282** B4
Penarth Pl ST5 ....**283** A1
Pencombe Dr WV4........**266** D5
Penda Gr WV6.............**254** F5
Pendeford Ave WV6......**255** E8
Pendeford Bsns Pk WV9 .**239** F3
Pendeford Cl WV6 ....**255** E8
Pendeford Hall La WV9 .**239** D5
Pendeford High Sch
  WV10......................**240** B2
Pendeford La WV9........**240** A3
Pendeford Mill La WV8..**239** C3
Pendeford Mill Nature
  Reserve* WV9 ....**239** E4
Pendene Ct WV4..........**266** A5
Penderel Cl WV10 ....**241** A6
Penderel St WS3..........**243** C1
Pendinas Dr WV8.........**239** B3
Pendine Gr ST4............73 B6
Pendle Hill WS12 ....**210** C4
Pendleton Cl WS6.........**242** F8
Pendrell Cl WV8..........**239** C2
Pendrell Hall Coll WV8..**238** C6
Pendrill Rd WV10.........**240** E3
Pendryl Cl ST19 ....**223** C7
Penfleet Ave ST3 ....74 A1
Pengrove Cl ST6...........41 E8
Penhallow Dr WV4........**266** E5
Penk Dr WS7..............**229** D6
Penk Dr N WS5............**178** C2
Penk Dr S WS5............**178** C2
Penkhull Cl 4 ST4........72 A7
Penkhull Ed Ctr ST4......72 A7
Penkhull New Rd ST4.....72 A6
Penkhull Terr ST4.........72 A6
Penk Rd ST11..............91 A7
Penkridge Bank WS12,
  WS15......................**196** B8
Penkridge Cl WS11.......**209** D1
Penkridge Ind Est ST19..**207** D2
Penkridge Mid Sch ST19 **193** A2
Penkridge Rd ST19.......**193** B7
Penkridge Sta ST19......**207** E8
Penkridge Wharf ST19...**207** F8
Penk Rise WV6............**255** B4
Penkside Wlk WV9.......**224** B3
Penkvale Rd ST17........**174** F6
Penkville St ST4..........72 A5

Penleigh Gdns WV5......**269** F7
Penmark Gr ST3 ....89 E8
Penmere Dr
  Newcastle-u-L ST5.........71 C1
  Werrington ST9............59 A3
Pennant Ct WV3..........**266** B8
Penn Bridge SK11 ....7 E1
Penn Cl WS3 ....**243** C1
Penn Common Rd WV4..**265** F1
Penn Croft ST18 ....**177** D8
Penn Croft La WV4......**266** A1
Penncroft WV4............**265** E4
Pennell St ST2 ....58 B4
Penn Fields Sch WV3....**265** F7
Penn Hall Sch WV4......**265** E3
Penn Hospl WV4..........**265** F5
Pennhouse Ave WV4....**265** F5
Pennine Dr
  Cannock WS11............**209** E2
  Dudley DY3 ....**271** D3
Pennine Way Biddulph ST8 .16 E1
  Newcastle-u-L ST5.........55 E3
  Tamworth B77 ....**262** C8
Pennington Cl ST3........74 C2
Penn Rd Sedgley DY3 ....**270** F8
  Wolverhampton WV2,WV3,
  WV4 ....**266** B8
Penn St WV3 ....**266** B8
Penns Wood Cl DY3 ......**266** C2
Pennwood Ct WV4........**265** D6
Pennwood La WV4........**265** F3
Penny Bank Ct WS15....**178** E1
Penny Bank Ho 6 ST13 ..30 F5
Pennycress Gdns WV10 .**241** C7
Penny Cress Gn WS11....**227** F4
Pennycroft La ST14 ......**111** C1
Pennycroft Rd ST14......**111** A1
Pennyfield Cl ST16 ....**285** C3
Pennycrofts ST16 ....**285** C3
Penny Ct WS6 ....**242** F8
Penny Farthing Arc DY3 .**271** D8
Pennyfields Ave ST6 .....41 D1
Pennyfields Rd ST7.......26 D2
Penny La ST10.............76 D3
Pennymoor Rd B77.......**262** B7
Pennymore Cl ST4.........88 B8
Penny Royal Cl DY3 ......**271** D2
Pennys Croft WS13......**214** E1
Penport Gr ST3...........**284** A2
Penrhyn Ave ST6..........42 B1
Penrith Cl ST4.............88 C6
Penrith Ct ST5.............71 B6
Pensett Trad Est The
  DY6 ....**271** A1
Pensford Gr ST1...........57 F5
Pensgreave Rd DE13.....**166** B6
Penshaw Cl WV9.........**240** A2
Pens Meadow Sch DY8..**275** E3
Pensnett Trad Est The
  DY6 ....**275** F8
Penstone Ave WV4.......**264** E4
Pentire Rd WS14.........**231** D6
Pentland Gdns WV6......**255** E2
Pentland Gr ST5...........55 E3
Penton Pl ST3.............**283** A1
Penton Wlk ST3 ....**88** E7
Pen-Y-Bont Wlk ST8......27 E6
Pen-Y-Bryn Way TF10...**168** F2
Penzance Way ST17......**156** E1
Penzer St DY6.............**275** D7
Peolsford Rd WS3 ....**244** A4
Peover La CW12 ....6 F6
Pepper St
  Newcastle-u-L,Silverdale
  ST5 ....**54** F1
  Newcastle-u-L ST5........**283** B2
Perceval St ST1............57 E5
Percival Dr ST9............43 C3
Percy St ST1 ....**282** B3
Peregrine Cl
  Burton u T DE15..........**167** D3
  Dudley DY1 ....**271** F1
  Whittington WS14 ....**232** F5
Peregrine Gr ST3..........90 A6
Perivale Cl ST1 ....58 A6
Periwinkle Cl WS8 ....**244** D6
Perkins St ST6.............41 C7
Perks Rd WV11 ....**242** A1
Perle Brook ST21.........**133** D7
Perott Dr B75.............**258** D2
Perrin Cl ST17............**174** F6
Perry Cl Hanley ST1......**282** C2
  Tamworth B79 ....**250** B6
Perrycrofts Cres B79.....**250** C7
Perrymount Cl ST4........71 F6
Pershore Cl WS3 ....**242** F2
Pershore Dr DE14.........**185** A8
Pershore Rd WS3.........**242** F2
Pershore Way WS3.......**242** F2
Persia Wlk 10 ST6........41 D3
Perth Cl DE15 ....**167** D2
Perth St ST4..............**284** A5
Perthy Gr ST4..............87 F7
Perton Brook Vale WV6..**254** F2
Perton Fst Sch WV6 .....**254** E5
Perton Gr WV6............**254** F2
Perton Mid Sch WV6.....**255** A5
Perton Rd WV6............**254** F2
Perton Sandown Fst Sch
  WV6 ....**254** F2
Perton Wood View ST3...72 F3
Pessall Farm Holding
  B79........................**217** C8
Pessall La B79............**217** C6
Petard Cl B77 ....**261** C8
Peterborough Dr WS12...**210** C1
Peterdale Dr WV4........**265** F3
Peterhead B77 ....**250** F5

Peter James Ct ST16.....**155** E6
Petersfield WS11 ....**209** F4
Petersfield Rd ST4........**72** C4
Petersfield Way CW2 .....37 D4
Petershouse Dr B74......**257** F5
Peter's La WS7 ....**230** A5
Peterson Ho 3 ST6........89 F8
Peters Wlk WS13 ....**214** A2
Pethills La ST13 ....48 C5
Petrel Gr ST3..............90 B7
Pettiford Cl WS13........**215** D6
Pevensey Gr ST3..........73 C6
Peverill Rd Perton WV6 ..**254** F4
  Wolverhampton WV4.....**266** E3
Pezenas Dr TF9............97 B1
Pheasant Way WS11 .....**210** A1
Pheasant Wlk TF9 ....99 D3
Philip Cl WS11 ....**209** E6
Philip La ST9 ....59 B8
Philip St ST4 ....72 E6
Phillips Ave WV11 ....**241** F1
Phillips Cl ST15..........**120** D7
Phillipson Way ST6.......57 D8
Phoenix Bank TF9.........97 D1
Phoenix Cl Kidsgrove ST7 ..26 C2
  Rugeley WS15 ....**178** F1
Phoenix Ctr WS11........**226** E6
Phoenix Pl WS11 ....**210** A2
Phoenix Rise WV2 ....**266** C6
Phoenix St
  4 Stoke-on-T ST6.........41 D3
  Wolverhampton WV2 .....**266** D6
Picasso Cl WS11 ....**210** D2
Picasso Rise ST3..........90 B7
Piccadilly Arc ST1........**282** B3
Piccadilly Cres B78......**261** F1
Piccadilly ST1 ....**282** B2
Piccadilly La DE6 ....**261** C8
  Piccadilly B78.............**261** F1
Pickwick Pl 7 ST6........41 D3
Pickering Cl ST3 ....**284** A1
Pickford Pl 8 ST3.........74 A1
Pickleys La DE6 ....**127** C8
Pickmere Cl ST2..........43 B3
Picknal La ST14 ....**126** A7
Picknalls Fst Sch ST14..**126** B7
Picknalls ST14............**126** B7
Pickstock TF10 ....**149** B2
Pickwick Gr ST13 ....31 A5
Pickwick Pl ST17 ....25 D2
Picton St Hanley ST1 ....**282** C2
  Leek ST13 ....30 D5
Piddocks Rd DE15........**186** B5
Pidduck St ST6............56 E7
Pierce Rd ST6.............41 D8
Pier St WS8 ....**244** F7
Pigeonhay La ST14 ......**110** C2
Piggott Gr ST2............58 A3
Pike Cl ST16...............**156** A5
Pike La WS15.............**198** A4
Pikelow La ST10 ....49 B3
Pilgrim Pl ST16...........**285** B2
Pilgrim St ST16 ....**285** B2
Pilkington Ave ST5........71 A6
Pillar Cl ST2...............73 D7
Pillaton Cl ST19..........**207** F7
Pillaton Dr WS12 ....**209** C6
Pillaton Hall Farm ST19..**208** C7
Pilsbury St ST5............56 D6
Pilsden Pl ST3.............90 C7
Pilstones Rd ST15 ....**103** B1
Pilstone Way ST15.......**103** C1
Pimlico Ct DY3 ....**271** D3
Pinch The DE6.............36 B2
Pine Cl Burton u T DE14 ..**185** A8
  Great Wyrley WS6........**226** F4
  Kingswinford DY6 ....**275** D5
  Kinver DY7.................**278** C3
  Market Drayton TF9.......97 B1
  Talke ST7..................40 D7
Pine Cl Blythe Bridge ST11 ..90 D8
  Loggerheads TF9 ....99 E4
Pine Cres ST17 ....**175** F6
Pine Ct Blythe Bridge ST11 ..90 D8
  Swadlincote DE11.........**186** F6
Pinehurst Cl ST5 ....71 B3
Pine Gr Burntwood WS7..**228** F5
  Cannock WS12............**195** A1
  Stoke-on-T ST4...........88 D7
Pine Leigh B74...........**258** B1
Pine Rd ST4...............72 C4
Pineside Ave WS15 ......**211** F5
Pines Park Home Est The
  WS12......................**209** D5
Pines The Lichfield WS14 .**231** F7
  Wolverhampton WV3......**255** D1
Pine Sq WS11.............**195** A1
Pine Tree Cl WS12 ....**195** A1
Pinetree Dr Aldridge B74..**256** D1
  Blythe Bridge ST11 ....90 D7
Pinetrees La TF9..........99 F5
Pinetrees WS15..........**196** F4
Pine View Rugeley WS15..**178** C3
  Smestow DY3..............**269** D3
Pineways Dr WV6.........**255** E4
Pineways Stourbridge DY8 **275** C2
  Sutton Coldfield B74 .....**257** C3
Pine Wlk Codsall WV8....**238** F2
  Uttoxeter ST14............**125** F8
Pinewood Ave
  Cannock WS11............**209** D4
  Wood End DY2 ....**262** C1
Pinewood Cl
  Brownhills WS8 ....**228** E2
  Wolverhampton WV3......**265** A8
  Woombourne WV5........**270** A6
Pinewood Cres ST3........74 C1
Pinewood Dr
  Colwich ST18..............**177** D8

Pinewood Dr continued
  Loggerheads TF9 ....99 E4
Pinewood Gr
  Blythe Bridge ST11........91 A6
  Newcastle-u-L ST5.........40 E1
Pinewood Rd
  Burton u T DE15..........**185** F6
  Loggerheads TF9 ....99 F5
Pinewoods Ave DY9......**281** F4
Pinewoods Cl DY9........**281** F4
Pinewoods Ct DY9........**281** F4
Pinewoods TF10 ....**168** E1
Pinewood Wlk DY6 ......**275** E8
Pinfold Ave ST6 ....42 D4
Pinfold Cl Tutbury DE13 .**146** C5
  Wheaton Aston ST19.....**205** B6
Pinfold Cres WV4 ....**265** D6
Pinfold Dr WS15 ....**198** C5
Pinfold Gr WV4...........**265** D6
Pinfold Hill WS14........**246** F6
Pinfold La
  Abbots Bromley WS15....**161** C3
  Blore TF9..................**98** C2
  Cheslyn Hay WS6.........**226** C2
  Norbury ST20 ....**151** B4
  Norton Canes WS11 ......**227** E4
  Penkridge ST19 ....**192** D1
  Wheaton Aston ST19.....**205** B6
  Wolverhampton WV4.....**265** E5
Pinfold Rd WS13..........**213** F1
Pinfold St ST14 ....**126** C7
Pingle Farm Rd DE11....**186** F5
Pingle La
  Hammerwich WS7 ....**229** D5
  Stone ST15 ....**120** B7
Pingle The WS15.........**196** B7
Pinhoe Pl ST3.............73 E3
Pinnox St ST6.............41 E2
Pintail Cl ST17...........**175** A7
Pioneer Pl ST6............42 C3
Pioneer Way ST17........**175** A7
Pipe Hall Farm Nature
  Reserve* WS13 ....**230** A8
Pipe Hay La DE6 ....**144** D5
Pipe La WS15.............**198** B8
Piper Cl WV6..............**254** F4
Piper Pl DY8...............**279** E8
Piper Rd WV6.............**265** C8
Pipers Croft WS13 ....**214** A2
Piper's La TF10 ....**168** A3
Piper's Lodge TF10 ......**168** A3
Pipe Wood La WS15......**180** B4
Pippins The
  Newcastle-u-L ST5.........71 C3
  Stafford ST17 ....**174** E5
Pireford Pl ST15...........41 A1
Pirehill La ST15...........**119** F5
Pirehill Prim Sch ST15...**119** F6
Pirehill Rd ST5.............41 B1
Pirie Cl CW12 ....6 A4
Pirie Rd CW12 ....6 A4
Pitchcroft La TF10 ....**187** A5
Pitcher La ST13............31 B5
Pitfield Ave ST5 ....56 D3
Pitgreen La ST5............56 C4
Pit La ST7..................40 C6
Pitlea Pl 1 ST3............73 C6
Pitmarsh View ST5........56 C5
Pitsford St ST3.............73 E2
Pitstone Cl ST16..........**136** D1
Pitt St E ST6...............57 A8
Pitt St W ST6..............57 A8
Pitts Hill Bank ST6.........41 D3
Pitt St Kidderminster DY10 **280** A1
  Stafford ST16 ....**155** C6
Plainfield Gr ST2...........73 D8
Plainview Cl WS9 ....**256** E2
Plaisaunce The ST5........71 B6
Plane Gr ST5...............40 E1
Planks La WV5............**269** F6
Plantation La Himley DY3 .**270** B3
  Hopwas B78 ....**249** B4
Plantation Pk ST5.........70 C6
Plantation Rd
  Cannock WS12............**195** A1
  Stoke-on-T ST4...........88 D7
Plant Cres ST17 ....**174** F7
Plant La WS7..............**228** E2
Plants Cl WS6 ....**243** A8
Plant St Cheadle ST10....76 E2
  Stourbridge DY8 ....**275** E2
Plant Way WS3...........**243** F4
Plardivick Rd ST17.......**171** B6
Platts Ave ST9..............43 B6
Platts Cres DY8 ....**279** E8
Platts Dr DY8..............**279** E8
Platts Rd DY8..............**279** E8
Platt St WS11.............**210** A5
Playdale TF10.............**168** B4
Pleasant Cl DY6 ....**275** C4
Pleasant St ST6............56 F7
Pleasant View DY3 ......**271** D2
Plex St ST6.................41 D3
Pleydell St ST1............57 F7
Plough Bank
  Weston-Under-Lizard
  TF11 ....**203** A6
  Wetley Rocks ST9..........60 B7
Plough La TF10............**168** F5
Ploughmans Croft TF10 .**169** A4
Ploughmans Pl B75......**258** D2
Ploughmans Wlk
  Kingswinford DY6 ....**275** A7
  Lichfield WS13............**214** C3
  Wolverhampton WV8......**239** F1
Plough Mews DY7 ....**278** A3
Plough St ST1 ....**282** C4

Plover Cl
Featherstone WV10 241 B7
Meir ST3 90 A7
Plover Dr ST8 27 E8
Plover Field CW3 68 D6
Plovers Rise WS15 178 D2
Plummer Rd DE11 186 F6
Plumtree Gr ST1 57 F6
Plymouth Gr ST5 55 F7
Pochard Cl ST6 42 C2
Podmore Ave ST7 54 F6
Podmore La ST7 54 E6
Podmore St ST6 57 A7
Pointon Gr ST6 43 A5
Polesworth High Sch B78 262 F7
Police Dr TF9 112 C8
Polperro Way 9 ST3 90 A7
Pomona Rise ST1 57 D8
Pond Cres WV2 266 E7
Pond Gr WV2 266 E7
Pond La WV2 266 D7
Ponesfield Rd WS13 214 B2
Ponesgreen WS13 214 B2
Pool Ave WS11 228 B5
Pool Cl WV10 225 D1
Pool Dam ST5 283 B2
Poole Ave ST2 43 B2
Poole Cres WS8 228 D2
Pooles Rd ST8 17 B1
Poole St DY8 279 E4
Poole's Way WS7 229 C7
Pooley La Gnosall TF10 188 C7
Polesworth B78 251 F2
Poolfield Ave ST5 70 F8
Poolfield Ave N ST5 71 A8
Poolfield Rd WS13 230 E6
Poolfields Ave ST6 43 C7
Poolfields Cl ST5 70 F8
Pool Gn WS9 256 A5
Pool Green Terr WS9 256 A5
Pool Hall Cres WV3 265 A8
Pool Hall Rd WV3 265 A8
Poolhill Cl ST3 284 A2
Pool House Rd WV5 269 D6
Pool La ST17 176 C4
Pool Mdw WS6 226 D1
Pool Meadow Cl WS15 196 D8
Pool Rd Brownhills WS7 228 E3
Burntwood WS7 228 E4
Poolside Cotts ST18 121 A1
Poolside CW3 68 E6
Pool Side
Newcastle-u-L ST5 283 A3
Scholar Green ST7 25 A8
Poolside ST3 88 F8
Pool St Longton ST4 73 B6
Newcastle-u-L ST5 283 A2
Wolverhampton WV2 266 C8
Pool View WS6 227 A4
Pope Gdns ST17 174 C7
Pope Gr WS12 209 F6
Pope Rd WV10 241 B1
Popes La WV6 255 A6
Poplar Ave
Brownhills WS8 245 A8
Burntwood WS7 228 F6
Cannock WS11 209 F4
Newcastle-u-L ST5 56 A3
Poplar Cl
Blythe Bridge ST11 91 A6
Eccleshall ST21 133 E6
Haughton ST18 172 E6
Newcastle-u-L ST5 56 A3
Stone ST15 119 F7
Uttoxeter ST14 110 F1
Wombourne WV5 270 B6
Poplar Cres DY8 279 D3
Poplar Ct ST5 56 A3
Poplar Dr Kidsgrove ST7 26 A1
Stoke-on-T ST3 72 F2
Poplar Gr Longton ST3 73 A1
Newcastle-u-L ST5 283 D3
Poplar La Bearstone TF9 82 F5
Cannock WS11 209 B1
Poplar Rd Brownhills WS8 245 A8
Great Wyrley WS6 227 A1
Kingswinford DY6 275 E5
Stourbridge DY8 279 E3
Wolverhampton WV3 266 A6
Poplar Rise B74 257 D6
Poplars Dr WV8 238 F2
Poplars Farm Way WV9 224 B2
Poplars Park Cvn Pk DE6 144 A7
Poplars Rd
Armitage WS15 198 C4
Burton u T DE13 166 C7
Poplars The
Cannock WS11 209 E4
Stourbridge DY8 275 F2
Poplar St
Norton Canes WS11 228 A6
Wolverhampton WV2 266 D6
Poplar Way ST17 174 E6
Poppit's La ST14 110 F4
Poppy Gdns DE13 201 A2
Porchester Cl WS9 245 A2
Porlock Ave ST17 175 D8
Porlock Gr ST4 88 B6
Portal Rd ST16 156 B5
Porters Farm Ct ST14 127 E2
Porters La ST13 31 F3
Porthill Bank ST5 56 C6
Porthill ST6 56 D7
Porthill Gn ST5 56 C6
Porthill Grange ST5 56 C6
Porthill Rd ST6 56 D7
Porthkerry Gr DY3 271 B7
Port La
Abbots Bromley WS15 160 E5
Brewood WV9 223 B3
Portland Ave
Aldridge WS9 256 B5
Burton u T DE14 185 A7
Tamworth B79 249 F8
Portland Cl ST11 90 D7
Portland Ct WS9 256 B6
Portland Dr Biddulph ST8 16 D2
Forsbrook ST11 91 B8
Market Drayton TF9 97 A1
Scholar Green ST7 25 E6
Portland Gr ST5 71 B3
Portland Mews ST5 56 B6
Portland Pl Barlaston ST12 88 F4
Cannock WS11 226 C7
Waterhouses ST10 48 F2
Portland Rd Aldridge WS9 256 B6
Longton ST3 284 B4
Portland St N ST13 30 F6
Portland St S ST13 30 F6
Portland St Hanley ST1 282 A4
Leek ST13 30 F6
Portleven Cl ST17 175 E7
Portleys La B78 260 D4
Portobello WS15 178 E2
Portrush Rd WV6 254 D4
Port St ST6 56 E7
Portswood Cl WV9 239 F1
Port Vale Ct ST6 42 A1
Port Vale St ST6 56 E8
Portway Cl DY6 275 E5
Portway Dr DE13 146 C5
Portway La B79 234 C7
Portway Pl DY10 280 A5
Portway The DY6 275 E5
Postern Rd DE13 165 B3
Post La ST9 43 F6
Post Office La
Gnosall TF10 188 D6
Gorstyhill CW2 37 F1
Rugeley WS15 196 B7
Post Office Rd
Alrewas DE13 201 A3
Seisdon WV5 263 F3
Post Office Row ST17 193 B8
Post Office Sq CW3 68 E5
Pothooks La ST13 33 F4
Potsmans La ST18 122 D7
Potteries Mus & Art Gall The* ST1 282 B2
Potteries Sh Ctr ST1 282 B3
Potteries Way ST1 282 C3
Potters Ave ST15 118 F6
Potters Croft B79 218 E2
Potters End ST8 16 C1
Potts La ST14 141 B7
Pouk La WS14 245 F7
Poulson St ST4 72 B7
Pound Gdns ST6 42 D4
Poundsgate Gr ST4 88 B8
Pound St WV5 267 C7
Pountney St WV2 266 C8
Pourbaix Ho WS13 231 B6
Povey Pl ST5 41 B1
Powderham Cl ST6 41 E8
Powell Pl TF10 168 F3
Powell St ST1 282 A4
Power Gr ST3 284 A4
Power Station Rd WS15 178 F1
Power Station Road Ind Est WS15 178 F1
Power Wash Ind Est ST8 27 B4
Pown St SK17 23 F6
Powy Dr ST7 26 B2
Poxon Rd WS9 245 A3
Poynings The WV6 255 C5
Precinct The B79 250 B5
Preedys Cl WS15 160 F5
Prescott Ave ST16 156 A4
Prescott Dr ST19 193 A1
Prestbury Ave ST5 71 B2
Preston St ST6 57 C8
Preston Vale La ST19 192 C1
Prestwick Rd DY6 275 C6
Prestwood Ct ST17 285 B1
Prestwood Dr
Stourbridge DY7 279 A7
Stourton DY7 278 F8
Prestwood La ST14 79 E1
Prestwood Rd DY7 278 E6
Pretoria Rd ST1 57 A3
Priam Cl ST5 41 B1
Priam Gr WS3 244 B5
Price Ave B78 249 D1
Price Cl TF9 99 D5
Price Ct Burton u T DE14 165 F4
Burton u T DE14 166 A4
Prices Rd DY3 271 C3
Price St Burslem ST6 56 F8
Cannock WS11 209 E1
Priestley Dr ST3 284 D4
Prime St ST1 57 E5
Primitive St ST7 26 C7
Primley Ave B77 261 F5
Primrose Ave WV10 240 D3
Primrose Cl Walsall WS3 244 A5
Wheaton Aston ST19 205 C7
Primrose Dell CW3 68 D6
Primrose Dr
Burton u T DE14 185 A8
Newport TF10 168 F1
Primrose Gdns
Codsall WV8 239 A3
Featherstone WV10 241 B7
Primrose Gr ST5 283 C4
Primrose Hill
Stoke-on-T ST4 72 A2
Stourbridge DY8 275 E1
Primrose Mdw 1 WS11 210 C2
Primrose Way ST14 126 B8
Prince Albert Terr ST15 135 A8
Prince Ave ST18 172 F5
Prince Charles Ave ST13 31 B7
Princefield Ave ST19 207 F8
Princefield Fst Sch ST19 207 F8
Prince George St ST10 76 D3
Prince Rupert Mews WS13 231 A8
Prince Rupert's Way WS13 231 A8
Princes Dr WV8 239 A2
Princes Gdns WV8 239 A2
Princes Rd Stoke-on-T ST4 71 F8
Stourbridge DY8 279 D3
Princess Ave Audley ST7 39 D1
Leek ST13 31 B8
Princess Cl WS7 228 E7
Princess Ct ST7 40 D5
Princess Dr ST3 74 B4
Princess Gdns TF10 168 F1
Princess Pl ST16 155 E5
Princes Sq ST6 56 D8
Princess Rd ST14 111 A1
Princess St Biddulph ST8 27 D7
Burntwood WS7 228 E8
Burton u T DE14 166 C4
Cannock WS11 209 F5
Newcastle-u-L ST5 283 C3
Talke Pits ST7 40 D5
Princes St ST16 285 B3
Prince's St ST15 105 A2
Princess Way DE13 166 E7
Prince St Brownhills WS9 244 F2
Cannock WS12 209 E6
Leek ST13 31 A6
Princeton Gdns WV9 239 F2
Princetown Cl ST3 90 A7
Priorfield Cl ST3 284 B4
Priors La TF9 97 A1
Priors Mill DY3 271 E5
Prior's Pl ST19 206 A6
Priory Ave ST13 31 A8
Priory CE Prim Sch ST4 87 F8
Priory Cl Congleton CW12 16 B7
Tamworth B79 249 F7
Tutbury DE13 146 B5
Priory Ct Brownhills WS9 245 A4
Market Drayton TF9 97 A1
Newcastle-u-L ST5 283 B2
Priory Dr ST18 177 D8
Priory Field Cl WV14 266 F1
Priory Green Prim Sch WV9 240 A2
Priory Lands DE13 147 F2
Priory La DY3 271 D7
Priory Pl ST7 26 A3
Priory Rd Bucknall ST2 58 B6
Cannock WS12 210 D4
Newcastle-u-L ST5 283 B1
Rugeley WS15 197 B5
Stone ST15 120 B7
Priory The Endon ST9 44 A8
Sedgley DY3 271 D8
Pritchett Ave WV4 266 F3
Probert Rd WV10 240 B1
Probyn Ct ST3 284 C2
Proctors Rd WS15 198 C4
Proffitt Cl WS8 245 A5
Progress Dr WS11 226 F6
Progress Ind Ctr WS11 226 F7
Prospect Dr WS13 231 F8
Prospect Manor Ct WS12 210 C3
Prospect Pk WS11 226 D7
Prospect Pl 9 Leek ST13 30 E5
Stafford ST17 175 A6
Prospect Rd
Burntwood WS7 229 B6
Dudley DY3 271 C2
Leek ST13 31 A5
Market Drayton TF9 97 B1
Stafford ST16 155 F5
Prospect St Burslem ST6 56 E7
Tamworth B79 250 A5
Prospect Terr ST5 283 A3
Prosper Mdw DY6 275 F7
Providence St ST1 282 C4
Provost Pl ST13 31 A7
Pruden Ave WV4 266 F3
Puddle Bank La CW12 15 F5
Puddle Hill ST18 139 D1
Puddy La ST9 44 A5
Pudsey Dr B75 258 C3
Pugh Rd WV4,WV14 266 F2
Pugin Cl WV6 254 D3
Pullman Cl B77 251 A2
Pullman Ct ST10 76 D2
Pulteney Dr ST16 155 B6
Pump Bank ST5 69 F7
Pump Ct ST7 39 E2
Pump La Doveridge DE6 127 B8
Rugeley WS15 178 C3
Pump St Leek ST13 31 A7
Stoke-on-T ST4 72 A7
Purbeck St ST6 57 B7
Purbrook Rd WV1 266 F8
Purbrook B77 261 E8
Purcell Ave WS13 214 C2
Purser Cres ST5 56 B5
Pyebirch La ST21 134 B5
Pye Green Rd WS11 209 E4
Pye Green Valley Prim Sch WS12 210 A7
Pyenest St ST1 282 A1
Pyrus Gr WS15 196 D6

Q

Quabbs La ST11 91 C8
Quadrangle The ST9 43 F7
Quadrant Rd ST1 282 B3
Quadrant The Hanley ST1 282 B3
Sedgley DY3 266 D1
Quadrille Lawns WV9 239 F2
Quail Gn WV6 254 F2
Quail Gr ST3 90 A7
Quantico Cl 12 ST17 175 A8
Quantock Cl WS8 245 A4
Quarry Ave ST4 71 F8
Quarry Bank
Hollington ST10 94 A4
Keele ST5 69 F8
Quarry Bank Rd Keele ST5 69 F8
Market Drayton TF9 112 B7
Quarry Berry La DE12 236 E7
Quarry Brow DY3 271 E6
Quarry Cl
Cheslyn Hay WS6 226 E3
Rugeley WS15 196 B8
Stoke-on-T ST9 43 C3
Werrington ST9 59 B4
Quarry Hills La WS14 231 D6
Quarry House La TF9 112 A7
Quarry La ST20 171 C4
Quarry Lodge WS14 231 D5
Quarry Pl TF9 112 B7
Quarry Rd Hollington ST10 94 A3
Stoke-on-T ST4 71 F8
Quarry Terr ST7 26 A1
Quarter La SK17 23 B2
Quayle Gr 2 DY8 275 D3
Quee La ST14 126 B1
Queen Anne St ST4 72 B8
Queen Elizabeth II Ct ST4 72 D6
Queen Elizabeth's Mercian Sch B79 250 C6
Queen Margaret's Rd TF9 99 D5
Queen Mary Rd ST4 72 A1
Queen Mary's Dr ST12 88 E3
Queen's Ave ST6 41 C1
Queensberry Rd ST3 73 D2
Queens Cotts ST19 206 B7
Queen's Croft Com Sch WS13 231 B7
Queens Ct
Burton u T DE14 185 B8
Caverswall ST11 74 D3
Longton ST3 73 B1
Newcastle-u-L ST5 283 C3
Queen's Dr ST8 27 D6
Queens Dr
Burntwood WS7 228 F5
Leek ST13 31 B8
Newport TF10 168 F1
Queens Gdns
Codsall WV8 238 F3
Talke Pits ST7 40 D5
Queen's Hospl DE13 166 A6
Queensland Cres DE15 167 C2
Queensmead Rd ST3 89 F7
Queens Park Ave ST3 73 B1
Queens Par WS3 243 B1
Queen's Prim Sch ST4 73 A5
Queens Rd Sedgley DY3 271 E8
Shareshill WV10 225 B6
Queen's Rd Stoke-on-T ST4 71 F7
Stourbridge DY8 279 F6
Queens Rise DE13 146 C6
Queen's Row ST12 88 F2
Queen's Sq 3 ST15 105 A2
Queens Sq WS11 209 E1
Queen St Audley ST7 39 C1
Brownhills WS9 244 F2
Burntwood WS7 228 F5
Burslem ST6 56 F8
Burton u T DE14 166 C1
Cannock,Blackfords WS11 209 D1
Cannock WS11 210 A5
Cheadle ST10 76 E4
Cheslyn Hay WS6 226 D3
Queens Terr ST1 57 E4
Queen St Kidsgrove ST7 26 A2
Kingswinford DY6 275 D7
Leek ST13 30 F6
Lichfield WS13 231 A7
Longnor SK17 13 B6
Market Drayton TF9 97 C1
Newcastle-u-L,Chesterton ST5 55 E7
Newcastle-u-L,Porthill ST5 56 B6
Newcastle-u-L ST5 283 C3
Rugeley WS15 196 F8
Stourbridge DY8 279 F6
Stourbridge,Wordsley DY8 275 E3
Uttoxeter ST14 126 C7
Queensville Ave ST17 156 A1
Queensville Bridge ST17 156 A1
Queensville Ret Pk ST17 175 A8
Queensville Stafford ST17 156 A1
Stafford ST17 175 B8
Queensway Ct 7 ST3 74 A1
Queens Way B78 262 F6
Queensway Ind Est ST6 56 C8
Queensway
Newcastle-u-L ST5 71 B6
Rugeley WS15 196 E7
Stafford ST16 285 B4
Stoke-on-T ST4 72 C6
Tamworth B79 250 A8
Queens Wlk ST3 74 B4
Queenswood Rd B75 258 B1
Queen Victoria Prim Sch DY3 271 E8
Quendale WV5 269 E6
Quillets Rd DY8 275 C3
Quince B77 251 B3
Quince Tree Sch B77 251 A3
Quinton Ave WS6 226 F3
Quinton Gr ST5 56 B4
Quinton Pl WS11 228 A4
Quinton Wlk ST6 42 C2
Quixhill Bank ST14 95 F8
Quixhill La ST14 95 E8
Quonians La WS13 231 B8
Quorn Cl DE15 167 A1
Quorn Cres DY8 275 C3

R

Rabbit La WV10 241 A8
Raby St WV2 266 D8
Racecourse La DY8 279 F1
Race Course ST5 55 C1
Racecourse Rd ST4 72 A4
Rachel Gr ST4 73 B6
Raddle La B79 217 E5
Radford Bank ST17 175 C8
Radford Cl ST15 105 A1
Radford Dr WS4 244 C2
Radford La WV3,WV4 264 F7
Radford Rd ST4 56 F1
Radford Rise ST17 175 C8
Radford St ST15 105 A1
Radhurst Rise DE13 183 C2
Radley Way ST9 59 B3
Radmore Cl WS7 228 D8
Radmore La
Abbots Bromley WS15 161 C7
Gnosall TF10,ST20 170 D7
Radnor Ct WS9 244 F4
Radnor Rd DY3 271 C8
Radnor Rise WS12 210 B4
Radstock Cl ST17 175 E6
Radstock Rd WV12 242 C1
Radstone Rise ST5 71 B3
Radway Green Rd
Barthomley CW2 38 D6
Barthomley CW2 38 E8
Ragees Rd DY6 275 F4
Raglan Ave WV6 254 F3
Raglan Cl
8 Burton u T DE13 166 D8
Aldridge WS9 256 F3
Sedgley DY3 271 B7
Raglan St ST4 72 D6
Raglan Wlk ST4 72 D6
Ragley Cl WS3 243 A1
Raikes La WS14 246 C7
Railswood Dr WS3 244 B3
Railton Ave ST3 73 A1
Railway Cotts
Colwich ST17 177 D7
Congleton CW12 6 A1
Cotes Heath ST21 102 D3
Cresswell ST11 91 D3
Egginton DE65 148 B7
Leek ST13 30 E1
Leek ST13 45 E8
Norton Bridge ST15 135 A8
Rugeley WS15 197 A5
Railway Ct ST9 43 F7
Railway Ent Ctr ST4 57 A1
Railway La WS7 211 E1
Railway Pas ST3 284 C4
Railway Rd ST3 73 E2
Railway St Cannock WS11 226 E8
Norton Canes WS11 228 A5
Stafford ST16 285 A3
Stoke-on-T ST6 41 E2
Railway Terr
Brocton ST17 176 C7
Kingsley Holt ST10 62 A3
Longton ST3 284 D3
Rainbow St 8 WV2 266 C8
Rainford Cl ST7 26 F1
Rainham Gr ST6 42 A8
Rainscar B77 262 B7
Rake End Ct WS15 179 F1
Rakegate Prim Sch WV10 240 B1
Rake Hill WS7 229 B8
Rakes La DE6 51 F6
Rakeway Rd ST10 76 F1
Raleigh Hall Ind Est ST21 117 E2
Ralph Ct ST17 174 B8
Ralph Dr ST1 57 F7
Ralston Cl WS3 243 A4
Ramage Gr ST3 73 D1
Rambleford Way ST16 155 D8
Ramillies Cres WS6 226 F1
Ramsay Cl ST12 88 E4
Ramsey Rd ST5 283 A4
Ramsey St ST4 72 C5
Ramshaw Gr 5 ST3 73 D6
Ramshaw View ST13 31 B8
Ramshorn Rd ST10 78 E8
Randall Cl DY6 275 F4
Randle Dr B75 258 C3
Randles La ST9 60 B6
Randle's View CW12 16 C8
Ranelagh Ho WV2 266 D7
Ranelagh Rd WV2 266 D6
Ranelagh St ST1 282 B2

Rangeley View ST15......104 E2
Rangemoor La DE6.......80 D6
Rangemore Hall Mews
DE13...................164 B1
Rangemore Hill DE13...183 B7
Rangemore St DE14.....166 B3
Rangemore Terr ST5.....56 D3
Ranger's Wlk WS15......178 B1
Rangeways Rd DY6......275 F4
Rangifer Rd B78........249 F1
Rank The ST20..........171 C5
Ranleigh Ave DY6......275 F4
Ranscombe Dr DY3......271 D2
Ransome Pl ST3.........73 E4
Ranton Park Area 3
WS11..................210 A2
Ranworth Cl ST5.........71 B2
Ratcliffe Rise WV4.....266 D4
Ratcliffe Ave DE14.....185 B8
Ratcliffe Cl DY3........271 F6
Rathbone Ave ST5......56 D3
Rathbone St 4 ST6......41 E3
Rathlin Cl WV9.........240 A3
Rathmore Cl DY8........279 E2
Rathwell Cl WV9........240 A1
Rattigan Dr ST3..........73 F4
Raton St ST1...........182 A2
Raven Cl Cannock WS12.210 E4
  Cheslyn Hay WS6......226 D2
  Huntington WS12......209 C7
Raven Ct
  Market Drayton TF9....97 C1
  Wolverhampton WV10..240 B3
Ravenhill Cl WS15......196 F6
Ravenhill Dr WV8.......239 A4
Ravenhill Terr WS15....196 F7
Ravenna Way ST15......73 E4
Raven Rd DE13.........182 A2
Ravensbank Mobile Home Pk
ST18..................137 D2
Ravens Cl ST7...........39 E3
Ravenscliffe Rd ST7.....41 A8
Ravenscroft DY8........279 C6
Ravens Cl WS8.........244 F7
Ravensholme WV6......254 F2
Raven's La ST17.........39 F3
Ravenslea Rd WS15....196 F6
Ravensmead Com Prim Sch
ST7...................39 E3
Ravenstone B77........262 B8
Ravens Way DE14......166 B4
Ravenswood Cl ST5.....71 B3
Ravenswood Crest 4
ST17..................175 C7
Rawle Cl ST10..........76 C3
Rawlett Sch
  Tamworth B79.........250 A8
  Wigginton B79........234 A1
Rawlins St ST1..........57 E5
Rawnsley Rd WS12.....210 E6
Ray Ct B74.............257 F3
Raygill B77............262 B8
Rayleigh Rd WV3.......266 A8
Rayleigh Way ST2.......58 D1
Raymond Ave ST1........57 D7
Raymond St ST1.......282 B1
Reacliffe Rd SK11,ST13...18 B4
Reade's La CW12........16 D8
Reading Way ST2.......58 D2
Reads Rd ST4...........72 F8
Reapers Wlk WV8......239 F1
Reason Rd ST17.......174 F5
Rebecca Gdns WV4.....265 F4
Rebecca St ST4..........72 B8
Recorder Gr ST6........42 B6
Recreation Rd ST3......73 E2
Rectory Cl
  Church Leigh ST10....109 A5
  Drayton Bassett B78..260 E5
Rectory Dr TF11........203 F2
Rectory Fields DE8....275 E2
Rectory Gdns
  Armitage WS15.......198 A4
  Talke Pits ST7........40 D6
Rectory La
  Armitage WS15.......197 F4
  Haughton ST18.......172 F5
Rectory Mews
  Eggington ST10.......148 B4
  Mucklestone TF9.......99 A7
Rectory Rd Hanley ST1..282 A1
  Hollington ST10.......94 C2
Rectory St Hanley ST1..282 A1
  Stourbridge DY8......275 E3
Rectory View ST7........40 D6
Redacres WV6...........255 C6
Red Bank La TF9.......112 B8
Red Bank Longton ST3...73 C1
  Market Drayton TF9...112 B8
Redbourne Dr CW2.......37 D1
Redbourn Rd WS3.......243 A4
Redbridge Cl ST4........71 F1
Redbrook Cl WS12.....210 D2
Redbrook La WS15....196 F5
Redcar Rd Stoke-on-T ST4.88 B7
Redcliffe Dr WV5......270 B8
Redcliff B77............250 F5
Redfern Dr WV7.........229 B5
Redfern Rd Stone ST15..119 F5
  Uttoxeter ST14.......111 A1
Redford Dr WV7.........237 B5
Redgrave Dr ST16......155 C2
Red Hall La ST4.........54 C5

Red Hall Prim Sch DY3..271 C3
Redhall Rd DY3.........271 C2
Redheath Cl ST15.......55 A2
Redhill Ave WV5.......270 A6
Redhill Cl B79.........250 A7
Redhill Dr ST10.........92 E5
Redhill Gdns ST15.....120 B8
Redhill Gorse ST16....155 C8
Red Hill DY7...........277 E4
Redhill La DE13........146 B5
Redhill Prim Sch WS11..209 F4
Redhill Rd Cannock WS11..209 F4
  Stone ST15...........105 C1
Redhills ST21..........133 E6
Redhills Rd Bucknall ST2..58 A7
  Stoke-on-T ST2........57 F8
Redhill ST16...........155 C8
Red Ho The
  Albrighton WV7.......237 A5
  Market Drayton TF9....97 C1
Red House Cres ST3....284 A3
Red House Ind Est WS9..256 A6
Redhouse Rd WV6......255 B5
Redhurst Dr WV10......240 B3
Red La WV11...........242 C3
Redlake B77............261 E8
Red La CW3.............68 E5
Redland Dr ST2..........58 D3
Redlands The ST15.....120 C7
Redlands Way B74......257 A1
Red La Sedgley DY3....271 B8
  Stoke-on-T ST3.......43 C2
Red Lion Ave WS11.....228 A4
Red Lion Cl ST7..........40 D7
Red Lion Cres WS11....228 A4
Red Lion La WS11......228 B4
Red Lion Pas ST1......282 C3
Red Lion St ST16.......285 B4
Redlock Field WS14....231 A5
Redman Gr ST6..........57 C7
Redmine Cl ST5..........56 A4
Redmond Cl WS15.....178 C2
Redmoor Cl DE15......167 B3
Redmoor Gdns WV4.....266 A5
Redmoor Rd WS15....211 F4
Rednall Dr B75.........258 C3
Red Rd ST15............78 C3
Redrock Cres ST7.......26 C1
Red Rock Dr WV8......238 F2
Redruth Cl DY6........275 D8
Redruth Dr ST17......156 D1
Redstone Way DY3....271 D4
Redwell Cl B77.........250 D5
Redwing Cl
  3 Packmoor ST7......26 F1
  Hammerwich WS7....229 D5
Redwing Dr Biddulph ST8..27 B8
  Huntington WS12......209 C7
Redwing B77...........262 A6
Redwood Ave Dudley DY1..271 F5
  Stone ST15...........120 B5
Redwood Cl B74........256 F2
Redwood Dr
  Burntwood WS7.......228 F8
  Burton u T DE15......186 A8
  Cannock WS11........210 A3
Redwood Pl ST3.........73 F1
Redwood Rd DY7......278 C3
Reedbed Gr ST6.........42 C3
Reedham Gdns WV4....265 D5
Reedham Way ST2......58 D2
Reedly Rd WV12.......242 C1
Reedmace B77.........250 C2
Rees Dr WV5...........270 B7
Reeve Cl WS15........198 B4
Reeve La WS13.........231 B8
Reeves Ave
  Newcastle-u-L ST5.....56 B3
  Stoke-on-T ST6........42 A3
Reeves Gdns WV8......239 A4
Refinery St ST5........283 C2
Regal Cl B77...........261 C8
Regency Cl ST7..........40 D6
Regency Dr ST9.........43 C4
Regency Wlk B74......257 D5
Regency Way DE13....166 D8
Regent Ave ST6.........41 F3
Regent Cl DY6.........275 C6
Regent Coll ST4.........57 A2
Regent Ct Ipstones ST10..62 A8
  Newcastle-u-L ST5.....56 B3
Regent Rd Hanley ST1..282 B1
  Wolverhampton WV4...265 E5
Regents Ho DE14......184 F7
Regent St Leek ST13....30 F6
  Stoke-on-T ST4.......72 A5
  Stone ST15...........104 F1
Regent Theatre* ST1..282 B2
Regina Cres WV6......255 B4
Reginald Mitchell Prim Sch
The ST7................25 D1
Reginald Mitchell Way
ST6....................41 C5
Reginald St 5 ST6......57 A8
Regina St ST6..........42 D2
Regis Beeches WV6....255 C5
Regis Rd WV6..........255 C5
Registry St ST4.........72 B8
Reid Cl WV12..........229 F7
Reid St ST6.............56 E8
Reindeer Rd B78.......249 E1
Relay Dr B77...........262 C7
Rembrandt Cl WS11....210 D2
Rembrandt Way ST3....90 B6
Remer St ST6...........57 B6

Remington Dr WS11....226 F8
Renard Way ST3.........90 B7
Rendel Gr ST15........104 E2
Rendermore Cl ST19...207 E7
Rene Rd B77............250 C5
Renfrew Cl
  Newcastle-u-L ST5.....70 F8
  Stourbridge DY8......275 C3
Renfrew Pl ST4..........72 A1
Rennie Cres ST13.......45 D5
Rennison Dr WV5......270 A6
Renown Ct ST2..........41 D6
Renshaw Dr DE11.....186 F5
Renshaw Wood La WV8..221 F2
Renton Gr WV10.......240 A1
Renton Rd WV10......240 A1
Repington Rd N B77...251 A5
Repington Rd S B77...251 A5
Repington Rd ST1........57 F8
Repton Ave WV6......254 E3
Repton Cl Cannock WS11..226 B8
  Stafford ST17........156 B1
Repton Dr ST5...........70 F5
Repton Rd DE15......167 E8
Reservoir Rd
  Burton u T DE14......165 F4
  Cannock WS12........210 D4
  Longton ST3...........73 E2
Retreat Gdns DY3......271 E7
Retreat Gdns The WV6..253 C3
Retreat St WV3........266 B8
Reva Rd ST6............174 E8
Revival St WS3........243 B1
Reynards La SK17......24 E4
Reynards Rise TF9.......99 D5
Reynolds Ave ST5.......55 E6
Reynolds Cl
  Lichfield WS13.......214 B2
  Swindon DY3..........269 E2
Reynolds Gr WV6......254 F5
Reynolds Rd ST6........42 A3
Rhein Way 2 ST17....175 A8
Rhodes Cl DY3.........271 A4
Rhodes Cl ST5...........56 C7
Rhodes Ho ST5.........167 C3
Rhodes St ST1..........57 D6
Rhondda Ave ST6........57 C7
Rialto Pl ST6...........41 D3
Ribble Cl Hilton DE65..157 A8
  Newcastle-u-L ST5.....71 B4
Ribble Dr ST8...........16 E1
Ribble Ind Est ST6......56 F6
Ribblesdale Ave CW12...6 A5
Ribblesdale B77.......262 B7
Ricardo St ST3..........73 C1
Riceyman Rd ST5........56 B8
Richard Clarke Fst Sch
WS15..................161 A6
Richard Cooper Rd
WS14..................246 F5
Richard Crosse CE Prim Sch
DE13..................199 C6
Richard Heathcote Com Prim
Sch The ST7...........54 E6
Richards Ave
  Stafford ST16........156 A4
  Stoke-on-T ST6........41 F3
Richards Cl WS11......227 F6
Richardson Dr WS7....228 E8
Richardson Dr DY8....279 E8
Richardson Pl ST6......42 B6
Richardson Way WS15..178 D3
Richard Wakefield CE Prim
Sch DE13.............146 C6
Richborough Dr DY1...271 F4
Riches St WV6.........255 F3
Richfield La ST17......193 F8
Richmere Ct WV6......255 B3
Richmond Ave
  Stoke-on-T ST1........57 D8
  Wolverhampton WV3..255 F1
Richmond Cl
  Cannock WS11........210 A5
  Chorlton CW2..........37 D1
  Newport TF10.........168 F1
  Stafford ST17........174 E7
  Tamworth B79.........250 A5
Richmond Dr
  Lichfield WS14.......231 D7
  Perton WV6...........254 F3
  Wolverhampton WV3..255 E1
Richmond Gdns
  Stourbridge DY8......279 F7
  Wombourne WV5......270 A5
Richmond Grove ST5...56 D3
Richmond Gr DY8......279 E8
Richmond Pk
  Kingswinford DY6.....275 C8
  Rugeley WS15.........196 F5
Richmond Rd
  Sedgley DY3..........271 E7
  Stoke-on-T ST4........72 A1
  Wolverhampton WV3..255 E1
Richmond St
  Burton u T DE14......166 C4
  Stoke-on-T ST4........72 A7
Richmond Terr ST1....282 A1
Rickerscote Ave ST17..175 A6
Rickerscote Hall La
ST17..................175 A5
Rickerscote Rd ST17..174 F6
Ridding Bank ST4........87 B7
Ridding La Denstone ST14..79 E2
  Gratwich ST14.......124 C3
Riddings Cres WS3....243 F4
Riddings La DE6.......144 D6
Riddings The B77......250 E5
Rider's Way WS15.....178 B1

Riversleigh Dr DY8.....279 E8
Riversmeade Way ST16.155 A5
Riversmead ST5.........71 B4
River View SK17........13 B2
Riverway ST17.........285 C2
River Way ST15........120 A7
Rivington Cl DY8......279 E4
Rivington Cres ST6.....42 A6
Rixdale Cl ST1.........282 B4
Roaches Sch ST8........27 C6
Roaches The* ST13....10 C2
Roach B77.............261 D6
Road One CW1..........37 D8
Road Two CW1..........37 C8
Robert Cl B79..........249 F7
Robert Heath St ST6....42 C2
Roberts Ave ST5.......283 B4
Roberts Cl
  Alsagers Bank ST7.....54 F6
  Brownhills WS9.......244 F2
Roberts Green Rd DY3..271 E4
Robertson Dr ST5........55 F3
Robertson Sq ST14......71 E4
Roberts Prim Sch DY3..271 D4
Robert St Dudley DY3..271 D4
  Stoke-on-T ST6........41 D4
Robert Sutton RC Sch
DE15..................186 A7
Robertville Rd ST2......58 B3
Robey's La B78.........251 D3
Robina Dr ST10..........76 E3
Robin Cl Huntington WS12.209 C7
  Stoke-on-T ST7........41 F8
  Tamworth B77........261 C8
Robin Croft 14 ST6......56 F8
Robin Hill ST8...........28 A7
Robin Hill Gr ST4......73 B5
Robinia B77............251 A4
Robin La TF10.........168 A4
Robins Cl WS6.........226 D1
Robins Croft WS11....210 A1
Robinson Ave ST6......57 D8
Robinson Cl B79.......249 E7
Robinson Ct ST3.........88 F8
Robinson Rd
  Burntwood WS7.......228 F8
  Swadlincote DE11....186 F6
  Trentham ST4..........87 F8
Robins Rd WS7.........228 E7
Robins The TF9..........99 D4
Robinswood ST17......175 C6
Robson Cl WS8.........244 F5
Robson St ST1.........282 A2
Rocester La ST10........49 A2
Roche Ave ST13.........31 A8
Roche Rd WS3..........242 F1
Rochester Ave WS7....229 A7
Rochester Rd ST3........73 C5
Rochester Way WS12..210 C1
Roche The
  Burntwood WS13.....230 A8
  Cheddleton ST13.......45 C4
  Creswell Green WS13..212 F1
Roche Way WS3.........242 F1
Rochford Cl ST13........30 C5
Rochford Gr WV4......265 D5
Rochford Way ST2......58 D1
Rock Cres ST15.........105 C4
Rock End Dr ST13.......45 B1
Rockeries The ST17....175 A6
Rock Farm Rd WS14...232 E6
Rockfield Ave ST10......43 D1
Rock Hill B78,WS14....248 C4
Rock House Dr ST12....88 D1
Rockhouse Dr ST18....158 B2
Rockhouse La ST7.......40 C7
Rockingham Cl
  Dudley DY3...........271 B3
  Walsall WS3..........243 B1
Rockingham Dr
  Cheadle ST10..........76 F3
  Perton WV6...........254 F3
Rock La Ashley TF9....100 C8
  Muckleston TF9........99 C7
Rocklands Cres WS13..214 D1
Rocklands ST5...........56 C7
Rocklands Sch WS13..231 D8
Rock La ST21...........102 B1
Rockmount Gdns DY7..278 B3
Rockrose Gdns WV10..241 A7
Rockside ST7...........26 C6
Rock St DY3............271 E5
Rocks The Brown Edge ST6.43 B8
  Standon ST21........102 C2
Rock The WV6..........255 D5
Rocky Wall DY7........277 E4
Rodbaston Coll ST19..207 E3
Rodbaston Dr ST19....207 E5
Roddam Ct TF10.......168 E2
Roddige La WS13......216 A8
Rode Hall* ST7.........58 F1
Rodenhurst House Flats 3
TF9....................97 C1
Rodger Ave CW3.........53 A6
Rodgers St ST6..........41 C7
Rodway La WV4........266 D3
Roebuck Cl ST15......106 D2
Roebuck Sh Ctr ST5...283 B2
Roebuck St ST4........175 B8
Roe Deer Grn TF10....168 E5
Roe La ST5.............71 A4
Roe Pk ST7.............15 E1
Roford Ct DY3..........271 E5
Rogate Cl ST4...........73 B6
Rogers Ave ST5..........55 F3

Rogers Cl WV11 . . . . 242 A2
Rogerson Rd WS13 . . . . 215 D6
Rogerstone Ave ST4 . . . . .71 E6
Rokewood Cl DY6 . . . . 270 D1
Rokholt Cres WS11 . . . . 209 C1
Rolfe Cl ST4 . . . . .72 A2
Rolleston La DE13 . . . . 146 D5
Rolleston Rd DE13 . . . . 166 C8
Rolling Mill Rd WS11 . . . . 227 F4
Rolt Cl ST15 . . . . 104 E3
Roma Cl ST3 . . . . .89 D8
Roman Ct WS8 . . . . 228 E2
Roman Cl Cannock WS11 . .226 E5
  Tamworth B77 . . . . 261 E7
Roman Dr ST5 . . . . .55 D5
Roman La B74 . . . . 257 B4
Roman Pk B74 . . . . 257 B4
Roman Pl B74 . . . . 257 B2
Roman Rd Coven WV9 . . . . 224 A3
  Little Aston B74 . . . . 257 C4
Roman Rd (Sandy La)
  DY8 . . . . 279 C3
Romans Grange B74 . . . . . 257 C5
Roman View WS11 . . . . . . 226 F5
Roman Way
  Lichfield WS14 . . . . 231 D7
  Tamworth B79 . . . . 249 E2
Roman Wlk WS14 . . . . 230 D2
Romany Way DY8 . . . . 279 C3
Romer Side ST2 . . . . .73 C8
Romesco Way
  7 Stafford ST17 . . . . . . 175 A4
  Stafford ST17 . . . . 175 A4
Romford Mdw ST21 . . . . . 133 D6
Romford Pl ST3 . . . . .90 B7
Romford Rd ST16 . . . . 155 E6
Romilly Cl Lichfield WS14 . 231 E7
  Stourbridge DY8 . . . . 279 E6
Romney Ave ST5 . . . . .55 B6
Romney Dr ST16 . . . . 155 B4
Romney Gr ST3 . . . . .89 C8
Romney B77 . . . . 261 F8
Romsey Cl ST2 . . . . .73 D8
Romsey Gr WV10 . . . . 240 C3
Romsey Rd WV10 . . . . 240 C3
Romsey Way WS4 . . . . 242 F3
Romsley Cl WS4 . . . . 244 C2
Romsley La WV15 . . . . 276 A2
Ronald St ST3 . . . . 284 C2
Ronaldsway Dr ST5 . . . . . 283 A4
Ronald Wlk ST3 . . . . 284 C2
Ronson Ave ST4 . . . . .71 E4
Rooker Ave WV2 . . . . 266 F6
Rooker Cres WV2 . . . . 266 F6
Rookery Ave ST3 . . . . .73 A1
Rookery Cl
  Armitage WS15 . . . . 198 C5
  Yoxall DE13 . . . . 182 A2
Rookery Cotts ST21 . . . . . 115 E6
Rookery Cres ST11 . . . . . . .91 C2
Rookery Ct
  Lichfield WS13 . . . . 230 E7
  Stoke-on-T ST4 . . . . .71 E3
Rookery La Aldridge WS4 . 256 B6
  Stoke-on-T ST4 . . . . .71 F3
  Weeford B75,B78 . . . . 248 C2
  Wolverhampton WV2 . . . . 266 B6
Rookery Par WS9 . . . . 256 B6
Rookery Rd
  Coldmeece ST15 . . . . 118 C2
  Kidsgrove ST7 . . . . .26 C3
  Wombourne WV5 . . . . 270 B6
Rookery Rise WV5 . . . . 270 B6
Rookery The
  Newcastle-u-L ST5. . . . . . .55 C1
  Stoke-on-T ST4 . . . . .71 E3
Rookswood Copse **2**
  ST17 . . . . 175 C6
Rookwood Dr WV6 . . . . . . 254 F2
Roper Way DY3 . . . . 271 F6
Roper Wlk DY3 . . . . 271 F6
Rope St ST4 . . . . .56 D1
Ropewalk The DE14 . . . . . 166 C1
Roseacre Gr ST3 . . . . .89 F6
Roseacre La ST11 . . . . .90 F6
Roseacre ST5 . . . . .55 F2
Rose Ave Burton u T DE13 . 148 A2
  Kingswinford DY6 . . . . . . 275 F5
Rose Bank Cres ST10 . . . . .78 B6
Rose Bank St ST13 . . . . . . .30 F6
Rose Bank Terr ST13 . . . . .30 F6
Rose Bay Mdw **2** WS11 . 210 C2
Roseberry Dr CW3 . . . . . . .68 E7
Roseberry Cl ST8 . . . . .27 E8
Rosebery Rd B77 . . . . 261 D4
Rosebery St ST6 . . . . .41 F5
Rosebury Gr WV5 . . . . 269 E6
Rose Cottage Dr **2** DY8 . 275 D3
Rose Cottage Gdns
  DE14 . . . . 166 D1
Rose Cotts TF11 . . . . 203 F8
Rosedale Wlk DY6 . . . . 275 E8
Rose Dr WS8 . . . . 244 E5
Rosehill WS12 . . . . 209 F8
Rosehill Cl ST12 . . . . .43 B1
Rose Hill ST16 . . . . 155 C3
Rose La WS7 . . . . 229 C2
Roseland Cres ST2 . . . . . . .43 B1
Roseleigh Cres DE11 . . . . 186 F6
Rosemary Ave
  Dudley DY1 . . . . 271 F6
  Wolverhampton WV4 . . . . 266 C6
Rosemary Cl WS8 . . . . 244 D6
Rosemary Cres
  Dudley DY1 . . . . 271 F6
  Wolverhampton WV4 . . . . 266 C5

Rosemary Cres W WV4 . .266 B5
Rosemary Ct B74 . . . . 257 D4
Rosemary Dr
  Huntingdon WS12 . . . . . . 209 D5
  Little Aston B74 . . . . 257 C3
  Uttoxeter ST14 . . . . 126 B6
Rosemary Ednam Cl ST4 . .71 E8
Rosemary La DY8 . . . . 279 D3
Rosemary Nook B74 . . . . . 257 D5
Rosemary Pl ST1 . . . . .57 E7
Rosemary Rd
  Cheslyn Hay WS6 . . . . 226 D3
  Tamworth B77 . . . . 250 F4
Rosemary St ST5 . . . . .55 E1
Rose Mill TF9 . . . . .99 E5
Rosemount Rd DE15 . . . . . 166 F3
Rosemount WV6 . . . . 255 D5
Rosendale Ave ST5 . . . . . . .55 F6
Rosendale Rd ST5 . . . . .56 A5
Roseneath Pl ST2 . . . . .43 B1
Rose St ST1 . . . . .57 E5
Rose Tree Ave ST4 . . . . . . .71 E2
Rose Tree La DE11 . . . . . . 186 F7
Rosevale Bsns Pk ST5 . . . .55 F8
Rosevale Ct ST5 . . . . .55 E8
Rosevale Rd ST5 . . . . .55 E8
Rosevale St ST2 . . . . .43 B1
Roseville Dr CW12 . . . . . . .16 B8
Roseville Gdns WV8 . . . . . 239 A4
Rose Way WS15 . . . . 176 F2
Rosewood Ave ST9 . . . . . . .43 C4
Rosewood Cl
  Little Aston B74 . . . . 257 D5
  Tamworth B77 . . . . 250 D4
Rosewood Ct B77 . . . . 250 D4
Rosewood Gdns
  Essington WV11 . . . . 242 B3
  Stafford ST16 . . . . 155 C3
Rosewood Pk WS6 . . . . 226 D2
Rosewood Rd DE15 . . . . . . 185 F6
Rosewood Sch DY1 . . . . . . 271 E1
Rosliston Rd DE15 . . . . . . 185 E7
Rosliston Rd S DE15 . . . . . 185 E5
Rosliston Rd
  Swadlincote DE15 . . . . . . 185 D3
  Walton-On-Trent DE12. . . 202 E8
Rossall Ave ST5 . . . . .70 F5
Ross Cl Longton ST3 . . . . . .74 A4
  Wolverhampton WV6 . . . . 255 E2
Ross Dr DY6 . . . . 275 C2
Rossett Gr ST6 . . . . .41 F8
Rosslyn Rd ST3 . . . . 284 C2
Ross Rd ST10 . . . . .62 C2
Rosvean Cl ST1 . . . . 282 B4
Rosy Bank ST9 . . . . .43 C3
Rosy Cross B79 . . . . 250 B5
Rotary Ho DY1 . . . . 271 F1
Rothay B77 . . . . 261 F8
Rothbury Gn WV12 . . . . . . 210 E2
Rother Wlk ST6 . . . . .42 A4
Rotherwood Dr ST17 . . . . 285 A1
Rothesay Ave ST5 . . . . .70 F7
Rothesay Cl Longton ST3 . .73 D2
  Newcastle-u-L ST5. . . . . . .70 F7
Rothesay Dr DY8 . . . . 271 E8
Rothesay Rd ST3 . . . . .73 D2
Rothley Gn ST13 . . . . .88 F7
Rothsay Ave ST1 . . . . .57 D8
Rothwell St ST4 . . . . .71 F6
Rotten Row WS14 . . . . 231 C7
Rotterdam St5 . . . . .55 F1
Rotterdam Rd ST5 . . . . . . .55 F1
Rough Bank CW12 . . . . . . .16 E8
Roughcote La ST11 . . . . . . .74 C5
Rough Hills Cl WV2 . . . . . . 266 F6
Rough Hills Rd WV2 . . . . . 266 F6
Roughley Dr B75 . . . . 258 C2
Roughley Farm Rd B75 . . 258 E3
Roughlow La DE6 . . . . .80 D1
Roundfields ST9 . . . . .43 C3
Round Hill DY3 . . . . 266 D2
Roundhill Way WS8 . . . . . 229 A2
Round House Rd DY3 . . . . 271 F4
Roundway Down WV6 . . . . 254 F3
Roundway ST3 . . . . .72 D2
Roundwell St ST4 . . . . .41 D3
Rouse Cl ST10 . . . . 155 C2
Rowallan Rd B75 . . . . 258 D2
Rowanburn Cl ST13 . . . . . .73 D5
Rowan Cl
  Biddulph Moor ST8 . . . . . .28 B8
  Kidsgrove ST7 . . . . .41 A8
  Lichfield WS14 . . . . 231 D8
  Stone ST15 . . . . 120 B6
Rowan Cres WV3 . . . . 265 E7
Rowan Ct ST14 . . . . .95 F4
Rowan Dr Armitage WS13 . 198 C3
  Essington WV11 . . . . 242 B3
  Newport TF10 . . . . 168 F1
Rowan Glade ST17 . . . . . . 175 C6
Rowan Gr Brewood ST19 . 223 D6
  Burntwood WS7 . . . . 228 F7
  Stoke-on-T ST3 . . . . .72 E3
Rowan La TF9 . . . . .99 F5
Rowan Pl ST5 . . . . .55 D8
Rowan Rd Cannock WS11 . 209 C2
  Market Drayton TF9 . . . . . .97 E2
  Sedgley DY3 . . . . 266 F1
Rowan Rise DY6 . . . . 275 E6
Rowbury Dr DE15 . . . . 167 B2
Rowena Gdns DY3 . . . . . . 266 C2
Rowhurst Cl ST5 . . . . .55 D7
Rowhurst Pl ST6 . . . . .42 C5
Rowland St ST3 . . . . .73 B1
Rowley Ave
  Newcastle-u-L ST5. . . . . . .55 F7
  Stafford ST17 . . . . 285 A1

Rowley Bank Gdns ST17. 174 E8
Rowley Bank Ho ST17. . . . 174 E8
Rowley Bank ST17 . . . . . . 174 E8
Rowley Cl Cannock WS12 . 210 B8
  Edingale B79 . . . . 217 C5
  Rugeley WS15 . . . . 197 A6
Rowley Gr ST17 . . . . 174 E8
Rowley Hall Cl ST17 . . . . . 174 C8
Rowley Hall Dr ST17 . . . . . 174 C8
Rowley Hall Hospl ST17 . 174 D8
Rowleyhill Dr ST19 . . . . . . 206 F4
Rowley La ST17 . . . . 155 C5
Row Moor Way ST6 . . . . . . .42 E2
Rownall Pl **2** ST3 . . . . . . .74 A2
Rownall Rd Meir ST3 . . . . .74 A1
  Werrington St9 . . . . .59 D5
Rownall View ST13 . . . . . . .30 C4
Rowney Cl TF9 . . . . .99 D4
Rownton Cl B74 . . . . 257 D4
Row The ST18 . . . . 137 F4
Rowton Ave WV6 . . . . 254 E3
Rowton St DE13 . . . . 166 C6
Roxall Cl ST10 . . . . 281 C2
Roxburghe ST3 . . . . 284 D2
Royal Cl Rugeley WS15 . . . 196 D7
  Stoke-on-T ST2 . . . . .43 A3
Royal Oak Dr ST3 . . . . 221 E8
Royal St ST4 . . . . 284 A5
Royal Way ST2 . . . . .43 A3
Royal Wlk ST10 . . . . .76 D3
Royal Wolverhampton Sch
  The WV3 . . . . 266 B7
Royce Ave ST8 . . . . .27 B5
Roycroft Cl ST5 . . . . .56 B8
Royden Ave ST1 . . . . .57 F4
Royds Cl ST18 . . . . 172 E6
Roylance St ST6 . . . . .41 D3
Royston Chase ST4 . . . . . . 257 A3
Royston Way ST3 . . . . 271 C8
Royston Wlk ST3 . . . . 284 C3
Royville Pl ST6 . . . . .57 D8
Rozel Ave DY10 . . . . 280 B1
Ruabon Cl ST8 . . . . .27 E6
Rubens Cl DY3 . . . . 271 D5
Rubens Way ST3 . . . . .90 B7
Rubian St ST4 . . . . .72 F6
Rudge Dale Rd TF9 . . . . . . 100 A4
Rudge Rd WV6 . . . . 263 B7
Rudgind Cl Stone ST15. . . 104 E2
  Wolverhampton WV10 . . . 240 E4
Rudyard Gr ST5. . . . . .56 C4
Rudyard Ho ST17 . . . . 174 E5
Rudyard Lake Steam Rly*
  ST13. . . . . .18 E2
Rudyard Lake Visitors Ctr*
  ST13. . . . . .18 E1
Rudyard Rd Biddulph ST8. .17 F1
  Poolend ST13 . . . . .19 A1
  Rudyard ST13 . . . . .29 E8
Rudyard Vale Cvn Pk
  ST13. . . . . .18 D2
Rudyard Way ST10 . . . . . . .76 F4
Ruelow Mdw ST10 . . . . . . .62 A7
Ruffin Cl ST15 . . . . 120 C7
Rufford B79 . . . . 249 E6
Rugby Cl Burton u T DE14. 166 C8
  Newcastle-u-L ST5. . . . . . .70 F4
Rugby Dr ST3 . . . . .73 C1
Rugby Rd DY8 . . . . 279 D2
Rugeley Rd
  Armitage WS15 . . . . 197 D5
  Burntwood,Chase Terrace
    WS7 . . . . 211 F2
  Burntwood,Gorstey Ley
    WS7 . . . . 229 C2
  Cannock WS12 . . . . 211 B7
  King's Bromley DE13 . . . . 199 A5
  Rugeley WS15 . . . . 196 D1
Rugeley Town Sta ST15 . . 196 E8
Rugeley Trent Valley Sta
  WS15 . . . . 178 F3
Ruiton St DY3 . . . . 271 D4
Rumbold Ave WS3 . . . . . . 215 D6
Rumer Hill Bsns Est
  WS11 . . . . 226 E7
Rumer Hill Rd WS11 . . . . . 226 F8
Running Hills WS15 . . . . . 197 F4
Runnymede Cl ST2 . . . . . . .58 B3
Runnymede ST15 . . . . 120 A6
Rupert St **1** ST8 . . . . .27 C8
Rushall Cl DY8 . . . . 279 E8
Rushall JMI Sch WS4 . . . . 244 B1
Rushall Rd WV10 . . . . 240 E2
Rushbrook Cl WS8 . . . . . . 244 D6
Rushcliffe Dr ST3 . . . . .90 B7
Rushes Mill WS3 . . . . 243 E3
Rushey La WV7 . . . . 252 D6
Rushford Ave WV5 . . . . . . 270 A6
Rush La
  Market Drayton TF9 . . . . . .97 A4
  Tamworth B77,B78 . . . . . . 261 D4
Rushmoor Gr **4** ST3 . . . . .90 B7
Rushton Cl ST5 . . . . .70 F8
Rushton CE Prim Sch SK11 .8 B2
  Tutbury DE13 . . . . 146 C6
Rushton Gr **11** ST6 . . . . . .57 A7
Rushton Mews ST12 . . . . . 211 C4
Rushton ST5 . . . . .70 F4
Rushton Rd ST6 . . . . .57 A7
Rushtons La ST15 . . . . 105 F6
Rushton Way ST11 . . . . . . .90 A6
Rushwater Cl WV5 . . . . . . 269 E6
Ruskin Ave Dudley DY3 . . 271 A5
  Wolverhampton WV4 . . . . 266 F7
Ruskin Cl ST3 . . . . 284 D5
Ruskin Dr ST18 . . . . 154 E2
Ruskin Glass Ctr* DY8 . .279 F7

Ruskin Pl DE14 . . . . 166 D6
Ruskin Rd WV10 . . . . 241 A1
Rusper Cl ST1 . . . . .57 F6
Russell Bank Rd B74 . . . . 257 E4
Russell Cl Congleton CW12 .16 A8
  Tamworth B77 . . . . 261 E6
  Uttoxeter ST14 . . . . 126 D8
  Wolverhampton WV11 . . . 241 F1
Russell Ct B74 . . . . 257 D3
Russell Gr ST9 . . . . .59 B4
Russell Ho B77 . . . . 250 F2
Russell Pl ST6 . . . . .41 D6
Russell Rd ST6 . . . . .41 D6
Russells Hall Prim Sch
  DY1 . . . . 271 E1
Russell's Hall Rd DY1 . . . 271 F1
Russell St
  Burton u T DE14 . . . . 166 D2
  Leek ST13 . . . . .30 E5
  Longton ST3 . . . . 284 B1
  Newcastle-u-L ST5. . . . . . .56 C5
Russel St ST16 . . . . 285 A3
Russet Cl **2** ST3 . . . . .90 A7
Russet Cl WS7 . . . . 229 A6
Russets The ST17 . . . . 174 F6
Russet Wlk WV8 . . . . 239 E1
Rustington Ave ST3 . . . . . .73 E3
Ruston Ave ST6. . . . . .42 B6
Rutherford Cl ST4. . . . . . . .71 B3
Rutherford Ct ST18 . . . . . 156 C5
Rutherford Pl ST14 . . . . . . .71 E7
Rutherglen Cl WS15. . . . . 178 C1
Ruthin Gr ST8 . . . . .27 E6
Ruthin Rd ST2 . . . . .58 D2
Rutland Ave
  Rugeley WS15 . . . . 196 D6
  Wolverhampton WV4 . . . . 265 D4
Rutland Cl DE15 . . . . 185 D6
Rutland Cres WS9 . . . . . . 245 B1
Rutland Dr B78 . . . . 250 A1
Rutland Pl
  Newcastle-u-L ST5. . . . . . .71 C4
  Stourbridge DY8 . . . . 279 D8
Rutland Rd
  Cannock WS12. . . . . 210 C1
  Kidsgrove ST7 . . . . .26 A2
  Longton ST3. . . . . 284 C4
  Rutland St ST1 . . . . 282 A4
  Ruxley Cl ST3 . . . . .57 F3
  Ruxley Rd ST2 . . . . .58 A3
Ryandra Bsns Pk ST10 . . .76 B2
Ryburn Cl CW2 . . . . .37 B3
Rycroft CE Mid Sch ST14. .95 E4
Rydal Cl Aldridge B74 . . . 256 F2
  Cannock WS12 . . . . 210 A8
Rydal Dr WV6. . . . . 254 F4
Rydal Est WS15 . . . . 178 F3
Rydal Ho ST16 . . . . 285 C3
Rydal B77 . . . . 262 A7
Rydal St ST5 . . . . .71 B4
Ryder Cl DE11 . . . . 186 E2
Ryder Rd ST3 . . . . .90 A8
Ryders Hayes Com Sch
  WS3 . . . . 244 A5
Ryders Hayes La WS3 . . . 244 A4
Ryder St DY8 . . . . 275 D2
Rye Bank Cres ST5 . . . . . . 283 B3
Rye Bank ST5 . . . . 283 B3
Ryebrook Gr ST6 . . . . .41 F6
Ryecroft Ave WV4. . . . . . . 266 B5
Ryecroft La Sedgley DY3. . 271 C8
  Upper Tean ST10 . . . . .92 F3
Ryecroft Dr **3** WS7 . . . . . 229 A8
Ryecroft ST5 . . . . 283 B3
Ryecroft Rd ST6 . . . . .42 E3
Ryecroft Sch Ctr WS7 . . . 229 A8
Rye Cl ST16. . . . . 155 A5
Ryedale Way CW12 . . . . . .16 C2
Ryefield WS4 . . . . 239 E1
Ryehills ST17 . . . . .39 E1
Ryeland Cl ST3 . . . . .89 C8
Ryhope Wlk WV9 . . . . 240 A3
Ryknield Prim Sch DE14 . 142 F2
Ryknield Cl WS13. . . . . . . 215 E7
Ryknild Cl B74. . . . . 257 F6
Ryknild St Alrewas DE13 . 201 A2
  Lichfield WS14 . . . . 231 E6
Rylands Dr WV4 . . . . 266 A4
Rylcroft **7** WV4 . . . . 266 F4
Rylestone Cl ST3 . . . . .90 B7
Ryle St WS3 . . . . 243 D1
Ryton B77 . . . . 262 A7
Ryton Way DE65 . . . . 147 D8

S

Sabine St ST17 . . . . 285 C1
Sabrina Rd WV6 . . . . 254 E1
Sackville St ST4 . . . . .56 E1
Saddlers Cl ST4 . . . . .56 B6
Saddlers Cres WS9 . . . . . 245 B1
Saddlers Ct WS4 . . . . .72 E5
Saddlestones The WV6 . . 254 D4
Saddleworth Rd WS3 . . . . 243 A4
Sadler Ctr WS8 . . . . 245 A8
Sadler Rd WS8 . . . . 245 A8
Sadlers Mill WS8 . . . . 245 A7
Saffron Cl
  Barton-u-N DE13 . . . . 183 C1
  Stafford ST16 . . . . .90 A6
Saffron Gdns WV4 . . . . . . 266 A4
Saffron B77 . . . . 251 B4
Sage Cl ST3 . . . . 282 B1
St Aidan's Cl DE13 . . . . . . 166 C8
St Aidan's Dr ST17 . . . . . . .26 C3
St Aidan's Rd WS11 . . . . . 209 E5

St Aidan's St ST6 . . . . .41 D4
St Albans Cl WV11 . . . . . . 242 A1
St Albans Cl DE13 . . . . . . 166 C7
St Albans Rd ST6 . . . . 155 E7
St Andrew Cl WS12 . . . . . 211 A5
St Andrews Ave WS3 . . . . 244 B4
St Andrew's CE Prim Sch
  B79 . . . . 218 E1
St Andrew's CE Prim Sch
  Weston ST18 . . . . 138 D2
  Wolverhampton WV6 . . . . 255 F4
St Andrew's Cl
  Clifton Campville B79 . . . . 218 F2
  Dudley DY3 . . . . 271 A3
St Andrews Cl DY8 . . . . . . 279 F2
St Andrew's Cres ST11 . . . .57 D7
St Andrew's Dr B13 . . . . . 166 E8
St Andrew's Dr ST7 . . . . . .26 C3
St Andrew's Dr ST5 . . . . . .70 F8
St Andrew's Rd WV6 . . . . 254 D5
St Andrews Rd ST17 . . . . 174 C7
St Andrew's Sq **3** ST4 . .72 A7
St Andrews B77 . . . . 251 B4
St Andrews Way TF10 . . . 168 E1
St Anne's CE Prim Sch
  ST6. . . . . .28 B1
St Anne's Cl WS7 . . . . 228 E4
St Anne's RC Prim Sch
  ST17. . . . . 175 D7
St Annes Rd WS13 . . . . . . 214 B3
St Anne's Rd WV10 . . . . . 240 B1
St Anne's Vale ST6. . . . . . .43 B8
St Ann St ST1 . . . . 282 C3
St Ann Wlk ST1 . . . . 282 C3
St Anthonys Cl WS15. . . . 196 F8
St Anthonys Ct ST14 . . . . .72 B5
St Anthony's Dr ST5 . . . . .71 A7
St Anthonys Dr WS3 . . . . 244 B5
St Anthony's RC Prim Sch
  WV10 . . . . 240 D3
St Augustine's CE Fst Sch
  DE6 . . . . 144 D5
St Augustines Dr CW2 . . . .37 E3
St Augustine's RC Prim Sch
  ST3. . . . . .89 F7
St Augustine's Rd WS15. . 196 E6
St Austell Cl
  Stafford ST17 . . . . 175 D8
  Tamworth B79 . . . . 250 A6
St Austin's RC Prim Sch
  ST17. . . . . 285 C2
St Barbara Ho WS15 . . . . 178 E1
St Barbara's Rd WS15 . . . 198 C5
St Bartholomew's CE Prim
  Sch SK17. . . . . .13 B7
St Bartholomews CE Prim
  Sch 265 E3
St Bedes Sch WS15. . . . . 178 A6
St Benedict Bishop CE Prim
  Sch WV6. . . . . 270 B7
St Benedict's Dr ST7 . . . . 177 D8
St Benedict's Rd WV5 . . . 229 B6
St Benedicts Rd WS7 . . . . 270 A6
St Bernadette's RC Prim Sch
  WS8 . . . . 244 F8
St Bernadettes RC Prim Sch
  WV5 . . . . 269 F6
St Bernard Pl ST12 . . . . . .58 A5
St Bernard's Cl WS12. . . . 211 D4
St Bernard's Rd ST5 . . . . .53 B3
St Bertelin St ST16 . . . . . 155 C6
St Blaise Rd B75 . . . . 258 D3
St Brides Cl Sedgley DY3 . 271 C8
  Wombourne WV5 . . . . 269 F6
St Catherine's Cl ST14 . . 126 D8
St Catherine's Cres WV4 . 265 F4
St Catherine's Rd WS13. . 214 B3
St Chad Cl B77 . . . . 250 F2
St Chad's CE Prim Sch
  Lichfield WS13 . . . . 231 C8
  Newcastle-u-L ST5. . . . . . .40 D2
St Chads CE Prim Sch
  WV6 . . . . 253 C8
St Chads Cl ST19 . . . . 223 D6
St Chad's Cl
  Donstone ST14 . . . . .95 D6
  Dudley DY3 . . . . 271 B3
St Chads Cl
  Lichfield WS13 . . . . 214 B1
  Pattingham WV6 . . . . 253 C2
St Chad's Cl ST15 . . . . . . 120 C7
St Chad's Cl WS13 . . . . . . 231 B8
St Chad's Pl ST6 . . . . 285 B3
St Chads RC Prim Sch
  DY3 . . . . 271 D7
St Chad's Rd Cl DE13 . . . 166 C7
St Chad's Rd ST21 . . . . . . 133 D6
St Chad's Rd WS13. . . . . . 214 C1
St Chad's Rd ST6. . . . . . . .41 E3
St Chads Way TF9 . . . . . . .82 C2
St Christopher Ave ST4 . . .71 E6
St Christopher Cl WV2 . . . .37 F3
St Christopher's Dr WS7 . 250 C1
St Christopher's RC Prim Sch
  WV8 . . . . 239 A3
St Clair St ST3 . . . . 284 C2
St Clements Cl CW2 . . . . . .37 B1
St David Cl WS12 . . . . 211 A6
St Davids Cl WS3 . . . . 244 B5

St David's Dr DE13. . . . . 166 D8
St Davids Pl WS3 . . . . 243 D2
St Davids Rd
  Clifton Campville B79 . . . . . .218 F2
  Stafford ST17 . . . . .174 D7
St Davids Way ST8. . . . . . . 27 E6
St Dominics Ct ST4 . . . . . . .72 A8
St Dominics Ind Jun Sch
  ST4. . . . . .71 F8
St Dominic's Priory Sch
  ST15. . . . . 104 F1
St Dominic's RC Prim Sch
  ST15. . . . . 105 A1
St Dominic's Sch ST19 . . . 223 C7
St Editha's Cl B79 . . . . .250 B5
St Editha's Ct
  Church Eaton ST20 . . . . . . .190 B8
  Tamworth B79 . . . . .250 B7
St Edmund's Ave ST5 . . . . .56 D6
St Edmund's Cl WV6 . . . . . .255 F3
St Edmunds RC Sch
  WV3 . . . . .255 E3
St Edward's CE Fst Sch
  ST13. . . . . .45 B5
St Edwards CE Mid Sch
  ST13. . . . . .30 C5
St Edwards Ct DE11. . . . . . .186 F5
St Edwards Gn WS15. . . . . .196 E7
St Edward's Hall ST11. . . . .45 C7
St Edward's Rd ST13. . . . . .45 C4
St Edward's St ST13 . . . . . .30 E5
Sainte Foy Ave WS13. . . . . 231 A6
St Elizabeth's RC Prim Sch
  B79. . . . . .249 F8
St Filumena's RC Prim Sch
  ST11. . . . . .74 E2
St Foy Ave WS13 . . . . .230 F5
St Francis Cl
  Burton u T DE13. . . . . 166 D8
  Cannock WS12. . . . . 211 A5
  Walsall WS3 . . . . .244 B5
St Francis of Assisi RC Sch
  WS9 . . . . 256 C5
St Francis RC Prim Sch
  WS4. . . . . 244 C1
St Gabriel's RC Prim Sch
  B77. . . . . .250 E1
St George Dr WS12 . . . . . . 211 A5
St George & St Martin's RC
  Prim Sch ST1 . . . . .282 C4
St Georges Ave ST9. . . . . .43 E6
St George's Ave N ST5. . . .56 B5
St George's Ave S ST5. . . .56 B5
St Georges Ave ST6. . . . . .42 B4
St George's Ave W ST5. . . .56 B5
St George's Cres ST4 . . . . .72 A1
St Georges Ct B74 . . . . . . .257 E5
St Georges Hospl ST16. . . 285 C4
St George's Rd
  Burton u T DE13. . . . . 165 F5
  Newcastle-u-L ST5. . . . . . . .283 A2
  Stafford ST17 . . . . .156 A2
  Stone ST15 . . . . 120 B8
  Stourbridge DY8 . . . . .279 D2
St George's St ☐ ST13. . . .30 E6
St George's Way B77 . . . . .250 F4
St Giles Gr ST18 . . . . 172 F6
St Giles' RC Prim Sch
  ST10. . . . . .76 D3
St Giles Rd WS7 . . . . 229 B6
St Gile's Rd ST5 . . . . .55 F2
St Giles & St George's CE
  Prim Sch ST5 . . . . .283 C2
St Gregory's RC Prim Sch
  ST3. . . . . .284 B2
St Gregory's Rd ST3 . . . . .284 A3
St Helens Rd WS13 . . . . . . 214 B3
St Helier Cl ST5 . . . . .70 F3
St Hilda's Ave ST13 . . . . . .45 C4
St Ives Cl Stafford ST17 . . 175 D8
  Tamworth B79 . . . . .250 B6
St James Cre Prim Sch
  Longdon WS15. . . . . 198 A2
  Stourbridge DY8 . . . . .279 D7
St James Cl
  Longdon WS15. . . . . 198 A1
  Walsall WS3 . . . . .244 B5
St James Cres ST17. . . . . 193 B8
St James Ct Audley ST7. . .39 D2
  Barton-u-N DE13 . . . . .183 D2
St James' Ct ST8 . . . . .16 E3
St James Gdns WS8 . . . . . 244 F7
St James Gn ST21 . . . . . . 102 E3
St James Pl ST4 . . . . .72 A1
St James Prim Sch WS8 . . 244 F8
St James' Rd DE13. . . . . . . 183 D1
St James Rd
  Cannock WS11. . . . . 209 C1
  Norton Canes WS11 . . . . . . .228 B5
  Sutton Coldfield B75 . . . . . .258 C2
St James' St DY3 . . . . 271 D3
St James St ST1. . . . . .282 A2
St James Wlk WS8. . . . . . . 244 F7
St John Cl B75 . . . . 258 D4
St John Fisher RC High Sch
  ST5. . . . . .283 A4
St John's Ave
  Newcastle-u-L ST5. . . . . .56 C4
  Oulton ST15. . . . . .105 C3
  Stoke-on-T ST4. . . . . .71 E4
St John's CE Fst Sch
  ST19. . . . . 221 E7
St Johns CE Prim Sch
  WS9 . . . . 245 A3

St John's CE Prim Sch
  Cheddleton ST9 . . . . .60 A7
  Essington WV11. . . . . .242 A4
  Keele ST5 . . . . .69 F7
  Stafford ST15 . . . . .156 B4
St John's Cl WS9 . . . . .244 F3
St Johns Cl WS7. . . . . .211 E1
St John's Cl
  Cannock WS11. . . . . 226 D8
  Lichfield WS13. . . . . 231 B6
St Johns Cl
  Rugeley WS15 . . . . 196 C8
  Stowe-by-Chartley ST18 . . .139 C3
St John's Cl DY3. . . . . .269 D2
St John's Ct
  Burton u T DE13. . . . . 166 C7
  Cannock WS12. . . . . 210 E1
  Walsall WS3 . . . . .243 B1
St John's Dr
  Shenstone WS14 . . . . .246 F5
  Swadlincote DE11 . . . . .186 E5
St John's Hill WS14 . . . . . .246 F5
St Johns Ho B74. . . . . .257 E3
St John's Pl ST8 . . . . .27 D7
St John's Pl Biddulph ST8 .27 D7
  Newcastle-u-L ST5 . . . . .55 F2
St John's Prep Sch
  WS15. . . . . 213 A8
St John's Prim Sch DY3. .269 E2
St John's RC Prim Sch
  ST10. . . . . .78 E1
St John's RC Prim Sch
  ST18. . . . . .158 B2
St Johns Rd ST9 . . . . .27 C7
St Johns Rd ST8 . . . . .27 D7
St John's Rd WS8 . . . . 245 A5
St John's Rd
  Burton u T DE13. . . . . 166 C7
  Cannock WS11. . . . . 226 E7
  Congleton CW12 . . . . 6 A5
St Johns Rd
  Essington WV11. . . . . .242 A3
  Stafford ST17 . . . . .174 D8
  Stafford Rd ST17 . . . . .174 D8
St Johns Rd WS3 . . . . .244 B1
St Johns Ret Pk ☐ WV2 266 C8
St Johns Sch WS13 . . . . . .231 B7
St John's Sq
  ☐ Burslem ST6. . . . . .56 F8
  Uttoxeter ST14 . . . . 110 F1
St John St Hanley ST1 . . . .282 C4
  Stafford St B79. . . . . .250 B5
  Lichfield WS13. . . . . 231 B7
St Johns Way ST6 . . . . 100 C5
St John's Wlk ST16 . . . . . .156 A3
St Johns Wood ST7 . . . . . . 25 F1
St Johns Wood WS14 . . . .247 A5
St John The Evangelist RC
  Prim Sch (Annexe) ST7 . .25 F1
St Joseph & St Theresa RC
  Prim Sch WS7. . . . . .228 C6
St Josephs Cl WS3. . . . . . .244 A4
St Joseph's Coll ST4. . . . .71 F3
St Joseph's Convent Sch
  WV6 . . . . .255 C6
St Josephs Ct WV4. . . . . . .265 D6
St Joseph's RC Prim Sch
  Cannock WS12. . . . . 210 C4
  Lichfield WS14. . . . . 231 C7
  Rugeley WS15 . . . . 196 F7
  Uttoxeter ST14 . . . . .126 B8
St Joseph St ST6 . . . . .41 D7
St Jude's CE Prim Sch
  WV3 . . . . .255 F3
St Jude's Ct ☐ WV6 . . . . . .255 F3
St Jude's Rd WV6. . . . . . . .255 F3
St Jude's Rd W WV6. . . . . .255 F3
St Jude's Way DE13. . . . . .166 C8
St Lawrence CE Prim Sch
  ST20. . . . . .171 E6
St Lawrence Dr WS11. . . .210 B2
St Lawrence View SK17 . .23 B2
St Lawrence Way ST20. . 171 D7
St Leonard's Ave
  Ipstones ST10 . . . . .62 A8
  Stafford ST17 . . . . .156 A1
St Leonard's CE Fst Sch
  Dunston ST18 . . . . .192 F8
  Ipstones ST10 . . . . .62 A8
St Leonard's CE Prim Sch
  B79. . . . . .234 C1
St Leonard's Prim Sch
  ST17. . . . . .156 A1
St Leonards View B78 . . .262 F8
St Leonard's Way CW3. . .67 C1
St Lucy's Dr ST5. . . . . .56 C7
St Lukes CE Prim Sch
  ST9. .43 E7
St Luke's CE Prim Sch
  Hanley ST1 . . . . .282 C2
  Newcastle-u-L ST5. . . . . .55 A2
St Luke's CE Prim Sch
  WV2. . . . . .266 B7
St Luke's Cl
  Cannock WS11. . . . . 226 D8
  Newcastle-u-L ST5. . . . . .55 B2
St Lukes Cl ST15. . . . . .135 A8
St Lukes Ct ST1. . . . . .282 C2
St Lukes Prim Sch (Inf Site)
  WV2 . . . . .282 B4
St Luke's Wlk WS15. . . . . .198 C4
St Margarets DE13 . . . . . . .165 F5

St Margaret's CE Jun Sch
  ST5. .56 D4
St Margarets Ct CW3 . . . . .53 B6
St Margaret's Ct
  Draycott in t M ST11. . . . . . .91 E5
  Newcastle-u-L ST5. . . . . .56 D5
St Margarets Dr ST1. . . . . .57 E8
St Margarets Gr ST3 . . . . .72 F3
St Margaret's Rd B79 . . . .250 B7
St Margarets Rd WS3 . . . .244 A4
St Margaret's B74. . . . . . . .257 C3
St Margaret Ward RC Sch &
  Arts Coll ST6. . . . . .41 F5
St Maria Goreti RC Prim Sch
  ST2. .58 C2
St Mark's CE Prim Sch
  ST1. . . . . .282 A1
St Marks Cl WS6. . . . . .226 F4
St Marks Cl ST1. . . . . .282 A2
St Marks Rd WS8 . . . . .245 A5
St Mark's Rd
  Burntwood WS7. . . . . .229 C6
  Burton u T DE13. . . . . 166 C8
St Marks Rd WS3 . . . . .244 A4
St Mark's St ST1. . . . . .282 A1
St Martin Noel's Almshouses
  ST16. . . . . .285 B3
St Martin's Cl
  Burton u T DE13. . . . . 166 C8
  Wolverhampton WV2. . . . . .266 E6
St Martin's La ST3. . . . . . .284 C4
St Martin's Pl ST16 . . . . . .285 B3
St Martin's Rd
  Newcastle-u-L ST5. . . . . .70 F8
  Talke Pits ST7 . . . . .40 E6
St Mary of the Angels RC
  Prim Sch WV9. . . . . .256 B5
St Mary & St Chad CE Fst
  Sch ST19. . . . . .223 C6
St Mary's CE Prim Sch
  Uttoxeter ST14 . . . . 111 B1
  Wheaton Aston ST19. . . . . .205 C7
St Marys CE Prim Sch
  WV7 . . . . .237 B5
St Mary's CE Prim Sch
  Bosley SK11. . . . . .7 D8
  Colton WS15 . . . . .178 F6
  Kingswinford DY6 . . . . .275 D7
  Mucklestone ST9 . . . . .99 A7
  Stoke-on-T ST6 . . . . .41 D3
St Marys Cl WV7 . . . . .237 A5
St Marys Cl ST18 . . . . .173 C1
St Mary's Cl
  Checkley ST10 . . . . .109 B8
  Newton Solney DE15 . . . . . .167 E8
  Sedgley WV3. . . . . .271 F8
St Marys Cl WV10 . . . . . . .225 C2
St Mary's Cres ST14 . . . . .111 B1
St Mary's Ct ☐ ST13 . . . . .173 C1
St Mary's Dr
  Burton u T DE13. . . . . 166 C8
  Newcastle-u-L ST5. . . . . .71 A8
  Stretton DE13 . . . . .147 F2
St Mary's Gate ST16 . . . . .285 B3
St Mary's Gr ST16 . . . . . . .236 D3
St Marys Mews ST16 . . . . .285 B3
St Mary's Pl ST16. . . . . . . .285 B3
St Marys RC Prim Sch
  ST19. . . . . .223 B6
St Mary's RC Prim Sch
  WS11. . . . . 226 E8
St Mary's RC Prim Sch
  Leek ST13 . . . . .30 E5
  Newcastle-u-L ST5. . . . . . . .283 A3
  Stoke-on-T ST6 . . . . .42 D3
St Mary's Rd
  Colwich ST18. . . . . .177 D8
  Lichfield WS13. . . . . 214 B3
  Loggerheads TF9 . . . . .99 D5
  Longton ST3 . . . . .73 D5
  Newcastle-u-L ST5. . . . . .56 D5
St Mary's & St John's Sch
  WV2. . . . . .266 D8
St Mary's St
  Market Drayton TF9 . . . . . . .97 D1
  Newport TF10 . . . . .168 F3
St Mary's Way
  Aldridge WS9. . . . . .256 B5
  Tamworth B77 . . . . .250 B4
St Matthew ST WS12 . . . . 211 A5
St Matthew's Ave WS7 . .229 F7
St Matthews Ct
  ST3. .89 E4
St Matthews Cl WS3 . . . . .244 B5
St Matthews Ct ST4. . . . . .72 F6
St Matthews Dr ST18 . . . .154 D2
St Matthew's Rd WS7 . . . .229 F7
St Matthew's St ST14 . . . .185 C8
St Matthew St WV7 . . . . . .237 A5
St Mawes Cl ST17. . . . . . . .175 D8
St Mawes Rd WV6 . . . . . . .255 A3
St Michael Rd WS13 . . . . .231 C8
St Michaels CE Fst Sch
  ST19. . . . . .192 E1
St Michael's CE Fst Sch
  Rudyard ST13 . . . . .18 C2
  Stone ST15 . . . . 120 C6
St Michael's CE Jun & Inf Sch
  WV6. . . . . .255 E5
St Michael's CE Prim Sch
  Annexe WS3 . . . . 244 A3
St Michael's CE Prim Sch
  Lichfield WS14. . . . . 231 C7
  Lichfield WS14. . . . . 231 C8
St Michaels CE Prim Sch
  WS3. . . . . .243 F2

St Michael's Cl
  Adbaston ST20 . . . . .131 C4
  Penkridge ST19 . . . . .207 E8
  Stafford ST17 . . . . .175 E8
St Michaels Cl ST15. . . . .120 B8
St Michaels Cl WS3 . . . . .244 A2
St Michaels Cl CV9 . . . . . .262 C1
St Michaels Cl ☐ ST15. . .120 A8
St Michaels Cl WV6 . . . . . .255 F5
St Michaels Ct WS3 . . . . .197 A5
St Michaels Dr WS12 . . . .211 A5
St Michael's Dr WS15. . . .197 A5
St Michael's Hospl
  WS13 . . . . .231 D8
St Michaels Mount WS15 .120 C6
St Michael's RC Prim Sch
  WV3 . . . . .265 D7
St Michaels Rd
  Burton u T DE13. . . . . 166 D8
  Dudley DY3 . . . . .270 F5
St Michael's Rd
  Newcastle-u-L ST5. . . . . .56 B3
  Penkridge ST19 . . . . .207 E8
  Rugeley WS15 . . . . 197 A5
  Stoke-on-T ST6 . . . . .41 F5
St Michael's Sq ST19 . . . .192 E1
St Mildred's CE Prim Sch
  ST10. . . . . .62 D3
St Modwena Way ST19 . . .207 F7
St Modwen's Cl WS13 . . . .166 C7
St Modwen's RC Prim Sch
  DE13 . . . . 166 B5
St Modwen's Wlk DE14 . . 166 E2
St Nicholas Ave ST6 . . . . .42 E4
St Nicholas CE Fst Sch
  WV8 . . . . .238 F4
St Nicholas Cl WS3 . . . . . .244 A4
St Nicholas Way WS15 . . .160 F6
St Oswald's CE Fst Sch
  DY10. . . . . .280 A1
St Patrick Cl WS12. . . . . . .211 A6
St Patrick's Dr ST5 . . . . . . .70 F8
St Patrick's Pl ST16 . . . . .285 B3
St Patrick's RC Prim Sch
  ST16. . . . . .155 E5
St Patricks Rd ☐ DE13. . 166 D8
St Patrick's Pl ST16. . . . . .285 B4
St Patrick's Rd ST16. . . . . .285 B4
St Paul's CE Fst Sch
  WV9. . . . . .224 B3
St Paul's CE Prim Sch
  ST7. . . . . .285 C2
St Pauls CE Prim Sch
  WV9 . . . . .240 A2
St Paul's Cl
  Cannock WS11. . . . . 210 B1
  Coven WV9 . . . . .224 C2
  Stoke-on-T ST6 . . . . .72 F2
  Tamworth B77 . . . . .261 C4
St Paul's Mews ☐ WS5 .196 F8
St Pauls Rd ☐ WS15. . . . .196 F8
St Paul's Rd
  Burntwood WS7. . . . . .229 C6
  Cannock WS12. . . . . 210 F3
  Newcastle-u-L ST5. . . . . . . .283 A2
St Paul's St W DE14. . . . . 166 B4
St Paul's Sq DE14. . . . . . . 166 B3
St Paul St ST6. . . . . .56 E8
St Peter & St Paul RC Prim
  Sch
  Lichfield WS13. . . . . 214 B1
  Newport TF10 . . . . .168 C3
St Peter's Bridge DE14. . 166 E1
St Peter's CE Fst Sch
  Alton ST10 . . . . .78 E1
  Marchington ST14 . . . . .127 F2
St Peter's CE High Sch &
  International Language Coll
  ST4. .71 F7
St Peter's CE Prim Sch
  WS12. . . . . 210 D4
St Peter's CE Prim Sch
  Caverswall ST11 . . . . .74 D2
  Edgmond TF10 . . . . .168 A4
St Peter's CE Prim Sch
  ST18. . . . . .158 B7
St Peter's CE Prim Sch
  Netherseal DE12 . . . . .219 F6
  Stonnall WS9 . . . . .245 E4
  Yoxall DE13 . . . . .182 A3
St Peter's Cl
  Stonnall WS9 . . . . .245 E4
  Tamworth B77 . . . . .250 D1
St Peter's Collegiate CE Sch
  WV3 . . . . .255 E3
St Peters Ct
  Burton u T DE15. . . . . 166 F1
  Lichfield WS13. . . . . 214 B2
St Peters Ct ST20 . . . . . . .151 A4
St Peters Dr WS3. . . . . . . .244 A4
St Peter's Gdns ST17 . . . .174 F5
St Peters La ST11. . . . . . . .91 A7
St Peter's RC Prim Sch
  Burslem ST6. . . . . .57 A6
  Walsall WS7. . . . . .229 F7
St Peter's Rd
  Burntwood WS7. . . . . .229 C6
  Cannock WS12. . . . . 210 D4
St Peter's St W ST5 . . . . . 166 F1
St Peter's Wlk ST6. . . . . . .57 A6
St Phillip's Ave WV3 . . . . .265 F7
St Phillips Ave WV3 . . . . . .265 F8
St Phillip's Gr WV3 . . . . . .265 F7

St Saviour's CE Prim Sch
  ST7. .25 D1
St Saviour's Cl WV2. . . . . .266 F6
St Saviour's St ST7 . . . . . .25 D1
St Stephens Ct
  Burton u T DE13. . . . . 166 C7
  Cannock WS12. . . . . 210 C4
  Great Haywood ST18. . . . . .158 B2
St Stephen's Prim Sch
  WS13. . . . . 215 D7
St Stephen's Rd WS7 . . . .229 C6
St Teresa's RC Prim Sch
  ST4. .71 F2
St Teresa's RC Prim Sch
  WV4 . . . . .266 E5
St Thomas Aquinas RC Prim
  Sch ST4. . . . . .56 F1
St Thomas CE Prim Sch
  ST7. .26 A1
St Thomas' Cl WS9 . . . . . .245 B1
St Thomas Dr WS12 . . . . . .211 A5
St Thomas La ST18. . . . . .156 D3
St Thomas More Coll
  ST3. .73 A3
St Thomas More RC Prim
  Sch WS6. . . . . .227 A4
St Thomas' Pl ST4. . . . . . .71 F7
St Thomas' RC Prim Sch
  ST10. . . . . .92 E4
St Thomas St Mow Cop ST7 .26 E7
  Stafford ST16 . . . . .156 A3
St Vincent Mews ST15. . . .104 D4
St Vincent Pl ST5 . . . . .56 F2
St Vincent Rd ST15. . . . . . .119 F7
St Werburgh's CE Prim Sch
  Hanbury DE13 . . . . 145 A4
  Kingsley ST10 . . . . .61 E2
St Wilfrid's RC Prim Sch
  ST16. . . . . .41 F3
St Wulstan's RC Prim Sch
  ST5. .56 D4
Salcombe Ave ST17 . . . . . 175 D8
Salcombe Cl WS11. . . . . . .226 C7
Salcombe Pl ST1 . . . . .57 D7
Sale La DE13 . . . . .200 C1
Salem St ST1. . . . . .56 F3
Sales La DE15 . . . . .167 C4
Salisbury Ave
  Burton u T DE15. . . . . 167 D3
  Hanley ST1 . . . . .282 B1
Salisbury Cl Dudley DY1. .271 F3
  Lichfield WS13. . . . . 214 C3
  Madeley CW3 . . . . .68 F7
  Rugeley WS15 . . . . 196 C6
Salisbury Dr
  Cannock WS12. . . . . 210 B1
  Stoke-on-T ST6 . . . . .156 B4
Salisbury Hill View TF9 . .112 B7
Salisbury Rd
  Market Drayton TF9. . . . . . .112 B8
  Stafford ST16 . . . . .156 B4
Salisbury St Leek ST13. . .30 E6
  Stoke-on-T ST6 . . . . .41 E3
Salkeld Pl ST6. . . . . .42 B5
Sallow Gr WS8. . . . . 229 A1
Sallyfield La DE6 . . . . .165 E1
Sally Ward Dr WS9 . . . . . .245 A4
Salmond Ave ST16. . . . . . .156 B5
Salop Dr WS11 . . . . .226 F8
Salop Gr ST5 . . . . .71 C4
Salop Pl ST7 . . . . .26 A3
Salt Ave ST17. . . . . .285 C1
Salt Banks ST18 . . . . 137 C3
Saltbrook La DE6 . . . . 144 F8
Saltdean Cl ST13 . . . . .73 C2
Salters Cl ST9 . . . . .59 B3
Salter's Ct TF10. . . . . .168 E3
Saltersford La ST10 . . . . . .94 F8
Salters Green Way DE13 .201 B3
Salter's La TF10 . . . . .168 E3
Salters La Tamworth B79 . .250 B6
  Werrington ST9 . . . . .59 B2
Salter's Mews TF10 . . . . . 168 E3
Salter's Rd WS9 . . . . .245 A4
Salter St ST16 . . . . .285 B3
Saltheath La ST18 . . . . . . .137 E3
Saltings Mobile Home Pk
  The ST18. . . . . 156 D2
Salt La ST18 . . . . .137 D5
Salt Rd Salt ST18. . . . . . . .137 E4
  Sandon ST18 . . . . .137 D3
Salt St La B78. . . . . .260 E5
Salt Works La ST18 . . . . . .138 D2
Sam Barber Ct WS12. . . . .210 E1
Sambar Rd B78. . . . . .249 F1
Sambrook Cres TF9 . . . . . .97 E2
Sampson St ST1. . . . . .282 A3
Samuel Cl WS13 . . . . 214 C2
Samuel Ho WS3 . . . . .243 B1
Samuel Johnson's Birthplace
  Museum WS13 . . . . .231 B8
Samuel Sq Packmoor ST7 . .26 F1
  Walsall WS3 . . . . .243 B1
Sancton Gn ☐ ST6 . . . . . .56 E8
Sandalwood Dr ST6. . . . . . .57 A5
Sandalwood Rd DE15 . . . .185 E6
Sandbach Rd ST6. . . . . .57 B7
Sand Bank WS3. . . . . 243 A4
Sandcrest St ST3 . . . . .73 F1
Sandcrest Wlk ST3. . . . . . .73 F1
Sanderling Cl WV10. . . . . .241 B7
Sanderling Rise WS27 . . . .228 B2
Sandfield Bridge DY5 . . . .271 B1
Sandfield Gr DY3 . . . . .271 B2
Sandfield Mdw WS15 . . . .231 A6

Sandfield Rd DY8	275 F2	Sandy Rd Biddulph ST8	16 C2	School La continued
Sandford Cl WS15	198 A8	Stoke-on-T ST6	41 D6	Longsdon ST9	30 A2
Sandford Cres CW2	37 D1	Stourbridge DY8	279 D1	Maer TF9	84 A7
Sandford Hill Prim Sch		Sandy Way B77	251 B3	Market Drayton TF9	112 A8
ST3	73 C6	Sangster La ST6	42 D2	School Lane Cl ST17	174 F5
Sandford Ho WS13	231 A7	Sankey Cres WS11	196 E7	School La
Sandford Rd DY1	271 E1	Sankey Rd WS11	209 F3	Norton Canes WS3	227 E2
Sandford Rise WV6	255 C6	Sankey's Cnr WS7	228 F7	Onneley CW3	68 A4
Sandford St		Sanstone Cl WS3	243 C3	Rolleston on D DE13	147 B4
Lichfield WS13	231 B7	Sanstone Rd WS3	243 C3	Sandon ST18	137 E7
Longton ST3	73 C5	Sant St ST6	56 E8	Shareshill WV10	225 D2
Newcastle-u-l ST5	55 E8	Sapling Rise ST10	92 E3	Shuttington B79	251 A7
Sandgate St ST3	73 D3	Saplings Cl ST19	192 F1	Stafford,Rickerscote ST17	174 F5
Sandhill St WS3	243 A1	Saplings The		Stoke-on-T ST3	89 A8
Sandhurst Ave 4 ST3	73 F1	Newcastle-u-l ST5	71 C3	Stretton ST19	206 C3
Sandhurst Cl ST5	56 C4	Penkridge ST19	192 F1	Sudbury DE6	128 E4
Sandhurst Dr WV4	266 A4	Stafford ST17	156 A1	Tamworth B77	261 D5
Sandhurst Gr DY8	275 E3	Sapperton La DE65	129 F8	Walsall WS3	243 F4
Sandhurst Pl ST3	89 F8	Sapphire Dr WS11	210 C3	Walton-on-t-H ST17	175 F6
Sandhurst Rd B74	257 F5	Saracen Way 10 ST3	74 A1	Warslow SK17	23 B1
Sandiford Cres TF10	168 E2	Sara Cl B74	258 A3	Weeford B78	248 D2
Sandiway DE13	201 E8	Sarah Challinor Cl 6		Weston-Under-Lizard TF11	203 E2
Sandiway Pl ST1	57 E6	WS15	196 E8	Wolverhampton WV10	240 E2
Sandmere Rise WV10	240 E1	Sarah Siddons Ho 2		School Pl ST16	155 E5
Sandon Ave ST5	71 A5	WS13	231 B7	School Rd Bagnall ST9	43 F2
Sandon Cl ST11	91 C2	Saredon Cl WS3	244 A1	Brewood ST19	223 C6
Sandon Ct ST3	89 F7	Saredon Rd		Bucknall ST2	58 A5
Sandon High Sch ST3	89 F8	Shareshill WV10	225 D2	Eccleshall ST21	133 D6
Sandon Ho WV6	255 E5	Wedges Mills WS6,WS11,		Edgmond TF10	168 A3
Sandon La ST5	122 C5	WV10	226 B3	Himley DY3	270 B3
Sandon Mews ST16	155 F6	Sargeant Ave ST6	42 A6	Norton Canes WS11	228 A6
Sandon Old Rd ST3	89 F7	Sark Cl ST5	70 E4	Rugeley WS15	178 D2
Sandon Rd Cresswell ST1	91 C3	Sark Pl 1 ST3	73 D6	Trysull WV5	269 C8
Hilderstone ST15	106 D1	Sarraine Ind Pk ST10	76 B2	Uttoxeter ST14	110 F1
Hopton ST18	137 C2	Sarver La ST10	75 D4	Wheaton Aston ST19	205 C5
Stafford ST16,ST18	155 F6	Sash St ST16	285 B4	Wolverhampton,Tettenhall
Stoke-on-T ST3	89 F7	Saturn Rd Cannock WS11	210 A5	WV6	255 B3
Wolverhampton WV10	240 B2	Stoke-on-T ST6	42 C1	Wombourne WV5	270 B7
Sandon St Hanley ST1	57 A3	Saul Ct ST14	126 B7	School St 3 Leek ST13	30 C4
Leek ST13	30 E3	Saunders Cl WS12	211 A6	Newcastle-u-L,Broad Meadow
Sandown Ave WS6	226 E3	Saunders Rd ST5	56 B4	ST5	55 F6
Sandown Cl		Saverley Green Rd WS11	106 E8	Newcastle-u-L ST5	283 C3
Burntwood WS7	211 F1	Savey La DE13	181 F2	Sedgley DY3	271 E8
Burton u T DE14	185 A7	Savoureuse Dr ST17	175 A8	Stoke-on-T ST4	71 E3
Cannock WS12	211 A6	Savoy Rd CW1	37 A8	Stourbridge DY8	279 F6
Cheadle ST10	76 E5	Sawpit La ST17	176 A3	Tamworth B77	250 E4
Sandown Dr WV6	254 F4	Sawyer Dr ST8	16 C1	Walsall WS4	244 D1
Sandown Pl ST2	43 C2	Saxifrage Dr ST15	120 C6	School View ST14	141 C8
Sandpiper Cl WS12	250 F5	Saxon Cl Burton u T DE15	185 F7	School Wlk
Sandpiper Ct ST7	26 C2	Great Wyrley WS6	227 A2	Burntwood WS7	228 D8
Sandpiper Dr ST14	126 B6	Polesworth B78	251 F1	Tamworth B79	250 B6
Sandpiper B77	262 A5	Tamworth B77	261 F6	Scimitar Cl B79	249 E7
Sandra Cl Aldridge WS9	256 B5	Saxoncourt WV6	255 C5	Scotch Orchard Prim Sch
Stoke-on-T ST6	42 A2	Saxon Ct WS13	230 E7	WS13	214 D1
Sand Rd DE13	164 C7	Saxondrive WV6	250 C5	Scotch Orch WS13	214 D1
Sandringham Ave DE15	167 A1	Saxonfields WV6	255 C5	Scot Hay Rd
Sandringham Cl		Saxon Hill Sch WS14	231 C6	Alsagers Bank ST7	54 E5
Burntwood WS7	211 E1	Saxon Mill La B79	250 C4	Newcastle-u-l ST5	54 F3
Market Drayton TF9	97 E2	Saxon Rd ST19	207 F8	Scotia Bsns Pk ST6	41 E2
Stafford ST17	175 C8	Saxon St DE15	185 F7	Scotia Rd Burslem ST6	41 F1
Sandringham Cres ST4	72 A1	Saxon Wlk WS13	230 E7	Cannock WS11	209 D3
Sandringham Dr WS9	245 B1	Saxton Dr B74	257 F6	Scott Ave WV4	265 E4
Sandringham Rd		Sayers Rd ST16	155 C7	Scott Cl WS14	231 B6
Pattingham WV6	253 C2	Scalpcliffe Cl DE15	166 F3	Scott Lidgett Ind Est ST6	56 D8
Stafford ST17	175 C8	Scalpcliffe Rd DE15	166 F3	Scott Lidgett Rd ST6	56 D7
Stourbridge DY8	275 D1	Scammerton B77	262 B7	Scott Rd Stoke-on-T ST6	41 F3
Wolverhampton WV4	266 A4	Scammell La ST21	134 E7	Tamworth B77	250 E4
Wombourne WV5	269 F6	Scampion Cl WV6	254 E5	Scotts Ho 8 ST16	155 D5
Sandsdown Cl ST8	16 C1	Scampton Way B79	250 C8	Scott's Rd DY8	279 F6
Sands La ST6	28 B2	Scarecrow La B75	258 E4	Scott St Cannock WS12	210 F3
Sands Rd ST7	26 E6	Scarlett St ST5	283 B2	Newcastle-u-L ST5	283 C3
Sandstone Cl DY3	271 D4	Scarratt Cl ST11	91 B8	Scott Way WS7	211 F1
Sandstone Ct B77	262 A7	Scarratt Dr ST11	91 B8	Scragg St ST7	41 F8
Sandwell Pl ST3	89 E8	Sceptre St ST1	282 B2	Scrimshaw Dr ST6	42 C3
Sandwell Rd WV10	240 B1	Schofield La B79	217 D5	Scrivener Rd ST4	71 C4
Sandwick Cres ST1	57 F6	Sch of St Mary & St Anne		Scropton Old Rd DE65	146 C8
Sandwood Cres ST3	73 C5	WS15	161 A6	Scropton Rd Hatton DE65	146 B8
Sandy Bank ST1	102 C4	Scholar Green Prim Sch		Scropton DE65	129 F1
Sandybrook Cl ST13	30 F3	ST7	25 E6	Sculthorpe Rd DY10	281 B2
Sandybrook La ST13	30 F2	Scholars Gate		Seabridge Jun & Inf Schs
Sandy Cres WV11	242 A1	Burntwood WS7	229 D7	ST5	71 A4
Sandy Croft TF10	168 F3	Rugeley WS15	197 A5	Seabridge La ST5	71 B4
Sandyfield Ct ST16	16 C1	Schoolacre Rise B74	256 E1	Seabridge Rd ST5	283 A1
Sandyfield Rd ST1	57 E5	School Ave WS8	244 F8	Seabrooke Rd WS15	197 A5
Sandyfields Rd DY3	271 B6	School Bank ST10	94 B2	Seafield Cl DY6	275 E4
Sandyfields ST5	85 C5	School Cl Audley ST7	40 A1	Seafield B77	250 F5
Sandyford Ct ST16	285 B4	Burntwood WS7	228 D8	Seaford St ST4	57 B1
Sandyford St ST16	155 E5	Codsall WV8	239 A4	Seaforth Gr WV11	242 B1
Sandy Gr WS8	228 F1	Dilhorne ST10	75 D4	Seagram Way ST14	126 D7
Sandy Hill ST9	59 C4	Leek ST13	30 C4	Seagrave Pl ST5	71 A6
Sandy Hollow WV6	255 C2	Norton Canes WS11	228 B6	Seagrave St ST5	283 C3
Sandy La Ashley TF9	100 E7	Trysull WV5	269 C8	Searchlight La ST21	134 E7
Biore TF9	98 C3	Wolverhampton WV3	265 B7	Searle Ave ST16	155 C2
Brewood ST19	223 C6	School Cres WS11	228 B6	Seaton Ave ST17	175 F8
Brown Edge ST6	43 B7	School Ct WS12	210 C6	Seaton Cl ST3	89 E8
Cannock WS11	209 B1	School Dr Oakamoor ST10	78 A7	Seaton Pl DY8	275 C2
Chapel Chorlton ST5	85 C4	Stourbridge DY8	279 F8	Seaton B77	261 F8
Codsall WV8	238 F4	Schoolfields Rd WS14	247 A5	Sebring Ave ST3	89 E8
Copmere End ST21	132 D7	Schoolgate Cl WS4	244 D1	Seckham Rd 4 WS13	231 A8
Cotes Heath ST21	102 D4	School Ground La TF10	169 A3	Seckington La B79	236 C3
Huntington ST10	9 E1	School Ho The WS7	229 D7	Second Ave
Kinver DY7,DY11	277 F1	School House La WS15	161 A6	Branston DE14	165 E1
Linton DE12	186 A1	School La		Brownhills WS8	229 A1
Longsdon ST9	44 F8	Admaston WS15	159 F3	Bucknall ST2	58 D4
Market Drayton TF9	112 D6	Ashley TF9	100 B6	Kidsgrove ST7	25 E1
Newcastle-u-L ST5	283 D4	Astbury CW12	15 B8	Kingswinford,Wall Heath
Newton Regis B79	236 D6	Biddulph ST8	17 B1	DY6	275 F8
Rugeley WS15	196 E8	Bradnop ST13	31 E3	Newcastle-u-L ST5	56 C7
Tean ST12	43 C2	Burntwood WS7	228 D8	Stafford ST16	155 C7
Weston ST18	138 C4	Caverswall ST3,ST11	74 D2	Sedberg Cl ST5	70 F4
Whittington WS14	232 D4	Colton WS15	178 F6	Seddon Ct ST1	282 C3
Wolverhampton,Bushbury		Coven WV9	224 B3	Seddon Rd ST3	73 C5
WV10	240 E1	Dunston ST18	192 D7	Sedgefield Cl DY1	271 E3
Wolverhampton,Tettenhall		Edingale B79	217 C5	Sedgefield Gr WV6	254 F4
WV6	255 E6	Gentleshaw WS15	212 A5	Sedgefield Rd DE14	184 F7
Sandy Mount WV5	270 B7	Great Haywood ST18	158 B2	Sedgemoor Ave WS7	229 B5
		Hill Ridware WS15	198 A8	Sedgefield Way WS11	228 B4
		Hopwas B78	249 B2	Sedgley Hall Ave DY3	271 C8

Sedgley Rd WV4	265 F2	San – She 325
Sedgley Cl WV2	266 C7	Sharpe St B77	251 A5
Sedgley Wlk ST3	284 C4	Sharplands TF9	99 D5
Seedcroft La WS15	160 F4	Sharrat Field B75	258 D2
Seedfields Rd ST3	72 E3	Sharron Dr ST13	31 B5
Seeds La WS8	244 F8	Shaver's La WS15	197 B1
Seedymill La WS13	213 E7	Shawbury Gr WV6	254 E5
Seesall The ST20	171 E7	Shaw Cl WS13	215 D8
Sefton Ave Congleton CW12	6 A1	Shaw Ct WS11	228 A5
Stoke-on-T ST1	57 E7	Shaw Dr Burntwood WS7	212 A1
Sefton Cl DE15	167 B1	Fradley WS13	215 C6
Sefton Rd Longton ST3	73 E2	Shawe Park Rd ST10	76 E8
Tamworth B77	261 E6	Shaw Gdns ST17	174 C7
Sefton St ST1	57 A3	Shaw Hall La WV9	240 C7
Seighford Rd ST18	154 D5	Shaw La Albrighton WV7	237 B5
Seisdon Rd WV5	264 A1	Armitage WS13	198 F2
Selborne Rd ST13	30 E4	Gentleshaw WS15	212 A4
Selbourne Dr ST6	41 F7	King's Bromley WS13	199 A4
Selby Cl ST5	71 A5	Lichfield WS13	231 A8
Selby St ST4	74 B5	Tong TF11	220 D5
Selby Way WS3	242 E2	Wolverhampton WV6	255 B3
Selby Wlk ST3	88 E7	Shawmans La ST18	172 E8
Selker Dr B77	250 F5	Shawms Crest ST17	175 D8
Sellman St ST20	171 E6	Shawm s The ST17	175 C8
Selmans Hill WS3	243 C2	Shaw Pl ST13	31 A6
Selman's Par WS3	243 C2	Shawport Ave ST5	56 A8
Selsdon Rd WS3	242 F3	Shaw Rd WV4	266 C6
Selwood Cl ST3	73 D1	Shaws La ST21	133 C6
Selworthy Dr ST17	175 E6	Shaw's La WS6	227 A2
Selworthy Rd ST17	175 E6	Shaw St Biddulph ST8	27 C7
Selwyn Cl Alrewas DE13	201 A3	Hanley ST1	282 A4
Wolverhampton WV6	266 C7	Newcastle-u-L ST5	283 B3
Selwyn Ct ST21	133 E7	Shaw-Wall La ST10	62 F7
Selwyn Rd WS7	229 F8	Shay La Foxt ST10	62 C6
Selwyn St ST4	72 B6	Weston Jones TF10	150 A4
Selwyn Wlk B74	257 C4	Shayler Gr WV2	266 D7
Semper Cl CW12	6 A4	Sheaf Pas ST3	284 C3
Senior Cl WV11	242 A3	Sheaf St ST1	282 A1
Serin Cl ST14	126 C6	Shearers Pl 4 ST5	258 E3
Seton Ho ST4	71 D4	Shearer St ST1	282 A1
Setterfield Way WS15	196 F6	Shearwater Ct WV10	240 B3
Settle Gr ST3	90 A7	Shebdon ST16	155 B7
Setton Dr DY3	271 E7	Sheepcote La B77	250 F4
Seven Acres WS9	256 B5	Sheep Fair WS15	178 E1
Seven Arches Way ST14	72 C7	Sheep Market ST13	30 E6
Sevenoaks Gr ST3	90 B6	Sheepwalks La DY7	277 B7
Seven Springs Nature Trail*		Sheepwash La DY11	277 C2
ST17	177 D5	Sheffield Cl ST14	110 F1
Severs Rd WS12	211 D3	Sheffield St ST14	166 C1
Severn Cl Biddulph ST8	16 E1	Shefford Rd ST5	70 F3
Congleton CW12	6 A1	Shelburne St ST4	72 A5
Stretton DE13	147 C1	Sheldon Ave CW12	6 A1
Uttoxeter ST14	126 C6	Sheldon Gr ST5	55 F6
Severn Dr		Sheldon Rd WV10	240 A1
Burntwood WS7	229 D6	Sheldrake Gr ST4	71 D4
Burton u T DE14	166 E3	Shelfield Sports & Com Coll
Hilton DE65	147 D8	WS4	244 C2
Newcastle-u-l ST5	54 B5	Shelford Rd ST6	41 D6
Perton WV6	254 B4	Shelley Ave DE14	166 D6
Severn Ho DY3	271 D3	Shelley Cl Armitage WS13	198 B4
Severn Rd		Burton u T DE14	166 D6
Brownhills WS8	228 C2	Colwich ST18	177 D8
Stourbridge DY8	279 F3	Dudley DY3	271 A5
Walsall WS3	243 E1	Kidsgrove ST7	41 A8
Severn St ST1	282 A4	Stafford ST16	156 A5
Seward Cl WV14	231 D6	Shelley Dr Cheadle ST10	76 C2
Seymour Ave DE14	166 E2	Sutton Coldfield B74	257 F6
Seymour Cl WS6	226 D1	Shelley Rd Bucknall ST2	58 B6
Seymour Gdns B74	257 E3	Burntwood WS7	212 A1
Seymour St ST1	57 E3	Cannock WS11	209 E5
Shackerley La WV7	221 B1	Tamworth B79	250 A7
Shackleton Dr		Wolverhampton WV10	240 D2
Perton WV6	254 E5	Shelmore Cl ST16	155 B8
Stoke-on-T ST6	41 C4	Shelmore Way ST20	171 D7
Shackleton Rd WS3	243 D2	Shelsley Cl ST19	193 A1
Shackleton Way ST16	136 B6	Shelsley St ST10	76 F4
Shackson Cl ST1	282 B1	Shelton Ent Ctr ST1	282 A1
Shadwell Dr DY3	271 D3	Shelton Farm Rd ST1	282 A1
Shaffalong La ST13	45 A5	Shelton New Rd ST4	56 E1
Shaftesbury Ave ST6	42 A2	Shelton Old Rd ST4	72 B8
Shaftesbury Dr WS12	210 C7	Shelton B77	261 F7
Shaftsbury Rd WS7	229 F7	Shemilt Cres ST6	42 C3
Shaftsbury Rd WS15	196 E6	Shendon Gr ST5	58 C2
Shakespeare Ave WS14	231 B6	Shenley Gr ST17	174 D6
Shakespeare Cl		Shenstone Ave DY8	279 D3
Kidsgrove ST7	41 A8	Shenstone Cl B74	257 E6
Stoke-on-T ST2	43 A2	Shenstone Ct WV3	266 A6
Tamworth B79	250 A6	Shenstone Dr WS9	256 A8
Shakespeare St ST6	27 C7	Shenstone Ho WS13	214 E1
Shakespeare Gr WS: 1	209 D4	Shenstone Lodge Sch
Shakespeare Rd		WS14	247 A3
Burntwood WS7	228 F8	Shenstone Sta WS14	246 F6
Burton u T DE14	166 D6	Shenton St ST3	284 D5
Dudley DY3	271 A4	Shephard Cl ST18	158 B3
Stafford ST17	175 C8	Shepherd Cl WS13	214 C3
Shaldon Ave ST9	43 C4	Shepherds Bush St16	155 E5
Shales The WV5	269 E5	Shepherds Ct TF10	169 A3
Shallcross La DY3	271 D3	Shepherds Fold ST17	175 C6
Shallowford Ct ST1	57 A3	Shepherds Pool Rd B75	258 E2
Shallowford Mews ST16	155 D5	Shepherd St ST8	27 C7
Shanklin Cl WS6	227 A3	Shepley Cl WS15	172 E8
Shannon App DE14	166 E2	Shepley Gr ST13	120 C7
Shannon Dr		Shepley St ST3	88 E7
Brownhills WS8	228 C2	Sheppard St ST4	72 A6
Stoke-on-T ST6	41 C7	Shepwell Gdns WV10	241 C7
Shannon Rd ST17	174 D6	Sheraton Cl Aldridge WS9	256 B6
Shannon's Mill B79	250 A5	Cannock WS12	210 A7
Shannon B77	261 F8	Sheraton Grange DY8	279 F2
Shannon Wlk WS8	228 C2	Sherborne Cl WV10	240 E1
Shanti Niketan WV2	266 D7	Sherborne St ST5	71 A5
Shardlow Cl Longton ST4	73 A6	Sherborne Gdns WV8	239 A3
Stone ST15	120 C6	Sherborne Rd WV10	240 D1
Sharman Cl ST14	71 F2	Sherborne Ave WS12	210 E4
Sharman Way ST20	171 E7	Sherbourne Dr DE14	185 A7
Sharnbrook Dr ST17	178 C2		
Sharon Cl WV4	266 E5		
Sharon Way WS12	210 D3		

Sherbrook Cl ST17 . . . . . . 176 A3
Sherbrooke Ave B77 . . . . . 261 E6
Sherbrook Rd WS11 . . . . . 209 C1
Sheridan Gdns
  Dudley DY3 . . . . 270 F5
  Stoke-on-T ST3 . . . . 72 F2
Sheridan St ST16 . . . . 156 A4
Sheridan Way ST15 . . . . . 120 D7
Sheriden Way ST5 . . . . 55 E2
Sheriffs Cl WS14 . . . . 231 E6
Sheriffs Way ST11 . . . . . . 133 D7
Sherifoot La B75 . . . . 258 B4
Sheringham Covert
  ST16 . . . . 156 C4
Sheringham Dr WS15 . . . . 178 B2
Sheringham Pl ST5 . . . . . . 56 D5
Sherington Dr WV4 . . . . . 266 D5
Sherracop La WS15 . . . . . 160 A1
Sherrans Dell WV4 . . . . . . 266 D4
Sherratt St ST6 . . . . 42 C3
Sherringham Dr WV11 . . . 242 C1
Shervale Cl WV4 . . . . 266 A6
Sherwin Rd ST6 . . . . 41 F3
Sherwood Ave ST17 . . . . . 174 E4
Sherwood Cl CV9 . . . . 262 C1
Sherwood Dr WS11 . . . . . 210 A3
Sherwood Rd
  Stoke-on-T ST3 . . . . 89 F7
  Stourbridge DY8 . . . . 279 E7
Shetland Ave B77 . . . . 261 F7
Shetland Rd ST3 . . . . 72 F3
Shillingford Dr ST4 . . . . . . 88 B8
Shilton Cl ST4 . . . . 71 F5
Shinwell Gr ST3 . . . . 90 A8
Shipley Cl DE14 . . . . 185 B8
Shipley Pl ST16 . . . . 42 C2
Shippy La ST18 . . . . 172 C8
Shipston Rd ST17 . . . . 156 D1
Shipton Cl DY1 . . . . 271 F3
Shipton Dr ST14 . . . . 110 F1
Shirburn Rd ST13 . . . . 31 A6
Shirebrook Cl ST13 . . . . . . 88 E7
Shirehall Rd WS11 . . . . . . 210 B2
Shire Lea WS8 . . . . 245 B6
Shirelea Cl WS7 . . . . 229 B8
Shire Oak Sch WS9 . . . . . 245 A5
Shireoaks Dr ST17 . . . . . . 175 C6
Shire Ridge WS9 . . . . 245 B4
Shires Ind Est WS14 . . . . . 231 A6
Shireview Gdns WS3 . . . . 244 B4
Shireview Rd WS3 . . . . . . 244 B4
Shirewood WS11 . . . . 209 B2
Shirley Ave ST9 . . . . 59 B4
Shirley Dr ST10 . . . . 94 E8
Shirley Rd ST1 . . . . 282 B1
Shirley St Burslem ST6 . . . . 56 D8
  Leek ST13 . . . . 30 D5
Shirleywich ST18 . . . . 138 E1
Shirley Wlk B79 . . . . 249 F7
Shirrall Dr B78 . . . . 259 E4
Shoal Hill Cl WS11 . . . . . . 209 B2
Shobnall Cl DE14 . . . . 166 B4
Shobnall Ct DE14 . . . . 166 B3
Shobnall Prim Sch DE14 . . 165 F4
Shobnall Rd DE14 . . . . 166 A3
Shobnall St DE14 . . . . 166 B4
Sholing Cl WV8 . . . . 239 F1
Shoobridge St ST13 . . . . . . 30 F5
Shooting Butts Rd WS15 . . 196 A8
Shop La Brewood ST19 . . . 223 C6
  Oaken WV8 . . . . 238 D2
  Trescott WV6 . . . . 265 D7
Shops The **B8** DY6 . . . . . . 275 D4
Short Bambury St ST3 . . . . 73 D6
Shortbutts La WS14 . . . . . 231 B5
Short La Barton-u-N DE13 . 183 D1
  Cheslyn Hay WS6 . . . . . . 126 A2
  Gratwich ST14 . . . . 124 D3
Shortlands La WS3 . . . . . . 243 F3
Short Rd WV10 . . . . 240 E1
Short St Brownhills WS8 . . 244 F7
  Burton u T DE15 . . . . 185 E7
  Cannock WS11 . . . . 209 F3
  Longton ST3 . . . . 284 D3
Short Street Com Inf Sch
  DE15 . . . . 185 E7
Short St Stourbridge DY8 . 279 F5
  Uttoxeter ST14 . . . . 126 B8
Shorwell Gr ST6 . . . . 41 E8
Shotsfield Pl ST2 . . . . 43 A1
Shotsfield St ST2 . . . . 43 A1
Shotwood Cl DE13 . . . . . . 147 A4
Shotwoodhill La DE13 . . . 147 A5
Showan Ave ST5 . . . . 56 D3
Showell La WV4 . . . . 265 B3
Shraleybrook Rd ST7 . . . . . 54 B7
Shredicote La ST18 . . . . . . 191 B7
Shrewsbury Dr
  Newcastle-u-L ST5 . . . . . . 40 E2
  Weston-Under-Lizard TF11 203 E2
Shrewsbury Mall WS15 . . 178 F1
Shrewsbury Rd
  Edgmond TF10 . . . . 168 A4
  Market Drayton TF9 . . . . 112 B8
  Stafford ST17 . . . . 285 B1
  Stretton DE13 . . . . 147 F2
Shrewsbury Way TF10 . . . 168 E2
Shropshire Brook Rd
  WS15 . . . . 198 B4
Shropshire St ST18 . . . . . . 97 C1
Shrubbery Cl DY10 . . . . . 280 A5
Shrubbery Hill DY10 . . . . 280 A5
Shrubbery The
  Elford B79 . . . . 216 E1

Shrubbery The continued
  Rugeley WS15 . . . . 197 B6
Shruggs La ST18 . . . . 121 C1
Shugborough Cl WS3 . . . . 243 B1
Shugborough Cotts
  ST18 . . . . 177 C8
Shugborough Dr DY1 . . . . 271 E2
Shugborough Farm Mus*
  ST17 . . . . 177 A8
Shugborough Hall*
  ST17 . . . . 158 A1
Shugborough Rd WS15 . . 178 C3
Shugborough Way
  WS11 . . . . 210 C1
Shughborough Cl ST9 . . . . 59 A2
Shuker's Cl TF10 . . . . 169 A2
Shut La ST11 . . . . 116 B6
Shutt Green La
  Brewood ST19 . . . . 223 B8
  Kiddemore Green ST19 . . 222 E8
Shuttington Rd B77,B79 . . 251 B6
Sich La DE13 . . . . 182 D4
Sidcot Pl ST11 . . . . 57 D8
Siddalls St DE15 . . . . 167 B3
Siddons Cl WS13 . . . . 213 F2
Sides La DE6 . . . . 81 B5
Sidestrand WV9 . . . . 239 F3
Sideway Rd ST4 . . . . 72 B5
Sidings Ind Est DE14 . . . . 166 E4
Sidings Pl ST3,ST4 . . . . . . 284 B4
Sidings The
  Cannock WS12 . . . . 210 C7
  Cheadle ST10 . . . . 76 D2
  Stone ST15 . . . . 120 B8
Sidmouth Ave
  Newcastle-u-L ST5 . . . . . 283 C3
  Stafford ST17 . . . . 156 D1
Sidney Ave ST17 . . . . 174 E1
Sidney Dr ST10 . . . . 62 A2
Sidney St WV2 . . . . 266 C8
Sidon Hill Way WS11 . . . . 210 C2
Siemens Rd ST17 . . . . 285 B1
Signal Gr WS3 . . . . 243 A1
Signal Wlk B77 . . . . 251 A2
Silica Rd B77 . . . . 251 B2
Silk Mill La DE13 . . . . 146 C6
Silkmore Cres ST17 . . . . . 175 A7
Silkmore La ST17 . . . . 175 A8
Silkmore Prim Sch ST17 . 174 F7
Sill St ST13 . . . . 30 E6
Sill Gn B79 . . . . 234 C1
Sillitoe Pl ST4 . . . . 72 A6
Silsden Gr ST3 . . . . 74 C2
Silva Ave DY6 . . . . 275 F4
Silver Birch Coppice
  B74 . . . . 257 D5
Silver Birch Dr
  Kinver DY7 . . . . 277 F5
  Wolverhampton WV6 . . . 266 B8
Silver Birch Rd
  Aldridge B74 . . . . 256 F1
  Huntington WS12 . . . . . . 209 D8
  Norton Canes WS11 . . . . 228 B5
  Wolverhampton WV2 . . . 266 E7
Silver Cl ST8 . . . . 27 C8
Silver Court Gdns WS8 . . 244 F7
Silver Ct WS8 . . . . 244 F7
Silverdale Bsns Pk ST5 . . . 55 D1
Silverdale Cl Chorlton CW2 37 C2
  Newport TF10 . . . . 168 E1
Silverdale Dr WV8 . . . . . . 228 D7
Silverdale Gdns DY8 . . . . 275 C3
Silverdale Prim Sch ST5 . . 55 C1
Silverdale Rd
  Newcastle-u-L,Knutton
  ST5 . . . . 55 B1
  Newcastle-u-L,Wolstanton
  ST5 . . . . 56 C5
Silverdale St ST5 . . . . 55 B8
Silver Fir Cl WS12 . . . . . . 210 A8
Silvergate Ct CW12 . . . . . . 15 E8
Silverhill Cl DE13 . . . . . . 166 C8
Silver La ST14 . . . . 127 E7
Silver Link Rd B77 . . . . . . 250 F1
Silvermine Cl **5** ST7 . . . . . 26 B2
Silver Poplars Mobile Homes
  Pk WV7 . . . . 237 E1
Silver Ridge ST12 . . . . . . 104 D8
Silver's Cl WS3 . . . . 243 F4
Silver St Brownhills WS8 . 244 F7
  Cheadle ST10 . . . . 76 E6
Silverstone Ave ST10 . . . . . 76 E3
Silverstone Cres ST6 . . . . . 41 E8
Silver St Stoke-on-T ST6 . . . 42 E4
  Uttoxeter ST14 . . . . 126 C8
Silverthorn Way ST17 . . . 175 C7
Silverton Cl ST5 . . . . 56 A8
Silvertrees Cvn Pk WS15 . 195 E7
Silverwood ST7 . . . . 26 B1
Silvester Way ST17 . . . . . 175 E6
Simcox St WS12 . . . . 210 D4
Simeon Way ST15 . . . . . . 120 C6
Simister Ct **10** ST6 . . . . . . 41 D3
Simmonds Cl WS3 . . . . . . 243 D3
Simmonds Rd WS3 . . . . . . 243 D3
Simmonds Way WS8 . . . . 245 A6
Simmons Cl DE18 . . . . 260 B1
Simmons Rd WV11 . . . . . 242 B1
Simonburn Ave ST4 . . . . . . 71 F6
Simon Pl ST14 . . . . 57 B1
Simons Rd TF9 . . . . 112 B8
Simpkins Cl WS9 . . . . 245 A3
Simpson Cl ST16 . . . . 155 B7
Simpson Rd WS3 . . . . 214 B2
Simpson St Hanley ST1 . . 282 C1
  Newcastle-u-L ST5 . . . . . . 56 B5

Sinai Cl DE13 . . . . 165 E4
Sion Ave DY10 . . . . 280 A1
Sion Hill Mid Sch DY10 . . 280 A1
Sir Graham Balfour High Sch
  ST16 . . . . 155 D8
Sir John Offley CE Prim Sch
  CW3 . . . . 68 E5
Sir Robert Peel Hospl
  B78 . . . . 249 D2
Sir Thomas Boughey High
  Sch ST7 . . . . 54 D7
Siskin Cl WS7 . . . . 229 D5
Siskin Pl ST13 . . . . 90 B7
Sister Dora Ave WS7 . . . . 229 F7
Sitwell Gr ST3 . . . . 284 D4
Six Ashes Rd
  Bobbington DY7 . . . . 267 F1
  Halfpenny Green DY7 . . . 268 B3
  Six Ashes WV15 . . . . 272 D7
Six Roads End DE6 . . . . . . 144 C4
Skeath La ST18 . . . . 137 C4
Skellern Ave ST6 . . . . 42 C3
Skellern St ST7 . . . . 25 D2
Skidmore Ave
  Tamworth B77 . . . . 261 C5
  Wolverhampton WV3 . . . 265 F8
Skipacre Ave ST6 . . . . 42 D1
Skipness B77 . . . . 250 E5
Skipton Pl WS11 . . . . 226 B7
Skye Cl Longton ST3 . . . . 284 B7
  Tamworth B77 . . . . 261 F7
Skylark Cl Dudley DY5 . . . 271 C1
  Huntington WS12 . . . . . . 209 C7
  Uttoxeter ST14 . . . . 126 C6
Slab La ST9,ST20 . . . . 190 B2
Slacken La ST7 . . . . 25 D2
Slack La Mayfield DE6 . . . . 81 C8
  Mayfield,Middle Mayfield
  DE6 . . . . 81 B7
Slacky La WS3 . . . . 243 F1
Slade Ave WS7 . . . . 229 A8
Slade Fields ST14 . . . . 111 B1
Slade Gdns WV8 . . . . 239 A4
Slade Hill **3** WV6 . . . . 255 F3
Sladehollow La DE6 . . . . . . 65 C1
Slade La
  Sutton Coldfield B75 . . . . 259 A3
  Tamworth B77 . . . . 261 C4
  Waterhouses ST10 . . . . . . 49 A5
Slade Rd
  Sutton Coldfield B75 . . . . 258 E3
  Wolverhampton WV10 . . 240 C3
Slade View Rise WS12 . . . 211 A6
Slaidburn Gr
  Birches Head ST1 . . . . 57 F5
  Stafford ST17 . . . . 175 C7
Slaney St ST5 . . . . 283 C1
Slang La WS15 . . . . 211 F5
Slapton Cl ST12 . . . . 57 F1
Slate La WV8 . . . . 238 D5
Slater St Biddulph ST8 . . . . 27 C7
  Burslem ST6 . . . . 56 D8
Sleeve The ST13 . . . . 30 C4
Sleigh Gr ST13 . . . . 30 E5
Slessor Rd ST16 . . . . 156 A5
Slindon ST17 . . . . 285 B1
Sling La ST19 . . . . 206 B4
Slingsby B77 . . . . 261 C7
Slippery La ST1 . . . . 282 A2
Slitting Mill Rd WS15 . . . . 196 B7
Sloane Way ST4 . . . . 73 B6
Smallbrook La WV5 . . . . . 270 B7
Smallcross Cl ST14 . . . . . . 126 C5
Smalley Cl WS11 . . . . 210 A5
Small La ST21 . . . . 133 E7
Smallman St ST16 . . . . . . 285 C4
Small Mdws DE13 . . . . . . 183 E2
Smallridge WS13 . . . . 213 F2
Smallshire Way DY8 . . . . . 279 E8
Smallthorne Prim Sch
  ST6 . . . . 42 D2
Smallwood Cl ST5 . . . . 40 D1
Smallwood Gr ST1 . . . . 57 F6
Smallwood Rd WV6 . . . . . 255 B6
Smarts Ave WS14 . . . . 258 A7
Smedley Ct DE65 . . . . 148 B5
Smestow Bridge Ind Est
  WV5 . . . . 269 C6
Smestow La DY3 . . . . 269 D5
Smestow Mews WV5 . . . . 269 D4
Smestow Sch WV3 . . . . . . 255 B1
Smillie Pl WS11 . . . . 209 F3
Smith Child St ST6 . . . . . . 41 D4
Smithfield Cl ST7 . . . . 97 D2
Smithfield Ct ST1 . . . . 282 B1
Smithfield Ctr The **4**
  ST13 . . . . 30 F5
Smithfield Ho **2** ST13 . . . . . 30 F5
Smithfield Rd
  Market Drayton TF9 . . . . . 97 D2
  Uttoxeter ST14 . . . . 126 B8
  Walsall WS13 . . . . 213 E2
Smithfield Rise WS13 . . . . 231 C8
Smith Ho WS3 . . . . 243 D8
Smithpool Rd ST4 . . . . 72 D5
Smiths Bldgs **4** ST3 . . . . . 74 A1
Smith's Cl WS7 . . . . 228 D6
Smiths Pas ST3 . . . . 73 A5
Smith St Longton ST3 . . . . 284 C5
  Wood End CV9 . . . . 262 C1
Smithy Bank ST10 . . . . 78 E1
Smithy Croft ST20 . . . . . . 190 B7
Smithy Ct ST4 . . . . 90 C3
Smithyfield Rd ST6 . . . . . . 42 D4
Smithy La Barthomley CW2 38 C6
  Barthomley CW2 . . . . 38 C6
  Bednall ST17 . . . . 193 H8
  Biddulph ST8 . . . . 16 D2

Smithy La continued
  Bosley SK11 . . . . 7 E6
  Bradley ST18 . . . . 191 C8
  Cheadle ST10 . . . . 92 D8
  Clifton Campville B79 . . . 218 E2
  Dudley DY5 . . . . 271 B1
  Eccleshall ST21 . . . . 117 B2
  Hixon ST18 . . . . 158 C8
  Knighton TF9 . . . . 83 B5
  Lichfield WS13 . . . . 214 A1
  Longdon WS15 . . . . 212 F8
  Longton ST3 . . . . 284 C3
  Norton Bridge ST15 . . . . 118 F1
  Seighford ST18 . . . . 154 B7
  Tamworth B77 . . . . 261 F7
  Weston CW2 . . . . 37 C5
  Whitmore ST5 . . . . 85 F6
Smokies Way ST8 . . . . 16 C1
Smout Cres WV4 . . . . 266 F2
Snape Hall Cl ST5 . . . . 85 D6
Snape Hall Rd ST5 . . . . 85 C7
Snape Hollow CW2 . . . . . . 37 E4
Snape La CW2 . . . . 37 E4
Snape Rd WV11 . . . . 242 B1
Snapes La DE6 . . . . 81 B1
Snead Cl ST16 . . . . 156 A4
Sneyd Cl ST13 . . . . 45 C4
Sneyd Ct ST16 . . . . 156 A4
Sneyd Green Prim Sch
  ST6 . . . . 57 C7
Sneyd Hall Rd WS3 . . . . . 243 A1
Sneyd Hill ST6 . . . . 57 C8
Sneyd Hill Ind Est ST6 . . . . 57 B8
Sneyd Ho WS3 . . . . 242 F1
Sneyd Ind Est ST6 . . . . 57 B8
Sneydlands WS15 . . . . . . 178 F1
Sneyd La Walsall WS3 . . . 243 B1
  Willenhall WV11 . . . . 242 C1
Sneyd Pl ST6 . . . . 41 C6
Sneyd St Hanley ST6,ST1 . 57 C6
  Leek ST13 . . . . 30 E5
Sneyd Terr ST5 . . . . 55 B2
Sneyd Wood View ST6 . . . 57 C7
Snipe Cl WV10 . . . . 241 B7
Snowberry Dr ST5 . . . . . . 271 C1
Snowdon Way ST3 . . . . . . 74 B2
Snowdon Rd
  Burnhill Green WV6 . . . . 252 B6
  Cannock WS11 . . . . 209 C6
Snowdon Rise DY3 . . . . . 271 C6
Snowdon Way WV12 . . . . 242 B1
Snowdrop Cl WS8 . . . . . . 244 D6
Snow Hill Hanley ST1 . . . . 282 A1
  Stafford ST16 . . . . 285 B4
Snows Ct TF10 . . . . 168 F2
Snowshill Gdns DY1 . . . . 271 F4
Snows Yd ST16 . . . . 285 A4
Soames Cres ST3 . . . . 73 C6
Solent Cl WV9 . . . . 239 F2
Solney Cl DE11 . . . . 186 F3
Solway Cl B79 . . . . 250 A7
Solway Gr ST3 . . . . 73 E4
Somerfield Cl WS4 . . . . . . 244 C2
Somerford Cl Coven WV9 . 224 B2
  Great Wyrley WS6 . . . . . 226 E1
Somerford Gdns WV10 . . 240 E2
Somerford La ST19 . . . . . 223 F5
Somerley Rd ST1 . . . . 57 F6
Somerset Ave
  Kidsgrove ST7 . . . . 25 C2
  Rugeley WS15 . . . . 196 D6
Somerset Dr DY8 . . . . 279 D7
Somerset Pl WS11 . . . . . . 209 F3
Somerset Rd
  Burton u T DE15 . . . . 185 D6
  Hanley ST1 . . . . 57 E4
  Stafford ST17 . . . . 174 C7
Somerton Rd ST9 . . . . 59 A3
Somerton Way ST3 . . . . . 284 D5
Somerville Rd ST7 . . . . . . 175 C6
Somerville Ave ST5 . . . . . . 56 D3
Somerville Rd B79 . . . . . . 249 D6
Somerville Rd DE13 . . . . . 201 A2
Somerville Sq ST17 . . . . . 174 F6
Somerville Terr **5** WS15 . . 196 D6
Sonning Dr WV9 . . . . 239 F2
Sophia Way ST5 . . . . 56 B8
Sopwith Cl ST15 . . . . 118 F5
Sorbus B77 . . . . 251 B4
Sorrel Ave ST10 . . . . 92 F3
Sorrel Cl Bucknall ST2 . . . . 58 A3
  Featherstone WV10 . . . . 241 B7
  Lichfield WS13 . . . . 230 C6
  Uttoxeter ST14 . . . . 126 C5
Sorrel B77 . . . . 251 B5
Sorrento Gr ST3 . . . . 73 E4
Sotherby Ho ST16 . . . . . . 285 A3
Souldern Way ST3 . . . . 73 D4
Southall Way ST2 . . . . 58 A1
Southampton St ST1 . . . . 282 C4
South Ave DY6 . . . . 279 F4
Southbank St ST13 . . . . . . 30 F5
Southbank View DY6 . . . . 275 C4
Southborough Cres ST6 . . . 42 C4
Southbourne Rd WV10 . . 240 C3
South Broadway St
  DE15 . . . . 185 C8
South Cl WS11 . . . . 210 A6
South Cres WV10 . . . . 240 A4
South Downs Cl ST3 . . . . . 89 C8
South Dr DE11 . . . . 186 F5
Southern Cl DY6 . . . . 275 F3

Southern Cross WS14 . . . 231 C7
Southern Ct **5** ST4 . . . . 72 A7
Southernhom Rd DY3 . . . . 271 B7
Southern Way ST6 . . . . 42 D1
Southfield Cl WV9 . . . . . . 239 A6
Southfield Gr WV3 . . . . . . 265 C7
Southfields Cl ST17 . . . . . 174 D5
Southfields Rd ST17 . . . . . 74 D6
Southfield Way WS6 . . . . 226 F2
Southgate Ave ST4 . . . . . . 88 C6
Southgate Brewood ST19 . 223 D7
  Cannock WS11 . . . . 226 B7
Southgate End WS11 . . . . 226 B7
South Gn WV4 . . . . 265 D5
South Hill DE11 . . . . 147 D4
Southlands Ave
  Longton WS3 . . . . 284 B1
  Newcastle-u-L ST5 . . . . . . 56 C5
Southlands Cl ST13 . . . . . . 30 C6
Southlands Rd CW12 . . . . . 16 A8
Southlowe Ave ST17 . . . . . 59 E4
Southlowe Rd ST9 . . . . 59 E4
South Oak St DE14 . . . . . 185 B8
South Oval DY3 . . . . 271 C5
South Pl ST6 . . . . 42 D6
South Rd Bucknall ST2 . . . 58 B5
  Coldmeece ST15 . . . . . . 118 D6
  Stourbridge DY8 . . . . . . 279 E4
  Wolverhampton WV4 . . . 265 C8
South Staffordshire Bsns Pk
  WS11 . . . . 226 C4
South St
  Mount Pleasant ST7 . . . . . 26 B6
  Stafford ST16 . . . . 285 A3
  Stoke-on-T ST6 . . . . 42 D6
South Terr
  Newcastle-u-L ST5 . . . . . . 56 C5
  Stoke-on-T ST4 . . . . 72 A5
South Uxbridge St DE14 . 185 B8
South View DE14 . . . . 27 C8
South View **4** ST18 . . . . . . 27 C8
South View Cl
  Codsall WV8 . . . . 239 B2
  Featherstone WV10 . . . . 241 B6
South View DE6 . . . . 81 D6
South View Rd DY3 . . . . . 271 C8
South View ST14 . . . . 126 B7
South View Wlk ST14 . . . . 95 F3
South Walls ST16 . . . . 285 B3
Southwark Cl WS13 . . . . . 214 C3
Southway Ct DY6 . . . . 275 F4
Southwell Est ST21 . . . . . 133 E6
South Wlk ST3 . . . . 74 B1
South Wolfe St ST4 . . . . . . 72 B7
Southwood Cl DY6 . . . . . . 275 E5
South Wood ST5 . . . . 85 A7
Sovereign Bsns Pk DE14 . 166 D5
Sovereign Dr
  Burton u T DE14 . . . . 185 B8
  Dudley DY1 . . . . 271 E2
Sovereign La TF9 . . . . 100 C3
Sovereign Works DY1 . . . 271 E4
Sowdley Gn ST19 . . . . 205 B4
Sowdley La ST19 . . . . 205 B4
Sowers Ct B75 . . . . 258 D4
Spalding Pl ST2 . . . . 73 E8
Sparch Ave ST5 . . . . 56 C4
Sparch Gr ST5 . . . . 56 C4
Sparch Hollow ST5 . . . . . . 56 C4
Spark St ST4 . . . . 72 A7
Spark Terr ST4 . . . . 72 A7
Sparrowbutts Gr ST7 . . . . . 26 C2
Sparrow Cl ST18 . . . . 177 D8
Sparrows End La ST19 . . . 223 D6
Sparrow St ST6 . . . . 42 D2
Spas St ST6 . . . . 56 B6
Spa St ST6 . . . . 57 C7
Speakman St ST3 . . . . 284 D2
Spearhill WS14 . . . . 231 E8
Spedding Rd ST4 . . . . 72 F8
Spedding Way ST8 . . . . 27 E8
Speechly Dr WS15 . . . . . . 178 D2
Speedwall St ST3 . . . . 73 C5
Speedwell Cl WV9 . . . . . . 256 A5
Speedwell Gdns WV13 . . 241 B8
Speedwell Rd ST5 . . . . 40 F1
Speedwell Rise ST16 . . . . 155 A5
Speedy Cl WS11 . . . . 209 E6
Speedymill Cotts WS15 . . 213 F8
Spencer Ave Endon ST9 . . . 43 E6
  Leek ST13 . . . . 30 D6
Spencer Cl Dudley DY3 . . . 271 A4
  Stretton DE13 . . . . 147 D1
  Uttoxeter ST14 . . . . 126 C5
  Weston ST18 . . . . 138 C2
Spencer Dr WS7 . . . . 228 E8
Spencer Pl ST5 . . . . 55 E6
Spencer Rd
  Lichfield WS14 . . . . 231 B6
  Stoke-on-T ST4 . . . . 72 C8
Spencroft Rd ST5 . . . . 56 A5
Spend La Mapleton DE6 . . . 66 F7
  Thorpe DE6 . . . . 53 E2
Spenser Cl B79 . . . . 254 F4
Spenser Cl Stafford ST17 . 174 C8
  Tamworth B79 . . . . 250 A6
Spens St ST6 . . . . 56 B7
Sperry Cl ST17 . . . . 90 B7
Spey Dr DY7 . . . . 275 C4
Spiceal Mews ST14 . . . . . 126 C7
Spicer's Cl WS15 . . . . 267 C8
Spills Mdw DY3 . . . . 271 E5
Spindlewood Cl **1**
  WS12 . . . . 210 D1
Spinney
  Burntwood WS7 . . . . 212 A1
  Endon ST9 . . . . 43 E8
  Norton Canes WS11 . . . . 227 F5

Spinney Cl *continued*
Polesworth B78 . . . . .262 F8
Stourbridge DY8 . . . . .275 C3
Walsall WS3 . . . . .244 A2
Spinney Dr CW2 . . . . .37 B5
Spinney Farm Rd WS11 . .226 B7
Spinneyfields ② ST17 . . .175 D5
Spinney La WS7 . . . . .211 F3
Spinney Lodge DE13 . . . .145 E6
Spinney Rd DE14 . . . . . . .184 F8
Spinney The Biddulph ST8 . .27 C6
  Dudley DY3 . . . . .271 C2
  Lawton-gate ST7 . . . . .25 E4
  Little Aston B74 . . . . .257 B6
  Madeley Heath CW3 . . . . . .69 A8
  Newcastle-u-L ST5 . . . . . . .71 C2
  Wolverhampton WV3 . . . .255 D1
Spinning School La B79 . .250 B5
Spiral Cl DY3 . . . . .271 D3
Spire Cl ST6 . . . . .42 E3
Spires Croft WV10 . . . . . .225 D1
Spires The WS14 . . . . . . .231 E6
Spitfire Cl ST16 . . . . .136 B1
Spitfire Way ST6 . . . . .41 C4
Splash La WS12 . . . . .210 C3
Spode Ave
  Armitage WS15 . . . . .198 C4
  Hopton ST18 . . . . .156 B8
Spode Cl Cheadle ST10 . . . .76 C2
  Stone ST15 . . . . .119 E5
Spode Gr ST5 . . . . .71 B3
Spode Mus* ST4 . . . . .72 B7
Spode Pl ST11 . . . . .210 B2
Spode St ST4 . . . . .72 A5
Spoutfield Rd ST4 . . . . .56 F1
Spout La ST2 . . . . .43 C1
Spragg House La ST6 . . . . .42 E3
Spratslade Dr ST3 . . . . . .284 B2
Spreadoaks Dr ST17 . . . .175 D5
Sprengers Cl ST19 . . . . . .193 A1
Springbank Ave ST19 . . . . .43 E6
Spring Bank Flats ST16 . .155 D6
Spring Bank ST7 . . . . .26 A7
Spring Cl Ty Hagley DY9 . .281 F4
  Kinver DY7 . . . . .277 F5
  Swadlincote DE11 . . . . . .186 F1
  Walsall WS4 . . . . .244 C2
Spring Cres ST6 . . . . .43 C7
Springcroft ST11 . . . . .90 F6
Springcroft Prim Sch
  ST11 . . . . .90 E7
Springdale Jun & Inf Schs
  WV4 . . . . .265 D5
Springfarm Rd DE15 . . . .167 A1
Springfield Ave
  Newport TF10 . . . . .168 E1
  Rugeley WS15 . . . . .196 F7
  Sedgley DY3 . . . . .266 E1
Springfield ST11 . . . . .90 E1
  Newcastle-u-L ST5 . . . . . . .55 F6
Springfield Com Specl Sch
  ST13 . . . . .31 A5
Springfield Cres ST3 . . . .284 B2
Springfield Ct Leek ST13 . .31 A6
  Stafford ST17 . . . . .174 C5
  Wolverhampton WV10 . . .240 D4
Springfield Dr
  Forsbrook ST11 . . . . .91 A8
  Leek ST13 . . . . .31 A6
  Stafford ST17 . . . . .174 E5
  Talke ST7 . . . . .40 E8
  Wheaton Aston ST19 . . . .205 C7
Springfield Gn DY3 . . . . . .266 E1
Springfield Gr
  Biddulph ST8 . . . . .27 D5
  Sedgley DY3 . . . . .266 D1
Springfield La WV10 . . . .240 D4
Springfield TF9 . . . . .99 E5
Springfield Mobile Home Pk
  ④ TF9 . . . . .112 A8
Springfield Prim Sch ST4 . .71 E6
Springfield Rd
  Biddulph ST8 . . . . .27 D7
  Leek ST13 . . . . .31 A6
  Tamworth B77 . . . . .261 D8
  Uttoxeter ST14 . . . . .126 B8
Springfield Rise WS12 . . .210 C6
Springfields Fst Sch
  ST15 . . . . .118 F6
Springfields Ind Est
  TF10 . . . . .168 F1
Springfields ST10 . . . . . . .168 F1
Springfields Rd
  Rugeley WS15 . . . . .178 D3
  Stoke-on-T ST4 . . . . .71 E6
Springfield Terr DE15 . . .167 A1
Spring Garden Rd ST3 . . .284 B2
Spring Gdns
  Forsbrook ST11 . . . . .91 B8
  Leek ST13 . . . . .30 D5
  Stone ST15 . . . . .120 A5
Springhead Cl ST7 . . . . .40 D6
Springhead Prim Sch ST7 .40 D6
Springhill Ave WV4 . . . . .265 C4
Springhill Cl WS4 . . . . . . .244 D1
Springhill Gr WV4 . . . . . . .265 B4
Springhill La WV4 . . . . . . .265 B4
Springhill Pk WV4 . . . . . . .265 B3
Springhill Prim Sch
  WS7 . . . . .229 B6
Springhill Rd
  Brownhills WS8 . . . . .245 A7
  Burntwood WS7 . . . . .229 A6
Springhill Terr WS15 . . . .196 F7
Spring Hollow ST21 . . . . .133 G6
Spring La
  Bishops Wood ST19 . . . . .221 E8

Spring La *continued*
  Walsall WS4 . . . . .244 C2
  Whittington WS14 . . . . . .232 E6
Spring Leasow ST20 . . . . .151 A4
Springle Styche La WS7 . .212 C1
Spring Mdw WS6 . . . . .226 D1
Spring Meadows Cl WV8 .239 B4
Springpool ST5 . . . . .70 C6
Spring Rd Lichfield WS13 .214 D2
  Longton ST3 . . . . .73 E2
  Walsall WS4 . . . . .244 D1
Springs Bank ST9 . . . . .44 A2
Springside Pl ST3 . . . . .88 E7
Spring St Cannock WS11 . .226 E8
  Stoke-on-T ST5 . . . . .56 D1
Spring Terrace Rd DE15 .166 F1
Spring Terr WS7 . . . . .228 E5
Springvale Prim Sch
  WS11 . . . . .226 E8
Springvale Rise ST16 . . . .155 D8
Spring View ST16 . . . . .43 C7
Springwater Dr CW2 . . . . .37 C1
Springwood Dr ST15 . . . .120 D7
Springwood Rd ST5 . . . . . .55 C8
Sprinkbank Rd ST6 . . . . . . .42 A5
Sprink La CW12 . . . . .6 D5
Sprinkswoods La DE6 . . . . .81 E5
Sprinkwood Gr ST3 . . . . . .74 A3
Sproston Rd ST6 . . . . .41 F4
Spruce Rd WS12 . . . . .194 F1
Spruces The DY9 . . . . .281 F4
Spruce St ST7 . . . . .251 B4
Spruce Way
  Stafford ST16 . . . . .155 C3
  Wolverhampton WV3 . . . .255 D1
Spruce Wlk WS15 . . . . . . .178 C3
Spur Lea ST18 . . . . .173 C1
Spur St ST1 . . . . .282 C1
Spur Tree Ave WV3 . . . . . .255 A1
Square The Aldridge WS9 .256 B6
  Caverswall ST11 . . . . .74 E2
  Checkley ST14 . . . . .109 E7
  Codsall WV8 . . . . .238 F4
  Derrington ST18 . . . . .154 D2
  Elford B79 . . . . .216 D2
  Fazeley B78 . . . . .261 A8
  Great Haywood ST18 . . . .158 B2
  Marchington ST14 . . . . . .127 E2
  Meir ST3 . . . . .74 B2
  Newcastle-u-L ST5 . . . . . . .71 B6
  Newport TF10 . . . . .168 F3
  Oakamoor ST10 . . . . .78 A6
  Pattingham WV6 . . . . .253 C2
  Whiston ST19 . . . . .62 D3
  Wolverhampton WV2 . . . .266 D8
  Woore CW3 . . . . .67 C1
Squires Gate WS7 . . . . . . .229 C8
Squires View WS7 . . . . .72 C7
Squirrel Cl
  Cannock WS12 . . . . .210 D2
  Huntington WS12 . . . . . . .209 C6
Squirrel Hayes Ave ST8 . . .27 E6
Squirrel Hayes Cotts DE13 .27 E6
Squirrel Hayes Fst Sch
  ST8 . . . . .27 D7
Squirrels Cnr DE13 . . . . . .162 F7
Squirrels Hollow WS7 . . . .212 A2
Squirrels The
  Lichfield WS14 . . . . .231 C7
  Newcastle-u-L ST5 . . . . . . .71 C3
Squirrel Wlk
  Little Aston B74 . . . . .257 C5
  Stafford ST17 . . . . .174 E4
  Wolverhampton WV4 . . . .266 A5
Stable Ct DY3 . . . . .271 E6
Stableford Bank ST5 . . . . . .86 A1
Stableford Cvn Pk ST5 . . . .86 B2
Stable La
  Market Drayton TF9 . . . . . .97 B1
  Shareshill WV10 . . . . .225 A7
  Wetton DE6 . . . . .35 B1
Stables The
  Great Haywood ST18 . . . .158 B2
  Lawton-gate ST7 . . . . .25 C4
Stacey Cl SK17 . . . . .23 B2
Stackhouse Cl WS9 . . . . . .245 A4
Stackhouse Dr WS3 . . . . .244 A4
Stackyard La TF10 . . . . . . .168 A4
Stadium Ct ST6 . . . . .57 A6
Stadmorslow La
  Harriseahead ST7 . . . . .26 F4
  Packmoor ST6,ST7 . . . . . . .27 A3
Stafford Ave ST5 . . . . .71 B4
Stafford Brook Rd WS15 .195 F8
Stafford Castle* ST16 . . .155 A1
Stafford Cl Stone ST15 . . .120 A5
  Walsall WS3 . . . . .243 B2
Stafford Coll ST16 . . . . . . .285 A3
Stafford Cres
  Newcastle-u-L ST5 . . . . . . .71 C4
  Whittington WS14 . . . . . .232 D3
Stafford Ct WV10 . . . . . . .240 C5
Stafford Gram Sch ST16 .174 C6
Stafford La
  Cannock WS12 . . . . .210 B5
  Codsall WV8 . . . . .238 E1
  Hanley ST1 . . . . .282 B3
Stafford Rd
  Brewood WV10 . . . . .224 C5
  Cannock WS11 . . . . .209 D1
  Coven Heath WV10 . . . . .240 D4
  Eccleshall ST21 . . . . .133 F6
  Gnosall ST20 . . . . .171 C6
  Huntington WS11,WS12 . .209 C5
  Lichfield WS13 . . . . .213 D2
  Newport TF10 . . . . .169 A3

Stafford Rd *continued*
  Penkridge ST19 . . . . .192 E2
  Stone ST15 . . . . .120 A6
  Stone ST15 . . . . .120 A7
  Uttoxeter ST14 . . . . .126 A6
  Walsall WS3 . . . . .243 B4
  Weston ST18 . . . . .138 C3
Staffordshire Ct ST18 . . .156 D4
Staffordshire Enamels*
  ST3 . . . . .72 A5
Staffordshire General Hospl
  ST16 . . . . .156 B4
Staffordshire Regiment Mus
  The* WS14 . . . . .232 C2
Staffordshire Tech Pk
  ST18 . . . . .156 C5
Staffordshire Univ WS13 .231 B7
Staffordshire Univ (Stafford
  Campus) ST18 . . . . .156 C5
Staffordshire Univ (Stoke
  Campus) ST4 . . . . .72 C8
Staffordshire Yeomanry
  Mus* ST16 . . . . .285 B3
Stafford Sta ST16 . . . . . . .285 A2
Stafford St Brewood ST19 .223 C6
  Burton u T DE14 . . . . . . .166 D5
  Cannock WS12 . . . . .210 E1
  Eccleshall ST21 . . . . .133 E7
  Hanley ST1 . . . . .282 B3
  Market Drayton TF9 . . . . . .97 D1
  Newcastle-u-L ST5 . . . . . .283 C2
  Newport TF10 . . . . .168 F3
  Stafford ST16 . . . . .285 B3
Stagborough Way WS12 .210 B4
Stag Cl WS15 . . . . .178 B1
Stag Cres WS11 . . . . .228 A6
Stag Dr WS12 . . . . .209 C6
Staines Ct ST15 . . . . .120 C7
Staite Dr WV10 . . . . .280 B5
Staite Terr DY10 . . . . .280 A5
Stakenbridge La DY10 . . .281 D4
Staley Croft WS12 . . . . . .209 C4
Stalling's La DY6 . . . . .275 D8
Stallington Cl ST11 . . . . . . .90 D4
Stallington Gdns ST11 . . . .90 F6
Stallington Rd ST11 . . . . . .90 C3
Stamer St ST1 . . . . .72 B6
Stamford Cres WS7 . . . . . .229 A8
Stamford St DY8 . . . . .279 F7
Stamford Way WS9 . . . . . .245 C1
Stamps Cl DE15 . . . . .167 C3
Standard St ST4 . . . . .72 D6
Standedge B77 . . . . .262 B7
Standersfoot Pl ST16 . . . . .42 B6
Standhills Rd DY6 . . . . . . .275 E8
Standing Butts Cl DE12 . .202 D8
Standon Ct ST21 . . . . .101 F4
Stanfield Rd ST6 . . . . .42 A1
Stanfield St ④ ST4 . . . . . . .73 D6
Stanford Cl ST19 . . . . .193 B1
Stanford Rd WV2 . . . . .266 C8
Stanhope Gn DE15 . . . . . .167 F1
Stanhope Ho B79 . . . . . . .250 A4
Stanhope St
  Burton u T DE15 . . . . . . .167 B3
  Hanley ST1 . . . . .282 A1
Stanier St
  Newcastle-u-L ST5 . . . . . .283 B3
  Stoke-on-T ST4 . . . . .72 E6
Stanley Bank ST9 . . . . .44 A5
Stanley Cl DE12 . . . . .219 F7
Stanley Cres ST14 . . . . . . .111 A2
Stanley Ct WV6 . . . . .254 E4
Stanley Dr
  Newcastle-u-L ST5 . . . . . . .40 D1
  Swindon DY3 . . . . .269 E2
Stanley Gr
  Newcastle-u-L ST5 . . . . . . .56 D2
  Stoke-on-T,Endon ST9 . . . .43 F7
  Stoke-on-T ST4 . . . . .72 B8
  Stone ST15 . . . . .104 F1
  Stowe-by-Chartley ST18 . .139 C4
Stanley Matthews Sports Ctr
  ST4 . . . . .72 C8
Stanley Matthews Way
  Stoke-on-T,Hem Heath
  ST4 . . . . .88 D7
  Stoke-on-T,Hollybush ST4 . .72 C3
Stanley Moss La ST9 . . . . .43 E5
Stanley Moss Rd ST9 . . . . .43 F5
Stanley Rd Biddulph ST8 . . .16 C2
  Cannock WS12 . . . . .210 A6
  Newcastle-u-L ST5 . . . . . . .56 E2
  Stoke-on-T,Hartshill ST4 . . .71 E8
  Stoke-on-T,Stanley Moor
  ST9 . . . . .43 E4
  Stourbridge DY8 . . . . .279 F3
  Wolverhampton WV10 . . .240 D1
Stanley St Biddulph ST8 . . .27 C8
  Burton u T DE14 . . . . . . .166 C2
  Leek ST13 . . . . .31 A5
  Stoke-on-T ST6 . . . . .41 E4
  Walsall WS3 . . . . .243 D1
Stansgate Pl ST1 . . . . .282 A4
Stanshope La DE6 . . . . .35 C2
Stansmore Rd ST3 . . . . .74 B2
Stanton Ave DY1 . . . . .271 F6
Stanton Cl ST14 . . . . .126 A6
Stanton La Ellastone DE6 . .80 C4
  Upper Mayfield DE6 . . . . . .66 A2
Stanton Prim Sch DE15 . .186 B5
Stanton Rd
  Burton u T DE15 . . . . . . .185 F7
  Meir ST3 . . . . .74 A1
Stanway Ave ST6 . . . . .57 C7
Stanway Cl ST14 . . . . .126 A6
Stanway La ST8 . . . . .37 B2
Stapenhill Rd DE15 . . . . . .166 F2
Stapleford Gdns WS7 . . . .229 D6

Stapleford Gr DY8 . . . . . . .275 E2
Stapleton Cres ST3 . . . . . . .73 A1
Star And Garter Rd ST3 . . .89 E8
Star Bank Cotton ST10 . . . .63 E1
  Oakamoor ST10 . . . . .78 C7
Star Cvn Site The WV9 . . .224 B1
Starkey's La ST19 . . . . . . .205 D7
Starling Cl ST7 . . . . .26 D3
Starling Ct WV10 . . . . .240 B3
Star St WV3 . . . . .265 E8
Startley La WS15 . . . . .196 F1
Starwood Rd ST3 . . . . .89 E8
Starwood Terr ST10 . . . . . .78 A6
Statfold La Airewas DE13 .200 F3
  Fradley WS13 . . . . .215 D8
Statham St ST1 . . . . .282 A2
Station App
  Lichfield WS13 . . . . .231 F8
  Stone ST15 . . . . .104 F1
  Sutton Coldfield,Hill Hook
  B74 . . . . .257 F6
Station Bridge Rd ST4 . . . .72 E5
Station Cl WV8 . . . . .238 F3
Station Cotts
  Sudbury DE6 . . . . .128 E2
  Whitmore ST5 . . . . .85 D5
Station Cres ST6 . . . . .42 D2
Station Ct Cannock WS11 .226 F8
  Newport TF10 . . . . .169 A1
Station Dr Armitage WS15 .198 B4
  Blakedown DY10 . . . . . . .281 C2
  Four Ashes WV10 . . . . . .224 C5
  Keele ST5 . . . . .69 D8
Stationfields Park Homes
  B79 . . . . .250 C5
Station Gr ST22 . . . . .43 A1
Station Ind Est ST11 . . . . . .57 F3
Station La
  Rushton Spencer SK11 . . . .8 B2
  Walton-on-T DE12 . . . . . .184 D1
Station Rd
  Albrighton WV7 . . . . .237 B5
  Aldridge WS9 . . . . .256 A5
  Alton ST10 . . . . .78 E1
  Barlaston ST12 . . . . .88 D1
  Barton-u-N DE13 . . . . . . .183 E2
  Biddulph ST8 . . . . .16 C1
  Cannock WS12 . . . . .210 C6
  Cheadle ST10 . . . . .76 D2
  Cheddleton ST13 . . . . .45 D6
  Codsall WV8 . . . . .238 F4
  Coleshill CW15 . . . . .118 C6
  Cotes Heath ST21 . . . . . .102 D3
  Draycott in t C DE6 . . . . .144 D8
  Four Ashes WV10 . . . . . .224 D5
  Gnosall ST20 . . . . .171 D6
  Great Wyrley WS6 . . . . . .226 F4
  Halmer End ST7 . . . . .54 D7
  Hammerwich WS7 . . . . . .229 E3
  Hatton DE65 . . . . .146 B8
  Haughton ST18 . . . . .172 E7
  Keele ST5 . . . . .69 E8
  Kidsgrove ST7 . . . . .25 F1
  Lichfield WS13 . . . . .231 C7
  Madeley CW3 . . . . .68 E5
  Madeley Heath ST5 . . . . . .69 D8
  Mow Cop ST7 . . . . .26 C8
  Newcastle-u-L ST5 . . . . . . .55 B2
  Newchapel ST7 . . . . .26 D6
  Newport TF10 . . . . .168 F1
  Norton Bridge ST15 . . . . .118 F1
  Onneley CW3 . . . . .68 B2
  Penkridge ST19 . . . . .192 E1
  Rolleston on D DE13 . . . .147 C4
  Rugeley WS15 . . . . .178 F2
  Scholar Green ST7 . . . . . . .26 A8
  Shenstone WS14 . . . . . . .246 F6
  Stafford ST16 . . . . .285 A2
  Stoke-on-T,Endon ST9 . . . .43 F7
  Stone ST15 . . . . .104 F1
  Stowe-by-Chartley ST18 . .139 C4
  The Bank ST7 . . . . .26 A8
  Uttoxeter ST14 . . . . .126 D7
  Walsall WS3 . . . . .244 A3
  Wombourne WV5 . . . . . . .270 A8
Station St Burslem ST6 . . . .56 D8
  Burton u T DE14 . . . . . . .166 D3
  Cheslyn Hay WS6 . . . . . . .226 E3
  Leek ST13 . . . . .30 D5
Station View WS3 . . . . .74 A1
Station Wlks ST7 . . . . .54 D7
Station Yd DE13 . . . . .201 B2
Staunton Rd WS3 . . . . .243 A3
Staveley Cl ST2 . . . . .58 A3
Staveley Rd ST5 . . . . .55 A1
Steadman Cres ST17 . . . .174 E6
Stedman St ST1 . . . . .282 C4
Steele Ave ST6 . . . . .42 B2
Steele Cl ST13 . . . . .45 D5
Steelhouse La WV2 . . . . . .266 E8
Steel St ST4 . . . . .71 E8
Steenwood La WS15 . . . . .160 A2
Steeple Way ST4 . . . . .72 A5
Steere Ave B79 . . . . .250 C7
Stellar St ST6 . . . . .42 C1
Stenbury Cl WV10 . . . . . . .240 F4
Stephanie Gr B77 . . . . . . .251 A6
Stephen Ave ST10 . . . . .61 D2
Stephen St ST4 . . . . .72 A5
Stephenson Dr WV6 . . . . .254 E5
Stephenson Way WS12 . . .210 B5
Stephens Gn DE14 . . . . . .185 B8
Stephens Rd ST17 . . . . .59 F7
Stephens Wlk WS13 . . . . .214 A2
Stepping Stones
  ④ Leek ST13 . . . . .30 E5

Stepping Stones *continued*
  Rugeley WS15 . . . . .178 D1
Step Row ① ST13 . . . . .30 E5
Steps Gdns ST18 . . . . .172 E6
Sterling Pk B77 . . . . .261 E7
Sterndale Dr Longton ST4 . .73 B6
  Newcastle-u-L ST5 . . . . . . .71 B3
Sterndale Moor SK17 . . . . . .5 E6
Sterrymere Gdns DY7 . . . .278 B4
Stevens Dr WS12 . . . . .210 D6
Stevens Gate ⑥ WV2 . . . . .266 C8
Stevenson Dr ST17 . . . . . .174 C7
Stevenson Rd Bucknall ST2 .58 A4
  Doveridge DE6 . . . . .127 B8
  Tamworth B79 . . . . .250 A6
Stevenson Wlk WS14 . . . .231 B6
Steventon Pl ① ST6 . . . . . .56 F8
Stewart Cl DE14 . . . . .185 A6
Stewart Ct ST2 . . . . .58 D1
Stewart Rd
  Brownhills WS9 . . . . .245 A3
  Kingswinford DY6 . . . . . . .275 D4
Stewart St Stoke-on-T ST4 . .72 D6
  Wolverhampton WV2 . . . .266 C8
Stewkins Ct ④ DY8 . . . . . .279 E8
Stewkins DY8 . . . . .279 E8
Stewponey The DY7 . . . . .278 E6
Stickley La DY3 . . . . .271 C4
Stile Cl Biddulph ST8 . . . . . .27 B5
  Rugeley WS15 . . . . .196 D4
Stile Cop Rd WS15 . . . . . .196 D4
Stile House La ST13 . . . . . .31 E6
Stirling Cl Bucknall ST2 . . . .73 E7
  Castle Gresley DE11 . . . . .186 F1
Stirling Pl WS11 . . . . .226 B8
Stirling Rise ⑦ DE13 . . . .166 D8
Stirling St ST8 . . . . .57 A8
Stitchings The DE6 . . . . . . .65 C1
Stockbridge Cl WV6 . . . . .254 F2
Stockfield Rd ST3 . . . . .89 F7
Stockford La WS13 . . . . . .216 A3
Stockhay La WS7 . . . . .229 D5
Stockholm Gr ST5 . . . . .57 E7
Stocking-Gate La ST13 . . .153 F2
Stocking La ST13 . . . . .153 B5
Stockings La
  Longdon WS15 . . . . .197 D2
  Wheaton Aston ST19 . . . .205 D5
Stock La ST14 . . . . .143 B8
Stocks La ST14 . . . . .125 C7
Stockton La ST17 . . . . .175 E7
Stockwell End WV6 . . . . . .255 D6
Stockwell Gr ST3 . . . . .73 D3
Stockwell Rd WV6 . . . . . . .255 D5
Stockwell St ST13 . . . . .30 F6
Stockwood Rd ST5 . . . . .71 A3
Stoke Bsns Pk ST4 . . . . . . .72 B6
Stoke Old Rd ST4 . . . . .56 E1
Stoke-on-Trent Coll
  (Burslem Campus)
  Burslem ST6 . . . . .57 B8
  Stoke-on-T ST6 . . . . .42 B1
Stoke-on-Trent Coll
  (Cauldon Campus) ST4 . .57 B1
Stoke-on-Trent Sta ST4 . . .72 B8
Stoke Rd DE14 . . . . .57 B1
Stoke Recn Ctr ST4 . . . . . . .72 B6
Stokesay Ave WV6 . . . . . .254 F3
Stokesay Dr ST10 . . . . .76 F3
Stokesay Gr ST6 . . . . .57 A7
Stokesay Rise DY1 . . . . . . .271 E3
Stoke Ski Ctr ST6 . . . . .56 F5
Stoke's La WS11 . . . . .227 F7
Stoneacre Cl WV3 . . . . . . .255 A1
Stone Bank Rd ST7 . . . . . . .41 B8
Stonebridge Rd ST19 . . . .223 D6
Stone Bsns Pk ST15 . . . . .120 B4
Stone Chair La ST7 . . . . . . .25 E7
Stone Cotts Clifton DE6 . . .81 E8
  Congleton CW12 . . . . .6 C3
  Weston-Under-Lizard
  TF11 . . . . .203 C4
Stonecrop Cl WS8 . . . . . . .244 D6
Stone Cross ST19 . . . . . . .192 E1
Stone Ent Ctr ST15 . . . . . .120 B4
Stonefield Ct ③ ST15 . . . .104 F2
Stonefield Sq ST15 . . . . . .105 A1
Stonehaven Gr ST3 . . . . . .282 C1
Stonehaven B77 . . . . .250 F5
Stonehill Wlk ⑤ B77 . . . . .261 F6
Stonehouse Cres ST9 . . . . .59 B3
Stonehouse Dr B74 . . . . . .257 C4
Stonehouse Rd
  Rugeley WS15 . . . . .178 A1
  Werrington ST9 . . . . .59 B3
Stone La DY7 . . . . .278 A4
Stone Sq WV6 . . . . .256 B5
Stoneleigh Ct ST18 . . . . . .174 C5
Stoneleigh Gdns WV8 . . . .238 F4
Stoneleigh Rd ST6 . . . . .42 A5
Stoneleigh Way DY3 . . . . .271 D6
Stone Pine Cl WS12 . . . . .209 F8
Stonepine Pl ST17 . . . . . . .271 E6
Stonepit B77 . . . . .250 C1
Stone Rd Eccleshall ST21 . .134 B7
  Stafford,Parkside ST16 . . .155 C4
  Stafford ST16 . . . . .155 D5
Tittensor ST4,ST12 . . . . . .71 F1
Tittensor ST4,ST12 . . . . . .88 A3
Tixall ST18 . . . . .87 F7
  Uttoxeter ST14 . . . . .126 B8
  Yarlet ST16,ST18 . . . . . .136 B2

Stuart Ave continued
Stoke-on-T ST4 .... 88 A7
Stuart Cl N ST15 .... 119 F6
Stuart Cl ST15 .... 119 F5
Stuart Gr ST5 .... 56 C4
Stuart Rd ST1 .... 57 E2
Stuart Way TF9 .... 97 B2
Stubbers Green Rd WS9 .. 206 A7
Stubbs Dr ST15 .... 120 D7
Stubbsfield Rd ST5 .... 283 C1
Stubbs' Gate ST5 .... 283 C2
Stubbs La Hanley ST1 .. 282 C2
Stanton DE6 .... 65 C2
Stubbs Rd WV3 .... 266 A6
Stubbs St S6 .... 56 E8
Stubbs' St ST5 .... 283 C2
Stubby La DE6 .... 144 B6
Stubwood Hollow ST14 .. 95 D5
Stubwood La ST14 .... 95 D4
Stud Farm Cotts B78 .. 249 E2
Studley Gate DY8 .... 279 D5
Studley Rd WV3 .... 265 C8
Sturgeon's Hill WS14 .. 231 C7
Sturgess St ST14 .... 72 A6
Stychbrook Gdns WS13 .. 214 B2
Stychfields ST17 .... 285 C1
Suckling Green La WV8 .. 238 F2
Sudbourne Cl ST6 .... 41 E8
Sudbury Hall & Mus of
  Childhood* DE6 .... 128 D5
Sudbury Pk DE6 .... 128 D7
Sudbury Prim Sch DE6 .. 128 E4
Sudbury Rd DE13 .... 182 A4
Sudeley Gdns DY1 .... 271 D2
Sudeley B77 .... 261 C8
Sudgrove Pl ST3 .... 90 B7
Sudlow St ST6 .... 57 B7
Suffolk Cl ST5 .... 71 D4
Suffolk Gr WS9 .... 256 B8
Suffolk Rd
  Burton u T DE15 .... 185 D7
  Stoke-on-T ST3 .... 89 C8
Suffolk Way B78 .... 250 A1
Sugar Loaf La DY10 .. 281 B7
Sugar St SK11 .... 8 C2
Sugnall Bsns Ctr ST21 .. 116 D2
Sullivan Way ST13 .... 214 C2
Sullivan Wlk WS13 .... 214 C2
Summerbank Prim Sch
  ST6 .... 41 D4
Summerbank Rd ST6 .. 41 D4
Summercourt Dr DY6 .. 275 C6
Summercourt Sq DY6 .. 275 C5
Summer Dr DY3 .... 271 C3
Summerfield Arc 6
  ST15 .... 120 A8
Summerfield Ave DY6 .. 275 C7
Summerfield Cl B77 .. 250 D4
Summerfield Dr ST14 .. 126 A8
Summerfield ST7 .... 26 B1
Summerfield Rd
  Burntwood WS7 .... 229 A5
  Tamworth B77 .... 250 D4
Summerfields ST15 .... 118 E6
Summergate DY3 .... 271 C4
Summer Gr WS13 .... 214 D2
Summerhill Dr ST5 .... 40 D1
Summerhill Gdns TF9 .. 112 C8
Summer Hill DY6 .... 275 C6
Summerhill La ST18 .. 135 C5
Summerhill Sch The
  DY6 .... 275 B6
Summerhill WS14 .... 245 E8
Summerhouse Gr TF10 .. 168 F4
Summerhouse La WS13 .. 212 E3
Summer La Dudley DY3 .. 271 C3
  Walsall WS4 .... 244 F2
Summer Row ST3 .... 284 C2
Summerside Ave WS12 .. 211 C4
Summer St
  Kingswinford DY6 .... 275 D6
  Stoke-on-T ST4 .... 72 A5
  Stourbridge DY8 .... 279 F5
Summerville Rd ST4 .. 71 E3
Summit Pl DY3 .... 271 B2
Sunbeam Dr WS6 .... 226 F3
Sunbeam St WV2 .... 266 C7
Sunbeam B77 .... 250 E3
Sunbury Ave WS14 .... 231 E7
Sunbury Cl ST14 .... 88 C6
Sundorne Pl ST2 .... 58 B2
Sundour Cres WV11 .. 241 B1
Sundown Dr ST17 .... 174 B7
Sundridge Wlk WV4 .. 265 C6
Sunfield Rd WS11 .... 209 B1
Suningdale Cl DE13 .. 147 C1
Suniley Dr WS12 .... 210 D7
Sunningdale Ave WV6 .. 254 D5
Sunningdale Cl
  Stoke-on-T ST5 .... 42 B3
  Stourbridge DY8 .... 279 F2
Sunningdale Dr ST16 .. 156 C3
Sunningdale Gr ST5 .. 55 D8
Sunningdale Rd DY3 .. 266 B1
Sunningdale Stone ST15 .. 120 A7
  Tamworth B77 .... 251 C5
Sunningdale View ST3 .. 89 E3
Sunningdale Way WS3 .. 243 A3
Sunny Bank ST6 .... 56 E6
Sunnybank Cl WS9 .. 256 E2
Sunnybank Ct ST6 .... 42 A3
Sunnybank Cvn Pk ST19 .. 205 E7
Sunny Bank DE6 .... 81 C7
Sunnybank Rd DY3 .. 271 F5
Sunnycroft Ave ST3 .. 284 A1
Sunnyfield Oval ST2 .. 43 C1
Sunny Gdns TF10 .... 168 F5
Stuart Ave
  Draycott in t M ST11 .. 91 C6

Sunny Hill Cl WV5 .. 270 B6
Sunnyhills Rd ST13 .. 30 D3
Sunny Hollow ST5 .... 56 A2
Sunnymead Rd 1 WS7 .. 229 A8
Sunnymede Rd 1 DY6 .. 275 F4
Sunnyside Ave ST4 .. 41 F4
Sunnyside WS9 .... 245 A2
Sunnyside Cl DE11 .. 186 F7
Sunny Side ST10 .... 61 D3
Sunnyside Rd ST14 .. 111 B1
Sunnyside DE11 .... 186 F7
Sunridge Ave WV5 .. 270 A7
Sunridge Cl ST2 .... 43 B2
Sunrise Hill WS12 .... 210 B6
Sunset Cl Coven WV9 .. 226 F3
  Great Wyrley WS6 .... 226 F3
  Tamworth B79 .... 250 A5
Sunset Pl WV4 .... 266 F3
Sun St Cheadle ST10 .. 76 E3
  Hanley ST1 .... 282 A2
Sunwell Gdns ST10 .. 76 E3
Surrey Cl Cannock WS11 .. 226 F8
  Rugeley WS15 .... 196 D6
Surrey Dr
  Kingswinford DY6 .... 275 F3
  Tamworth B78 .... 250 A1
  Wolverhampton WV3 .... 255 C1
Surrey Ho 2 DY8 .... 279 F8
Surrey La Kidsgrove ST7 .. 26 A2
  Stafford ST17 .... 174 C8
Surrey Wlk WS9 .... 245 A1
Surtees Gr ST4 .... 73 B5
Sussex Ave WS9 .... 256 A8
Sussex Dr Cannock WS12 .. 210 B5
  Kidsgrove ST7 .... 26 A2
  Wolverhampton WV3 .... 255 E1
Sussex Pl ST3 .... 73 D1
Sussex Rd DE15 .... 185 E6
Sutherland Ave
  Longton ST3 .... 284 B1
  Wolverhampton WV2 .... 266 F8
Sutherland Cres ST11 .. 90 E6
Sutherland Dr
  Newcastle-u-L ST5 .... 70 F5
  Wombourne WV5 .... 265 A1
Sutherland Gr WV6 .. 254 F4
Sutherland Prim Sch ST3 .. 72 F1
Sutherland Rd
  Cheslyn Hay WS6 .... 226 E2
  Longsdon ST9 .... 30 A1
  Longton ST3 .... 284 C3
  Stone ST15 .... 120 C7
  Tittensor ST12 .... 88 A1
  Wolverhampton WV4 .... 266 B5
Sutherland St ST4 .. 72 C6
Sutton Ave B78 .... 250 A4
Sutton Cl WS15 .... 196 E2
Sutton Ct Forton TF10 .. 169 C8
  Wolverhampton WV4 .... 266 E2
Sutton Dr Stafford ST16 .. 155 A4
  Stoke-on-T ST4 .... 71 F4
  Stoke-on-T ST4 .... 71 F4
Sutton La TF9 .... 112 C4
Sutton Pl ST6 .... 56 E2
Sutton Rd Aldridge WS9 .. 256 A1
  Mile Oak B78 .... 260 A4
  Tamworth B78 .... 249 C1
Sutton St
  Newcastle-u-L ST5 .... 55 E6
  Stourbridge DY8 .... 275 F1
Sutton Way TF9 .... 112 B7
Swadlincote La DE11 .. 186 E2
Swaffham Way ST2 .. 58 D2
Swaffield Pl WS11 .... 210 B3
Swainsfield Rd DE13 .. 182 A2
Swainsley Cl 3 ST6 .. 42 A7
Swaledale Ave CW12 .. 6 A5
Swallow Cl
  1 Kidsgrove ST7 .... 26 B2
  Huntington WS12 .... 209 C7
  Meir ST3 .... 90 A7
  Rugeley WS15 .... 178 D2
  Uttoxeter ST14 .... 126 B6
Swallow Croft Leek ST13 .. 30 D1
  Lichfield WS14 .... 214 A1
Swallow Ct Alrewas DE13 .. 201 A2
  Wolverhampton WV10 .... 240 B3
Swallowdale
  5 Stafford ST17 .... 175 D6
  Brownhills WS9 .... 245 B4
  Wolverhampton WV6 .... 254 F2
Swallowfall Ave DY8 .. 279 C4
Swallowfields Dr WS12 .. 210 B3
Swallowfields Rd DY3 .. 266 C2
Swallowfield B79 .... 249 E6
Swallowmore View ST7 .. 40 C8
Swallow Rd 4 ST17 .. 266 F1
Swallows Cl WS3 .... 244 A5
Swallowsreach WS13 .. 213 F1
Swallow Wlk ST8 .... 27 D7
Swanage Cl ST3 .... 90 B7
Swan Bank Talke ST7 .. 40 D7
Swan Cl Blakedown DY10 .. 281 B1
  Cheslyn Hay WS6 .... 226 D2
Swancote Dr WV4 .... 265 C6
Swan Cotts WS14 .... 232 E6
Swan Ct Burton u T DE14 .. 166 F3
Swan Dr WS8 .... 244 E7
Swan Farm La CW3 .. 67 B1
Swanfield Rd DY8 .... 275 F1

Swanfields WS7 .... 229 C6
Swan Gr ST6 .... 41 D1
Swanholme Way ST5 .. 85 C4
Swan La WS15 .... 161 A6
Shareshill WV10 .... 225 C1
Stoke-on-T ST4 .... 71 E3
Stourbridge DY8 .... 275 F2
Swanmere TF10 .... 168 F5
Swan Mews WS13 .... 231 A8
Swanmore Cl WV3 .. 265 E8
Swanmote B79 .... 249 F5
Swannington St DE13 .. 166 B6
Swan Pas ST11 .... 90 F7
Swan Rd B77 .... 250 C3
Swan Pool Gr WS4 .. 244 D1
Swan Rd
  Draycott in t C DE6 .... 144 D6
  Lichfield WS13 .... 231 A7
  Whittington WS14 .... 232 E6
Swansmoor Dr ST18 .. 139 D1
Swan Sq ST6 .... 56 F8
Swan St Stoke-on-T ST4 .. 72 B8
  Stourbridge DY8 .... 279 E5
Swanton B77 .... 87 F7
Swan Wlk DE14 .... 166 D2
Swarbourn Cl DE13 .. 182 A2
Swaythling Gr ST2 .. 58 D1
Sweetbriar Way
  Cannock WS12 .... 210 D2
  Stafford ST17 .... 175 C6
Sweetbrier Dr 4 WV8 .. 275 E1
Sweetman St WV6 .. 255 F4
Sweetplace La ST20 .. 189 E2
Sweetpool La DY8 .. 281 F5
Swift Cl Kidsgrove ST7 .. 26 B2
  Uttoxeter ST14 .... 126 B6
Swift Dr ST8 .... 27 E8
Swift Pl ST3 .... 73 F5
Swift B77 .... 250 E3
Swinburne Cl
  Stafford ST17 .... 174 C8
  Stoke-on-T ST3 .... 72 F2
Swindale Dr B77 .... 262 B7
Swindon Rd DY6 .... 275 B6
Swinfen Broun Rd WS13 .. 231 A8
Swinford Leys WV5 .. 269 D5
Swin Forge Way DY3 .. 269 C2
Swingle Hill Rd ST3 .. 72 F3
Swinscoe Cl ST14 .. 96 A3
Swiss Dr DY8 .... 275 F2
Swiss Lodge Dr B78 .. 260 F8
Swithin Dr ST3 .... 73 B6
Swynnerton Dr WV11 .. 241 F4
Sycamore Cl Biddulph ST8 .. 16 E2
  Burton u T DE15 .... 185 E5
  Meir Heath ST3 .... 90 A5
  Stourbridge DY8 .... 279 D2
  Talke ST7 .... 40 E8
  Uttoxeter ST14 .... 126 B8
Sycamore Cres WS15 .. 197 A6
Sycamore Dr Hixon ST18 .. 158 C8
  Wolverhampton WV3 .... 255 D1
Sycamore Gdns ST6 .. 56 D8
Sycamore Gn
  Cannock WS11 .... 209 E6
  Dudley DY1 .... 271 F5
Sycamore Green Prim Sch
  DY1 .... 271 F5
Sycamore Gr
  Newcastle-u-L ST5 .... 56 D3
  Stoke-on-T ST3 .... 72 E3
Sycamore Hill WS15 .. 211 F5
Sycamore La WS17 .. 174 B8
Sycamore Pl WS7 .... 228 F7
Sycamore Rd
  Burntwood WS7 .... 228 F7
  Burton u T DE15 .... 185 F6
  Cannock WS12 .... 210 F4
  Kingswinford DY6 .... 275 E6
  Mayfield DE6 .... 81 C7
  Stone DE6 .... 120 B8
Sycamores The
  Hagley DY9 .... 281 F5
  Lichfield WS14 .... 231 B5
  Sutton Coldfield B74 .. 257 F2
Sycamore B77 .... 261 E7
Sycamore Way
  Huntington WS12 .... 209 D8
  Market Drayton TF9 .. 97 D2
Sydenham Pl ST2 .... 73 D8
Sydnall La TF9 .... 112 F1
Sydney St
  Burton u T DE14 .... 166 D6
  Stoke-on-T ST4 .... 72 E2
Syerscote La
  Clifton Campville B79 .. 218 B1
  Wigginton B79 .... 234 C2
Sykesmoor B77 .... 262 B7
Sylvan Gr ST4 .... 71 E3
Sylvan Way ST17 .... 175 C5
Sylvester St ST6 .... 57 A8
Sytch La WV5 .... 270 A5
Sytch Rd ST6 .... 43 B7

Talbot Fst Sch ST14 .. 141 C8
Talbot Rd Rugeley WS15 .. 196 F6
  Stafford ST17 .... 285 B1
  Wolverhampton WV2 .... 266 C6
Talbotshill La DY10 .. 280 C4
Talbot St 5 Leek ST13 .. 30 F5
  Hanley ST1 .... 282 C1
  Rugeley WS15 .... 196 F8
Talbot St B77 .... 250 E3
Talbot Way TF9 .... 97 C2
Talke Rd
  Newcastle-u-L,Red Street
  ST7 .... 40 D4
  Newcastle-u-L ST5 .... 55 F8
Talland Ave B77 .... 250 E5
Tall Ash Ave CW12 .. 6 A4
Tallis Gr ST1 .... 57 F5
Tallpines ST17 .... 175 C7
Tall Trees Cl B74 .. 257 D4
Tally Cl ST3 .... 73 D7
Talsarn Gr ST4 .... 88 C6
Tamar Cl WS8 .... 228 C2
Tamar Dr DY3 .... 271 F6
Tamar Gr Cheadle ST10 .. 76 F1
  Perton WV6 .... 254 E4
  Stafford ST17 .... 174 B8
Tamar Rd Kidsgrove ST7 .. 26 B2
  Tamworth B77 .... 262 A5
Tame Ave WS7 .... 229 D6
Tame Cl ST8 .... 16 D1
Tame Ct Fazeley B78 .. 261 B8
  Tamworth B79 .... 250 A5
Tamedrive B78,B79 .. 250 A4
Tame Dr WS3 .... 244 A1
Tame Gr WS11 .... 226 D8
Tame St B77 .... 250 C3
Tame Valley Bsns Pk
  B77 .... 261 E6
Tame Valley Ind Est B77 .. 261 E6
Tame Wlk ST3 .... 74 A4
Tamworth Bsns Ctr B77 .. 251 B3
Tamworth Bsns Pk B77 .. 251 B3
Tamworth Castle Mus*
  B79 .... 250 B4
Tamworth Castle* B79 .. 250 B4
Tamworth Cl WS8 .... 228 F2
Tamworth & Lichfield Coll
  (Tamworth Campus)
  B79 .... 250 B6
Tamworth Rd (Amington)
  B77 .... 250 F5
Tamworth Rd B77 .. 250 F5
Tamworth Rd (Dosthill)
  B77 .... 261 C6
Tamworth Rd Elford B79 .. 233 E8
  Lichfield WS14 .... 231 C5
  Polesworth B78 .... 251 E1
  Sutton Coldfield B75 .. 259 A2
  Tamworth,Mount Pleasant
  B77 .... 250 C1
  Tamworth,Two Gates B77 .. 261 D8
  Whittington WS14 .... 232 B3
  Wood End CV9 .... 262 C1
Tamworth Sta B79 .. 250 C5
Tamworth St WS13 .. 231 B8
Tan Bank TF10 .... 168 F3
Tanfield Cl WV6 .... 255 B3
Tanglewood Gr DY3 .. 266 C2
Tangmere Cl WV6 .. 254 E5
Tanhill B77 .... 262 B7
Tanners Rd ST22 .... 58 B7
Tannery Cl WS15 .... 178 F1
Tansey Cl ST2 .... 58 A3
Tansey Green Rd DY6 .. 271 A1
Tansley View WV2 .. 266 D7
Tansy Sutton Coldfield B74 .. 257 F4
  Tamworth B77 .... 250 C3
Tanyard WS3 .... 231 C8
Tapby St ST10 .... 76 D3
Taplin Cl ST16 .... 155 D7
Taplow Pl WS11 .... 209 E4
Tapper Cl ST3 .... 243 C3
Tara Gr ST2 .... 43 A3
Targate Ct WS15 .... 198 A5
Target Cl ST7 .... 40 E6
Tarleton Rd ST1 .... 57 E4
Tarporley Gr ST4 .... 71 E5
Tarquin Cl DE13 .... 147 E2
Tarragona Dr ST17 .. 175 A8
Tarragon Dr ST3 .... 90 A6
Tarrant B77 .... 261 F8
Tarvin Gr ST6 .... 41 F6
Tasman Dr ST18 .... 156 C5
Tasman Gr WV6 .... 254 E5
Tasman Sq ST1 .... 57 E5
Tatenhill Comm DE13 .. 164 E1
Tatenhill La
  Burton u T DE14 .... 184 D7
  Rangemore DE13 .... 164 C2
  Tatenhill DE13 .... 184 A8
Tatlowfold La ST10 .. 48 F4
Tatton Cl ST13 .... 30 B5
Tatton St ST3 .... 284 C2
Taunton Ave WV10 .. 240 D4
Taunton Pl ST5 .... 55 F7
Taunton Way ST2 .. 58 D2
Taurus Gr ST6 .... 41 F6
Taverners Cl WV12 .. 242 C1
Taverners Dr ST5 .. 120 D6
Tavistock Ave ST17 .. 156 D1
Tavistock Cl B79 .... 250 D4
Tavistock Cres ST5 .. 71 A5
Tavistock Pl ST4 .... 56 B2
Tawney Cl ST7 .... 26 B2
Tawney Dr DY3 .... 266 B2
Tay Cl Biddulph ST8 .. 16 E1
  Cheadle ST10 .... 76 F1
  Longton ST3 .... 284 C5

T

Tack Farm Rd DY8 .. 275 D1
Tadgedale Ave TF9 .. 99 D5
Tagg La DY8 .... 275 C7
Tag La Cheswardine TF9 .. 113 F3
  Chipnall TF9 .... 114 A3
Talaton Cl WV9 .... 240 A2
Talbot Ave B74 .... 257 B3
Talbot Cl TF10 .... 168 D1

Taylor Ave ST5. . . . . .56 C4
Taylor Rd Bucknall ST2 . . . . .58 B6
  Wolverhampton WV4. . . . .266 F5
Taylors La ST14. . . . . .95 D4
Taylor's La WS15. . . . . . .178 E1
Taylor St
  Newcastle-u-L ST5. . . . . . .56 C4
  Stoke-on-T ST6 . . . . .41 C7
Taylor Wlk ST17 . . . . . . .174 C7
Taynton Cl ST6 . . . . .42 B8
Teal Cl ST5. . . . . .85 C5
Teal View ST6 . . . . .42 D2
Tean Cl Burntwood WS7 . . .229 D6
  Burton u T ST15. . . . . . . .167 A1
Teanhurst Cl ST10 . . . . . . .92 F2
Teanhurst Rd ST10. . . . . . .92 F2
Tean Rd ST10. . . . . .76 D1
Teasel Gr WV10 . . . . .241 B7
Tebworth Cl WV9 . . . . . . .239 F2
Tedder Rd ST16. . . . . . . .156 B5
Teddesley Ct WS11. . . . . .209 E3
Teddesley Rd
  Acton Trussell ST19 . . . . .193 B6
  Penkridge ST19 . . . . .192 F2
Tellwright Gr ST5. . . . . . . .175 D1
Teddesley Way WS12. . . . .209 C6
Teign B77 . . . . .262 A5
Telegraph St ST17 . . . . . .285 B1
Telford Ave
  Albrighton WV7 . . . . .237 B6
  Great Wyrley WS6 . . . . . .226 F3
Telford Cl
  Burntwood WS7 . . . . .229 C8
  Congleton CW12 . . . . .6 B2
  Stone ST15 . . . . .120 C6
  Talke ST7 . . . . .40 E8
Telford Dr ST16. . . . . . . .155 F8
Telford Gdns
  Brewood ST19 . . . . .223 C7
  Wolverhampton WV3 . . . .265 D7
Telford Gr WS12 . . . . . . .210 B7
Telford La ST20. . . . . . . .171 C5
Telford Rd B79 . . . . .249 F8
Telford Way ST6 . . . . .42 A4
Tellwright Gr ST5. . . . . . . .56 B7
Tellwright St ST6 . . . . .42 A1
Telmah Cl DE13. . . . . . . .147 D1
Teme Rd DY8. . . . . .279 F3
Temperance Pl ST6 . . . . . .41 D7
Tempest St B79. . . . . . . .250 A5
Templar Cres ST5. . . . . . . .56 B6
Templars Way ST19 . . . . .207 F8
Templar Terr ST5 . . . . .56 B6
Temple Cl DE14 . . . . .166 E7
Temple St Dudley DY3. . . .271 D3
  Stoke-on-T ST4 . . . . .72 D6
Templeton Ave ST2 . . . . . .73 C8
Tenacre La DY3 . . . . .271 E6
Tenbury Cl WS9. . . . . . . .256 C8
Tenbury Ct WV4 . . . . . . .265 D5
Tenbury Gdns WV4. . . . . .265 D5
Tenbury Gn ST2 . . . . .58 C1
Ten Butts Cres ST17 . . . . .174 F5
Tenby Dr ST11. . . . . .155 F6
Tenby Gr ST5. . . . . .55 F7
Tenford La ST10 . . . . .92 E5
Tennant Pl ST5 . . . . .56 B7
Tennscore Ave WS6. . . . . .226 E3
Tennyson Ave
  Burntwood WS7 . . . . .212 A1
  Kidsgrove ST7 . . . . .41 A8
  Sutton Coldfield B74. . . . .257 F6
  Tamworth B79 . . . . .250 A6
Tennyson Cl Cheadle ST10. .76 B2
  Market Drayton TF9. . . . . .112 A7
Tennyson Gdns ST3 . . . . . .72 F2
Tennyson Rd
  Burton u T DE14. . . . . . . .166 D7
  Dudley DY3 . . . . .271 A4
  Stafford ST17 . . . . .174 C8
Tenterbanks ST16. . . . . . .285 A3
Tercel Gr ST3. . . . . .90 A7
Terence Wlk ST8 . . . . .27 B2
Tern Ave ST7 . . . . .26 C2
Tern Cl Biddulph ST8 . . . . .27 E8
  Wolverhampton WV4 . . . .266 D3
Tern Gr TF9 . . . . .99 E5
Tern Ridge TF9 . . . . .97 D1
Tern View TF9 . . . . .97 C2
Terrace The Cheadle ST10 . .76 D3
  Wolverhampton WV3 . . . .255 C1
Terrington Dr ST4 . . . . .71 B2
Terry Cl Lichfield WS13 . . .213 F2
  Meir ST3 . . . . .74 B3
Terson Way ST3 . . . . .73 F4
Tettenhall Ave WV6 . . . . .255 D5
Tettenhall Coll WV6 . . . . .255 D4
Tettenhall Rd WV1,WV3,
  WV6. . . . . .255 F4
Tettenhall Wood Sch
  WV6. . . . . .255 B3
Teveray Dr ST19 . . . . . . .207 F7
Teviot Gdns WV8. . . . . . .239 A5
Tewe Pl WS13 . . . . .231 A6
Tewkesbury Ct ST2 . . . . . .58 A4
Tewkesbury Rd WS3 . . . . .242 E2
Tewnals La WS13 . . . . . . .213 E5
Tewson Gn ST6 . . . . .57 C7
Thackeray Dr Longton ST3. .73 A2
  Tamworth B79 . . . . .250 A7
Thackeray Wlk ST17 . . . . .174 C7
Thames Dr Biddulph ST8 . . .27 E8
  Cheadle ST10. . . . . .76 B1
Thames Ho DY3 . . . . .271 D3
Thames Rd
  Newcastle-u-L ST5. . . . . . .71 B4
  Walsall WS3 . . . . .243 E1

Thames Way ST17 . . . . . .174 B8
Thanet Cl DY6 . . . . .275 C7
Thanet Gr ST3. . . . . .284 A3
Thatcham Gn ST3. . . . . . . .88 F7
Thatcher Gr ST8 . . . . .27 B8
Thatchers Ct WV5 . . . . . .264 C1
Thatchmoor La DE13. . . . .182 C7
Thelma Ave ST4 . . . . .43 B7
Theodore Rd ST2 . . . . .58 B3
Theresa Cl ST14 . . . . .72 A2
Third Ave Branston DE14 . .165 F1
  Brownhills WS8 . . . . .229 A1
  Bucknall ST2 . . . . .58 D4
  Kidsgrove ST7 . . . . .25 F1
  Kingswinford DY6 . . . . . .275 F8
Thirlmere Cl
  Cannock WS11. . . . . .209 E1
  Wolverhampton WV6. . . . .255 D8
Thirlmere Dr WV11 . . . . . .242 A2
Thirlmere Gr Longton ST3 . .73 E3
  Perton WV6 . . . . .254 F4
Thirlmere Pl ST5 . . . . .71 B5
Thirlmere Rd WV6 . . . . . .255 D8
Thirlmere Way ST17 . . . . .174 E7
Thirsk Pl ST5. . . . . .56 B8
Thistleberry Ave ST5 . . . . .70 F7
Thistle Cl Dudley DY3 . . . .271 F6
  Rugeley WS15 . . . . .178 C2
Thistledown Ave WS7 . . . .229 A6
Thistle Down Cl B74 . . . . .257 A2
Thistledown Dr
  3 Cannock WS12 . . . . . . .210 D1
  Featherstone WV10 . . . . .241 A7
Thistledown Wlk DY3 . . . .266 C1
Thistles The ST5 . . . . .70 F7
Thistley Hough High Sch
  ST4. . . . . .71 E6
Thistley Hough ST4 . . . . . .71 F6
Thistley Nook WS13 . . . . .214 A1
Thomas Alleyne's High Sch
  ST14. . . . . .126 C8
Thomas Ave
  Newcastle-u-L ST5. . . . . . .56 A4
  Stafford ST16 . . . . .155 B3
  Stone ST15 . . . . .120 C6
Thomas Barnes Prim Sch
  B78. . . . . .249 B7
Thomas Greenway
  WS13 . . . . .214 A2
Thomas Hardy Ct B79. . . .250 A7
Thomas Ho WS3 . . . . . . .243 D3
Thomas Russell Inf Sch
  DE13 . . . . .183 E1
Thomas Russell Jun Sch
  DE13 . . . . .183 E1
Thomas St Biddulph ST8. . .16 D1
  Leek ST13 . . . . .30 D6
  Packmoor ST7 . . . . .26 F1
  Talke ST7 . . . . .40 D8
  Tamworth B77 . . . . .250 D4
  Wolverhampton WV2 . . . .266 C8
Thompson Ave WV2. . . . . .266 E6
Thompson Cl ST17 . . . . . . .73 C6
Thompson Rd WS15. . . . .197 B6
Thompstone Ave ST5 . . . . .55 F3
Thor Cl WS11 . . . . .210 A5
Thoresby Croft DY1 . . . . .271 F3
Thoresby B79. . . . . .249 E6
Thorley Dr ST10 . . . . .76 F2
Thorley's Hill WS15 . . . . .212 C6
Thornbridge Gr WS9. . . . .244 F3
Thornburrow Dr ST4 . . . . .71 E8
Thornbury Ct WV6 . . . . . .255 A3
Thornby Ave B77 . . . . . . .261 E8
Thorncliffe View WS13. . . .31 B8
Thorncliff Gr ST11 . . . . . . .57 F5
Thorncliff Rd WS13. . . . . .31 C7
Thorn Cl WS15. . . . . .197 A7
Thorndyke St ST1. . . . . . .282 A1
Thorne Pl ST3 . . . . .74 B3
Thornescroft Gdns DE14 .185 B8
Thornes Croft WS9 . . . . . .245 E4
Thornewill Dr DE13 . . . . .147 F1
Thorneycroft Ave ST6 . . . . .42 B2
Thorneyfields La
  Stafford ST17 . . . . .174 A8
  Stafford ST17 . . . . .174 B7
Thorney Lanes
  Gorsty Hill DE13 . . . . . . .143 B2
  Newborough DE13. . . . . .162 D6
Thorney Rd B74. . . . . . . .256 F1
Thornfield Ave ST13 . . . . .31 B5
Thornfield Cres WS3 . . . . .229 A8
Thornfield Croft DY3. . . . .271 E7
Thornham Cl ST5. . . . . . . .71 B2
Thornham Gn ST2 . . . . . . .58 C1
Thornhill Cl DE13 . . . . . .183 C2
Thornhill Dr CW3 . . . . . . .68 E7
Thornhill Rd Bucknall ST2 . .73 E8
  Cannock WS12. . . . . . . .209 F7
  Leek ST13 . . . . .30 C4
  Little Aston B74 . . . . .257 B1
Thornleigh DY3. . . . . . . .271 D5
Thornley Cl WV11. . . . . . .241 F1
Thornley Croft WS6. . . . . .226 D1
Thornley Rd
  Stoke-on-T ST6 . . . . .42 A3
  Wolverhampton WV11. . . .241 F1
Thornley St ST14 . . . . . . .166 D5
Thornton Rd ST4 . . . . .72 C8
Thornton Way ST7 . . . . . .261 C8
Thorn Tree La DE11. . . . . .186 F8
Thornyedge Rd
  Bagnall ST9. . . . . .44 A1
  Bagnall,Tompkin ST9 . . . .44 C1
Thornyhurst La WS14 . . . .246 A6
Thorny Rd ST15. . . . . . . .118 B6
Thorpe Ave WS7 . . . . . . .228 D8

Thorpe Cl
  Burntwood WS7 . . . . .228 D8
  Burton u T DE15. . . . . . . .167 C2
Thorpe Dr WS13 . . . . . . .215 E8
Thorpe Gn ST3 . . . . .88 F7
Thorpe Rise ST10. . . . . . . .76 E6
Three Mile La ST5 . . . . . . .69 F4
Three Spires Sh Ctr
  WS13 . . . . .231 B7
Three Tuns La WV10 . . . . .240 D1
Three Tuns Par WV10 . . . .240 C2
Thrift Rd DE14. . . . . .185 B8
Thurlstone Dr WV4 . . . . . .265 F4
Thurlstone Rd WS3 . . . . . .243 B3
Thurlwood Dr ST6 . . . . . . .42 F2
Thurne B77 . . . . .261 F8
Thursfield Ave ST7. . . . . . .26 C3
Thursfield Pl ST6 . . . . .42 D4
Thursfield Prim Sch ST7 . .26 E3
Thursfield Wlk ST6 . . . . . . .42 D5
Thurso B77. . . . . .250 E5
Thurston Way ST2 . . . . . . .73 C8
Thurvaston Rd DE6 . . . . . .96 F1
Thyme Gr ST3 . . . . .90 B6
Tibberton Cl WV3. . . . . . .265 D7
Tibb St ST7. . . . . .39 F2
Tiber Dr ST5 . . . . .55 D5
Tickhill La ST10,ST11. . . . .74 F5
Tidebrook Pl ST6 . . . . .41 E7
Tideswell Gn DE11. . . . . .186 E5
Tideswell Rd ST3 . . . . . . .284 C5
Tierney St ST11. . . . . . . .282 C4
Tiffany La WV9 . . . . .239 F2
Tilbrook Cl ST2 . . . . .73 C8
Tilbury Cl WV3 . . . . .265 A8
Tilcon Ave ST18 . . . . . . .156 D2
Tildesley Cl ST19 . . . . . .207 E8
Tildesley Ct ST19 . . . . . .207 E8
Tilehurst Pl ST3 . . . . .72 E1
Tilery La ST3 . . . . .88 D8
Tilewright Cl ST7 . . . . .26 B2
Tilia Rd B77 . . . . .251 B5
Tiller Gr B75 . . . . .258 D8
Tillett Gn ST3 . . . . .74 B3
Tilling Dr ST15 . . . . .120 A6
Tillington Manor Prim Sch
  ST16. . . . . .155 C6
Tillington St ST16. . . . . . .155 D5
Till Wlk ST3 . . . . .73 D6
Tilson Ave ST4. . . . . .71 F7
Tilstone Cl ST17 . . . . .41 A8
Timberfields Rd ST16 . . . .155 C4
Timberfields ST15 . . . . . .118 E6
Timber Gr ST19. . . . . . . .223 D6
Timber La ST14. . . . . . . .126 B6
Timber Pit La ST19 . . . . .205 B4
Timble Cl ST2 . . . . .73 C8
Times Sq ST3 . . . . .284 B4
Timmis St ST1 . . . . .57 A3
Timor Gr ST4. . . . . .88 A8
Timothy Cl ST3 . . . . .73 C6
Tinacre Hill WV6. . . . . . . .254 E2
Tinker's Castle Rd WV5 . .263 D1
Tinkers Green Rd B77. . . .261 F6
Tinkers La Ashley TF9 . . . .100 A4
Tinsley St WS10 . . . . .219 E3
Tinsell Brook DE65 . . . . . .147 E8
Tintagel Cl Perton WV6 . . .254 F3
  Stretton DE13 . . . . .147 E2
Tintagel Dr DY1 . . . . .271 E2
Tintagel Pl ST2 . . . . .73 D8
Tintern Cres WS3 . . . . . . .242 F2
Tintern Ct WV6 . . . . .254 E4
Tintern Pl ST5. . . . . .55 F7
Tintern St ST1. . . . . .57 E3
Tintern Way WS3 . . . . . . .242 F2
Tipping Ave ST3 . . . . .78 F1
Tipping St ST16. . . . . . . .285 B3
Tipton Rd DY3 . . . . .271 F7
Tipton St DY3 . . . . .271 E7
Tirley St ST4 . . . . .72 E5
Tissington Pl ST3 . . . . . . .90 C7
Titan Way WS13 . . . . . . .231 F8
Titchfield Cl WV10 . . . . . .240 E4
Tithe Barn Cl ST16. . . . . .156 A4
Tithe Barn La WS13,
  WS15. . . . . .212 C5
Tithebarn Rd WS15. . . . . .178 E2
Tithe Barn Rd ST16. . . . . .156 A4
Tittensor CE Fst Sch ST12 .88 A1
Tittensor Rd
  Barlaston ST12 . . . . .104 B8
  Newcastle-u-L ST5. . . . . . .71 C5
Titterton La ST13 . . . . . . .33 B4
Titterton St ST4 . . . . .72 C6
Tittesworth Ave ST13 . . . .31 A7
Tittesworth Est ST13. . . . .20 E4
Tiverton Ave ST17 . . . . . .175 D8
Tiverton Cl WS11 . . . . . . .210 B3
Tiverton Rd ST2 . . . . .73 C8
Tixall Cl ST18. . . . . .157 E3
Tixall Mews ST18 . . . . . . .157 D3
Tixall Rd Stafford ST18. . . .156 D3
  Tixall ST18. . . . . .157 B2
Toby's Hill DE6 . . . . .144 C7
Toft End Rd ST5. . . . . .41 B1
Tolkien Way ST4 . . . . .72 A8
Toll Bar Rd ST9. . . . . .59 D4
Tolldish La ST18. . . . . . . .158 C4
Tollgate Ave ST5 . . . . .85 D5
Tollgate Cl ST7 . . . . .40 C8
Tollgate Cotts DE6. . . . . . .81 E8
Tollgate Dr ST16. . . . . . . .155 F8
Tollgate Ind Est ST16 . . . .155 F8
Tollgate La B79. . . . . .233 E4

Tollgate Rd ST13. . . . . . . .29 C6
Tollhouse Way WV5 . . . . .269 E7
Tolman Dr B77 . . . . .250 D3
Tolson Ave B78 . . . . .261 B8
Tolson Cl B77 . . . . .261 D5
Tolworth Gdns WV2. . . . . .266 E7
Tom Fields ST7 . . . . .39 F1
Tomkinson Cl TF10. . . . . .169 A4
Tom La DY7 . . . . .268 E5
Tomlinson Bsns Pk DE65 .129 F4
Tomlinson St ST6 . . . . .56 D8
Tommy's La CW12 . . . . . . .6 A4
Tompkin Rd ST9 . . . . .44 B4
Tom Williams Way B77. . .261 C8
Tonadine Cl WV11. . . . . . .242 A1
Tonbridge Ave ST6. . . . . . .42 B4
Toney Pl ST2 . . . . .57 F7
Tong Cl ST19 . . . . .221 E8
Tong Dr TF11 . . . . .203 F1
Tong Rd ST19. . . . . .221 F7
Tongue Ave B78 . . . . . . .261 A8
Tongue La ST6. . . . . .27 F1
Tontine Sq ST1 . . . . .282 B3
Tontines Sh Ctr The ST1. .282 B3
Tontine St ST1. . . . . .282 B3
Tony Waddington Pl ST4 .72 D4
Toothill Rd ST14 . . . . . . .126 C4
Top Chapel La ST6. . . . . . .28 B1
Topham Pl ST2 . . . . .57 F3
Top Heath Row ST6. . . . . .43 B8
Top La Beech ST4. . . . . . .103 C8
  Beech ST4 . . . . .87 C1
Top Rd
  Acton Trussell ST17 . . . . .175 B1
  Biddulph ST8 . . . . .17 D3
Top Station Rd ST19 . . . . .26 D7
Topsey Cl ST4 . . . . .284 C4
Torbay B77 . . . . .250 E5
Torc Ave B77 . . . . .250 E4
Torc High Sch B77. . . . . .250 F1
Torfield WV8 . . . . .239 E2
Torrance Cl DE14 . . . . . .185 A6
Torrance Gr ST14 . . . . . . .110 F2
Torres Wlk ST1. . . . . .57 E5
Torridge Dr ST17 . . . . . . .174 B8
Torridge B77 . . . . .262 A5
Torridon Cl ST4. . . . . .88 C6
Torridon Rd WV11 . . . . . .242 B1
Torrington Ave ST17 . . . . .175 E8
Torside B77 . . . . .262 B7
Tor St ST1. . . . . .57 D7
Torvale Rd WV6. . . . . . . .255 A2
Torville Dr ST8 . . . . .27 E8
Tor Way WS3 . . . . .243 F3
Totness Cl DE13 . . . . . . .166 D7
Tower Bsns Pk WS15. . . . .197 B5
Tower Cl Biddulph ST8 . . . .27 B6
  Market Drayton TF9. . . . . .97 B1
Tower Crane Dr ST10 . . . . .76 B1
Tower Hill Rd
  Biddulph ST8 . . . . .27 A6
  Mow Cop ST7 . . . . .26 F7
Tower Rd Burton u T DE15 .167 B2
  Stoke-on-T ST4 . . . . .194 F1
  Loggerheads TF9 . . . . . . .99 F4
  Sutton Coldfield B75 . . . .258 B3
Tower Sq ST6 . . . . .41 D3
Tower St DY3 . . . . .266 D1
Tower View Prim Sch
  DE15 . . . . .167 C3
Tower View Rd WS6. . . . . .242 F8
Town End ST10 . . . . .76 C3
Townend ST11. . . . . .106 E8
Townend La Swinscoe DE6. .65 E5
  Waterhouses ST10 . . . . . .48 F4
Townfield Cl ST7 . . . . .25 D2
Townfields WS13. . . . . . .231 A7
Townfold WS3 . . . . .244 A4
Town Head ST10. . . . . . . .78 F1
Town Head Farm ST10 . . . .78 F1
Town Hill DE13 . . . . .182 B2
Town Meadows Way
  ST14. . . . . .126 C8
Town Rd ST1. . . . . .282 B4
Townsend Ave DY3. . . . . .271 D8
Townsend Cl B79 . . . . . . .236 D4
Townsend Ho B79 . . . . . .250 A4
Townsend La ST17. . . . . . .25 A8
Townsend Pl Bucknall ST2 .58 B3
  Kingswinford DY6 . . . . . .275 D6
Town Wells Mews ST10. . .168 E6
Town Yard Ind Est ST13 . . .30 D5
Toy Cl WS15 . . . . .178 D1
Trade St ST14 . . . . .72 B7
Trafalgar Cl WS12. . . . . . .210 E4
Trafalgar Ct 6 ST6 . . . . . .57 A7
Trafalgar Ho WS12. . . . . .210 E4
Trafalgar Rd ST4. . . . . . . .71 E8
Trafalgar St ST1 . . . . .282 B4
Tramway The DE11 . . . . .186 F7
Transport La ST3 . . . . . . .284 B3
Tranter Cres WS11 . . . . . .210 B3
Tranter Rd ST2 . . . . .58 B6
Tranwell Cl WV9 . . . . . . .239 F2
Travellers Cl WS7 . . . . . . .229 A5
Travers Ct ST4. . . . . .72 D6
Travers St ST6 . . . . .56 E7
Treacastle Cl B77 . . . . . . .250 E4
Trecastle Gr ST3 . . . . .73 E1
Treetops 7 ST17 . . . . . . .175 C7
Tree Tops WV5. . . . . .269 E8
Trefoil Cl ST7 . . . . .251 B5
Tregaron Ct ST2 . . . . .59 A3
Tregenna Cl 8 ST3 . . . . . .90 A7
Tregew Pl ST5. . . . . .55 D2
Tregony Rise WS14 . . . . .231 D6
Tregowan Cl ST6 . . . . .42 B3
Trenance Cl WS14 . . . . . .231 D7

Trenchard Ave ST16. . . . .156 A5
Trent Bridge Cl ST4. . . . . .88 D7
Trent Bridge Ho DE14. . . .166 F3
Trent Cl Burntwood WS7 . .229 D6
  Cheadle ST10. . . . . .76 E1
  Great Haywood ST18. . . . .158 B2
  Perton WV6 . . . . .254 E4
  Stafford ST17 . . . . .174 F6
  Stone ST15 . . . . .119 F8
Trent Ct ST15. . . . . .119 F8
Trentfield La ST18 . . . . . .137 D5
Trentfields Rd ST2 . . . . . . .43 B2
Trent Gr Biddulph ST8 . . . .27 D6
  Newcastle-u-L ST5. . . . . . .71 A3
Trentham Bsns Ctr ST4. . . .88 D7
Trentham Cl WS11 . . . . . .210 B1
Trentham Ct ST4. . . . . . . .87 E7
Trentham Gardens Sch ST4 .87 F7
Trentham Gdns* ST4 . . . .87 F6
Trentham Gr ST5 . . . . .56 C4
Trentham High Sch ST4 . .87 F8
Trentham Rd
  Hanchurch ST5. . . . . .86 E8
  Newcastle-u-L ST5. . . . . . .71 A1
  Stoke-on-T ST4,ST3 . . . . .88 E7
Trentham Rise WV2 . . . . .266 F7
Trent Ho Cannock WS12 . .210 C5
  Dudley DY3 . . . . .271 E3
Trent Ind Est DE14 . . . . . .166 E4
Trent La
  Great Haywood ST18. . . . .158 B2
  Hixon ST18 . . . . .157 E8
  Newton Solney DE15 . . . .167 D8
Trentley Dr ST8. . . . . .28 B8
Trentley Rd ST4. . . . . .88 A7
Trentmill Rd ST1. . . . . . . .57 E2
Trent Rd
  Blythe Bridge ST11 . . . . . .91 A7
  Cannock WS11. . . . . . . .209 E5
  Stone ST15 . . . . .104 E1
  Walsall WS3 . . . . .244 A1
Trentside Rd ST6 . . . . .43 A5
Trent St Bucknall ST2 . . . . .57 F3
  Burton u T DE14. . . . . . . .166 C1
Trent Terr
  Burton u T DE14. . . . . . . .166 C1
  Stoke-on-T ST6 . . . . .43 A5
Trent Vale CE Prim Sch
  ST4. . . . . .71 E3
Trent Valley Cotts WS13 . .214 F1
Trent Valley Rd
  Lichfield WS13,WS14. . . . .231 D8
  Stoke-on-T ST4 . . . . .71 F5
Trent Valley Trad Est
  WS15 . . . . .178 F2
Trent View Cl WS15 . . . . .197 A7
Trentway Cl ST2 . . . . .58 A3
Trent Wlk Hanley ST1. . . .282 C1
  Ingestre ST18 . . . . .137 F7
Tresham Rd 2 DY6 . . . . .275 D8
Trevelyan's Gn ST16 . . . . .155 C8
Trevelyn Cl DE15. . . . . . .167 C2
Trevithick Cl Bucknall ST2 .73 D7
  Burntwood WS7. . . . . . . .229 C8
Trevor Ave ST4. . . . . .227 A3
Trevor Dr ST11 . . . . .74 D3
Trevor Rd WS3. . . . . .243 F5
Trevose Ct WS3. . . . . .242 F3
Trimley Way ST2. . . . . . . .58 B2
Trimpley Gdns WV4 . . . . .265 E3
Trimpos ST10. . . . . .76 A4
Triner Pl ST4. . . . . .42 E4
Tring Cl ST2. . . . . .73 C8
Tring Ct WV6 . . . . .255 F4
Trinity Cl Cannock WS11. .226 E8
  Shenstone WS14 . . . . . . .246 F6
  Stourbridge DY8 . . . . . . .275 D2
Trinity Ct Congleton CW12. .6 B1
  Newcastle-u-L ST5. . . . . . .55 E7
  Tamworth B79 . . . . .249 D6
Trinity Gorse ST16 . . . . . .155 B8
Trinity Pl Bucknall ST2. . . .58 B4
  Congleton CW12 . . . . .16 B8
Trinity Rd Ecclesshall ST21. .133 D5
  Sutton Coldfield B75 . . . .258 C1
  Uttoxeter ST14 . . . . .126 C7
  Wood End B78,CV9 . . . . .262 B3
Trinity Rise ST16. . . . . . . .155 B8
Trinity St ST1 . . . . .282 B3
Trinity Wlk ST14 . . . . . . .126 C7
Tristram Gr DE13 . . . . . . .147 E2
Triton Cl WS6. . . . . .226 F1
Triton Wlk ST6 . . . . .42 D2
Triumph B77 . . . . .250 E3
Trojan B77 . . . . .250 E3
Troon Cl Stretton DE13. . .147 C1
  Walsall WS3 . . . . .243 A3
Troon Gr WS6. . . . . .254 D5
Troon Pl DY8 . . . . .275 D3
Troon B77 . . . . .251 C4
Troutdale Cl ST4. . . . . .73 B6
Trowbridge Cres ST2 . . . . .58 D8
Trubshaw Cl ST18. . . . . . .177 E8
Trubshaw Cross ST6 . . . . .56 D8
Trubshaw St ST6 . . . . .56 D8
Trubshawe Pl ST4 . . . . . . .72 B8
Trubshaw Pl ST5 . . . . .55 F6
Truro Cl Congleton CW12 . .15 E8
  Lichfield WS13 . . . . .214 B3
  Rugeley WS15 . . . . .196 D6
Truro Pl Bucknall ST2 . . . . .58 B2
  Cannock WS12. . . . . . . .227 C8

Truro Way ST17 . . . . 156 D1
Trussel Grange ST17 . . . 175 B1
Trussell CI ST17 . . . . 175 A1
Trustley CI DE14 . . . . 185 B7
Trysull Gdns WV3 . . . . . . 265 D7
Trysull Holloway WV5 . . 264 C3
Trysull Rd Orton WV5 . . . 264 E1
 Wolverhampton WV3 . . . 265 D7
 Wombourne WV5 . . . . . . 269 E8
Tuckers PI TF10 . . . . 168 E3
Tudor CI Burntwood WS7 229 C6
 Cheslyn Hay WS6 . . . . . . 226 E3
 Lichfield WS14 . . . . 231 F6
 Market Drayton TF9 . . . . . 97 B2
 Newport TF10 . . . . 169 A4
 Stoke-on-T ST4 . . . . 72 A6
 Stone ST15 . . . . 119 F6
Tudor Cres Tamworth B77 250 F4
 Wolverhampton WV2 . . . 266 B6
Tudor Ct Essington WV11 . 241 H4
 Fulford ST11 . . . . 90 E1
 Newcastle-u-L ST5 . . . . . . 56 B6
 Sutton Coldfield B74 . . . 258 A2
Tudor Gdns DY8 . . . . 279 E5
Tudor Gr ST5 . . . . 56 C4
Tudor Hollow
 2 Burton u T DE13 . . . . . . 166 D8
 Fulford ST11 . . . . 90 E1
Tudor Park Ct B74 . . . . . . 257 F3
Tudor Park Gdns WS7 . . . 229 C6
Tudor PI DY3 . . . . 271 E6
Tudor Rd Burntwood WS7 229 C6
 Cannock WS12 . . . . 209 F8
 Dudley DY3 . . . . 271 E6
Tudor Rise
 Clifton Campville B79 . . . 218 E2
 Stafford ST16 . . . . 155 C8
Tudor Rose Ct ST6 . . . . . . 42 E2
Tudor Rose WV6 . . . . 42 E2
Tudor Row 8 WS13 . . . . . 231 B7
Tudors The ST6 . . . . 41 E4
Tudor Vale DY3 . . . . 271 E6
Tudor Way
 Cheslyn Hay WS6 . . . . . . 226 D1
 Stafford ST17 . . . . 155 B1
Tuke PI WS13 . . . . 213 F1
Tulip Gr ST5 . . . . 283 C4
Tulley PI ST2 . . . . 58 A1
Tullis CI ST16 . . . . 155 C2
Tulsa CI ST2 . . . . 58 A1
Tunbridge Dr ST5 . . . . 54 F2
Tunley St ST15 . . . . 104 F1
Tunnicliffe CI ST3 . . . . 73 E3
Tunnicliffe St WS11 . . . . 178 D1
Tunnicliffe Way ST14 . . . 110 F2
Tunstall La ST20 . . . . 131 F2
Tunstall Rd Biddulph ST8 . 27 C5
 Bosley CW12,SK11 . . . . . . 7 C7
 Congleton CW12 . . . . 6 F2
Tunstall Road Ind Est 8 27 B4
Tuppenhurst La WS15 . . . 198 D3
Turf CI WS11 . . . . 228 A4
Turf Cotts WV4 . . . . 265 F2
Turf Pitts La B75 . . . . 258 F4
Turin CI ST3 . . . . 73 F4
Turn Dr ST5 . . . . 70 E6
Turls Hill Rd Sedgley DY3 271 E8
 Sedgley WV14 . . . . 271 F8
Turls St DY3 . . . . 271 E8
Turnberry Dr ST4 . . . . 88 A8
Turnberry Gr WV6 . . . . . . 254 D5
Turnberry Rd WS3 . . . . . . 243 A4
Turnberry B77 . . . . 251 C5
Turnbull Rd WS13 . . . . . . 215 C6
Turnbury CI DE14 . . . . . . 185 A7
Turner Ave Audley ST7 . . . 40 A1
 Wolverhampton WV4,
 WV14 . . . . 266 F2
Turner CI WS11 . . . . 210 D2
Turner Cres ST5 . . . . 55 E6
Turner Croft WS13 . . . . . 215 D8
Turner Gr WV6 . . . . 255 A4
Turner's Gr DY3 . . . . 271 C4
Turner's Hill Rd DY3 . . . . 271 C4
Turners La TF10 . . . . 168 A3
Turner St
 Dudley,Gornalwood DY3 . 271 D3
 Hanley ST1 . . . . 57 E5
Turney Gr ST17 . . . . 174 C8
Turney Rd DY8 . . . . 279 F6
Turnham Gn WV6 . . . . . . 254 E3
Turnhill CI ST18 . . . . 174 C6
Turnhill Gr ST5 . . . . 56 B7
Turnhurst Rd ST7 . . . . 41 F7
Turnlea CI ST18 . . . . 27 B6
Turnock St ST2 . . . . 58 C4
Turnpike Way WV9 . . . . . 224 C1
Turnstone Dr WV10 . . . . . 241 B7
Turquoise Gr ST1 . . . . . . 210 C3
Turton CI Alrewas DE13 . . 201 A2
 Walsall WS3 . . . . 243 A4
Tuscan CI ST10 . . . . 76 D1
Tuscan Ho ST3 . . . . 284 B2
Tuscan St ST3 . . . . 284 C4
Tuscan Way ST5 . . . . 55 D6
Tutbury Ave WV6 . . . . . . 255 A3
Tutbury Castle* DE13 . . . 146 B7
Tutbury CI WS11 . . . . 210 C3
Tutbury Gr ST3 . . . . 73 D4
Tutbury & Hatton Sta
 DE65 . . . . 146 D8
Tutbury Rd
 Burton u T DE13 . . . . . . 166 B8
 Stretton DE13 . . . . 147 A1
Tutbury B77 . . . . 261 C7

Tutehill WS13 . . . . 262 B7
Twayblade DE14 . . . . 185 B8
Tweed Gr ST5 . . . . 71 A4
Tweed St ST4 . . . . 72 E4
Twemlow CI ST18 . . . . . . 154 D2
Twemlow St ST1 . . . . 57 A3
Twentylands DE13 . . . . . 147 D4
Twickenham Ct DY8 . . . . 279 C7
Twigg St ST2 . . . . 58 B2
Twizles La B79 . . . . 218 A1
Two Gates Com Prim Sch
 Tamworth B77 . . . . 261 C8
 Tamworth,Mount Pleasant
 B77 . . . . 250 C1
Two Gates Ind Est B77 . . 261 D7
Two Oaks Ave WS7 . . . . . 228 D8
Two Trees CI B78 . . . . . . 249 B6
Twyford CI Aldridge WS9 . 256 B5
 Swadlincote DE11 . . . . . 186 F2
Twyning Gn ST3 . . . . 88 F7
Tylecote Cres ST18 . . . . . 158 B2
Tyler Gr 5 Burslem ST6 . . 56 E8
 Stone ST15 . . . . 119 C7
Tyndall PI ST14 . . . . 71 E7
Tyne CI WS8 . . . . 228 C2
Tynedale Cres WV4 . . . . . 266 E3
Tyneham Gr ST2 . . . . 43 A2
Tyne Way ST5 . . . . 71 B4
Tyning CI WV9 . . . . 240 A2
Tyninghame Ave WV6 . . . 255 D7
Tynings La WS9 . . . . 256 A5
Tynsel Parkes CE Fst Sch
 ST14 . . . . 110 F1
Tynwald Grange ST15 . . . 56 A3
Tyrell Gr ST1 . . . . 57 F8
Tyria Way 8 ST17 . . . . . . 175 A8
Tyrley CI WV6 . . . . 255 B2
Tyrley Rd TF9 . . . . 112 F5
Tyrol CI DY8 . . . . 279 D6
Tyson CI ST2 . . . . 73 D8
Tythebarn Dr DY6 . . . . . . 275 A7

U

Ubberley Gn ST2 . . . . 58 C2
Ubberley Rd ST2 . . . . 58 C1
Uffington Par ST2 . . . . . . 73 C8
Ufton CI ST3 . . . . 88 F7
Ullswater Ave WV6 . . . . . 56 E7
Ullswater Dr Cheadle ST10 76 F4
 Stone ST15 . . . . 120 D7
Ullswater Gdns DY6 . . . . 275 D6
Ullswater Ho ST17 . . . . . 174 E6
Ullswater PI WS11 . . . . . . 209 E1
Ullswater Rd WV11 . . . . . 242 B1
Ullswater B77 . . . . 262 B7
Ulster Dr Dr DY6 . . . . 275 E4
Ulster Terr ST14 . . . . 12 C3
Ulverston Rd ST3 . . . . 88 F7
Umberleigh Rd ST3 . . . . . 88 F7
Underhill CI TF10 . . . . . . 168 F3
Underhill La WV10 . . . . . 241 A2
Underhill Prim Sch
 WV10 . . . . 241 B1
Underhill Wlk DE14 . . . . 166 D2
Underley CI DY6 . . . . 275 B7
Under Rainow Rd CW12 . . . 6 E1
Under The Hill ST8 . . . . . . 17 A2
Undertown La DE6 . . . . . . 96 D6
Underwood CI ST16 . . . . 155 D8
Underwood Rd ST5 . . . . . . 55 A1
Unicorn Ind Est ST5 . . . . . 56 D8
Unicorn PI ST6 . . . . 41 F5
Union CI ST1 . . . . 282 B4
Union La WV5 . . . . 264 D2
Union St Burntwood WS7 . 228 E5
 Burton u T DE14 . . . . . . 166 D2
 Cannock WS11 . . . . 226 E6
 Hanley ST1 . . . . 282 B4
 Leek ST13 . . . . 30 F6
Unity Ave ST1 . . . . 57 D7
Unity Way ST1 . . . . 40 D8
University Ct ST18 . . . . . 156 C5
University Way CW1 . . . . . 37 A8
Univ of Sheffield SK17 . . . 4 B8
Univ of Wolverhampton
 Compton Park Campus
 WV6 . . . . 255 E2
Unwin Cres DY8 . . . . 279 E5
Unwin St ST6 . . . . 42 B3
Upfield Cotts WS7 . . . . . . 229 E7
Upfield Way WS15 . . . . . 178 C2
Uplands Ave
 Stoke-on-T ST6 . . . . 41 F6
 Werrington ST9 . . . . 59 B3
 Wolverhampton WV3 . . . 265 D8
Uplands CI
 Cannock Wood WS15 . . . 211 F5
 Penkridge ST19 . . . . 192 E2
Uplands Croft ST9 . . . . . . 59 A4
Uplands Dr Sedgley DY3 . 271 D8
 Werrington ST9 . . . . 59 A3
 Wolverhampton WV3 . . . 265 E8
 Wombourne WV5 . . . . . . 270 A6
Uplands Gn WS15 . . . . . . 196 D6
Uplands Jun Sch WV3 . . . 265 D8
Uplands Rd Bucknall SP2 . . 58 B7
 Stafford ST16 . . . . 174 D6
Uplands The Biddulph ST8 . 16 E2
 Great Haywood ST18 . . . 158 B2
 Newcastle-u-L ST5 . . . . . 283 C4
Upneaudowns Dr ST16 . . 155 B1
Upper Ave
 Codsall Wood ST19 . . . . . 222 F2
 Coven WV9 . . . . 223 B3
Upper Bar TF10 . . . . 168 F2

Upper Belgrave Rd ST3 . . 73 D1
Upper Brook St 2 WS15 . 196 E8
Upper Cres ST4 . . . . 71 E8
Upper Cross Rd WS15 . . 196 E7
Upper Cross St ST3 . . . . 284 C4
Upper Furlong St ST4 . . . 72 D6
Upper Gn WV6 . . . . 255 D5
Upper Gungate B79 . . . . 256 B6
Upper Hattons Cotts
 WV9 . . . . 239 D5
Upper Hillchurch St ST2 . 282 C3
Upper Huntbach St ST1 . 282 C3
Upper Keys Bsns Pk
 WS12 . . . . 210 E3
Upper Landywood La
 Cheslyn Hay WS6 . . . . . . 226 D1
 Great Wyrley WS6 . . . . . 242 D8
Upper Lodge Rd WS15 . . 197 F4
Upper Market Sq ST1 . . . 282 B3
Upper Marsh ST5 . . . . 56 D3
Upper Normacot Rd 1
 ST3 . . . . 73 D2
Upper St John St WS14 . . 231 B6
Upper Sneyd Rd WV11 . . 242 B2
Upper St WV6 . . . . 255 D5
Upper Villiers St WV2 . . . 266 C6
Upper Way WS15 . . . . . . 197 B2
Upper Zoar St WV3 . . . . . 266 B8
Upton CI TF9 . . . . 97 D1
Upton PI WS15 . . . . 178 D2
Urmston PI ST3 . . . . 88 F7
Usam Trad Est WV10 . . . 240 D2
Usuiwall CI ST1 . . . . 133 D6
Utterby Side ST2 . . . . 73 C8
Uttoxeter Heritage Ctr*
 ST14 . . . . 126 C7
Uttoxeter Race Course*
 ST14 . . . . 126 E6
Uttoxeter Rd
 Abbots Bromley WS15 . . 160 E6
 Alton ST10 . . . . 94 E8
 Armitage WS15 . . . . 198 C4
 Blithbury WS15 . . . . 180 A5
 Blythe Bridge ST11 . . . . . 90 E7
 Checkley ST10,ST14 . . . 109 D8
 Foston DE65 . . . . 129 E4
 Foston,HM Detention Ctr
 DE65 . . . . 129 C4
 Fradswell ST18 . . . . 123 B6
 Hilderstone ST15 . . . . . . 121 D7
 Hill Ridware WS15 . . . . . 198 A8
 Longton ST3 . . . . 284 C3
 Meir ST3 . . . . 74 A1
 Milwich ST18 . . . . 122 D5
 Scropton DE65 . . . . 129 F3
 Stone ST15 . . . . 120 E7
Uttoxeter Sta ST14 . . . . . 126 D7
Uxbridge CI DY3 . . . . 271 D2
Uxbridge Ct
 Burntwood WS7 . . . . 228 F5
 Cannock WS12 . . . . 210 C5
Uxbridge St
 Burton u T DE14 . . . . . . 166 C1
 Cannock WS12 . . . . 210 C4

V

Vale Ave Aldridge WS9 . . 256 D3
 Dudley DY3 . . . . 271 D6
Vale CI WS13 . . . . 214 B1
Vale Gdns ST19 . . . . 207 E8
Vale Head Dr WV6 . . . . . . 255 A2
Valentine Rd ST7 . . . . 26 A1
Vale Park (Port Vale FC)*
 ST6 . . . . 42 A1
Vale Pleasant ST5 . . . . 55 C2
Vale PI ST11 . . . . 282 A4
Valerian B74 . . . . 257 F4
Valerian Way ST3 . . . . 90 A6
Vale Rise ST19 . . . . 207 F8
Vale Row DY3 . . . . 271 D5
Vale St Dudley DY3 . . . . . 271 D5
 Newcastle-u-L,Chesterton
 ST5 . . . . 55 E8
 Newcastle-u-L,Silverdale
 ST5 . . . . 55 B2
 Stoke-on-T ST4 . . . . 72 B7
Vale View Aldridge WS9 . 256 B4
 Cheddleton ST13 . . . . 45 D5
 Newcastle-u-L ST5 . . . . . . 56 D7
Valley Dr ST13 . . . . 30 B5
Valley Gn WS6 . . . . 226 E2
Valley Heritage Ctr*
 WS12 . . . . 210 D6
Valley La Lichfield WS13 . 231 D8
 Tamworth B77 . . . . 261 C7
Valley Park Nature Reserve*
 WV6 . . . . 255 D3
Valley Park Way ST3 . . . . . 72 F3
Valley Prim Sch ST10 . . . . 78 A7
Valley Rd
 Cannock,Hazelslade
 WS12 . . . . 211 A6
 Cannock,Hednesford
 WS12 . . . . 210 D6
 Coldmeece ST15 . . . . . . 118 B7
 Dudley DY3 . . . . 271 E6
 Meir ST3 . . . . 74 B3
 Stone ST15 . . . . 120 B6
 Walsall WS3 . . . . 243 D1
Valley Side WS3 . . . . 243 F2
Valley The WS7 . . . . 228 D8
Valley View
 Brownhills WS8 . . . . 245 A4
 Market Drayton TF9 . . . . 112 A7
Valley View Wlk ST14 . . . 96 A3
Vanbrugh Ct WV6 . . . . . . 254 E3

Vancouver Dr DE15 . . . . . 167 C3
Van Diemans Rd WV5 . . . 269 F5
Van Gogh CI WS11 . . . . . 210 D2
Vanguard B77 . . . . 261 D6
Vanity CI ST15 . . . . 105 C4
Vanity La ST15 . . . . 105 C4
Varden Cres ST5 . . . . 178 E1
Vardon CI ST16 . . . . 156 C3
Vaudrey Cres CW12 . . . . . . 6 A3
Vaughan CI B74 . . . . 257 F6
Vaughan Gdns WV8 . . . . 238 F4
Vaughan's La ST5 . . . . . . 159 C6
Vaughan Way ST17 . . . . . 155 C1
Vauxhall Terr TF10 . . . . . 168 E3
Vauxhall Terr TF10 . . . . . 168 E3
Venice CI ST5 . . . . 70 E7
Venn PI ST1 . . . . 57 E2
Ventnor Gr ST3 . . . . 88 F6
Venton CI ST6 . . . . 42 E4
Ventura Park Rd B78.. . . 249 F3
Ventura Pk Rd B78. . . . . . 250 A3
Ventura Pk B78. . . . . 250 A3
Venture Way ST6 . . . . 42 C2
Vercourt B74 . . . . 257 B3
Verdi CI ST13 . . . . 214 C2
Verdon CI ST19 . . . . 208 A7
Verity Wlk DY8 . . . . 275 E1
Vermont Gn 4 WS11 . . . 210 A3
Verney CI ST14 . . . . 125 C7
Verney Way ST3 . . . . 88 F7
Vernon Ave Audley ST7 . . . 39 D2
 Brownhills WS8 . . . . 245 A8
 Congleton CW12 . . . . 15 F8
Vernon CI Audley ST7 . . . . 39 D2
 Essington WV11 . . . . 241 F4
 Sutton Coldfield B74 . . . 257 E5
Vernon Ho ST14 . . . . 126 C7
Vernon Lodge Prep Sch
 ST19 . . . . 206 C3
Vernon Rd ST4 . . . . 72 B8
Vernons PI WV10 . . . . . . 225 D1
Vernon Terr DE13 . . . . . . 166 C4
Vernon Way WV3 . . . . . . 242 E1
Verona Gr ST3 . . . . 73 E5
Veronica Ave WV4 . . . . . 266 E5
Verulam CI ST16 . . . . 155 E7
Verulam Rd ST16 . . . . . . 155 E7
Verwood CI ST16 . . . . . . 156 C4
Vesey CI B74 . . . . 257 F2
Vessey Terr ST5 . . . . 283 C2
Vestry Ct DY8 . . . . 279 E6
Vicarage Bank ST18. . . . . 138 E6
Vicarage CI
 Brownhills WS8 . . . . 245 A7
 Burton u T DE15 . . . . . . 167 B4
 Dordon B78 . . . . 262 F5
 Eccleshall ST21 . . . . 133 D7
Vicarage Cres
 Caverswall ST11 . . . . 74 D3
 Newcastle-u-L ST5 . . . . . 283 C1
 Tittensor ST12 . . . . 88 A1
 Upper Tean ST10 . . . . 92 E3
Vicarage Croft DE13 . . . . 199 D6
Vicarage Ct
 Burntwood WS7 . . . . 228 F6
 Kinver DY7 . . . . 278 A3
Vicarage Dr Kinver DY7 . . 278 A3
 Stramshall ST14 . . . . . . 110 F4
Vicarage Field DE15 . . . . 166 F1
Vicarage Hill B78 . . . . . . 260 B1
Vicarage La Barlaston ST12 88 F2
 King's Bromley DE13 . . . 199 D6
 Madeley CW3 . . . . 68 E5
 Stoke-on-T ST4 . . . . 71 E4
Vicarage Rd
 Brewood ST19 . . . . 223 D6
 Brownhills WS8 . . . . 245 A7
 Dudley,Woodsetton DY3 . 271 F5
 Four Ashes WV10 . . . . . . 224 F6
 Leek ST13 . . . . 30 F6
 Stoke-on-T ST4 . . . . 71 F8
 Stourbridge DY8 . . . . . . 279 D7
 Upper Tean ST10 . . . . 92 E3
 Walsall WS3 . . . . 244 B2
 Wolverhampton,Blakenhall
 WV2 . . . . 266 D8
 Wolverhampton,Penn WV4 265 E3
Vicarage Row ST10 . . . . . 78 E1
Vicarage Way Hixon ST18 139 C1
 Stafford ST17 . . . . 285 A1
Vicar's CI Lichfield WS13 . 231 A8
 Oulton ST15 . . . . 105 C4
Vicars Croft WS15 . . . . . 178 F2
Vicar St DY3 . . . . 271 D8
Vichy CI ST5 . . . . 70 E7
Vickers Rd ST6 . . . . 42 A5
Victoria Ave
 Halmer End ST7 . . . . 54 E7
 Hanley ST1 . . . . 282 B1
 Kidsgrove ST7 . . . . 25 F2
 Walsall,Wallington Heath
 WS3 . . . . 243 C1
Victoria CI ST5 . . . . 55 C1
Victoria Com Sch DE14.. 166 C4
Victoria Cotts ST14 . . . . . 61 A2
Victoria Cres DE14.. . . . . 166 C5
Victoria Ct
 8 Kidsgrove ST7 . . . . 26 A2
 Biddulph ST8 . . . . 27 B4
 Leek ST13 . . . . 30 D5
 Market Drayton TF9.. . . . 112 B8
 Newcastle-u-L ST5 . . . . . . 56 C3
 Norton Canes WS11 . . . . 228 B5
 Stoke-on-T ST4 . . . . 72 B8
Victoria Dr B78 . . . . 261 A8
Victoria Gdns WS5 . . . . . 230 F6
Victoria Gr WV5 . . . . 270 A8
Victoria Ho 2 ST4 . . . . . . 71 F8

Victoria Hospl WS13 . . . . 231 A6
Victoria Ind Complex
 ST4 . . . . 284 A5
Victoria Mdw DE13 . . . . . 199 D6
Victoria Park Rd ST6. . . . . 41 E4
Victoria Pk TF10 . . . . 168 F3
Victoria PI
 Newcastle-u-L,Chesterton
 ST5 . . . . 55 E7
 Newcastle-u-L,Wolstanton
 ST5 . . . . 56 D5
 Stoke-on-T ST4 . . . . 72 E6
Victoria Rd
 Burton u T DE14 . . . . . . 166 C4
 Market Drayton TF9 . . . . . 97 B1
 Newcastle-u-L ST5 . . . . . 283 C2
 Sedgley DY3 . . . . 271 E8
 Stafford ST16 . . . . 285 A3
 Stoke-on-T ST4 . . . . 72 E4
 Tamworth B79 . . . . 250 C5
 Walsall WS3 . . . . 244 A3
 Wolverhampton,Penn WV3 265 E7
 Wolverhampton,Tettenhall
 WV6 . . . . 255 C5
Victoria Row ST8 . . . . 27 C4
Victoria Sq Hanley ST1.. . 282 A1
Victoria St
 Broomhill WS11 . . . . 209 E4
 Burton u T DE14 . . . . . . 166 C4
 Cannock,Bridgtown WS11 . 226 D8
 Cannock WS12 . . . . 210 C6
 Cheadle ST10 . . . . 76 E3
 Kingswinford DY6 . . . . . 270 B1
 Leek ST13 . . . . 31 A6
 Newcastle-u-L,Chesterton
 ST5 . . . . 55 E7
 Newcastle-u-L,Silverdale
 ST5 . . . . 55 C2
 Newcastle-u-L ST5 . . . . . 283 C2
 Stafford ST16 . . . . 285 B4
 Stoke-on-T ST4 . . . . 56 D1
 Stone ST15 . . . . 105 A1
 Yoxall DE13 . . . . 182 A3
Victoria Terr ST16. . . . . . 155 E5
Victoria Way ST17 . . . . . 175 E5
Victor St Stone ST15. . . . 104 F1
 Walsall WS3 . . . . 244 A1
Victory Ave WS7 . . . . 228 F7
Victory CI WS12. . . . . 210 F4
Victory Cres ST10 . . . . . . 76 E3
Victory Terr B78 . . . . 261 B8
Vienna PI ST5 . . . . 70 F6
Vienna Way ST3 . . . . 73 E5
Viewfield Ave WV12 . . . . 209 F7
Viewfield Cres DY3 . . . . . 271 D6
Viewlands Dr WV6 . . . . . 255 A2
View St WS12. . . . . 209 F6
Viggars PI ST5 . . . . 55 F2
Vigo CI WV9 . . . . 244 F2
Vigo PI WS9 . . . . 256 A8
Vigo Rd WS9 . . . . 244 F2
Vigo Terr WS9 . . . . 244 F2
Viking B77 . . . . 261 D7
Villa CI Biddulph ST8 . . . . 27 C7
Shareshill WV10 . . . . 225 D1
Village Gdns ST17 . . . . . 175 F7
Village Mews The WV6. . . 255 B3
Village The Astbury CW12 . 15 B8
 Endon Bank ST9 . . . . 29 A1
 Keele ST5 . . . . 69 F7
 Kingswinford DY6 . . . . . 275 E7
 Walton-on-t-H ST17. . . . 175 F6
Villa Melita ST11 . . . . 90 D7
Villa Rd ST13 . . . . 45 C8
Villas The Foxt ST10 . . . . . 62 C5
 Stoke-on-T ST4 . . . . 72 A5
Villa St ST14 . . . . 72 A5
Villiers Ind Est WV2 . . . . 266 B7
Villiers St ST3 . . . . 284 B1
Vincent St ST1. . . . . 57 E5
Vine Bank Rd ST7. . . . . . . 26 A1
Vinebank St ST4 . . . . 72 A6
Vine CI Hixon ST18 . . . . . 158 B8
 Wolverhampton WV10 . . 240 D3
Vinegar Hill ST21 . . . . . . 132 C7
Vine La WS11. . . . . 226 D5
Vine Row WS7 . . . . 72 A6
Vine St DY9 . . . . 275 E1
Vineyard Dr TF10 . . . . . . 168 F3
Vineyard Rd TF10 . . . . . . 168 F3
Violet La DE15. . . . . 185 F8
Violet Lane Inf Sch DE15 185 F8
Violet Way DE15 . . . . 186 A8
Virginia Ave ST17 . . . . . . 175 A8
Virginia Dr WV4 . . . . 265 F4
Virginsalley La DE6 . . . . . 82 F2
Viscount Rd WV2 . . . . . . 211 E1
Viscount Wlk 8 ST5 . . . . . 90 A7
Vista The DY3. . . . . 266 D2
Vivian Rd ST4 . . . . 72 F6
Vowchurch Way ST2 . . . . . 58 C1
Voyager Dr WS11 . . . . . . 226 F6
Vulcan Rd WS13 . . . . 214 E1

W

Waddell CI WV14 . . . . . . 266 F2
Wadden La ST18. . . . . 138 E4
Wade Ave ST5 . . . . 56 D6
Wadebridge Rd ST2. . . . . . 58 B1
Wade CI Cheadle ST10 . . . 76 D1
 Hill Ridware WS15. . . . . . 197 F8
Wade Croft WS15. . . . . . . 179 F1
Wade CI ST7 . . . . 26 A1
Wade La WS15. . . . . 197 F8
Wadesmill Lawns WV10 . 240 E4

Wade St Lichfield WS13. . . .231 B7
Stoke-on-T ST6 . . . . .42 B1
Wadham St ST4 . . . . .72 A7
Waggon Cotts ST7. . . . . . . .38 E1
Waggoner's La B78 . . . . . .259 E8
Waggon La DY10. . . . . 281 A3
Wain Ave
Newcastle-u-L ST5. . . . . .70 F8
Stoke-on-T ST6 . . . . .42 E5
Wain Dr ST4. . . . . .71 E5
Wainrigg B77. . . . . .262 B7
Wain St ST6. . . . . .41 F1
Wainwood Rise ST4. . . . . . .71 F5
Wainwright Cl DY6. . . . . . 275 A8
Wainwright Wlk ST1 . . . . 282 C3
Wakefield Ave DE13. . . . . .146 B6
Wakefield Rd ST4. . . . . .71 F4
Wakelams Fold DY3. . . . . 271 C3
Wakeley Hill WV4. . . . . . . .265 F4
Wakeman Ct WV11. . . . . . .241 F3
Walcot Cl B75 . . . . .258 B3
Walcot Gr ST2. . . . . .58 A2
Waldale Cl WV11 . . . . 242 C1
Walden Ave ST16 . . . . 155 D6
Walden Gdns WV4 . . . . . . .265 E6
Wales La DE13. . . . . 183 D1
Walford Ave WV3 . . . . .265 F8
Walford Back La ST21. . . 117 C8
Walford Rd DE13. . . . . 147 D3
Walhouse CE Jun Sch
WS11. . . . . 209 C1
Walhouse Dr ST19 . . . . . . .207 F7
Walhouse St WS11. . . . . . .226 E8
Walker Dr DY10. . . . . 280 A1
Walker Rd ST6. . . . . .71 F4
Walkers Croft WS13. . . . . 214 C2
Walkersgreen Rd ST5 . . . . .40 D2
Walkers Rise WS12 . . . . . . 210 D8
Walker St Burton u T DE14 .166 B1
Stoke-on-T ST6 . . . . .41 D2
Walkfield Rd DE13 . . . . . . .200 F2
Walklate Ave ST5 . . . . .56 D3
Walk La WV5 . . . . 270 A6
Walkley Bank TF10. . . . . . 169 C4
Walkmill Bsns Pk
Cannock WS11. . . . . 226 D5
Market Drayton TF9. . . . . . 112 C7
Walkmill Dr TF9 . . . . 112 D8
Walkmill La WS11. . . . . . . 226 D5
Walkmill Marsh Nature Reserve* TF9. . . . . 112 C7
Walkmill Rd TF9 . . . . 112 C8
Walkmill Way WS11. . . . . 226 D5
Walks The ST13. . . . . .30 D5
Walk The DY3. . . . . 266 D1
Wallace Cl WS11. . . . . .227 F5
Wallace Ct WS6. . . . . 226 D1
Wallace Rd WS8 . . . . .244 E8
Walland Gr ST16. . . . . .155 B4
Wallash DE6. . . . . .81 C7
Wallbridge Cl ST13 . . . . . . .30 D4
Wallbridge Dr ST13 . . . . . . .30 C4
Wallbridge Prec ST13. . . . . .30 C4
Wallbrook Rd ST18 . . . . . .122 F3
Wall Croft WS9 . . . . .256 B7
Wall Ditch DE6 . . . . .35 B2
Wall Dr B74 . . . . .257 F4
Walley Dr ST6 . . . . .41 D6
Walley Pl ST6 . . . . .57 A7
Walley's Dr ST5. . . . . .56 D2
Walley St Biddulph ST8. . . . .27 C8
Burslem ST6 . . . . .57 A7
Wallfield Cl ST10 . . . . .92 D4
Wallheath Cres WS14 . . . . .245 E5
Wallheath La WS14 . . . . . .245 F5
Wallhill Ct ST13 . . . . .30 E3
Wallington Cl WS3. . . . . . . .243 B2
Wallington Heath WS3 . . .243 B2
Wallis Pl ST2. . . . . .58 B5
Wallis St ST4 . . . . .72 F6
Wallis Way ST2. . . . . .43 B2
Wall Lane Terr ST13. . . . . . .45 C6
Wall La WS13,WS14. . . . . . .230 D3
Wall (Letocetvm) Roman Site (Town)* WS14 . . . . .230 E2
Wallnut Wlk WS13 . . . . . . .230 F6
Wallows Wood DY3 . . . . . 271 A4
Wall Rd DE14. . . . . 185 A7
Wall Roman Site (Letocetvm) Mus* WS14. . . . . 230 D2
Wallshead Way TF10 . . . . .168 F1
Walls Wood ST5 . . . . .85 B7
Walmer Mdw WS9 . . . . . . .256 B7
Walmer Pl ST4 . . . . .284 B5
Walmers The WS9 . . . . . . .256 B7
Walmsley Ct DY7 . . . . .278 B3
Walney Gr ST1. . . . . .282 B4
Walnut Ave WV8. . . . . .239 B3
Walnut Cl Cannock WS11 . .209 F3
Newport TF10 . . . . .168 F1
Walnut Crest ST18 . . . . . . 158 C8
Walnut Ct WS15 . . . . 197 A6
Walnut Dr Cannock WS11. .209 F3
Wolverhampton WV3. . . . . . 255 D1
Walnut Gr Lichfield WS14. .231 F7
Newcastle-u-L ST5. . . . . .55 D8
Walnut Tree La TF10 . . . . .188 B7
Walpole St ST3 . . . . 284 D5
Walrand Cl B79. . . . . .234 B1
Walsall Acad WS3 . . . . . . 243 C2
Walsall Rd Aldridge WS9 . 256 A5
Brownhills WS9. . . . . .244 E2
Cannock WS11. . . . . .226 E7
Great Wyrley WS6 . . . . 227 A2
Leamonsley WS13 . . . . .230 E6
Lichfield,Christ Church WS13 . . . . 231 A7

Walsall Rd *continued*
Lichfield,Pipehill WS13, WS14 . . . . 230 C5
Norton Canes WS11 . . . . . .227 F4
Stonnall WS14. . . . . .245 E8
Sutton Coldfield B74 . . . . . 257 D4
Walsall WS3 . . . . 244 A1
Walsall Wood Rd WS9. . . .256 B7
Walsall Wood Sch WS8. . 245 A4
Walsingham Gdns ST5 . . . .71 B2
Walter St WS3. . . . . 244 A1
Waltonbury Cl ST17. . . . . .175 F6
Walton Cres
Stoke-on-T ST4 . . . . .72 C6
Wolverhampton WV4. . . . . .266 E5
Walton Cross ST15. . . . . . 120 A7
Walton Gdns WV8. . . . . . . .238 F4
Walton Grange ST15 . . . . 120 A7
Walton Gr ST7. . . . . .40 C8
Walton Hall ST21 . . . . .134 B5
Walton Hall Sch ST21 . . . .134 B5
Walton Heath WS3. . . . . . .242 F3
Walton High Sch ST17 . . .175 E6
Waltonhurst La ST21. . . . 134 C4
Walton Ind Est ST15 . . . . 120 A6
Walton La ST17. . . . . .176 B5
Walton Lodge ST17 . . . . . .175 F6
Walton Mead Cl ST17 . . . .175 F7
Walton-on-Trent CE Prim Sch DE12 . . . . 202 D8
Walton Pl ST5 . . . . .55 F6
Walton Priory Mid Sch
ST15. . . . . .119 F6
Walton Rd Aldridge WS9. . 245 A1
Stoke-on-T ST4 . . . . .71 F3
Swadlincote DE15 . . . . 185 D5
Wolverhampton WV4. . . . . .266 F5
Walton Way Stone ST15. . .119 F7
Talke ST7. . . . . .40 C8
Wanderers Ave WV2 . . . . 266 C6
Wandsbeck B77 . . . . .261 E8
Wannerton Rd DY10. . . . . .281 B1
Wansbeck Wlk DY3 . . . . . .271 F6
Warburton Ct 10 ST6. . . . . .57 A7
Warburton St 7 ST6. . . . . .57 A7
Ward Cl WS13 . . . . 215 D6
Ward Gr WV4. . . . . .266 F3
Wardle Cl B75 . . . . 258 A4
Wardle Cres ST13. . . . . .30 E4
Wardle La ST2. . . . . .43 C1
Wardle Pl WS11 . . . . .209 E5
Wardles La WS6 . . . . .226 F2
Wardle St Stoke-on-T ST6. . .41 E3
Tamworth B79. . . . . 250 A5
Wardlow Cl WV4. . . . . .266 B6
Ward Pl ST6 . . . . .42 B5
Ward Rd Codsall WV8 . . . . .238 F3
Wolverhampton WV4. . . . . 266 D5
Wards La CW12. . . . . .16 C8
Ward St WS12 . . . . .209 F6
Warings The WV5. . . . . . . .269 F4
Warm Croft ST15 . . . . 120 C7
Warminster Pl ST3. . . . . . 284 A3
Warmson Cl ST3. . . . . .73 C6
Warner Rd WV8. . . . . .238 F3
Warner St ST1. . . . . .282 B2
Warnford Wlk WV4 . . . . . 265 C6
Warren Cl Cannock WS12. 211 A5
Lichfield WS14. . . . . .231 E7
Stretton DE13 . . . . .147 E1
Warren Croft WS15 . . . . . 198 C4
Warren Ct 5 TF9 . . . . .97 C1
Warren Dr DY3 . . . . 266 C1
Warren Gdns DY6. . . . . . . 275 C6
Warren Hill DE11 . . . . .186 E5
Warren La DE14 . . . . .184 F7
Warren Pl
Brownhills WS8. . . . . 245 A7
Longton ST3. . . . . 284 D2
Warren Rd
Burntwood WS7. . . . . 229 A5
Stoke-on-T ST6 . . . . .42 B6
Warrens La ST16. . . . . .155 B6
Warren St ST3. . . . . 284 D2
Warrilow Cl 1 ST3 . . . . .90 A7
Warrilow Heath Rd ST5 . . .40 C1
Warrington Dr ST13. . . . . . .30 C5
Warrington Rd ST1 . . . . . . .57 D1
Warrington St ST4. . . . . . . .72 F6
Warsill Gr ST3. . . . . .73 D4
Warstone Hill Rd WV6 . . . .253 F4
Warstone Rd WS6 . . . . 242 C7
Warstones Cres WV4. . . . 265 D5
Warstones Dr WV4. . . . . . 265 C6
Warstones Gdns WV4 . . . 265 C6
Warstones Jun & Inf Sch
WV4. . . . . .265 E6
Warstones Rd WV4 . . . . . 265 D5
Wartell Bank Ind Est
DY6 . . . . 275 D7
Wartell Bank DY6. . . . . . . 275 D7
Warwick Ave
3 Longton ST3. . . . . .73 F1
Cheadle ST10. . . . . .76 C2
Newcastle-u-L ST5. . . . . .71 C4
Perton WV6 . . . . .254 F3
Warwick Cl
Burton u T DE14. . . . . .184 F8
Cannock WS11. . . . . .226 F8
Kidsgrove ST7 . . . . .26 A3
Market Drayton TF9. . . . . . . .97 D2
Warwick Ct
6 Wolverhampton WV4 . . .266 F4
Dudley DY3 . . . . 271 D3
Warwick Dr WV8. . . . . .238 E3
Warwick Gr ST5 . . . . .56 E3
Warwick Rd
Stafford ST17 . . . . .175 B8

Warwick Rd *continued*
Stourbridge DY8 . . . . 275 D1
Tamworth B77 . . . . .250 E4
Warwick St Biddulph ST8. . .27 C7
Burton u T DE13. . . . . 166 C6
Hanley ST1 . . . . .57 A3
Newcastle-u-L ST5. . . . . .55 E7
Warwick Way WS9. . . . . . . 245 A1
Wasdale Dr DY6 . . . . .275 E6
Wasdale Rd WS8. . . . . 244 D6
Washbrook La
Norton Canes WS11 . . . . . 227 D5
Thorpe DE6 . . . . .51 F4
Wash Dale La ST15 . . . . . 105 A6
Washerwall La ST9 . . . . . . .59 A4
Washerwall St ST2. . . . . . . .73 D8
Washford Rd DE65 . . . . . . .147 E8
Washington Cl ST8 . . . . .16 C2
Washington Ct WV3. . . . . 255 D1
Washington Dr ST17 . . . . 175 A8
Washington St ST6 . . . . . . .41 E2
Waste La DE6. . . . . .79 D4
Wastwater Ct WV6 . . . . . . .254 F4
Watchfield Cl ST3 . . . . .73 F1
Waterbeck Gr ST4 . . . . .88 C5
Waterbridge La WV5. . . . . .269 E7
Waterbrook Cl ST19. . . . . .207 E7
Waterbrook Way WS11. . .226 E6
Waterdale Gr ST3. . . . . .73 E3
Water Dale WV3 . . . . .255 E2
Waterdale WV5 . . . . .269 E5
Water Eaton La ST19. . . . .207 B5
Waterfall La ST10. . . . . .48 F2
Waterford Dr TF10 . . . . . . .168 E1
Waterford Rd DY6 . . . . . . 275 D7
Watergate St ST6. . . . . .41 D3
Water Glades Cl 2 ST1 . . . .56 F2
Waterhead Cl WV10 . . . . . 241 A2
Waterhead Dr WV10 . . . . .241 B2
Waterhead Grange WS8. .244 E7
Waterhead Rd ST3. . . . . . . .73 F1
Waterhouses CE Prim Sch
ST10. . . . . .48 F2
Watering Cl ST5 . . . . .85 C4
Watering Trough Bank
CW3. . . . . .69 B8
Water La Bobbington DY7 . 268 D2
Newport TF10 . . . . .168 F3
Waterlily Cl WS12. . . . . . . .210 E3
Water Lily Gr WS8 . . . . . . .244 E7
Waterloo Bvd WS12. . . . . .210 E4
Waterloo Ct ST13 . . . . .30 D5
Waterloo Gr ST7. . . . . .26 A2
Waterloo Ho WS15. . . . . . .197 B6
Waterloo Rd
Burslem ST6,ST1 . . . . .57 A6
Edgmond TF10. . . . . 168 A6
Waterloo St
Burton u T DE14. . . . . 166 C4
Hanley ST1 . . . . 282 C2
Leek ST13 . . . . .30 D5
Watermeadow Dr WS4 . . 244 D1
Watermeadow Gr 3 ST1. . .56 F2
Watermeet Gr ST1. . . . . .56 F3
Watermill Cl WV10. . . . . . . 240 D3
Watermint Cl WS12 . . . . . .210 E4
Waterpark Rd DE6 . . . . . . .127 B8
Water Rd DY3 . . . . 271 C2
Waters Dr B74. . . . . 257 D3
Waters Edge WS15. . . . . . 198 C5
Watersedge Gr 4 ST1 . . . .56 F2
Waterside Bsns Pk
WS15 . . . . 197 A7
Waterside DE15. . . . . .185 E7
Waterside Cl Madeley CW3 68 E6
Slade Heath WV10. . . . . . . .224 E2
Wolverhampton WV2. . . . . 266 D7
Waterside Com Jun Sch
DE15 . . . . .185 E7
Waterside Ct
Branston DE14. . . . . .165 F1
Gnosall ST20. . . . . 171 C5
Tamworth B77 . . . . .250 F5
Waterside Dr
Market Drayton TF9. . . . . . . .97 E2
Stoke-on-T ST3 . . . . .88 E7
Waterside Mews TF10. . . .168 E3
Waterside Rd DE15 . . . . . 185 D7
Waterside WS15 . . . . .196 F6
Waterside Way
Brownhills WS8. . . . . 228 D2
Wolverhampton WV9. . . . . . 240 A3
Watersmead Cl WS12 . . . .210 F4
Watersmeet Ct ST15 . . . . 120 C6
Watersmeet Ho B78 . . . . .261 B8
Waters Rd WS15. . . . . .160 F3
Water St Burntwood WS7 . .228 E8
Kingswinford DY6 . . . . 275 D7
Newcastle-u-L,Red Street ST5 . . . . .40 D2
Newcastle-u-L ST5. . . . . . . 283 C3
Stafford ST16 . . . . .285 B3
Stoke-on-T ST4 . . . . .72 A5
Waters View WS3 . . . . .244 B5
Waterton Cl DE13. . . . . 148 A1
Waterways Gdns DY8 . . . .275 E1
Waterworks Cotts DY6 . . .274 F4
Watery La
Abbots Bromley WS15. . . . 160 D4
Astbury CW12. . . . . .15 C5
Clifton DE6. . . . . .81 E7
Codsall WV8 . . . . 239 A5
Ellastone DE6 . . . . .80 B4
Gentleshaw WS7,WS15. . . .212 B3
Hangingbridge DE6 . . . . .81 F8
Haughton ST18 . . . . .172 F5
Kingstone ST14 . . . . .125 B2
Lichfield WS13. . . . . 214 C4

Watery La *continued*
Longton ST3. . . . . .73 D1
Scropton DE65. . . . . .129 E2
Stourbridge DY8 . . . . .275 E2
Swadlincote DE11 . . . . 186 D5
Uttoxeter ST14 . . . . 110 C6
Watford Gap Rd WS14. . . 258 A7
Watford Gap WS14. . . . . . 258 A7
Watford St ST4 . . . . .72 C8
Wathan Ave WV14 . . . . . . .266 F1
Watkin St ST4 . . . . .72 D6
Watkiss Dr WS15 . . . . 178 D1
Watlands Ave ST5 . . . . .56 C6
Watlands Rd ST7 . . . . .39 E2
Watlands View ST5. . . . . . . .56 B6
Watling St
Blymhill Lawn TF11 . . . . . . 204 C2
Brownhills WS8. . . . . 228 D1
Cannock WS11. . . . . 226 D6
Dordon B77,B78 . . . . 262 D6
Hints B78. . . . . 248 D3
Norton Canes WS11 . . . . . 227 D3
Watling Street Bsns Pk
WS11. . . . . 228 A2
Watling Street Prim Sch
WS8 . . . . .228 E1
Watling St
Tamworth,Bonehill B78 . . . .249 E1
Tamworth,Two Gates B77 . 261 D7
Tamworth,Wilnecote B77, B78. . . . . .261 E7
Watson Cl Fradley WS13. . .215 E8
Rugeley WS15 . . . . 178 D3
Watson Rd Stoke-on-T ST4. . .71 F4
Wolverhampton,Lanesfield WV14 . . . . .266 F2
Wolverhampton,Pendeford WV10 . . . . .240 B2
Watson St
Burton u T DE14. . . . . 166 D1
Stoke-on-T ST4 . . . . .72 A8
Wattfield Cl WS15 . . . . . . 197 A5
Watt Ho DY6. . . . . .275 F7
Wattles La ST17 . . . . .175 B2
Watt Pl ST10 . . . . .76 D3
Watts Cl ST17 . . . . .174 B8
Wat Tyler Cl WS15 . . . . . . 178 D3
Waveney Ave WV6 . . . . . . .254 E4
Waveney Ct ST5 . . . . .71 B4
Waveney Gr
Cannock WS11. . . . . .209 B1
Newcastle-u-L ST5. . . . . .71 B4
Waveney B77 . . . . .261 E8
Waveney Wlk N ST6 . . . . . .42 A4
Waveney Wlk S ST6. . . . . . .42 A4
Wavenham Cl B74 . . . . .257 E5
Waverley Cres
Wolverhampton,Goldthorn Hill WV4 . . . . .266 B6
Wolverhampton,Lanesfield WV4 . . . . .266 F3
Waverley Gdns
Rugeley WS15 . . . . .178 B2
Wombourne WV5. . . . . .270 B7
Waverley La DE14. . . . . . . .166 B4
Waverley Pl ST5 . . . . .71 B5
Waverley Rd WS3. . . . . .242 F2
Waverley Wlk WS14. . . . . .231 B6
Waverton Rd ST2. . . . . .73 E7
Wavertree Ave ST7 . . . . .25 E7
Waybutt La CW2. . . . . .52 D8
Wayfield Dr ST16 . . . . 155 D8
Wayfield Gr ST4 . . . . .71 D8
Wayside Acres WV8. . . . . .238 F2
Wayside Ave ST5 . . . . .56 C4
Wayside Dr B74 . . . . 257 C3
Wayside WV8. . . . . .239 F2
Wayte St ST1. . . . . 282 A4
Wealden Hatch WV10 . . . .240 E4
Wealdstone Dr DY3 . . . . . 271 D2
Weathercock La CW12 . . . . . 6 E3
Weatheroaks WS9 . . . . . . .245 B4
Weaver Cl Biddulph ST8 . . . .16 D1
Cheadle ST10. . . . . .76 E5
Weaver Ct 8 B75. . . . . .258 E3
Weaver Dr ST17 . . . . .174 B8
Weaverlake Dr DE13 . . . . .181 F3
Weaver Pl ST5. . . . . .71 B4
Weaver Rd ST14 . . . . .111 B2
Weavers La ST15 . . . . 120 C7
Weaver St ST1. . . . . .282 B3
Weavers The ST14 . . . . .95 D6
Weavers Wlk ST15 . . . . . . 103 C4
Weaving Gdns 1 WS11 . . .209 E1
Webb Ave WV6 . . . . .254 E5
Webb Cl WS13. . . . . 215 C6
Webberley La ST3 . . . . . . 284 C3
Webb St ST3 . . . . .74 B3
Webley Rise WV10 . . . . . . .240 F4
Webster Ave ST3 . . . . .73 E5
Webster St ST5 . . . . 283 C2
Webster Wlk WS11. . . . . . 210 A4
Wedgewood Ave ST15. . . .119 E6
Wedgewood Cl
Burntwood WS7. . . . . 229 C7
Burton u T DE15. . . . . .167 B1
Wedgewood Ct WS4 . . . . 244 C1
Wedgwood Ave
Audley ST7. . . . . .40 A1
Newcastle-u-L ST5. . . . . .71 A7
Wedgwood Cl WV5. . . . . . .269 F7
Wedgwood Ct ST1 . . . . .57 A3
Wedgwood Dr ST12. . . . . . .88 E4
Wedgwood Halt ST12 . . . . .88 D3
Wedgwood La
Barlaston ST12 . . . . .88 E4
Biddulph ST8 . . . . .16 C2
Biddulph ST8 . . . . .16 C3

Wedgwood Pl 1 ST6 . . . . .56 F8
Wedgwood Rd
Cheadle ST10. . . . . .76 D1
Hopton ST18 . . . . .156 B8
Stoke-on-T ST4 . . . . .72 F6
Talke ST7. . . . . .40 D7
Wedgwood St
4 Burslem ST6. . . . . .56 F8
Newcastle-u-L ST5. . . . . .56 D5
Wedgwood Story The* ST12. . . . . .88 D4
Weeford Dell 2 B75 . . . . . .258 E3
Weeford Rd B75 . . . . .258 F3
Weeping Cross ST17 . . . . 175 D7
Weetman Cl ST6. . . . . .41 C7
Weighton Gr ST2 . . . . .58 E1
Weir Bank DE15 . . . . .185 E6
Weir Gr ST7 . . . . .26 B2
Weirside DE6 . . . . .81 D7
Welbeck Pl ST2. . . . . .58 C5
Welbury Gdns WV6 . . . . . .255 F5
Welby St ST4 . . . . .72 D5
Welch St ST4 . . . . .72 B7
Weldon Ave ST3 . . . . .74 B4
Welford Gr B74 . . . . .257 F3
Welford Rd B77. . . . . 261 C5
Welford Rise DE13 . . . . . . 166 A6
Welland Cl DE15 . . . . 167 A5
Welland Gr ST5. . . . . .71 A3
Welland Rd DE65 . . . . 147 D8
Wellbury Cl ST4 . . . . .88 C5
Wellcroft Grange DE6. . . . . .65 D1
Weller Cl ST11. . . . . .90 D3
Weller Ct WV3. . . . . 255 D1
Weller St ST4. . . . . .71 E8
Wellesbourne Cl WV3 . . . .265 B8
Wellesbourne B79 . . . . . . 250 C8
Wellesley St ST1. . . . . 282 A1
Wellfield Cl WS11. . . . . . . .226 B7
Wellfield Rd
Aldridge WS9. . . . . .256 B8
Alrewas DE13 . . . . 201 A2
Bucknall ST2 . . . . .58 C1
Wellington Ave WV3 . . . . .265 F7
Wellington Cl
Kingswinford DY6 . . . . .275 E4
Stafford ST16 . . . . .155 E5
Wellington Cres WS13 . . .215 B4
Wellington Ct
2 Leek ST13. . . . . .30 E5
Hanley ST1 . . . . 282 C3
Wellington Dr
Cannock WS11. . . . . .226 B8
Rugeley WS15 . . . . .196 E8
Wellington Mill 1 ST13. . . .30 E5
Wellington Rd
Albrighton WV7 . . . . .220 F1
Burton u T,Branston DE14 . .184 E8
Burton u T DE14. . . . . 166 A2
Hanley ST1 . . . . 282 C2
Kidsgrove ST7 . . . . .26 A2
Newport TF10 . . . . .168 E1
Wellington St W DE14. . . .166 B3
Wellington St
1 Newcastle-u-L ST5. . . . . .56 C5
Burton u T DE14. . . . . .166 B3
Hanley ST1 . . . . 282 C2
Leek ST13 . . . . .30 E6
Wellington Terr ST1. . . . . 282 C2
Well La Biddulph ST8. . . . . . .16 D3
Great Wyrley WS6. . . . . 227 A1
Walsall WS3 . . . . .243 E1
Warslow SK17. . . . . .22 B2
Weston Jones TF10. . . . . . . 150 C4
Wells Cl Biddulph ST8 . . . . . .27 D8
Cannock WS11. . . . . .209 E6
Perton WV6. . . . . 254 D4
Rugeley WS15 . . . . 196 C6
Wells Dr ST17 . . . . .175 E7
Wells La ST18 . . . . 191 C8
Wells Rd WV4 . . . . .265 F5
Well St Biddulph ST8 . . . . . . .27 D7
Cheadle ST10. . . . . .76 E3
Forsbrook ST11. . . . . .91 A8
Hanley ST1 . . . . 282 C2
Leek ST13 . . . . .30 F5
Mow Cop ST7. . . . . .26 D7
Newcastle-u-L ST5. . . . . . . 283 C2
Wellyards Cl ST18. . . . . . . 138 D2
Welney Gdns WV9 . . . . . . 240 A3
Welsh Cl ST3 . . . . .89 D8
Wembley La WS7 . . . . 228 D8
Wembury B77 . . . . .250 E5
Wem Gr ST5. . . . . .40 E2
Wendell Crest WV10 . . . . .240 F4
Wendling Cl ST2. . . . . .58 D1
Wendover Gr ST2. . . . . .58 C1
Wendover Rd WV4 . . . . . . .266 F2
Wendy Cl ST2 . . . . .58 B1
Wenger Cres ST4 . . . . .88 A7
Wenham Dr ST3 . . . . .90 B7
Wenlock Ave WV3 . . . . . . .265 E8
Wenlock Cl
Newcastle-u-L ST5. . . . . .40 E2
Sedgley DY3. . . . . 271 C7
Stoke-on-T ST6 . . . . .42 B8
Wenlock Dr TF10 . . . . .168 E2
Wenlock B77 . . . . 250 D3
Wensleydale Ave CW12. . . . . 6 A5
Wensleydale Cl ST1. . . . . . .57 D7
Wentlows Ave ST10 . . . . . . .92 D5
Wentlows Rd ST10. . . . . . . .92 D5
Wentworth Cl WS7. . . . . . 229 C7
Wentworth Ct B75 . . . . . . .258 B1

Wentworth Dr
Kidsgrove ST7 . . . . .26 C3
Lichfield WS14 . . . . .231 D5
Stafford ST16 . . . . .156 C3
Stretton DE13 . . . . .147 D1
Wentworth Gr
Perton WV6 . . . . .254 D5
Stoke-on-T ST1 . . . . .57 F8
Wentworth Rd
Stourbridge DY8 . . . . . . .279 E2
Walsall WS3 . . . . .242 F3
Wolverhampton WV10 . . . .240 F3
Werburgh Dr ST4 . . . . . . .88 A7
Wereton Rd ST7 . . . . .39 D1
Wergs Dr WV6 . . . . .255 A7
Wergs Hall WV8 . . . . . . .254 F7
Wergs Hall Rd
Codsall WV8 . . . . .254 F8
Wolverhampton WV6,WV8. .255 A7
Wergs Rd Codsall WV8 . . . .254 F7
Wolverhampton WV6 . . . . .255 B6
Werneth Gr WS3 . . . . . . .243 A4
Werrington Prim Sch ST9 .59 B3
Werrington Rd ST2 . . . . . . .58 B4
Wesker Pl ST3 . . . . .73 F4
Wesleyan Ct ⑤ ST13 . . . . .30 D6
Wesleyan Rd TF9 . . . . . . .100 A6
Wesley Ave
Cheslyn Hay WS6. . . . . . .226 D3
Codsall WV8 . . . . .239 B2
Wesley Cl Burntwood WS7 .211 F1
Wombourne WV5. . . . . . .269 F5
Wesley Ct
⑤ Wolverhampton WV4 . . .266 F4
Betley CW3 . . . . .53 A6
Cannock WS11. . . . . .209 E1
Wesley Dr ST15. . . . . . . .120 C6
Wesley Gdns ⑦ ST7 . . . . .26 A2
Wesley Pl Cannock WS12 . .210 C7
Halmer End ST7. . . . . .54 D7
Newcastle-u-L ST5. . . . . . .70 F8
Wesley Rd WV8 . . . . .239 B2
Wesley St Audley ST7 . . . . .40 A1
Blythe Bridge ST11 . . . . . . .91 A7
Stoke-on-T ST6 . . . . .41 D3
Wesley Way B77 . . . . .250 F4
Wessenden B77 . . . . .262 B7
Wessex Cl WS8 . . . . .244 F7
Wessex Ct B79. . . . . .251 F7
Wessex Dr Cannock WS11 .209 F2
Stoke-on-T ST4 . . . . .88 A8
Wessex Rd WV2. . . . . . . .266 F6
Westacre ST1. . . . . .57 F3
Westacre Cres WV3 . . . . .255 C1
Westacre Dr DE11 . . . . . .186 F2
Westacre Inf Sch WV3 . . . .255 C1
West Acres ST14. . . . . . . .141 C8
West Ave Kidsgrove ST7 . . .25 C1
Newcastle-u-L ST5. . . . . . .56 D2
Stoke-on-T ST4 . . . . .71 F8
Weston CW2 . . . . .37 B5
West Bank ST4 . . . . .72 A6
West Beeches WV9 . . . . .224 B2
Westbeech Rd WV6 . . . . .253 D5
Westbook Way WV5. . . . . .269 F5
Westbourne Ave
Cannock WS11. . . . . .209 D3
Cheslyn Hay WS6. . . . . . .226 E3
Westbourne Cl ST13 . . . . . .30 C6
Westbourne Cres WS7 . . .229 B7
Westbourne Dr ST6. . . . . . .41 E5
Westbourne Rd WV4 . . . . .266 A5
Westbourne Villas ST6. . .285 B4
West Brampton ST5. . . . . .283 B3
Westbrook Ave WS9. . . . . .256 A5
Westbury Cl ST1. . . . . .57 F5
Westbury Hayes ST17 . . . .174 A8
Westbury Rd ST5 . . . . .71 B3
West Butts Rd WS15 . . . . .178 B1
West Cannock Way
WS12 . . . . .195 D1
Westcliffe ST13. . . . . .30 D6
Westcliffe Ave ST5. . . . . . .71 A3
Westcliffe Hospl ST6. . . . . .41 F7
West Cl Stafford ST16 . . . . .156 A3
Stone ST15 . . . . .119 F7
West Coppice Rd WS8 . . .244 C8
Westcott Cl DY6 . . . . .275 F3
Westcott La TF9 . . . . .130 A7
West Cres ST1. . . . . .57 E8
Westcroft Ave WV10 . . . . .241 A1
Westcroft Rd
Sedgley DY3. . . . . .266 B2
Wolverhampton WV6. . . . .254 F6
Westcroft Sch WV10 . . . . .240 F2
West Dr Cheddleton ST13 . . .45 C7
Fazeley B78 . . . . .249 E2
West End Ave ST13 . . . . . . .30 D5
Westerby Dr ST9. . . . . .59 A3
Westerham Cl ST4 . . . . . . .87 F7
Westering Parkway
WV10. . . . . .240 F4
Western Ave DY3 . . . . . . .271 B8
Western By Pass WS13. . .213 E1
Western By-Pass WS13 . . .230 F8
Western Rd
Cannock WS11. . . . . .210 B6
Stourbridge DY8 . . . . . . .279 F4
Western Springs Prim Sch
WS15 . . . . .178 D2
Western Springs Rd
WS15 . . . . .178 D2
Westfield Ave ST7 . . . . .39 C2
Westfield Dr
Aldridge WS9. . . . . .256 A6

Westfield Dr continued
Wombourne WV5. . . . . . .269 F7
Westfield Gr WV3 . . . . . . .265 C8
Westfield Manor B75 . . . . .258 A4
Westfield Prim Sch WV5 .269 F7
Westfield Rd Bucknall ST2. .58 B3
Burton u T DE13. . . . . . . .166 B6
Mow Cop ST7 . . . . .26 C7
Sedgley DY3. . . . . .266 E1
Westfields
Cauldon Lowe ST10. . . . . . .63 E4
Leek ST13 . . . . .30 F5
Westfields Rd WS15. . . . . .197 F4
Westfields Rise CW3 . . . . . .67 C1
Westfields B78 . . . . .262 D8
Westgate Brewood ST19 . .223 D7
Cannock WS12. . . . . .210 F6
Westgate Cl DY3 . . . . .271 E7
West Gn WV4 . . . . .265 C5
Westhall Cl ST19. . . . . . . .223 D6
Westhall Gate WS3 . . . . . .243 B2
Westhead Ave ST16 . . . . .156 A4
Westhead Rd DY10. . . . . . .280 A4
Westhead Rd N DY10. . . . .280 A4
Westhead Wlk ST1. . . . . . .282 A2
West Hill Ave WS12 . . . . . .210 B6
West Hill Prim Sch
WS12 . . . . .210 B6
West Hill ST14 . . . . .126 C6
Westhill WV3 . . . . .255 C2
Westhouse La ST14 . . . . . .79 F3
Westland Ave WV3. . . . . . .255 F2
Westland Gdns DY8 . . . . .279 F7
Westland Rd
Market Drayton TF9. . . . . . .97 B1
Wolverhampton WV3. . . . .255 F2
Westlands ST1. . . . . .39 F2
Westlands Ave ST5. . . . . . .70 F7
Westlands Prim Sch ST5 . .70 F6
Westlands Rd ST14 . . . . . .126 B6
Westlands The ST14. . . . . .95 D6
Westland St ST4. . . . . .72 A7
Westlands CW3 . . . . .83 B7
Westleigh Rd WV5. . . . . . .269 F5
Westley Cl DY10 . . . . .280 C5
Westmarsh Gr ST6. . . . . . .42 A4
Westmead Rd DE13 . . . . . .183 C1
Westmere Cl CW2 . . . . .37 B5
Westmill St ST1 . . . . .282 C1
Westminster Ave WV4. . . .266 B5
Westminster Cl ST17 . . . . .175 C8
Westminster Dr
④ Burton u T DE13. . . . . .166 D8
Market Drayton TF9. . . . . .112 A7
Westminster Pl ST4. . . . . . .72 A1
Westminster Rd
Cannock WS11. . . . . .209 E6
Leek ST13 . . . . .31 A7
Stourbridge DY8 . . . . . . .275 D2
Westmorland Ave ST7. . . . .40 F7
Westmorland Cl
Stoke-on-T ST6 . . . . .42 A8
Tamworth B78 . . . . .250 A1
Weston Bank Cl TF11 . . . .203 E2
Weston Bank
Thurvaston DE6 . . . . .96 F1
Weston ST18 . . . . .37 A6
Weston-Under-Lizard TF11 .203 E2
Weston Cl
Bishops Wood ST19. . . . . .221 E8
Cannock WS11. . . . . .210 C1
Newcastle-u-L ST5 . . . . . . .55 F3
Werrington ST2. . . . . .59 A4
Weston Coyney Inf Sch
ST3. . . . . .74 B5
Weston Coyney Jun Sch
ST3. . . . . .74 A3
Weston Coyney Rd
Longton ST3. . . . . .73 E3
Meir ST3 . . . . .74 A4
Weston Cres WS9 . . . . . . .256 A4
Weston Ct ST3. . . . . .74 A4
Weston Dr
Great Wyrley WS6 . . . . . . .226 F1
Meir ST3 . . . . .74 A4
Westonfields Dr ST3 . . . . . .73 E3
Weston Ho WV6 . . . . .255 E5
Weston La Bowers ST21. . .102 A4
Standon ST21 . . . . .101 F6
Weston CW2 . . . . .37 A6
Weston Park Ave DE14. . .166 D7
Weston Park* TF11 . . . . . .203 F1
Weston Rd
Albrighton WV7 . . . . .237 B5
Hopton ST16,ST18. . . . . .156 C4
Lichfield WS13. . . . . .214 A2
Meir ST3 . . . . .74 A3
Stowford CW1. . . . . .37 B8
Weston Road High Sch
ST18. . . . . .156 D5
Weston St Leek ST13 . . . . . .31 A6
Longton ST3. . . . . .73 D6
Westonview Ave ST3 . . . . . .73 D5
Westover Dr ST15. . . . . . .120 C7
West Par ST4. . . . . .72 C5
Westport Lake Rd ST6 . . . .41 D1
Westport Rd ST6. . . . . .41 E1
West Prec ST4. . . . . .282 B2
West Rd WV4. . . . . .266 F5
Westridge DY3 . . . . .271 C8
Westsprink Cres ST3 . . . . .73 E2
West St Biddulph ST8. . . . . .27 C7
Burton u T DE15. . . . . . . .167 B3
Cannock WS11. . . . . .210 E6
Leek ST13 . . . . .30 E6
Meir ST3 . . . . .74 B5

West St continued
Mount Pleasant ST7 . . . . . .26 B6
Newcastle-u-L,Porthill ST5 . .56 D7
Newcastle-u-L,Silverdale
ST5. . . . . .55 B1
Newcastle-u-L ST5. . . . . . .283 C2
Stourbridge DY8 . . . . . . .279 F5
Tamworth B79 . . . . .250 C5
Tamworth,Kettlebrook
B77. . . . . .250 C3
West Terr ST6 . . . . .42 B6
West View ST14. . . . . .125 C7
Westview Cl ST13. . . . . . . .30 C6
West View Dr DY6. . . . . . .275 E5
West View Mayfield DE6 . . .81 D6
Newcastle-u-L ST5. . . . . . .56 B5
Rocester ST14 . . . . .96 A3
Newcastle-u-L ST5. . . . . . .89 F4
Westward Cl ST14 . . . . . . .111 B1
West Way Gn ST17. . . . . . .155 C1
Westway Ho WS4 . . . . . . .244 B1
West Way Stafford ST17 . . .174 C8
Uttoxeter ST14 . . . . .110 F1
Walsall WS4 . . . . .244 B2
Westwick Cl WS9 . . . . . . .245 E4
West Winds WV10. . . . . . .241 C7
Newcastle-u-L ST5. . . . . . .89 F4
Westwood Cl
Cheddleton ST13 . . . . .45 C4
Chorlton CW2 . . . . .37 B1
Westwood Ct
⒀ Leek ST13 . . . . .30 D6
Hanley ST1. . . . . .282 C3
Westwood Fst Sch ST13 . . .30 C5
Westwood Gr ⒁ ST13 . . . . .30 C6
Westwood Heath Rd ST13 .30 C6
Westwood High Sch ST13 .30 C5
Westwood Holdings
WS12 . . . . .209 B6
Westwood Park Ave ST13 . .30 B5
Westwood Park Dr ST13 . . .30 B5
Westwood Pk DE11 . . . . . .186 F5
Westwood Rd Leek ST13. . .30 D5
Meir ST3 . . . . .74 A2
Newcastle-u-L ST5. . . . . . .56 D6
Westwoods Hollow WS7 . .229 B8
Westwood Terr ⒄ ST13 . . .30 D6
Westwood View ⒁ ST13 . . .30 D6
Wetherall Cl WS15 . . . . . .178 D2
Wetherby Cl Cheadle ST10. .76 E5
Newcastle-u-L ST5. . . . . . .55 E7
Wolverhampton WV10 . . . .240 D5
Wetherby Ct DE14 . . . . . . .184 F7
Wetherby Rd
Stoke-on-T ST4 . . . . .88 B7
Walsall WS3 . . . . .243 A4
Wetheral Rd DE15 . . . . . . .167 C2
Wetley Ave ST9 . . . . .59 F4
Wetley La ST13 . . . . .33 A2
Wetmore La ST14. . . . . . . .166 F6
Wetmore Rd
Burton u T DE14. . . . . . . .166 E5
Burton u T DE14. . . . . . . .166 E6
Wettenhall Dr ST13 . . . . . . .30 B4
Wetton Rd ST13 . . . . .34 B5
Wexford Cl DY1. . . . . .271 F2
Weybourne Ave ST2. . . . . . .43 B3
Weyhill Cl WV9 . . . . .239 F2
Weymouth Dr B74 . . . . . . .257 F4
Weymouth Ho B79 . . . . . . .250 B5
Whalley Ave ST4. . . . . .71 B6
Wharf Cl WS14 . . . . .231 C7
Wharfe Cl ST14 . . . . .126 C8
Wharfedale Rd DY6 . . . . . .275 B7
Wharfedale Rd CW12 . . . . . .6 A5
Wharf Hos DE13 . . . . .184 A1
Wharf La Astbury CW12 . . . .15 B3
Burntwood WS8. . . . . . . .228 F3
Wharf Pl ST14 . . . . .77 A4
Wharf Rd Biddulph ST8. . . . .27 C8
Burton u T DE14. . . . . . . .166 E5
Gnosall ST20 . . . . .171 C5
Rugeley WS15 . . . . .196 E7
Wharf Road Ind Est DE14 .166 E5
Wharf St ST5 . . . . .283 D3
Wharf Terr WV3 . . . . .69 B8
Wharmadine La
Ashley TF9. . . . . .100 E7
Maer TF9 . . . . .84 F1
Wharwell La WS6. . . . . . . .227 A1
Whateley La B77,B78. . . . .261 F4
Whateley Villas CV9. . . . . .262 A2
Whatmore St ST6. . . . . .42 C1
Wheat Breach Cl DE13 . . .166 B6
Wheatcroft Cl
⒀ Sutton Coldfield B75 . . .258 E3
Burntwood WS7. . . . . . . .229 A5
Penkridge ST19 . . . . .207 F8
Wheatfields ST6 . . . . .42 D1
Wheathill Cl WV4 . . . . .265 E3
Wheatland Gr WS9. . . . . . .256 B4
Wheatlands Cl ⒀ WS12. . .210 C1
Wheatlands Rd DE15. . . . .185 E7
Wheatlands The WV6 . . . . .254 D3
Wheatley Ave ST4 . . . . .71 E6
Wheatley Cl ST5. . . . . .258 C3
Wheatley Gr WS6 . . . . .227 A2
Wheatley La DE15 . . . . . . .167 A5
Wheatley St WV2 . . . . .266 F6
Wheatmill Cl DY10 . . . . . . .281 B2
Wheatridge Cl DY6 . . . . . .275 A8
Wheatsheaf Cl B75 . . . . . .258 E4
Wheatsheaf Rd WV8 . . . . .239 E1
Wheatstone Cl DY3 . . . . . .271 E6
Wheel Ave WV8. . . . . .238 F3
Wheel Ct The WV8 . . . . . . .238 F3
Wheeler Cl WV8 . . . . .238 F4

Wheeler St DY8. . . . . .279 F5
Wheelfield WV8 . . . . .238 F3
Wheelhouse Rd WS15. . . .197 B6
Wheel La WS13 . . . . .213 F1
Wheelock Way ⒄ ST7 . . . .26 B2
Wheelwrights La ST21 . . .134 D7
Whetstone Field Prim Sch
WS9 . . . . .256 B4
Whetstone Gn WV10 . . . . .240 D1
Whetstone La WV9 . . . . . . .256 B4
Whetstone Rd ST6. . . . . . . .16 C2
Whieldon Cres ST4 . . . . . . .72 C5
Whieldon Ind Est ST4. . . . .72 C6
Whieldon Rd ST4 . . . . .72 C6
Whilmot Cl WV10 . . . . .241 B6
Whimple Side ST2. . . . . . . .58 B1
Whimster Sq ST17 . . . . . . .174 A8
Whinberry Rise DY5 . . . . .271 C2
Whinyates Rise WS11 . . . .226 F8
Whisper La ST4,ST5 . . . . . . .86 E7
Whiston Cl WV7 . . . . .237 A5
Whiston Eaves La ST10 . . .62 D2
Whitacre La WS14 . . . . . . .245 E7
Whitaker Rd ST3. . . . . .72 F3
Whitbread Dr ST8 . . . . .27 E8
Whitburn Cl WV9 . . . . .240 A2
Whitby Cl Stafford ST17. . .174 C7
Walsall WS3 . . . . .242 F3
Whitby Way WS11 . . . . . . .226 C8
Whitchurch Gr ST5 . . . . . . .40 E2
Whitcliffe Pl ST3 . . . . .72 F3
Whitcombe Rd ST3 . . . . . . .74 A2
White Bark WS12 . . . . . . .210 A8
Whitebeam Cl
Brownhills WS8 . . . . .244 E6
Dudley DY3 . . . . .271 C4
Newcastle-u-L ST5. . . . . . .40 D1
Whitebridge Ind Est
ST15. . . . . .104 F2
Whitebridge La ST15. . . . .104 E2
Whitebridge Way ST15. . . .104 F2
White Farm Rd B74. . . . . .257 E4
Whitefield Cl WV8 . . . . . . .239 B2
Whitefields La ST10. . . . . . .49 B2
Whitegates CW12 . . . . .16 D4
Whitehall Ave ST7 . . . . .25 F2
Whitehall Cl ST14 . . . . . . .141 C8
Whitehall Ct WV3. . . . . . . .265 F6
Whitehall Rd
Kingswinford DY6 . . . . . . .275 C6
Wolverhampton WV4. . . . .266 B5
White Harte Cvn Pk DY7 .278 A3
Whitehaven Dr ST1 . . . . . .282 B4
Whitehead Rd ST6. . . . . . . .42 B5
Whiteheart Mews DE13 . . .201 A2
Whitehill Ave ST7 . . . . .26 B2
Whitehill Rd ST7 . . . . .26 B2
White Hollies WS3. . . . . . .243 F4
White Horse Rd WS8. . . . .228 E2
Whitehouse Ave WV3 . . . .265 D8
Whitehouse Cres
Burntwood WS7. . . . . . . .229 B7
Wolverhampton WV11. . . .241 F1
Whitehouse Dr WS13 . . . . .230 F6
White House La DY7. . . . . .268 F1
Whitehouse La
Codsall WV8 . . . . .238 D7
Sandon ST15 . . . . .121 B7
White House La DY3. . . . . .269 B1
Whitehouse Rd
Bucknall ST2 . . . . .58 B5
Newcastle-u-L ST5. . . . . . .56 B3
Whitehouse Rd N ST5. . . . . .56 B4
Stoke-on-T ST6 . . . . .262 F7
White Houses WV10. . . . . .241 B5
Whitehurst La ST10. . . . . . .75 D6
White Ladies Priory*
TF11. . . . . .221 D4
White Lion St ST17 . . . . . .285 B2
Whitemill La ST15 . . . . . . .119 F7
White Oak Dr
Kingswinford DY6 . . . . . . .275 C6
Wolverhampton WV3. . . . .255 C1
Whiteoaks Dr ST19 . . . . . .221 E8
White Oaks ST17 . . . . .175 D5
Whiteridge Rd ST7 . . . . . . .26 B2
White Row WV5 . . . . .264 C1
Whitesands Cl B77. . . . . . .250 E5
Whitesands Gr ST3 . . . . . . .74 A2
White's Dr DY3 . . . . .271 E8
Whites La CW2 . . . . .37 B6
White's Mdw ST18. . . . . . .153 D4
Whitesmiths Cl DY3. . . . . .271 D8
Whitestone Rd ST3 . . . . . . .90 B6
Whites Wood WV5. . . . . . .270 A5
Whitesytch La ST15. . . . . .121 B8
Whitethorn Ave ST12 . . . . . .88 D1
Whitethorn Cl WS12 . . . . .210 A8
Whitethorn Cres B74. . . . . .256 D1
Whitethorn Rd ⒄ DY8 . . .275 F1
Whitethorn Way ST5. . . . . .40 E1
Whitfield Ave WS5 . . . . . . .283 A1
Whitfield Rd
Cannock WS11. . . . . .210 C7
Kidsgrove ST7 . . . . .26 B2
Stoke-on-T ST6 . . . . .42 D6
Stoke-on-T ST13 . . . . .30 E4
Whitfield Valley Prim Sch
ST6. . . . . .42 B7
Whitgreave Ave WV10. . . .241 B7
Whitgreave Ct
Featherstone WV10. . . . . .241 B6
Stafford ST18 . . . . .155 D5
Whitgreave La
Great Bridgeford ST18 . . .135 D3
Rugeley WS15 . . . . .196 E6
Whitgreave ST18. . . . . . . .136 A4

Whitgreave Prim Sch
WV10. . . . . .241 B7
Whiting B77 . . . . .261 D7
Whitley Ave B77. . . . . .250 E5
Whitley Cl WV6 . . . . .255 B2
Whitley Rd ST6 . . . . .42 D6
Whitmore Ave ST9. . . . . . . .59 B4
Whitmore Rd
Hanchurch ST4 . . . . .87 D8
Newcastle-u-L ST5. . . . . . .70 D4
Stourbridge DY8 . . . . . . .279 D5
Whitmore ST5 . . . . .86 B8
Whitmore St ST1 . . . . .57 A2
Whitney Ave DY8 . . . . .279 D6
Whitridge Gr ST2 . . . . .73 D8
Whittaker Mews ST14. . . . .95 F3
Whittaker St WV2. . . . . . . .266 E6
Whittingham Dr ST17 . . . .174 B8
Whittington Common Rd
WS14 . . . . .232 B5
Whittington Hall La
Kinver DY7. . . . . .278 E2
Stourbridge DY7 . . . . . . .279 B3
Whittington Ho WS13 . . . .214 E1
Whittington Prim Sch
WS14 . . . . .232 E4
Whittle Cl ST1. . . . . .282 C4
Whittle Rd ST3 . . . . .90 B8
Whitty La
Blackshaw Moor ST13. . . . .20 C6
Upper Hulme ST13 . . . . . . .20 D6
Whitworth La WS15. . . . . .178 B1
Whygate Gr ST1 . . . . .57 F6
Whytmore The WS13 . . . . .230 F5
Wickenlow La SK17 . . . . . . .3 C1
Wickensones Ct ST8 . . . . . .27 D7
Wicket La DY7. . . . . .274 E1
Wickets The DE15. . . . . . .185 F8
Wickstead Row CW3 . . . . . .53 A6
Widecombe La ST17 . . . . .175 E7
Widecombe Rd ST1. . . . . . .57 F5
Widgeon Gr WV10 . . . . . . .241 B7
Widney Ave WS9. . . . . . . .245 B1
Wigford Rd B77 . . . . .266 C5
Wiggin Ho WS3 . . . . .243 C3
Wigginton Rd B79 . . . . . . .250 B7
Wightman Cl WS14 . . . . . .231 E6
Wightwick Bank WV6 . . . .255 A2
Wightwick Cl WS3 . . . . . . .243 B1
Wightwick Ct WV6. . . . . . .255 A2
Wightwick Hall Rd
WV6. . . . . .254 E2
Wightwick Manor* WV6 .254 F1
Wigley Bank Rd DY7 . . . . .277 D6
Wigmore Pl ST3 . . . . .73 C6
Wignall Rd ST6 . . . . .41 D6
Wilbraham's Wlk ST7 . . . . .39 D2
Wilcox Ave ST12 . . . . .210 B7
Wildacres DY3. . . . . .279 C6
Wildowl Wlk ST5. . . . . .85 C2
Wild Goose Ave ST7 . . . . . .26 C3
Wildhay La Stanton DE6. . . .80 C7
Wootton DE6. . . . . .80 A7
Wilding Rd ST6. . . . . .42 D6
Wildtree Ave WV10. . . . . . .241 A2
Wildwood Dr
Stafford ST17 . . . . .175 C6
Stafford ST17 . . . . .175 C7
Wildwood Gate ⒁ ST17 . .175 D6
Wildwood Lawns ST17 . . . .175 C7
Wildwood Sh Ctr ST17 . . . .175 D6
Wileman Pl ST4 . . . . .72 E6
Wileman St ST4 . . . . .72 F6
Wilfred Owen Cl TF9 . . . . .112 A7
Wilfred Pl ST4 . . . . .71 F8
Wilkes Cl WS3 . . . . .243 E3
Wilkes Croft DY3 . . . . .271 D7
Wilkes Rd WV8 . . . . .238 F3
Wilke's Wood ST18 . . . . . .154 F8
Wilkin Rd WS8. . . . . .228 C2
Wilkins Croft DE13. . . . . . .200 F2
Wilkins Ho WS3 . . . . .243 A1
Wilkinson Cl WS7 . . . . . . .229 B8
Wilkinson St ST6 . . . . .41 D2
Wilkinson Wlk ⒀ TF9 . . . . .97 C1
Wilks St ST6. . . . . .41 E4
Willatt Pl ST17 . . . . .43 A1
Willcock Rd
Burton u T DE14. . . . . . . .185 A7
Wolverhampton WV2. . . . .266 F2
Willdale Gr ST1. . . . . .57 F5
Willerby Fold WV10. . . . . . .240 F4
Willeton St ST2. . . . . .58 A3
Willett Ave WS7. . . . . .228 E5
Willey La ST20. . . . . .171 C6
Willfield La ST6,ST9 . . . . . . .43 C6
William Allitt Sch DE11 . . .186 E7
William Ave Biddulph ST8 . . .27 D7
Meir ST3 . . . . .90 C8
William Baxter Sch
WS12 . . . . .210 A8
William Birch Ct ST2. . . . . .58 A1
William Birch Rd ST2. . . . . .58 A1
William Cl ST11. . . . . .91 B7
William Clowes St ST6. . . . .56 F8
William Coltman Way
ST6. . . . . .41 C5
William Fiske Ct ST4. . . . . .71 F4
William Hutson Jun Sch
DE13 . . . . .166 B8
William IV Rd DE13 . . . . . .201 A3
William Lunn's Homes ⒁
WS14 . . . . .231 C8
William MacGregor Prim Sch
B77. . . . . .250 D4

William Mews WV10 . . . . 225 C2
William Morris Ct WS15 . 178 D3
William Morris Gr WS11 . 209 E4
William Nadin Way DE11 . 186 E3
William Newton Cl DE65 . 148 B5
William Rd ST7 . . . . 26 A2
William Ruston Rd ST6 . . 42 D2
Williams Ave WS13 . . . . . 215 C6
Williams Cl ST16 . . . . 155 B3
Williams Ct ST16 . . . . 155 F7
William Shrewsbury Prim
  Sch DE13 . . . . 147 F2
Williamson Ave
  Prospect Village WS12 . 211 C4
  Stoke-on-T ST6 . . . . 42 E6
Williamson St ST6 . . . . . . 41 E2
William St
  Burton u T DE14. . . . . . 166 C5
  Congleton CW12 . . . . 6 A4
  Stoke-on-T ST4 . . . . 72 E6
Williams Wlk ST15 . . . . . 103 C4
William Terr ST16 . . . . . . 155 A5
William Tolson's Ind Est
  B78 . . . . 261 A8
William Wiggin Ave
  WS3 . . . . 243 B2
Willington Rd B79 . . . . . . 250 B7
Williscroft Pl WS15 . . . . 179 A6
Willmer Cres ST7 . . . . 26 B6
Willmott Cl B75 . . . . 258 D3
Willmott Rd B75 . . . . 258 D3
Willotts Hill Rd ST5 . . . . . 40 D1
Willoughby Cl ST17 . . . . 207 F7
Willoughby Ct ST14 . . . . 125 C7
Willoughby Rd B79 . . . . 249 E7
Willoughby St ST6 . . . . . . 41 D7
Willow Ave WS7 . . . . 229 C6
Willowbank B78 . . . . 250 B1
Willow Bank WV3 . . . . . . 255 C1
Willow Bottom La B79 . . 234 B7
Willowbrook ST18 . . . . . 154 E2
Willowbrook Dr ST16 . . . . 42 E1
Willow Cl Coven WV9 . . . 224 B2
  Fradley WS13 . . . . 215 E8
  Hagley DY9 . . . . 281 F5
  Kidsgrove ST7 . . . . 41 A7
  Newcastle-u-L ST5. . . . . . 40 D1
  Penkridge ST19 . . . . 207 F6
  Upper Tean ST10 . . . . 92 D5
  Walton-on-t-H ST17. . . . 175 F6
Willowcroft Rise ST11 . . . 90 D7
Willowcroft Way ST7. . . . 26 E4
Willowcroft ST17 . . . . . . 151 E7
Willow Ct WS14. . . . . 231 C5
Willowdale Ave ST4. . . . . 72 C5
Willowdale Grange WV6. 255 E6
Willow Dale ST15 . . . . . . 120 C3
Willow Dr Cheddleton ST13 . 45 C8
  Codsall WV8 . . . . 239 B3
  Swadlincote DE11 . . . . . 186 F7
Willowfield Ct ST4. . . . . . . 88 D7
Willowfield Dr ST4. . . . . . . 88 C7
Willow Gr
  Essington WV11. . . . . . . 242 B3
  Stoke-on-T ST5 . . . . 72 E2
Willowherb Cl WS11 . . . . 210 C2
Willow Ho WS4 . . . . 244 D1
Willowmoor ST17. . . . . . 174 E5
Willowood Gr ST3 . . . . . . 72 C1
Willow Pl Biddulph ST8. . . 17 B1
  Burton u T DE15. . . . . . 185 E7
Willow Rd
  Barton-u-N DE13 . . . . . 183 D1
  Kinver DY7 . . . . 278 C3
  Stone ST15 . . . . 120 B7
  Wolverhampton WV3 . . 265 D8
Willow Row ST3 . . . . 284 B3
Willows Dr ST3 . . . . 90 A4
Willowsmere Dr WS14. . 231 F7
Willows Prim Sch WS13 . 214 B2
Willows Prim Sch The
  ST4. . . . . 71 F7
Willows The
  Burton u T DE14. . . . . . 166 D2
  Cannock WS11. . . . . 209 C1
  Leek ST13 . . . . 30 C5
  Rugeley WS15 . . . . 197 A5
  Stoke-on-T ST5 . . . . 120 B6
  Sutton Coldfield,Streetly
    B74 . . . . 257 C2
  Wombourne WV5. . . . . . 269 F5
  Wrinehill CW3 . . . . 53 A3
  Yarnfield ST15 . . . . 118 E6
Willowtree Cl WS13 . . . . 214 B2
Willow Tree Gr ST4 . . . . . 72 E4
Willow Way ST11 . . . . 91 A8
Willow Wlk WS12 . . . . . . 210 C2
Willridding La D66. . . . . . 80 C7
Willsford Ave ST14. . . . . 126 D7
Wilmcote Dr B75 . . . . . . 258 B3
Wilmore Ct ST18. . . . . . . 137 D1
Wilmore Hill La ST18 . . . 137 D1
Wilmore La DE13 . . . . . . 164 B3
Wilmot Cl ST5 . . . . 55 F3
Wilmot Dr ST5. . . . . 55 F3
Wilmot Gr ST3 . . . . 73 C6
Wilmott Cl WS13 . . . . 55 F2
Wilnecote High Sch B77 . 261 F6
Wilnecote Jun Sch B77 . 261 F7
Wilnecote La B77. . . . . . . 250 D2
Wilnecote Sta B77 . . . . . 261 D7
Wilner's View WS3 . . . . . 243 F5
Wilson Ct WS15 . . . . 210 C2
Wilson Keys Ct WS15. . . 178 F2
Wilson Rd ST4. . . . . 71 F1
Wilson St
  Newcastle-u-L ST5. . . . . 283 B3

Wilson St continued
  Stoke-on-T ST6 . . . . 42 B2
Wilson Way ST6 . . . . 41 C6
Wiltell Rd Ind Est WS14 . 231 B7
Wiltell Rd WS14 . . . . 231 B6
Wilton Ave ST9 . . . . 59 F4
Wilton Cl DY3 . . . . 271 E7
Wilton St ST5. . . . . 283 A4
Wiltshire Gr ST5 . . . . 71 C4
Wiltshire Ho 3 DY8 . . . . 279 F8
Wimberry Dr ST5 . . . . 40 D1
Wimblebury Rd WS12 . . 210 F2
Wimborne Ave ST3 . . . . . . 88 F7
Wimhurst Mdw WV10 . . 240 F4
Winburn Cl WV6 . . . . 254 F3
Winchcombe Cl DY1 . . . . 271 E3
Winchcombe Dr DE15. . . 167 B1
Winchester Ave ST2 . . . . . 58 D1
Winchester Cl
  Armitage WS15 . . . . 198 B4
  Lichfield WS13. . . . . 214 C3
Winchester Ct
  Stafford ST17 . . . . 175 D6
  Sutton Coldfield B74 . . . 257 F2
Winchester Dr
  Burton u T DE14. . . . . . 185 C8
  Newcastle-u-L ST5. . . . . . 70 F4
Winchester Mews WV4. . 256 B4
Winchester Rd
  Cannock WS11. . . . . 210 A3
  Tamworth B78 . . . . 249 F3
  Wolverhampton WV10. . 240 C3
Wincote Dr WV6 . . . . 255 C4
Wincote La ST21. . . . . . . 133 C3
Windermere Way ST10. . . 76 C4
Windermere Dr
  Aldridge B74 . . . . 256 F3
  Kingswinford DY6 . . . . . 275 D6
Windermere Ho ST16 . . . 285 C3
Windermere Pl WS11 . . . 209 E1
Windermere Rd
  Newcastle-u-L ST5. . . . . . 71 B4
  Wolverhampton WV6. . . 255 D8
Windermere St ST1 . . . . . 282 A4
Windermere St WV6 . . . . 277 F2
Winding The WS13 . . . . . 214 A1
Windmill Ave ST7. . . . . . . 41 A8
Windmill Bank
  Gentleshaw WS15 . . . . . 212 B5
  Wombourne WV5. . . . . . 270 A7
Windmill Cl
  4 Uttoxeter ST14. . . . . 111 B1
  Lichfield WS13. . . . . 214 A2
  Stoke-on-T ST3 . . . . 89 F4
  Tamworth B79 . . . . 250 A8
Windmill Cres WV3 . . . . . 255 A1
Windmill Dr ST14 . . . . . . 127 E3
Windmill Gr DY6 . . . . 275 B8
Windmillhill La WS14 . . . 232 E5
Windmill Hill ST3 . . . . 89 F4
Windmill La Croxton ST21 . 114 F2
  Gentleshaw WS15 . . . . . 212 A4
  Lichfield WS13. . . . . 214 A2
  Snelston DE6. . . . . 81 E2
  Wolverhampton WV3 . . 255 A1
Windmill St
  Dudley,Gornalwood DY3 . 271 D5
  Hanley ST1 . . . . 282 C3
Windmill View ST10 . . . . . 59 C4
Windrow The WV6 . . . . . 254 D4
Windrush Cl
  Stoke-on-T ST4 . . . . 88 C5
  Walsall WS3 . . . . 244 A1
Windrush Dr
  Cannock WS11. . . . . 209 E6
  Hilton DE65 . . . . 147 D8
Windsmoor St ST4. . . . . . . 72 B5
Windsor Ave
  Cannock WS12. . . . . 210 B6
  Longton ST3. . . . . 284 D2
  Wolverhampton WV4. . . 265 E6
Windsor Cl
  Burntwood WS7. . . . . . . 211 C1
  Dudley DY3. . . . . 271 B2
  Rugeley WS15 . . . . 196 D7
  Stone ST15 . . . . 119 F5
  Tamworth B79 . . . . 250 C7
Windsor Cres DY7 . . . . . . 277 F4
Windsor Ct
  Cannock WS12. . . . . 210 B6
  Lichfield WS14. . . . . 231 B6
Windsor Dr
  Burton u T DE15. . . . . . 166 F1
  Leek ST13 . . . . 31 B7
  Market Drayton TF9. . . . . 97 E2
Windsor Gdns
  Codsall WV8 . . . . 238 F3
  Wolverhampton WV3 . . 265 A8
Windsor Gr
  Stourbridge DY8 . . . . . . 275 E1
  Walsall WS4 . . . . 244 C2
Windsor Holloway DY7. . 278 C1
Windsor Ho ST7 . . . . 40 D6
Windsor Ind Est DE14. . . 166 F4
Windsor Park CE Mid Sch
  ST14. . . . . 126 B8
Windsor Rd
  Albrighton WV7. . . . . . . 237 A6
  Cheslyn Hay WS6 . . . . . 226 E4
  Pattingham WV6. . . . . . 253 C2
  Stafford ST17 . . . . 175 B8
  Stoke-on-T ST4 . . . . 72 A1
  Stourbridge DY8 . . . . . . 279 E3
  Uttoxeter ST14 . . . . 111 A1
  Wolverhampton WV4. . . 265 F6
Windsor St ST5. . . . . 283 C3
Windy Arbour ST10 . . . . . 76 E4

Windy Arbour La WV10. . 225 E4
Windycote La ST10 . . . . . . 60 B2
Windyridge SK17 . . . . 13 B6
Winford Ave DY6. . . . . . . 275 E4
Wingate CB74. . . . . 257 E4
Wingate Wlk ST3 . . . . 88 F7
Wingay Cl ST16. . . . . 56 C8
Winghay Pl ST6. . . . . 42 B5
Winghay Rd ST7 . . . . 26 B2
Winghouse La ST15. . . . . 103 E7
Wingrove Ave 1 ST3 . . . . 73 D1
Winifred Gdns ST3. . . . . . 88 B8
Winifred St ST1. . . . . 282 A4
Winnipeg Cl ST4 . . . . 88 B8
Winnipeg Rd ST5 . . . . 55 F8
Winrush Cl DY3. . . . . 271 D3
Winscar Croft DY3 . . . . . 271 D3
Winsford Ave ST3 . . . . 73 E2
Winsford Cres ST17 . . . . 175 E6
Winslow Dr WV6. . . . . . . 255 C4
Winslow Gn ST2 . . . . 58 C1
Winsor Ave WS12 . . . . . . 210 B6
Winstanley Cl WS15. . . . 178 D2
Winstanley Rd WS15 . . . 178 D2
Winston Cl DE11. . . . . . . 186 E5
Winston Pl ST2 . . . . 58 A3
Winston Rd Cookley DY11 . 280 A6
  Swindon DY3 . . . . 269 E2
Winston Terr ST5 . . . . 56 C6
Winterbourne Gr ST3 . . . . 73 E3
Winter Cl WS13. . . . . 214 D2
Wintercroft La DE6 . . . . . . 51 E1
Winterfield La ST3 . . . . . . 74 B7
Winterley Gdns DY3. . . . . 271 E6
Winterside Cl ST5 . . . . 40 D1
Wintonfield St ST4. . . . . . 72 C7
Winton Sq ST4 . . . . 72 C8
Winwood Cl DY8. . . . . . . 279 F4
Wiscombe Ave ST19 . . . . 193 A1
Wise St ST13 . . . . 284 C1
Wissage Ct WS13 . . . . . . 231 D8
Wissage La WS13 . . . . . . 214 D1
Wissage Rd WS13 . . . . . . 231 D8
Wisteria Dr WS8 . . . . 228 C2
Wistmans Cl DY1 . . . . . . 271 E2
Wistwood Hayes WV10 . 240 F4
Witchford Cres ST3 . . . . . . 88 F7
Witham Way ST13 . . . . . . 16 E1
Withern Way DY3 . . . . . . 271 D3
Withers Rd WV8 . . . . 239 B3
Withies Rd ST4 . . . . 71 E4
Withington Rd ST6. . . . . . 42 A8
Within La ST18 . . . . 137 D1
Withnell Gn ST6 . . . . 42 A6
Withymere La WV5 . . . . . 270 C8
Withystakes Rd ST9 . . . . . 59 D4
Withywood Cl WV12 . . . 242 C1
Witley Dr 1 WS13 . . . . . . 231 E8
Witney Cl B79 . . . . 249 F7
Witney Gr WV10 . . . . 240 B3
Witney Rd ST17 . . . . 156 D1
Witney Wlk ST3 . . . . 88 F7
Witton Rd WV4 . . . . 266 A6
Witton St DY8 . . . . 279 F4
Wobaston Ct WV10. . . . . 240 B3
Wobaston Rd
  Codsall WV9 . . . . 239 E4
  Wolverhampton WV9,
    WV10 . . . . 240 B4
Woburn Cl ST4 . . . . 88 C5
Woburn Dr CW12 . . . . 16 B8
Woburn B77. . . . . 250 D3
Wodehouse Cl WV5. . . . . 269 E5
Wodehouse Cotts WV5. . 270 E8
Wodehouse La WV5,DY3 . 270 E8
Woden Cl WV5. . . . . 269 F7
Wogan St ST16 . . . . 155 E5
Wold The WV5 . . . . 267 D7
Wolfe St ST14 . . . . 72 B6
Wolfscote Dale DE11. . . . 186 F7
Wolgarston High Sch
  ST19 . . . . 208 A8
Wolgarston Way ST19. . . 207 F7
Wollaston Ct DY8 . . . . . . 279 C6
Wollaston Rd
  Stourbridge DY8 . . . . . . 279 E8
  Stourton DY7 . . . . 278 C4
Wollery La TF11 . . . . 204 C2
Wolmer Rd WV11 . . . . . . 242 A2
Wolmore La WV5 . . . . . . 263 B2
Wolseley Ctr The* ST17 . 178 A5
Wolseley Ct
  Rugeley WS15 . . . . 197 B6
  Stafford ST18 . . . . 156 D5
Wolseley Rd
  Newcastle-u-L ST5. . . . . . 56 B5
  Rugeley,Cannock Chase Ctry Pk
    WS15 . . . . 177 E1
  Rugeley WS15 . . . . 178 E2
  Stafford ST16 . . . . 156 C3
  Stoke-on-T ST4 . . . . 71 F4
Wolsey Rd WS13 . . . . 213 F2
Wolstanton High Sch ST5 . 56 C4
Wolstanton Rd ST5 . . . . . . 56 C4
Wolstanton Ret Pk ST5 . . 56 C4
Wolstern Rd ST3. . . . . 73 D5
Wolverhampton Bsns Airport
  DY7 . . . . 268 C2
Wolverhampton Coll Wulfrun
  Campus WV6. . . . . 255 E3
Wolverhampton Girls' High
  Sch WV6. . . . . 255 F2
Wolverhampton Gram Sch
  WV3. . . . . 255 F2
Wolverhampton Rd
  Cannock WS11. . . . . 226 D8

Wolverhampton Rd continued
  Cheslyn Hay WV10,WS6 . 226 B2
  Codsall WV8 . . . . 239 A3
  Cookley DY10. . . . . 280 B3
  Essington WV11. . . . . . . 242 A3
Wolverhampton Rd E
  WV4 . . . . 266 D5
Wolverhampton Rd
  Kingswinford DY6 . . . . . 270 C1
  Nurton WV6 . . . . 254 A3
  Pattingham WV6 . . . . . . 253 E3
  Penkridge WS11 . . . . . . 207 E8
  Sedgley DY3. . . . . 266 D2
  Stafford ST17 . . . . 285 B1
  Stoke-on-T ST4 . . . . 278 F7
  Walsall,Pelsall WS3. . . . 243 F3
  Walsall,Wallington Heath
    WS3 . . . . 243 B1
  Wedges Mills WS11. . . . 226 B6
Wolverley Ave
  Stourbridge DY8 . . . . . . 279 C6
  Wolverhampton WV4. . . 265 D5
Wolverley Ct WV7. . . . . . 223 E8
Wolverley Rd DY10. . . . . 280 A2
Wolverson Rd WV9 . . . . . 245 A4
Wombourne Cl DY3 . . . . 271 C8
Wombourne Ent Pk
  WV5. . . . . 269 D5
Wombourne Pk WV5. . . . 269 C5
Wombourne Rd DY3,WV5 . 269 F3
Wombrook Dale WV5 . . . 269 D6
Wombrook Ind Est WV5. . 269 E6
Woodall St ST1 . . . . 57 B6
Wood Ave Coven WV9 . . 224 B3
  Dudley DY3 . . . . 271 C4
  Kingsley ST10 . . . . 61 D2
Wood Bank La ST19 . . . . 193 B2
Wood Bank Rd WV3 . . . . 271 C7
Wood Bank Rd ST4 . . . . . 265 A8
Woodbank St ST6 . . . . 56 F8
Woodberry Ave ST4. . . . . 71 F5
Woodberry Cl
  Stafford ST17 . . . . 174 F4
  Stoke-on-T ST4 . . . . 71 E5
Woodbine Cl DE14. . . . . . 184 E6
Woodbridge Cl
  Walsall,Wallington Heath
    WS3 . . . . 243 A3
  Walsall WS4 . . . . 244 D1
Woodbridge Rd ST5 . . . . . 71 B2
Woodburn Rd ST6 . . . . . . 42 C2
Woodcock Gdns WV10 . . 241 B7
Woodcock La ST7 . . . . 26 C6
Woodcock Rd WS15. . . . . 178 C1
Woodcocks' Well CE Prim
  Sch ST7 . . . . 26 C6
Wood Common Grange
  WS3 . . . . 243 F4
Woodcote Rd WV6 . . . . . 255 C4
Woodcote The 3 ST17 . . 175 C7
Wood Cres Stafford ST16 . 155 B6
  Stone ST15 . . . . 119 F5
Woodcroft ST17 . . . . 40 A1
Woodcroft Ave
  Tamworth B79 . . . . 250 B8
Woodcroft Fst Sch ST13 . 30 C4
Woodcroft La ST13 . . . . . . 30 D4
Woodcross La WV14 . . . . 266 F2
Woodcross St WV14. . . . . 266 F2
Wood Ct DE14 . . . . 166 C1
Wooddisse La ST13 . . . . . . 33 E2
Wood Eaton Rd ST20. . . . 190 A7
Woodedge La ST14 . . . . . 143 F6
Wood End La
  Fradley WS13 . . . . 215 A5
  Lichfield WS13. . . . . 214 B7
Woodend Pl WV6 . . . . . . 255 B4
Wood End Prim Sch CW9 262 C1
Wood End Rd WV11. . . . . 241 C1
Woodend St ST4. . . . . 72 F6
Wood End Way WS9 . . . . 245 B1
Woodfield Ave ST4 . . . . . 265 F6
Woodfield Cl WS11 . . . . . 227 F7
Woodfield Ct ST13 . . . . . . 31 A6
Woodfield Ho WS3. . . . . . 244 B3
Woodfield Hts WV6 . . . . . 255 D4
Woodfield Jun & Inf Schs
  WV4 . . . . 265 F6
Woodfield Rd DY3 . . . . . . 271 C4
Woodfields Dr WS14 . . . . 231 E5
Woodfold Croft WS9 . . . . 256 B7
Woodford Cl WV9. . . . . . 239 F2
Woodford Cres WS7 . . . . 229 B7
Woodford Rd 1 WS11 . . 209 F4
Woodford La WV5 . . . . . . 269 D8
Woodford Way
  Cannock WS12. . . . . 210 D1
  Wombourne WV5. . . . . . 269 D6
Woodgate Ave ST7. . . . . . 25 A5
Woodgate St ST4 . . . . 74 A1
Woodgreen WS6 . . . . 226 E5
Woodhall Pl ST5. . . . . 54 F7
Woodhall Rd
  Kidsgrove ST7 . . . . 26 C3
  Wolverhampton WV4. . . 265 E5
Woodham Warsall WV4 . 244 D1
  Wedges Mills WS11. . . . 226 B5
  Woodseaves ST20. . . . . . 151 E7
Wood Hayes Croft WV10 241 C2
Wood Hayes Rd WV11. . . 241 C1
Woodhead Rd ST22 . . . . . 58 C8
Woodhead Yd ST10 . . . . . 76 E5
Woodheyes Lawns
  WS15 . . . . 178 C1
Woodhill Cl WV5. . . . . . . 269 D6
Wood Hill Dr WV5 . . . . . . 269 F5

Woodhouse High Sch
  B77. . . . . 250 F4
Woodhouse La
  Albrighton WV7 . . . . . . 237 C2
  Biddulph Moor ST8 . . . . . 17 A1
  Biddulph ST8 . . . . 16 F2
  Brown Edge ST6 . . . . 42 F6
  Foston DE65 . . . . 129 F7
  Haughton ST18 . . . . 172 D8
  Norton in H CW3. . . . . . . 82 A7
  Tamworth B77 . . . . 251 A5
Woodhouse Mid Sch ST8 . 16 E2
Woodhouse Rd N WV6 . . 255 B4
Woodhouse Rd WV6 . . . . 255 B4
Woodhouses La WS7. . . . 229 F6
Woodhouses Rd WS7 . . . 230 A7
Woodhouse St ST4. . . . . . 72 B6
Woodhurst Cl B77 . . . . . . 250 F5
Woodingdean Cl 3 ST3 . . 73 D5
Woodkirk Cl ST6. . . . . 42 A8
Wood La Aldridge B74 . . 256 E2
  Cannock WS12. . . . . 210 C4
  Cheslyn Hay WS11. . . . . 225 F6
  Gratwich ST14 . . . . 124 D2
  Hanbury DE13 . . . . 144 F3
  Maer ST5. . . . . 84 D3
Woodland Ave
  Cheddleton ST13 . . . . . . 45 B1
  Hagley DY8 . . . . 281 F5
  Newcastle-u-L ST5. . . . . . 56 C5
  Stoke-on-T ST6 . . . . 42 F4
  Wolverhampton WV6. . . 255 B3
Woodland Cl
  Albrighton WV7 . . . . . . 237 A6
  Cannock WS12. . . . . 210 B8
  Leek ST13 . . . . 30 F2
Woodland Cres WV3 . . . . 265 D7
Woodland Ct
  Cannock WS12. . . . . 209 C4
  Shenstone WS14 . . . . . . 258 A7
Woodland Dr
  Cheslyn Hay WS6. . . . . . 226 E4
  Foston DE65 . . . . 129 D4
  Rocester ST14 . . . . 95 F3
Woodland Gr Dudley DY3 . 271 B3
  Kidderminster DY10 . . . 280 C3
  Stoke-on-T ST6 . . . . 42 B2
Woodland Hills CW3 . . . . 68 E8
Woodland Rd
  Stanton DE15. . . . . 186 B4
  Tamworth B77 . . . . 251 A4
  Wolverhampton WV3. . . 265 D7
Woodlands Ave
  Kidsgrove ST7 . . . . 25 D1
  Stone ST15 . . . . 119 F8
Woodlands Cl
  Stafford ST16 . . . . 155 C7
  Stone ST15 . . . . 119 E8
  Thorpe DE6 . . . . 51 D1
Woodlands Com Prim Sch
  The B77 . . . . 250 E4
Woodlands Cotts WV4 . . 265 F4
Woodlands Cres WS3 . . . 243 F5
Woodlands Dr
  Chorlton CW2 . . . . 37 C3
  Coven WV9. . . . . 224 B3
  Stone ST15 . . . . 120 C3
Woodlands Gr ST3. . . . . . . 90 A4
Woodlands La
  Cheslyn Hay WS11. . . . . 225 B8
  Forsbrook ST11 . . . . 91 B6
Woodlands Paddock
  WV4 . . . . 265 E4
Woodlands Rd
  Cookley DY10. . . . . 280 A4
  Stafford ST16 . . . . 155 B7
  Stoke-on-T ST4 . . . . 71 E4
  Wombourne WV5. . . . . . 270 A5
Woodlands Rise DE6. . . . 144 A7
Woodland St ST8 . . . . 27 D6
Woodlands The
  Coldmeece ST15 . . . . . . 118 C6
  Kidsgrove ST7 . . . . 25 E3
  Lichfield WS13. . . . . 231 D8
  Stoke-on-T ST4 . . . . 71 E4
  Tatenhill DE13 . . . . 184 A8
  Wood End CW9 . . . . 262 C1
Woodlands View DE12. . . 219 F3
Woodlands Views ST14. . 127 E2
Woodland View DY3. . . . 269 C4
Woodland Way
  Burntwood WS7. . . . . . . 229 A6
  Polesworth B78 . . . . 262 F8
Wood Lane Prim Sch ST7 . 40 A1
  Stone ST15 . . . . 119 F5
  Stretton ST19 . . . . 206 C4
  Swadlincote DE11 . . . . . 186 F7
  Uttoxeter ST14 . . . . 126 E6
  Walsall WS3 . . . . 243 F4
  Wedges Mills WS11. . . . 226 A6
Woodlawn Gr DY6 . . . . . 275 D5
Wood La
  Wolverhampton WV10. . 240 D2
  Yoxall DE13 . . . . 182 A6
Woodleighton Gr ST14. . 126 C6
Woodleighton Gr ST14. . 126 C6
Woodleyes Cres ST17 . . . 175 D6
Woodman Gr 5 B75. . . . 258 E3
Woodman La WS14. . . . . 226 E4
Woodman St ST2 . . . . 43 B1
Woodmill La WS15. . . . . . 161 B7
Woodpark La ST3. . . . . 89 D7

Woodpecker Dr
Packmoor ST7 . . . . .26 E1
Stoke-on-T ST7 . . . . .41 E8
Woodpecker View TF9 . . . .99 C3
Woodpecker Way WS11 . 210 C3
Wood PI ST3 . . . . .74 B2
Wood Rd Codsall WV8 . . . .238 E4
Dudley DY3 . . . . .271 C4
Longsdon ST9 . . . . .45 A8
Wolverhampton WV6 . . . . .255 C3
Wombourne WV5 . . . . .270 B7
Woodridge CI TF10 . . . . . .168 A4
Wood Ridings WS13 . . . . .214 A1
Woodroffe's Cliff ST14 . .143 C5
Woodrow Way
Ashley TF9 . . . . .100 C5
Newcastle-u-L ST5 . . . . .40 F1
Woodruff CI ST7 . . . . .27 A1
Woods Croft WS13 . . . . . .214 A1
Woodseat Gr ST14 . . . . . . .96 A4
Woodseaves CE Prim Sch
ST20 . . . . .151 E7
Woodsetton Sch The
DY3 . . . . .271 F7
Woodshot Ave WS15 . . . . .198 C4
Woodshutt's St ST7 . . . . . .25 E1
Woodside Ave
Brown Edge ST6 . . . . .43 B6
Kidsgrove ST7 . . . . .26 A1
Woodside ST5 . . . . .85 C3
Woodside CI
Colwich ST18 . . . . .177 D8
Wood End CV9 . . . . .262 C1
Woodside Cotts ST10 . . . . .77 F7
Woodside Cres ST5 . . . . . . .71 C2
Woodside Dr
Little Aston B74 . . . . .257 C5
Meir Heath ST3 . . . . .90 A4
Woodside Gr WV8 . . . . . . .239 B2
Woodside La ST13 . . . . . . .30 C2
Woodside Lawton-gate ST7 .25 E4
Madeley CW3 . . . . .68 E7
Woodside PI
Cannock WS11 . . . . .209 E5
Stoke-on-T ST2 . . . . .43 B1
Woodside B74 . . . . .257 E2
Woodside Villas ST3 . . . . .284 D4
Woodside Way WS9 . . . . .256 B5
Woods La
Burton u T DE15 . . . . .167 A1
Burton u T DE15 . . . . .167 B1
Woodsorrel Rd DY1 . . . . .271 F4
Wood St Audley ST7 . . . . . .39 E3
Burton u T DE14 . . . . .166 C1
Woodstile CI B75 . . . . .258 D3
Wood St Leek ST13 . . . . . . .30 F5
Longton ST3 . . . . .284 C4
Mow Cop ST7 . . . . .26 D7
Woodstock CI
Newcastle-u-L ST5 . . . . .56 C3
Stourbridge DY8 . . . . .275 C1
Woodstock Dr
Huntington WS12 . . . . .209 C7
Stourbridge DY8 . . . . .275 C2
Sutton Coldfield B74 . . . . .257 D4
Woodstock Rd
Kidsgrove ST6 . . . . .41 A7
Stafford ST17 . . . . .156 D1
Woodstock St ST6 . . . . .41 C8
Woodstone Ave ST9 . . . . . .43 E6
Wood St Stourbridge DY8 .279 D6
Wood End CV9 . . . . .262 C1

Wood Terr ST1 . . . . .282 A1
Wood The ST3 . . . . .74 C2
Woodtherne CI ST19 . . . . .207 F7
Woodthorne CI
Dudley DY1 . . . . .271 D2
Rugeley WS15 . . . . .178 C2
Woodthorne Prim Sch
WV6 . . . . .255 B4
Woodthorne Rd S WV6 . .255 A5
Woodthorne Rd WV6 . . . .255 A6
Woodthorne Wlk DY6 . . . .275 E8
Woodvale Cres ST9 . . . . . .43 E8
Wood View ST7 . . . . .40 A1
Woodview Rd DE11 . . . . . .186 E5
Wood View WS15 . . . . .196 F6
Woodville Gdns DY3 . . . . .266 F1
Woodville PI ST3 . . . . .74 A2
Woodville Rd ST3 . . . . .74 A2
Woodville Terr ST3 . . . . . . .74 B2
Woodward St ST1 . . . . .57 D6
Woodyard Dr B79 . . . . . . .217 C5
Woodyard La DE65 . . . . . .129 F5
Woody Bank WS6 . . . . . . .226 E2
Woolliscroft Ave ST5 . . . . .56 D3
Woolliscroft Rd ST2 . . . . . .58 B3
Woolrich St ST6 . . . . .56 E7
Woolridge Ct ST6 . . . . .42 D1
Woolston Ave CW12 . . . . . .6 A2
Woore Prim Sch CW3 . . . . .67 C1
Woosnam CI DE14 . . . . . . .185 A6
Wootton CI WS11 . . . . .210 B3
Wootton Dr ST16 . . . . .155 A7
Wootton La
Eccleshall ST21 . . . . .133 E3
Oakamoor ST10 . . . . .78 E4
Wootton Rd WV3 . . . . .265 D8
Woottons Ct WS11 . . . . . .209 F1
Worcester CI
Cannock WS11 . . . . .226 F8
Lichfield WS13 . . . . .214 C3
Rugeley WS15 . . . . .196 C6
Sutton Coldfield B75 . . . . .258 D3
Talke ST7 . . . . .40 D7
Worcester Ct WV3 . . . . . . .266 A6
Worcester Gr WV6 . . . . . . .254 D4
Worcester La B75 . . . . .258 D4
Worcester PI ST2 . . . . .58 D2
Worcester Rd
Burton u T DE15 . . . . .185 E6
Hagley DY9 . . . . .281 F3
Whittington WS14 . . . . . . .232 C3
Wordsley Ct DY8 . . . . .275 E3
Wordsley Green Sh Ctr
DY8 . . . . .275 D2
Wordsley Hospl DY8 . . . . .275 E3
Wordsley Sch The DY8 . .275 F3
Wordsworth Ave
Stafford ST17 . . . . .174 C8
Tamworth B79 . . . . .250 A6
Wolverhampton WV4 . . . . .266 F4
Wordsworth CI
Armitage WS15 . . . . .198 A4
Burton u T DE14 . . . . .166 D6
Cannock WS11 . . . . .209 D4
Cheadle ST10 . . . . .76 C2
Lichfield WS14 . . . . .231 B5
Wordsworth Ct WV6 . . . . .254 E4
Wordsworth Dr TF9 . . . . .112 A7
Wordsworth Rd
Burntwood WS7 . . . . .229 A8
Dudley DY3 . . . . .271 B5
Worfield Gdns WV5 . . . . . .265 F6
Worsley Dr CW12 . . . . .6 B1
Worston La ST15,ST18 . . .135 B5
Worth CI ST3 . . . . .73 D4

Worthing PI ST3 . . . . .284 B3
Worthington Rd WS13 . . .215 D6
Worthington Way DE14 . .166 D3
Wraggs CI WV9 . . . . .240 B3
Wraggs La ST8 . . . . .17 B1
Wrekin Ave TF10 . . . . .168 E2
Wrekin Ct B74 . . . . .257 F2
Wrekin Dr
Wolverhampton,Penn
WV3 . . . . .265 E8
Wolverhampton,Tettenhall
WV6 . . . . .255 A5
Wrekin Gr WV11 . . . . .242 B1
Wrekin La WV6 . . . . .255 A5
Wrekin View
Brownhills WS8 . . . . .245 A5
Huntington WS12 . . . . .209 C7
Wrekin View Rd DY3 . . . . .271 C8
Wren Ave WV6 . . . . .254 D3
Wrenburry CI ST5 . . . . .40 D1
Wrenbury Cres ST2 . . . . . .58 B1
Wren CI ST8 . . . . .27 E8
Wrens Croft WS11 . . . . . . .210 B1
Wrenswood ST17 . . . . .175 C6
Wren View
Loggerheads TF9 . . . . .99 C4
Longton ST3 . . . . .284 D2
Wrexham CI ST8 . . . . .16 D1
Wright Ave ST5 . . . . .57 F7
Wrighton CI ST2 . . . . .57 F2
Wrighton Dr DY5 . . . . .271 C1
Wrighton Gr B78 . . . . .261 A8
Wright's Ave WS11 . . . . . .209 F5
Wright St Kidsgrove ST7 . . .25 D1
Stafford ST16 . . . . .155 E5
Wrinehill Rd CW5 . . . . .52 A6
Wrottesley Ct WV8 . . . . . .254 C8
Wrottesley Park Rd WV6,
WV8 . . . . .254 D5
Wrottesley Rd WV6 . . . . . .255 B5
Wrottesley Rd W
Perton WV6 . . . . .254 F6
Wolverhampton WV6 . . . . .255 A6
Wroxham Way ST5 . . . . . . .71 B2
Wulfad Ct ST15 . . . . .120 C7
Wulfric CI ST19 . . . . .208 A8
Wulfruna Gdns WV3 . . . . .255 F1
Wulstan Dr ST5 . . . . .56 C3
Wulstan Rd ST6 . . . . .57 A6
Wyatt St ST6 . . . . .41 C7
Wychall Dr WV10 . . . . .240 E4
Wychbold CI WV12 . . . . . .242 D1
Wychbold Way WV12 . . . .242 D1
Wychbury Rd WV3 . . . . . . .265 C2
Wych Elm Rd WS8 . . . . . . .244 E5
Wycherwood Gdns ST17 .175 D5
Wychwood Pk
Chorlton CW2 . . . . .37 B2
Gorstyhill CW2 . . . . .37 E2
Wycliffe Rd ST6 . . . . .56 F8
Wye CI Cheadle ST10 . . . . . .76 E1
Hilton DE65 . . . . .147 D8
Perton WV6 . . . . .254 F4
Wye Dale DE11 . . . . .186 F2
Wye Ho DY3 . . . . .271 D3
Wye Rd Newcastle-u-L ST5 . .71 A3
Walsall WS3 . . . . .243 E1
Wyggeston St DE13 . . . . . .166 C6
Wykeham Gr WV6 . . . . . . .254 D3
Wyllie Mews DE14 . . . . . .166 D3
Wymondley Gr ST4 . . . . . . .88 B6
Wynbank CI ST7 . . . . .54 E8
Wynchcombe Ave WV4 . .265 D4
Wyndham Cres DE15 . . . . .167 C3
Wyndham Rd ST3 . . . . .88 F7

Wyndham Wood CI
WS13 . . . . .215 D7
Wyndley CI B74 . . . . .257 F6
Wyndley Manor B74 . . . . .258 A6
Wynd The DY3 . . . . .266 D1
Wynford PI ST2 . . . . .58 B1
Wynne Cres WV4 . . . . .265 C3
Wynn Rd WV4 . . . . .265 F5
Wynstay Ave ST9 . . . . .59 A3
Wynstay Ct ST5 . . . . .71 C1
Wynyates B79 . . . . .249 E6
Wyre CI WS9 . . . . .244 F4
Wyre Rd DY8 . . . . .279 E7
Wyrley Brook Pk WS11 . .226 D5
Wyrley Brook Ret Pk
WS11 . . . . .226 D6
Wyrley CI Burntwood WS8 .228 F3
Lichfield WS14 . . . . .231 A5
Wyrley La WS3 . . . . .243 E8
Wyrley Rd B75 . . . . .258 D1
Wyvern Gr WS12 . . . . .210 A5
Wyvern B77 . . . . .250 F3
Wyvis CI WV6 . . . . .255 E2

Y

Yale St ST6 . . . . .56 E7
Yardley PI ST3 . . . . .88 F6
Yardley St ST6 . . . . .42 F5
Yardley Wlk ST3 . . . . .88 F6
Yarlet Croft ST16 . . . . .155 D6
Yarlet La ST18 . . . . .136 D5
Yarlet St ST18 . . . . .136 C7
Yarmouth Wlk ST3 . . . . . .284 D5
Yarnbrook Gr ST6 . . . . .42 D3
Yarner CI DY1 . . . . .271 E2
Yarnfield CI ST3 . . . . .74 A2
Yarnfield La ST15 . . . . .119 B8
Yarrow CI
Burton u T DE15 . . . . .167 B2
Walsall WS3 . . . . .244 A5
Yateley CI ST2 . . . . .58 B2
Yates Croft B74 . . . . .257 F6
Yates Ind Est WS3 . . . . . . .227 F2
Yates St ST1 . . . . .282 A2
Yaxley Ct ST5 . . . . .71 B2
Yaxley PI ST3 . . . . .88 F6
Yeadon Gdns WV3 . . . . . .265 D8
Yeager Ct ST15 . . . . .118 F6
Yeaman St ST4 . . . . .72 B6
Yeatsall Rd WS15 . . . . . . .160 E5
Yeldham PI ST3 . . . . .88 F6
Yelt La DE6 . . . . .127 D8
Yelverton Ave ST17 . . . . . .175 D8
Yelverton CI WS3 . . . . .243 B4
Yemscroft WS6 . . . . .243 A8
Yenton CI B78 . . . . .250 A1
Yeoman Ind Est DE14 . . . .166 E5
Yeoman Way WS15 . . . . . .198 A4
Yeovil PI ST3 . . . . .88 F6
Yeovilton B79 . . . . .250 C8
Yerley Hill DE6 . . . . .66 C5
Yew CI WS15 . . . . .198 A4
Yew PI ST5 . . . . .55 D8
Yew Tree Ave
Lichfield WS14 . . . . .231 E8
Stoke-on-T ST3 . . . . .72 E2
Yew Tree CI
Derrington ST18 . . . . .154 E2
Norton Canes WS11 . . . . . .228 A5
Stoke-on-T ST3 . . . . .43 D1
Yewtree Cres DE15 . . . . . . .185 F7
Yew Tree Ct ST17 . . . . .174 E4
Yew Tree Dr ST19 . . . . . . .205 C6

Yew Tree Gdns WV8 . . . . .239 A4
Yew Tree La Astbury CW12 . .15 C3
Bridgemere CW5 . . . . .67 A6
Wolverhampton WV6 . . . . .255 A5
Yew Tree PI WS3 . . . . .243 D3
Yew Tree Rd
Pattingham WV6 . . . . .253 D2
Rugeley WS15 . . . . .196 F6
Yewtree Rd DE11 . . . . .186 F7
Yew Tree Rd WS4 . . . . . . .244 B8
Yew Tree Terr ST7 . . . . .41 A8
York Ave Fulford ST11 . . . . .90 E1
Wolverhampton WV3 . . . . .255 E1
York CI Biddulph ST8 . . . . . .16 C2
Forsbrook ST11 . . . . .91 B8
Lichfield WS13 . . . . .214 C3
Rugeley WS15 . . . . .196 D6
Talke ST7 . . . . .40 D7
York Cres
Stourbridge DY8 . . . . .279 D7
Wolverhampton WV3 . . . . .255 E1
Yorkdale CI DY3 . . . . .271 D3
York Gdns WV3 . . . . .255 E1
York PI ST5 . . . . .283 B3
York Rd Cannock WS11 . . .226 F7
Meir ST3 . . . . .74 B3
Stafford ST17 . . . . .175 B8
Wolverhampton WV3 . . . . .265 B8
Yorksand Rd B78 . . . . .260 F8
Yorkshire Way WS7 . . . . . .229 F8
York St Burton u T DE14 . .166 C4
Hanley ST1 . . . . .282 B3
Leek ST13 . . . . .30 F6
Newcastle-u-L ST5 . . . . . . .283 D3
Stone ST15 . . . . .105 A2
Youlgreave Ave ST2 . . . . . . .58 B2
Youlton PI ST2 . . . . .58 B2
Young Ave ST16 . . . . .155 C6
Younger St ST4 . . . . .72 D6
Young St Cheadle ST10 . . . .76 E3
Stoke-on-T ST6 . . . . .41 F6
Yoxall Ave ST4 . . . . .71 F8
Yoxall Rd
King's Bromley DE13 . . . . .199 D7
Newborough DE13 . . . . . . .162 E7

Z

Zamenhof Gr ST6 . . . . .42 C1
Zennor Gr ST2 . . . . .58 B2
Zetland PI ST3 . . . . .88 F6
Zetland Wlk ST3 . . . . .88 F6
Zion WS6 . . . . .226 D3
Zion St ST6 . . . . .57 A8
Zoar St DY3 . . . . .271 C3
Zodiac Dr ST6 . . . . .41 E6
Zouche CI DY8 . . . . .279 E8